# Marriage Notices from Washington County New York Newspapers

## 1799-1880

*Mary S. Jackson and Edward F. Jackson*

HERITAGE BOOKS
2006

# HERITAGE BOOKS
## AN IMPRINT OF HERITAGE BOOKS, INC.

### Books, CDs, and more—Worldwide

For our listing of thousands of titles see our website
at
www.HeritageBooks.com

Published 2006 by
HERITAGE BOOKS, INC.
Publishing Division
65 East Main Street
Westminster, Maryland 21157-5026

Copyright © 1995 Mary S. Jackson and Edward F. Jackson

Other books by the authors:

*1850 Census for the Town of Howard, Steuben County, New York
and Genealogical Data on the Families Who Lived There*

*Death Notices from Steuben County, New York Newspapers, 1797-1884*

*Death Notices from Washington County, New York Newspapers, 1799-1880*

*Marriage and Death Notices from Schuyler County, New York Newspapers*

*Marriage and Death Notices from Seneca County, New York Newspapers, 1817-1885*

*Marriage Notices from Steuben County, New York Newspapers, 1797-1884*

Other books by Mary S. Jackson:

*Marriages and Deaths from Tompkins County, New York Newspapers*

International Standard Book Number: 978-0-7884-0342-7

# Introduction

Newspapers are probably one of the most valuable and interesting sources for genealogy and are too often overlooked by researchers. Not only for the marriage and death notices that are published but many other articles are a valuable source of information. Some newspapers carry family histories of many of the local people. They also print sale of properties, notices of probate, advertising, personal items such as who is ill this week or who visited who, reunions, etc. They can be very entertaining as well as informative.

This volume contains marriage notices from Washington County New York newspapers from 1799 to 1880 abstracted from microfilm copies available at the New York State Library. Other copies may be available elsewhere. Although these newspapers were published in Washington County, they include notices for all the surrounding counties and the state of Vermont. They also include many notices for those people who moved to other towns in New York or to other states.

Vital records were being recorded by the Town Clerks in New York State beginning in 1880. However, recording was not mandatory until 1906. Before 1880 one of the best sources for these vital records are local newspapers for that time period. Verification of the information contained in these newspapers should be made by using a primary source whenever possible. Sometimes mistakes were made in printing and these newspapers are very old and sometimes very difficult to read. It is still one of the best sources available.

Notices may have been printed in more than one newspaper and occasionally there is a difference in either the age of the person or in the date given. When this happened it is indicated by giving both dates such as (May 1/7, 1850) rather than using duplicate notices. With this volume and its companion "Death Notices from Washington County Newspapers," it is possible to find information on three and four generations for some families.

# List of Newspapers

| | |
|---|---|
| County Post and North Star | 1837 |
| Granville Sentinel | 1875 - 1877 |
| Local Observer | August 1865 |
| Northern Centinel | 1799 - 1800 |
| Northern Post | 1804 - 1821 |
| Salem Press | 1850 - 1855 |
| Salem Weekly Review | 1877 - 1880 |
| Sandy Hill Herald | 1829 - 1876 |
| Washington County Chronicle | 1864 - 1870 |
| Washington County Journal | 1845 - 1850 |
| Washington County News | 1871 |
| Washington County People's Journal | 1854 - 1880 |
| Washington County Post | 1837 - 1879 |
| Whitehall Chronicle | 1851 - 1877 |
| Whitehall Times | 1864 - 1877 |

## COUNTY POST AND NORTH STAR
### January 4, 1837 - May 10, 1837

| | |
|---|---|
| **FITCH** James H. of Salem, NY | December 29, 1836 |
| **BAKER** Catherine of Jackson, NY | Salem, NY |
| | |
| **BRADLEY** Ephraim L. of Union Village, NY | January 9, 1837 |
| **GRIFFIN** Emily of Union Village, NY | Salem, NY |
| | |
| **BRISTOL** Albert G. of Whitehall, NY | January 12, 1837 |
| **TAFT** Sophia A. of Whitehall, NY | Whitehall, NY |
| | |
| **RICE** Roswell Jr. of White Creek, NY | January 30, 1837 |
| **HORTON** Orra of White Creek, NY | White Creek, NY |
| | |
| **LOOMIS** Amos of Granville, NY | January 29, 1837 |
| **WILSON** Polly Ann of Whitehall, NY | Whitehall, NY |
| | |
| **MC NISH** Thomas of Salem, NY | February 8, 1837 |
| **BINNINGER** Frances Maria of Salem, NY | Salem, NY |
| | |
| **FISHER** Gerritt of Jackson, NY | February 9, 1837 |
| **SHERMAN** Eunice of Cambridge, NY | Cambridge, NY |
| | |
| **WHITE** Albert C. of Union Village, NY | December 28, 1836 |
| **BINNINGER** Catherine of New York City | New York City |
| | |
| **SWEET** Almon of Salem, NY | March 2, 1837 |
| **HETH** Maria of Salem, NY | Salem, NY |
| | |
| **AYLSWORTH** Edward of Arlington, Vt. | February 21, 1837 |
| **MARTIN** Sarah V. of Salem, NY | Salem, NY |
| | |
| **ROBERTSON** David of Jackson, NY | March 2, 1837 |
| **MC FARLAND** Catherine of Cambridge, NY | Cambridge, NY |
| | |
| **BROWN** Solomon of Salem, NY | March 9, 1837 |
| **HUGGINS** Abigail | Salem, NY |
| | |
| **MILLER** Gerritt of Easton, NY | February 28, 1837 |
| **LEE** Hannah of Argyle, NY | Argyle, NY |
| | |
| **STEVENS** Mathew Howe | March 15, 1837 |
| **CHURCH** Caroline Maria dau of L. C. of Salem, NY | Salem, NY |
| | |
| **BOWEN** David of Salem, NY | March 23, 1837 |
| **CARSWELL** Jane | Salem, NY |

WHELDON Phillip G. of Easton, NY — March 15, 1837 — Pittstown, NY
AUSTIN Ann G. of Pittstown, NY

WHITE Thomas of Rupert, Vt. — April 6, 1837 — Salem, NY
WYMAN Aurelia of Rupert, Vt.

HATCH Elisha of Whitehall, NY — April 6, 1837 — Whitehall, NY
ALLBRIGHT Mrs. Sally of Whitehall, NY

VOLENTINE Elias Jr. of Jackson, NY — April 11, 1837 — Jackson, NY
FINEL Lydia Ann of Jackson, NY

BOYD James of Salem, NY — April 25, 1837 — Salem, NY
ROUSE Jane of Argyle, NY

DURKEE Harrison of New York City — April 26, 1837 — Troy, NY
HART Mary A. dau of R. P. of Troy, NY

OSBORN Daniel of Ft. Edward, NY — May 1, 1837 — Ft. Edward, NY
GREEN Christina of Ft. Edward, NY

## GRANVILLE SENTINEL
### September 17, 1875 - September 6, 1877

WOODSTOCK James H. of Iowa City, Iowa — September 8, 1875 — Putnam, NY
MC LAUGHLIN Nellie of Putnam, NY

BROWN Denom C. of Danby, Vt. — September 28, 1875 — Granville, NY
KELLEY Esther G. of Tinmouth, Vt.

OWEN Frank of Eagle Bridge, NY — October 16, 1875 — Cambridge, NY
BENTLEY Maggie of Cambridge, NY

TOWNSEND C. W. of Poultney, Vt. — October 20, 1875 — Rochester, NY
RUSSELL Annie of Cambridge, NY

MC LAUGHLIN William B. of Putnam, NY — October 20, 1875 — Putnam, NY
WILLIAMSON Alice of Putnam, NY

LEE George N. — October 26, 1875 — Granville, NY
POTTER Mary E.

POTTER David S. of Granville, NY — October 26, 1875 — Granville, NY
CARPENTER Fanny E. of Granville, NY

CONE Judson F. of Wells, Vt. — November 3, 1875 — Granville, NY
PARK Lydia M. of Wells, Vt.

STICKNEY Lewis of Granville, NY — November 10, 1875

DE KALB Georgie of Granville, NY — M. Granville, NY

KING H. V. of Salem, NY
HAYNES Katie of Bowling Green, Ohio — November 15, 1875
Granville, NY

CLARK Peter of Hartford, NY
BURTON Nora E. of Hartford, NY — November 25, 1875
Granville, NY

WOOD Ames of Wallingford, Vt.
CHASE Ella M. of Wallingford, Vt. — November 25, 1875
Granville, NY

BROWN Robert F. of Duffield, England
HILLS E. G. of Hartford, NY — November 20,1875
Pittsfield, Mass.

NORTON George W. of Jay, NY
PRESTON Sarah S. of N. Granville, NY — November 25, 1875
N. Granville, NY

BEECHER George W. of E. Poultney, Vt. (newspaper date) December 31, 1875
NELSON Chloe — W. Pawlet, Vt.

DENIO Fayette
WINCHESTER Emma dau of Norman — December 29, 1875
Pawlet, Vt.

GAINER Edgar F. of Castleton, Vt.
GATES Delia E. of Castleton, Vt. — December 28, 1875
Granville, NY

BARKER D. M. of Granville, NY
GRIFFIN Lizzie of Granville, NY — December 9, 1875
Middlebury, Vt.

WRIGHT Allen of Putnam, NY
SHEAR Ella of Putnam, NY — December 29, 1875
Putnam, NY

BUTTON John H. of Granville, NY
WOODARD Laura A. of Hebron, NY — January 17, 1876
Hebron, NY

WHITTEMORE Charles of Adamsville, NY
SLOCUM M. Louisa dau of Warren of S. Hartford, NY — January 19, 1876
S. Hartford, NY

JOHNSON William M. of Hartford, NY
MACBETH Jennie — January 27, 1876
N. Hartford, NY

NICHOLSON L. E. of Cambridge, NY
MC KIE Mary L. of Cambridge, NY — January 26, 1876
Cambridge, NY

GILES Daniel F. of Pawelt, Vt.
GRUET Frances of Ft. Edward, NY — December 30, 1875
Argyle, NY

LEE John J. of Granville, NY
IVES Martha E. dau of P. Ives of Granville, NY — February 2, 1876
N. Granville, NY

GREY I. W. of Slateville, NY                          January 26/27, 1876
MC COTTER Mrs. Sophrona of Hebron, NY                 Hebron, NY

REED W. of Hebron, NY                                 March 8, 1876
WELCH Helen A. of Hebron, NY                          Hebron, NY

WINTER Allen M. of Arcadia, Iowa                      March 16, 1876
HILL Ellen of Pawlet, Vt.                             Granville, NY

MOORE Allen R. of Ft. Ann, NY                         March 8, 1876
VAUGHN Nancy of Putnam, NY                            Westhaven, Vt.

WALLACE John of Castleton, Vt.                        March 27, 1876
LEE Ellen of Castleton, Vt.                           Hampton, NY

BAILEY Rollon E. of Wallingford, Vt.                  April 30, 1876
PARRY Leva of Danby, Vt.                              Granville, NY

JOHNSTON William of S. Hartford, NY                   April 26, 1876
SCHERMERHORN Mrs. Julia of Sandy Hill, NY             Sandy Hill, NY

BUTLER Charles S. of Poultney, Vt.                    May 16, 1876
BEEBE Agnes S. of Dorset, Vt.                         Granville, NY

MORRIS Richard P. of Poultney, Vt.                    May 20, 1876
JONES Elizabeth D. of M. Granville, NY                M. Granville, NY

HOYT A. G. of Fremont Ctr., Mi.                       June 2, 1876
GILES Mary E. of N. Pawlet, Vt.                       N. Pawlet, Vt.

HALEY Thomas S. of Sherburne, Vt.                     June 10, 1876
COLTON Mary A. of Sherburne, Vt.                      Granville, NY

LAVIEGNE Henry C. of Poultney, Vt.                    June 13, 1876
POTTER Edna of Granville, NY                          Granville, NY

HOLLAND Charles H. of Manchester, Vt.                 June 15, 1876
RICHIE Fannie H. of Dorset, Vt.                       Granville, NY

SIMONDS Frederick of Weston, Vt.                      June 15, 1876
BURROUGHS Hattie of Weston, Vt.                       Pawlet, Vt.

POWELL Joseph of Wallingford, Vt.                     June 29, 1876
WELLMAN Mrs. Anna J. of Wallingford, Vt.              Greenwich, NY

HIGGINS David E. Md. of Putnam, NY                    August 21, 1876
CRAMMOND Maggie of Putnam, NY                         Putnam, NY

WETHERBEE Andrew of Benson, Vt.                       October 14, 1876
MANLY Hannah Maria of Benson, Vt.

BROWN Amos of Danby Vt.                                    November 22, 1876
TARBELL Harriet E. of Mt. Tabor, Vt.                       Granville, NY

MEERWARTH George of E. Artlington, Vt.(newspaper date)    December 1, 1876
BLIVEN Josephine of Pharsalia, NY                          Granville, NY

HEATH John W. of Granville, NY                             November 28, 1876
GOULD Marion L. of Granville, NY

NELSON Bernice of Hebron, NY                               December 6, 1876
WARNER Myra of Pawlet, Vt.                                 Pawlet, NY

COLER Charles                                              November 19, 1876
SHATTUCK Lydia                                             Whitehall, NY

MASON Charles F. of N. Granville, NY                       December 4, 1876
NORTHUP Nellie E. dau of George                            W. Granville, NY

BROWN Isaac H. of Danby, Vt.                               December 15, 1876
HULETT Laura D. of Danby Vt.

GRAHAM Oscar F. of Ft. Ann, NY                             January 1, 1877
PARISH Roxanna M. of Ft. Ann, NY                           M. Granville, NY

WALLER Comfort of Hebron, NY                               December 24, 1876
STARBUCK Deborah of W. Pawlet, Vt.                         N. Hebron, NY

BEDELL Nathaniel of Granville, NY                          December 27, 1876
KENYON Lucinda of New Hampshire                            N. Hebron, NY

MC ARTHUR Arthur of Troy, NY                               January 9, 1877
GRIFFIN Ella E. of Cohoes, NY                              Cohoes, NY

WRIGHT Henry A.                                            January 1, 1877
CUMMINGS Carrie D.                                         Hartford, NY

LILLIE Robert M. of Putnam, NY                             January 3, 1877
CRAIG Emma of Putnam, NY                                   Putnam, NY

POTTER John D. of Granville, NY                            January 15/17, 1877
WHITING Gertrude of Pawlet, Vt.                            Pawlet, Vt.

SHELDON George W. of E. Rupert, Vt.                        February 1, 1877
HULETT Ida of Pawlet, Vt.                                  Pawlet, Vt.

JONES Joseph of Jamesville, NY                             February 12, 1877
DILLON Amelia of Jamesville, NY                            Granville, NY

PEABODY Edwin of Putnam, NY                                February 10/12 1877

MC INTYRE Emma of Putnam, NY — Putnam, NY

SANBORN Charles of Shuylerville, NY — February 6, 1877
REYNOLDS Sarah E. of Greenwich, NY — Greenwich, NY

SIMONDS Edgar A. of Hampton, NY — January 30, 1877
CISCO Ida of New Hampshire

BLACK James B. of Poulteny, Vt. — March 15, 1877
SPAULDING Jessie A. of Poultney, Vt.

WOODELL Frederick of Hartford, NY — March 5, 1877
BUMP Annie M. of Hartford, NY — Wells, Vt.

WILSON James of E. Salem, NY — April 12, 1877
RANSBOTTOM Abbie of Jackson, NY — Shushan, NY

HARWOOD N. A. — April 26, 1877
CARUTHERS Ann/Abbie — Salem, NY

THORNTON Allison of Ira, NY — May 2, 1877
AMES Alice of W. Rutland, Vt. — Granville, NY

CARR Albert of Arlington, Vt. — April 21, 1877
MARBLE Eva of Sunderland, Vt.

ROWELL John W. of Pittsfield, Ohio — May 1, 1877
HULETT Adde of Danby, Vt. — Danby, Vt.

KELLY Dexter G. of Pawlet, Vt. — May 23, 1877
COMSTOCK Jennie A. of Pawlet, Vt. — Granville, NY

KING Charles of Ft. Edward, NY — May 28, 1877
MC CURDY Belle of Ft. Edward, NY — Granville, NY

GREGORY Addis L. of Ft. Edward, NY — May 28, 1877
BULL Zilphia D. of Ft. Edward, NY — Granville, NY

ALEXANDER William — May/June 30, 1877
RANDLES Ettie dau of James I. — Lakeville, NY
(paper gives date of June 30, 1877, date of issue June 7, 1877)

MOSHER Byron C. of Schaghticoke, NY — August 1, 1877
DILLINGHAM Lydia J. dau of Henry of Granville, NY — Granville, NY

ROGERS Deliverance of Granville, NY — August 7, 1877
PRATT Carrie E. dau fo James E. — Granville, NY

DAGGETT William E. of M. Granville, NY — August 14, 1877
WELCH Mary of M. Granville, NY — M. Granville, NY

BURT George L. of Pawlet, Vt.                          August 21, 1877
COMSTOCK Minnie A. of Pawlet, Vt.                      Granville, NY


LOCAL OBSERVER (FT. EDWARD)
August 1865

MC DOUGAL Alex                                         August 8., 1865
NELSON Mary                                            Argyle, NY


Northern Centinel (Salem, NY)
April 23, 1799 - December 23, 1800

COWAN Moses of Cambridge, NY                           October 28, 1800
YOUNGLOVE Betsey dau of John                           Cambridge, NY


Northern Post (Salem, NY)
May 29, 1804 - April 5, 1821

MC CLARY Dr. Samuel of Watervliet, NY                  May 21, 1804
SCOTT Polly of Salem, NY                               Salem, NY

MONTGOMERY William              (newspaper date)       October 25, 1804
CONKEY Sally                                           Salem, NY

HURD Daniel                                            November 1, 1804
GLEASON Sylvia dau of Jacob                            Benson, Vt.

MARTIN William                                         December 2, 1804
BEMAN Lydia dau of Samuel                              Hampton, NY

PROUDFIT Robert of Broadalbin, NY                      December 18, 1804
LAW Eliza dau of David of Albany, NY                   Albany, NY

JACKSON Robert of Hebron, NY                           December 27, 1804
GAULT Lydia of Salem, NY

BOYD Robert of Salem, NY                               January 14, 1805
ANDREWS Margaret of Hebron, NY

MARTIN Joseph of Lisbon, NY                            January 18, 1805
ARMSTRONG Margaret of Hebron, NY

HAMEL John of Hartford, NY                             January 23, 1805
PROUDFIT Jane dau of Dr. Andrew Proudfit               Argyle, NY

ARMSTRONG Thomas of Hebron, NY   (newspaper date)      February 7, 1805

GIBSON Mary of Argyle, NY                                    Argyle, NY

BAKER Abishal of Salem, NY                                   January 24, 1805
LYTLE Martha of Argyle, NY

SAFFORD Perry of Cambridge, NY                               January 29, 1805
MC KILLIP Margaret of Cambridge, NY

HAWLEY Joseph of Salem, NY                                   February 5, 1805
GRAY Sally dau of Col. David Gray of Camden, NY

TRACY Gardner of Lansingburgh, NY                            February 9, 1805
LANSING Catherine dau of Cornelius                           Lansingburgh, NY

RUSSELL David of Salem, NY                                   February 19, 1805
LANSING Alida dau of Cornelius of Lansingburgh, NY           Lansingburgh, NY

NEVINS John of Salem, NY                                     February 18, 1805
SEARS Betsey of Salem, NY                                    Salem, NY

BOSTWICK Jared of Salem, NY          (newspaper date)        September 26, 1805
PLYMPTON Lucretia dau of Oliver of Sturbridge, Mass.         Sturbridge, Mass.

CAMPBELL Cap. James of Augusta, Canada   (news. date)        October 10, 1805
MOORE Sally widow of St. John HONEYWOOD of Salem, NY

COOPER Joseph of Salem, NY                                   October 1, 1805
EASTLING Hannah of Salem, NY

STREETER Lemuel son of Dr. John of Granville, NY             October 13, 1805
FRENCH G. dau of Maj. Peter P. of Hampton, NY

MC MURRAY Robert Jr. of Salem, NY                            November 14, 1805
BARBER Betsey dau of George of Cambridge, NY                 Cambridge, NY

CLARK Isaac                                                  November 25, 1805
FAIRLEY Mary dau of John                                     Salem, NY

BARBER George of Cambridge, NY                               December 2, 1805
MOORE Jane dau of late John of Shodac, NY

CORNELL Paul of Cambridge, NY        (newspaper date)        December 12, 1805
RAWLEY Abigail of Cambridge, NY                              Cambridge, NY

STONE Reuben of Cambridge, NY        (newspaper date)        January 2, 1806
FAIRCHILD Nancy of Cambridge, NY                             Cambridge, NY

GRAY Robert of Heborn, NY                                    December 31, 1805
LYTLE Mary of Hebron, NY                                     Hebron, NY

WRIGHT Thomas of Salem, NY                                January 23, 1806
CREIGHTON Agnes of Hebron, NY

ROWAN Stephen of Salem, NY                                March 18, 1806
MERRILL Mrs. Sally of Salem, NY

WATSON James Y.                      (newspaper date)     March 27, 1806
STONE Susan dau of Abner                                  Salem, NY

BEATTY John of Salem, NY                                  April 3, 1806
BEATTY Miss ____ of Salem, NY

BARBER Thomas of Cambridge, NY                            April 7, 1806
ADAMS Betsey R of Salem, NY

LAWTON John of Cambridge, NY                              August 14, 1806
DAVIS Sarah W. of Cambridge, NY                           Cambridge, NY

FULLERTON Walter of Hebron, NY                            October 9, 1806
GREGORY Martha dau of L. GANSEVORT of Milton, NY          Stillwater, NY

ROSS Theodorus of Willsborough, NY    (newspaper date)    October 16, 1806
GANSEVORT Eliza dau of L.                                  Salem, NY

ROBERTSON Alexander of Argyle, NY                         December 15, 1806
MC FARLAND Margaret dau of William of Salem, NY

BRANARD Daivd of Fairhaven, Vt.                           January 4, 1807
WELLS Rocksena widow of Gen. H. OLDS of Poultney, Vt.

LYTLE Clark of Camden, NY                                 February 12, 1807
HOLMES Reliance of Camden, NY

CAMPBELL John of Cambridge, NY                            December 22, 1807
WALKER Polly of Greenwich, NY                             Greenwich, NY

BILLINGS Jesse L. of Salem, NY                            January 18, 1810
WARFORD Margaret of Salem, NY                             Albany, NY

MC MURRAY Robert of Cambridge, NY                         July 3, 1810
WHITESIDE Ann R. of Cambridge, NY

GANTZ George of Salem, NY                                 May 30, 1810
MC COY Sally of Salem, NY

DAKE Arnold of Argyle, NY                                 January 1, 1811
STEWART Margaret of Argyle, NY                            Argyle, NY

THOMPSON James of Argyle, NY                              January 1, 1816

**LEIGH** Amy of Argyle, NY                                          Argyle, NY

**BAKER** Nathaniel                                                  January 24, 1811
**HYER** Sally                                                       Salem, NY

**DOIG** John of Cambridge, NY          (newspaper date)             January 31, 1811
**DUNN** Margaret of Cambridge, NY                                   Cambridge, NY

**HUNT** Levi of Martinsburgh, NY                                    February 6, 1811
**SMITH** Roxy dau of Thadeus of Salem, NY

**MC CLEARY** John                                                   May 28, 1811
**MC KILLIP** Sally                                                  Salem, NY

**POWERS** Isaac                                                     July 2, 1811
**RUSSELL** Orphana dau of Capt. William Russell

**LEE** Martin Atty. of Granville, NY    (newspaper date)            November 14, 1811
**WENDELL** Ann dau of Gerritt of Cambridge, NY                      Cambridge, NY

**SWETLAND** William Atty. of Plattsburgh, NY                        November 19, 1811
**KIRTLAND** Henrietta J. dau of John                                Fair Vale, NY

**STEELE** Alexander of Salem, NY                                    February 10, 1812
**MC NISH** Betsey dau of Alexander of Salem, NY                     Salem, NY

**MATHEWS** Capt. David of Salem NY                                  February 27, 1812
**MC CRACKEN** Azuba of Salem, NY

**MONCRIEF** William of Salem, NY                                    March 5, 1812
**BAKER** Sally of Salem, NY

**BAKER** Thomas of Salem, NY                                        March 12, 1812
**GREENO** Betsey M. of Salem, NY

**WILCOX** Loami                                                     April 14, 1812
**PADDOCK** Hannah                                                   Greenwich, NY

**TODD** Jonathan of Westhaven, Vt.                                  May 21, 1812
**LAWRENCE** Phebe of Salem, NY

**MC FARLAND** Daniel of Salem, NY                                   June 18, 1812
**STEELE** Mary dau of Capt. John Steele of Salem, NY

**GUNNISON** John                                                    October 1, 1812
**PIERCE** Prudence                                                  Salem, NY

**COOK** Elutherus of Salem, NY                                      December 13, 1812
**CARSWELL** Martha of Salem, NY

| | |
|---|---|
| **SEELEY** Loring of Salem, NY | December 16, 1812 |
| **FRAZIER** Margaret of Hebron, NY | Hebron, NY |
| | |
| **WILLARD** Heman of Stockbridge, Mass. | February 3, 1813 |
| **MILLARD** Jane of Ballston, NY | Ballston, NY |
| | |
| **HEERMANS** Dr. Cornelius P. | January 22, 1813 |
| **CURTIS** Mrs. Susan | Lansingburgh, NY |
| | |
| **REID** John of Whitehall, NY | March 29, 1813 |
| **PROUDFIT** Mary of Salem, NY | Salem, NY |
| | |
| **MC DONALD** James | March 24, 1813 |
| **CARSWELL** Polly | |
| | |
| **WARFORD** Charles of Salem, NY | May 12, 1813 |
| **HILL** Betsey | Cambridge, NY |
| | |
| **WEBSTER** James of Hebron, NY | September 21, 1813 |
| **BECKER** Catherine of Salem, NY | Hebron, NY |
| | |
| **VAIL** George of Troy, NY | October 7, 1813 |
| **THOMAS** Jane dau of David | Salem, NY |
| | |
| **BOICE** Joseph of Greenwich, NY | October 13, 1813 |
| **EIGHTS** Ann dau of Abraham of Albany, NY | Albany, NY |
| | |
| **ELLIOTT** John of Salem, NY | December 14, 1813 |
| **GRAHAM** Rebecca of Salem, NY | |
| | |
| **THOMPSON** John C. of Ticonderoga, NY | January 12, 1814 |
| **GIBSON** Maria of Salem, NY | Salem, NY |
| | |
| **GRAY** David D. | February 2, 1814 |
| **MC KILLIP** Sally | Salem, NY |
| | |
| **STEELE** Thomas | February 3, 1814 |
| **MC NISH** Sally dau of Alexander | Salem, NY |
| | |
| **GRAY** James S. of Salem, NY | February 3, 1814 |
| **SHELDON** Pouella dau of John | Rupert, Vt. |
| | |
| **SHELDON** Josiah of Greenwich, NY (newspaper date) | February 10, 1814 |
| **BENEDICT** Mary of Albany, NY | Albany, NY |
| | |
| **STEVENSON** James | February 22, 1814 |
| **CARSON** Isabella | Salem, NY |
| | |
| **MARTIN** Adam | March 7, 1814 |

**FITCH** Almira dau of Asa                                        Salem, NY

**STODDARD** Eleazor of Pawlet, Vt.                               March 9, 1814
**SILL** Emily of Moreau, NY                                      Moreau, NY
  (twin brothers and twin sisters)
**STODDARD** Josiah of Pawlet, Vt.                                March 9, 1814
**SILL** Almira of Moreau, NY                                     Moreau, NY

**BOYD** Robert                                                   April 11, 1814
**ROWAN** Betsey                                                  Salem, NY

**WILLIAMS** Israel Atty. of Union Village, NY                    May 23, 1814
**EIGHTS** Rachel of Albany, NY                                   Albany, NY

**MARTIN** William B. Middlebury, Vt.                             June 19, 1814
**BELL** Roxanna of Middlebury, Vt.

**GILLESPIE** John of Hebron, NY                                  July 7, 1814
**POOL** Eliza of Salem, NY                                       Salem, NY

**CLARK** William                                                 July 7, 1814
**FELT** Lucinda                                                  Hebron, NY

**ROWAN** Abraham                        (newspaper date)         September 22, 1814
**CRUIKSHANK** Susan                                              Salem, NY

**SAFFORD** Mayhew of Salem, NY                                   September 21, 1814
**FITCH** Maria dau of Col. Fitch of Vergennes, Vt.              Vergennes, Vt.

**HOPKINS** David of Hebron, NY                                   October 6, 1814
**SMITH** Susan dau of Thomas of Hebron, NY                       Hebron, NY

**PRINDLE** Abram                                                 November 28, 1814
**KIMBERLY** Betsey Ann                                           Sandgate, Vt.

**SEYMOUR** James H. of Salem, NY                                 November 26, 1814
**ANDREWS** Eliza of Stillwater, NY                               Stillwater, NY

**HITCHCOCK** Mr. ____ age 74 yrs        (newspaper date)         December 22, 1814
**MOORE** Hannah age 74 yrs                                       Woodstock, NY

**GRAY** David Jr.                                                January 8, 1815
**WEBB** Jane                                                     Salem, NY

**TOMB** Joseph                                                   January 8, 1815
**COOLEY** Betsey                                                 Salem, NY

**STEVENS** Lieut. late of U. S. Army                             January 9, 1815
**PIERCE** Mary                                                   Salem, NY

REYNOLDS Linus J. of Glens Falls, NY     January 1, 1815
BAKER Alice of Ft. Ann, NY     Ft. Ann, NY

MARTIN Aaron Jr. of Salem, NY     February 27, 1815
LINN Artemicia of Greenwich, NY     Greenwich, NY

HISCOCK Whitney of Cambridge, NY     March 20, 1815
CARLEY Polly     Salem, NY

SMITH William, Warren Co. Clerk     September 23, 1815
WHALLEN Margaret dau of Reuben of Essex, NY     Essex, NY

TOMB Henry     November 16, 1815
MC FARLAND Nancy     Salem, NY

CHAPPELL Elias S.     January 8, 1816
FREEMAN Charity     Salem, NY

MC MILLAN John of Salem, NY     January 22, 1816
LYTLE Jane dau of David of Salem, NY     Salem, NY

MC FARLAND William son of William C. of Salem, NY     January 30, 1816
TILFORD Betsey dau of George of Argyle, NY     Argyle, NY

MC FARLAND David of Saratoga, NY (newspaper date)     February 1, 1816
STONE Eunice dau of Abner of Salem, NY     Salem, NY

WHITNEY William H. of Salem, NY     February 13, 1816
MC NAUGHTON Hannah of Salem, NY     Salem, NY

HARVEY James of Cambridge, NY     February 13, 1816
GOODALE P. of Salem, NY     Salem, NY

RYAN Dr. Alvin of Virgil, NY (newspaper date)     February 15, 1816
PORTER Harriet dau of John of Cambridge, NY     Cambridge, NY

HART Richard P. of Troy, NY (newspaper date)     February 15, 1816
HOWARD Betsey Amelia dau of William of New York City     New York City

KNICKERBOCKER Derick of Schaghticoke, NY     February 13, 1816
DE RIDDER Anna dau of Gen. Simon De Ridder of Easton     Easton, NY

FINEL Luther of Salem, NY     March 17, 1816
PARKER Phebe of Salem, NY     Salem, NY

LYTLE Samuel V. of Salem, NY     March 28, 1816
ROWAN Mary dau of John of Salem, NY     Salem, NY

MC FARLAND Capt. William M. of Salem, NY     May 2, 1816

| | |
|---|---|
| **FITCH** Mary dau of Asa of Salem, NY | Salem, NY |
| **YOULEN** Benjamin of Salem, NY<br>**BLOWERS** Rachel of Salem, NY | May 6, 1816<br>Salem, NY |
| **GANTZ** George of Salem, NY<br>**MC COY** Sally of Salem, NY | June 4, 1816<br>Salem, NY |
| **WILLIAMS** Col. John of Salem, NY<br>**SMITH** Almira of Whitehall, NY | July 6, 1820<br>Whitehall, NY |
| **WELLER** Sidney of Salem, NY<br>**MEACHAM** Laura M. of Salem, NY | July 6, 1820<br>Salem, NY |
| **JONES** Charles of Brockville, Ontario, Canada<br>**SMITH** Florilla of Burlington, Vt. | September 20, 1820<br>Salem, NY |
| **STREETER** Salmon of Salem, NY<br>**CHATTIN** Sophia of Salem, NY | November 18, 1820<br>Salem, NY |
| **DUNLAP** Peter C. of Salem, NY<br>**FITCH** Barbara J. dau of Asa of Salem, NY | March 29, 1821<br>Salem, NY |

## SALEM PRESS
### May 21, 1850 - December 25, 1855

| | |
|---|---|
| **DICKEY** Oliver H. of Sandy Hill, NY<br>**BURT** Clarissa of Granville, NY | June 29, 1850<br>Granville, NY |
| **GARDINER** Col. Stephen of Columbia, Ill.<br>**INGALLS** L. S. formerly of Granville, NY | June 28, 1850<br>Griffin, Ga. |
| **PIERCE** A. of Horicon, NY<br>**OSBORN** Mary B. dau of late Miron of Glens Falls, NY | August 1, 1850<br>Glens Falls, NY |
| **BROWNELL** James of Hoosick, NY<br>**CHASE** Freelove of Cambridge, NY | July 21, 1850<br>Cambridge, NY |
| **MARTIN** George of Whitehall, NY<br>**HITCHENS** Jane of Whitehall, NY | August 6, 1850<br>Whitehall, NY |
| **DUEL** Melancton of Pawlet, Vt.<br>**BROOKINS** Laura of Pawlet, Vt. | August 11, 1850<br>Pawlet, Vt. |
| **EPPS** John of Salem, NY<br>**LIVINGSTON** Eliza of Troy, NY | August 6, 1850<br>Salem, NY . |
| **WEEKS** Thomas of Cambridge, NY<br>**HOGABOOM** Phebe Elizabeth of Salem, NY | August 6, 1850<br>Salem, NY |

| | |
|---|---|
| **BURTIS** John D. of Schuylerville, NY | August 4, 1850 |
| **HILL** Louisa W. of Cohoes, NY | Waterford, NY |
| | |
| **CHASE** Nicolas S. of White Creek, NY | August 28, 1850 |
| **RICH** Clarissa A. of White Creek, NY | |
| | |
| **SMITH** Henry of S. Granville, NY | August 27, 1850 |
| **OSBORN** Mary of S. Granville, NY | S. Granville, NY |
| | |
| **PARIS** Urias of Sandy Hill, NY | September 4, 1850 |
| **ROGERS** Cordelia E. dau of Charles of Sandy Hill, NY | Sandy Hill, NY |
| | |
| **THOMPSON** Albert of Castleton, Vt. | September 11, 1850 |
| **RICE** Sarah Elizabeth of Jackson, NY | Jackson, NY |
| | |
| **BEEBE** Justine E. of E. Greenwich, NY | September 12, 1850 |
| **MARTIN** Elizabeth D. of Fitchs Point, NY | Salem, NY |
| | |
| **MERCHANT** Henry of Albany, NY (newspaper date) | September 24, 1850 |
| **OLIPHANT** Caroline F. of W. Granville, NY | W. Granville, NY |
| | |
| **WARNER** De Witt of Reading, NY | September 26, 1850 |
| **COON** Charlotte of Salem, NY | Salem, NY |
| | |
| **JOHNSON** Edwin of N. White Creek, NY | September 25, 1850 |
| **HENDERSON** Jane E. of N. White Creek, NY | White Creek, NY |
| | |
| **BUCK** Horace M. of Kingsbury, NY | September 29, 1850 |
| **SMITH** Nancy M. of Kingsbury, NY | Kingsbury, NY |
| | |
| **WHITE** Charles A. of Sandy Hill, NY | September 17, 1850 |
| **BEACH** Deborah of Easton, NY | Easton, NY |
| | |
| **INGALLS** David T. | September 23, 1850 |
| **SIMONS** Samantha of Pittsford, Vt. | Belcher, NY |
| | |
| **CHUBB** Bezaleel of Union Village, NY | September 25, 1850 |
| **BENNETT** Emily L. of Union Village, NY | Troy, NY |
| | |
| **GUNNISON** William of Troy, NY | October 1, 1850 |
| **SHEPARD** Mary E. dau of Samuel | Troy, NY |
| | |
| **NASH** Harvey B. of Kingsbury, NY | October 3, 1850 |
| **DUNHAM** Mary Jane dau of Samuel of Kingsbury, NY | Kingsbury, NY |
| | |
| **NORTON** Henry of Greenwich, NY | September 13, 1850 |
| **ROOD** Diana of Greenwich, NY | Union Village, NY |
| | |
| **MORSE** Stephen of Litchfield, Conn | September 25, 1850 |

**BEDELL** Sarah E. of St. Lawrence Co. NY — Greenwich, NY

**MORSE** Artemus of Greenwich, NY — October 15, 1850
**BRYANT** Elizabeth of Greenwich, NY — Greenwich, NY

**MC DOUGAL** Alexander of Argyle, NY — October 10, 1850
**KING** Julia of Argyle, NY — Union Village, NY

**DODD** Walter of Cambridge, NY — October 10, 1850
**THOMPSON** Harriet of Cambridge, NY — Cambridge, NY

**EDDY** James M. of Greenwich, NY — October 23, 1850
**BARNARD** Elizabeth R. dau of John — Greenwich, NY

**HOWARD** Archibald of Greenwich, NY — October 16, 1850
**RUGG** Mary of Milton, NY

**RICH** Lafayette of White Creek, NY — October 24, 1850
**GRIFFITH** Louisa of Manchester, Vt. — Manchester, Vt.

**CHAMBERLAIN** William of Salem, NY — November 12, 1850
**CARSWELL** Martha of Salem, NY — Salem, NY

**DURPHEE** Isaac W. of Cambridge, NY — November 6, 1850
**SISSON** Sarah M. dau of Ira & Betsey M. — White Creek, NY

**KENYON** Andrew of Greenwich, NY — November 7,1850
**YOUNG** Mary of Easton, NY — Easton, NY

**MC NABB** James of Greenwich, NY — November 7, 1850
**EMERSON** Lorinda of Easton, NY — Easton, NY

**COZZENS** Earl M. of Greenwich, NY — November 7, 1850
**RHODES** Martha M. of Granville, NY — Granville, NY

**TABER** Lewis of Easton, NY — November 12, 1850
**CRANDALL** Sarah P. of Easton, NY — Easton, NY

**MC NAUGHTON** Malcolm of Argyle, NY — November 13, 1850
**BOYD** Elizabeth of Argyle, NY — Argyle, NY

**CARTER** Francis — November 14, 1850
**SMITH** Caroline M. — Whitehall, NY

**SHERMAN** Josiah R. of Salem, NY — November 27, 1850
**WALKER** Lydia S. of Salem, NY — Salem, NY

**WHEDON** P. of Pawlet, Vt. — October 31, 1850
**STAPLES** Ruth of Pawlet, Vt.

CRONIN Timothy of Salem, NY      December 3, 1850
LARKIN Helen M. of Salem, NY      White Creek, NY

CHAMBERS Thomas of Union Village, NY      November 29, 1850
HOWE Hannah of Easton, NY

ROSS Jacob of Northumberland, NY      December 5, 1850
SMITH Margaret of Argyle, NY      Argyle, NY

BRATT Nicolas of Easton, NY      December 11, 1850
GORSLINE Janette of Schaghticoke, NY      Schaghticoke, NY

JOHNSON Franklin of Landgrove, Vt.      December 19, 1850
COOK Hannah dau of Seth of Granville, NY      Granville, NY

SHIRLAND Seneca G. of W. Haven, Vt.      January 3, 1851
MOTT Martha A. of Salem, NY      Poultney, Vt.

EVEREST Sedgewick of M. Granville, NY      January 9, 1851
SUMMER Amanda of M. Granville, NY

GRAHAM Robert of Jackson, NY      January 1, 1851
MAXWELL Mary of Jackson, NY      Jackson, NY

FOSTER Allen      December 27, 1850
CAMPBELL Jane      Cambridge, NY

BAILEY Henry M. of E. Otto, NY      January 1, 1851
LARKIN Sarah A. dau of Nathan formerly of Shushan, NY      E. Otto, NY

KING Joseph of Argyle, NY      January 9, 1851
HARSHA Jane of Argyle, NY

POND Alembert of Elizabethtown      January 29, 1851
LESTER Elizabeth C. of Saratoga Springs, NY      Saratoga Spr. NY

LAPHAM Joseph B. of Danby, Vt.      January 29, 1851
STAPLES Lydia of M. Granville, NY      M. Granville, NY

STEVENS Henry of Shushan, NY      February 5, 1851
COOPER Ann Maria of Shushan, NY      Salem, NY

HULL Dorr of N. White Creek, NY      February 4, 1851
RICE Susan A. of N. White Creek, NY      Schuylerville, NY

GUY Charles B. of Kingsbury, NY      January 21, 1851
BROWN Mary O. of Granville, NY      Castleton, Vt.

FERGUSON John of Syracuse, NY      February 10, 1851

**JOHNSON** Sarah W. of Hebron, NY

| | |
|---|---|
| **HUSTED** Daniel M. of Pittstown, NY | February 12, 1851 |
| **WILSON** Emily N. dau of William of Cambridge, NY | Cambridge, NY |
| | |
| **FAULKENBURY** W. H. of Whitehall, NY | February 6, 1851 |
| **NOBLE** Mary A. of Whitehall, NY | Granville, NY |
| | |
| **GILLIS** Seneca of Argyle, NY | February 12, 1851 |
| **HOWARD** Elinor Crary of E. Greenwich, NY | Sandy Hill, NY |
| | |
| **ROOKER** Mathison | February 26, 1851 |
| **GRANT** Mary Eliza dau of Peter of Granville, NY | Whitehall, NY |
| | |
| **PARK** Joseph Esq. of Wells, NY | March 12, 1851 |
| **WILCOX** Phebe of Pawlet, Vt. | Pawlet, Vt. |
| | |
| **WILSON** Charles of Sandy Hill, NY | March 5, 1851 |
| **COOPER** Fidelia of Moreau, NY | Moreau, NY |
| | |
| **BARNES** Henry Jr. of Salem, NY | March 18, 1851 |
| **MC LEAN** Helen of Jackson, NY | Jackson, NY |
| | |
| **TABOR** Russell of Easton, NY | March 16, 1851 |
| **SHELDON** Elizabeth of Easton, NY | Easton, NY |
| | |
| **HULETT** Alanson A. | March 13, 1851 |
| **BREWSTER** Harriet of Dresden, NY | Dresden, NY |
| | |
| **LAMPHERE** Leander of Dresden, NY | March 16, 1851 |
| **CONGDON** Julia Ann of Putnam, NY | Putnam, NY |
| | |
| **CLARK** Orange | March 17, 1851 |
| **M'CANE** Sarah | Whitehall, NY |
| | |
| **MYLOTT** Robert | March 17, 1851 |
| **M'NALL** Ann | Whitehall, NY |
| | |
| **LOOMIS** Henry of Granville, NY | March 5, 1851 |
| **WHITE** Mary of Ft. Ann, NY | Pawlet, Vt. |
| | |
| **LAMB** George of S. Granville, NY | March 4, 1851 |
| **DUEL** Olive of S. Granville, NY | |
| | |
| **SMART** James of Salem, NY | March 25, 1851 |
| **BOYD** Mrs. Jane of Salem, NY | Salem, NY |
| | |
| **HOLMAN** Cyrus L. of Glens Falls, NY | March 22, 1851 |
| **BRIERLY** Marie of Whitehall, NY | Whitehall, NY |

| | |
|---|---|
| PRATT Leroy D. of Cambridge, NY | March 20, 1851 |
| WILLETT Amie of Cambridge, NY | White Creek, NY |
| | |
| WARNER Calvin P. of White Creek, NY | April 25, 1851 |
| HARWOOD Elizabeth L. of New Lebanon, NY | White Creek, NY |
| | |
| BAKER Albert of Sandy Hill, NY | April 22, 1851 |
| HENRY Mrs. Clary of Whitehall, NY | Whitehall, NY |
| | |
| BLANCHARD Andrew H. of Greenwich, NY | May 4, 1851 |
| WENTWORTH Elizabeth of Greenwich, NY | Center Falls, NY |
| | |
| HEGEMAN Jerry | April 29, 1851 |
| PERRINE Elizabeth formerly of Union Village, NY | Racine, Wis. |
| | |
| CURTIS Abram of Schaghticoke, NY | May 5, 1851 |
| ADAMS Rebecca of White Creek, NY | White Creek, NY |
| | |
| CLEVELAND David A. of Salem, NY | May 12, 1851 |
| DRAPER Delia of Salem, NY | Salem, NY |
| | |
| CHEESBRO Martin V. of Union Village, NY | May 10, 1851 |
| BENNETT Olive of Easton, NY | Schuylerville, NY |
| | |
| WOODIN J. L. of New York City | May 27, 1851 |
| MILLIMAN Harriet of Salem, NY | Salem, NY |
| | |
| BREWER Albert of Union Village, NY | May 25, 1851 |
| POTTER Jane of Union Village, NY | Saratoga Spr., NY |
| | |
| CHASE Leroy | May 21, 1851 |
| GREEN Rebecca of Cambridge, NY | Cambridge, NY |
| | |
| ROGERS James of Greenwich, NY | June 11, 1851 |
| KETCHUM Isabella M. of Greenwich, NY | Salem, NY |
| | |
| M'GEE James of Whitehall, NY | June 10, 1851 |
| MILLER Margaret R. of Ft. Ann, NY | Ft. Ann, NY |
| | |
| HALL George A. | June 11, 1851 |
| DAYTON Helen dau of Gaius | Whitehall, NY |
| | |
| BALDWIN Jonathan of New York City | June 11, 1851 |
| WHEELER Elizabeth | Whitehall, NY |
| | |
| STREET Schuyler of Greenwich, NY | May 29, 1851 |
| BROWN Nancy of Greenwich, NY | E. Greenwich, NY |
| | |
| REICHEL William C. of Bethlehem, Pa. | June 26, 1851 |

**GRAY** Mary Jane dau of Levi of E. Salem, NY

**DIBBLE** Wakefield of Sandy Hill, NY                June 18, 1851
**BRUSH** Elizabeth of Sandy Hill, NY

**MINOR** David W. of Union Village, NY             June 21, 1851
**BABCOCK** Sarah of Union Village, NY             Union Village, NY

**BUMP** Thomas of Hartford, NY                    July 3, 1851
**GREGORY** Mrs. Prudence of Belcher, NY           Belcher, NY

**MEADER** George H. of Union Village, NY          July 1, 1851
**TINGUE** Maria of Cambridge, NY                  Galesville, NY

**LIVINGSTON** John E. of Chester, Ohio            July 3, 1851
**BAIN** Nancy of Argyle, NY                       Union Village, NY

**MC MANN** Michael of Salem, NY                   July 16, 1851
**SMITH** Ann of Salem, NY                         Union Village, NY

**HAWLEY** David of New York City                  August 7, 1851
**WHITESIDE** Louisa Maria dau of late James       Cambridge, NY
     (stepdaughter of officiating clergy Rev. Peter **GORDON**)

**HOLMES** William Mowry son of Henry of Greenwich, NY    August 26, 1851
**STEVENS** Frances E. dau of Ira C. of Jackson, NY       Jackson, NY

**HAZZARD** John W. of Sandy Hill, NY              August 24, 1851
**LATIMER** Sarah E. of Sandy Hill, NY             Sandy Hill, NY

**HASTINGS** George of Cohoes, NY                  August 18, 1851
**BARKER** Betsey R. of Salem, NY                  Salem, NY

**BOYD** William C. of Salem, NY                   August 27, 1851
**MC LEARY** Jane of Salem, NY                     Salem, NY

**RAMSEY** Hugh of Salem, NY                       September 3, 1851
**BROWN** Mary Jane of Hebron, NY

**ACKLEY** John of Jackson, NY                     September 3, 1851
**CLEVELAND** Frances E. dau of James              Jackson, NY

**CARSWELL** James H. of Salem, NY                 September 15, 1851
**CLARK** Isabel of Salem, NY

**PARRY** John of Ft. Edward, NY                   September 1, 1851
**MC INTYRE** Lucy dau of James of Ft. Edward, NY  Ft. Edward, NY

**HASTINGS** Pomeroy of Shaftsbury, Vt.            September 10, 1851
**ELWELL** Melona of Bennington, Vt.               White Creek, NY

BACHELDER Moses age 72y 9m     August 2, 1851
STEARNS Margaret age 18y 7m     Deerfield, NY

REED Rev. Levi H. of Fayetteville, NY     September 17, 1851
FULLER Maria Louisa Dau of John R. of Kent, Conn.     Kent, Conn.

HILLMAN Leroy of Jackson, NY     September 17, 1851
FOSTER Mary A. of Easton, NY     Easton, NY

BOARDMAN William P. Esq. of Albany, NY     September 23, 1851
MORRIS Catherine V. N. of Cambridge, NY     Cambridge, NY

THOMPSON Charles of Salem, NY     September 13, 1851
FULLERTON Martha of Hebron, NY     Hebron, NY

REA John of Hebron, NY     September 7, 1851
CHRISTIE Grace of Greenwich, NY     Greenwich, NY

SANFORD Milo of Whitehall, NY     September 14, 1851
COREY Mary R. of Crown Point, NY     Albany, NY

TIPLADY William N. of Hebron, NY     October 23, 1851
CHAMBERLAIN Sarah J. of Ballston Spa, NY     Rupert, Vt.

LITTLEFIELD Moses A. of Rutland, Vt.     October 28, 1851
FIELDING Jane dau of John of Union Village, NY     Union Village, NY

BAIN George W.     October 21, 1851
KELLIE Elizabeth     Ft. Edward, NY

BROOKS Nathan of Hague     October 29, 1851
SHATTUCK Abigail of W. Rutland, Vt.     S. Granville, NY

FINCH James C. Esq. of Kingsbury, NY     October 30, 1851
MARTIN Catherine A. of Kingsbury, NY     Kingsbury, NY

WILEY John W. of Buskirks Bridge, NY     November 3, 1851
EASTON Sarah of Pittstown, NY     White Creek, NY

WOODARD William W. of Sunderland, Vt.     November 2, 1851
LITTLE Sophia of Sunderland, Vt.     Jackson, NY

DANFORTH Edward M. of Summit, NY     November 12, 1851
HARSHA N. Anna dau of George C. of Argyle, NY     Oconomowoe, Wis.

WOODWORTH Ira of N. White Creek, NY     November 11, 1851
BALDWIN Charlotte of Cambridge, NY     Cambridge, NY

NORTON Malcom of Salem, NY     December 10, 1851

| | |
|---|---|
| ROSE Catherine of N. White Creek, NY | White Creek, NY |
| HADWIN Oliver R. V. of Danby, Vt. | December 10, 1851 |
| BAKER Sarah Jane dau of Benjamin of Granville, NY | Granville, NY |
| RICH A. A. of Salem, NY | December 1, 1851 |
| BEATY Margaret of Salem, NY | Salem, NY |
| SHELDON Titus of Rupert, Vt. | December 24, 1851 |
| BAKER Eliza of Rome, NY | Granville, NY |
| MACUMBER John of Granville, NY | December 24, 1851 |
| STEWART Lucretia of Granville, NY | Granville, NY |
| BISHOP Stephen T. of Granville, NY | January 8, 1852 |
| CHAPMAN Helen E. of Granville, NY | Granville, NY |
| BETTS O. F. of Pawlet, Vt. | December 29, 1851 |
| ANDRUS Minerva E. of Granville, NY | Granville, NY |
| PARKER Isaac G. of Greenwich, NY | January 11, 1852 |
| ELDRIDGE Mrs. Cornelia dau of John GAVETT | Greenwich, NY |
| MOREY Mathew of Hebron, NY | January 1, 1852 |
| HAY Clarissa of W. Rupert, Vt. | W. Rupert, Vt. |
| PRATT M. V. B. of Cambridge, NY | January 12, 1852 |
| RISING Mary M. of W. Rupert, Vt. | W. Rupert, Vt. |
| KELSEY Charles of Troy, NY | January 12, 1852 |
| HOUGHTON Laura of Troy, NY | W. Rupert, Vt. |
| CHAPMAN Perry of Salem, NY | January 12, 1852 |
| WHITCOMB Ann of Salem, NY | Hebron, NY |
| BURDICK John V. of White Creek, NY | January 22, 1852 |
| WELLS Judith of Coila, NY | Coila, NY |
| RISING Jacob L. of Buskirks Bridge, NY | January 3, 1852 |
| STILES Mrs. Sarah C. of Pittstown, NY | Buskirks Br. NY |
| PRATT Rev. J. H. of Granville, NY | January 19, 1852 |
| MASON Phebe Jane of Granville, NY | Granville, NY |
| SHURTLEFF Lewis of California | January 22, 1852 |
| WITBECK Charlotte of Easton, NY | Union Village, NY |
| HODGE J. N. of N. White Creek, NY | January 26, 1852 |
| MILLIMAN Harriet of N. White Creek, NY | White Creek, NY |

HULL Nelson of Granville, NY
DILLINGHAM Hannah K. dau of Otis

February 2, 1852
Granville, NY

BLAKEMAN Theodore of Ballston, NY
CHAMBERLAIN Maria Louisa dau of Dr. J. F.

February 7, 1852
Ballston, NY

CLARK Fitch of Rupert, Vt.
ELWELL Laura of Rupert, Vt.

February 10, 1852
Rupert, Vt.

OSTRANDER Alexander A. of Albany, NY
WRIGHT Julia A. of Hebron, NY

March 1, 1852
Hebron, NY

OSTRANDER Lawrence of Salem, NY
SMITH Mary L. of Hampton, NY

March 1, 1852
Hampton, NY

ROBERTSON James D. of N. White Creek, NY
KING Sarah A. of Troy, NY

February 17, 1852
Hoosick Falls, NY

ROBERTSON George of Cambridge, NY
GRAVES Susan J. of N. Hebron, NY

February 17, 1852
Hoosick Falls, NY

STEVENS M. B. of Shushan, NY
LYMAN A. of Shushan, NY

February 24, 1852
Shushan, NY

MILLER Nicolas of Argyle, NY
WHITE Margaret Ann of Argyle, NY

February 17, 1852
Argyle, NY

WHITE Alexander of Salem, NY
MUNSON Edetha M. of Hebron, NY

March 9, 1852
Hebron, NY

CHAMBERS Wiliam of Cambridge, NY
DUNLOP Jane of Cambridge, NY

March 3, 1852
Cambridge, NY

MOORE James of Albany, NY
MEADER Mary Y. of N. Easton, NY

March 29, 1852
N. Easton, NY

YOUNG Zadoc T. of Easton, NY
TANNER Nancy of Bolton, NY

March 11, 1852
Glens Falls, NY

COREY Allen of Saratoga Springs, NY
PATRICK Cordelia C. of Saratoga Springs, NY

March 18, 1852
Saratoga Spr. NY

BLASHFIELD James of Salem, NY
HEATH M. M. of Kingsbury, NY

April 13, 1852
Salem, NY

BAXTER George W. of Ft. Ann, NY
HAMMOND Mary E. of Ticonderoga, NY

March 30, 1852

BLAKE J. W. of Chicopee Falls, Mass.

April 11, 1852

WILDS L. A. dau of T. B. of Grafton, NY formerly Salem     Grafton, NY

LAMBERTSON Albert of Salem, NY     April 25, 1852
KANE Mrs. Jane of Salem, NY     Salem, NY

PRATT Lott of Adamsville, NY     April 5, 1852
KILMER Elizabeth of Adamsville, NY     Adamsville, NY

ROCHFORD Peter of Greenwich, NY     May 23, 1852
GERO Mary of Greenwich, NY     Salem, NY

STEVENS Archibald of Coeymans, NY     May 19, 1852
DILLINGHAM Sylvia S. of Granville, NY     Troy, NY

MITCHELL George of Granville, NY     May 19, 1852
DILLINGHAM Sarah of Granville, NY     Troy, NY

HAYDORN Edward of Cambridge, NY     May 22, 1852
WOODWARD Almira K. of Schaghticoke, NY     Schuylerville, NY

ROBERTSON Gilbert Jr. of Troy, NY     June 10, 1852
DAGGETT Angeline dau of Joseph     Troy, NY

PATTISON John of Ft. Ann, NY     June 4, 1852
MASON Deborah of Ft. Ann, NY     Ft. Ann, NY

SANDBORN J. K. of Sandy Hill, NY     June 1, 1852
BALDWIN Ellen R. of Sandy Hill, NY     Sandy Hill, NY

TEFFT Dr. M. of W. Poulteney, Vt.     June 8, 1852
SCOTT A. M. of W. Poulteney, Vt.     W. Poulteney, Vt.

DORSEY Patrick of White Creek, NY     June 13, 1852
KILMARTIN Mary of Troy, NY     White Creek, NY

CROCKER Rev. James W. of N. White Creek, NY     June 17, 1852
DILLON Mary A. of Albany, NY     Albany, NY

BROWN Daniel A. of Cambridge, NY     May 17, 1852
HUNT Mary Ann dau of John P. of White Creek, NY     Pittstown, NY

ROBERTSON William of Greenwich, NY     June 14, 1852
HENRY Ann of Greenwich, NY     Greenwich, NY

LEWIS Amos of Easton, NY     June 30, 1852
WATSON Hannah of Centre Falls, NY     Centre Falls, NY

GOODMAN H. M. of New Haven, Conn.     June 24, 1852
HAWLEY Eliza M. of N. White Creek, NY     White Creek, NY

INGALLS Charles R. of Union Valley, NY
STEVENS Lorinda of Troy, NY

June 30, 1852
Troy, NY

WEAVER Charles of Ft. Miller, NY
ANTHONY Elizabeth W. of Ft. Miller, NY

July 7, 1852
Ft. Miller, NY

HARSHA D. S. formerly of Argyle, NY
DONALDSON Margaret S. of Wisconsin

June 10, 1852
Waupun, Wis.

HOPKINS George N. of Salem, NY
BARNES Eleanor of Hebron, NY

July 21, 1852
Hebron, NY

CULVER Azor of Cambridge, NY
PRATT Mary Caroline of Cambridge, NY

August 31, 1852
Cambridge, NY

FOWLER P. of Cambridge, NY
VAN VECHTEN Martha M. of N. White Creek, NY

September 1, 1852
White Creek, NY

VAN WORMER William of W. Ft. Ann, NY
BLOOD Harriet dau of Samuel of W. Ft. Ann, NY

September 1, 1852
W. Ft. Ann, NY

BLACKMER Lovander of Dorset, Vt.
COOK Lydia Ann of Granville, NY

September 1, 1852

BROWN William O. of Hartford, NY
SMITH Mary Ann of Hartford, NY

August 21, 1852

KETCHUM Earl M. of Cambridge, NY
REYNOLDS Susan of Easton, NY

August 29, 1852
White Creek, NY

TABER John M. of Easton, NY
RICE Mary P. of Easton, NY

August 29, 1852
White Creek, NY

MONTGOMERY James of Cambridge, NY
FERGUSON Mary of Cambridge, NY

August 27, 1852
Cambridge, NY

BARBER William P. of N. White Creek, NY
SWANZY Mary of N. White Creek, NY

September 30, 1852

BURCH Josiah of White Creek, NY
GREGG Sarah Ann of White Creek, NY

September 22, 1852
White Creek, NY

FROST Western of Ft. Ann, NY
WESTERN Luna of Whitehall, NY

September 26, 1852
Whitehall, NY

BARLOW Lewis of Jackson, NY
GOULD Frances E. of Knox, NY

October 19, 1852

CLARK Henry of Salem, NY

November 4, 1852

| | |
|---|---|
| **WRIGHT** Cornelia of Salem, NY | Salem, NY |
| | |
| **LAKIN** William H. of Salem, NY | November 8, 1852 |
| **ROBERTSON** Jane of Salem, NY | Salem, NY |
| | |
| **BEEBE** George of Salem, NY | November 8, 1852 |
| **WATKINS** Eunice of Salem, NY | Salem, NY |
| | |
| **CUNNINGHAM** R. C. of Salem, NY | December 1, 1852 |
| **SPRAGUE** Lydia of Salem, NY | Troy, NY |
| | |
| **WRIGHT** Franklin H. of Jackson, NY | January 25, 1853 |
| **DEMING** Amelia M. of Huron, Ohio | Huron, Ohio |
| | |
| **POLLOCK** Joseph of Argyle, NY | February 9, 1853 |
| **ASHTON** Lydia of Salem, NY | Salem, NY |
| | |
| **RAYMOND** S. P. of Rupert, Vt. | February 9, 1853 |
| **DEWEY** Laura of Salem, NY | Salem, NY |
| | |
| **TOMB** Rev. J. S. L. | January 25, 1853 |
| **ABBOTT** Kate M. dau of Uriah of Brunswick, NY | Brunswick, NY |
| | |
| **MAY** Charles A. of US Army | February 11, 1853 |
| **LAW** Josephine dau of George of New York City | New York City |
| | |
| **CORBETT** Henry of New York City | February 18, 1853 |
| **JAGGER** Cora E. dau of Ira of Albany, NY | Albany, NY |
| | |
| **CAMERON** Alexander of Greenwich, NY | January 27, 1853 |
| **DAVISON** Sarah of Greenwich, NY | Greenwich, NY |
| | |
| **RICE** Robert of N. White Creek, NY | February 22, 1853 |
| **COOK** Emeline of Jackson, NY | Salem, NY |
| | |
| **BARKER** Phineas of Salem, NY | February 23, 1853 |
| **SHAW** E. Amelia of Rupert, Vt. | Rupert, Vt. |
| | |
| **WILSON** Chester H. of Hebron, NY | February 23, 1853 |
| **KINNE** Elizabeth S. of Rupert, Vt. | Rupert, Vt. |
| | |
| **WALKER** B. F. of Madison, NY | February 18, 1853 |
| **PIERCE** S. J. of Jackson, NY | White Creek, NY |
| | |
| **HARRINGTON** I. of Salem, NY | March 12, 1853 |
| **CLAPP** Sarah M. of Salem, NY | Ft. Hamilton, NY |
| | |
| **MORRISON** Robert of Brunswick, NY | March 13, 1853 |
| **WILDS** Clarissa of Grafton, NY | Grafton, NY |

WILLIAMS John W. of Greenwich, NY     March 24, 1853
BRIGGS Harriet M. of Salem, NY     Salem, NY

BURCH Platt of Hebron, NY     March 17, 1853
POTTER Hannah of Saratoga, NY     Greenfield, NY

MONTGOMERY George of Salem, NY     March 29, 1853
SNYDER Elizabeth of Salem, NY     Easton, NY

SHAW Beaman of White Creek, NY     April 2, 1853
SKINNER Sara M. of Jackson, NY     Salem, NY

MARBLE Ezra of Sunderland, Vt.     March 28, 1853
LARKIN Mrs. Mary of Salem, NY

PRESTON Harvey of Granville, NY     April 6, 1853
HALL Betsy of Salem, NY

CAMERON D. A.     April 7, 1853
HAY G. A. of Coila, NY

MACK Thomas D. of Argyle, NY     March 22, 1853
ARMSTRONG Jane E. of Argyle, NY     Argyle, NY

GUILD J. Henry of Sandusky, Ohio     May 15, 1853
BURTON Jane M. of Rupert, Vt.     Rupert, Vt.

HUNT Ward of Utica, NY     (newspaper date)     January 21, 1853
TAYLOR Maria dau of James of Albany, NY     Albany, NY

LATTIMORE E. C. of Whitehall, NY     June 9, 1853
GATINGS Elizabeth of Whitehall, NY     Whitehall, NY

SMITH Phipps of Granville, NY     July 4, 1853
THOMPSON Minerva of Granville, NY     Granville, NY

GETTY Ebenezer     June 30, 1853
RIPLEY Mrs.     Wells, Vt.

BRALEY Israel of Salem, NY     July 4, 1853
ELDRIDGE Sarah A. of Adamsville, NY     Ft. Edward, NY

MC NAUGHTON Franklin of Ontario, NY     July 4, 1853
LIDDLE Elizabeth of Hebron, NY     Hebron, NY

STREETER Roswell of Jay, NY     July 16, 1853
MORRISON Mary of Salem, NY     Union Village, NY

NOBLE John T. of Glens Falls, NY     August 11, 1853

GODDARD Anna J. of Macon, Ga.                          Saratoga, NY

KANE William of Salem, NY                              August 15, 1853
BEATY Elizabeth of Salem, NY                           Salem, NY

HINES Henry of Cincinnati, Ohio                        September 1, 1853
WOODWORTH Mary F. of Salem, NY                         Salem, NY

HEDGES George W.                                       September 6, 1853
DOIG Jane A. of Jackson, NY

LARKIN Archilaus of Shushan, NY                        September 9, 1853
SHARP Mary E. of Shushan, NY                           Salem, NY

SCOTT Darius O. of N. White Creek, NY                  September 7, 1853
WARD Mary A. of N. White Creek, NY                     White Creek, NY

ARMSTRONG D. M. Md. of Red Creek, NY                   September 22, 1853
FITCH Hannah of Salem, NY                              Salem, NY

FREEMAN Harvey of Salem, NY                            September 27, 1853
ATWOOD Eliza of Salem, NY                              Salem, NY

THOMPSON Egbert of Georgia                             October 5, 1853
NORTON Susan dau of William S. of Ft. Edward, NY       Ft. Edward, NY

HAYES Harmon E. of Shushan, NY                         October 5, 1853
REYNOLDS Helen M. of Shushan, NY                       Shushan, NY

BILLINGS Samuel of Salem, NY                           September 14, 1853
KUMENSBY Mary of Lansingburgh, NY                      Waterford, NY

INGALLS Truman of Hebron, NY                           October 11, 1853
WHITCOMB Abigail of Granville, NY                      Hebron, NY

LENDRUM George of Argyle, NY                           October 12, 1853
BAIN Julia of Argyle, NY                               Argyle, NY

PATTERSON John of Caledonia, NY                        September 28, 1853
GLOVER Esther of Jackson, NY

PINKERTON Robert of Greenwich, NY                      November 2, 1853
MC ALLISTER Rachael of Hebron, NY                      Hebron, NY

WALLS John of Greenwich, NY                            October 20, 1853
CAMERON Margaret of Greenwich, NY                      Greenwich, NY

CAMPBELL John of Salem, NY                             November 13, 1853
MORROW Jane of Argyle, NY

SHIPLEY Sumner B. of Salem, NY
ROBERTS Ella W. of Williamstown, Mass.

November 5, 1853
Troy, NY

PORTER George of Salem, NY
CLAPP E. H. of Salem, NY

January 2, 1854
Salem, NY

BURNETT Allen A. of Rockwell's Mills, Ill.
ROCKWELL Sarah A. of Rockwell's Mills, Ill.

December 15, 1853

SHAW Henry of Rupert, Vt.
PORTER Margaret A. of Hebron, NY

December 28, 1853
Hebron, NY

RUSSELL William of Ft. Covington, NY
ROBINSON Lucina E. A. of Ft. Covington, NY

December 29, 1853
Ft. Covington, NY

CHERRY James of Jackson, NY
MC FARLAND Elison of Greenwich, NY

January 26, 1854
Greenwich, NY

MASON Rev. H. G. of N. Granville, NY
PECK Eugenia dau of Darius of Glens Falls, NY

January 21, 1854
E. Greenwich, NY

MC CLARTY Robert of Salem, NY
MACKLIN Mary Jane formerly of Hebron, NY

February 2, 1854
Hebron, NY

WHITE John of Salem, NY
MUNSON Dorcas J. of Hebron, NY

March 23, 1854
White Creek, NY

LIDDLE George of Salem, NY
CARUTHERS Jane of Whitehall, NY

March 7, 1854
Pawlet, Vt.

SHERMAN Albert M. of Salem. NY
BURTON Charlotte of W. Rupert, Vt

March 23, 1854
W. Rupert, Vt.

RIDER James Everest of Peru, NY
THURSTON Mary Jane of Salem, NY

May 17, 1854
Salem, NY

MARTIN John H. of Salem, NY
MONTGOMERY Mary Jane of Salem, NY

May 18, 1854
Salem, NY

HOPKINS Cornelius S. of Salem, NY
WILSON Emeline of Centre Falls, NY

May 18, 1854
Centre Falls, NY

PITCHER William of S. Branch, NJ
MC LEAN Mary Ann dau of Thomas R. of Jackson, NY

June 7, 1854
Jackson, NY

DUNHAM Dewey of Bennington, Vt.
BEEBE Maria of Jackson, NY

May 4, 1854
Jackson, NY

BILLINGS Henry of Jackson, NY

June 7, 1854

**MC FARLAND** Margaret M. of Salem, NY

| | |
|---|---|
| **SELFRIDGE** John O. of Sparta, Ill, | June 7, 1854 |
| **BELL** Jennette of Argyle, NY | Argyle, NY |
| | |
| **BEATTIE** John of Salem, NY | June 14, 1854 |
| **AUSTIN** Lydia of Salem, NY | Salem, NY |
| | |
| **FERGUSON** William of Sharron, Vt. | July 5, 1854 |
| **LYMAN** Jane E. of Shushan, NY | Bennington, Vt. |
| | |
| **WARREN** Joseph R. of Ludlow, Vt. | July 4, 1854 |
| **SPAULDING** Harriet A. of Salem, NY | Salem, NY |
| | |
| **ADAMS** William of White Creek, NY | July 5, 1854 |
| **SMITH** Kate A. of Jackson, NY | Jackson, NY |
| | |
| **POTTER** Benjamin of Jackson, NY | July 26, 1854 |
| **WING** Juliaette of White Creek, NY | White Creek, NY |
| | |
| **GRAY** David of Camden Valley, NY | August 2, 1854 |
| **LAMBERT** Rebecca of Salem, NY | Salem, NY |
| | |
| **HARRIS** Charles of Ft. Miller, NY | August 16, 1854 |
| **WAIT** Elvina of Troy, NY | Troy, NY |
| | |
| **GRAY** Henry C. of N. White Creek, NY (newspaper date) | September 19, 1854 |
| **WILLARD** M. Clara dau of Levi of Keene, NH | Lynn, Mass. |
| | |
| **REED** Villeroy D. of Lansingburgh, NY | October 18, 1854 |
| **UNDERWOOD** Jennie M. dau of Joseph | Lansingburgh, NY |
| | |
| **WELLS** James S. of Cambridge, NY | October 7, 1854 |
| **HANKS** Aurelia of Cambridge, NY | |
| | |
| **DOUGLAS** Dr. Horace of Cambridge, NY | November 2, 1854 |
| **WELLS** Mrs. Mary J. of Cambridge, NY | |
| | |
| **DAVIS** Oscar F. of Whitehall, NY | November 22, 1854 |
| **ROWE** Charlotte F. dau of late Rufus of Whitehall, NY | Whitehall, NY |
| | |
| **BULL** M. V. of Hebron, NY | November 14, 1854 |
| **STOWELL** Hannah Jane dau of Horace of Whitehall, NY | Whitehall, NY |
| | |
| **KELLY** Joseph of Salem, NY | November 27, 1854 |
| **CARUTHERS** Elizabeth of Salem, NY | Salem, NY |
| | |
| **AUSTIN** Lewis of Salem, NY | January 10, 1855 |
| **BILLINGS** Ellen E. of Salem, NY | Salem, NY |

| | |
|---|---|
| **HASTINGS** G. F. of New York City | January 15, 1855 |
| **CARPENTER** Mrs. Prudence of Troy, NY | Troy, NY |
| | |
| **FERGUSON** John F. of Salem, NY | January 17, 1855 |
| **ROSS** Eliza Jane of Salem, NY | Jackson, NY |
| | |
| **HOWE** Henry G. of N. White Creek, NY | January 17, 1855 |
| **COOK** Helen M. dau of Dr. O. Cook of White Creek, NY | White Creek, NY |
| | |
| **FRENCH** Orrin | January 17, 1855 |
| **RANDALL** Betsey | Shushan, NY |
| | |
| **BILLINGS** Christopher of Salem, NY | February 12, 1855 |
| **AUSTIN** Sally of Salem, NY | Salem, NY |
| | |
| **BROWNELI** Smith of Pittstown, NY | February 14, 1855 |
| **SMART** Isabella of Salem, NY | Salem, NY |
| | |
| **ASHTON** Michael of Salem, NY | January 31, 1855 |
| **MC NAB** Jennie of Greenwich, NY | Greenwich, NY |
| | |
| **WOODWORTH** George of Shushan, NY | February 14, 1855 |
| **CURTIS** Mary of E. Greenwich, NY | E. Greenwich, NY |
| | |
| **MC NITT** Asa of Salem, NY (newspaper date) | March 27, 1855 |
| **SHERMAN** Maria M. of Rupert, Vt. | Rupert, Vt. |
| | |
| **MAWHINNEY** Alexander of Rupert, Vt. | March 14, 1855 |
| **TOWSLEY** Laura of Rupert, Vt. | Rupert, Vt. |
| | |
| **WILLIAMS** Melancton B. of Brooklyn, NY | March 22, 1855 |
| **BINNINGER** Nancy of Camden Valley, NY | Camden Valley, NY |
| | |
| **WILLIAMS** William of Salem, NY | March 28, 1855 |
| **FINCH** Esther A. of Pawlet, Vt. | Pawlet, Vt. |
| | |
| **OVIATT** Clark of Salem, NY | March 15, 1855 |
| **LAMB** Amanda F. of Penfield, NY | |
| | |
| **CRAIG** James F. of Hebron, NY | March 28, 1855 |
| **STEWART** Lydia of Greenwich, NY | Greenwich, NY |
| | |
| **WESTON** T. R. of Salem, NY | April 12, 1855 |
| **ATWOOD** Jane Ann of Salem, NY | Salem, NY |
| | |
| **SIMPSON** William of England | March 4, 1855 |
| **MC CLENATHAN** Chloe of W. Rupert, Vt. | W. Rupert, Vt. |
| | |
| **WELLS** Henry of Salem, NY | April 7, 1855 |

PARKS Adeline of Jackson, NY

Ft. Edward, NY

MC INDUE Joseph of Salem, NY
BEATY Jane of Salem, NY

April 19, 1855
Troy, NY

SMART John of Salem, NY
FAIRLEY Susannah of Salem, NY

May 7, 1855
Salem, NY

BREWER Leroy of Easton, NY
SMITH Menemah of Easton, NY

May 9, 1855
Greenwich, NY

FITCH Charles L. of Salem, NY
CLAGHORN Cynthia E. of Salem, NY

June 11, 1855
Salem, NY

WEAVER Junius B. of Schuyler Falls, NY
HARDY Alice A. of Schuyler Falls, NY

July 5, 1855
Salem, NY

LARKIN H. H. of Salem, NY
WHITCOMB Melissa of Salem, NY

July 23, 1855
Salem, NY

PRINDLE John S. of Salem, NY
THOMPSON Jane H. of Salem, NY

August 31, 1855
Salem, NY

MC FARLAND Rev. A. of Brookville, Ind.
MOREY Jennie A. of Cambridge, NY

September 20, 1855
Cambridge, NY

PARRY John of Ft. Edward, NY
STILES H. E. dau of Ransom of Argyle, NY

October 3, 1855
Argyle, NY

DICKSON William G. of Savannah, Ga.
WILSON Sarah dau of Nathan W. of Salem, NY

October 11, 1855
Salem, NY

SHIPLEY S. B. of New York City
KILMER Mary H. of Clifton Park, NY

September 22, 1855
Clifton Park, NY

CULVER James S. of E. Greenwich, NY
HASTINGS Elsia Maria of Salem, NY

October 30, 1855
Salem, NY

HOLSTON V. Y. o Quincey, Ill.
TAYLOR Lottie M. dau of William of Cambridge, NY

November 8, 1855
Cambridge, NY

STEARNS William of Sandgate, Vt.
FLOWERS Mary of Algiers

October 25, 1855

ADAMS James of Milan, Ohio
WRIGHT Sophronia J. of Jackson, NY

December 12, 1855
Jackson, NY

WAIT A. D.
DARROW Celina dau of Hiram of Cambridge, NY

December 11, 1855
Cambridge, NY

CRANDALL Simeon of Cambridge, NY     December 5, 1855
WHITE Elizabeth of Warrensburgh, NY     Warrensburgh, NY

GLOVER Charles B.     December 6, 1855
PATTERSON M. E., formerly of Union Village, NY     Charleston, SC

CLARK Jed P. Jr. formerly of Salem, NY     December 12, 1855
FISH Sarah of Sheldon, Vt.     Sheldon, Vt.

ALLEN Henry of Ludlow, Vt.     November 14, 1855
FOSTER Alida M. of Shushan, NY     Shushan, NY

BARTLETT Joel of Shushan, NY     November 14, 1855
CORSE Mary E. dau of William of Shushan, NY     Shushan, NY

PIKE Norman of Ft. Edward, NY     December 20, 1855
CLARK Phebe of Hebron, NY     Ft. Edward, NY

## Salem Weekly Review
### December 8, 1877-December 30, 1879

MC HUGH Edward T. of Salem, NY     November 29, 1877
BURNS Mary of Cambridge, NY     Cambridge, NY

BEATTIE John J. of Salem, NY     December 19, 1877
TOWNSEND Eva of Salem, NY     Salem, NY

SCRIBNER Chipman of Somerville, Mass.     December 24, 1877
MC WHORTER M. H. dau of G. A. SAFFORD of Salem     Boston, Mass.

BALDWIN Hiram of Jackson, NY     January 7, 1878
BAKER Lucy of Jackson, NY     Cambridge, NY

COON Edwin F. of Lake, NY     January 15, 1878
TOWSLEY Florence C. of Dorset, Vt.     Granville, NY

HARWOOD James of Washington, Iowa     January 23, 1878
FISHER Elizabeth of Greenwich, NY     Greenwich, NY

COPELAND James     January 16, 1878
MC DOUGAL Mary Frances     N. Argyle, NY

BURTON Willard E.     January 17, 1878
PARKERSON Ida E.     N. Argyle, NY

SHAW Robert of Salem, NY     January 22, 1878
STEWART Sarah M. of S. Argyle, NY     S. Argyle, NY

| | | |
|---|---|---|
| FOSTER Frank R. of Greenwich, NY | | January 24, 1878 |
| RALSTON Mary A. of Greenwich, NY | | Salem, NY |
| | | |
| MARTIN Robert of Hebron, NY | (newspaper date) | February 2, 1878 |
| CAREY Susan of New York City | | Cambridge, NY |
| | | |
| HALL Austin J. of Poulteney, Vt. | | January 19, 1878 |
| ORCUTT Nellie of Hartford, NY | | Granville, NY |
| | | |
| POTTER William H. of Granville, NY | | January 23, 1878 |
| PERRY Helen E. of Granville, NY | | Granville, NY |
| | | |
| HEDGES James F. of Jackson, NY | | February 5, 1878 |
| WRIGHT Helen M. of E. Salem, NY | | |
| | | |
| FARRELLY Owen of Salem, NY | | February 13, 1878 |
| SULLIVAN Maggie of Salem, NY | | Salem, NY |
| | | |
| DOOLEY Michael | | January 8, 1878 |
| MC CABE Margaret | | Grenwich, NY |
| | | |
| LANNARD Patrick | (newspaper date) | February 16, 1878 |
| GRINNAN Mary | | White Creek, NY |
| | | |
| MULLIGAN James | | February 5, 1878 |
| O'DONNELL Mary | | Cambridge, NY |
| | | |
| TRACY Timothy | | February 11, 1878 |
| MILLETT Mary | | Cambridge, NY |
| | | |
| MC GARTH John | | February 13, 1878 |
| MURRAY Ellen | | Cambridge, NY |
| | | |
| ROGERS Myron of Greenwich, NY | | February 7, 1878 |
| EDIE Delia of Greenwich, NY | | N. Greenwich, NY |
| | | |
| MC DONNELL Patrick of Cambridge, NY | | February 19, 1878 |
| KEARNS Mary of Boston, Mass. | | Boston, Mass. |
| | | |
| DAVIS William Jr. of Cambridge, NY | | February 19, 1878 |
| SHAW Phebe of Cambridge, NY | | S. Hartford, NY |
| | | |
| ALLEN Nelson R. of Greenwich, NY | | February 2, 1878 |
| DANTZ Flora E. of Greenwich, NY | | Glens Falls, NY |
| | | |
| PETTEYS Frederick of Cambridge, NY | | February 25, 1878 |
| MC CUE Maggie of Easton, NY | | Cambridge, NY |
| | | |
| JOHNSTON John W. | | March 13, 1878 |
| BEATTIE Nettie dau of Robert | | |

STEELE Donald T.
BROWN Georgia B. dau of Rev. Hugh Brown

March 13, 1878
Shushan, NY

PRIEST Josiah
SNYDER Mary J.

March 7, 1878
Shushan, NY

BRAINARD Mr. of E. Salem, NY
CAREY Miss of E. Salem, NY

March 8, 1878
Shushan, NY

STEWART W. Herbert
HAY Maggie S.

March 20, 1878
Lakeville, NY

ROGERS Frank of Hebron, NY
CROSIER Ella of Hebron, NY

March 18, 1878
Hebron, NY

RACE Marvin E. of Granville, NY
MARTIN Amelia H. dau of Robert

April 10, 1878

MC INTYRE Henry of Hoosick Falls, NY
WARREN Mary E. of Buskirks Bridge, NY

April 23, 1878
Pittstown, NY

WRIGHT George of Greenwich, NY
HAY Elizabeth of Greenwich, NY

May 9, 1878
Salem, NY

YOULEN David O. of Salem, NY
DELAMANO Alice of Schenectady, NY

May 1, 1878
Schenectady, NY

GREEN Sanford
WILCOX Mrs. Mary A. formerly of Greenwich, NY

May 1, 1878
Fox Lake, Wis.

THURBER Volentine W. of Cambridge, NY (newspaper date) May 18, 1878
AKIN Helen L. of Cambridge, NY

Cambridge, NY

THOMPSON O. F.
AMIDON Sarah A.

May 18, 1878
Granville, NY

AXTELL Emery of Winhall, Vt.          (newspaper date)
STILES Edith of Winhall, Vt.

May 25, 1878
W. Hebron, NY

CAPRON S. S. of Albany, NY          (newspaper date)
HIGGINS Addie Frances of Rutland, Vt.

May 25, 1878
W. Pawlet, Vt.

MURPHY John
COX Ellen

May 28, 1878

WATERS Frank J. of Rupert, Vt.
WOODARD Hattie A. of Rupert, Vt.

May 24, 1878
W. Rupert, Vt.

QUA Charles H. of Cambridge, NY

May 29, 1878

| | |
|---|---|
| **HORTON** Ruth M. of Cambridge, NY | Cambridge, NY |
| **ROBINSON** John A. of Hebron, NY<br>**HALL** Sarah M. formerly of Argyle, NY | June 4, 1878<br>Havana, NY |
| **GOULDER** W. A.<br>**MC CULLOUGH** Ann J. | May 23, 1878<br>Salem, NY |
| **BANNISTER** Allen W. of Brattleboro, Vt.<br>**RUSSELL** Fannie | June 9, 1878<br>Hoosick Falls, NY |
| **LACKEY** C. H. of Hebron, NY      (newspaper date)<br>**SPRAGUE** Susan of Wallingford, Vt. | June 15, 1878<br>Cambridge, NY |
| **MORGAN** Simon L.<br>**WILBUR** Hannah E. | June 19, 1878<br>Jackson, NY |
| **HORTON** David of Richfield Springs, NY<br>**HORTON** Mrs. Harriet of Cambridge, NY | June 19, 1878<br>Cambridge, NY |
| **WOOD** Lyman B. of Eagle Bridge, NY<br>**ATWOOD** Alice J. of Hoosick Falls, NY | June 20, 1878<br>Cambridge, NY |
| **SUTHERLAND** O. K. of Shushan, NY<br>**GRAHAM** Emma of Salem, NY | June 20, 1878<br>Bondville, Vt. |
| **HEWITT** H. M.<br>**BARNARD** Mary A. dau of J. H. of Greenwich, NY | June 6, 1878<br>Fox Lake, Wis. |
| **SEARLES** Myron of Pawlet, Vt.<br>**LA POINTE** Sarah of Pawlet, Vt. | July 2, 1878<br>Salem, NY |
| **ELY** Alfred<br>**KENYON** Sylvia | June 26, 1878<br>Hebron, NY |
| **MARSH** Oscar of Eagle Bridge, NY<br>**SULLIVAN** Mary of M. Granville, NY | July 1, 1878<br>N. Granville, NY |
| **BARRINGER** Henry C. of Middle Falls, NY<br>**MOSHER** Amelia of Greenwich, NY | July 2, 1878<br>Greenwich, NY |
| **GORHAM** Henry of Poultney, Vt.<br>**CRITTENDEN** Mary E. of Poultney, Vt. | August 3, 1878<br>W. Rupert, Vt. |
| **POWELL** William of Ft. Edward, NY<br>**SEELEY** Elizabeth of Belcher, NY | July 29, 1878<br>Belcher, NY |
| **MC EACHRON** Robert of Grand Junction, Iowa<br>**MADISON** Maggie dau of J. H. | August 8, 1878<br>W. Hebron, NY |

PILLING Robert of Greenwich, NY
SPAINE Maggie A. of Greenwich, NY

August 11, 1878
Salem, NY

MC CLELLAN George R. of Shushan, NY
ROBERTSON Sarah M. of Cambridge, NY

August 21, 1878
Greenwich, NY

CURTIS Benjamin of E. Greenwich, NY
LEWIS Hannah of Salem, NY

September 3, 1878

POTTER James S. of Argyle, NY
TEMPLE Lottie E. of Granville, NY

September 3, 1878
Granville, NY

LANGDON Nathan S. of Greenwich, NY
CARTER Etta F. dau of C. B. of Jackson, NY

September 4, 1878
Jackson, NY

ERWIN Dr. S. B. of W. Hebron, NY
MC EACHRON Cassie L. of Argyle, NY

September 3, 1878
Argyle, NY

COLE George of Arlington, Vt.
WHITE Sabra of White Creek, NY

August 29, 1878
White Creek, NY

SHERMAN Daniel son of Jesse S. of Salem, NY
BRAYMER Nettie dau of Jacob of Hebron, NY

August 29, 1878
Minnesota

ODBERT George E. of Salem, NY
ROBERTS Ann dau of Dexter of Manchester, Vt.

September 5, 1878
Manchester, Vt.

AINSLEE Rev. George of Argyle, NY
SHANNON Mary Mc Lean of Argyle, NY

September 12, 1878
Argyle, NY

GILCHRIST Theodore
WARD Mattie of Granville, NY

September 5, 1878
Granville, NY

OATMAN Isaac Jr. of Hebron, NY
WILSON Hattie of Hebron, NY

September 17, 1878
Hebron, NY

DONGAN Mathew of Hebron, NY
LONG Mrs. Eliza of S. Granville, NY

September 19, 1878
S. Granville, NY

SHEPHERD Levi R. of N. Dorset, Vt.
THOMPSON Anna M. of N. Dorset, Vt.

September 19, 1878
Salem, NY

LINDSAY William John
HILL Josie

September 18, 1878
E. Greenwich, NY

TALLMADGE George H. of Greenwich, NY
WILLARD Ella of Greenwich, NY

September 22, 1878
Saratoga, NY

HENRY Walter V. V. of Eagle Bridge, NY

October 3, 1878

**LARMON** Ruth E. of Salem, NY

| | |
|---|---|
| **INGALLS** David of Troy, NY, formerly of Salem, NY | September 24, 1878 |
| **VASEY** Helena V. dau of Edward | Richmond, Canada |
| | |
| **CONKEY** John F. of E. Salem, NY | October 1, 1878 |
| **MARSH** Lucy A. of W. Arlington, Vt. | Cambridge, NY |
| | |
| **FULLERTON** William H. of Manchester, Vt. | October 8, 1878 |
| **FULLERTON** Kate A. of Argyle, NY | Argyle, NY |
| | |
| **CLEVELAND** Herbert | October 23, 1878 |
| **CHAMBERLAIN** Mary | Salem, NY |
| | |
| **POTTER** Horace of Greenwich, NY | October 7, 1878 |
| **TEFFT** Mrs. Esther E. of Greenwich, NY | Schuylerville, NY |
| | |
| **GETTY** Andrew of Salem, NY | October 30, 1878 |
| **CARRIER** Anna C. dau of Levi of Phoenix, NY | Phoenix, NY |
| | |
| **HENRY** Ralph of N. Adams, Mass. | November 4, 1878 |
| **JOHNSON** Mary D. sister of Moses of Salem, NY | Brattleboro, Vt. |
| | |
| **PALMER** Robert C. of Pawlet, Vt. | October 29, 1878 |
| **CLAY** Mary E. of Tinmouth, Vt. | Granville, NY |
| | |
| **HOLCOMB** I. H. of N. Creek, NY | October 29, 1878 |
| **GERMAN** Mary M. of Greenwich, NY | Cambridge, NY |
| | |
| **HOLLISTER** Horatio of Pawlet, Vt. | November 6, 1878 |
| **SCOTT** Mrs. Clarissa of Hebron, NY | Hartford, NY |
| | |
| **MC DOWELL** Robert Ewens of Rutland Vt. | November 18, 1878 |
| **COMEGYS** Mrs. Isabella of Salem, NY | Salem, NY |
| | |
| **BAIN** James P. | November 13, 1878 |
| **DONALDSON** Maggie | Argyle, NY |
| | |
| **MC WHORTER** James formerly of Hebron, NY | November 20, 1878 |
| **BRADY** Mary E. formerly of Hebron, NY | Plattmouth, Neb. |
| | |
| **FULLER** George E. of Amherst, Mass. (newspaper date) | December 7, 1878 |
| **WALSH** Jennie of Cambridge, NY | Cambridge, NY |
| | |
| **STETSON** Ralph of Ashfield, Mass. | November 27, 1878 |
| **BRONSON** Lucy M. of Ashfield, Mass. | Shushan, NY |
| | |
| **MC ARTHUR** John R. of Jackson, NY | December 11, 1878 |
| **TELFORD** Sarah of Jackson, NY | |

ALLEN Charles of Hartford, NY  
MURRAY Maggie of Hartford, NY  
December 18, 1878  
Salem, NY

JONES Robert T. of Salem, NY  
JONES Janie of Salem, NY  
December 14, 1878  
Salem, NY

LOOMIS George B.        (newspaper date)  
MARKS Ida dau of Ira  
December 21, 1878  
Pawlet, Vt.

WAUGH Rev. A. D. of Plattsburgh, NY  
AGAN Mary B.  
December 17, 1878  
Granville, NY

PERRY David of Pawlet, Vt.  
WILLIAMS Ellen  
December 25, 1878  
Salem, NY

PERKINS Joseph of Rupert, Vt.  
SHERMAN Julia  
December 25, 1878  
Hebron, NY

FAIRBANKS Edward of Sandgate, Vt.  
RAYBROOKS Nellie of Sandgate, Vt.  
December 19, 1878  
Shushan, NY

WALLACE Thomas N. of Greenwich, NY  
HUTCHINS Mary E. of Greenwich, NY  
December 24, 1878  
Greenwich, NY

SHANNON George B. of Salem, NY  
HOPKINS Libbie of Rupert, Vt.  
January 1, 1879  
Rupert, Vt.

AMIDON A. S. of Hebron, NY  
TAYLOR Emily E. of E. Dorset, Vt.  
January 1, 1879  
Hebron, NY

KEGLER Fred T. of New York City  
OATLEY Hattie M. formerly of Salem, NY  
December 27, 1878  
Greenwich, NY

SHIELDS Thomas  
MOLLMAN Clara  
December 2, 1878  
Salem, NY

CRAMER Patrick  
WILSON Mrs. Rebecca  
December 29, 1878  
Salem, NY

FAIRLEY George A. of Argyle, NY  
SAFFORD Libbie A. of Salem, NY  
January 1, 1879  
Salem, NY

HARWOOD H. G. of Dorset, Vt.  
FARWELL Mary A. of Dorset, Vt.  
December 26, 1878  
Dorset, Vt.

HILL H. D. W. C. of Whitehall, NY  
WHEELER Mrs. A. J. of Sudbury, Vt.  
December 23, 1878  
Sandy Hill, NY

ROBERTS Brooks W. of Rupert, Vt.  
January 7, 1879

| | |
|---|---|
| WESTCOTT Alice R. of Fairhaven, Vt. | Fairhaven, Vt. |
| CURTIS James H. of N. Greenwich, NY<br>WIGGINS Mrs. Ziphora R. | January 1, 1879<br>E. Greenwich, NY |
| CHASE Chester of Salem, NY<br>ORCUTT Henrietta of Jackson, NY | January 6, 1879<br>Saratoga, NY |
| LEWIS Barden O. of Wells, Vt.<br>COOK Louisa of Rupert, Vt. | January 1, 1879<br>Rupert, Vt. |
| KENNEDY James of W. Pawlet, Vt.<br>DOOLEY Lizzie of Granville, NY | January 1, 1879<br>M. Granville, NY |
| CUTHBERT Alexander of Argyle, NY<br>MC DOUGAL Annie of Argyle, NY | January 1, 1879<br>N. Argyle, NY |
| SIMONDS Warren of Pawlet, Vt.<br>WINSLOW Ida of Cambridge, NY | January 9, 1879<br>Cambridge, NY |
| WILLIAMSON Varnum of Greenwich, NY<br>MC MULLEN Hattie of Easton, NY | January 1, 1879<br>Easton, NY |
| ALDRICH Herbert of Bennington, Vt.<br>SQUARES Nellie of Woodford, Vt. | December 24, 1878<br>White Creek, NY |
| LEWIS Thomas of E. Greenwich, NY<br>CARTER Lizzie of Salem, NY | January 20, 1879<br>E. Greenwich, NY |
| BURT Kneeland A. of Greenwich, NY<br>PORTER Nellie M. of Middle Falls, NY | January 5, 1879<br>Schuylerville, NY |
| FOWLER Deerling V. of Cambridge, NY<br>GREEN Sarah M. of Jackson, NY | January 8, 1879<br>Cambridge, NY |
| WATROUS Eddie H. of Pawlet, Vt.<br>MOORE Nellie of Pawlet, Vt. | January 16, 1879<br>Pawlet, Vt. |
| POTTER John of Granville, NY<br>DENNISON Alida of Granville, NY | January 22, 1879<br>Granville, NY |
| WARD Walter of N. Granville, NY<br>HERRICK Mary E. of Poultney, Vt. | January 20, 1879<br>Granville, NY |
| SAFFORD Gideon Leroy of Greenwich, NY<br>ROBINSON Mary E. of Argyle, NY | January 15, 1879<br>N. Argyle, NY |
| IRWIN James of S. Argyle, NY<br>TINKEY Sarah A. of S. Argyle, NY | December 25, 1878<br>S. Argyle, NY |

| | | |
|---|---|---|
| **FAIRLEY** Hugh E. of Hebron, NY | | January 22, 1879 |
| **LEE** Mrs. Betsey of Hebron, NY | | Hebron, NY |
| | | |
| **GUTHRIE** Lester of Hebron, NY | | January 22, 1879 |
| **CROSIER** Maggie of Hebron, NY | | Hebron, NY |
| | | |
| **COLE** John E. of Pittsford, Vt. | | January 27, 1879 |
| **ROGERS** Leify A. of Pittsford, Vt. | | Hampton, NY |
| | | |
| **WOODARD** D. D. of Granville, NY | (newspaper date) | February 8, 1879 |
| **WESCOTT** Lillie of Saratoga, NY | | Saratoga Springs, NY |
| | | |
| **REID** William of Belcher, NY | | February 5, 1879 |
| **RUSSELL** Mary C. of Belcher, NY | | Belcher, NY |
| | | |
| **CLARK** Alvah W. of Salem, NY | | February 4, 1879 |
| **SMITH** Julia E. of Jackson, NY | | Shushan, NY |
| | | |
| **ROBERTSON** Clifford P. of Cambridge, NY | | February 4, 1879 |
| **LARKIN** Hattie of E. Greenwich, NY | | Shushan, NY |
| | | |
| **HAY** Chauncey of W. Hebron, NY | | January 29, 1879 |
| **BULLOCK** S. E. of Lake, NY | | Lake, NY |
| | | |
| **CARL** Patrick | | February 21, 1879 |
| **TRUMBULL** Maggie | | Salem, NY |
| | | |
| **CLEVELAND** Henry of Shushan, NY | | February 25, 1879 |
| **BILLINGS** Mary dau of Samuel of Salem, NY | | Salem, NY |
| | | |
| **VANCE** William of Jackson, NY | | February 19, 1879 |
| **LEE** Mrs. Esther of Cambridge, NY | | Greenwich, NY |
| | | |
| **BARBER** Nelson H. of Shaftsbury, Vt. | | February 24, 1879 |
| **STOVER** Emma Josephine of Cambridge, NY | | Cambridge, NY |
| | | |
| **NELSON** Austin J. of Hebron, NY | | February 26, 1879 |
| **ROGERS** Mary J. of Hebron, NY | | Cambridge, NY |
| | | |
| **SHANNON** Charles of Argyle, NY | | February 18, 1879 |
| **HALL** Ella of Argyle, NY | | Argyle, NY |
| | | |
| **COLLINS** Michael of Salem, NY | | February 25, 1879 |
| **MULLEN** Catherine of Salem, NY | | Hebron, NY |
| | | |
| **HAYES** William R. of Cambridge, NY | | March 14, 1879 |
| **SWEET** Mary D. of Bennington, Vt. | | White Creek, NY |
| | | |
| **HALL** Austin of Cambridge, NY | | March 18, 1879 |

| | |
|---|---|
| **GEDDES** Lizzie E. of Cambridge, NY | Cambridge, NY |
| | |
| **COLE** Charles of Somonauk, Ill. | March 20, 1879 |
| **BEVERIDGE** Maggie of Hebron, NY | Hebron, NY |
| | |
| **GREEN** Henry of Cambridge, NY | March 26, 1879 |
| **RIDER** Sarah E. of Cambridge, NY | Cambridge, NY |
| | |
| **JONES** William of Pawlet, Vt. | March 22, 1879 |
| **SMITH** Alemeda of Granville, NY | Poultney, Vt. |
| | |
| **ORCUTT** Charles A. D. of Shushan, NY | March 11, 1879 |
| **BREWER** Caroline J. of Shushan, NY | Shushan, NY |
| | |
| **HASTINGS** Edward F. of Jackson, NY | April 8, 1879 |
| **WILSON** Jennie L. of Shushan, NY | Greenwich, NY |
| | |
| **CAREY** Dennis E. of Shaftsbury, Vt. | April 8, 1879 |
| **EDIE** Sarah M. of Shushan, NY | Greenwich, NY |
| | |
| **FERGUSON** James M. of Argyle, NY | April 2, 1879 |
| **MACKLIN** Mattie of Argyle, NY | W. Hebron, NY |
| | |
| **CARSWELL** Benjamin | April 9, 1879 |
| **MC DOUGAL** Julia dau of David H. | Argyle, NY |
| | |
| **BARNETT** Volney R. of Salem, NY | April 17, 1879 |
| **CLARK** Mary dau of Charles H. of Salem, NY | N. Bennington, Vt. |
| | |
| **QUA** Henry A. of Cambridge, NY | April 16, 1879 |
| **KING** Alma of Coila, NY | Coila, NY |
| | |
| **SWAIN** Sheldon O. of Waukesha Co. Wis. | April 13, 1879 |
| **GOULD** Katie S. formerly of Washington Co. NY | Blooming Prairie, Mn. |
| | |
| **BEATTIE** Charles E. of Salem, NY | April 26, 1879 |
| **FLOWERS** Emma of W. Rupert, Vt. | E. Greenwich, NY |
| | |
| **EDDY** Samuel M. formerly of Greenwich, NY | April 23, 1879 |
| **DOWNER** Inez L. of Auburn, NY | Auburn, NY |
| | |
| **FLYNN** John of Cambridge, NY | May 8, 1879 |
| **COLTON** Margaret of Salem, NY | Salem, NY |
| | |
| **HILL** Thomas E. of Chicago, Ill. | May 10, 1879 |
| **WHITCOMB** Mrs. Ella M. | Shushan, NY |
| | |
| **LINSENBARTH** F. E. | May 29, 1879 |
| **LAKIN** Maggie G. dau of W. H. of Salem, NY | Salem, NY |

| | |
|---|---|
| **ROBERTSON** Charles S. of Cambridge, NY | April 28, 1879 |
| **MESSER** Lorraine C. of Troy, NY | Cambridge, NY |
| | |
| **MOORE** Rev. W. W. of Shushan, NY | May 25, 1879 |
| **JENKINS** Josephine of Shushan, NY | Shushan, NY |
| | |
| **MARCELLUS** W. H. of Schenectady, NY | June 5, 1879 |
| **SNOWDEN** Lillie of Salem, NY | Salem, NY |
| | |
| **GUTHRIE** John of Hebron, NY | June 3, 1879 |
| **BLACK** Sarah of Hebron, NY | W. Hebron, NY |
| | |
| **MOSHER** F. D. of Eagle Bridge, NY | May 23, 1879 |
| **SISSON** Frankie L. of Eagle Bridge, NY | Hoosick, NY |
| | |
| **HOLLISTER** George of N. Granville, NY | June 8, 1879 |
| **WALLACE** Emma of Hebron, NY | Hebron, NY |
| | |
| **OLMSTEAD** Rev. I. G. of Moreau, NY | June 11, 1879 |
| **CHASE** Fannie dau of Samuel of Easton, NY | Easton, NY |
| | |
| **PIKE** Charles B. | June 17, 1879 |
| **BRISTOL** Mary Elizabeth of Whitehall, NY | Whitehall, NY |
| | |
| **SMITH** Edgar A. of Greenwich, NY | June 23, 1879 |
| **DE WITT** Lizzie E. of Augusta, Maine | Salem, NY |
| | |
| **ANDREWS** Morgan H. of Pawlet, Vt. | June 28, 1879 |
| **WATERS** Fannie J. of Pawlet, Vt. | Granville, NY |
| | |
| **DANFORTH** Fred A. of E. Salem, NY | March 3, 1879 |
| **DODD** Hattie of E. Salem, NY | Cambridge, NY |
| | |
| **HATCH** Mr. of Hebron, NY | July 16, 1879 |
| **HANNIBAL** Mary E. of Hebron, NY | Hebron, NY |
| | |
| **COPELAND** Oliver J. | July 19, 1879 |
| **HILL** Emma | Salem, NY |
| | |
| **HALE** Dr. F. E. of Shushan, NY | August 6, 1879 |
| **RICE** Ida M. dau of N. E. of Cambridge, NY | Cambridge, NY |
| | |
| **PLOTKE** Lewis of Salem, NY | August 5, 1879 |
| **ROBINSON** Betsey of Troy, NY | Troy, NY |
| | |
| **BEATTIE** Rev. Wesley of Kingsbury, NY | August 26, 1879 |
| **BURT** Libbie of Ticonderoga, NY | Ticonderoga, NY |
| | |
| **FRENCH** Levi B. of Yankton, Dakota | August 20, 1879 |

WELLS Jeannette L. dau of Franklin of Constantine, Mi.          Constantine, Mi.

TRUMBULL Henry of Hoosick Falls, NY          August 16, 1879
FROST Mrs. Carrie of Hoosick Falls, NY          Salem, NY

HANNA Joseph of Argyle, NY          September 2, 1879
ALLEN Lydia of Argyle, NY          Salem, NY

ALLEN William of Salem, NY          August 15, 1879
ALLEN Jane of Salem, NY          W. Hebron, NY

ELLIS Wilbur J. of Poultney, Vt.          August 26, 1879
MATTISON Florence of Poultney, Vt.

TREVETT Rev. J. B. of Cambridge, NY          September 9, 1879
PARSONS Mrs. Hattie S. dau of Mrs. Phebe SEARING          Dover, NJ

WATSON Nelson of N. Hebron, NY          September 10, 1879
MC MILLAN Maggie J. of Salem, NY          Ft. Edward, NY

RYAN John T. of Salem, NY          September 24, 1879
YOUNG Estella E. of Salem, NY          Salem, NY

WELLS Thomas of Salem, NY          September 23, 1879
FLYNN Rosa of Salem, NY          Salem, NY

BUCK James Henry of Arlington, Vt.          September 24, 1879
TURNER Ella M. of Sandgate, Vt.

EDIE George H. of Buskirks Bridge, NY          September 18, 1879
WOODWORTH Anna M. of Greenwich, NY          Greenwich, NY

BAILLIE Thomas E. of Troy, NY          October 1, 1879
ALEXANDER Lizzie A. of Jackson, NY

DONAHUE Robert of Greenwich, NY          September 28, 1879
RANDALL Sarah E. of Greenwich, NY          Salem, NY

MC CLELLAN Andrew of Hebron, NY   (newspaper date)          October 11, 1879
GREGORY Alice of Ft. Edward, NY

MILLIMAN Jarvis W. of Ft. Edward, NY          September 30, 1879
ANDREWS Libbie of Ft. Edward, NY          Ft. Edward, NY

LILLIE Thomas A. of Whitehall, NY          October 1, 1879
BROUGHTON Florence of Whitehall, NY          Whitehall, NY

GRAY Levi H. formerly of Salem, NY          October 16, 1879
WHEELER Elizabeth of Troy, NY          Troy, NY

| | |
|---|---|
| LEE Walter of Salem, NY | October 8, 1879 |
| FAIRLEY Bell of Salem, NY | E. Greenwich, NY |
| | |
| WENDELL John of Schenectady, NY | October 15, 1879 |
| BROWNELL Anna H. of Shushan, NY | Shushan, NY |
| | |
| RYAN Michael of Salem, NY | October, 19, 1879 |
| RYAN Nellie of Salem, NY | Salem, NY |
| | |
| MC CLELLAN Joseph P. of Jackson, NY | October 4, 1879 |
| HAY Sarah M. of Coila, NY | Schuylerville, NY |
| | |
| CAMPBELL John A. of Washington DC | October 30, 1879 |
| CLEVELAND Fannie of Shushan, NY | Shushan, NY |
| | |
| FLOWERS Gardner H. | November 6, 1879 |
| HATCH Emma L. dau of John | Salem, NY |
| | |
| HATCH Albert | November 6, 1879 |
| BOYD Jennie dau of Thomas | Salem, NY |
| | |
| DONNELLY John H. formerly of Salem, NY | November 12, 1879 |
| CONNOR Anna of Johnsonville, NY | Schaghticoke, NY |
| | |
| SMART Lafayette of Hebron, NY | November 12, 1879 |
| WILLIAMSON Alta of Hebron, NY | Hebron, NY |
| | |
| DODD Francis M. of E. Salem, NY | November 1, 1879 |
| ROBERTS Mary L. of E. Salem, NY | Cambridge, NY |
| | |
| MOWRY Henry L. of Greenwich, NY | November 20, 1879 |
| DOWD Jennie F. | E. Berlin, Conn. |
| | |
| SKEELS Hinman of Whitehall, NY | November 12, 1879 |
| WALLER Dora of Hartford, NY | Hartford, NY |
| | |
| GIBSON John of Belcher, NY | November 19, 1879 |
| WHITE Mary of Belcher, NY | Belcher, NY |
| | |
| TIERNEY James of Salem, NY | November 16, 1879 |
| WALL Catherine of Troy, NY | Troy, NY |
| | |
| COLVIN William of Pawlet, Vt. | December 3, 1879 |
| CHAPIN Ella of Pawlet, Vt. | Shushan, NY |
| | |
| BAIN H. C. of Lake, NY | November 6, 1879 |
| STARR Cordelia of Green Island, NY | Green Island, NY |
| | |
| CASSELS Dorastus F. of Belcher, NY | December 3, 1879 |

| | |
|---|---|
| **WILBUR** Emma A. of Greenwich, NY | Greenwich, NY |
| **RANDLES** Sylvester of Lake, NY<br>**WIGGINS** Mary of Belcher, NY | December 3, 1879<br>Belcher, NY |
| **GILMAN** John B. of Troy, NY<br>**BOWEN** Jennie of Hartford, NY | December 9, 1879<br>Hartford, NY |
| **BROWN** Wilbur of Pawlet, Vt.<br>**CULVER** Addie dau of Samuel of Pawlet, Vt. | December 9, 1879<br>Pawlet, Vt. |
| **RANDALL** Ransom B. of Sandgate, Vt.<br>**HAYES** Sarah of Sandgate, Vt. | December 16, 1879<br>Cambridge, NY |
| **MANLY** Leroy of Arlington, Vt.<br>**HAYES** Maggie A. of Sandgate, Vt. | December 14, 1879<br>Cambridge, NY |
| **BROWN** Luther F. of Greenwich, NY<br>**FLOWERS** Flora A. of Salem, NY | December 15, 1879<br>Salem, NY |
| **MORRIS** Henry D.<br>**BEATTIE** Grace dau of Walter B. of Salem, NY | December 24, 1879<br>Salem, NY |
| **BAKER** Nicolas<br>**KERSLAKE** Eva dau of Thomas | December 29, 1879 |
| **PENNIMAN** William H. of Battenville, NY<br>**HILL** Ellen of Battenville, NY | December 11, 1879<br>Greenwich, NY |
| **CALHOUN** James of Lake, NY<br>**POTTER** Jennie of Middle Falls, NY | December 23, 1879<br>Middle Falls, NY |
| **PARIS** Charles R. of Sandy Hill, NY<br>**BIGGART** Alma of Sandy Hill, NY | December 23, 1879<br>Adamsville, NY |
| **BURKE** A. A. of Hebron, NY<br>**WOODARD** Mary of Hebron, NY | December 25, 1879<br>Hebron, NY |
| **ROCKWOOD** Frank of Bennington, Vt.<br>**MEARS** Sarah of Manchester, Vt. | December 24, 1879<br>Sandgate, Vt. |

## SANDY HILL HERALD
### May 12, 1829 - December 28, 1876

| | |
|---|---|
| **HERRINGTON** Seth P.<br>**NASH** Harriet | December 16, 1830<br>Sandy Hill, NY |
| **SLADE** Mason H. of Hartford, NY<br>**HOLBROOK** Lucina of Hartford, NY | December 15, 1830<br>Hartford, NY |

BULKLEY Hiram of Williamstown, Mass.          December 10, 1834
OLIPHANT Mary J. dau of R. W. of Granville, NY    N. Granville, NY

WILSON Hiram F. formerly of Troy, NY           October 8, 1839
WEEKS Elizabeth dau of Joseph of Sandy Hill, NY    Sandy Hill, NY

MC CLAUGHRY E. C. of Kortwright, NY            January 19, 1841
CLARK Mary S. of Argyle, NY                    Argyle, NY

MURPHY Rev. Jeremiah                           February 10, 1841
CONKLIN Elizabeth                              Sandy Hill, NY

VAUGHN Thomas of Whitehall, NY                 February 10, 1841
ROBERSON Jane dau of Alexander of Ft. Edward, NY

REID Archibald W. of Argyle, NY                February 11, 1841
GLEASON Laura of Milton, Saratoga Co. NY       Milton, NY

POTTER Thomas of Greenwich, NY                 March 6, 1841
MOSHER Judith S. of Sandy Hill, NY             Argyle, NY

GATES Jacob                                    March 20, 1841
PARKER Eliza Ann                               Sandy Hill, NY

HYDE Dan of Sandy Hill, NY                     April 21, 1841
FOLLETT Lucy J. of Sandy Hill, NY              Sandy Hill, NY

BROWN John A.                    (newspaper date)  May 11, 1841
BERRY Maria Louisa dau of late Simeon of Sandy Hill, NY  Sandy Hill, NY

MC COY John of Ft. Edward, NY                  May 12, 1841
SHAW Jane of Ft. Edward, NY                    Ft. Edward, NY

HITCHCOCK Preston                              May 25, 1841
MURPHY Ann late of Sandy Hill, NY              Hawley, Mass.

BARKER Porter of W. Ft. Ann, NY                August 11, 1841
MASON Helen of Sandy Hill, NY                  Sandy Hill, NY

NICHOLS George D. of W. Ft. Ann, NY            August 12, 1841
FORBES Clarissa of W. Ft. Ann, NY              W. Ft. Ann, NY

GRIMWOOD Joseph C. of Albany, NY               September 2, 1841
WING Susan A. dau of D. W. of Ft. Edward, NY   Ft. Edward, NY

PARKER I. R. of Sandy Hill, NY                 September 20, 1841
SCOFIELD Eliza Ann of Glens Falls, NY          Glens Falls, NY

JACKSON Reuben H.                              September 1, 1841

**ALVORD** Elizabeth     Edinburgh, NY

**SHERWOOD** Winfield S. of Glens Falls, NY     September 14, 1841
**WORTHINGTON** Sarah of Rome, NY     Rome, NY

**DOUBLEDAY** Danvers of Sandy Hill, NY     September 29, 1841
**STONE** Olledine dau of Charles of Kingston, NY     Kingston, NY

**SMITH** Justin A. of Whitehall, NY     October 6, 1841
**WAINWRIGHT** Eliza of Montpelier, Vt.     Montpelier, Vt.

**BOSTWICK** Samuel B. of Vermont     October 12,, 1841
**WOOD** Harriet R. dau of Col J. B.     New York City

**PRESTON** Dr. of Schuylerville, NY     October 19, 1841
**DIBBLE** Cornelia E. of Sandy Hill, NY     Sandy Hill, NY

**VIELE** Francis of Moreau, NY     October 21, 1841
**CARLTON** Betsey Maria dau of Clark of Sandy Hill, NY     Sandy Hill, NY

**PHILLIPS** Burdin     October 26, 1841
**DURKEE** Mrs. Nancy of Ft. Edward, NY     Sandy Hill, NY

**WOODWORTH** S. P. of Rome, NY     November 18, 1841
**BROWNELL** Lydia Ann of Sandy Hill, NY     Sandy Hill, NY

**HOLLAND** Park of Sandy Hill, NY     November 10, 1841
**VAUGHN** Harriet of Kingsbury, NY     Kingsbury, NY

**BALDWIN** Charles of Ft. Edward, NY     December 15, 1841
**HARRIS** Jane Maria of Queensbury, NY     Queensbury, NY

**KINGSLEY** Levi     December 19/26 1841
**BAKER** Lodema dau of E. D. of Queensbury, NY     Ft. Ann, NY

**DERBY** George F. of Sandy Hill, NY     January 25, 1844
**HOWLAND** Jane F. dau of Stephen of Galway, NY     Galway, NY

**WILSON** David of Whitehall, NY     January 25, 1844
**DIBBLE** Caroline dau of late Carmi of Sandy Hill, NY     Sandy Hill, NY

**HOLBROOK** Newell W. of Sandy Hill, NY     February 20, 1844
**MC COY** Margaret of Argyle, NY     Argyle, NY

**ESTEY** James P. of Granville, NY     May 30, 1844
**HALL** Emily dau of William of Rutland, Vt.     Rutland, Vt.

**SHERRILL** Charles H. of Sandy Hill, NY     June 18, 1844
**RICE** Eliza dau of Sylvester of Sandy Hill, NY     Sandy Hill, NY

BAKER Marcus A.                                         June 20, 1844
CHALMERS Emeline                                        Whitehall, NY

NORTHUP John H. of Troy, NY                             July 8, 1844
HOLMAN Sarah of Glens Falls, NY                         Glens Falls, NY

MILLIMAN N. B.                                          August 6, 1844
BARNEY Celina dau of Throop of Sandy Hill, NY           Sandy Hill, NY

AXTELL Alanson of Ft. Ann, NY                           September 10, 1844
HILLIBERT Aura Ann of Ft. Ann, NY                       Ft. Ann, NY

MOSS Ai of Sandy Hill, NY                               September 16, 1844
WELLMAN Laura of Sandy Hill, NY                         Glens Falls, NY

GRIFFITH Samuel R. of Sandy Hill, NY                    September 24, 1844
HARRINGTON Susan C. of Sandy Hill, NY                   Sandy Hill, NY

HARRIS Refine ot Sandy Hill, NY                         December 5, 1844
PARKER Harriet dau of Squire                            Ft. Ann, NY

BEACH Charles H. of Sandy Hill, NY                      December 25, 1844
CRONKHITE Martha of Sandy Hill, NY

HOWLAND Enos of Sandy Hill, NY                          February 6, 1845
MURPHY Susan of Sandy Hill, NY                          Sandy Hill, NY

LEMON A. R. of Whitehall, NY                            February 27, 1845
PENFIELD Harriet D. of Whitehall, NY                    Whitehall, NY

MATHEWS William H. of Sandy Hill, NY                    March 16, 1845
WEEKS Margaret dau of Joseph of Sandy Hill, NY          Sandy Hill, NY

CRONKHITE William W. of Sandy Hill, NY                  May 12, 1845
MC MASTERS Emeline of Seneca, Ontario Co. NY            Seneca, NY

BUCK Charles A. of Sandy Hill, NY                       June 3, 1845
WOODWORTH Mary Jane dau of Abel of Sandy Hill, NY       Sandy Hill, NY

HUGHES Charles of Sandy Hill, NY                        June 25, 1845
STONE Lucy A. of Kingston, NY                           Kingston, NY

FOILS John                                              September 14, 1845
WEST Sophia                                             Hartford, NY

PARISH Seth of Ft. Edward, NY                           October 2, 1845
PAYNE Ann of Ft. Edward, NY                             Ft. Edward, NY

CRONKHITE M. F. of Sandy Hill, NY                       October 16, 1845

SARGENT L. B. dau of S. B.        Sandy Hill, NY

NILES John M. of Spencertown, NY    October 15, 1845
WHITE Charlotte P. of Sandy Hill, NY   Sandy Hill, NY

FERRIS Lemuel W. of Sandy Hill, NY   October 8, 1845
WASHBURN Nancy A. of Hartford, NY   Hartford, NY

DYER Benjamin J. of Troy, NY     October 31, 1845
JUDD Aurelia of Sandy Hill, NY    Sandy Hill, NY

SMITH Abraham of Sandy Hill, NY   December 17, 1845
HARRIS Emma Ann of Queensbury, NY  Queensbury, NY

TALLMAN Benjamin Franklin of Sandy Hill, NY  January 14, 1846
KIMBLE Aliena of Sandy Hill, NY     Sandy Hill, NY

GRAVES Gaylord of E. Troy, NY    December 9, 1845
FREEMAN Keziah of Sandy Hill, NY   E. Troy, NY

EASTMAN Phillip of Ft. Ann, NY    January 25, 1846
HASKINS Catherine of Ft. Ann, NY   Sandy Hill, NY

EASTWOOD Martin Jr.       February 5, 1846
VAUGHN Mary Ann

ASHBY John B. of Sandy Hill, NY (newspaper date) December 29, 1846
MILLER Eliza J. of Minerva, NY     Minerva, NY

REYNOLDS William H. of Moreau, NY   March 25, 1847
PIALEY Emeline of Moreau, NY     Moreau, NY

LEE John T. of Troy, NY      June 2, 1847
HARDER Jane A. dau of John J. of Kinderhook, NY Kinderhook, NY

MURPHY George of Utica, NY     September 16, 1847
COLLAMER Melissa A. dau of late Doty of Sandy Hill, NY Sandy Hill, NY

HAMBLIN James T. of Jamesport, Long Island December 2, 1847
PARRY Harriet Eliza of Ft. Edward, NY

SIMMONS Amos of Sandy Hill, NY   December 8, 1847
KING Matilda dau of Jesse of Sandy Hill, NY Sandy Hill, NY

CARLTON Orville N. of Sandy Hill, NY  March 16, 1848
BROWN Fanny E. of Whitehall, NY   Whitehall, NY

DEAN George F.         March 11, 1848
WRIGHT Margaret E. dau of Maj. James Wright of Sandy Hill, NY

PASCO Edward L. of Sandy Hill, NY — April 6, 1848 — Albany, NY
SAGER Barbara Ann of Albany, NY

SHERRILL George B. of Sandy Hill, NY — May 11, 1848 — Ft. Edward, NY
BENNETT Angelina of Ft. Edward, NY

NASH Harvey B. of Sandy Hill, NY — August 31, 1848 — Luzerne, NY
HASKELL Aurelia dau of Nathaniel of Sandy Hill, NY

FOILS John of Sandy Hill, NY — September 12, 1848 — Sandy Hill, NY
GILLIS Catherine E. of Sandy Hill, NY

OWNES Hugh of Johnsburg, NY — October 8, 1848 — Sandy Hill, NY
CARL Catherine dau of Owen of Queensbury, NY

HOLLEY Benjamin of Adamsville, NY — October 25, 1848 — Sandy Hill, NY
STANTON Mrs. Sarah of Sandy Hill, NY

HOLMAN Dewitt C. of Sandy Hill, NY — November 16, 1848 — Sandy Hill, NY
SHURTLEFF Lucina of Sandy Hill, NY

BEACH James of Sandy Hill, NY — November 16, 1848 — Sandy Hill, NY
MERCHANT Catherine of Saratoga Co. NY

WING Asahel of Sandy Hill, NY — December 7, 1848 — Schuylerville, NY
HASKINS Juliette of Schuylerville, NY

WEEKS E. T. of Sandy Hill, NY — December 26, 1848 — Warrensburgh, NY
WILSON Catherine dau of Henry of Warrensburgh, NY

PARKS Henry — February 22, 1849 — Newark, NY
BLANEY Mrs. Jane formerly of Sandy Hill, NY

PRATT Benjamin P. of Troy, NY — August 30, 1849 — Ft. Edward, NY
TAYLOR Caoline W. dau of Lansing G.

KIMBALL Hollis S. of Sandy Hill, NY — October 11, 1849 — Sandy Hill, NY
FISH Mary E. of Sandy Hill, NY

HARRIS Noel of Queensbury, NY — October 21, 1849 — Adamsville, NY
GRIFFIN Cordelia of Queensbury, NY

THOMPSON James of Ft. Ann, NY — October 25, 1849 — Ft. Ann, NY
ANDREWS Betsey of Kingsbury, NY

WALLACE Laurens of Warrensburgh, NY — November 4, 1849 — Glens Falls, NY
QUINN Sarah

SARGENT H. G. of Comstocks Landing, NY — December 10, 1849

| | |
|---|---|
| **HYDE** Emma V. dau of Roswell of Sandy Hill, NY | Sandy Hill, NY |
| **HYDE** Roswell of Sandy Hill, NY<br>**DUNHAM** Mrs. Betsey dau of Rufus **CHURCH** | December 4, 1849<br>Sandy Hill, NY |
| **FLAGLER** Titus of Adamsville, NY<br>**FOX** Alida of Ballston Spa, NY | December 7, 1849<br>Adamsville, NY |
| **STRONG** Marcellus of Glens Falls, NY<br>**HOPKINS** Miriam of M. Granville, NY | January 7, 1850<br>M. Granville, NY |
| **EMMONS** Andrew C. of Brooklyn, NY<br>**BANCROFT** Juliette of Saratoga Springs, NY | February 27, 1850<br>Sandy Hill, NY |
| **BACHELDER** Ira of Ft. Ann, NY<br>**VAUN** Helen M. of Kingsbury, NY | February 27, 1850<br>Kingsbury, NY |
| **BARKER** H. W. of Adamsville, NY<br>**WINSHIP** Ann of Queensbury, NY | March 31, 1850<br>Queensbury, NY |
| **CLARK** Noble W. of Sandy Hill, NY<br>**FERRIS** Maria dau of Cyrus of Sandy Hill, NY | April 14, 1850<br>Granville, NY |
| **CHURCH** Charles D. of Sandy Hill, NY<br>**MC KIBBEN** Celia C. of Auburn, NY | April 10, 1850<br>Auburn, NY |
| **TEFFT** Henry of Sandy Hill, NY<br>**HARRIS** Mrs. Susan C. of Sandy Hill, NY | May 6, 1850<br>Sandy Hill, NY |
| **MOORE** Albert W. of Ft. Ann, NY<br>**GAMBLE** Matilda of Greenwich, NY | May 12, 1850<br>Sandy Hill, NY |
| **PIERSON** Henry Begordus<br>**GREEN** Lydia J. of Queensbury, NY | May 15, 1850 |
| **DOUBLEDAY** Harvey M. of Sandy Hill, NY<br>**CARY** Mary G. of Stillwater, NY | May 21, 1850<br>Stillwater, NY |
| **FERRIS** Lyman R. of Sandy Hill, NY<br>**MILLER** Minerva A. of Sandy Hill, NY | May 31, 1850<br>Ft. Ann, NY |
| **SIMONDS** O. H. of Pawlet, Vt.<br>**STRONG** Melissa M. of Sandy Hill, NY | May 27, 1850<br>Sandy Hill, NY |
| **WING** Abraham of Glens Falls, NY<br>**ROBERTSON** Mrs. Angeline B. of New York City | June 12, 1850<br>New York City |
| **HOLBROOK** Amariah of Sandy Hill, NY<br>**STRONG** Helen May dau of John of Sandy Hill, NY | June 23, 1850<br>Sandy Hill, NY |

| | |
|---|---|
| FREEMAN Ralph P. of Sandy Hill, NY | July 27, 1850 |
| PIKE Susan E. of Ft. Edward, NY | Ft. Edward, NY |
| | |
| WING George W. of Ft. Edward, NY | September 3, 1850 |
| COLEMAN Martha Ann dau of William of Sandy Hill, NY | Sandy Hill, NY |
| | |
| KIDDER Edward A. of Whitehall, NY | September 10, 1850 |
| MOSS Louisa Helen of Sandy Hill, NY | Sandy Hill, NY |
| | |
| DE WOLF William of Ft. Edward, NY | September 11, 1850 |
| MARTIN Mary J. of Ft. Ann, NY | Ft. Ann, NY |
| | |
| BROWNELL Isaac of Sandy Hill, NY | October 9, 1850 |
| HARRIS Catherine of Ft. Edward, NY | Ft. Edward, NY |
| | |
| IVES James O. Morrisville, NY formerly of Sandy Hill | October 9, 1850 |
| BASSETT Abby S. of Lee, Mass. | Lee, Mass. |
| | |
| ATHERTON Archibald P. of Queensbury, NY | October 24, 1850 |
| AUSTIN Cornelia of Queensbury, NY | Queensbury, NY |
| | |
| WELLS Caleb of Ft. Edward, NY | December 17, 1850 |
| HUBBELL Cornelia S. of Ft. Edward, NY | Ft. Edward, NY |
| | |
| BRECKENRIDGE John Y. of Bennington, Vt. | February 1, 1851 |
| PICKERING Hannah S. of Northumberland, NY | Northumberland, NY |
| | |
| CARPENTER Daniel of Pittstown, NY | February 20, 1851 |
| FINN Hannah of Northumberland, NY | Northumberland, NY |
| | |
| MELHINCH Andrew of Utica, NY | March 17, 1851 |
| CARPENTER Ellen of Sandy Hill, NY | Sandy Hill, NY |
| | |
| TAYLOR Tracy of Troy, NY | April 23, 1851 |
| WING Ellen M. dau of Abraham of Glens Falls, NY | Glens Falls, NY |
| | |
| HOLDEN Dr. A. W. of Warrensburgh, NY | May 1, 1851 |
| BUELL Elizabeth of Glens Falls, NY | Glens Falls, NY |
| | |
| WEEKS John of Palming, Mi. | April 26, 1851 |
| WILSON Mary A. of Warrensburgh, NY | Warrensburgh, NY |
| | |
| VAUGHN Edwin A. of Sandy Hill, NY | May 8, 1851 |
| STRONG Anna E. dau of John of Sandy Hill, NY | Sandy Hill, NY |
| | |
| WOODIN J. L. of New York City | June 3, 1851 |
| MILLIMAN Harriet of Salem, NY | Salem, NY |
| | |
| MADISON Elijah of Ft. Ann, NY | July 8, 1851 |

| | |
|---|---|
| **KEECH** Lovina of Ft. Ann, NY | Sandy Hill, NY |
| **BRAGG** George Henry of Ft. Miller, NY<br>**SHEPHERD** Sarah Margaret of Ft. Miller, NY | September 23, 1851<br>Ft. Miller, NY |
| **FREEMAN** Adolphus of Kingsbury, NY<br>**MASON** Mrs. Cynthia A. of Kingsbury, NY | September 21, 1851<br>Sandy Hill, NY |
| **GREEN** Isaac W. P. of Boston, Mass.<br>**BLAWIS** Mercy Ann of Easton, NY | November 9, 1851<br>Galesville, NY |
| **FOX** William A. of Ft. Edward, NY<br>**HEIST** Mary A. of Glens Falls, NY | October 23, 1851<br>Glens Falls, NY |
| **DIXSON** Stewart Truman of Hebron, NY<br>**POTTER** Harriet of N. Argyle, NY | October 8, 1851<br>Belcher, NY |
| **WHITTAKER** Garry H. of Troy, NY<br>**SEARS** Mary M. of Lenox, Mass. | November 17, 1851<br>Cambridge, NY |
| **MOTT** George of Glens Falls, NY<br>**COLLAMER** Eliza Jane of Sandy Hill, NY | December 9, 1851<br>Sandy Hill, NY |
| **HOLMES** Lemuel G. of Sandy Hill, NY<br>**HAWLEY** Naoma of Moreau, NY | December 9, 1851<br>Moreau, NY |
| **HOUGHTON** R. L.          (newspaper date)<br>**WYMAN** Eliza J. | December 16, 1851<br>White Creek, NY |
| **WALES** Lewis Henry of Rutland, Vt.<br>**BAUMES** Mary A. of Greenwich, NY | November 27, 1851<br>Union Village, NY |
| **KILMORE** Charles of Rock City<br>**PARKS** Julia of Sandy Hill, NY | December 30, 1851<br>Sandy Hill, NY |
| **VAUGHN** William M. of Sandy Hill, NY<br>**PHETTEPLACE** Ann D. of Schuylerville, NY | January 4, 1852<br>Schuylerville, NY |
| **LATIMER** Banjamin T. of Troy, NY<br>**VAN VRANKEN** Ellen of Salem, NY | January 15, 1852<br>Salem, NY |
| **JOHNSON** Charles M. of Hoosic, NY<br>**BRYANT** Amanda of Hoosic, NY | December 31, 1851<br>White Creek, NY |
| **PRATT** Simeon of Greenwich, NY<br>**LAMB** Catherine Y. V. of Cambridge, NY | December 25, 1851<br>Cambridge, NY |
| **CURTIS** Leroy of White Creek, NY<br>**HERRINGTON** Patience of White Creek, NY | January 1, 1852<br>White Creek, NY |

| | |
|---|---|
| **LYTLE** Abram of Salem, NY | January 1, 1852 |
| **MC MILLAN** Mary A. of Argyle, NY | Argyle, NY |
| | |
| **GAMBOL** Albert A. | January 20, 1852 |
| **TOWSEY** Helen | Sandy Hill, NY |
| | |
| **COLLAMER** Edward L. of Shelbourne, Vt. | January 25, 1852 |
| **JONES** Mary C. D. dau of Walter | Whitehall, NY |
| | |
| **PARKS** S. A. of Sandy Hill, NY | February 12, 1852 |
| **HEWITT** Harriet of Stillwater, NY | Stillwater, NY |
| | |
| **MC AULEY** Thomas of Cambridge, NY | December 18, 1851 |
| **MILLER** Helen Maria of Jackson, NY | Hebron, NY |
| | |
| **COOK** William H. of Sandy Hill, NY | February 7, 1852 |
| **FOSTER** Sally M. of Sandy Hill, NY | Jackson, NY |
| | |
| **SIMPSON** Simeon D. W. of Shushan, NY | February 11, 1852 |
| **QUA** Margaret of N. White Creek, NY | |
| | |
| **WHITE** Alanson F. of Union Village, NY | February 24, 1852 |
| **BURTON** Lydia dau of Simon of Easton, NY | Easton, NY |
| | |
| **RIST** Joel of Saratoga Springs, NY | February 25, 1852 |
| **STEVENSON** Susan of Glens Falls, NY | Glens Falls, NY |
| | |
| **LYTLE** David of Salem, NY | February 19, 1852 |
| **PIERCE** Edna M. of Jackson, NY | Jackson, NY |
| | |
| **WALKER** John of Troy, NY | February 27, 1852 |
| **FOX** Augusta of Ballston Spa, NY | Adamsville, NY |
| | |
| **HARDEN** William of Adamsville, NY | March 14, 1852 |
| **CLOUGH** Phebe of Hartford, NY | Hartford, NY |
| | |
| **BRISBIN** William of Saratoga, NY | March 18, 1852 |
| **COULTER** Anna Maria of Cambridge, NY | Cambridge, NY |
| | |
| **ANDREWS** Haney of Hoosick, NY | March 16, 1852 |
| **BLAKE** Sally D. of Hoosick, NY | N. White Creek, NY |
| | |
| **YOUNG** Arnold of Easton, NY | March 4, 1852 |
| **LINCOLN** Lucy of Hebron, NY | Hebron, NY |
| | |
| **BARBER** George W. of Ft. Ann, NY | March 30, 1852 |
| **HAMMOND** Mary of Ticonderoga, NY | Ticonderoga, NY |
| | |
| **CARSWELL** William J. of Ft. Edward, NY | April 7/14, 1852 |

| | |
|---|---|
| **PAYNE** Mary dau of George of Moreau, NY | Moreau, NY |
| **DURKEE** Daniel of Ft. Edward, NY<br>**DAVIS** Elizabeth of Queensbury, NY | April 14, 1852 |
| **CHANDLER** Norman V. of Salem, NY<br>**PARKS** Matilda J. of Wheatland, Wis. | April 3, 1852<br>Wheatland, Wis. |
| **BARBER** Hiram of Ft. Ann, NY<br>**DUNHAM** Cornelia T. dau of Daniel of Sandy Hill, NY | April 26, 1852<br>Sandy Hill, NY |
| **SMITH** James of Glens Falls, NY<br>**INMAN** Caroline of Union Village, NY | April 20, 1852<br>Argyle, NY |
| **WILSON** Horace H. of White Creek, NY<br>**TANNER** Caroline L. of Troy, NY | May 1, 1852 |
| **OSTRUM** William M. of Troy, NY<br>**VIELE** Caroline H. of Ft. Miller, NY | May 5, 1852 |
| **LEE** Francis of Union Village, NY<br>**RIVERS** Clarissa of Union Village, NY | May 6, 1852 |
| **FREEMAN** Rush of Kingsbury, NY<br>**BUCKLIN** Mary W. of Eatonville, NY | May 17, 1852<br>Sandy Hill, NY |
| **SHAW** John of Ft. Edward, NY<br>**JOHNSON** Catherine of Sandy Hill, NY | May 21, 1852<br>Sandy Hill, NY |
| **STONE** Dr. Luther of Charlotte, Vt.<br>**WEBB** Amanda M. of Sandy Hill, NY | June 9, 1852<br>Sandy Hill, NY |
| **PARKER** George<br>**SMITH** Ellen | June 9, 1852<br>Sandy Hill, NY |
| **ROBSON** Thomas K. of Easton, Md.<br>**NORTHUP** Julia E. dau of H. B. of Sandy Hill, NY | June 6, 1852<br>Easton, Md. |
| **POTTER** Leroy of Easton, NY<br>**DUEL** Clarissa of Hebron, NY | June 12, 1852<br>Hebron, NY |
| **DUEL** B. M. of White Creek, NY<br>**QUACKENBUSH** Alida of Cambridge, NY | June 2, 1852<br>Cambridge, NY |
| **STEVENS** John D. of Wells, Vt.<br>**ATWELL** Mary J. of Wells, Vt. | June 29, 1852<br>Sandy Hill, NY |
| **DUNN** James of Hebron, NY          (newspaper date)<br>**MC EACHRON** Margaret of Argyle, NY | July 6, 1852<br>Hebron, NY |

FOSTER William O. of Salem, NY                        July 1, 1852
HILL Emily of Salem, NY                               Salem, NY

CRONKHITE Leonard W. of Sandy Hill, NY                July 21, 1852
GREENE Betsey Ann dau of Henry of Queensbury, NY      Sandy Hill, NY

FINCH Rev. Horace W. of Mt. Hope, NY                  July 20, 1852
WILSON Electa A. dau of Lemuel of E. Whitehall, NY    Whitehall, NY

ADAMS James Jr. of Westhaven, Vt.    (newspaper date) July 27, 1852
HOWE Charlotte E. of Whitehall, NY                    Whitehall, NY

KING John of Sandy Hill, NY                           August 21, 1852
TISDALE Flora of Sandy Hill, NY                       Sandy Hill, NY

OGDEN Edward of Albany, NY                            September 22, 1852
HAND Juliette E. dau of Josiah of Sandy Hill, NY      Sandy Hill, NY

SARGENT A. J. of Troy, NY                             September 23, 1852
HARRIS Helen M. dau of C. of Sandy Hill, NY           Sandy Hill, NY

SAYLES Dr. Cyrus of White Creek, NY                   September 14, 1852
WATKINS Lydia A. of Jackson, NY

CARR Joseph of Welton, NY                             September 5, 1852
HAIGHT Mrs. Betsey Marie of Saratoga, NY              Saratoga, NY

CLARK Col. Almon of Sandy Hill, NY                    October 4, 1852
ABEEL Catherine W. dau of Christopher of Coveville, NY  Coveville, NY

SHERMAN Dr. F. A. of Sandy Hill, NY                   October 14, 1852
CLARK Mary dau of Col. Almon Clark of Sandy Hill, NY  Sandy Hill, NY

OGDEN Lucius D. of Sandy Hill, NY                     October 30, 1852
HOLLEY Loretta Jane of Sandy Hill, NY                 Sandy Hill, NY

HAMLIN Rev. James T. of Mattituck, NY                 November 11, 1852
PARRY Sophia of Ft. Edward, NY                        Ft. Edward, NY

NELSON Samuel                                         November 11, 1852
BUCK Abby                                             Sandy Hill, NY

THOMPSON Albert A. of New York City                   November 16, 1852
COLEMAN Maria Jane dau of William of Sandy Hill, NY   Sandy Hill, NY

PHILBRICK William R. of Canada East                   November 20, 1852
NOBLE Eleanor D. of Ft. Ann, NY                       Sandy Hill, NY

CLUFF Thomas of Hartford, NY                          November 14, 1852

PRATT Harriet of Adamsville, NY                               Adamsville, NY

STUART James T. of Argyle, NY                                 October 18, 1852
COBINE Elizabeth of Hebron, NY                                Hebron, NY

WILLIAMS Martin of Salem, NY                                  December 12, 1852
WHEATON Mary A. of Sandy Hill, NY                             Sandy Hill, NY

COFFIN J. W. of New York City                                 December 25, 1852
GRIFFIN Sarah I. of Sandy Hill, NY                            Sandy Hill, NY

JUCKET Alvea of Whitehall, NY                                 December 29, 1852
BOOMER Phebe A. of Hartford, NY                               Hartford, NY

HEATH Jacob of Argyle, NY          (newspaper date)           January 18, 1853
STEWART Mary Jane of Argyle, NY                               Argyle, NY

LOCKE I. E. of Sandy Hill, NY                                 January 19, 1853
RICE Lydia dau of Sylvester                                   Sandy Hill, NY

HUTTON Andrew of Greenwich, NY                                January 19, 1853
CONLEE Caroline of Queensbury, NY                            Queensbury, NY

BOYD Thomas of Salem, NY                                      January 12, 1853
PARISH Ellen of Hebron, NY                                    Salem, NY

BARTHOLOMEW Charles of Dresden, NY                            January 12, 1853
SNODY Angeline of Dresden, NY                                 Dresden, NY

BAKER Alexander of Ft. Ann, NY                                January 12, 1853
THOMPSON Polly of Ft. Ann, NY                                 Ft. Ann, NY

FERRIS Walter A. of Sandy Hill, NY                            February 22, 1853
DILLOWAY Eliza Jane of Ft. Ann, NY                            Ft. Miller, NY

STRAIT Thomas of Ft. Edward, NY                               March 24, 1853
SPRING Mary of Hartford, NY                                   Hartford, NY

WRIGHT James C. of New York City                              March 29, 1853
MILLER Maria L. dau of Hugh of Brooklyn, NY

SYLVESTER N. B. of Lowville, NY                               January 18, 1853
TAYLOR Sarah Jane of Argyle, NY                               Argyle, NY

WING Nehemiah of Queensbury, NY                               April 26, 1853
SISSON Sarah Jane of Sandy Hill, NY                           Sandy Hill, NY

ABBOTT Harrison                                               May 26, 1853
WALLING Mary                                                  Hartford, NY

NORTHUP Joseph of Hartford, NY                    May 26, 1853
WALLING Martha of Hartford, NY                    Hartford, NY

WATTS Alfred of Danville, Vt.                     June 4, 1853
STURDEVANT Sarah of Sandy Hill, NY                Ft. Edward, NY

WOART Rev. John of Great Barrington, Mass.        September 8, 1853
DEWEY Eliza Newton dau of Stephen LEE of Sandy Hill    New York City

CLARK Guy W. of Sandy Hill, NY                    October 17, 1853
HOWLAND Deborah A. dau of Stephen of Galway, NY   Galway, NY

HUGHES Charles of Sandy Hill, NY    (newspaper date)    November 1, 1853
HUTCHINSON Anna E. dau of William of Bustleton, Pa.    Bustleton, Pa.

MILLER Augustine S. of Sandy Hill, NY             July 23, 1853
BUCK Adeline H. of Sandy Hill, NY                 Sandy Hill, NY

INGALSBEE Horace H. of Hartford, NY               December 25, 1853
AUSTIN Maria N. of Hartford, NY                   Hartford, NY

BAILEY James H. of Sandy Hill, NY                 January 1, 1854
PERRY Susan C. of Syracuse, NY                    Syracuse, NY

BENNETT H. W. of Sandy Hill, NY                   January 11, 1854
CLARK Charlotte of Sandy Hill, NY                 Sandy Hill, NY

WIEDMAN Henry of Sandy Hill, NY                   January 22, 1854
GRIFFITH Hulda Jane of Sandy hill, NY             Glens Falls, NY

SKINNER C. G. of Whitehall, NY                    February 15, 1854
THOMAS Mary J. dau of Samuel of Ft. Ann, NY       Ft. Ann, NY

KINNEY Morris of Argyle, NY                       March 6, 1854
ROUSE Sarah of Argyle, NY                         Argyle, NY

CARY John of Argyle, NY                           March 16, 1854
POLLOCK Mary of Argyle, NY                        Argyle, NY

NELSON William A. of Ft. Ann, NY                  April 26, 1854
NORTHUP Louisa A. dau of N. C. of Sandy Hill, NY  Sandy Hill, NY

SPAULDING George of Luzerne, NY                   May 11, 1854
BURNER Mrs. Sarah of Luzerne, NY                  Sandy Hill, NY

NELSON M. B. of Sandy Hill, NY                    May 6, 1854
HARDEN Mrs. Martha of Sandy Hill, NY              Saratoga Springs, NY

Issues missing from May 1854 - May 1855

BROMLEY Charles H. of Sandy Hill, NY      May 19, 1855
VAN TASSEL Mary of Sandy Hill, NY

SUTHERLAND John of Ft. Ann, NY      July 1, 1855
MC FARLAND Eliza dau of Henry of Kingsbury, NY

MC COY John of Argyle, NY      July 3, 1855
MC MILLEN Mary of Warrensburgh, NY      Warrensburgh, NY

WILKINSHAW Thomas of New York City      July 3, 1855
THOMAS Mary of Sandy Hill, NY      Sandy Hill, NY

KEENE F. J. J. of Ft. Edward, NY      July 4, 1855
LORD Lucy of Ft. Edward, NY      Ft. Edward, NY

CHURCHILL Charles P. of Ft. Edward, NY      July 3, 1855
BEEBE Emeline B. of Hartford, NY      Hartford, NY

LITTLE Alden of Ft. Edward, NY    (newspaper date)      August 14, 1855
DERBY Jane of Ft. Edward, NY      Ft. Edward, NY

SHERMAN Franklin of Ft. Edward, NY      September 1, 1855
DICKINSON Jerusha J. of Northumberland, NY      Ft. Edward, NY

HILON Nicolas of Ft. Edward, NY      July 8, 1855
KING Ann of Ft. Edward, NY      Sandy Hill, NY

HARRIS Hiram M. of Glens Falls, NY      September 21, 1855
ROWLEY Delia dau of late Col. Lee T. of Granville, NY      Pawlet, Vt.

BURGESS Walter of New York City      October 3, 1855
GUY Sophia T. of Kingsbury, NY      Kingsbury, NY

LADOO John      October 2, 1855
HORSLEY Mary Ann      Sandy Hill, NY

BROWN Joseph of Sandy Hill, NY      October 24, 1855
CROSS Ida of Sandy Hill, NY      Sandy Hill, NY

BUCK Charles of Toledo, Ohio, formerly Sandy Hill, NY      November 1, 1855
DURFEE Louisa of Sylvania, Ohio      Adrian, Mi.

MASON O. K. of Sandy Hill, NY      December 27, 1855
HINES Eve E. dau of Samuel of Adamsville, NY

GUY William of Sandy Hill, NY      December 25, 1855
FERRIS Elvira of Sandy Hill, NY      Sandy Hill, NY

| | |
|---|---|
| **BOND** Barnet | December 25, 1855 |
| **GILLIS** Fanny Eliza | Sandy Hill, NY |
| | |
| **MADISON** Michael | January 1, 1856 |
| **SWEET** Marinda Maria | Sandy Hill, NY |
| | |
| **BUTTERFIELD** Jeremiah of Michigan City, Ind. | January 1, 1856 |
| **WOODRUFF** Caroline E. dau of Walter of Ft. Ann, NY | |
| | |
| **DAVIS** Arthur B. of Sandy Hill, NY | February 4, 1856 |
| **PROAL** Charlotte Evalina of Utica, NY | Utica, NY |
| | |
| **CHOATE** Ossian W. of New York City | February 27, 1856 |
| **WING** Emma S. dau of D. W. | Ft. Edward, NY |
| | |
| **WAINWRIGHT** E. W. of Chicago, Ill. | February 27, 1856 |
| **WILLIAMS** Jane | Ft. Edward, NY |
| | |
| **COLBURN** Charles of Warrensburgh, NY | February 23, 1856 |
| **TRUE** Sarah of Ft. Edward, NY | Ft. Edward, NY |
| | |
| **CURTIS** John W. of Union Village, NY | February 21, 1856 |
| **WHITE** Hannah dau of late Moses of Union Village, NY | Union Village, NY |
| | |
| **WHITMORE** George R. | March 4, 1856 |
| **NIMS** Ann dau of Warren | Ft. Ann, NY |
| | |
| **GOSS** Lauriston H. | March 6, 1856 |
| **WILSON** Barbara J. | Ft. Ann, NY |
| | |
| **BUCK** John C. | April 18, 1856 |
| **HENRY** Mary C. dau of late Robert | Sandy Hill, NY |
| | |
| **HALL** David of Hartford, NY | April 10, 1856 |
| **WASHBURN** Jane of Hartford, NY | Hartford, NY |
| | |
| **HITCHCOCK** Rev. P. M. of Sandy Hill, NY | May 22, 1856 |
| **PIERSON** Henrietta dau of Bogordus | Sandy Hill, NY |
| | |
| **MARTIN** Byron | June 3, 1856 |
| **WALL** Sarah | Sandy Hill, NY |
| | |
| **STUART** John Y. of Sandy Hill, NY | June 28, 1856 |
| **GILLIS** Margaret Ann of Sandy Hill, NY | Ft. Edward, NY |
| | |
| **ALDEN** Jesse of Glens Falls, NY | July 23, 1856 |
| **JONES** Harriet dau of Lynds of Fonda, NY | Fonda, NY |
| | |
| **NASH** Danvers T. of Sandy Hill, NY | August 5, 1856 |

**FAXON** Mary of Sandy Hill, NY

**VAN TASSEL** William of Sandy Hill, NY   (newspaper date)   September 9, 1856
**BIXBY** S. A. of Corning, NY                                 Corning, NY

**MILLER** Alfred A. of Gansevort, NY                          September 25, 1856
**REYNOLDS** Sarah C. of Gansevort, NY

**MILLS** John N. of Ft. Edward, NY                            September 20, 1856
**FULLER** Maria of Ft. Edward, NY                             Troy, NY

**ROSELL** Marlow W. of Moreau, NY                             September 24, 1856
**TAYLOR** Elizabeth dau of late L. G. of Ft. Edward, NY       Ft. Edward, NY

**ANDREWS** Johnson P. of Ft. Edward, NY                       September 24, 1856
**BARBER** Mary of Ft. Edward, NY                              Ft. Edward, NY

**NORTON** Daniel of Queensbury, NY                            October 9, 1856
**DANTZ** Jane of Queensbury, NY                               Sandy Hill, NY

**VETTER** Jacob                                               October 16, 1856
**HENSLER** Lissie                                             Sandy Hill, NY

**SHEFFERS** William of Glens Falls, NY                        October 28, 1856
**FISH** Helen of Sandy Hill, NY                               Sandy Hill, NY

**TEFFT** O. A. of Redford, NY                                 November 23, 1856
**CARLISLE** Mary of Sandy Hill, NY                            Sandy Hill, NY

**HUNT** George M.                                             December 3, 1856
**LESTER** Jane E. of Ft. Edward, NY                           Sandy Hill, NY

**DURKEE** Merit of Ft. Edward, NY                             December 17, 1856
**DURKEE** Maryette of Ft. Edward, NY                          Ft. Edward, NY

**PIKE** Jacob of Ft. Edward, NY        (newspaper date)       January 5, 1857
**WILLIAMS** Mary                                              Ft. Miller, NY

**DOUBLEDAY** Danvers of Sandy Hill, NY                        January 17, 1857
**CHALK** Anna dau of Thomas of Sandy Hill, NY                 Troy, NY

**INGALLS** Truman S. of Hartford, NY                          January 27, 1857
**NORTON** Adeline dau of Col. John of Hartford, NY            Hartford, NY

**HAWLEY** Auselmo                                             February 4, 1857
**GREEN** Mrs. Emily J.                                        Glens Falls, NY

**OVIATT** Wilson of Salem, NY                                 February 5, 1857
**HUBBARD** Margaret of N. White Creek, NY                     N. White Creek, NY

| | |
|---|---|
| **ALDEN** Henry of Vergennes, Vt. | February 20, 1857 |
| **CAVIENOR** Catherine of Sandy Hill, NY | Sandy Hill, NY |
| | |
| **BALLOU** Henry of Sandy Hill, NY | October 25, 1857 |
| **WEEKS** Eliza M. of Sandy Hill, NY | Sandy Hill, NY |
| | |
| **BEMAN** Samuel S. | October 22, 1857 |
| **WHITTEN** Caroline W. dau of late Ebenezer of Elryia, Oh. | Carolia, M. T. |
| | |
| **HATCH** Kenyon C. of Jackson, NY | December 31, 1857 |
| **FOSTER** Mary of Saratoga Springs, NY | Saratoga Springs, NY |
| | |
| **SCOVILLE** Edward of Cambridge, NY | December 24, 1857 |
| **EASTMAN** Malvina of Cambridge, NY | Cambridge, NY |
| | |
| **BAIN** John of Argyle, NY | January 23, 1858 |
| **WENDLE** Mary of Argyle, NY | Sandy Hill, NY |
| | |
| **KING** Valentine of Russelton, Canada | January 4, 1858 |
| **CLEMENT** Martha A. of Ft. Edward, NY | Ft. Edward, NY |
| | |
| **WHITFORD** Daniel D. of Saratoga Springs, NY | January 13, 1858 |
| **CHURCHILL** Adelia dau of Jacob of Ft. Edward, NY | Ft. Edward, NY |
| | |
| **RHODES** Francis N. of Dresden, NY | January 17, 1858 |
| **HESELTON** Eliza of Glens Falls, NY | Ft. Edward, NY |
| | |
| **MACKINTOSH** C. C. of Kingsbury, NY | January 20, 1858 |
| **RICH** Esther J. of Ft. Edward, NY | Ft. Edward, NY |
| | |
| **ROBERSON** Barber of Greenwich, NY | January 20, 1858 |
| **FOSTER** Harriet of Greenwich, NY | Greenwich, NY |
| | |
| **ROBERTSON** John | January 27, 1858 |
| **RICE** Minnie S. dau of Daniel | Easton, NY |
| | |
| **PIKE** William of Ft. Edward, NY | January 20, 1858 |
| **HATHAWAY** Mary J. dau of Peter | Salem, NY |
| | |
| **CARSWELL** Abner of Salem, NY | January 20, 1858 |
| **MC EACHRON** Harriet of Argyle, NY | Argyle, NY |
| | |
| **STOCKWELL** Henry of Dresden, NY    (newspaper date) | February 2, 1858 |
| **LINCOLN** Sarah of Dresden, NY | Dresden, NY |
| | |
| **TANNER** John R. of Granville, NY | January 18, 1858 |
| **SLOCUM** Charlotte J. of Granville, NY | Granville, NY |
| | |
| **WATSON** James G. of Whitehall, NY | December 29, 1857 |

WATSON Almira of Salem, NY

Whitehall, NY

MOTT John W. of Ft. Edward, NY
STOUGHTON Almira W. of Ft. Edward, NY

February 3, 1858
Ft. Edward, NY

SWEARIN Albert of Glens Falls, NY
BOMBURGH Caroline of New York City

February 5, 1858
New York City

WILLIAMS Oliver of Detroit, Mi.
WALKER Mary dau of Hiram of Salem, NY

January 29, 1858
Salem, NY

WILSON L. M. of Cambridge, NY
LIVINGSTON Sarah M. of Cambridge, NY

February 2, 1858
White Creek, NY

PATTEN Alexander of Sandy Hill, NY
BETTS Rhoda E. of Moreau, NY

January 27, 1858
Ft. Edward, NY

SPRING Hannibal of Whitehall, NY
KING Julia Ann of Whitehall, NY

February 9, 1858
Whitehall, NY

TEFFT John B. of Greenwich, NY
TABOR Emily of W. Hebron, NY

February 4, 1858
W. Hebron, NY

SEELYE Justin F. of Queensbury, NY
CHENEY Mary P. of Glens Falls, NY

February 14, 1858
Glens Falls, NY

MC CARTY Jeremy of Glens Falls, NY
SWANEY Bridget of Glens Falls, NY

February 14, 1858
Glens Falls, NY

BAKER Evret C. of Union Village, NY
RICHARDS Mrs. Kate of Union Village, NY

February 24, 1858
Union Village, NY

STREETER Benjamin of Castleton, Vt.
MILLER Hannah E. dau of G. L. of Argyle, NY

February 17, 1858
Argyle, NY

SEARS Thomas of Salem, NY
ROGERS Mary C. of Battenville, NY

February 17, 1858
Union Village, NY

MORRIS Joseph Gifford of Rochester, NY
NELSON Josephine A. dau of Luther of Hartford, NY

April 7, 1858
Hartford, NY

LARAWAY Stephen of Kingsbury, NY
LARAWAY Mrs. Jane of Kingsbury, NY

April 19, 1858
Kingsbury, NY

WHIPPLE George Edgar of Ft. Edward, NY
GROESBECK Margaret of Ft. Edward, NY

April 29, 1858
Ft. Edward, NY

LITTLE Meredith B. of Glens Falls, NY
PECK Amanda E. dau of Herman of Glens Falls, NY

June 2, 1858
Glens Falls, NY

IRISH George W. of Sandy Hill, NY — June 5, 1858 — Sandy Hill, NY
MOSS Alvira of Sandy Hill, NY

RAINEY Charles H. of Argyle, NY — June 16, 1858 — Sandy Hill, NY
COTTRELL Sarah E. of Argyle, NY

TILFORD W. H. of Ft. Edward, NY — July 15, 1858 — Ft. Edward, NY
WESTON Lizzie A. dau of R. F. of Ft. Edward, NY

KING E. W. Md. of Ft. Edward, NY — July 19, 1858
PALMER Eliza A. of Hartford, NY

PATRICK Robert James of Glens Falls, NY — September 1, 1858 — Sandy Hill, NY
CROSSETT Jane of Glens Falls, NY

CHAPIN James of Vicksburg, Miss. — September 9, 1858 — Hartford, NY
COWEN Mary E. dau of Judge S. S. of Hartford, NY

ORTON Wallace of Glens Falls, NY — September 11, 1858 — Sandy Hill, NY
NORTON Maria of Glens Falls, NY

FINCH Daniel J. of Sandy Hill, NY — September 14, 1858 — Sandy Hill, NY
LEWIS Delia M. dau of Henry of Sandy Hill, NY

ROBERTS Harry of Sandy Hill, NY — September 13, 1858 — Sandy Hill, NY
BULL Mary J. of Sandy Hill, NY

GREEN John C. of Sandy Hill, NY — September 14, 1858 — Sandy Hill, NY
BARTLETT Mary Milcena dau of Albert of Sandy Hill, NY

PHETTEPLACE George C. of Sandy Hill, NY — September 22, 1858 — Sandy Hill, NY
BIGGART Eliza dau of James of Sandy Hill, NY

MONTOUR Joseph of Sandy Hill, NY — September 23, 1858 — Sandy Hill, NY
BARRETT Orilla of Plattsburgh, NY

VAUGHN Amos C. of Sandy Hill, NY — September 26, 1858 — Sandy Hill, NY
HINES Aseneth P. of Sandy Hill, NY

MORSE John of Sandy Hill, NY — October 5, 1858
BROWN Sylvia Jane of Sandy Hill, NY

BAKER John H. of Sandy Hill, NY — October 19, 1858 — Sandy Hill, NY
FERRIS Helen M. dau of Benjamin of Sandy Hill, NY

MARR William T. of Canada — October 25, 1858 — Ft. Edward, NY
ELLISON Catherine of Northumberland, NY

BRATT Merchant H. of Ft. Edward, NY — October 20, 1858

| | |
|---|---|
| STEWART Susan S. of Ft. Edward, NY | Ft. Edward, NY |
| MC EACHRON Alexander of Glens Falls, NY<br>CORLEY Mary E. of Syracuse, NY | October 25, 1858<br>Ft. Edward, NY |
| MANLY W. E. of Buffalo, NY<br>LEWIS Cornelia of Sandy Hill, NY | October 26, 1858<br>Richfield Springs, NY |
| BAXTER William E. of Carver, Minn.<br>WING Jennie dau of J. of Kingsbury, NY | November 9, 1858<br>Kingsbury, NY |
| MILLER Jeremiah F. of Sandy Hill, NY<br>NELSON Harriet of Sandy Hill, NY | November 10, 1858 |
| AMIDON Sidney G. of Sandy Hill, NY<br>KNAPP Susan M. of Sandy Hill, NY | November 18, 1858<br>Sandy Hill, NY |
| CULVER Charles D. of New York City<br>BELLAMY Louisa A. dau of late Julius of Sandy Hill, NY | December 28, 1858<br>Sandy Hill, NY |
| HILL Edwin<br>RICHARDSON Mary D. C. dau of late A. B. | January 12, 1859<br>Argyle, NY |
| BEACH Orville of Oshkosh, Wis.<br>THOMPSON Helen A. dau of Lewis B. of Northumberland | January 19, 1859<br>Northumberland, NY |
| COLE Charles of Sandy Hill, NY<br>THOMPSON Ann dau of B. of Northumberland, NY | January 19, 1859<br>Northumberland, NY |
| BAKER Guilford D. of Rochester, NY<br>GRAVES Orrie E. adopted dau of G. M. Baker | January 20, 1859<br>Queensbury, NY |
| NORTON Alonzo of Hartford, NY<br>GATES Nancy of Hartford, NY | January 20, 1859 |
| JACOBIE William Jr. of E. Greenwich, NY<br>CLARK Mariese Y. S. of S. Hartford, NY | February 18, 1859<br>Saratoga Springs, NY |
| HOLLEY Prof. William A. of Ft. Edward, NY<br>BATES Mary T. dau of Rev. Merritt Bates | March 10, 1859<br>N. White Creek, NY |
| HARRINGTON Orrin D.<br>VAUGHN Loretta S. | March 6, 1859<br>Whitehall, NY |
| STARKS Simon Peter of Ft. Ann, NY<br>ELLSWORTH Sarah of Ft. Ann, NY | February 20, 1859<br>Ft. Ann, NY |
| BROADWAY John of Ft. Ann, NY<br>MC CONHIE Henrietta of Hartford, NY | February 6, 1859<br>Ft. Ann, NY |

MAHAFFY Samuel of Salem, NY                       February 22, 1859
MOORE Lydia L. of Sandgate, Vt.                    Salem, NY

WILLIAMSON Daniel R.                               March 3, 1859
CRAMMOND Jennett                                   Putnam, NY

IRONS Willis of S. Hartford, NY                    March 18, 1859
BARRELL Sarah A. of S. Hartford, NY

LEE S. Barry of Sandy Hill, NY                     March 16, 1859
CARMAN Adeline of New York City                    New York City

WARREN John W. of Sandy Hill, NY                   April 6, 1859
WHITE Prudence A. of Sandy Hill, NY                Sandy Hill, NY

WROTH John of Sandy Hill, NY                       April 21, 1859
BRIERLY Louisa of Sandy Hill, NY                   Sandy Hill, NY

MOBBS James F. of Sandy Hill, NY                   May 5, 1859
BLISS Addie step dau of H. Y. MIDDLEWORTH          Sandy Hill, NY

HARDEN George W. of Hartford, NY                   May 2, 1859
DEANE Helen M. of Hartford, NY                     Hartford, NY

ROWE Andrew D. of Elizabeth, NJ                    May 3, 1859
HARDEN Sarah L. of Hartford, NY                    Hartford, NY

COLE Hiram                                         May 25, 1859
HOLLEY Esther dau of Daniel                        Sandy Hill, NY

VAN TASSEL Eugene D. of Sandy Hill, NY             May 25, 1859
BRIERLY Ann of Sandy Hill, NY                      Sandy Hill, NY

BACHELDER Isaac of Sandy Hill, NY                  June 5, 1859
COVEY Mary E. of Sandy Hill, NY                    Moreau, NY

MEEKER Hiram Jr. Md. of Sandy Hill, NY             June 16, 1859
LANGWORTHY Julia M. of Middlebury, Vt.             Middlebury, Vt.

HICKOK Rev. Henry F. of Sandy Hill, NY             June 16, 1859
CLEAVER Lizzie T. of Saratoga Springs, NY

FISK Edwin of Caldwell, NY                         August 17, 1859
HOY Elizabeth of Caldwell, NY                      Sandy Hill, NY

BROWNELL William of Sandy Hill, NY                 September 8, 1859
STUART Mary of Sandy Hill, NY                      Queensbury, NY

LOVELAND George of Thurman, NY                     September 28, 1859

POTTER Elizabeth of Thurman, NY — Sandy Hill, NY

BURDICK Frederick C. of Sandy Hill, NY — October 26, 1859
MIDDLEWORTH Ella J. dau of H. V. — Sandy Hill, NY

BEVAN John S. of Logansport, Ind. — November 9, 1859
CORNELL Kate A. dau of N. P. of Ft. Ann, NY — Ft. Ann, NY

DICK William of Greenwich, NY — November 17, 1859
PRINTER Mrs. Margaret of Greenwich, NY — Greenwich, NY

CLARK John M. of Salem, NY — November 17, 1859
GARNSEY Mary dau of A. of Saratoga, NY — Saratoga Springs, NY

DAY Edwin W. formerly of N. Granville, NY — October 12, 1859
INGALLS Harriet E. of Saratoga, Minn. — Saratoga, Minn.

BRUNDAGE Clinton D. of Pittstown, NY — December 22, 1859
REED Eliza Jane dau of Hugh of Pittstown, NY — Pittstown, NY

CRANDALL Harvey of Caldwell, Vt. — November 25, 1859
HUBBELL Eveline of Caldwell, Vt. — Sandy Hill, NY

BAKER R. W. of Easton, NY — December 10, 1859
MICKEL Henrietta of Glens Falls, NY — Sandy Hill, NY

FERGUSON Augustus of Sandy Hill, NY — December 17, 1859
WHITING Martha of Sandy Hill, NY — Sandy Hill, NY

BALDWIN J. P. of Queensbury, NY — January 1, 1860
KING Eliza A. of Queensbury, NY — Sandy Hill, NY

BALDWIN Charles A. of Sandy Hill, NY — January 2, 1860
WRIGHT Isabella of Sandy Hill, NY — Sandy Hill, NY

DEAN Caleb J. of Kingsbury, NY — January 2, 1860
SISSON Mary of Kingsbury, NY — Kingsbury, NY

RICH John G. of Sandy Hill, NY — December 31, 1859
HANCOCK Cornelia A. of Sandy Hill, NY — Sandy Hill, NY

CRANDALL Calvin of Pittstown, NY — January 4, 1860
BRUNDAGE Phebe of Pittstown, NY — Pittstown, NY

WRIGHT William of Warrensburgh, NY — January 4, 1860
MATTISON Sarah P. of Kingsbury, NY — Kingsbury, NY

SMITH Alfred of Pittstown, NY — January 11, 1860
HALL Ruth A. of Pittstown, NY — Pittstown, NY

BARRELL Henry of Hartford, NY
FOWLER Roxanna of Argyle, NY
February 15, 1860
Argyle, NY

WATERS John of Horicon, NY
GRAVES Olive dau of Rev. Oliver Graves of Bolton, NY
February 22, 1860
Bolton, NY

HARRINGTON Ormus of Alburgh, Vt.
SNOW Laura of Comstocks Landing, NY
February 22, 1860
Comstocks Landing

TUPPER James of Jersey City, NJ
TALLMADGE Mary of Whitehall, NY
February 28, 1860
Whitehall, NY

EDMONDS Richard of Whitehall, NY
WINTERS Ann E. of Whitehall, NY
February 28, 1860
Whitehall, NY

SHEAR Jonathan
FRENCH Charlotte
February 21, 1860
Putnam, NY

ANDERSON William Jr.
SIMPSON Agnes
February 22, 1860
Putnam, NY

DUERS M. A. of Sandy Hill, NY
BUCK Lucy Jane of Sandy Hill, NY
March 3, 1860
Sandy Hill, NY

RUSSELL William A. of Salem, NY
CALDWELL Ada of Westchester Co. NY
February 27, 1860
Sandy Hill, NY

SMITH Ebenezer of Albany, NY
CULVER Harriet J. of Cambridge, NY
February 22, 1860
Cambridge, NY

SCRIPTURE John of Moreau, NY
PARKS Olive P. dau of Hiram of Moreau, NY
June 28, 1864
Moreau, NY

SMITH Henry A. of Chatham, NY
WHITE Sarah S. of Sandy Hill, NY
June 29, 1864
Sandy Hill, NY

SKELLIE John P. of Sandy Hill, NY
HOGLE Sarah Jane of Sandy Hill, NY
July 31, 1864
Sandy Hill, NY

GUY Zina C.
VAUGHN Angie C. dau of Dewitt C. of Kingsbury, NY
January 12, 1865
Kingsbury, NY

MURPHY Elijah W. of Sandy Hill, NY
HULBERT Helen A. dau of Chauncey of Philadelphia, Pa.
January 16, 1865
Philadelphia, Pa.

NORTHUP Lieut. Edward B. of Sandy Hill, NY
SEELYE Mattie of Niagara Co. NY
January 12, 1865
Niagara Co. NY

STOWELL John N. of Sandy Hill, NY
March 6, 1865

**DEWEY** Helen Mary of Sandy Hill, NY                      Sandy Hill, NY

**NELSON** James S. of Sandy Hill, NY                       March 1, 1865
**MALCOM** Jennie A. dau of Lewis of Albany, NY            Albany, NY

**MC MILLAN** James of N. Argyle, NY                        March 14, 1865
**MC DOUGAL** Mary Ann of N. Argyle, NY                    N. Argyle, NY

**HOLMES** Lemuel C. of Whitehall, NY                       March 16, 1865
**NEWCOMB** Mrs. Fannie of Whitehall, NY                   Whitehall, NY

**BENWAY** Edward of Sandy Hill, NY                         March 22, 1865
**TANNER** Mrs. Sarah of Glens Falls, NY                   Kingsbury, NY

**MURDOCK** D. W.                                           March 26, 1865
**BLIVEN** Julia O.                                         Sandy Hill, NY

**COVEY** John H. formerly of Sandy Hill, NY                June 17, 1865
**KINGSLEY** Mary J. of Philadelphia, Pa.                  Phildelphia, Pa.

**NELSON** N. F. of Sandy Hill, NY                          July 29, 1865
**MOORE** Cornelia of Ft. Edward, NY                       Glen's Falls, NY

**ALLEN** William H. of Granville, NY                       September 7, 1865
**SMITH** Helen E. of Sandy Hill, NY                       Sandy Hill, NY

**MANNING** Gilbert H. of Fultonville, NY                   September 5, 1865
**MARTIN** Frances E. of Ft. Edward, NY                    Ft. Edward, NY

**ABEEL** J. C. of Washington DC                            October 22, 1867
**WHITE** Hattie A. of Sandy Hill, NY                      Sandy Hill, NY

**COTY** Paul of Sandy Hill, NY                             February 24, 1868
**NAILOR** Zelia M. of Glens Falls, NY                     Glens Falls, NY

**TABER** Horace of Easton, NY                              March 6, 1868
**CONKLIN** Amanda of Sandy Hill, NY

**JOHNSTON** James B. of Glens Falls, NY                    May 22, 1868
**VIELE** Louisa M. of Glens Falls, NY                     Sandy Hill, NY

**ALLEN** George Henry of Sandy Hill, NY                    August 10, 1868
**AMIDON** Adelaide of Queensbury, NY

**STEARNS** Asahel of Owego, NY                             June 8, 1869
**GRACE** Eva L. of Glens Falls, NY                        Sandy Hill, NY

**PIKE** George H. of Ft. Edward, NY                        December 28, 1870
**ALLEN** Eliza J. of Ft. Edward, NY                       Ft. Edward, NY

WELLS Josiah of W. Ft. Ann, NY
DE BOICE Sarah Ann of W. Ft. Ann, NY

December 24, 1870
Glens Falls, NY

WELLS Bethuel of Sandy Hill, NY
VAN DEUSEN Mrs. Mary of Sandy Hill, NY

December 28, 1870
Glens Falls, NY

MILLER Isaiah of Sandy Hill, NY
BUCK Ann Eliza dau of James P.

January 10, 1871
Kingsbury, NY

MAHAFFY William J. of Salem, NY
GREEN Anna M. of Jackson, NY

January 2, 1871
Jackson, NY

O'HARA Bartlett of Glens Falls, NY
KEYES Eliza U. of Glens Falls, NY

December 29, 1870
Glens Falls, NY

BLISS Charles E. of Poultney, Vt.
O'DONALD Mary J. of Hampton, NY

December 28, 1870
Hampton, NY

BURDICK Lewis H. of Easton, NY
CRANDALL Louise E. of Greenwich, NY

January 3, 1871
Greenwich, NY

MC LAREN L.
PREWETT Hattie F.

January 2, 1871
Yazoo, Miss.

LAPHAM Benjamin of Onarga, Ill.
FULLER Lizzie of Glens Falls, NY

January 19, 1871
Glens Falls, NY

SMITH Joseph of Hebron, NY
CLARK Mary E. of Hebron, NY

January 11, 1871
Greenwich, NY

PRATT Howard of Cambridge, NY
RICE Lucy M. of Cambridge, NY

January 19, 1871
Cambridge, NY

DAVIDSON James of Johnsburg, NY
SOMERVILLE Sarah Maria of Johnsburg, NY

January 2, 1871
Johnsburg, NY

REILLY John of Sandy Hill, NY
FLANAGAN Catherine of Sandy Hill, NY

January 31, 1871
Glens Falls, NY

COPELAND Franklin of Caldwell, Vt.
THOMPSON Annie L. of S. Glens Falls, NY

January 26, 1871
S. Glens Falls, NY

RYAN John of Ft. Edward, NY
BUCKLEY Lizzie dau of Patrick

January __, 1871

MC WOODARD James of Hebron, NY
BOCKES Georgie of Cambridge, NY

January 26, 1871

HAGER Charles M. of Wallingford, Vt.

January 14, 1871

SHIPPA Mary E. of Tinmouth, Vt.     Granville, NY

SAVAGE Charles B. of Granville, NY     January 25, 1871
DE KALB Martha of Granville, NY     Granville, NY

HOLLEY J. B.     January 18, 1871
CLARK Frances M. dau of James     Salem, NY

SHAW Bryant of Cambridge, NY     January 11, 1871
WOLFE Melissa of Greenwich, NY     Greenwich, NY

STEWART George of S. Argyle, NY     January 25, 1871
TIMMERMAN Julia E. of S. Argyle, NY     S. Argyle, NY

MARTIN George W. of Harts Falls, NY     February 1, 1871
LAMBERT Sarah G. dau of Rev. A. B. of S. Hartford, NY     S. Hartford, NY

GILCHRIST James H. of N. Argyle, NY     January 26, 1871
REYNOLDS Mary C. of N. Argyle, NY     N. Argyle, NY

SMITH Timothy of Glens Falls, NY     January 27, 1871
LINARD Josephine of Glens Falls, NY     Glens Falls, NY

WOODCOCK John of Ft. Ann, NY     January 29, 1871
BROWN Esther N. of Ft. Ann, NY     Glens Falls, NY

ALLISON John W. of Glens Falls, NY     January 31, 1871
LEE Mary of Greenwich, NY     Greenwich, NY

THURSTON Daniel P.     February 8, 1871
COBURN Ellen T. of Greenwich, NY     Greenwich, NY

NOYES Hiram of Troy, NY     February 9, 1871
HEGEMAN Marion of Glens Falls, NY     Glens Falls, NY

HINCKLEY Dymick of Ft. Edward, NY     February 9, 1871
DECKER Hattie of Troy, NY

SHEPHERD Juline P. of Vienna, Iowa     February 2, 1871
SPRAGUE Victoria S. of Greenwich, NY     Greenwich, NY

MEADER William H. of Quaker Springs, NY     February 6, 1871
HAY Fidelia of Greenwich, NY     Greenwich, NY

PARKS Daniel E. of Sandy Hill, NY     February 22, 1871
ASHLEY Emma of Galway, NY

HALL Charles W. of Caldwell, Vt.     February 19, 1871
STAATS Mary of Caldwell, Vt.     French Mountain, NY

| | |
|---|---|
| **HADDEN** Thomas J. of Caldwell, Vt.<br>**GLYNN** Mary H. of Caldwell, Vt. | February 19, 1871<br>French Mountain, NY |
| **FARR** John of Ft. Ann, NY<br>**CLEMENTS** Mrs. Jane of Ft. Ann, NY | February 11, 1871<br>Ft. Ann, NY |
| **BROWN** William T. of Sunbeam, Ill.<br>**WOOD** Sarah M. of Hebron, NY | February 8, 1871<br>Salem, NY |
| **TEARSE** William P. of Eau De Claire, Wis.<br>**DE LONG** Ione of Glens Falls, NY | February 13, 1871<br>Glens Falls, NY |
| **REYNOLDS** James M. of Glens Falls, NY<br>**MILLS** Maggie of Pottersville, NY | February 8, 1871<br>Glens Falls, NY |
| **NORTHUP** J. M.<br>**SILL** Harriet dau of Zachariah | February 8, 1871<br>Hartford, NY |
| **WING** H. Mc Kie son of late Halsey R. of Glens Falls, NY<br>**MINER** Wilhelmina H. of Manchester, Vt. | February 16, 1871<br>Manchester, Vt. |
| **HALL** Edward of Luzerne, NY<br>**SCHOOLCRAFT** Gussie of Luzerne, NY | February 18, 1871<br>Luzerne, NY |
| **KENYON** Hiram of Jackson, NY<br>**ANTHONY** Martha J. of Cambridge, NY | February 16, 1871<br>Greenwich, NY |
| **HENRY** James of Argyle, NY<br>**WIGGINS** Maggie of Argyle, NY | February 14, 1871<br>Argyle, NY |
| **HYDE** Alonzo of Middletown, Vt.<br>**GREGORY** Emma of Sandy Hill, NY | February 28, 18/1<br>Glens Falls, NY |
| **HYDE** Charles of Greenwich, NY<br>**BREWER** Rebecca of Greenwich, NY | February 16, 1871<br>Greenwich, NY |
| **BOYLE** Lewis H. of Albany, NY<br>**WEST** Hattie A. of Glens Falls, NY | March 8, 1871<br>Glens Falls, NY |
| **PLUE** Andrew<br>**GROOME** Jennie | March 5, 1871<br>South Bay, NY |
| **CONNELLY** William<br>**BENTON** Lucinda | February 19, 1871<br>Ft. Ann, NY |
| **MILLER** William H. H. of Baltimore, Md.<br>**FOSTER** Nellie F. dau of Dr. Fordyce F. of Sandy Hill, NY | March 9, 1871<br>Sandy Hill, NY |
| **MC INTYRE** John of Hebron, NY | March 9, 1871 |

MC EACHRON Mary of E. Greenwich, NY — Hebron, NY

BROWN E. G. of Sandy Hill, NY — March 23, 1871
SMALLEY Hattie A. of Sandy Hill, NY — Sandy Hill, NY

BENNETT Albert of Moreau, NY — March 24, 1871
CRANDALL Adeline of Moreau, NY — Glens Falls, NY

MURRAY George S. of Luzerne, NY — March 15, 1871
RAWSON Frances E. of W. Glens Falls, NY — Glens Falls, NY

STRONG N. J. of Ashtabula, Ohio — March 9, 1871
HAMILTON E. A. — Moreau, NY

SWIFT George W. of Ft. Ann, NY — March 14, 1871
WILSON Martha J. of Whitehall, NY — Whitehall, NY

WILSON Thomas D. of Dresden, NY — March 14, 1871
NOBLE Mary J. of Dresden, NY — Whitehall, NY

EARLE John D. of Ft. Ann, NY — March 16, 1871
RISDEN Frankie J. of Texas, Mi. — Ft. Ann, NY

BLAKELEY George A. of Cambridge, NY — March 20, 1871
RUSS Martha dau of John P. of Albany, NY — Albany, NY

MILLER Stephen A. of Glens Falls, NY — March 21, 1871
STEVENSON Sarah M. of Glens Falls, NY — Glens Falls, NY

FOWLER William F. of Argyle, NY — March 22, 1871
BRAYMAN Mary J. of Argyle, NY — Greenwich, NY

IRVING James of Cambridge, NY — March 16, 1871
WEIR Maggie A. of Cambridge, NY — Cambridge, NY

LOY Charles — March 30, 1871
TRIPP Ada — Chester, NY

DOUGAN Mathew W. of Danby, Vt.      (newspaper date) — April 7, 1871
NORTON Adelina A. H. N. dau of Isaac of Granville, NY — Granville, NY

MONTY John C. of Sandy Hill, NY — April 9, 1871
NULTY Mary Elizabeth of Sandy Hill, NY — Glens Falls, NY

LAPHAM Oberon of Glens Falls, NY — April 9, 1871
MERRILL Dora V. of Glens Falls, NY

HELTON William of New York City — March 28, 1871
MC AULEY Maggie of Hartford, NY — Hartford, NY

| | |
|---|---|
| **BULLIS** Freeling H. of Glens Falls, NY | April 4, 1871 |
| **STEERE** Emma A. | Edinburgh, NY |
| | |
| **PORTER** J. Eddy | April 5, 1871 |
| **SANDERSON** Helen | Cambridge, NY |
| | |
| **MC LAUGHLIN** James of Dresden, NY | March 30, 1871 |
| **LOUGEE** Mrs. ____ widow of Louis of Dresden, NY | Dresden, NY |
| | |
| **PARTRIDGE** Frederick of Putnam, NY | April 9, 1871 |
| **PEABODY** Mary Jane of Putnam, NY | Putnam, NY |
| | |
| **WEAVER** George of Ft. Edward, NY | March 29, 1871 |
| **WHALEY** Mary formerly of Salem, NY | Ft. Edward, NY |
| | |
| **WHITCOMB** A. J. | April 12, 1871 |
| **HAWKINS** Sarah C. | Cambridge, NY |
| | |
| **SMITH** James H. of Sandy Hill, NY | April 24, 1871 |
| **PARTRIDGE** Mary of Sandy Hill, NY | Sandy Hill, NY |
| | |
| **RIFENBURG** Wesley of Sandy Hill, NY | April 26, 1871 |
| **DEWEY** Minnie S. of Ft. Edward, NY | Sandy Hill, NY |
| | |
| **COLLETT** John of Troy, NY | April 16, 1871 |
| **LAMPSON** Delia A. of Glens Falls, NY | Warrensburgh, NY |
| | |
| **MUNGER** Charles of Glens Falls, NY | April 16, 1871 |
| **SCHERMERHORN** Miss ____ of Glens Falls, NY | Warrensburgh, NY |
| | |
| **HAWKINS** Sylvester M. of Shaftsbury, Vt. | April 19, 1871 |
| **SPENCER** Ella J. of N. Granville, NY | Cambridge, NY |
| | |
| **ELY** Reuben of Hebron, NY | March 30, 1871 |
| **WOODARD** Mrs. Laura of W. Pawlet, Vt. | Granville, NY |
| | |
| **BEAUREGARD** John H. of Sandy Hill, NY | May 1, 1871 |
| **CROUKE** Nellie of Ft. Edward, NY | Glens Falls, NY |
| | |
| **MILLARD** George W. of Glens Falls, NY | April 16, 1871 |
| **KELLY** Gloriannah of Glens Falls, NY | Glens Falls, NY |
| | |
| **MASON** Herman of Sandy Hill, NY | May 11, 1871 |
| **NORTON** Lizzie of Sandy Hill, NY | Sandy Hill, NY |
| | |
| **DICKINSON** Reuben of Glens Falls, NY | April 29, 1871 |
| **BENTLEY** Mrs. Lenora of Glens Falls, NY | Glens Falls, NY |
| | |
| **BRUMAGIM** Benjamin of Moreau, NY | April 29, 1871 |

CHURCH Ida B. of Glens Falls, NY                    Glens Falls, NY

AMIDON William Franklin of Hebron, NY              May 9, 1871
ROBBINS Augusta of Peru, Vt.                       Salem, NY

HERRICK Eleazor of Bolton, NY                      May 5, 1871
MIDDLETON Helen of Warrensburgh, NY                Warrensburgh, NY

MANNING George of Buffalo, NY                      May 11, 1871
SKIFF U. Frances of Easton, NY                     Easton, NY

HARVEY Gustavus D. of Sandy Hill, NY               May 18, 1871
WILCOX Lottie A. of Sandy Hill, NY                 Sandy Hill, NY

BERRIGAN Thomas of Sandy Hill, NY                  May 20, 1871
HIGGINS Olivia A. of Sandy Hill, NY                Sandy Hill, NY

REA John M. of Hebron, NY                          May 16, 1871
KENYON Jane of Hebron, NY                          Jackson, NY

CAMPBELL Jeremiah of Shushan, NY                   May 17, 1871
IRWIN Jennie of Argyle, NY                         Argyle, NY

WARREN William of Sandy Hill, NY                   May 17, 1871
ACKLEY Libbie of Glens Falls, NY                   Glens Falls, NY

DORR J. Reed of Glens Falls, NY                    May 3, 1871
TEARSE Mary L. of Glens Falls, NY                  Glens Falls, NY

HARRIS Frank J. of Sandy Hill, NY                  June 1, 1871
SHERRILL Julia H. of Sandy Hill, NY                Sandy Hill, NY

LAUDER David D. of Moreau, NY                      May 21, 1871
BAKER Libbie of Moreau, NY                         Glens Falls, NY

HICKEY Patrick of Salem, NY                        May 22, 1871
WALSH Bridget of Ansenta, Conn.                    Ansenta, Conn.

LAW William of Shushan, NY        (newspaper date) June 9, 1871
DUFF Mary of E. Salem, NY                          E. Salem, NY

JENKINS Dr. of M. Granville, NY                    May 25, 1871
WILLIAMS Louisa of Fairhaven, Vt.                  Fairhaven, Vt.

BARBER Simeon T. Jr. of Glens Falls, NY            June 7, 1871
JOHNSON Nora of Glens Falls, NY                    Glens Falls, NY

MARSH Albert M. of Ft. Ann, NY                     June 8, 1871
PARDO Lucy of Ft. Ann, NY                          Ft. Ann, NY

| | |
|---|---|
| ARCHIBALD A. Jr. of Cattaraugus Co. NY<br>BENNETT Fannie of Ft. Edward, NY | June 7, 1871<br>Ft. Edward, NY |
| MADISON Charley of Center Creek, NY<br>GOODNOW Mandy of Center Creek, NY | June 4, 1871<br>Glens Falls, NY |
| JAMES Jeremiah S. of Sandy Hill, NY<br>REMINGTON Ella M. of Sandy Hill, NY | June 28, 1871 |
| GILMAN E. T. of Williamsport, Pa.<br>TRUE Eliza M. of S. Glens Falls, NY | June 15, 1871<br>Glens Falls, NY |
| RUSSELL Melvin of Queensbury, NY<br>MC DONALD Janette of Queensbury, NY | June 20, 1871 |
| BOWKER Charles of Schroon Lake, NY<br>WORTHINGTON Olive of Schroon Lake, NY | July 4, 1871<br>Sandy Hill, NY |
| OLDENHOUSE Charles of Albany Co. NY<br>O'DELL Flora of Putnam, NY | July 5, 1871<br>Putnam, NY |
| HUDSON Charles of Hebron, NY<br>MUNSON Celia of Hebron, NY | June 21, 1871<br>Ft. Edward, NY |
| ALLEN Horace C. of Hartford, NY<br>MARTIN Georgie C. of Hartford, NY | July 3, 1871<br>Hartford, NY |
| GRIFFIN Alonzo W. of Kingsbury, NY<br>PHILLIPS M. Viola of Sandy Hill, NY | July 20, 1871<br>Sandy Hill, NY |
| JUDD Evin R. K. of Whitehall, NY<br>GREEN Eliza of Troy, NY | June 10, 1871<br>Whitehall, NY |
| DERBY Sheldon C. of E. Rupert, Vt.<br>FILCH Eliza of E. Rupert, Vt. | July 5, 1871<br>Granville, NY |
| RUMBARD Alfred of Sandy Hill, NY<br>SENECAL Delia of Sandy Hill, NY | July 24, 1871<br>Glens Falls, NY |
| BEAULAC Phillip of Sandy Hill, NY<br>SOMERSETTE Philomene of Sandy Hill, NY | July 24, 1871<br>Glens Falls, NY |
| DELORREA Joseph of Jessups Landing, NY<br>STURDEVANT Clorinda of Jessup Landing, NY | July 16, 1871<br>Glens Falls, NY |
| POTTER Albert G. of Kansas<br>NUMAN Delia A. dau of Orange of Sandy Hill, NY | July 5, 1871<br>Glens Falls, NY |
| BREWER William of Greenwich, NY | July 13, 1871 |

SMITH Elizabeth of Greenwich, NY          Schuylerville, NY

DE LONG C. J. of Sandy Hill, NY          July 27, 1871
CLENDON Mary of Sandy Hill, NY          Glens Falls, NY

PATTEE David of Ft. Edward, NY          July 26, 1871
WILCOX Lorina L. of Greenwich, NY          Greenwich, NY

BERRY Sheldon C. of E. Rupert, Vt.          July 5, 1871
FILCH Eliza C. of E. Rupert, Vt.          Granville, NY

CASAVANT Charles of Glens Falls, NY          August 2, 1871
GREEN Laura of Glens Falls, NY          Glens Falls, NY

HOWARD E. W. of Warrensburgh, NY          July 31, 1871
FENTON Mrs. Adelia C. of Glens Falls, NY          Glens Falls, NY

WEST James of Glens Falls, NY          July 30, 1871
FLEWALLING Mrs. Sarah of Glens Falls, NY          Caldwell, NY

SCOTT Charles of Salem, NY          July 29, 1871
GREEN Nancy M. of Jackson, NY          Cambridge, NY

COOK Sanford M. of Granville, NY          August 8, 1871
GRIFFITH Kate of Granville, NY          Granville, NY

MALTHANER Martin          July 29, 1871
JOHNSON Ellen          Salem, NY

INGALLS Silas          August 12, 1871
STYLES Lucy          S. Hartford, NY

HULL L. L. D. of Oak Forest          August 13, 1871
SWEET Melissa          Moreau, NY

COOPE John E. of Blackington, Mass.          August 17, 1871
WHITNEY Ursala E.          Center Falls, NY

BENSON Lewis E. of Sudbury, Vt.          September 7, 1871
BLOOD Lucy A. of Forestdale, Vt.          Putnam, NY

HARTMAN Exra of Glens Falls, NY          August 31, 1871
PECK Julia Ann of Queensbury, NY          Glens Falls, NY

BAKER Lansing of Shushan, NY          September 5, 1871
MC BATH Margaret of Salem, NY          Salem, NY

PRICE Rev. James of Frankford, Pa.          September 7, 1871
CANNON Anna R.          Coila, NY

| | |
|---|---|
| HALE Levi of Putnam ,NY<br>BURDETT Jane of Whitehall, NY | September 11, 1871<br>Putnam, NY |
| MERRILL Henry E. of Bridgeport, Vt.<br>MURDOCK Anna B. of Crown Point, NY | September 12, 1871<br>Crown Point, NY |
| FINCH Lewis H. of E. Greenwich, NY<br>DONAHUE Mary A. of Easton, NY | September 18, 1871<br>Greenwich, NY |
| COON Daniel F. of Salem, NY<br>PERRY Sarah M. of Salem, NY | September 13, 1871<br>Salem, NY |
| MC FARLAND Henry<br>COX Emma dau of Lyman | September 20/27, 1871<br>Ft. Edward, NY |
| HARRIS S. P.<br>WILLIAMS Cora | September 24, 1871<br>Sandy Hill, NY |
| QUA Charles<br>DOWNS Olive | September 24, 1871<br>Hartford, NY |
| MILLS Edward E. of Schroon, NY<br>RUSSELL Edna of Glens Falls, NY | September 26, 1871<br>Glens Falls, NY |
| QUINLIN Timothy of Glens Falls, NY<br>BYRNE Winifred of Glens Falls, NY | September 13, 1871<br>Glens Falls, NY |
| HERBERT Irving<br>INGALLS Sarah dau of D. C. | October 4, 1871<br>N. Granville, NY |
| CRANDALL James of French Mountain, NY<br>BROWN Sarah Jane dau of George | October 5, 1871<br>French Mountain, NY |
| VIELE Phillip of Glens Falls, NY<br>VARNIA Delia of Wilton, NY | October 3, 1871<br>Wilton, NY |
| REILLY James of Stony Creek, NY<br>WALSH Jane A. of Cambridge, NY | October 4, 1871<br>Cambridge, NY |
| HOWARD Warren L. of Hebron, NY<br>ROOT Flora of Hebron, NY | September 19, 1871<br>Hebron, NY |
| GUNDRY Thomas of Ft. Edward, NY<br>LENNON Julia of Ft. Edward, NY | October 12, 1871<br>Sandy Hill, NY |
| WRIGHT Silas formerly of Sandy Hill, NY<br>CLARK Nellie B. formerly of Sandy Hill, NY | October 8, 1871<br>Glens Falls, NY |
| NOBLE Charles E. son of Rev. Edward Noble | October 26, 1871 |

| | |
|---|---|
| **WAIT** Lydia P. dau of N. W. | Sandy Hill, NY |
| **COOLIDGE** J. M. of Glens Falls, NY | October 18, 1871 |
| **MC EACHRON** Hannah M. of Glens Falls, NY | Glens Falls, NY |
| **WHITNEY** Walter Scott of Glens Falls, NY (newspaper date) | October 27, 1871 |
| **VAN TASSEL** Lovina of Glens Falls, NY | Glens Falls, NY |
| **WHITE** T. of Verona, Iowa | October 23, 1871 |
| **MITCHELL** C. M. dau of Sardis of Whitehall, NY | Whitehall, NY |
| **DANIELS** William (newspaper date) | October 27, 1871 |
| **GERM** Mrs. Elizabeth of Sandy Hill, NY | Salem, NY |
| **OWENS** F. Monroe of W. Ft. Ann, NY | October 2, 1871 |
| **DE GOLYER** Gertie D. of W. Ft. Ann, NY | W. Ft. Ann, NY |
| **DOWNING** Jacob of Denver, Col. | November 1, 1871 |
| **ROSEKRANS** Carrie E. of Clifton Park, NY | Glens Falls, NY |
| **PATTERSON** S. A. of New York City | October 26, 1871 |
| **HOOKER** Frances L. dau of late Daniel of Poultney, Vt. | Poultney, Vt. |
| **HALL** Robert E. of Argyle, NY | November 9, 1871 |
| **BARKLEY** Annie M. of Argyle, NY | Argyle, NY |
| **PRAY** Rev. W. T. of Centreport, NY | November 8, 1871 |
| **BARDEN** Adelia M. of Queensbury, NY | Queensbury, NY |
| **GILBERT** John W. of Stony Creek, NY | October 15, 1871 |
| **REVERE** Mary of Stony Creek, NY | Stony Creek, NY |
| **AGAN** Charles W. of White Creek, NY | November 2, 1871 |
| **BUTTERFIELD** Maggie J. of White Creek, NY | White Creek, NY |
| **BARTHOLOMEW** George O. of Whitehall, NY | November 8, 1871 |
| **INMAN** Iola of Hampton, NY | Hampton, NY |
| **YOUNG** John M. of Smiths Basin, NY | November 9, 1871 |
| **SHAW** Julia of Smiths Basin, NY | Smiths Basin, NY |
| **SHIELDS** Charles of Moreau, NY | November 8, 1871 |
| **WHIPPLE** Julia M. of Moreau, NY | Glens Falls, NY |
| **HAVILAND** Joseph age 78 yrs | November 2, 1871 |
| **HAVILAND** Mrs. Hannah age 74 yrs | Queensbury, NY |
| **THOMPSON** James F. formerly of Ft. Ann, NY | October 18, 1871 |
| **RAINEY** Lucelia C. dau of late Samuel of Georgetown, DC | Georgetown, DC |

| | |
|---|---|
| BENTLEY W. H. of White Creek, NY | October 22, 1871 |
| AELITT Mrs. Martha of White Creek, NY | White Creek, NY |
| | |
| STEVENSON Wellington of Glens Falls, NY | November 16, 1871 |
| ROBINSON W. M. of Glens Falls, NY | Sandy Hill, NY |
| | |
| INGALLS Milo H. of N. Granville, NY | November 14, 1871 |
| NORTHUP Louisa J. of Hartford, NY | Hartford, NY |
| | |
| GRANT Charles H. of Whitehall, NY | November 20, 1871 |
| HUBBARD Sarah C. of Ft. Ann, NY | Smiths Basin, NY |
| | |
| MORTON Clark A. of Sudbury, Vt. | November 6, 1871 |
| HOFF Mary O. of Brandon, Vt. | Hampton, NY |
| | |
| HATFIELD John W. of New York City | November 29, 1871 |
| DOUBLEDAY Mary of Sandy Hill, NY | Sandy Hill, NY |
| | |
| ROSEKRANS Clinton | November 23, 1871 |
| BRIGGS Fannie E. of Albany, NY | Albany, NY |
| | |
| BISSELL George S. of Glens Falls, NY | November 8, 1871 |
| BALDWIN Clara R. of Luzerne, NY | Johnstown, NY |
| | |
| FITZGERALD David of Ft. Edward, NY | November 18, 1871 |
| DONOVAN Margaret of Glens Falls, NY | Glens Falls, NY |
| | |
| PIKE Thomas of Ft. Edward, NY | November 9, 1871 |
| POWELL Mrs. Maria M. of Ft. Edward, NY | Ft. Edward, NY |
| | |
| GRIFFIN Edward of Albany, NY (newspaper date) | December 15, 1871 |
| WOOD Emma A. dau of William of Whitehall, NY | Whitehall, NY |
| | |
| FINCH Isaac of Ft. Ann, NY | November 28, 1871 |
| NORRIS Maria of Ft. Ann, NY | Ft. Ann, NY |
| | |
| COLE Leander of N. Hebron, NY | December 9, 1871 |
| SMITH Ella P. of N. Hebron, NY | Granville, NY |
| | |
| SAWYER E. R. of Sandy Hill, NY | December 21, 1871 |
| LORD Sarah E. dau of J. D. Lord of Leyden, NY | Leyden, NY |
| | |
| HOWLAND Lansing M. of Ft. Edward, NY | December 25, 1871 |
| O'DELL Hattie C. of Ft. Edward, NY | Ft. Edward, NY |
| | |
| WILLARD George of Glens Falls, NY | December 20, 1871 |
| WING Mrs. Edgar M. of Glens Falls, NY | Glens Falls, NY |
| | |
| CHAPMAN Charles C. of Whitehall, NY | December 21, 1871 |

| | |
|---|---|
| **WILSON** Annie M. of Whitehall, NY | Whitehall, NY |
| **WILLIAMS** Albert of Sandy Hill, NY<br>**ELMS** Fanny of Queensbury, NY | December 24, 1871<br>Sandy Hill, NY |
| **HENRY** George of Granville, NY<br>**BISHOP** Lucy dau of John Bishop of Granville, NY | December 28, 1871<br>Granville, NY |
| **WHITTEMORE** E. C. of Hartford, NY<br>**BULL** Fannie of Granville, NY | December 29, 1871<br>Granville, NY |
| **REED** James E. of Middletown, Vt.<br>**WHITE** Mary B. of Putnam, NY | November 1, 1871<br>Putnam, NY |
| **WOOD** J. W. of Whitehall, NY<br>**DYER** Emma L. of Hampton, NY | January 2, 1872<br>Hampton, NY |
| **ROUNDS** James of Greenfield, NY<br>**WELLS** Emma of Queensbury, NY | December 31, 1871<br>Glens Falls, NY |
| **BELL** Lewis W. of Ft. Edward<br>**SANDERS** Kate E. of Ft. Edward, NY | January 2, 1872<br>Ft. Miller, NY |
| **WILLIAMS** Erastus T.<br>**DENNISON** Sarah E. | December 28, 1871<br>Salem, NY |
| **WILLIAMS** Dewitt<br>**DENNISON** Matilda F. | December 28, 1871<br>Salem, NY |
| **ROGERS** Wilson of Hebron, NY<br>**HAY** Evelyn of W. Rupert, Vt. | January 3, 1872<br>Rupert, Vt. |
| **WHITNEY** Benjamin of Sandy Hill, NY<br>**SMITH** Maria of Sandy Hill, NY | January 18, 1872<br>Sandy Hill, NY |
| **SIMPSON** John Jr. of Putnam, NY<br>**GRAHAM** Jennie of Putnam, NY | December 31, 1871<br>Putnam, NY |
| **WHEELER** D. G. of Pawlet, Vt.<br>**ACKLEY** Emma C. of Salem, NY | January 17, 1872<br>Sandy Hill, NY |
| **WEST** J. F. of Hebron, NY<br>**BELL** Janie of Hebron, NY | December 14, 1871<br>Hebron, NY |
| **HOWES** L. of Ft. Ann, NY<br>**WILSEY** Alice of Ft. Ann, NY | January 2, 1872<br>Ft. Ann, NY |
| **DURHAM** Albert of Hebron, NY<br>**FOSTER** Lucretia M. of Hebron, NY | January 11, 1872<br>Hebron, NY |

MASON Charles L.       (newspaper date)     February 1, 1872
BARBOUR Julia E.                                   W. Granville, NY

WILLIAMS Martin of Shushan, NY             January 16, 1872
STILES Eliza H. of Shushan, NY             Shushan, NY

CRAWFORD Charles V. of Ft. Edward, NY(newspaper date) February 1, 1872
SMITH Anna of Granville, NY                     Granville, NY

MOREHOUSE H. C. of Salem, NY             January 23, 1872
STICKLES Lillie E. of Valley Falls, NY        Valley Fall, NY

MIDDLETON Joseph H. of Hartford, NY       January 21, 1872
PARISH Sophia N. E. of Saratoga Springs, NY   Glens Falls, NY

COX Orlando of Hebron, NY               January 25, 1872
PATTEN Mary of Hebron, NY              Hebron, NY

MC CONNELL James A.                February 1, 1872
MILLIMAN Mary dau of Pierce of N. Argyle, NY   Argyle, NY

WILLIAMSON William J. of Hebron, NY       January 30, 1872
POWELL Mary of Hebron, NY             Belcher, NY

EVANS W. L. of Ft. Edward, NY            January 30, 1872
FELL Flora M. of Ft. Edward, NY          Glens Falls, NY

ALLEN Charles L. of Whitehall, NY        January 30, 1872
TIERNEY Abbie of Whitehall, NY         Whitehall, NY

BALDRIDGE Dr. J. of Shushan, NY        January 31, 1872
KEEFER M. J. of Shushan, NY           Shushan, NY

HEATH William                     January 30, 1872
MC MULLEN Margaret               Argyle, NY

MERRIMAN Simeon of Whitehall, NY     February 14, 1872
GOSS Mary L. of Whitehall, NY         Whitehall, NY

JILLSON Henry C. of Whitehall, NY      February 14, 1872
BOWEN Susie C. of Plattsburgh, NY      Plattsburgh, NY

WRIGHT Samuel                   February 8, 1872
GRANT Mary J.                   N. Granville, NY

SAVILLE Myron                  February 13, 1872
COOK Hattie A.                 N. Granville, NY

ELLIS John S. of Cambridge, NY         February 8, 1872

| | |
|---|---|
| **BURNY** S. Alvira of N. Granville, NY | N. Granville, NY |
| | |
| **LISCOMBE** Frank of Brattleboro, Vt. | February 21, 1872 |
| **MASON** Dollie dau of O. T. Mason of N. Granville, NY | N. Granville, NY |
| | |
| **MANLY** R. E. of Granville, NY | February 16, 1872 |
| **JOHNSON** R. of New York City | Albany, NY |
| | |
| **FOWLER** David D. of Argyle, NY | February 22, 1872 |
| **NILES** H. Abbie of Sandgate, Vt. | |
| | |
| **ORCUTT** William S. of Salem, NY | February 20, 1872 |
| **LYON** Mary J. of E. Salem, NY | E. Salem, NY |
| | |
| **ROBBINS** Franklin S. of W. Glens Falls, NY | February 14, 1872 |
| **NEWCOMB** Mary Jane of W. Glens Falls, NY | W. Glens Falls, NY |
| | |
| **NORTON** Martin F. | February 22, 1872 |
| **WILKINS** E. E. F. of E. Rupert, Vt. | Granville, NY |
| | |
| **NELSON** Frank of Hebron, NY | February 15, 1872 |
| **GOURLEY** Grace dau of Alexander of Hartford, NY | W. Pawlet, Vt. |
| | |
| **ALSTON** Edward J. of Queensbury, NY | February 28, 1872 |
| **LANDON** Esther of Queensbury, NY | |
| | |
| **MOORE** Charles B. of Saratoga, NY | February 20, 1872 |
| **PATTERSON** Louisa M. of Ft. Ann, NY | Ft. Ann, NY |
| | |
| **KNOWLTON** Edward of Crown Point, NY | February 21, 1872 |
| **WRIGHT** Mary of Putnam, NY | Putnam, NY |
| | |
| **BROWN** Julius A. of Dresden, NY | March 2, 1872 |
| **WILSEY** Josephine A. of Dresden, NY | Whitehall, NY |
| | |
| **RUSSELL** Thomas Jr. of W. Ft. Ann, NY | February 22, 1872 |
| **BISHOP** Maria of W. Ft. Ann, NY | |
| | |
| **WELLS** H. H. Jr. of Richmond, Va. (newspaper date) | March 21, 1872 |
| **MORGAN** Kate E. | Glens Falls, NY |
| | |
| **MC KERROW** Robert of N. Argyle, NY | March 14, 1872 |
| **FORBES** Almira of Ft. Edward, NY | Ft. Edward, NY |
| | |
| **WAIT** Franklin of Granville, NY | March 14, 1872 |
| **STEWART** Laura of Granville, NY | Granville, NY |
| | |
| **MC NEIL** Dr. James | March 12, 1872 |
| **CLARK** Josephine G. dau of R. G. Clark | Argyle, NY |

| | | |
|---|---|---|
| WILSON Robert K. of Salem, NY | | March 14, 1872 |
| BOYD Frank L. of Salem, NY | | Salem, NY |
| | | |
| SPOCK Howard of New York City | | March 23, 1872 |
| MURDOCK Naomi H. of Glens Falls, NY | | Glens Falls, NY |
| | | |
| LAMB Oscar of Ft. Ann, NY | | March 14, 1872 |
| SKINNER Lillie of Ft. Ann, NY | | Ft. Ann, NY |
| | | |
| MC DOUGAL James of Argyle, NY | | March 20, 1872 |
| GILCHRIST Esther of Argyle, NY | | Argyle, NY |
| | | |
| COON Rufus of Salem, NY | | March 19, 1872 |
| WILSON Helen of Salem, NY | | Salem, NY |
| | | |
| HARVEY Samuel of Whitehall, NY | | March 11, 1872 |
| PIERCE Angelia of Benson, Vt. | | Benson, Vt |
| | | |
| STEVENS Henry A. | | March 13, 1872 |
| SWIFT Ruth | | N. Granville, NY |
| | | |
| CURTIS Harmon H. of San Jose, Cal. | | March 21, 1872 |
| PEELER Louisa | | Cambridge, NY |
| | | |
| BARBER James P. of Red Oak, Iowa | | March 13, 1872 |
| MC LAUGHLIN Mary of Putnam, NY | | Putnam, NY |
| | | |
| FERRIS Louis of Glens Falls, NY | (newspaper date) | April 4, 1872 |
| ADAMS Julia of Glens Falls, NY | | Sandy Hill, NY |
| | | |
| PHILLIPS Benjamin F. | | March 27, 1872 |
| HERRINGTON Julia M. | | Greenwich, NY |
| | | |
| COTY Clements of Sandy hill, NY | | April 8, 1872 |
| PREVILLE Adeline of Sandy Hill, NY | | Glens Falls, NY |
| | | |
| BRUNETT F. of Sandy Hill, NY | | April 8, 1872 |
| CROSS Matilda of Sandy Hill, NY | | Glens Falls, NY |
| | | |
| NORTON Benjamin T. | | March 20, 1872 |
| NORTHUP Almira T. | | Granville, NY |
| | | |
| O'DELL Augustus D. of Ft. Edward, NY | | April 1, 1872 |
| WILLIS Sarah A. of Ft. Edward, NY | | Ft. Edward, NY |
| | | |
| HOLLISTER Sorena of Whitehall, NY | | April 2, 1872 |
| BARRETT Julia A. of Dresden, NY | | Dresden, NY |
| | | |
| RIPLEY Charles of Dresden, NY | | April 3, 1872 |

| | |
|---|---|
| **ADAMS** Anna dau of Edward Adams of Westhaven, Vt. | Westhaven, NY |
| **FLYNN** John of Cambridge, NY<br>**CARR** Libbie of Greenwich, NY | April 3, 1872<br>Salem, NY |
| **JOHNSON** Rev. C. A. of Whitehall, NY   (newspaper date)<br>**SCOTT** Sarah E. of Whitehall, NY | April 18, 1872<br>Whitehall, NY |
| **COLTON** George of Salem, NY<br>**TIERNEY** Maggie of Salem, NY | March 31, 1872<br>Salem, NY |
| **HATCH** John of Cambridge, NY<br>**HILL** Martha E. of E. Greenwich, NY | April 10, 1872<br>E. Greenwich, NY |
| **HILL** Merritt of E. Greenwich, NY<br>**CARSWELL** Ida F. of E. Greenwich, NY | April 10, 1872<br>E. Greenwich, NY |
| **WILLIS** Silas of Sandy Hill, NY<br>**LITTLE** Susie of Sandy Hill, NY | April 16, 1872<br>Ft. Edward, NY |
| **GRAVES** R. A. of Salisbury, Vt.<br>**GRAVES** Mary E. dau of Dr. H. **MEEKER** of Granville | April 27, 1872<br>Granville, NY |
| **HUBBS** Paul K. of Valejo, Cal.<br>**DILLINGHAM** Mary A. of Glens Falls, NY | April 14, 1872<br>Valejo, Cal. |
| **PLUNKETT** Thomas of White Creek, NY<br>**MC MAHON** Mary Ann of Greenwich, NY | April 21, 1872<br>Salem, NY |
| **AUSTIN** Judson H. of Granville, NY<br>**DARBY** Flora A. of Granville, NY | April 20, 1872<br>Granville, NY |
| **LILLIE** John S. of Putnam, NY<br>**DEDRICK** Emma of Lowell, Mass. | May 2, 1872<br>Putnam, NY |
| **SHEDD** G. W. of Filchville, NY<br>**MAGRATH** Jane E. of Filchville, Vt. | May 1, 1872<br>Ft. Edward, NY |
| **VAUGHN** John of Glens Falls, NY<br>**QUINLIN** Ellen of Glens Falls, NY | May 2, 1872<br>Glens Falls, NY |
| **THOMPSON** John of Glens Falls, NY<br>**CHAMPAYNE** Mary of Luzerne, NY | April 28, 1872<br>Luzerne, NY |
| **CODMAN** A. M. of Salem, NY<br>**HENSHAW** Fannie M. of Hillsborough, NH | April 25, 1872<br>Hillsborough, NH |
| **WAKEMAN** Dr. Harwood of Sandy Hill, NY<br>**MURPHY** Sophia L. of Sandy Hill, NY | May 15, 1872<br>Sandy Hill, NY |

GRIFFITH E. P. of Sandy Hill, NY — May 9, 1872 — Sandy Hill, NY
NEWTON Mrs. B. of Glens Falls, NY

HULETT George S. of Pawlet, Vt. — May 1, 1872 — Granville, NY
ROBINSON Fannie L. of Pawlet, Vt.

MELLEN John of Dresden, NY — May 1, 1872 — Dresden, NY
BENJAMIN Cornelia of Dresden, NY

SHERMAN Henry L. of Greenwich, NY — May 1, 1872 — Greenwich, NY
MAY Katie of Greenwich, NY

ANDRESS Franklin E. of Hartford, NY — May 1, 1872 — Saratoga, NY
BROWN Libbie M. of Saratoga Springs, NY

AMES Austin of Whitehall, NY — May 16, 1872 — Whitehall, NY
CHAPIN Mattie of Whitehall, NY

HOWARD Dr. Daniel B. — May 15, 1872 — Warrensburgh, NY
GRIFFIN Louise F. dau of Duncan

ROBIN William H. of Winhall, Vt. (newspaper date) — May 23, 1872 — Hebron, NY
AMIDON Caroline of Hebron, NY

ROSS George of Whitehall, NY — May 2, 1872 — Whitehall, NY
RYAN Mary of Whitehall, NY

HUGHES Charles H. — May 11, 1872 — Argyle, NY
LANT Annie

CLEMENTS Edgar A. of Stony Creek, NY — May 8, 1872 — Stony Creek, NY
BRADLEY Adila of Stony Creek, NY

SIMPSON Wellesley B. of Ft. Edward, NY — May 22, 1872 — Ft. Edward, NY
LISCOMB Alza S. of Ft. Edward, NY

KEECH Oscar D. of Ft. Ann, NY — May 19, 1872 — Ft. Ann, NY
GRANGER Josephine of Ft. Ann, NY

BROWNELL Horace of Cambridge, NY — May 22, 1872 — Cambridge, NY
GALWAY Sarah of Cambridge, NY

BROMLEY Robert of Danby, Vt. — May 17, 1872 — Granville, NY
MADISON Ada of Danby, Vt.

STEVENSON Daniel W. of Argyle, NY — June 12, 1872 — Argyle, NY
BARKLEY Maggie of Argyle, NY

CALL Andrew S. of Glens Falls, NY — June 12, 1872

BAKER E. Jennie adopted dau of H. B. VAUGHN          Sandy Hill, NY

MC DONALD L. G. of Glens Falls, NY
TWINING Clara M. dau of Thomas late of Berkshire, Mass.          Lansingburgh, NY

REED Chauncey of Greenwich, NY          June 13, 1872
ROMAN Mary R. of Cambridge, NY          Cambridge, NY

ROUSE Charles          June 3, 1872
BARTON Libbie          Whitehall, NY

BARSS Frederick of Chester, NY          June 9, 1872
JONES Olive of Chester, NY          Pottersville, NY

NORTON John M. of Whitehall, NY          May 20, 1872
MARIAR Jennie M. of N. Granville, NY          Whitehall, NY

WHIPPLE Edward of Dresden, NY          June 3, 1872
CHASE Lydia A. of Dresden, NY          Whitehall, NY

SIMPSON Henry of Greenwich, NY          May 26, 1872
REED Fannie S. of Greenwich, NY          Greenwich, NY

MURRAY John of Whitehall, NY          May 26, 1872
TROTIER Mrs. Aurelia of Whitehall, NY          Whitehall, NY

BARDEN Asahel of Argyle, NY          June 19, 1872
CROSS Alvira P. dau of S. O. Cross of Kingsbury, NY          Kingsbury, NY

CROWLEY John of Gansevort, NY          June 28, 1872
MC GOWAN Lucinda of Gansevort, NY          Sandy Hill, NY

HARRIS Ira of Kingsbury, NY          June 16, 1872
HARRIS Clara A. of Kingsbury, NY          Sandy Hill, NY

COWAN Fred S.          June 16, 1872
GRISWOLD Cora C.          Whitehall, NY

AGATE John of Pittsford, NY          June 19, 1872
AUSTIN Mary of Glens Falls, NY          Glens Falls, NY

WOOD J. M. of Albany, NY          June 12, 1872
MIDDLETON Cary Jane of Warrensburgh, NY          Warrensburgh, NY

POTTER Sanford of Whitehall, NY          June 5, 1872
WEBSTER Annie of Plattsburgh, NY          Plattsburgh, NY

BENNETT Hazen W. Jr. of Ft. Edward, NY          June 19, 1872
PAYNE Lucy A. of Ft. Edward, NY          Ft. Edward, NY

| | | |
|---|---|---|
| WOOD William of Milwaukee, Wis. | | June 27, 1872 |
| SEELYE Fannie | | Glens Falls, NY |
| | | |
| WILSON Charles H. of Whitehall, NY | | June 24, 1872 |
| HARRIS Maggie of Whitehall, NY | | N. Granville, NY |
| | | |
| KITISON George A. | | June 27, 1872 |
| TISDALE Ellen B. dau of Capt. H. G. of Whitehall, NY | | Whitehall, NY |
| | | |
| STEVENSON Donald M. formerly of Cambridge, NY | | June 3, 1872 |
| DE MARIE Helen of Chicago, Ill. | | Chicago, Ill |
| | | |
| HILLMAN John M. of Jackson, NY | | June 12, 1872 |
| SMITH Jennie of Greenwich, NY | | Saratoga, NY |
| | | |
| CLARK Seth of Salem, NY | | June 26, 1872 |
| RUSSELL Sarah A. of Salem, NY | | Salem, NY |
| | | |
| MILLER Hill | (newspaper date) | July 4, 1872 |
| CURTIS Eliza sister of John W. Curtis | | Greenwich, NY |
| | | |
| GILCHRIST William | | June 12, 1872 |
| MC MINN Mary Ann | | N. Argyle, NY |
| | | |
| YARTER Mitchell of Kingsbury, NY | | July 3, 1872 |
| AMOREUX Azelia L. of Kingsbury, NY | | |
| | | |
| QUINLIN Norman of Glens Falls, NY | | July 8, 1871 |
| WEST Mary A. of Glens Falls, NY | | |
| | | |
| SMITH Frederick of Hebron, NY | | July 3, 1872 |
| NEFF Ann of Rupert, Vt. | | Salem, NY |
| | | |
| MOSHER Reuben H. of Ft. Plain, NY | | July 4, 1872 |
| HEATH Amanda of Northville, NY | | Whitehall, NY |
| | | |
| HYATT Jesse H. of Battenville, NY | | July 4, 1872 |
| VANCE Ada of Battenville, NY | | Greenwich, NY |
| | | |
| MILES Henry B. of Easton, NY | | July 4, 1872 |
| LENT Alice A. of Easton, NY | | Greenwich, NY |
| | | |
| HAMMOND Arthur of Caldwell, NY | | July 4, 1872 |
| HAMMOND Anna M. of Caldwell, NY | | Caldwell, NY |
| | | |
| WEIR Charles of Jackson, NY | | October 19, 1871 |
| WILSON Rosalthie V. dau of Osborn of Greenwich, NY | | Shushan, NY |
| | | |
| COOLEY James S. of Ft. Edward, NY | | June 20, 1872 |

CLARK M. Reba of Willsborough, NY                                    Willsborough, NY

MC KERNON David of Granville, NY                                     July 4, 1872
WOODARD Emma of Hebron, NY                                           N. Argyle, NY

WYMAN Albert H. of Ft. Ann, NY                                       July 4, 1872
SMITH Mary M. of Ft. Ann, NY                                         Glens Falls, NY

FARR Edgar A. of Greenfield, NY        (newspaper date)    July 25, 1872
DRAPER Deborah of Ft. Edward, NY                                     Ft. Edward, NY

FLAGG Anthony of Poultney, Vt.                                       July 7, 1872
SCUDDER Mattie J.                                                    S. Granville, NY

ANTHONY Clarence of Amsterdam, NY                                    August 4, 1872
JACKSON Mary A. of Sandy Hill, NY                                    Sandy Hill, NY

JUCKET Olif of Whitehall, NY                                         August 2, 1872
SNODY Clara of Dresden, NY                                           Hartford, NY

PITCHER A. D.                                                        July 18, 1872
POTTER Josie                                                         Ft. Edward, NY

KETCHUM Dr. T. J. of Pittsford, Vt.                                  July 30, 1872
SLAUSON Mary dau of Rev. J. L. of Troy Conference          Ticonderoga, NY

MEEHAN John of Salem, NY                                             July 18, 1872
KETRANS Bridget of Salem, NY                                         Cambridge, NY

WATSON William of Union Village, NY                                  July 30, 1872
CARSWELL Mary A. dau of A. Carswell of Ft. Miller, NY      Ft. Miller, NY

ROTCH William of Glens Falls, NY                                     August 5, 1872
FRAZIER Mehetable R. of Madoc, Canada W.                             Queensbury, NY

JENKINS Lyman J. son of Dr. Samuel Jenkins                           August 11, 1872
MURRAY Almira of Kingsbury, NY                                       Glens Falls, NY

WHITE Will S. of Glens Falls, NY                                     August 19, 1872
BENNETT Mary E. of Glens Falls, NY                                   Glens Falls, NY

GRAHAM F. H. of Ft. Plain, NY                                        August 17, 1872
NORTHUP Ada W. dau of George                                         W. Granville, NY

SPRIGER Henry of Gloversville, NY                                    September 10, 1872
MARIHEW Mary A. of Gloversville, NY                                  Sandy Hill, NY

LEE Napoleon of Glens Falls, NY                                      September 3, 1872
HARP Jennie                                                          Argyle, NY

**DODD** Henry S.                                              July 21, 1872
**TILFORD** Mary J.                                            Argyle, NY

**HAVILAND** Joseph D. of Glens Falls, NY                      August 27, 1872
**DE LONG** Maggie E. of Glens Falls, NY                       Glens Falls, NY

**THOMAS** Stephen of Glens Falls, NY                          September 3, 1872
**KENYON** Emma of S. Glens Falls, NY                          S. Glens Falls, NY

**REARDON** Daniel of Salem, NY                                August 16, 1872
**BOYLEN** Ann E. of Salem, NY                                 Whitehall, NY

**MILLETT** George of Whitehall, NY                            August 2, 1872
**MANSFIELD** Mary A. of Whitehall, NY                         Whitehall, NY

**SOUPER** Alonza A. of Granville, NY                          August 18, 1872
**TILL** Martha A. of Granville, NY                            Whitehall, NY

**ORCUTT** Calvin B. of Elizabeth, NJ                          September 28, 1872
**WILLETT** Minnie H. dau of Addison of N. Granville, NY       N. Granville, NY

**BRAYMER** Albert E. of Chicago, Ill.     (newspaper date)    September 19, 1872
**CROSBY** Minnie C. of Granville, NY                          Granville, NY

**BROWN** Clayton of Granville, NY                             September 15, 1872
**NORTHUP** Amanda dau of Thomas of Granville, NY              Granville, NY

**TALLMADGE** Edwin of Hoosick, NY                             September 7, 1872
**WALLER** Mary of Greenwich, NY                               Greenwich, NY

**DEWEY** George of Sandy Hill, NY                             September 29, 1872
**CORNELL** Sarah J. of Sandy Hill, NY                         Sandy Hill, NY

**JACKWAY** Frank A. of Westhaven, Vt.     (newspaper date)    October 3, 1872
**BARRETT** Mattie dau of Joseph Barrett of Dresden, NY        Dresden, NY

**YOUNG** Benjamin of Corinth, NY                              September 11, 1872
**ARLING** Mary E. of Corinth, NY                              Glens Falls, NY

**LONG** Able E. of N. Cambridge, Mass.                        September 26, 1872
**WILKINS** Sarah L. of N. Cambridge, Mass.                    Salem, NY

**LARAVEA** Stephen of Sandy Hill, NY                          September 16, 1872
**BAILEY** Frances of Sandy Hill, NY                           Whitehall, NY

**BALL** James B. of Boston, Mass.                             September 24, 1872
**ACKERMAN** Harriet of Boston, Mass.                          Argyle, NY

**WOODELL** Harvey of Hartford, NY                             September 19, 1872

DE KALB Emma of Granville, NY     N. Granville, NY

MC ARTHUR Thomas of Putnam, NY     September 10, 1872
MC LAUGHLIN Ellen of Putnam, NY     Putnam, NY

BOPREY William H. of Whitehall, NY     September 24, 1872
COLLINS Florence E. of Whitehall, NY     Saratoga Springs, NY

SHARP Charles H. of Argyle, NY     October 9, 1872
NASBEET Flora of Argyle, NY     Sandy Hill, NY

GRAY Charles of Burlington, Vt.     October 8, 1872
BRIGGS Louise dau of Rev. B. O. MEEKER of Sand Lake     Sand Lake, NY

GOWRAN Frank of Kingsbury, NY     October 5, 1872
CLEMENTS Lucy of Queensbury, NY     Queensbury, NY

WILCOX John B. of Troy, NY     October 9, 1872
ARCHIBALD Clara of Lake George, NY     Lake George, NY

JUCKET Byron G. of Whitehall, NY     October 3, 1872
JOHNSON Sarah of Whitehall, NY     N. Granville, NY

BECKWITH C. D. of Whitehall, NY     October 20, 1872
PARTRIDGE C. J. of Putnam, NY     E. Whitehall, NY

FOX Charles J. of Salem, NY     October 16, 1872
LIDDLE Grace A. of Salem, NY     Salem, NY

GREGORY Thomas C. of Salem, NY     October 3, 1872
FLOWERS Mrs. A. of Salem, NY     Kingsbury, NY

CUNNINGHAM F. D. of Binghamton, NY     October 15, 1872
WELLS Mary Louise of N. Greenwich, NY     N. Greenwich, NY

MC LEAN Sames of Jackson, NY     October 24, 1872
FOSTER Ella dau of Robert L. Foster     Shushan, NY

WAUGH James of Hartford, NY     October 30, 1872
MOORE Sarah of Canada West     N. Argyle, NY

SLIGHT Charles H. of S. Glens Falls, NY     October 23, 1872
ROSE Mary Jane of N. Ft. Ann, NY

WIGGINS Edward of S. Argyle, NY     September 26, 1872
BAIN Lana of S. Argyle, NY     N. Argyle, NY

TABER Charles L. of Easton, NY     October 27, 1872
NORTON Almira A. of Greenwich, NY     Greenwich, NY

SPRING John of Ft. Edward, NY
MAYHEW Hattie U. of Ft. Edward, NY

October 31, 1872
Ft. Edward, NY

COLE George of Whitehall, NY
CASE Delia of Ft. Edward, NY

November 17, 1872
Ft. Edward, NY

CUMMINGS James L.
HUTTON Jennie B. dau of William

November 14, 1872
Putnam, NY

WALKER Frank of Whitehall, NY
MC FERRON Aselath of Whitehall, NY

October 5, 1872
Granville, NY

RENAUD Napoleon of Whitehall, NY
JOHNSON Eliza of Whitehall, NY

November 3, 1872
Whitehall, NY

GODFREY Samuel F. of Ft. Edward, NY
ANDREWS Carolina S. of S. Glens Falls, NY

November 27, 1872
S. Glens Falls, NY

MANVILLE Orville A. of Whitehall, NY
SPOONER Dolly of Whitehall, NY

November 26, 1872
Whitehall, NY

KETCHUM Theodore S. of Glens Falls, NY
HAWLEY Frances S. of Bennington, Vt.

November 20, 1872
Bennington, Vt.

ROBERTSON George of White Creek, NY
MC ARTHUR Jennette of Jackson, NY

November 21, 1872
White Creek, NY

STILL James L. of Galway, NY
MOSHER Almeda of Galway, NY

September 2, 1872
Sandy Hill, NY

SMITH John E. of Caldwell, NY
COMSTOCK Fannie of Caldwell, NY

September 25, 1872
Sandy Hill, NY

WROATH John of Sandy Hill, NY
STEWART Margaret of Sandy Hill, NY

December 5, 1872
Sandy Hill, NY

MC GANN Mason of Hartford, NY
BUMP Emeline R. of Hartford, NY

November 28, 1872
N. Hebron, NY

HILLS Charles of S. Granville, NY
DURKEE Mary of Hartford, NY

November 28, 1872
N. Hebron, NY

PHILLIPS Seth of Montreal, Canada
BREWSTER Mary of Whitehall, NY

December 3, 1872
Whitehall, NY

DICKINSON Truman of Bolton, NY
CORNELL Jeanette of S. Glens Falls, NY

December 10, 1872
S. Glens Falls, NY

RUGAT Harmon B. of Chicago, Ill.

December 4, 1872

PRINDLE Margaret V. of Whitehall, NY | Whitehall, NY

ROGERS Adin B. of M. Granville, NY | December 11, 1872
CONANT Martha Helena of M. Granville, NY | Granville, NY

ROBERTS Alden of Ft. Edward, NY | December 6, 1872
DE LONG Pyrenia A. of Wilton, NY | Wilton, NY

HELMERS Simon of Herkimer, NY | December 2, 1872
GUNNING Mary of Factory Village, NY | Factory Village, NY

BOYCE Joseph C. of Poultney, Vt. | December 22, 1872
LANGDON Ida of Sandy Hill, NY | Sandy Hill, NY

ELLIOTT James B. of Kingsbury, NY | December 25, 1872
GUY Myraette of Kingsbury, NY | Sandy Hill, NY

ARCHIBALD W. H. of Salem, NY | December 18, 1872
WHITMAN Isabella M. of Salem, NY | Cambridge, NY

KILBURN Francis of Ft. Ann, NY | December 10, 1872
BAKER Hattie E. | N. Granville, NY

ROGERS A. B. of Granville, NY | December 11, 1872
CONANT Minnie of Granville, NY | Granville, NY

CARPENTER W. F. of Sandy Hill, NY | December 30, 1872
YARTER Minnie dau of Antoine of Sandy Hill, NY | Sandy Hill, NY

VANDENBURGH M. W. of Cromwell, Conn. | December 13, 1872
KING Mary E. of Ft. Edward, NY | Utica, NY

MC CLELLAN John T. of W. Hebron, NY | December 11, 1872
FOSTER Hattie E. of W. Hebron, NY | Hebron, NY

DAVIS Henry of S. Hartford, NY | December 25, 1872
HORTH Fannie J. of S. Hartford, NY | S. Hartford, NY

MANN Charles of Ft. Edward, NY | December 25, 1872
FLINT Cora M. of Ft. Edward, NY | Ft. Edward, NY

EMERSON Charles H. of Yonkers, NY | January 1, 1873
WILSON Flora P. dau of Joseph of Whitehall, NY | Whitehall, NY

HAY Clark W. of Hebron, NY | January 1, 1873
CHURCHILL Eva D. of Ft. Edward, NY | Ft. Edward, NY

SKELLIE William of Ft. Edward, NY | January 1, 1873
WHITING Silva I. of Kingsbury, NY | Ft. Edward, NY

| | |
|---|---|
| **EASTMAN** Edgar of Ft. Ann, NY | December 25, 1872 |
| **KEECH** Ella of Ft. Ann, NY | Ft. Edward, NY |
| | |
| **BROWN** Harvey of Greenwich, NY | January 1, 1873 |
| **GILCHRIST** Nancy J. dau of William of W. Hebron, NY | W. Hebron, NY |
| | |
| **FANEUF** Clemma of Gansevort, NY | December 18, 1872 |
| **HOLMES** Libbie of W. Ft. Ann, NY | W. Ft. Ann, NY |
| | |
| **FISHER** George of Ft. Ann, NY | December 21, 1872 |
| **AYLIFFE** Letitia of Ft. Ann, NY | Ft. Ann, NY |
| | |
| **DEWEY** J. H. A. of Ft. Ann, NY | December 24, 1872 |
| **HALL** Maria L. of Ft. Ann, NY | Ft. Ann, NY |
| | |
| **BARBER** Alexander of Dedham, Canada | December 24, 1872 |
| **POTTER** Charlotte M. of Ft. Ann, NY | |
| | |
| **CLEMENTS** Charles M. | January 15, 1873 |
| **UNDERWOOD** Kate dau of David | Ft. Edward, NY |
| | |
| **MEEKER** D. H. of N. Granville, NY | December 21, 1872 |
| **DAILEY** Kate of N. Granville, NY | N. Granville, NY |
| | |
| **SHAUGNESSY** John of Hampton, NY | December 25, 1872 |
| **HONEY** Agnes of Hampton, NY | N. Granville, NY |
| | |
| **MACKLIN** James | January 2, 1873 |
| **LASHER** Sarah | S. Argyle, NY |
| | |
| **GRAY** David S. of Salem, NY | January 7, 1873 |
| **WALLACE** Jane of Cambridge, NY | Salem, NY |
| | |
| **CURTIS** David of Ft. Edward, NY | January 1, 1873 |
| **TRIPP** Augusta of Chester, NY | Warrensburgh, NY |
| | |
| **CLEVELAND** George H. of Bellows Falls, Vt. | December 25, 1872 |
| **HISCOCK** Sopronia dau of D. C. of Whitehall, NY | Whitehall, NY |
| | |
| **STEVENSON** W. S. of Trenton, NJ | January 11, 1873 |
| **SAFFORD** Rosa A. formerly of Sandy Hill, NY | Trenton, NJ |
| | |
| **BROUGHAM** John H. of Ft. Edward, NY | January 15, 1873 |
| **HARRIS** Kate Angeline of Ft. Edward, NY | Troy, NY |
| | |
| **UPTON** James of Whitehall, NY | January 18, 1873 |
| **JOHNSON** Jane of Whitehall, NY | Whitehall, NY |
| | |
| **RICKETS** Richard | January 18, 1873 |

ANDERSON Eliza of Queensbury, NY

HASKINS George C. of Jackson, Mi.
BLIVEN Alice R. of Kingsbury, NY

JACKSON George P. of Kingsbury, NY
COLVIN Zilphia M. of Kingsbury, NY

VAN DEUSEN Ransom of Queensbury, NY
FINCH Mary A. of Queensbury, NY

SCOTT George of Troy, NY
FINN Lizzie A. of Ft. Edward, NY

VAN DEUSEN Sidney of Queensbury, NY
IRISH Matilda S. of Caldwell, NY

TRYON Cyrus of Westhaven, Vt.
LYONS Etta M. of Westhaven, Vt.

NORTHAM S. B. of Ripley, NY
BRAYTON M. L. of Hartford, NY

BAKER William C. of Schenectady, NY
ROGERS Ella S. of Bald Mountain, NY

CONWAY John J. of S. Trenton, NY
COONEY Jennie A. of Salem, NY

IRISH George S. of Glens Falls, NY
PURDY Martha A. of French Mountain, NY

WOODWARD Arthur S. of Corinth, NY
ALLEN Helen R. of Corinth, NY

SCOTT John Jr. of N. Argyle, NY
COY Mrs. Cornelia of Sandwich, Ill.

DIKEMAN Edward B. of Grand Rapids, Mi.
STEWART Mrs. Alice dau of Zenas VAN DEUSEN

COFFIN William M. of Glens Falls, NY
WACKLE Mary A. of S. Glens Falls, NY

BOYCE James H. of Hadley, NY
KENYON Emma dau of Stephen

GAILEY Joseph W. of Luzerne, NY
HAVENS Jennie E. of Day, NY

S. Glens Falls, NY

January 22, 1873
Sandy Hill, NY

January 24, 1873
Sandy Hill, NY

January 30, 1873
Sandy Hill, NY

January 28, 1873
Ft, Edward, NY

January 24, 1873
Whitehall, NY

January 23, 1873
Westhaven, Vt.

January 28, 1873
Hartford, NY

January 22, 1873
Bald Mountain, NY

January 23, 1873
Taunton, Mass.

February 1, 1873
Glens Falls, NY

January 14, 1873
Corinth, NY

February 13, 1873
Sandwich, Ill.

February 13, 1873
Glens Falls, NY

February 11, 1873
S. Glens Falls, NY

February 4, 1873
Luzerne, NY

February 11, 1873
Day, NY

BOYNE William H. of Brooklyn, NY     February 6, 1873
OSGOOD Ida of Glens Falls, NY     Jersey City, NJ

GOODRICH Warren D. of Whitehall, NY     February 19, 1873
HARDY Sarah of Whitehall, NY     Whitehall, NY

FREEMAN Albert O. of Ft. Ann, NY     February 19, 1871
WHITE Frankie of Ft. Ann, NY     Ft. Ann, NY
(newspaper date February 27, 1873, 1871 could be misprint)

ADAMS Darwin W. of Westhaven, Vt.     February 19, 1873
BENJAMIN Hattie S. of Whitehall, NY     Whitehall, NY

WOOD James M. of Orwell, Vt     February 20, 1873
PETERS Emma J. of Whitehall, NY     Whitehall, NY

REILLY James of Whitehall, NY     February 25, 1873
DEMPSEY Katie of Whitehall, NY     Whitehall, NY

ELLIS Robert T.     February 13, 1873
GREEN Sarah L.     Argyle, NY

CHASE George M. of Kingsbury, NY     October 23, 1872
SMITH Jennie S. of Kingsbury, NY     Sandy Hill, NY

HARRIS Freedom M. of Queensbury, NY     March 3, 1873
SEELYE Julia E. of Queensbury, NY     Sandy Hill, NY

STONE Joseph B. of Granville, NY     February 23, 1873
HOLLAND Lizzie of Poultney, Vt.     N. Granville, NY

CUMMINGS Thomas B. of Putnam, NY     February 27, 1873
WILLIAMSON Mary dau of Daniel of Putnam, NY     Putnam, NY

HOLLISTER E. W.     February 27, 1873
MC MULLEN Julia F.

THOMAS Henry of Whitehall, NY     January 2, 1873
MULHOLLAND Katie of Whitehall, NY     N. Granville, NY

GRANGE David of Canada East     February 25, 1873
RICE Hattie dau of David of Ft. Ann, NY     Ft. Ann, NY

ROBERTS John of Ft. Edward, NY     February 13, 1873
FREDENBURGH Helen M. of Fortsville, NY     Fortsville, NY

DEWEY Charles of Sandy Hill, NY     March 11, 1873
OATMAN Susan of Sandy Hill, NY     Glens Falls, NY

| | |
|---|---|
| **SMITH** J. Frank of Fairhaven, Vt.<br>**RISING** Mary D. of Fairhaven, Vt. | March 5, 1873<br>Glens Falls, NY |
| **HALE** Hiram D. of Hebron, NY<br>**GILCHRIST** Lucy E. of Hartford, NY | February 13, 1873<br>N. Argyle, NY |
| **CHAPMAN** Hiram W. of Hebron, NY<br>**LA BOSHIER** Josephine L. of Hebron, NY | February 20, 1873<br>N. Argyle, NY |
| **GRANGER** Edgar A. of Ft. Ann, NY<br>**COREY** Louisa dau of Charles of Hartford, NY | March 9, 1873<br>Hartford, NY |
| **CARPENTER** Henry C. of Glen's Falls, NY<br>**NORRIS** Carrie H. of Glens Falls, NY | March 20, 1873<br>Glens Falls, NY |
| **KENYON** James H. of Hadley, NY<br>**MORGAN** Ellen of Glens Falls, NY | March 19, 1873<br>Glens Falls, NY |
| **STEINER** Lambert D. of Cohoes, NY<br>**LONG** Fannie S. of Greenwich, NY | March 15, 1873<br>Greenwich, NY |
| **HILL** Moses A. of Cambridge, NY<br>**BALCH** Fannie M. of Cambridge, NY | March 18, 1873<br>Cambridge, NY |
| **ROSS** William of Mechanicsville, NY<br>**NUTT** Mary A. of Greenwich, NY | March 17, 1873<br>Greenwich, NY |
| **MC CLELLAN** John F. of Cambridge, NY<br>**GREEN** Harriet R. of Cambridge, NY | March 20, 1873 |
| **FULLER** George of Warrensburgh, NY<br>**COMER** Anna of Warrensburgh, NY | March 18, 1873<br>Caldwell, NY |
| **WOODARD** Clarence P.<br>**SHELDON** Theodosia T. | March 19, 1873<br>Hebron, NY |
| **SHELDON** D. A.<br>**DARROW** Amelia F. | March 19, 1873<br>Hebron, NY |
| **BROOKS** James G. of Feeder Dam, NY<br>**PHILO** Susan F. of Feeder Dam, NY | March 26, 1873<br>Glens Falls, NY |
| **EDDY** William B. of Elliott, NY<br>**BROWN** Minerva J. of Glens Falls, NY | March 26, 1873<br>Glens Falls, NY |
| **BELGARD** Michael of Whitehall, NY<br>**MOTT** Rosa of Port Henry, NY | March 25, 1873<br>Whitehall, NY |
| **ADAMS** Frank of Poultney, Vt.<br>**WOOD** Demas L. of Castleton, Vt. | March 25, 1873<br>Castleton, NY |

| | | |
|---|---|---|
| **STICKNEY** John Henry of Ft. Edward, NY | | March 19, 1873 |
| **DURKEE** Martha J. of Ft. Edward, NY | | Ft. Edward, NY |
| | | |
| **CRIPPIN** Charles of Granville, NY | | March 19, 1873 |
| **BARKER** Frank of Ft. Ann, NY | | Ft. Ann, NY |
| | | |
| **SMITH** Harvey of Kingsbury, NY | (newspaper date) | April 3, 1873 |
| **LOWELL** Alice M. of Granville, NY | | Granville, NY |
| | | |
| **HYDE** Melville of Sandy Hill, NY | | April 3, 1873 |
| **OATMAN** Sarah M. of Sandy Hill, NY | | Sandy Hill, NY |
| | | |
| **VINCENT** James S. of Sandy Hill, NY | | March 27, 1873 |
| **BURTON** Susannah C. of Sandy Hill, NY | | Sandy Hill, NY |
| | | |
| **CUMMINGS** George of E. Hartford, NY | | April 2, 1873 |
| **SCOTT** Blanche of E. Hartford, NY | | Granville, NY |
| | | |
| **SCOTT** Oscar of Whitehall, NY | | March 30, 1873 |
| **JOSEPH** Phebe J. of Whitehall, NY | | Whitehall, NY |
| | | |
| **DURKEE** William of E. Hartford, NY | | April 9, 1873 |
| **BUMP** Martha Jane of E. Hartford, NY | | N. Hartford, NY |
| | | |
| **BAKER** Charles M. of Stony Creek, NY | | March 30, 1873 |
| **DICKINSON** Mary E. of Stony Creek, NY | | Stony Creek, NY |
| | | |
| **BROWN** Benjamin O. of French Mountain, NY | | March 18, 1873 |
| **HAGGART** Lottie A. of Gloversville, NY | | Gloversville, NY |
| | | |
| **LAMB** James of Lakeville, NY | | March 12, 1873 |
| **GRAHAM** Elizabeth dau of John of N. Argyle, NY | | N. Argyle, NY |
| | | |
| **LA ROSE** Napoleon | | April 21, 1873 |
| **COTY** Cordelia | | Sandy Hill, NY |
| | | |
| **GREER** Donaldson of Glens Falls, NY | | April 17, 1873 |
| **SMITH** Mary of Sandy Hill, NY | | Sandy Hill, NY |
| | | |
| **MOORE** George M. of Ft. Ann, NY | | April 9, 1873 |
| **CADY** Esther of Ft. Ann, NY | | Ft. Ann, NY |
| | | |
| **POTTER** Dewane of Queensbury, NY | (newspaper date) | April 24, 1873 |
| **TAYLOR** Harriet A. of Ft. Ann, NY | | Sanfords Ridge, NY |
| | | |
| **GOODMAN** E. W. of Potsdam Junction, NY | | April 16, 1873 |
| **COOL** Anna F. dau of Joseph B. of Glens Falls, NY | | Glens Falls, NY |
| | | |
| **WHITCOMB** Morrison of Ft. Ann, NY | | March 29, 1873 |

| | |
|---|---|
| **RIST** Priscilla of Luzerne, NY | Luzerne, NY |
| **SCOVILLE** Addison P. of Luzerne, NY<br>**BROWN** Anna dau of Geroge of French Mountain, NY | April 10, 1873<br>French Mountain, NY |
| **YOUNG** Alexander of Argyle, NY<br>**BARDEN** Eleanor of Argyle, NY | April 24, 1873<br>Argyle, NY |
| **BROWN** George C. of Johnsburgh, NY<br>**SANDERS** Alvina of Johnsburgh, NY | April 12, 1873<br>N. River, NY |
| **BURROUGHS** Alonzo of N. Whitehall, NY<br>**VAN WAGNER** Sarah of Gansevort, NY | April 24, 1873<br>Glens Falls, NY |
| **HILL** Charles Henry of Cambridge, NY<br>**LYONS** Anna of Cambridge, NY | April 28, 1873<br>Cambridge, NY |
| **SMITH** Byron G. of Elgin, Ill.        (newspaper date)<br>**CROSS** Mrs. Caroline E. of Luzerne, NY | May 8, 1873<br>Luzerne, NY |
| **PASCO** John H. of Thurman, NY<br>**BLACKWOOD** Ella of Hadley, NY | April 26, 1873<br>Thurman, NY |
| **HARRIS** George R. of Glens Falls, NY<br>**MOTT** Millie S. of Glens Falls, NY | May 1, 1873<br>Glens Falls, NY |
| **BELVILLE** Alfred of Whitehall, NY<br>**ST CLAIR** Sapronia dau of Louis | April 30, 1873<br>Whitehall, NY |
| **RICE** Samuel of Cold Springs, NY<br>**BARTHOLOMEW** Mattie of N. Granville, NY | May 15, 1873<br>N. Granville, NY |
| **MANNIS** Dewey of Ft. Edward, NY<br>**SWIFT** Elizabeth of Dresden, NY | May 18, 1873<br>Dresden, NY |
| **RAYMOND** Rufus of Webster, Mass.<br>**CONVERSE** Mary J. of Moreau, NY | May 7, 1873<br>Moreau, NY |
| **SPRAGUE** Norman B. of Glens Falls, NY<br>**WEST** Nannie A. of Glens Falls, NY | May 14, 1873<br>Glens Falls, NY |
| **CUNNINGHAM** J. L.<br>**FOWLER** Lizzie | May 14, 1873<br>Chester, NY |
| **SAFFORD** J. G. of Sandy Hill, NY<br>**CORNELL** Theresa A. of Sandy Hill, NY | May 22, 1873<br>Sandy Hill, NY |
| **YARTER** James D. of Sandy Hill, NY<br>**MURRAY** Hattie L. of Whitehall, NY | May 21, 1873<br>Whitehall, NY |

| | |
|---|---|
| **RODD** John H. of Whitehall, NY<br>**BUEL** Addie E. of Whitehall, NY | May 14, 1873<br>Whitehall, NY |
| **VINETTE** Arthur of Troy, NY<br>**WILDE** Lillian E. of Bacon Hill, NY | May 18, 1873<br>Schuylerville, NY |
| **HOFFMAN** N. D. of Addison, NY<br>**RUSSELL** Ellen L. of Warrensburgh, NY | May 19, 1873<br>Chester, NY |
| **OWENS** William of Galesville, NY<br>**BURROUGHS** Catherine | May 10, 1873<br>Greenwich, NY |
| **BUMP** Almeron P. of Hartford, NY<br>**WRIGHT** Mrs. Marilla S. of Hartford, NY | June 4, 1873<br>Sandy Hill, NY |
| **CLEMENTS** A. J. of Queensbury, NY<br>**SISSON** Alice A. of S. Glens Falls, NY | June 1, 1873<br>E. Lake George, NY |
| **SHAW** Dudley E. of Glens Falls, NY<br>**CAMP** Ella of Glens Falls, NY | May 15, 1873<br>Westville, Conn. |
| **JUCKET** Abisor of Whitehall, NY<br>**INGALLS** Helen of Granville, NY | June 4, 1873<br>N. Granville, NY |
| **LEAVENS** Thurlow C.<br>**CONERY** Mary A. | June 4, 1873<br>Glens Falls, NY |
| **LEE** Adolphus of Glens Falls, NY<br>**FARMER** Sarah of Glens Falls, NY | June 3, 1873<br>Glens Falls, NY |
| **VAN HEUSEN** Garrett A.<br>**MEAD** Helen Jane | May 1, 1873<br>Queensbury, NY |
| **GATES** George A. of Saratoga Springs, NY<br>**POATES** Sarah E. dau of Dr. Asa **FITCH** | May 29, 1873<br>Fitchs Point, NY |
| **KNICKERBOCKER** Henry of Warrensburgh, NY<br>**JONES** Eliza of Chester, NY | June 7, 1873<br>Caldwell, NY |
| **AMIDON** Eugene W. of Queensbury, NY<br>**THOMAS** Laura of Bolton, NY | June 5, 1873<br>Bolton, NY |
| **SCHERMERHORN** Isaac of Caldwell, NY<br>**MYERS** Roxy of Caldwell, NY | June 7, 1873<br>Caldwell, NY |
| **EVERTS** John<br>**NORTON** Alice M. | June 5, 1873<br>Granville, NY |
| **WILLIAMS** James E. of Granville, NY | May 31, 1873 |

| | | |
|---|---|---|
| JONES Julia H. of Poultney, Vt. | | Fairhaven, Vt. |
| ALLISON Charles J. of Rochester, NY | | June 24, 1873 |
| SMITH Ida H. of Ft. Edward, NY | | Sandy Hill, NY |
| IRVING Charles H. of Ft. Edward, NY | | June 24, 1873 |
| CARTER Jennie L. of Ft. Edward, NY | | Sandy Hill, NY |
| NASH Melvin A. of Ft. Edward, NY | | June 17, 1873 |
| MONTGOMERY Mrs. Edith J. of Ft. Edward, NY | | Ft. Edward, NY |
| JONES Robert M. of Granville, NY | (newspaper date) | June 26, 1873 |
| ROBERTS Jane | | Rutland, Vt. |
| BARKLEY James J. of Ft. Edward, NY | | June 17, 1873 |
| HENRY Mary of Argyle, NY | | Argyle, NY |
| ORTON George E. of Glens Falls, NY | | June 19, 1873 |
| FOWLER Julia M. of Glens Falls, NY | | Glens Falls, NY |
| CARRINGTON L. H. of Whitehall, NY | | June 12, 1873 |
| LOWENTHAL Mrs. J. A. of Charlston, SC | | |
| WARD B. L. of Cambridge, NY | | June 12, 1873 |
| MC MURRAY Anne of Cambridge, NY | | Cambridge, NY |
| TAYLOR Daniel O. of S. Hartford, NY | | June 11, 1873 |
| WHITE Mrs. Chloe of Hartford, NY | | Hartford, NY |
| EDWARDS Griffith of Granville, NY | | June 14, 1873 |
| HAMBLET Wilhelmina of Granville, NY | | Rutland, Vt. |
| RUSSELL William | | June 23, 1873 |
| SHAW Matilda | | Caldwell, NY |
| SISSON Edwin | | June 23, 1873 |
| CRANDALL Julia | | Caldwell, NY |
| THOMPSON David of Hebron, NY | | June 19, 1873 |
| KING Emma of Argyle, NY | | Argyle, NY |
| WILBUR Rollin | | June 24, 1873 |
| RIAL Amelia | | Poultney, Vt. |
| MC FARLAND William | | June 25, 1873 |
| MC FARLAND Margaret | | Salem, NY |
| SIMMONS Thomas E. of Eagle Bridge, NY | | June 18, 1873 |
| OUBIT Emma L. of Greenwich, NY | | Greenwich, NY |

| | |
|---|---|
| **HOLDING** Prof. William J. | July 2, 1873 |
| **JONES** Lodesia E. | Glens Falls, NY |
| | |
| **FINCH** Henry T. of New York City | July 2, 1873 |
| **BARKER** Sarah M. dau of M. C. of Glens Falls, NY | Glens Falls, NY |
| | |
| **THURBER** Franklin of Arlington, Vt. | June 28, 1873 |
| **BREED** Roby A. of Arlington, Vt. | Shushan, NY |
| | |
| **BENTLEY** Edward A. of Sandgate, Vt. | July 2, 1873 |
| **CONGER** Mary S. of Sandgate, Vt. | Shushan, NY |
| | |
| **DIXON** Robert | July 4, 1873 |
| **LYTLE** Mary | Hartford, NY |
| | |
| **MONROE** Dr. J. T. of W. Pawlet, Vt. | July 4, 1873 |
| **BURCH** Ida of N. Hebron, NY | Schuylerville, NY |
| | |
| **BLANCHARD** Amos of Ft. Ann, NY | June 29, 1873 |
| **MC CABE** Laury of Ft. Ann, NY | Bolton, NY |
| | |
| **ELETHORPE** Wesley of Hague, NY | July 3, 1873 |
| **PUTNAM** Antha of Hague, NY | Hague, NY |
| | |
| **FITCH** Roswell R. of Coxsackie, NY | July 17, 1873 |
| **ELDRIDGE** Mrs. Helen E. of Ft. Edward, NY | Ft. Edward, NY |
| | |
| **KNAPP** William R. of Glens Falls, NY | July 3, 1873 |
| **RICE** Mary C. dau of Nathaniel of Fortsville, NY | Fortsville, NY |
| | |
| **WILDY** John E. of Northumberland, NY | July 10, 1873 |
| **MC GREGOR** Mary E. of Glens Falls, NY | Schuylerville, NY |
| | |
| **TABER** H. Sheldon | July 9, 1873 |
| **BURDICK** Libbie M. | Easton, NY |
| | |
| **SISSON** Edgar P. of Sandy Hill, NY | July 15, 1873 |
| **BENACH** Mary Ann of Sandy Hill, NY | Glens Falls, NY |
| | |
| **DURHAM** Anson of Galesville, NY | July 9, 1873 |
| **MAYNARD** Hannah A. formerly of Cambridge, NY | Hebron, NY |
| | |
| **SEELEY** Myron R. of Corinth, NY | July 19, 1873 |
| **MALLERY** Jennie of Corinth, NY | Luzerne, NY |
| | |
| **STANTON** Almond P. of Bolton, NY | July 4, 1873 |
| **WALKER** Elizabeth C. of Bolton, NY | Caldwell, NY |
| | |
| **OATMAN** Henry W. of Sandy Hill, NY | July 29, 1873 |

PARTRIDGE Eliza M. of Sandy Hill, NY — Glens Falls, NY

COLLINS Avery A. of Schroon Lake, NY
SHUTE Emma M. of Schroon Lake, NY — July 24, 1873 Schroon Lake, NY

DOOLAN John of Ft. Edward, NY
CARY Lizzie of Glens Falls, NY — August 7, 1873 Ft. Edward, NY

WILLIAMS Charles Henry of Stillwater, NY
BADGLEY Lydia Melissa of Stillwater, NY — August 5, 1873 Stillwater, NY

MC MURRAY Charles of Cambridge, NY
BOWE Annie F. of Cambridge, NY — July 31, 1873 Cambridge, NY

HALL Edgar S. of Sandy Hill, NY
WARREN Cornelia M. of Sandy Hill, NY — August 25, 1873 Sandy Hill, NY

NEVERS Phineas of Charlestown, NH
FRENDON Cornelia of Vermont — August 13, 1873 Whitehall, NY

MC NEIL John S. of Moreau, NY
CODAIR Lucy of W. Ft. Ann, NY — August 16, 1873 Glens Falls, NY

BROWN Hiram L. of Ft. Edward, NY
BUTLER Emma L. of West Mountain, NY — August 19, 1873 Glens Falls, NY

HALL E. S. of Sandy Hill, NY
WARREN Corny of Sandy Hill, NY — August 25, 1873 Sandy Hill, NY

SIMPSON Arthur P. of Fairport, NY
ROUSE Jennie M. of Northumberland, NY — September 4, 1873 Northumberland, NY

PRATT Edward C. of Whitehall, NY
COLLINS Miriam of Whitehall, NY — August 6, 1873

PATTEE Herbert of Sandy Hill, NY
MORRIS Emma of Sandy Hill, NY — September 21, 1873 Sandy Hill, NY

KING Fred A. of Salem, NY
LUCE Carrie W. of Cambridge, NY — September 7, 1873 Greenwich, NY

TOOLE John of Sandy Hill, NY
GANLEY Kate of Ft. Edward, NY — September 23, 1873 Ft. Edward, NY

COFFIN John B. of Queensbury, NY
HUBBELL Carrie of Queensbury, NY — September 15, 1873 Queensbury, NY

HOUGHTON S. A. of Cambridge, NY
GAMBLE Mattie of Cambridge, NY — September 4, 1873 Cambridge, NY

| | |
|---|---|
| KEMPSHALL Richard W. of Chicago. Ill. | October 1, 1873 |
| FORBES Emily A. of Ft. Edward, NY | Ft. Edward, NY |
| | |
| BURDICK George C. of Ft. Edward, NY | March 30, 1873 |
| HOLMAN Mary C. of Ft. Edward, NY | Ft. Edward, NY |
| | |
| MICKLEJOHN A. C. of Putnam, NY | September 25, 1873 |
| WILSON A. Amelia of N. Granville, NY | N. Granville, NY |
| | |
| DUNWICK W. H. of Ft. Edward, NY | September 22, 1873 |
| BISHOP Mary E. of Huntington, NY | Springfield, Mass. |
| | |
| FARRINGTON Alvin M. | September 28, 1873 |
| GREEN Emma G. dau of Simon of Whitehall, NY | Whitehall, NY |
| | |
| SMITH Eugene R. of Salem, NY | September 24, 1873 |
| DENISON Libbie M. of Salem, NY | Salem, NY |
| | |
| DIXON J. B. of Hebron, NY | September 16, 1873 |
| LIVINGSTON Maggie of Salem, NY | Salem, NY |
| | |
| BARKER Abram of Granville, NY | September 18, 1873 |
| ROBLEE Rhoda of Granville, NY | Granville, NY |
| | |
| CORLEW Leonard of Day Center, NY | September 28, 1873 |
| HOLLAND Adelia of Glens Falls, NY | Glens Falls, NY |
| | |
| SKEELS H. B. of Whitehall, NY | September 24, 1873 |
| WATSON Emma of Salem, NY | Whitehall, NY |
| | |
| SAFFORD Edwin of Salem, NY | October 1, 1873 |
| JOHNSTON Alice of Salem, NY | Salem, NY |
| | |
| BARNETT J. C. | September 23, 1873 |
| HURD Florence A. | Cambridge, NY |
| | |
| PETERS William of Rochester, NY | September 24, 1873 |
| RICE Augusta | Greenwich, NY |
| | |
| CRAWFORD John M. of Argyle, NY | September 24, 1873 |
| SMITH Sarah E. of Argyle, NY | Argyle, NY |
| | |
| GODFREY William of Ft. Edward, NY | September 16, 1873 |
| CASE Mary of Utica, NY | Utica, NY |
| | |
| WELLS A. H. of Sandy Hill, NY | October 2, 1873 |
| WENTWORTH Nellie of Troy, NY | Troy, NY |
| | |
| SHELDON Frank of Copake, NY | October 9, 1873 |

| | |
|---|---|
| **HARRIS** Mary E. dau of Joseph H. | Smiths Basin, NY |
| **COBB** M. L. of Sing Sing, NY | October 8, 1873 |
| **GRAY** Annie dau of H. C. of Cambridge, NY | Cambridge, NY |
| **FLACK** Albert W. of Cornwall, Canada | October 8, 1873 |
| **POWELL** Fannie of Ft. Edward, NY | Ft. Edward, NY |
| **CRONKHITE** H. P. of Ft. Edward, NY | October 8, 1873 |
| **MILLIMAN** Mary E. of Ft. Edward, NY | Ft. Edward, NY |
| **LAWRENCE** Clinton I. of Gansevort, NY | October 8, 1873 |
| **PORTER** Effie of Gansevort, NY | Gansevort, NY |
| **WITHERELL** Edwin of Glens Falls, NY | October 8, 1873 |
| **MC MULLEN** Margaret of Glens Falls, NY | Glens Falls, NY |
| **HUFTY** James of Crawford Co., Ohio | October 15, 1873 |
| **WRIGHT** Elizabeth V. of Washington Co., NY | Ft. Edward, NY |
| **SHAFER** Mitchell of Blairstown, Ill. | October 15, 1873 |
| **BEATTIE** Almira of Salem, NY | Salem, NY |
| **BAKER** C. A. of Plattsburgh, NY | October 23, 1873 |
| **WHITE** Hattie of Lock Haven, Pa. | Lock Haven, Pa. |
| **ATWOOD** M. D. of Hartford, NY | October 29, 1873 |
| **ANDRESS** S. M. of Hartford, NY | Hartford, NY |
| **CARR** Samuel W. of Whitehall, NY | October 22, 1873 |
| **BUEL** Mattie C. of Whitehall, NY | Whitehall, NY |
| **JEWETT** Truman of Whitehall, NY | October 23, 1873 |
| **HICKS** Philia dau of Orlando of N. Granville, NY | N. Granville, NY |
| **SCRIBNER** William H. H. of Castleton, Vt. | October 15, 1873 |
| **MORGAN** Mrs. Electa of Castleton, Vt. | E. Poultney, Vt. |
| **MC GANN** Patrick of Warrensburgh, NY | October 28, 1873 |
| **MANNING** Ella of Warrensburgh, NY | Glens Falls, NY |
| **OGDEN** Benjamin | October 30, 1873 |
| **DAY** Addie of Glens Falls, NY | Glens Falls, NY |
| **LITTLE** Russell A. | October 28, 1873 |
| **BROWN** Addie | Glens Falls, NY |
| **TAYLOR** William A. | October 29, 1873 |
| **WILSON** Minnie L. | Salem, NY |

| | |
|---|---|
| HAVILAND James M. of Glens Falls, NY | October 25, 1873 |
| RUGG Annie S. of Glens Falls, NY | Glens Falls, NY |
| | |
| GODIN Prosper | November 3, 1873 |
| GAYETTE Rosalie | Whitehall, NY |
| | |
| GALLUP Eugene S. of Greenwich, NY | October 26, 1873 |
| MALBY Clemmie E. of Greenwich, NY | Salem, NY |
| | |
| SEVERANCE Junius E. of Middlebury, Vt. | November 18, 1873 |
| BIGGART Dora D. dau of James of Kingsbury, NY | Kingsbury, NY |
| | |
| POND Oscar J. of Castleton, Vt. | November 12, 1873 |
| BROWN Eveline of Sandy Hill, NY | Sandy Hill, NY |
| | |
| STATIA Henry of Sandy Hill, NY | November 16, 1873 |
| MC HUGH Martha of Sandy Hill, NY | Lake George, NY |
| | |
| CUNNINGHAM John of Sandy Hill, NY | November 18, 1873 |
| KELLY Mary of Glens Falls, NY | Glens Falls, NY |
| | |
| COFFIN Sidney B. of Glens Falls, NY | November 19, 1873 |
| PHILO Mary Adsit dau of Hiram of Glens Falls, NY | Glens Falls, NY |
| | |
| PERRY D. C. of Plattsburgh, NY | November 18, 1873 |
| BOUDWIN Celina of Sandy Hill, NY | Whitehall, NY |
| | |
| ALLEN Gordon | November 18, 1873 |
| WIGGINS Mrs. Margaret of Fairhaven, Vt. | Whitehall, NY |
| | |
| SPINK William of Whitehall, NY | November 12, 1873 |
| HICKS Delia dau of Orlando of Granville, NY | Granville, NY |
| | |
| ALLEN Elias of Whitehall, NY | November 12, 1873 |
| SPINK Lucy D. dau of Amos of Whitehall, NY | Whitehall, NY |
| | |
| GARRETT Augustus of Ballston, NY | November 25, 1873 |
| HILLS Mattie E. of Ballston, NY | Glens Falls, NY |
| | |
| SEWARD Charles Andrew | November 25, 1873 |
| MANLY Eliza Jane | Whitehall, NY |
| | |
| AUSTIN F. A. of Whitehall, NY | November 27, 1873 |
| SHATTUCK Aurelia of Whitehall, NY | Whitehall, NY |
| | |
| GREEN O. H. of the Glen, NY | November 27, 1873 |
| HALL E. M. dau of Rev. A. Hall | Johnsburgh, NY |
| | |
| GAGE Adelbert of Luzerne, NY | November 27, 1873 |

108     *Marriage Notices*

| | |
|---|---|
| **TOOLEY** Olive H. of Luzerne, NY | Luzerne, NY |
| **VAN SCHAICK** George of Kingsbury, NY<br>**FERRIS** Adah F. of Kingsbury, NY | December 4, 1873<br>Glens Falls, NY |
| **KIPP** John G. of Cambridge, NY<br>**THOMAS** Julia E. of Cambridge, NY | November 22, 1873<br>Buskirks Bridge, NY |
| **BURROUGHS** George W. of Cambridge, NY<br>**MC KERNON** Mary J. of Cambridge, NY | November 26, 1873<br>Cambridge, NY |
| **IRVINE** William James of Argyle, NY<br>**GRANT** Estella E. of Windsor, Conn. | December 2, 1873<br>Argyle, NY |
| **JACKWAY** Edgar C. of Westhaven, Vt.<br>**CLARK** Ida M. | December 10, 1873<br>E. Whitehall, NY |
| **SCRIVER** Norman of Warrensburgh, NY (newspaper date)<br>**BARRETT** Mary L. of Johnsburgh, NY | December 18, 1873<br>Thurman, NY |
| **LAPHAM** John J. of Brooklyn, NY<br>**WALKER** Lizzie of Salem, NY | December 3, 1873<br>Salem, NY |
| **WILLIAMS** William<br>**WEEKS** Melvina | December 2, 1873<br>Sandy Hill, NY |
| **MOSHER** Isaac F. of Sandy Hill, NY<br>**STARKS** Alice E. of Ft. Edward, NY | December 17, 1873<br>Ft. Edward, NY |
| **BROWN** Joseph H. of Chicago, Ill.<br>**PARISH** Mary of Saratoga, NY | December 11, 1873<br>Ft. Ann, NY |
| **BARKER** C. H. of Adamsville, NY<br>**INGRAHAM** Jennie of Adamsville, NY | December 20, 1873<br>Glens Falls, NY |
| **LARKIN** H. B. of E. Greenwich, NY<br>**DYER** Ella of E. Greenwich, NY | December 15, 1873<br>Ft. Edward, NY |
| **SARGENT** Marvin D.<br>**CLARK** Julietta E. | December 11, 1873<br>Ft. Ann, NY |
| **DANFORTH** Oliver of Rupert, Vt.<br>**HILLS** Sarah of Rupert, Vt. | December 20, 1873<br>N. Granville, NY |
| **O'DELL** Baker of Putnam, NY<br>**LYONS** Julia E. of Putnam, NY | December 22, 1873<br>Putnam, NY |
| **DE KALB** George of M. Granville, NY<br>**DODGE** Sarah of M. Granville, NY | December 24, 1873<br>M. Granville, NY |

| | |
|---|---|
| VAN VRANKEN George W. | January 1, 1874 |
| LORD Phebe A. | Sandy Hill, NY |
| | |
| SAWYER Horace A. of Woodstock, Vt. | December 15, 1873 |
| MAHAN Ella A. of Bridgewater, Vt. | Sandy Hill, NY |
| | |
| MC GANN Thomas of Hartford, NY | December 25, 1873 |
| WELSH Eliza W. of Hartford, NY | Sandy Hill, NY |
| | |
| LA FOY John of Pennsylvania | December 27, 1873 |
| HUNTINGTON Emma of Dresden, NY | Dresden, NY |
| | |
| MOTT Charles M. of Glens Falls, NY | December 26, 1873 |
| OAKLEY Emma of Hoboken, NI | Hoboken, NJ |
| | |
| KENNEDY William A. of Hebron, NY | December 28, 1873 |
| KING Maggie A. | Ft. Edward, NY |
| | |
| ANDERSON Andrew of Blue Earth, Minn. | December 26, 1873 |
| EASTON Annie dau of George | Putnam, NY |
| | |
| NORTON Charles A. of Ft. Ann, NY | December 24, 1873 |
| BROWN Sarah E. of Hartford, NY | Greenwich, NY |
| | |
| WILLIS Rollin L. of Sandy Hill, NY | January 7, 1874 |
| SEELEY Emma A. of Sandy Hill, NY | Sandy Hill, NY |
| | |
| SMITH John H. of Glens Falls, NY | January 7, 1874 |
| ROSS Lucinda A. of Bolton, NY | Glens Falls, NY |
| | |
| HATCH Leroy T. of S. Hartford, NY | January 1, 1874 |
| WELLWOOD Phebe E. ot S. Hartford, NY | S. Hartford, NY |
| | |
| BARBER Horatio | January 1, 1874 |
| BENNETT Louisa | White Creek, NY |
| | |
| WHITE Charles E. of W. Hebron, NY | January 1, 1874 |
| TEFFT Emma A. of N. Petersburgh, NY | W. Hebron, NY |
| | |
| GRIFFIN W. H. of Bolton, NY | December 30, 1873 |
| TANNER Mary of Bolton, NY | Glens Falls, NY |
| | |
| FINN Cornelius | January 7, 1874 |
| LEARY Ellen | Glens Falls, NY |
| | |
| WILKINS W. A. | September 16, 1873 |
| GRISWOLD Hattie E. | Whitehall, NY |
| | |
| SHAW Wilfred C. of N. Pawlet, Vt. | January 14, 1874 |

WILLIAMS Mary Jane dau of Benjamin of Granville, NY          Granville, NY

REID Andrew of E. Greenwich, NY          December 26, 1873
HILL Sarah M. of E. Greenwich, NY          Cambridge, NY

LARONE Carliste of Sandy Hill, NY          January 26, 1874
ANDETTE Olive of Sandy Hill, NY          Sandy Hill, NY

HATHAWAY Adelbert of Dresden, NY          January 1, 1874
ST CLAIR Emma of Dresden, NY          Dresden, NY

RICE Walter of Shaftsbury, Vt.          January 16, 1874
MOONEY Esther of Shaftsbury, Vt.          Cambridge, NY

MARTIN F. D. of Ft. Ann, NY          January 30, 1874
AUSTIN Almira E. of Ft. Ann, NY          Whitehall, NY

SMITH Henry A.          February 4, 1874
GOODALE Mary W.          Whitehall, NY

O'DELL Harrie of Ticonderoga, NY          January 26, 1874
FRASER Miss ____          Putnam, NY

PACKARD Webster B. of Tinmouth, Vt.          January 22, 1874
CRAWFORD Matilda C. of Hartford, NY          Glens Falls, NY

CONNOR Patrick of Glens Falls, NY          February 1, 1874
NOONAN Catherine of Glens Falls, NY          Glens Falls, NY

SMITH Robert of Johnsburgh, NY          January 22, 1874
BROWN Carrie of Chester, NY          Glens Falls, NY

WILCOX George B. of Luzerne, NY          January 27, 1874
BUTTLE Lutheria of Luzerne, NY          Hadley, NY

ANDREWS James E. of Hebron, NY          January 28, 1874
DERMONT Marion M. of S. Adams, Mass.          Salem, NY

RUSSELL Walter of White Creek, NY          January 10, 1874
SHAVER Hettie of Granville, NY          N. Granville, NY

WELLING Herman D. of S. Cambridge, NY          January 22, 1874
DURFEE Libbie B. of S. Cambridge, NY          S. Cambridge, NY

YARTER Cyril of Sandy Hill, NY          February 8, 1874
POTVIN Louise of Sandy Hill, NY          Sandy Hill, NY

CASEY Patrick of Glens Falls, NY          February 7, 1874
SULLIVAN Margaret of Glens Falls, NY          Glens Falls, NY

| | |
|---|---|
| **DIBBLE** Oscar I. of S. Granville, NY | February 3, 1874 |
| **BROWN** Laura dau of David | M. Granville, NY |
| | |
| **BROTT** Hermon R. of Hadley, NY | January 29, 1874 |
| **MOORE** Eunice R. of Luzerne, NY | Luzerne, NY |
| | |
| **BRIGGS** Eli of Stillwater, NY | February 21, 1874 |
| **CONGDON** Helen E. of Hartford, NY | Hartford, NY |
| | |
| **SINGLETON** Jeremiah of Glens Falls, NY | February 12, 1874 |
| **CAREY** Maggie of Glens Falls, NY | Glens Falls, NY |
| | |
| **SIMPSON** George of Burlington, Vt. | February 16, 1874 |
| **MILLER** Mary of Burlington, NY | Whitehall, NY |
| | |
| **DEAL** Edward of Troy, NY | February 12, 1874 |
| **CUMMINGS** Libbie of Whitehall, NY | Whitehall, NY |
| | |
| **HOPKINS** Albert of Rupert, Vt. | February 11, 1874 |
| **GOOKINS** Eliza M. of Rupert, Vt. | Hartford, NY |
| | |
| **MC MURRAY** R. James | February 17, 1874 |
| **LINDSAY** Ann | Argyle, NY |
| | |
| **TOOMBS** Joseph of Hoosick Falls, NY | February 10, 1874 |
| **CAMPBELL** Mary A. of Cambridge, NY | Cambridge, NY |
| | |
| **BARKLEY** John D. son of John of Argyle, NY | February 12/14. 1874 |
| **SHILAND** Fannie of Ft. Edward, NY | Ft. Miller, NY |
| | |
| **AMBLER** Silas B. of Sandy Hill, NY | March 11, 1874 |
| **HOWE** Julia A. of Sandy Hill, NY | Sandy Hill, NY |
| | |
| **BETTERLY** George | February 18, 1874 |
| **HAVILAND** Mrs. Phebe formerly of Glens Falls, NY | Battle Creek, Mi. |
| | |
| **MOSHER** Charles A. of Glens Falls, NY | March 3, 1874 |
| **THOMPSON** Mary Jane of Glens Falls, NY | Glens Falls, NY |
| | |
| **GREEN** Ambrose of Cambridge, NY | March 5, 1874 |
| **WELLING** Jennie M. of Cambridge, NY | Greenwich, NY |
| | |
| **TEMPLE** John of Albany, NY | February 16, 1874 |
| **PALMER** Martha R. of Hoosick Falls, NY | Hartford, NY |
| | |
| **MC LEAN** John M. of Cambridge, NY | March 4, 1874 |
| **ROBERTSON** Anna of Cambridge, NY | Cambridge, NY |
| | |
| **GALWAY** Jonas of Hoosick Falls, NY | March 17, 1874 |

| | |
|---|---|
| CLEGG Alice of Argyle, NY | Argyle, NY |
| SIMPSON John of Glens Falls, NY<br>PARKS Elizabeth of Glens Falls, NY | February 26, 1874<br>Glens Falls, NY |
| EPHAM James P. of Boston, Mass.<br>SCHERMERHORN Catherine A. of Lake George, NY | March 7, 1874<br>Warrensburgh, NY |
| NORTON Samuel B. of Greenwich, NY<br>WILLIAMS Lydia C. of Salem, NY | March 5, 1874<br>Salem, NY |
| KINGSLEY Sewell of Luzerne, NY<br>MILLS Sarah Louisa of Luzerne, NY | March 15, 1874<br>Luzerne, NY |
| RAMSEY Samuel of Luzerne, NY<br>HILL Sarah of Corinth, NY | March 18, 1874<br>Luzerne, NY |
| WELLS Frank D. of Greenwich, NY<br>MORSE Susie E. of Greenwich, NY | March 20, 1874<br>Greenwich, NY |
| WASHBURN Platt of Easton, NY<br>HAMMOND Augusta | March 5, 1874<br>Bacon Hill, NY |
| TAYLOR Charles W.<br>RICHARDS Julia | March 26, 1874<br>Argyle, NY |
| COFFIN Elvin of Lake Goerge, NY<br>MYERS Maggie J. of Maltaville, NY | March 22, 1874<br>Maltaville, NY |
| SLOCUM Josiah of Johnsonville, NY<br>PETTEYS Mrs. Jane of Lake, NY | March 18, 1874<br>Lake, NY |
| HUGGINS John W. of Argyle, NY<br>FULLER Lucina J. of Cambridge, NY | March 25, 1874<br>Cambridge, NY |
| LANCHEVIN J. of Ft. Edward, NY<br>COUTURE Philomele of Ft. Edward, NY | April 5, 1874<br>Sandy Hill, NY |
| STEWART John W. of Sandy Hill, NY<br>NORTHUP Mary C. of Sandy Hill, NY | April 5, 1874<br>Sandy Hill, NY |
| KELLY Michael of Sandy Hill, NY<br>FINN Mary A. of Sandy Hill, NY | April 8, 1874<br>Sandy Hill, NY |
| IRVIN Alexander<br>FRENCH Mary | March 31, 1874<br>Lakeville, NY |
| CONWAY John<br>SELFRIDGE Elizabeth | April 1, 1874<br>Argyle, NY |

OBLENIS Charles of New York City
STODDARD Julia A. of Glens Falls, NY

March 31, 1874
Glens Falls, NY

SAFFORD Charles B. of Greenwich, NY
WRIGHT Anna of Greenwich, NY

March 29, 1874
Greenwich, NY

ANDRUS Edwin D. of Poultney, Vt.
NEWBERRY Grace A. of Ft. Ann, NY

March 25, 1874
Ft. Ann, NY

CONNELLY William of Sandy Hill, NY
TABER Jenevieve of Saratoga Springs, NY

April 8, 1874
Saratoga Springs, NY

PRUYN Edward F. of Glens Falls, NY
COOL Alice G. of Glens Falls, NY

April 14, 1874
Glens Falls, NY

SMITH Benjamin of Holland, Vt.
ALLEN Libbie of Hartford, NY

April 13, 1874
Hartford, NY

PARKE James C. of Whitehall, NY
KELLY Julia of New York City

April 8, 1874
Whitehall, NY

FISHER Warren of Cambridge, NY
FISHER Mrs. Alvina of Cambridge, NY

March 31, 1874
Cambridge, NY

DWYER William of Wilton, NY          (newspaper date)
CARR Clara J. of Wilton, NY

April 16, 1874
Greenfield, NY

BAILEY Lyman R. of Ft. Ann, NY
SKINNER Harriet of Ft. Ann, NY

March 31, 1874
Glens Falls, NY

GOURLEY Oliver of Glens Falls, NY
STEVENSON Ida of Glens Falls, NY

April 12, 1874
Glens Falls, NY

NICHOLS Henry
BURLINGHAM Mrs. Polly of Victory Mills, NY

April 11, 1874
Schuylerville, NY

HATCH John Q.
INGERSOLL Mary E.

April 16, 1874
Hebron, NY

DOUGAN Frank of Cambridge, NY
MENGEA Alice of Greenwich, NY

April 13, 1874
Cambridge, NY

MALOY Duncan          (newspaper date)
WOODELL Mary

April 23, 1874
Jackson, NY

FOX James of Poultney, Vt.
DEWEY Matella L. of Poultney, Vt.

April 28, 1874
Sandy Hill, NY

HARFORD John of Kingsbury, NY

April 28, 1874

WARNOCK Mary J. of Argyle, NY                        Sandy Hill, NY

MORRIS Alfred of Pawlet, Vt.                         April 11, 1874
WINSLOW Sarah of Pawlet, Vt.                         Granville, NY

LEWIS James of Sandgate, Vt.                         March 12, 1874
BELL Lizzie of Hebron, NY                            Hebron, NY

DELAY Denis of Greenwich, NY                         April 13, 1874
SMITH Julia of Greenwich, NY                         Cambridge, NY

WHITNER Leonard of Schuylerville, NY                 April 21, 1874
SMITH Mary J. of Schuylerville, NY                   Schuylerville, NY

BROMLEY Nelson R.                                    May 6, 1874
TEFFT Ella E.                                        Sandy Hill, NY

PARKMAN Truman of Salem, NY                          April 27, 1874
RUSSELL Julia A. of Salem, NY                        Greenwich, NY

JOHNSON J. George of Hebron, NY                      April 15, 1874
CAMPBELL Rachel of Hebron, NY                        N. Argyle, NY

JENKS L. H. of Pottersville, NY                      March 25, 1874
SCOTT B. A. of Worcester, Mass.                      Worcester, Mass.

BLAKE Frank of Victory Mills, NY                     April 27, 1874
DWYER Maggie of Victory Mills, NY                    Schuylerville, NY

CULVER Ensign S. of Cambridge, NY                    April 29, 1874
RICE Catherine of Cambridge, NY                      Cambridge, NY

DUGAS Arthur of Castleton, Vt.                       May 4, 1874
CARROLL Kitty of Castleton, Vt.                      Fairhaven, Vt.

STOCKWELL Isaac of Dresden, NY                       April 23, 1874
MC DONNELL Ellen of Dresden, NY                      Dresden, NY

SINNOTT William of Whitehall, NY                     May 5, 1874
WELCH Ellen of Whitehall, NY                         Whitehall, NY

CORBETT Patrick of Whitehall, NY                     May 5, 1874
CASTLE Ellen of Whitehall, NY                        Whitehall, NY

GILCHRIST James H. of Ft. Edward, NY                 May 6, 1874
GALLAGHER Mary of Ft. Edward, NY                     Ft. Edward, NY

BAILEY William M. of Brooklyn, NY                    May 6, 1874
RUSSELL Minnie of Ft. Edward, NY                     Ft. Edward, NY

MOORE Henry of Milton, Vt.
GRIFFIN Estelle E. of Whitehall, NY

May 4, 1874
Whitehall, NY

GRAHAM Samuel of Argyle, NY
STEVENSON Mary of Argyle, NY

May 7, 1874
Argyle, NY

BLANCHARD Henry of E. Arlington, Vt.
SANBORN Anna Maria of E. Arlington Vt.

May 7, 1874
Shushan, NY

MEARS W. J. of Kingsbury, NY
BENTLEY Tinnie of Kingsbury, NY

May 14, 1874
Kingsbury, NY

WARNOCK Robert
NICHOLS Sarah Maria dau of late John Nichols

May 7, 1874
Hartford, NY

LYONS William of M. Granville, NY
HANNETT Eliza of M. Granville, NY

May 12, 1874
M. Granville, NY

JORDAN George of Glens Falls, NY
WILCOX Ida Maud of Glens Falls, NY

May 19, 1874
Glens Falls, NY

PATTERSON Dr. J. F. of Glens Falls, NY
ALLEN Flora of Whitehall, NY

May 21, 1874
Whitehall, NY

BROWN Clinton of Tinmouth, Vt.      (newspaper date)
MOONEY Ellen of Castleton, Vt.

May 28, 1874
Hampton, NY

MATTISON Alonzo
MC NUTT Mary F. of Ft. Ann, NY

May 20, 1874
Ft. Ann, NY

FLEMING William J. of New York City
LACEY Gertrude E. of Syracuse, NY

May 2, 1874
Salem, NY

DUEL Scott of Horicon, NY
LA FLURE May Ann of Dresden, NY

May 20, 1874
Dresden, NY

MOYER John of Granville, NY
RYAN Margarette of Hydesville, Vt.

May 31, 1874
Sandy Hill, NY

LANSING U. J. of Greenwich, NY
WISWELL Ellen M. of Gloversville, NY

May 30, 1874
Albany, NY

SULLIVAN Mr. ____ of Comstocks Landing, NY
HEFFERMAN Hannah of Granville, NY

May 31, 1874
Granville, NY

EICHORN G. Hermance of Luzerne, NY
PORTEAU Jennie M. dau of Andrew of Luzerne, NY

June 2, 1874
Luzerne, NY

DIMMICK William of Cambridge, NY

May 28, 1874

|---|---|
| UPTON Fidelia H. of Pittsfield, Mass. | Pittsfield, Mass. |
| MURDOCK Hudson I. of Glens Falls, NY<br>HILKINS Sarah A. of Glens Falls, NY | June 19, 1874<br>Glens Falls, NY |
| JACKWAY Adelbert G. of Westhaven, Vt.<br>HULETT Mary E. of Dresden, NY | June 3, 1874<br>Dresden, NY |
| JOHNSON Nathan of Thurman, NY<br>MEAD Bessie of Johnsburgh, NY | June 2, 1874<br>Warrensburgh, NY |
| DRAKE Eugene of Easton, NY<br>GAMBLE Anna of Easton, NY | June 8, 1874<br>Easton, NY |
| SHEPHERD H. J. of Caldwell, NY<br>GLEASON Kate of Caldwell, NY | May 28, 1874<br>Saratoga Springs, NY |
| VAN KLEECK William of Arlington, Vt.<br>LACKEY Olive of Rupert, Vt. | June 15, 1874<br>Shushan, NY |
| BROWNELL Alanson W.<br>SEWELL Sue M. dau of William of S. Easton, NY | June 11, 1847<br>S. Easton, NY |
| STEWART George S. of Memphis, Mi.<br>LEIGHTON B. of Salem, NY | June 9, 1874<br>Salem, NY |
| BUREN James of Glens Falls, NY<br>FANCHER Ida M. of Glens Falls, NY | June 18, 1874<br>Glens Falls, NY |
| JONES Robert R. of Granville, NY<br>DAVIS Mary W. of Granville, NY | June 29, 1874<br>Granville, NY |
| NEWCOMB George E. of Glens Falls, NY<br>ANGELL Antoinette Isabell of Glens Falls, NY | July 2, 1874<br>Glens Falls, NY |
| RUSSELL S. W. of Glens Falls, NY<br>ZIMMERMAN Nellie of Glens Falls, NY | July 2, 1874<br>Glens Falls, NY |
| SMITH Abram of Sandy Hill, NY<br>KIRBY Maria of Sandy Hill, NY | July 16, 1874<br>Sandy Hill, NY |
| POUCHER David H. of Sandy Hill, NY<br>WHITE Alice of Ft. Ann, NY | July 5, 1874<br>Ft. Ann, NY |
| GLIS Frederick<br>OLSCHEOSKY Annie of New York City | July 11, 1874<br>Glens Falls, NY |
| CHAPIN William of Keene, NH<br>LORD Rosa of Glens Falls, NY | July 4, 1874<br>Glens Falls, NY |

| | |
|---|---|
| WALLACE J. H. of Whitehall, NY<br>BATES Ella of Whitehall, NY | July 4, 1874<br>Whitehall, NY |
| CORNELL Allen of Easton, NY<br>HARRINGTON Maggie of Easton, NY | July 1, 1874<br>Easton, NY |
| HILL Ezra of Putnam, NY<br>CONGLOND Annie of Putnam, NY | July 1, 1874<br>Putnam, NY |
| BICKFORD Philander J. of E. Middlebury, Vt.<br>JOHNDRO Maria of E. Middlebury, Vt. | July 1, 1874<br>Ticonderoga, NY |
| CROSIER David of Hebron, NY<br>ANDREWS Emma of Hebron, NY | July 4, 1874<br>Granville, NY |
| CLARK Fisher M.<br>TRIPP Mrs. Stephen formerly of Sandy Hill, NY | July 1, 1874<br>Boston, Mass. |
| AUSTIN German of Queensbury, NY<br>KEYES Lizzie of Weavertown, NY | July 3, 1874<br>Glens Falls, NY |
| ROSS Jacob of Rondout, NY<br>THOMPSON Hannah of Schuylerville, NY | July 11, 1874<br>Schuylerville, NY |
| SUDDARD David H. of Ticonderoga, NY<br>BENSON Harriet M. of Fairhaven, Vt. | July 14, 1874<br>Ticonderoga, NY |
| KENT Lorenzo F. of Kingsbury, NY<br>MEAD Waitsey L. of Kingsbury, NY | July 1, 1874<br>Kingsbury, NY |
| WILMARTH Clarence M. of Sandy Hill, NY<br>DE WOLF Kate Finch of Sandy Hill, NY | July 23, 1874<br>Glens Falls, NY |
| BENNETT William of Eagle Bridge, NY<br>EDDY Alvah of Easton, NY | July 15, 1874<br>Easton, NY |
| GRAY Edwin of Toronto, Canada<br>COLEMAN Agnes of Glens Falls, NY | July 22, 1874<br>Glens Falls, NY |
| POTTER William F. of Warrensburgh, NY<br>WOOD Caroline of Warrensburgh, NY | July 27, 1874<br>Glens Falls, NY |
| BALL Phillip of Luzerne, NY<br>POTTER Nellie of Luzerne, NY | July 20, 1874<br>Luzerne, NY |
| ANDREWS Warden of Queensbury, NY<br>MORSE Laura J. of Luzerne, NY | July 25, 1874<br>Luzerne, NY |
| YOUNG Henry | July 15, 1874 |

THOMPSON Minnie A.                                    Stony Creek, NY

BROWN Thomas of Granville, NY                         July 21, 1874
DOBBIN Bridget of Granville, NY                       Granville, NY

DAVIS Arthur B. of Sandy Hill, NY                     August 11, 1874
BOSTWICK Mary E. of Sandy Hill, NY                    Sandy Hill, NY

ANDREWS Sylvester of Howell, Mi.                      August 12, 1874
ESMOND Helen A. of Stillwater, NY                     Stillwater, NY

LESSON Peter of Ft. Ann, NY                           July 31, 1874
PALMER Clara of Granville, NY                         Granville, NY

LAMPHERE William H. of Whitehall, NY                  July 30, 1874
KNIGHT Eliza of Whitehall, NY                         Whitehall, NY

FEARY William of Albany, NY                           August 5, 1874
SHILAND Anna E. of Cambridge, NY                      Cambridge, NY

TOOMEY Michael of Greenwich, NY                       August 3, 1874
LEPPERMAN Eva J. of Greenwich, NY                     Greenwich, NY

DE GRUSH James E. of Sandy Hill, NY                   August 12, 1874
STOWELL Phebe E. of Sandy Hill, NY                    Glens Falls, NY

POTTER W. E. of Whitehall, NY US Navy Master          August 13, 1874
CARTER Sarah of Whitehall, NY                         Whitehall, NY

MINER Phillip of Glens Falls, NY                      August 11, 1874
DE VIGNON Agnes of Glens Falls, NY                    Glens Falls, NY

VIELE Charles E. of Glens Falls, NY                   August 6, 1874
ROGERS Mrs. Elizabeth Ann of Glens Falls, NY          Glens Falls, NY

MC CALL William H. of Greenwich, NY                   August 11, 1874
CULVER Sarah M. of Greenwich, NY                      Greenwich, NY

COOL Hiram M. of Glens Falls, NY                      August 18, 1874
FINCH Mrs. Catherine A. of Glens Falls, NY            Glens Falls, NY

WEST Chandler A. of Glens Falls, NY                   August 17, 1874
BULLARD Hattie A. of Glens Falls, NY                  Glens Falls, NY

BUCKLEY Edward of Schaghticoke, NY                    August 20, 1874
RATHBUN Emma J. of Easton, NY                         Easton, NY

DEAN Horace of Hartford, NY                           August 22, 1874
NORTHUP Eunice of Hartford, NY                        Hartford, NY

RACINE Joseph of Whitehall, NY  
BENNETT Ellen of Whitehall, NY  
August 23, 1874  
Whitehall, NY

GRANT Franklin E. of Ft. Edward, NY  
COLVIN Anna S. of Warrensburgh, NY  
August 20, 1874  
Luzerne, NY

ROGERS George H. of Glens Falls, NY  
PERRY Mary A. of North Creek, NY  
August 20, 1874  
Glens Falls, NY

REYNOLDS J. of Hartford, NY  
DURKEE Mattie of Hartofrd, NY  
August 29, 1874  
N. Hebron, NY

SHERMAN Charles H. of Sandy Hill, NY  
PHETTEPLACE Emma E. of Sandy Hill, NY  
September 3, 1874  
Sandy Hill, NY

CORNING Edward of Ft. Ann, NY  
AXTELI, Eliza of Ft. Ann, NY  
September 1, 1874  
Ft. Ann, NY

RILEY John W. of Ft. Edward, NY  
SALSBURY Helen J. of Hadley, NY  
August 31, 1874  
Luzerne, NY

LEWIS Allen S. of Schuylerville, NY  
HOWLAND Edith S. of Schuylerville, NY  
August 30, 1874  
Greenwich, NY

JOHNSON Andrew of Glens Falls, NY  
POTTER Ida of Glens Falls, NY  
September 6, 1874  
Glens Falls, NY

JENKINS Fayette of Queensbury, NY  
CHESTNUT Jennie C. of Queensbury, NY  
August 30, 1874  
Queensbury, NY

MC GEOCH Alexander  
BAIN Ella  
September 8, 1874  
S. Argyle, NY

PERRY M. A. of Salem, NY  
SHIELDS Annie M. of Salem, NY  
September 1, 1874  
Salem, NY

MURRAY Thomas C. of Rutland, Vt.  
THOMPSON Hattie A. of Glens Falls, NY  
September 3, 1874

ST MARY Joseph of Hartford, NY  
SWEET Edna E. of Salem, NY  
September 9, 1874  
Sandy Hill, NY

FREEMAN James J. of Corinth, NY  
LAWRENCE Irene I. of Glens Falls, NY  
September 13, 1874  
Glens Falls, NY

BENTLEY Gardner C. of Albany, NY  
FRATZ Eliza D. of Cambridge, NY  
September 14, 1874  
Cambridge, NY

BAKER Edmond W. of Sandy Hill, NY   (newspaper date)   October 1, 1874

| | | |
|---|---|---|
| BRISTOL Mrs. Amy of Sandy Hill, NY | | Sandy Hill, NY |
| DONNELLY Robert J. of Sandy Hill, NY | | September 29, 1874 |
| MC GOUGH Rose C. of Sandy Hill, NY | | Sandy Hill, NY |
| HILL James M. of Horicon, NY | (newspaper date) | October 1, 1874 |
| NELSON Betsey A. of Stockford, NY | | Sandy Hill, NY |
| HAYES Daniel of Stony Creek, NY | | September 29, 1874 |
| DINGMAN Helen of Stony Creek, NY | | Stony Creek, NY |
| OSGOOD Starks of Elizabeth, NY | | September 23, 1874 |
| FRANCE Samantha of Argyle, NY | | Argyle, NY |
| FLYNN John of Easton, NY | | September 25, 1874 |
| POUCHER Susie of Easton, NY | | Easton, NY |
| MOSS Chester age 78 yrs | | September 24, 1874 |
| PALMER Ella age 18 yrs | | Hague, NY |
| WRIGHT Leonard S. of New York City | | September 30, 1874 |
| VAN LOON Emma J. of Ft. Edward, NY | | Ft. Edward, NY |
| BOWTELL Charles W. of Rutland, Vt. | | September 30, 1874 |
| WOODSTOCK Annie B. of Ft. Edward, NY | | Ft. Edward, NY |
| BRODIE John of French Mountain, NY | | September 24, 1874 |
| BENSON Mrs. Margaret of Frence Mountain, NY | | French Mountain, NY |
| WILLIAMS Albert P. of Granville, NY | | September 23, 1874 |
| RASEY Delia E. of Granville, NY | | Warrensburgh, NY |
| ROGERS E. H. of New York City | | October 10, 1874 |
| COLEMAN Ella of Sandy Hill, NY | | Sandy Hill, NY |
| SAWYER Allen C. of Whitehall, NY | | October 8, 1874 |
| GAYLORD Anna W. of Whitehall, NY | | Whitehall, NY |
| BUTLER John of Brooklyn, NY | | October 7, 1874 |
| MC EWEN Mary O. of Luzerne, NY | | Luzerne, NY |
| MAGEE Charles B. of Salem, NY | | October 7, 1874 |
| BRYAN Lizzie of Salem, NY | | Salem, NY |
| DAILEY Charles A. of Ft. Miller, NY | | October 21, 1874 |
| DICKINSON Mrs. Harriet C. of Sandy Hill, NY | | Sandy Hill, NY |
| SMITH George of Amsterdam, NY | | October 14, 1874 |
| TOUSLEY Libbie of Ft. Edward, NY | | Ft. Edward, NY |

FLETCHER Leonard
HOWE Cornelia P. dau of Judge L. J. Howe

October 20, 1874
Cambridge, NY

VAN DEUSEN Hiram of Queensbury, NY
BLOOD Jane I. of Ft. Ann, NY

September 23, 1874
Ft. Ann, NY

ROBERTS Amos
WHITMORE Gertie C.

October 22, 1874
Rathboneville, NY

JONES Robert of N. Granville, NY
DAVIS Mrs. Ellen of N. Granville, NY

October 20, 1874
N. Granville, NY

MANN Charles B. of N. Granville, NY
CLARK Lottie D. of N. Granville, NY

October 20, 1874
N. Granville, NY

CROCKER R. K. of Cambridge, NY
TAYLOR Abbie Sherman of Cambridge, NY

October 22, 1874
Cambridge, NY

LOCKHART George E. of Glens Falls, NY
STEPHENS Allie M. of Luzerne, NY

October 28, 1874
Sandy Hill, NY

NORRIS H. W. of Glens Falls, NY
DAY Flora M. of Glens Falls, NY

October 29, 1874
Glens Falls, NY

HUTTON Andrew
WHITE Emeline

October 18, 1874
Granville, NY

MAY George H. of Chestertown, NY
ROSS Betsey B. of Horicon, NY

October 11, 1874
Horicon, NY

TAYLOR George E. of Luzerne, NY
GREENSLETE Ellen M. of Hadley, NY

October 11, 1874
Chester, NY

ALLEN Avery P. of Glens Falls, NY
PITCHER Mary E. of Warrensburgh, NY

November 8, 1874
Glens Falls, NY

ORGAN John of Troy, NY
MURPHY Mary of Granville, NY

October 29, 1874
Granville, NY

EATON Charles A. of Middletown, Vt.
ORCUTT Ann of Jackson, NY

October 28, 1874
Pawlet, Vt.

SWAN William H. of Chester, NY
NOBLE Ella of Warrensburgh, NY

October 28, 1874
Warrensburgh, NY

BEADNELL William of Chester, NY
HILL Ellen of Chester, NY

November 1, 1874
Warrensburgh, NY

HEFNER Frederick of Utica, NY

November 8, 1874

JOHNSON Julia of Whitehall, NY                                    Whitehall, NY

FARR Daniel of Creek Center, NY        (newspaper date)    November 19, 1874
COMBS Susan of Luzerne, NY                                 Lens Lake, NY

WILKINSON Dr. A. of Alpena, Mi.                            November 18, 1874
SHEPARDSON Frankie of Whitehall, NY                        Whitehall, NY

PARKER Edward A. of Kingsbury, NY                          November 19, 1874
MURRAY Rose Ellen of Argyle, NY                            Sandy Hill, NY

COOK Jay of Glens Falls, NY                                November 17, 1874
MORGAN Jennie H. of Moreau, NY                             Glens Falls, NY

STOLIKER G. L. of Granville, NY                            November 17, 1874
WANDLE Amanda of Argyle, NY                                Argyle, NY

JOHNSON Martin of Cambridge, NY                            November 19, 1874
WOOD Helen J. of Cambridge, NY                             Cambridge, NY

DONALDSON John of N. Greenwich, NY                         November 19, 1874
RICHARDS Jennie of N. Greenwich, NY                        Cambridge, NY

VAUGHN Carmi B.                                            November 10, 1874
WILKINSON Dora M. dau of Judge E. S.                       Prickly Pine Val, Mt.

DE LONG John B. of Glens Falls, NY                         November 28, 1874
THOMPSON Emma dau of Smith of Glens Falls, NY              Glens Falls, NY

PERKINS John H. of Glens Falls, NY                         November 24, 1874
CHAPMAN Mary Jane of Glens Falls, NY                       Glens Falls, NY

MEAD James of Glens Falls, NY                              November 26, 1874
MOYNIHAN Sarah of Glens Falls, NY                          Glens Falls, NY

WRIGHT Darwin of Ticonderoga, NY                           November 24, 1874
GRAHAM M. of Putnam, NY                                    Putnam, NY

GANNON James H. of Ft. Ann, NY                             November 24, 1874
RICE Adelaide of Ft. Ann, NY                               Ft. Ann, NY

LEWIS William H. of Pittstown, NY                          November 19, 1874
JOHNSON Delia H. of Cambridge, NY                          Jackson, NY

GARNER Edward T. of Beckert, Mass.                         November 25, 1874
MC DOWELL Libbie of Coila, NY                              Coila, NY

HAWLEY Hiram of W. Arlington, Vt.                          November 24, 1874
HUTCHINS Mrs. Jane of Cambridge, NY                        Cambridge, NY

MC NEARNEY Timothy of Cambridge, NY
FLYNN Ellen of Cambridge, NY

November 26, 1874
Cambridge, NY

HILL Hodges H. of Warrensburgh, NY
HARRINGTON Ida E. of Warrensburgh, NY

December 7, 1874
Sandy Hill, NY

HILL Goerge W. of Warrensburgh, NY
HARRINGTON Florence J. of Warrensburgh, NY

December 8, 1874
Sandy Hill, NY

BURCH Lyman of Hebron, NY
MC HUGH Sarah J. of Hartford, NY

December 5, 1874
Argyle, NY

MC EACHRON F. A. of Argyle, NY
CAMPBELL Jane of Argyle, NY

December 2, 1874
Argyle, NY

MOREHOUSE William of Hebron, NY
SMITH Deborah of Granville, NY

December 2, 1874
Granville, NY

MOORE James of Salem, NY
MADISON Charlotte M. of Salem, NY

November 24, 1874
Salem, NY

SHANKS Robert of Greenwich, NY
PIAGET Sophie of Albany, NY

November 26, 1874
Albany, NY

MOSS J. Carlton of Fredonia, NY
MOSS Mary E. of Sandy Hill, NY

December 9, 1874
Sandy Hill, NY

FRAZIER James A. of White Creek, NY
DAILEY Anna of White Creek, NY

November 26, 1874
Cambridge, NY

WELLS Edward of Cambridge, NY
PAUL Jennie of Greenwich, NY

December 8, 1874
Salem, NY

ANDREWS George E. of Salem, NY
SUTHERLAND Mary A. of Shushan, NY

December 9, 1874
Salem, NY

BABCOCK Clarence Nathan of Argyle, NY
MC MURRAY Nettie of Argyle, NY

December 16, 1874
Argyle, NY

STEVENSON Charles W. of Kingsbury, NY
STARKS Rosa A. of Ft. Ann, NY

December 12, 1874
Ft. Ann, NY

MC ALL George of S. Hartford, NY
LEE Sarah of S. Hartford, NY

December 1, 1874
S. Hartford, NY

BAILEY Loudon of Kingsbury, NY
SNEDECKER Mrs. Violetta of Glens Falls, NY

December 16, 1874
Glens Falls, NY

WILBUR Joseph L. of Easton, NY

November 25, 1874

WILSON Ellen of Easton, NY

Greenwich, NY

SMART Plinny of Hebron, NY
MOREHOUSE Ann of Hebron, NY

December 16, 1874
Hebron, NY

MOORE David L. of Sandy Hill, NY
SUPERNANT Anna of Sandy Hill, NY

December 28, 1874
Sandy Hill, NY

MORRIS Alfred A.
HAINES Susie L. dau of D. T.

December 14, 1874
Coxsackie, NY

GRAY Charles H. of Hartford, NY
SMITH Calista of Ft. Edward, NY

December 15, 1874
Ft. Edward, NY

NORTON Charles of Glens Falls, NY
BEVERLY Carrie of Glens Falls, NY

December 24, 1874
Glens Falls, NY

LUNDY John S. of Salem, NY
MC NAUGHTON Esther A. of Salem, NY

December 22, 1874
N. Argyle, NY

BROWN Amos of Bald Mountain, NY
HILLMAN Nettie F. of Bald Mountain, NY

December 22, 1874
Cambridge, NY

WOLCOTT Erastus of Copake, NY
CARROLL Hattie of E. Arlington, Vt.

December 22, 1874
Cambridge, NY

JONES John H. of Westfield, NY
SAFFORD Eva M. of Sandy Hill, NY

December 24, 1874
Westfield, NY

WHITTEMORE Myron of Sandy Hill, NY
WELLWOOD Emma of Sandy Hill, NY

December 23, 1874
S. Hartford, NY

WHEADON George H. of S. Hartford, NY
DILLINGHAM Ettie L. of S. Newbury, NH

December 31, 1874
S. Hartford, NY

STEELE Oliver L. of Dresden, NY
MANVILLE Barbara of Benson, Vt.

December 23, 1874
Whitehall, NY

WOODRUFF Myron of Ft. Ann, NY
BEECHER Laura of W. Granville, NY

December 29, 1874
W. Granville, NY

MAJORY Mr. ____ of Albany, NY
BEECHER Martha of W. Granville, NY

December 29, 1874
W. Granville, NY

STROUP Milo O. of Willington, Ohio
STEELE Louisa A. of Willington, Ohio

January 5, 1875
Salem, NY

CLARK Jerome T. of Greenwich, NY
WRIGHT Ida M. of Greenwich, NY

December 24, 1874
Greenwich, NY

BAKER R. W.
VAUGHN Ruth A.

January 27, 1875
Kingsbury, NY

HUMPHREY D. J. of Granville, NY
WHIDDON Henrietta H. of Hoosick Falls, NY

January 29, 1875
Hoosick Falls, NY

BLAKE William J. of Ft. Edward, NY
METCALF Jennie E. of Ft. Edward, NY

January 20, 1875
Ft. Edward, NY

RICE Adelbert
OSGOOD Celina

January 27, 1875
Glens Falls, NY

RENEY Frank of Glens Falls, NY
RICE Louisa of Glens Falls, NY

February 1, 1875
Glens Falls, NY

SLORAH Richard of Rome, NY
GETTY Maggie O. of N. Hebron, NY

February 2, 1875
N. Hebron, NY

ADAMS Marvin E. of Gansevort, NY
JACOBIE Helen E. of Moreau, NY

January 13, 1875
Moreau, NY

TAYLOR James of Ft. Ann, NY
CUDNEY Nora of Stony Creek, NY

January 19, 1875
Stony Creek, NY

MILLER Fred A. of Fairhaven, Vt.
RICE Emma N. of Castleton, Vt.

February 11, 1875
Schaghticoke, NY

WORTLEY William of Sunderland, Vt.
BARNES Eliza of Sunderland, Vt.

February 22, 1875
Shushan, NY

PHILO Jacob of Queensbury, NY
ASHLEY M. L. of Glens Falls, NY

March 14, 1875
Glens Falls, NY

COLTON Silas of Bolton, NY
GEORGE Delia of Bolton, NY

February 24, 1875
Bolton, NY

TRIPP Gardner D. of Pattens Mills, NY
GATES Joanna C. of Kingsbury, NY

March 18, 1875
Sandy Hill, NY

THOMPSON S. R.
SMITH Martha of Rupert, Vt.

March 23, 1875
Ft. Edward, NY

MASON John
MALOY Mrs. Katie

March 17, 1875
Glens Falls, NY

THAYER Edgar B. of Moreau, NY
HOWE Mrs. Helen J. of Moreau, NY

March 18, 1875
Glens Falls, NY

BROUGH Damas of the Troy Conference

February 23, 1875

WALDEN Almira E. dau of Hiram of Gallupville, NY                Gallupville, NY

POTTER Nathan                                                   March 23, 1875
KEMP Charlotte                                                  W. Newberry, NY

LADUE Cassius M. of Ticonderoga, NY                             March 21, 1875
PECK Nettie of Ticonderoga, NY                                  Ticonderoga, NY

SWEET Daniel of Kingsbury, NY                                   March 24, 1875
KINGSLEY Delia A. of Queensbury, NY                             Harrisenia, NY

HARRIS Walter G. of Queensbury, NY                              March 13, 1875
DICKINSON Alice of Queensbury, NY                               Queensbury, NY

KING John C. Of Hoosick Falls, NY                               March 27, 1875
BAIN Nettie of Hoosick Falls, NY                                Cambridge, NY

PENFIELD Charles M. of Saratoga, NY                             March 29, 1875
MOORE Maria F. of Bolton, NY                                    Lake George, NY

COPELAND Emmett of Middletown, Vt.                              April 7, 1875
SMITH Hattie M. of Poultney, Vt.                                Poultney, Vt.

LASHER John A.                                                  March 25, 1875
EDGAR Sarah M.                                                  Salem, NY

WOLFE James D. of Bristol, RI formerly Sandy Hill, NY           April 18, 1875
PERRY Minnie dau of late William of New York City              Phildelphia, Pa.

HALL David                                                      April 7, 1875
GRAHAM Ella                                                     Ft. Edward, NY

ADAMS A. W. of New York City                                    April 13, 1875
ROBERTS Sarah E. of Glens Falls, NY                             Glens Falls, NY

MONROE Califf of Poultney, Vt.                                  April 14, 1875
HYDE Lucy of Poultney, Vt.                                      Poultney, NY

ROBBINS William H. of Glens Falls, NY                           April 15, 1875
COOL Blanche E. of Glens Falls, NY                              Glens Falls, NY

GULLY Michael of Whitehall, NY                                  April 26, 1875
WINN Miss _____ of Rutland, Vt.                                 Rutland Vt.

WILCOX Sanford of Glens Falls, NY                               March 13, 1875
BAKER Luella of Horicon, NY                                     Horicon, NY

FRAZIER Stephen                                                 March 30, 1875
BAKER Julia of Bolton, NY                                       Horicon, NY

YATTAN Robert of Glens Falls, NY
HINDS Anna R. of Glens Falls, NY

April 27, 1875
Ft. Edward, NY

DOTY Lemuel A. of Glens Falls, NY
HALL Julia A. of Glens Falls, NY

May 13, 1875
Glens Falls, NY

MATHEWS Samuel of Schuylerville, NY
CLARK Julia E. of Victory Mills, NY

May 12, 1875
Schuylerville, NY

CHASE Platt N.
SMITH Mary L. of Windham, NY formerly Sandy Hill, NY

May 19, 1875
Windham, NY

VAUGHN Dallas of Sandy Hill, NY
GRIFFIN Fayetta of Bolton, NY

May 23, 1875
Bolton, NY

PETTIT Isaac of Ft. Miller, NY
SHEPPARD Mary of Ft. Miller, NY

May 19, 1875
Ft. Edward, NY

BAKER George A. of Wilton, NY
HEATH Maria A. of Corinth, NY

May 15, 1875
Luzerne, NY

MOSS Edward C. of Sandy Hill, NY
TANNER Caroline of Sandy Hill, NY

May 19, 1875
Glens Falls, NY

VAN TASSEL Harmon of Glens Falls, NY
CARR Katie A. of Glens Falls, NY

May 14, 1875
Glens Falls, NY

BEMIS Daniel D. of Granville, NY
MAGINOR Ellen G. of Granville, NY

May 31, 1875
Hartford, NY

BEATTIE James W. of Salem, NY
IRWIN Margaret of Salem, NY

May 20, 1875
W. Hebron, NY

BARRETT Harnabus of Whitehall, NY
SEENY Mary of Whitehall, NY

May 24, 1875
Fairhaven, Vt.

HUGGINS James of Schastian, Pa.
WILEY Maggie of Putnam, NY

June 2, 1875
Putnam, NY

MADOW Zebulon of Sandy Hill, NY
PARTRIDGE Dorah B. of Sandy Hill, NY

June 6, 1875
Granville, NY

STODDARD A. L. of Glens Falls, NY
WAIT Emma M. of Oxford, Mi.

June 3, 1875
Oxford, Mi.

CARLOW George Jr. of Albany, NY
KNIGHT Anna of Whitehall, NY

June 15, 1875
Whitehall, NY

ROOK A. S. of Detroit, Mi.

June 8, 1875

WILSON Katie of Salem, NY                                    Salem, NY

FAIRLEY C. J. of Sandy Hill, NY                              June 20, 1875
DUER Mary of Kingsbury, NY                                   Pattens Mills, NY

SUMNER Alfred C. of Bristol, Vt.                             June 16, 1875
TAYLOR Cornelia A. of Ft. Edward, NY                         Ft. Edward, NY

SAUL Henry of Hampton, NY        (newspaper date)            June 24, 1875
FAULK Emma of N. Granville, NY                               N. Granville, NY

NICHOLS Charles A. of Whitehall, NY                          June 20, 1875
DIGMAN Julia A. of Whitehall, NY                             Granville, NY

GRAHAM Charles of Coila, NY                                  June 10, 1875
JONES Amelia of Cambridge, NY                                Schuylerville, NY

DAVIS Oscar V. of Austin, Texas                              June 22, 1875
WARNER Ella of Sandy Hill, NY                                Troy, NY

SEELEY Benjamin of Queensbury, NY                            June 28, 1875
BATES Alida of Queensbury, NY                                Sandy Hill, NY

UNDERWOOD Gregory of Ft. Edward, NY                          June 23, 1875
GREGORY Jennie of Ft. Edward, NY                             Ft. Edward, NY

SMITH Albert of Moreau, NY                                   June 15, 1875
COOK Martha of Ft. Ann, NY                                   Glens Falls, NY

NELSON George H.                                             June 20, 1875
VAUGHN Ida J.                                                Ft. Ann, NY

DUEL Hiram S.                                                July 2, 1875
HILL Elizabeth of S. Granville, NY                           Sandy Hill, NY

ELLIS Henry L. of Schuylerville, NY                          May 23, 1875
HALL Mrs. Clementine of Schuylerville, NY                    Sandy Hill, NY

WARWICK W. P. of Oshkosh, Wis.                               July 7, 1875
BEACH Cornelia E. of Sandy Hill, NY                          Sandy Hill, NY

SMITH Joseph H.                                              June 9, 1875
PHELPS Emma                                                  W. Granville, NY

BROOKS Thomas of South Bay, NY                               June 13, 1875
MC MORE Hattie E. of South Bay, NY                           South Bay, NY

OWENS Charles L. of Ft. Ann, NY                              June 27, 1875
BANE Mary E. of Ft. Ann, NY                                  Comstocks, NY

| | |
|---|---|
| MURRAY Peter of Sandy Hill, NY | July 8, 1875 |
| DOYLE Mary of Sandy Hill, NY | Sandy Hill, NY |
| LEWIS D. L. of Wells, Vt. | June 26, 1875 |
| SEARLES Lucinda of Granville, NY | Granville, NY |
| HICKS Julius F. of Hoosick Tunnel, NY | July 4, 1875 |
| ROBERTS Ella C. of Hoosick Tunnel, NY | Glens Falls, NY |
| WEST Samuel of Northumberland, NY | July 7, 1875 |
| VANDERWERCKER Miss ____ of Northumberland, NY | Ft. Edward, NY |
| STREETER Mifflin H. Md. of Pawlet, Vt. | July 6, 1875 |
| TINGUE Mrs. Emma of Pawlet, Vt. | Salem, NY |
| DODGE Marshall B. of Smiths Basin, NY | July 11, 1875 |
| WIGGINS Lizzie of Hartford, NY | Smiths Basin, NY |
| MC LAUGHLIN William of Putnam, NY | July 8, 1875 |
| CUMMINGS Jennie of Putnam, NY | Putnam, NY |
| LLOYD Daniel G. of Sandy Hill, NY | July 12, 1875 |
| FENNELL Lydia A. of Sandy Hill, NY | Sandy Hill, NY |
| LORD Mahlon J. of Glens Falls, NY | July 13, 1875 |
| VAN VLECK Penelope of Northville, NY | Northville, NY |
| COUMEY Edward of Whitehall, NY | July 18, 1875 |
| DONAHUE Mary Ann of Whitehall, NY | Whitehall, NY |
| HOYT W. D. of Cambridge, NY | July 8, 1875 |
| O'DELL Almira T. of Cambridge, NY | Cambridge, NY |
| ROBERTSON Charles B. of Howard, NY | June 2, 1875 |
| GLOVER Lydia of Howard, NY | Howard, NY |
| TENANT Charles W. of Fairhaven, Vt. | July 14, 1875 |
| BARRETT Mattie L. of Ft. Ann, NY | Ft. Ann, NY |
| EVERTS Evan D. of Salem, NY | July 20, 1875 |
| PRITCHARD Margaret of Salem, NY | Salem, NY |
| WARREN Frank G. of Hampton, NY | July 31, 1875 |
| WILSON Susie dau of Jesse of Round Lake, NY | Hampton, NY |
| NORTHUP B. K. of Schuylerville, NY | July 25, 1875 |
| PRATT Lucy of Schuylerville, NY | Schuylerville, NY |
| HOLMES George H. of Kingsbury, NY | August 5, 1875 |

HENRY Elizabeth of Kingsbury, NY

Sandy Hill, NY

WILSON Samuel of Hebron, NY
SUTHERLAND Alexina of Dundee, Scotland

August 10, 1875
Salem, NY

WOOD Albert M. of Pawlet, Vt.          (newspaper date)
MYERS Mariah of Warrensburgh, NY

August 19, 1875
Warrensburgh, NY

FOSTER William H. of Sandy Hill, NY
STANNARD Mrs. Fannie M. of Sandy Hill, NY

August 18, 1875
Sandy Hill, NY

REEVES James M. of Ft. Edward, NY
RICHARDS Julia W. of Moreau, NY

August 17, 1875
Ft. Edward, NY

WILEY Thomas of Hebron, NY
LENDRUM Mary of Newburgh, NY

August 3, 1875
Newburgh, NY

BROWN Chester C. of Cape Vincent, NY
BROWN Mary Elizabeth of Ticonderoga, NY

August 17, 1875
Ticonderoga, NY

UHL Arthur M. of Poughkeepsie, NY
CROSS Lottie E. dau of A. K. & Charlotte of Sandy Hill

September 1, 1875
Kingsbury, NY

NOBLE Wesley D. of N. Adams, Mass.
MITCHELL Mary E. of Sandy Hill, NY

August 31, 1875
Sandy Hill, NY

SHERMAN William D. of Kingsbury, NY
BUCK Rosamond L. of Kingsbury, NY

September 1, 1875
Kingsbury, NY

THOMPSON D. S. of Glens Falls, NY
GARDNER Maggie of Falkirk, Scotland

August 10, 1875
Falkirk, Scotland

CONKLIN Edward of Sandy Hill, NY
FISH Betsey of Ft. Ann, NY

August 22, 1875
Dresden, NY

CARY C. W. of Ft. Edward, NY
MC KEAN Carrie of Ft. Edward, NY

September 2, 1875
Ft. Edward, NY

WOOD Samuel of Glens Falls, NY
FANCHER Mariette of Glens Falls, NY

September 11, 1875
Glens Falls, NY

QUEENY L. I. of Conklingville, NY
WILLIAMS Emma J. of Conklingville, NY

October 6, 1875
Luzerne, NY

MERRILL Cyrus of Albany, NY
GRIFFIN Mary E. of Warrensburgh, NY

October 12, 1875
Warrensburgh, NY

KETCHUM Andrew of Argyle, NY
MILLER Mary of New York City

October 27, 1875
Sandy Hill, NY

| | |
|---|---|
| **VAUGHN** Edmond A. of New Haven, Conn. | October 20, 1875 |
| **ROOSA** Annie E. of Glens Falls, NY | New Haven, Conn. |
| | |
| **REYNOLDS** Henry of Glens Falls, NY | October 16, 1875 |
| **PARKS** Carrie A. of Glens Falls, NY | Glens Falls, NY |
| | |
| **DE FOREST** Alfred E. of Ft. Edward, NY | November 3, 1875 |
| **BARBER** Edith M. of Coldwater, Mi. | Coldwater, Mi. |
| | |
| **BELTER** Frederick of W. Meridan, Conn. | November 3, 1875 |
| **JONES** Sarah of Glens Falls, NY | Glens Falls, NY |
| | |
| **AURINGER** Cyrus of French Mountain, NY | November 4, 1875 |
| **HENDRIX** Mrs. Eva of French Mountain, NY | French Mountain, NY |
| | |
| **ROBINSON** A. C. of Cambridge, NY | November 11, 1875 |
| **KENYON** Mary S. of Cambridge, NY | Cambridge, NY |
| | |
| **AUBERY** William of Ft. Edward, NY | November 21, 1875 |
| **MONTENY** Mary of Ft. Edward, NY | Sandy Hill, NY |
| | |
| **FARLAN** Alfred C. of Glens Falls, NY | November 18, 1875 |
| **SHERMAN** Belle of Glens Falls, NY | Glens Falls, NY |
| | |
| **HOWARD** H. A. of Glens Falls, NY | October 18, 1875 |
| **ROBBINS** Mary E. formerly of Boston, Mass. | Boston, Mass. |
| | |
| **DICKERSON** C. R. | November 11, 1875 |
| **SAFFORD** Helen D. of Ft. Edward, NY | Easton, NY |
| | |
| **MC DOUGAL** Alexander | December 1, 1875 |
| **THOMPSON** Ella C. of Adamsville, NY | Adamsville, NY |
| | |
| **DEAN** Elwin F. of Glens Falls, NY | November 27, 1875 |
| **BROWN** Lucy of Glens Falls, NY | Glens Falls, NY |
| | |
| **BARKER** Walter of Warrensburgh, NY | November 28, 1875 |
| **HERRICK** Adeline of Warrensburgh, NY | Warrensburgh, NY |
| | |
| **BRAYTON** Walter | December 7, 1875 |
| **WINSHIP** Jessie of Glens Falls, NY | Glens Falls, NY |
| | |
| **WEST** John C. of Springfield, Mass. | December 4, 1875 |
| **HARTMAN** Mira of Glens Falls, NY | Glens Falls, NY |
| | |
| **HUBBELL** Jerome | December 5, 1875 |
| **CROMWELL** Mary | Lake George, NY |
| | |
| **STEARNS** Janus of Stony Creek, NY | December 2, 1875 |

| | |
|---|---|
| DUNLAP Mary of Stony Creek, NY | Warrensburgh, NY |
| GREEN James W. formerly of Cambridge, NY<br>BARNES May S. of Lawrence, Kansas | December 8, 1875<br>Lawrence, Kansas |
| JONES Dr. J. M. of Canada<br>OSGOOD Florence M. of Ft. Edward, NY | December 23, 1875<br>Ft. Edward, NY |
| DWYER Howard H.<br>HUBBS Mary dau of Wm. ROBINSON formerly Glens Falls | December 12, 1875<br>Vallejo, Cal. |
| GRANT John L.<br>VAUGHN Flora of Kingsbury, NY | December 25, 1875<br>Ft. Ann, NY |
| TUCKER Horace of Greenwich, NY<br>BAIN Mary L. of S. Argyle, NY | December 22, 1875<br>S. Argyle, NY |
| GAUTHIER Arthur of Ticonderoga, NY<br>SNOW Minnie of Ticonderoga, NY | December 23, 1875<br>Ticonderoga, NY |
| SHAW Charles of E. Greenwich, NY<br>SCOTT Mary of E. Greenwich, NY | December 21, 1875<br>Salem, NY |
| LUTHER Joseph of Sandy Hill, NY<br>GOODNESS Josephine of Sandy Hill, NY | December 15, 1875<br>Luzerne, NY |
| MORRIS Erskine E. of Argyle, NY<br>SKELLIE Mary of Argyle, NY | December 15, 1875<br>Argyle, NY |
| CHENEY Albert E. formerly of Glens Falls, NY<br>WELCH Libbie dau of Horace of Lake George, NY | January 4, 1876<br>Lake George, NY |
| SHERMAN William of Hoosick, NY<br>MOREHOUSE Cynthia J. of Warrensburgh, NY | December 18, 1875<br>Warrensburgh, NY |
| KELLEHER John of Ft. Edward, NY<br>MACK Kate of Ft. Edward, NY | December 30, 1875<br>Ft. Edward, NY |
| FOSTER Franklin of Glens Falls, NY<br>EDDY Libbie of Greenwich, NY | December 28, 1875<br>Warrensburgh, NY |
| COOK George of Sheffield, Mass.<br>STEWART Ella of Argyle, NY | January 6, 1876<br>S. Argyle, NY |
| STEVENSON Albert J. of Argyle, NY<br>FULLERTON Eva of Argyle, NY | January 5, 1876<br>Argyle, NY |
| REID Donald<br>REID Hattie | January 5, 1876<br>Argyle, NY |

| | |
|---|---|
| MC MORE Norman of Ft. Ann, NY<br>MC KINNEY Ann Jane of Ft. Ann, NY | January 2, 1876<br>Ft. Ann, NY |
| BRUCE Hollis of Camden, NY<br>GRAY Jane M. of Camden, NY | December 29, 1875<br>Shushan, NY |
| TRIPP Cornelius F. of Cambridge, NY<br>HERRINGTON Anna L. of Jackson, NY | December 29, 1875<br>Cambridge, NY |
| HENDEE Charles of Kingsbury, NY<br>FAXON Lydia A. of Kingsbury, NY | January 11, 1876<br>Kingsbury, NY |
| LIDDLE William J. of Argyle, NY<br>FENTON Mrs. Emeline of Argyle, NY | January 5, 1876<br>Ft. Edward, NY |
| SAFFORD Leroy of Ft. Miller, NY<br>GRIFFIN Jennie of Gansevort, NY | January 4, 1876<br>Gansevort, NY |
| MATHEWS William H. of Ft. Edward, NY<br>COLEMAN Lina of Whitehall, NY | January 5, 1876<br>Whitehall, NY |
| BROWN William G. of Dresden, NY<br>WILSON Arville A. of Dresden, NY | January 9, 1876<br>Whitehall, NY |
| CLARK John C.<br>MERRIAM Fannie E. | January 5, 1876<br>Whitehall, NY |
| BURNETT J. W. of Salem, NY<br>IRWIN L. M. of W. Hebron, NY | January 5, 1876<br>W. Hebron, NY |
| RILLER Charles of Long Lake, NY<br>PARKER Emily H. of Chester, NY | January 4, 1876<br>Glens Falls, NY |
| LUDLAM David of Johnsburgh, NY<br>PHILLIPS Eunice A. of Johnsburgh, NY | January 6, 1876<br>Glens Falls, NY |
| DEE Patrick of Glens Falls, NY<br>MC KINSTRY Elvira of Speedletown, NY | January 13, 1876<br>Speedletown, NY |
| WOODCOCK F. J. of Pittsford, Vt.<br>HENDEE M. A. of Kingsbury, NY | January 26, 1876<br>Kingsbury, NY |
| TAYLOR William of Hebron, NY<br>RAMSEY Katie of S. Hartford, NY | January 15, 1876<br>S. Hartford, NY |
| HUBBELL John D. of Queensbury, NY<br>JENKINS Emeline of Queensbury, NY | January 16, 1876<br>The Onieda, NY |
| MC MAHON Dennis of Glens Falls, NY | January 19, 1876 |

| | |
|---|---|
| LEARY Mary of Glens Falls, NY | Glens Falls, NY |
| PARKE James H. of Whitehall, NY<br>HOLCOMB Cora C. of Whitehall, NY | January 19, 1876<br>Whitehall, NY |
| REA John of Jackson, NY<br>BEEBE Lottie of E. Greenwich, NY | January 13, 1876<br>E. Greenwich, NY |
| UNDERWOOD Harry of Hadley, NY<br>TAYLOR Ann of Luzerne, NY | January 18, 1876<br>Luzerne, NY |
| YOUNG Truman B.<br>HEATH Alice | January 13, 1876<br>Corinth, NY |
| NOLAN John W.<br>PARKS Ellen P. | January 26, 1876<br>Moreau, NY |
| IRISH Byron J. of Hague, NY<br>LEACH Nettie of Horicon, NY | January 17, 1876<br>Horicon, NY |
| SHIPPY Reglus of Glens Falls, NY<br>STANTON Emma J. of Albany, NY | January 24, 1876<br>Albany, NY |
| HARRIS George D. of Ft. Edward, NY<br>BARKLEY Marion M. dau of Alexander | February 3, 1876<br>Argyle, NY |
| ROUSE Clarence H. of N. Hoosick, NY<br>DEAN Fannie L. of Cambridge, NY | February 2, 1876<br>Cambridge, NY |
| BENNETT W. H. of S. Glens Falls, NY<br>ELLSWORTH Hettie M. of S. Glens Falls, NY | February 2, 1876<br>S. Glens Falls, NY |
| LA POINTE George of Moreau, NY<br>SWEET Eveline of Moreau, NY | February 3, 1876<br>Moreau, NY |
| KINNEY George H. of Argyle, NY<br>STREEVER Ellanora of Argyle, NY | February 16, 1876<br>Argyle, NY |
| COZZENS William of Hartford, NY<br>PERCY Ellen of Hartford, NY | February 5, 1876<br>Hartford, NY |
| DENTON Richard of Moreau, NY<br>DAVENPORT Altia of Moreau, NY | February 10, 1876<br>Glens Falls, NY |
| MILLS Thomas of Cambridge, NY<br>KILMER Mrs. Ruth P. of Argyle, NY | February 2, 1876<br>Argyle, NY |
| HERRINGTON Frederick of Easton, NY<br>DOORIS Charlotte J. of Easton, NY | February 12, 1876<br>Greenwich, NY |

WHITCOMB Milo of Granville, NY — February 16, 1876 — Greenwich, NY
WILLIAMSON Alma of Greenwich, NY

HALL Orrin of Cambridge, NY — February 16, 1876 — Coila, NY
GIFFORD Elizabeth of Coila, NY

ORCUTT Lorenzo S. of Hastings, Neb. — February 9, 1876 — Horicon, NY
BARTON Hannah of Horicon, NY

BUCK James O. son of J. P. — February 22, 1876 — Kingsbury, NY
MEAD Minnie

HAVILAND Willis — February 22, 1876 — Kingsbury, NY
ANDREWS Belle dau of Squire

RICH Henry of Whitehall, NY — February 23, 1876 — Whitehall, NY
CLANCY Mary of Whitehall, NY

TRULL William C. of New York City — February 23, 1876 — Salem, NY
BLANCHARD Jennie of Salem, NY

PALMER Jesse — February 22, 1876 — Greenwich, NY
CONLEE Mary

MOREY Sheldon H. of Rupert, Vt. — February 17, 1876 — Greenwich, NY
THOMPSON Anna E. of Rupert, Vt.

TRACY Dennis of Cambridge, NY — February 23, 1876 — Cambridge, NY
HURTON Annie of Cambridge, NY

CAREY Frank of Shaftsbury, Vt. — February 18, 1876 — White Creek, NY
MASON Eunice of Shaftsbury, Vt.

WICKES Charles H. of Lake George, NY — February 20, 1876 — Warrensburgh, NY
LAUDER Mary T. of Lake George, NY

MUNGER Orville of Queensbury, NY — March 1, 1876 — Queensbury, NY
PHILO Alvina of Queensbury, NY

SELBY E. C. of Ft. Edward, NY — March 1, 1876 — Ft. Edward, NY
HARRINGTON Laura A. of Ft. Edward, NY

STEWART John of Caldwell, NY — March 2, 1876 — S. Glens Falls, NY
STAATS Sarah E. of Caldwell, NY

O'DONNELL John of Salem, NY — February 28, 1876 — Salem, NY
MC DONALD Mary of Salem, NY

ARNOTT George of Salem, NY — February 24, 1876

CRUIKSHANK Emma of Salem, NY                         Salem, NY

HALL John B. of Warrensburgh, NY                     February 29, 1876
CAMERON Minnie E. of Rock City, NY                   Warrensburgh, NY

SMITH Edwin B. of Caldwell, NY                       March 1, 1876
GEORGE Anna L. of Bolton, NY                         Warrensburgh, NY

COOLIDGE T. F. of Glens Falls, NY                    February 24, 1876
SEELYE C. A. of Glens Falls, NY                      Horicon, Wis.

MERRIHEW Frank A. of Sandy Hill, NY                  March 8, 1876
CORNELL Allie of Sandy Hill, NY                      Sandy Hill, NY

JONES Dr. M. R. of Sandy Hill, NY                    March 10, 1876
HANNA Ellen G. of Sandy Hill, NY                     Sandy Hill, NY

KIMBALL Charles of New York City                     March 9, 1876
COFFIN Mary of Glens Falls, NY                       Glens Falls, NY

HAYES Freeman                                        March 6, 1876
LA PRARIE Philetta                                   Luzerne, NY

CLUTE Levi of Granville, NY                          March 10, 1876
RAYMOND Betsey of Hebron, NY                         Slateville, NY

BAKER Orson of Horicon, NY                           March 2, 1876
SHERMAN Almira M. of Horicon, NY                     Warrensburgh, NY

COON Thomas B. of Horicon, NY                        March 2, 1876
HASKINS Emily E. of Horicon, NY                      Warrensburgh, NY

NICHOLS John                                         March 15, 1876
DAVIDSON Ellen dau of late John                      Sandy Hill, NY

HILL E. W. of Glens Falls, NY                        March 11, 1876
CLAPP Sarah of Salem, NY                             Salem, NY

MOREY S. H. of Rupert, Vt.                           March 17, 1876
THOMPSON Ann Eliza of Rupert, Vt.                    E. Greenwich, NY

STOVER C. H.                                         March 2, 1876
BENNETT Ida M.                                       Greenwich, NY

NILES Henry G. of White Creek, NY                    March 11, 1876
CHURCH Ella F. of Shaftsbury, Vt.                    Greenwich, NY

FORD P. C.                                           March 2, 1876
MC CREA Jennie C. of Schuylerville, NY               Greenwich, NY

| | |
|---|---|
| MATTISON Nelson of Glastenbury, Vt. | March 9, 1876 |
| ELWELL Eliza A. of Glastenbury, Vt. | White Creek, NY |
| | |
| CHAMBERS W. G. of Kingsbury, NY | March 26, 1876 |
| HACKETT Mattie of Moreau, NY | Sandy Hill, NY |
| | |
| BEATTIE R. J. of Ft. Edward, NY | March 22, 1876 |
| KEELEY Mrs. Susan of Ft. Edward, NY | Ft. Edward, NY |
| | |
| SHAW David M. of Argyle, NY | March 16, 1876 |
| WATTS Mary T. of Argyle, NY | Salem, NY |
| | |
| AUSTIN George of Cambridge, NY | March 21, 1876 |
| AKIN Florence L. of Cambridge, NY | Cambridge, NY |
| | |
| ANDERSON Allen of Bolton, NY | March 19, 1876 |
| WOODS Hattie L. of Putnam, NY | Warrensburgh, NY |
| | |
| FINKLE Oscar G. of Bolton, NY | March 15, 1876 |
| ROBERTS Anna E. of Warrensburgh, NY | Warrensburgh, NY |
| | |
| DURHAM Frank of Fortsville, NY | March 23, 1876 |
| SHERMAN Anna of Ft. Miller, NY | Bacon Hill, NY |
| | |
| SWIFT Merritt of Ft. Ann, NY | March 31, 1876 |
| ATKINS Clara C. of Sandy Hill, NY | Sandy Hill, NY |
| | |
| VAUGHN Dewitt C. of Kingsbury, NY | March 29, 1876 |
| VAUGHN Mrs. Sarah of Rutland, Vt. | Rutland, Vt. |
| | |
| WELLS Joseph of Queensbury, NY | March 29, 1876 |
| MC EACHRON Ida of Queensbury, NY | Queensbury, NY |
| | |
| MC CRACKEN William of Windsor, Conn. | March 30, 1876 |
| MONTE Maggie L. of Argyle, NY | Argyle, NY |
| | |
| GIFFORD Dr. J. J. of Prairie Du Chien, Wis. | March 28, 1876 |
| CULVER Fannie E. of Cambridge, NY | Cambridge, NY |
| | |
| PATTERSON B. S. | March 26, 1876 |
| EDSON Mrs. Susan O. | Greenwich, NY |
| | |
| BROWN Clark J. (newspaper date) | April 6, 1876 |
| NICHOLS Eliza D. of Lake George, NY | Lake George, NY |
| | |
| ANDERSON Wesley of Luzerne, NY | April 2, 1876 |
| PRICE Annis J. of W. Glens Falls, NY | W. Glens Falls, NY |
| | |
| JAMES Charles H. of Cambridge, NY | March 29, 1876 |

| | |
|---|---|
| THOMAS Mary of Cambridge, NY | N. Cambridge, NY |
| MASON Alexander of Pawlet, Vt.<br>BRADFORD Pattie of Hebron, NY | April 5, 1876<br>Belcher, NY |
| HAMLIN Edwin R. of Ft. Edward, NY<br>CLARK Sarah E. of Troy, NY | April 15, 1876<br>Sandy Hill, NY |
| GAILEY Alexander of Luzerne, NY<br>MARTIN Lina of Glens Falls, NY | April 13, 1876<br>Ft. Edward, NY |
| POOL Calvin<br>HARRINGTON Sarah Ann | April 9, 1876<br>Easton, NY |
| SCHERMERHORN William of Lake George, NY<br>SMITH Augusta E. of Chester, NY | April 6, 1876<br>Warrensburgh, NY |
| BARBER Cicero W. of Ft. Edward, NY<br>GRAHAM Arminda B. of Albany, NY | April 13, 1876<br>Albany, NY |
| FLAGLER John D. of Adamsville, NY<br>MC AULEY Frances E. of Sandy Hill, NY | April 26, 1876<br>Sandy Hill, NY |
| SMITH Si E. of Dunhams Basin, NY<br>GATES Carrie of Dunhams Basin, NY | April 20, 1876<br>Sandy Hill, NY |
| STEERE Edwin R. of Whitehall, NY<br>SUTHERLAND Kate of Whitehall, NY | April 24, 1876<br>Whitehall, NY |
| RICHARDS Charles of Salem, NY<br>HIGGINS Sarah of Salem, NY | April 20, 1876<br>Salem, NY |
| MONTE William Henry<br>PAIR Louisa | April 18, 1876<br>Glens Falls, NY |
| HAZLETON Charles D. of Glens Falls, NY<br>INGLAS Ruana of Glens Falls, NY | April 17, 1876<br>Glens Falls, NY |
| SULLIVAN J. J.<br>KENNEDY Rose | April 26, 1876<br>Cambridge, NY |
| HUNT John E. of Dresden, NY<br>ALLEN Lillie of Dresden, NY | May 1, 1876<br>Whitehall, NY |
| HUNT Hibbard of Dresden, NY<br>TRACY Addie of Dresden, NY | May 1, 1876<br>Whitehall, NY |
| JAMES A. C. of Georgetown, Col.　(newspaper date)<br>ROBERSON Mrs. Mabel Ann of Greenwich, NY | May 4, 1876<br>Greenwich, NY |

| | |
|---|---|
| ROBINSON Melvin H. of Greenwich, NY | April 25, 1876 |
| RICE Edna J. of Greenwich, NY | Troy, NY |
| | |
| HAWKINS Edmond Palmer | April 25, 1876 |
| PAGE Miriam Hurley dau of H. C. formerly of Greenwich | Brooklyn, NY |
| | |
| MC FARLAND E. S. of Salem, NY | April 26, 1876 |
| MAXWELL C. A. of Boston, Mass. | Portland, Maine |
| | |
| SEELEY B. C. W. of Jersey City, NJ | April 24, 1876 |
| BEACH F. A. of Poultney, Vt. | Poultney, Vt. |
| | |
| TURNER Hiram E. of Irondale, NY | April 16, 1876 |
| PEASLEY Celia of Irondale, NY | Irondale, NY |
| | |
| LOCKHART John of Glens Falls, NY | May 4, 1876 |
| DAY Elise Estelle of Glens Falls, NY | Glens Falls, NY |
| | |
| ELWELL Franklin of Shaftsbury, Vt. | April 27, 1876 |
| HILL Mary E. of Bennington, Vt. | White Creek, NY |
| | |
| KETCHUM Charles L. of Ft. Edward, NY | May 11, 1876 |
| CRANE Eliza of Ft. Edward, NY | Ft. Edward, NY |
| | |
| NEWHALL James T. | May 1, 1876 |
| PROUDFIT M. Theresa | Santa Fe, NM |
| | |
| TAYLOR Dr. James of Cincinnati, Ohio | May 24, 1876 |
| ROGERS Susan A. dau of late Charles of Sandy Hill, NY | Sandy Hill, NY |
| | |
| GARRETT James S. of Glens Falls, NY | May 17, 1876 |
| MILLINGTON Annette B. of Glens Falls, NY | Glens Falls, NY |
| | |
| ABBOTT A. P. of Rutland, Vt. | May 25, 1876 |
| BUEL Mary R. of Whitehall, NY | Whitehall, NY |
| | |
| KELLY John N. formerly of Salem, NY | May 10, 1876 |
| CAIN Elizabeth of Rockburn, Quebec | Salem, NY |
| | |
| BENNETT Fayette of Easton, NY | April 23, 1876 |
| ROBINSON Sarah M. of Greenwich, NY | Greenwich, NY |
| | |
| YARTER Antoine A. of Sandy Hill, NY | June 4, 1876 |
| LA POINTE Rose of Sandy Hill, NY | Sandy Hill, NY |
| | |
| MC CARTHY Dennis of Warrensburgh, NY | June 1, 1876 |
| DONOVAN Mary Ann of Warrensburgh, NY | Warrensburgh, NY |
| | |
| BENNETT Peter R. of Greenwich, NY | May 20, 1876 |

**HIZER** Eliza of S. Adams, Mass.

Jackson, NY

**MORELY** Grant of Rupert, Vt.
**THOMPSON** Laura of Rupert, Vt.

May 10, 1876
Rupert, Vt.

**CAMPBELL** J. M. of Poultney, Vt.
**CARSWELL** Addie of Ft. Edward, NY

June 8, 1876
Ft. Edward, NY

**DOWNS** Edward T. of Ticonderoga, NY
**PRESCOTT** Mary L. of Ticonderoga, NY

June 8, 1876
Ticonderoga, NY

**SACKETT** William A.
**MARVIN** Mary L.

May 30, 1876
Saratoga Springs, NY

**SKINNER** Charles of New York City
**KENYON** Caroline Elizabeth dau of Hiram of Sandy Hill, NY

June 15, 1876
Sandy Hill, NY

**TRAVER** E. H. of Glens Falls, NY
**TRAVER** Jennie of Glens Falls, NY

June 13, 1876
Glens Falls, NY

**NEWMAN** John of Greenwich, NY
**BIGGART** Maggie of Greenwich, NY

June 7, 1876
Cambridge, NY

**BEAULAC** Paul of Sandy Hill, NY
**ANDREWS** Emeline of Sandy Hill, NY

June 25, 1876
Sandy Hill, NY

**OWEN** Robert Dale
**KELLOGG** Maggie (**WALTON**) formerly of Brooklyn, NY

June 22, 1876
Lake George, NY

**JONES** Elmer E. of Brandon, Vt.
**VAN SLEET** Ada of Herkimer, NY

June 14, 1876
Herkimer, NY

**WHITNEY** Leroy of Sandy Hill, NY
**YARTER** Elizabeth of Sandy Hill, NY

July 3, 1876
Sandy Hill, NY

**MEAD** Harvey E. of Johnsburgh, NY
**RAND** Helen L. of Sandy Hill, NY

June 28, 1876
Glens Falls, NY

**ROBINSON** Morris L. of Ft. Ann, NY
**BAKER** Ada T. dau of Alexander of Ft. Ann, NY

June 29, 1876
Ft. Ann, NY

**CLEMMONS** James H. of Dresden, NY
**BARTHOLOMEW** Arabella of Dresden, NY

June 15, 1876
Dresden, NY

**COPELAND** Edward G. of Detroit, Mi.
**RANDLES** Maggie of Hebron, NY

June 28, 1876
Hebron, NY

**DYER** Joseph H. of W. Troy, NY
**MAIER** Anna M. of Troy, NY

June 11, 1876
Greenbush, NY

| | |
|---|---|
| **BEEBE** Charles of New York City | June 28, 1876 |
| **YOUNGLOVE** Nettie M. of Glens Falls, NY | Glens Falls, NY |
| | |
| **JOHNSTON** Dudley of Sandy Hill, NY | July 2, 1876 |
| **MOORE** Azueena C. of Glens Falls, NY | Glens Falls, NY |
| | |
| **BENNETT** S. S. of Ft. Edward, NY | June 12, 1876 |
| **NIBLOCK** Jennie M. of Adams, NY | Adams, NY |
| | |
| **NELSON** Samuel of Hebron, NY | July 4, 1876 |
| **AYERS** Mary of Hebron, NY | Granville, NY |
| | |
| **MOORE** Solomon of Salem, NY | June 8, 1876 |
| **SMITH** Almira D. of Rupert, Vt. | Rupert, Vt. |
| | |
| **DELANEY** John C. of Arlington, Vt. | July 1, 1876 |
| **WRIGHT** Jennie of Rupert, Vt. | Rupert, Vt. |
| | |
| **GRAVES** Fayette N. of Burlington, Vt. | July 3, 1876 |
| **WHEADON** Jennie M. of Pawlet, Vt. | Rupert, Vt. |
| | |
| **MEAD** Madison of Easton, NY | July 3, 1876 |
| **MEAD** Mrs. Mary Ann of Schuylerville, NY | Greenwich, NY |
| | |
| **POTTER** Lyman H. of Queensbury, NY | July 2, 1876 |
| **HUBBELL** Lydia E. of Queensbury, NY | Queensbury, NY |
| | |
| **COLTON** Arthur of Lake George, NY | July 2, 1876 |
| **BURTON** Amanda Louise of Lake George, NY | |
| | |
| **MILLER** John of Glens Falls, NY | July 2, 1876 |
| **DARROW** Fannie of Lake George, NY | Warrensburgh, NY |
| | |
| **HEFFERMAN** John of Warrensburgh, NY | July 6, 1876 |
| **ASHE** Bridget of Thurman, NY | Warrensburgh, NY |
| | |
| **WHIPPLE** Edward of Granville, NY | July 4, 1876 |
| **NORTHUP** Viola M. of Granville, NY | Argyle, NY |
| | |
| **MC MULLEN** Thomas of Galway, NY | June 28, 1876 |
| **AUSTIN** Alice | Paris, NY |
| | |
| **RICE** Charles L. formerly of Greenwich, NY | June 28, 1876 |
| **CARSON** Sarah H. of Indianapolis, Ind. | Indianapolis, Ind. |
| | |
| **ENGLISH** William F. | July 13, 1876 |
| **ENGLISH** Levina of Vly Summit, NY | Greenwich, NY |
| | |
| **BENNETT** Peter R. of Greenwich, NY | July 9, 1876 |

| | |
|---|---|
| HISER Alice E. of Greenwich, NY | Greenwich, NY |
| NICHOLS Warren L. of Dorset, Vt. | July 17, 1876 |
| ELDRIDGE Mary E. of Warrensburgh, NY | Warrensburgh, NY |
| DRAKE Alphonso of Hebron, NY | July 4, 1876 |
| VAN BENTHUYSEN Gertrude A. M. of Hebron, NY | |
| SMITH Willard of Horicon, NY | July 12, 1876 |
| BAKER Mrs. Mercy of Warrensburgh, NY | |
| JARRARD W. J. of Plattsburgh, NY | August 8, 1876 |
| SMALLEY Louise C. of Sandy Hill, NY | Sandy Hill, NY |
| AVERY R. E. of Poultney, Vt. | August 2, 1876 |
| BULLARD Julia E. of Glens Falls, NY | Glens Falls, NY |
| FLUALLEN Thomas of Stony Creek, NY | July 23, 1876 |
| WINTERS Hattie of Sandy Hill, NY | Stony Creek, NY |
| PERRY Peter of Glens Falls, NY | August 13, 1876 |
| NAILOR Mary of Sandy Hill, NY | Glens Falls, NY |
| NAILOR Simeon of Sandy Hill, NY | August 12, 1876 |
| BENWAY Mary of Sandy Hill, NY | Glens Falls, NY |
| DUMAS Fred of Victory Mills, NY | August 5, 1876 |
| LUSSIER Julia of Victory Mills, NY | Schuylerville, NY |
| FRAZIER Ira E. of Lansingburgh, NY | July 23, 1876 |
| WILSON Ruth A. of Lansingburgh, NY | Warrensburgh, NY |
| WORCESTER Frank of Lake George, NY | August 15, 1876 |
| HUBBELL Belzora of Lake George, NY | Queensbury, NY |
| BURDICK E. D. of Thurman, NY | August 12, 1876 |
| HALL Mrs. Lucinda of Thurman, NY | Thurman, NY |
| WELLS W. H. of Ft. Edward, NY | August 22, 1876 |
| LESTER hattie E. of Hartford, NY | Sandy Hill, NY |
| WILLIAMS A. E. of Glens Falls, NY | August 26, 1876 |
| COOK Lizzie of Sandy Hill, NY | Sandy Hill, NY |
| DODD Charles of S. Cambridge, NY | August 22, 1876 |
| SEWELL Emma of S. Easton, NY | Cambridge, NY |
| FLOWERS Dr. B. F.                    (newspaper date) | August 31, 1876 |
| BENEDICT Addie P. formerly of Glens Falls, NY | Detroit, Mi. |

LYON William of Kingsbury, NY  
HANNA Elizabeth of Queensbury, NY  
August 30, 1876  
West Mountain, NY

DICKINSON Edward J. of New York City  
BENEDICT Ella C. dau of Ezra formerly of Glens Falls, NY  
August 28, 1876  
Lake George, NY

CUBIT Richard of Greenwich, NY  
HARTNETT Helen of Greenwich, NY  
August 31, 1876  
Greenwich, NY

WEST Landon  
SHIPLEY Eliza J.  
August 24, 1876  
Salem, NY

TUCKER John of Sandy Hill, NY  
PLANTZ Ellen of Cohoes, NY  
September 9, 1876  
Sandy Hill, NY

KENNEDY Peter of Ft. Edward, NY  
BENNETT Mary of Ft. Edward, NY  
September 12, 1876  
Ft. Edward, NY

MURRAY David of Sandy Hill, NY  
COTY Victoria of Sandy Hill, NY  
September 5, 1876  
Glens Falls, NY

BENJAMIN Charles of Dresden, NY  
PERRY Mary of Benson, Vt.  
September 5, 1876  
Putnam, NY

ACKLEY Albert of Jackson, NY  
KENYON Loie of Jackson, NY  
August 30, 1876  
Argyle, NY

MARTIN Willima M. of Hartford, NY  
WARREN Ida F. of Hartford, NY  
August 30, 1876  
Hartford, NY

CROSS E. J. of Sandy Hill, NY  
KEITH Alvira of Brookton, NY  
September 20, 1876  
Brookton, NY

PRATT Fred G. of Greenfield, Mass.  
WOODARD Libbie A. of Easton, NY  
September 6, 1876  
Easton, NY

CRAW D. H. of Schuylerville, NY  
LANNON F. A. of Schuylerville, NY  
September 12, 1876  
Schuylerville, NY

SMITH S. C. of La Grange, NY  
CRANDALL Ella D. formerly of Greenwich, NY  
August 10, 1876  
Portage Br., NY

FAXON T. F. of Hartford, NY  
GATES Minnie L. of Sandy Hill, NY  
September 26, 1876  
Sandy Hill, NY

MITCHELL Marcus of Chester, NY  
HIGLEY Maria of Glens Falls, NY  
September 19, 1876  
Glens Falls, NY

SAGE Enrique of Glens Falls, NY  
September 2, 1876

| | |
|---|---|
| **SANDS** Matilda of Glens Falls, NY | Glens Falls, NY |
| **HARRINGTON** Thomas of Warrensburgh, NY<br>**WOOD** Mrs. Mary of Warrensburgh, NY | September 20, 1876<br>Glens Falls, NY |
| **BENNETT** H. W. of Sandy Hill, NY<br>**ESMOND** Mrs. Nellie of Saratoga, NY | September 27, 1876<br>Saratoga Springs, NY |
| **GLYNN** Thomas H. of Whitehall, NY<br>**WOODARD** Maggie of Whitehall, NY | September 12, 1876<br>Whitehall, NY |
| **SHAW** John<br>**BROWN** Julia | September 14, 1876<br>Hebron, NY |
| **MILLER** Hugh R. of Shushan, NY<br>**BROWN** Libbie L. of Shushan, NY | September 11, 1876<br>Shushan, NY |
| **HAY** Ebenezer D. of Greenwich, NY<br>**RATHBUN** Lois E. of Greenwich, NY | September 20, 1876<br>Greenwich, NY |
| **HOWE** Rollin A. of Luzerne, NY<br>**SCOFIELD** Libbie E. of Hadley, NY | September 13, 1876<br>Luzerne, NY |
| **YOUNG** Charles A. of St Joseph, Pa.<br>**LANGWORTHY** Jane of Sandy Hill, NY | October 3, 1876<br>Sandy Hill, NY |
| **MATTISON** Zina H. of Saratoga Co. NY<br>**DUERS** Mrs. Matilda of Sandy Hill, NY | October 4, 1876<br>Sandy Hill, NY |
| **KENYON** D. R. of Johnsburgh, NY<br>**THOMAS** Emma of Glens Falls, NY | October 2, 1876<br>Glens Falls, NY |
| **GOURLEY** William of Putnam, NY<br>**EASTON** Emma of Putnam, NY | September 26, 1876<br>Putnam, NY |
| **DURKEE** Eleazor A. of Ft. Edward, NY<br>**CULVER** Alice B. of Pawlet, Vt. | September 20, 1876<br>Pawlet, Vt. |
| **KENDRICK** Samuel D. of Glens Falls, NY<br>**CADWELL** Lillie E. of Glens Falls, NY | September 28, 1876<br>Glens Falls, NY |
| **BARKER** Orville R. of Bolton, NY (newspaper date)<br>**PHELPS** Sylvia D. of Lake George, NY | October 5, 1876<br>Queensbury, NY |
| **BROWN** Rev. Oliver A. of Gloversville, NY<br>**STOVER** Nellie J. of Valley Falls, NY | September 27, 1876<br>Valley Falls, NY |
| **BIBBEY** Leonard of Glens Falls, NY<br>**KELLY** Emma A. of Glens Falls, NY | October 13, 1876<br>Sandy Hill, NY |

WHITNEY Halsey B. of Schroon, NY
BUTLER Ella M. of Schroon, NY

November 1, 1876
Chester, NY

CHENEY George W. formerly of Glens Falls, NY
MERCER Libbie of Westville, Conn.

November 7, 1876
Westville, Conn.

COLVIN Albert N. of Ripley, NY
CHENEY Luella J. of Whitehall, NY

November 15, 1876
Whitehall, NY

HOWE Barker M. of Alden, Vt.
CRONK Clara C. late of Sandy Hill, NY

November 2, 1876
Albert Lea, Minn.

ALLEN Henry M. of Watertown, NY
MILLER Frances E. of Sandy Hill, NY

December 13, 1876
Sandy Hill, NY

WATSON N. of Troy, NY
ABRAMS Nancy of Lansingburgh, NY

December 14, 1876
Lansingburgh, NY

DEARSTYNE H. A. of Bolton, NY
PALMATEER Fannie C. of Bolton, NY

December 18, 1876
Bolton, NY

## WASHINGTON COUNTY CHRONICLE (Whitehall, NY)
### December 23, 1864 - October 28, 1870

BALDWIN David H. of Whitehall, NY
HEAP Mary J. of Whitehall, NY

January 4, 1866
Whitehall, NY

TAFT Andrew J. of Whitehall, NY
SNOW Cynthia of Whitehall, NY

December 27, 1866
Whitehall, NY

NICHOLS T. of Whitehall, NY
WHITNEY E. H. of Whitehall, NY

September 16, 1868
Whitehall, NY

PATTERSON Thomas A. of Whitehall, NY
BENJAMIN Nellie M. of Whitehall, NY

October 7, 1868
Whitehall, NY

WALDRON L. F. of Whitehall, NY
TAFT Mary A. of Whitehall, NY

December 23, 1868
Whitehall, NY

WHITE Cordon of Killingly, Conn.
MC CLURE Henrietta K. of Ft. Ann, NY

December 29, 1868
Ft. Ann, NY

MC ADAMS S. T. of Whitehall, NY
DENNIS S. O. of Whitehall, NY

February 8, 1870
Whitehall, NY

KELSEY Albert of Whitehall, NY    (newspaper date)
FACTO Celia of Whitehall, NY

February 11, 1870
Whitehall, NY

| | | |
|---|---|---|
| **TILFORD** John of Cold Springs, NY | (newspaper date) | February 25, 1870 |
| **WHALEY** Sarah A. of Scranton, Vt. | | Whitehall, NY |
| | | |
| **BENJAMIN** James E. | | February 21, 1870 |
| **BEEBE** Olive dau of Joseph of Dresden, NY | | Dresden, NY |
| | | |
| **COATS** Robert E. of Benson, Vt. | | February 21, 1870 |
| **COATS** Mrs. Polly of Benson, Vt. | | Putnam, NY |
| | | |
| **RICHARDS** Frank of Whitehall, NY | | February 24, 1870 |
| **EARLE** Susan of Whitehall, NY | | Whitehall, NY |
| | | |
| **BLANCHARD** Eli of Whitehall, NY | | February 28, 1870 |
| **FLOOD** Maggie of Houses Point, NY | | |
| | | |
| **BLANCHARD** Alfred of Whitehall, NY | | February 23, 1870 |
| **MC COTTER** Libbie of Whitehall, NY | | Whitehall, NY |
| | | |
| **STEVENS** William B. of Shushan, NY | | February 24, 1870 |
| **STILES** Mary J. of Shushan, NY | | Whitehall, NY |
| | | |
| **ADAMS** Joseph A. of Pawlet, Vt. | | March 8, 1870 |
| **WEST** Achsah I. of Pawlet, Vt. | | Whitehall, NY |
| | | |
| **CLARK** Warren O. of Whitehall, NY | | March 3, 1870 |
| **MINER** Ella C. dau of late Dr. E. L. | | Lithopolis, Ohio |
| | | |
| **MORRIS** Charles W. | | March 9, 1870 |
| **PRENTISS** Kate | | Greenwich, NY |
| | | |
| **HUNT** T. G. of W. Haven, Vt. | | March 15, 1870 |
| **MC FERRON** Lucinda A. dau of Seth of Whitehall, NY | | Whitehall, NY |
| | | |
| **BUTTS** William D. of New York City | | March 22, 1870 |
| **BILLETT** Elizabeth of Whitehall, NY | | Whitehall, NY |
| | | |
| **WETHERBEE** Robbins of Dresden, NY | | April 9, 1870 |
| **MC LAUGHLIN** Mary | | Putnam, NY |
| | | |
| **SMITH** George of Putnam, NY | | April 14, 1870 |
| **TIMBLE** Jennie of Yellow Head, Ill. | | Putnam, NY |
| | | |
| **BROWN** Warren H. of Hartford, NY | | April 20. 1870 |
| **BULLIONS** Julia S. of Cambridge, NY | | New York City |
| | | |
| **MC NUTT** Elijah of Ft. Ann, NY | | April 17, 1870 |
| **HUNT** Sally of Ft. Ann, NY | | Ft. Ann, NY |
| | | |
| **WOOD** Warren Md. of Brasher Falls, NY (newspaper date) | | May 6, 1870 |
| **CARPENTER** Carrie of Lawrenceville, NY | | Whitehall, NY |

| | |
|---|---|
| **MIDDLEWORTH** Warren E. of Sandy Hill, NY | April 27, 1870 |
| **SCOVILLE** Eunie A. of Luzerne, NY | Luzerne, NY |
| | |
| **BELL** John of Lake City, Iowa | March 15, 1870 |
| **WOOD** Eunice of Argyle, NY | W. Hebron, NY |
| | |
| **GERROW** Mr. ____ of Putnam Co. NY | June 1, 1870 |
| **TUPPER** Frankie dau of Dr. Tupper of N. Granville, NY | N. Granville, NY |
| | |
| **MC MURRAY** E. of Salem, NY | May 26, 1870 |
| **MC FARLAND** Mary Grace of Salem, NY | S. Hartford, NY |
| | |
| **FARRINGTON** A. H. | June 8, 1870 |
| **COPELAND** Etta | Ft. Ann, NY |
| | |
| **MANVILLE** Sherman T. of Whitehall, NY | June 15, 1870 |
| **CHAPMAN** Nettie J. of Whitehall, NY | Whitehall, NY |
| | |
| **WILSON** (or **WILCOX**) Nelson G. of Omaha, Neb. | June 2, 1870 |
| **KING** Hettie E. | Argyle, NY |
| | |
| **MILLER** Rev. J. R. of Philadelphia, Pa. | June 2, 1870 |
| **KING** Lanie dau of Mrs. C. J. of Argyle, NY | Argyle, NY |
| | |
| **SNOW** W. A. of Ticonderoga, NY | June 30, 1870 |
| **CONGDON** Jane of Putnam, NY | Putnam, NY |
| | |
| **SAWYER** Chester D. of Port Kent, NY | August 3, 1870 |
| **KINGSLEY** Delia of Whitehall, NY | N. Granville, NY |
| | |
| **HASKINS** B. F. | August 4, 1870 |
| **SIGNOR** Elizabeth A. | Ft. Ann, NY |
| | |
| **FORKEY** Napoleon | August 8, 1870 |
| **FORREST** Celia | Whitehall, NY |
| | |
| **SKEELS** Edrick W. of Whitehall, NY | August 11, 1870 |
| **NORTON** Martha of Whitehall, NY | Whitehall, NY |
| | |
| **FINK** Isaac of Whitehall, NY | August 17, 1870 |
| **WRIGHT** Fanny of Whitehall, NY | Whitehall, NY |
| | |
| **WEBSTER** Henry M. of Hubbardton, Vt. | August 23, 1870 |
| **MALONE** Lillie E. of Hubbardton, Vt. | Whitehall, NY |
| | |
| **RENO** Henry | August 28, 1870 |
| **COFFINGER** Sophia | Whitehall, NY |
| | |
| **NYE** Henry C. of Whitehall, NY | September 15, 1870 |

| | |
|---|---|
| **BOARDMAN** Mary dau of late Cyrus | Whitehall, NY |
| **AMES** Frederick H. | September 30, 1870 |
| **GAYLORD** Mary T. dau of H. T. of Whitehall, NY | Whitehall, NY |
| **GILLIGAN** Anderson | October 4, 1870 |
| **GALVIN** Maggie J. | Albany, NY |
| **CARPENTER** James H. of Cambridge, NY | October 19, 1870 |
| **NEHER** Anna J. dau of Phillip S. of Troy, NY | Troy, NY |
| **STATIA** Charles W. of Hartford, NY | October 24, 1870 |
| **GANEY** Mary of Hartford, NY | Greenwich, NY |
| **PARKE** Henry Clay of Whitehall, NY | October 25, 1870 |
| **DUNN** Alice W. of Plainfield, NJ | Plainfield, NY |

## WASHINGTON COUNTY JOURNAL
### January 2, 1845 - December 26, 1850

| | |
|---|---|
| **LITTLEFIELD** Simeon of Union Village, NY | December 31, 1844 |
| **GREEN** Cinderella dau of Merritt of Union Village, NY | Union Village, NY |
| **SHERMERHORN** Alexander of Union Village, NY | December 31, 1844 |
| **SAFFORD** Gertrude of Union Village, NY | Union Village, NY |
| **STONE** Thomas N. of Jackson, NY | December 31, 1844 |
| **BURROUGHS** Maria dau of Ephraim of Jackson, NY | Jackson, NY |
| **CURTIS** James of Union Village, NY | January 1, 1845 |
| **BUCK** Beth dau of Cyrus of Union Village, NY | Union Village, NY |
| **SMITH** Joseph of Union Village, NY | January 4, 1845 |
| **TEFFT** Dorcas E. of Union Village, NY | Union Village, NY |
| **LOVE** William of Williamstown, Mass. | January 1, 1845 |
| **MARSH** Maria M. of Union Village, NY | Union Village, NY |
| **WOOSTER** John C. of Troy, NY | January 18, 1845 |
| **STARKS** Eliza Ann of Troy, NY | Union Village, NY |
| **PIERCE** William of W. Troy, NY | January 16, 1845 |
| **WHELDON** Maria dau of Jabez of Easton, NY | Easton, NY |
| **CROSBY** Dr. J. B. of Union Village, NY | January 31, 1845 |
| **ROBINSON** Almira S. of Union Village, NY | Union Village, NY |
| **LANGWORTHY** Phineas S. of Union Village, NY | February 19, 1845 |
| **POTTER** Sarah D. of Union Village, NY | Union Village, NY |

HOUGHTON Capt. Alfred
FENTON Julia A. of N. White Creek, NY
NY

March 3, 1845
N. White Creek,


FILLMORE Isaac O. of Cambridge, NY
PARMALEE Julia dau of Zalmon of Lansingburgh, NY

March 5, 1845
Lansingburgh, NY


MC CLELLAN William W. of W. Hebron, NY
MC WHORTER Esther Maria dau of Alexander of Hebron

March 18, 1845
W. Hebron, NY


BARR James of Pittstown, NY
MILLER Eliza M. of Easton, NY

February 27, 1845
Easton, NY


TUBBS Harvey of Easton, NY
HARRINGTON Ruth of Easton, NY

March 19, 1845
Easton, NY


LILLY Martin of Easton, NY
ADAMS Eleanor of Lansingburgh, NY

March 19, 1845
Easton, NY


MC DURFEE Amos of Battenville, NY
THORPE Betsey of Battenville, NY

March 27, 1845
Centre Falls, NY


NORCROSS Calvin T. of Easton, NY
BEADLE Betsey Ann of Easton, NY

May 26, 1845
Easton, NY


SANDERSON E. L. of Union Village, NY
BURTON Mary E. of Union Village, NY

June 19, 1845


CARPENTER Harvey of Troy, NY
LIVINGSTON Mary E. of Cambridge, NY

August 13, 1845
Cambridge, NY


MOSHER Eugene of Easton, NY
ANTHONY Hannah L. Centre Falls, NY

September 4, 1845
Centre Falls, NY


WATSON David R. of Greenwich, NY
BROWN Lydia F. of Greenwich, NY

September 31, 1845
Lakeville, NY


VAN SCHAICK Andrew J.
WILCOX Anna May dau of William of Coveville, NY

October 15, 1845
Coveville, NY


FREEMAN Henry of Northumberland, NY
DICKINSON Ann Maria of Schuylerville, NY

October 23, 1845
Union Village, NY


BARBER Gardner of Greenwich, NY
CAMPBELL Eleanor of Greenwich, NY

October 23, 1845
Greenwich, NY


SELLICK Perry of Union Village, NY
DEAN Adeline M. of Union Village, NY

December 10, 1845
Union Village, NY

MILLER Joseph of Easton, NY
SHAW Susan of Easton, NY

December 6, 1845

BIGELOW Anson of Easton, NY
NORTON Lydia of Easton, NY

December 23, 1845
Easton, NY

DENNIS William of Easton, NY
BLAWIS Chloe of Easton, NY

December 13, 1845
Easton, NY

ENGLISH Abraham J. of Easton, NY
WHELDON Cornelia M. of Easton, NY

January 1, 1846
Easton, NY

WHITE Thomas B. of Union Village, NY
POTTER Mary of Union Village, NY

January 1, 1846
Schuylerville, NY

BROWN Luther of Union Village, NY
HANES Alvira of Union Village, NY

January 14, 1846

CARR Stratton G. of Manchester, Vt.
HOVER Clarissa S. of White Creek, NY

January 6, 1846
White Creek, NY

BURCH Henry Jr. of Easton, NY
DURFEE Phebe Ann of Easton, NY

December 24, 1845
Union Village, NY

BROWNELL Esek of Cambridge, NY
HILL Margaret Ann of Cambridge, NY

January 15, 1846
Union Village, NY

WYMAN John of White Creek, NY
HEATH Laura of White Creek, NY

January 25, 1846
White Creek, NY

RYON George of Wilton, NY
WILCOX Maria of Moreau, NY

February 14, 1846
Moreau, NY

CRAW David of Schuylerville, NY
PROUTY Lucina R. of Easton, NY

February 17, 1846

BROWN John
HUGGINS Jane of Argyle, NY

February 5, 1846
Argyle, NY

MONCRIEF Alexander of Union Village, NY
LOSEE Ann of Schaghticoke, NY

February 13, 1846
Schaghticoke, NY

ADAMS Frederick of Easton, NY
KENYON Esther Ann of Greenwich, NY

February 5, 1846
Union Village, NY

WAIT Job S. of Cambridge, NY
WILSON Mary of Union Village, NY

February 19, 1846
Union Village, NY

DENNIS John of New London, Conn.
FITCH Lucinda of Salem, NY

February 25, 1846
Salem, NY

HALL Pliny F. of Salem, NY
ATWOOD Hannah G. of Salem, NY

February 19, 1846
Salem, NY

DOBBIN John of Greenwich, NY
GRAHAM Phebe of Jackson, NY

April 2, 1846
Jackson,NY

LATHROP Alvin of Poughkeepsie, NY
YOUNGLOVE Anna of Union Village, NY

April 14, 1846

PAUL John of Argyle, NY
MC DOUGAL Mary of Argyle, NY

April 16, 1846

COON James S. of Argyle, NY
CLEGG Jane dau of William of Schaghticoke, NY

May 11, 1846
Schaghticoke, NY

GARDNER William of Horicon, NY
YOUNG Aurelia of Horicon, NY

May 4, 1846
Horicon, NY

HARSHA William W.
SMITH Catherine L. of Ticonderoga, NY

May 7, 1846
Ticonderoga, NY

PROUDFIT Alexander M.
BLANCHARD Maria dau of John MC LEAN

June 10, 1846
Salem, NY

MATTOON Rev. S. formerly of Sandy Hill, NY
LOURIE Mary of Cambridge, NY

June 3, 1846
Cambridge, NY

GARVIN Peter of Centre Falls, NY
MINOR Elizabeth of Union Village, NY

June 16, 1846
Union Village, NY

WOODWORTH Calvin V. K.        (newspaper date)
FENWICK Jennett

June 25, 1846
Salem, NY

STEVENSON James of Salem, NY
VAN BENTHUYSEN Catherine dau of Barrent of Chester

June 23, 1846
Glendale, NY

DE LONG Abram of Easton, NY
BAIN Elizabeth of Argyle, NY

July 2, 1846
Argyle, NY

MOORE Nelson G. of Northumberland, NY
SMITH S. of Northumberland, NY
NY

July 9, 1846
Northumberland,

FERRIS Wesley L. of Chester, NY
EGGLESTON Mary E. of Union Village, NY

July 8, 1846
Union Village, NY

TILFORD Francis of Greenwich, NY
DOBBIN Ann of Jackson, NY

July 2, 1846
Jackson, NY

| | |
|---|---|
| **STILES** Joshua of Granville, NY | July 23, 1846 |
| **COWAN** Eliza Ann of Granville, NY | Granville, NY |
| | |
| **WILSON** David of Whitehall, NY | July 28, 1846 |
| **ROSS** Mary E. dau of late William D. of Essex, NY | Essex, NY |
| | |
| **MERRILL** Henry W. of Schuylerville, NY | July 30, 1846 |
| **GEORGE** Valerie of Schuylerville, NY | Saratoga Springs, |
| NY | |
| | |
| **POTTER** Leroy of Union Village, NY | August 23, 1846 |
| **WELLWOOD** Phebe of Union Village, NY | Argyle, NY |
| | |
| **FINCH** William of Clinton Co. NY | September 3, 1846 |
| **MC KILLIP** Mary Jane of Jackson, NY | Jackson, NY |
| | |
| **WING** Archibald of Schuylerville, NY | September 2, 1846 |
| **HARRIS** Grace of Schuylerville, NY | Saratoga Springs, |
| NY | |
| | |
| **INGALLS** Charles of Union Village, NY | September 9, 1846 |
| **MOSHER** Mary E. dau of Dr. C. Mosher of Easton, NY | Easton, NY |
| | |
| **HERRINGTON** Allen of Union Village, NY | September 9, 1846 |
| **BALDWIN** Henrietta of Union Village, NY | Union Village, NY |
| | |
| **HALL** Robert of Argyle, NY | September 16, 1846 |
| **FLACK** Eliza of Argyle, NY | Argyle, NY |
| | |
| **CURTIS** Edwin of Saratoga Springs, NY | October 14, 1846 |
| **KAPPLE** Ann of Arlington, Vt. | Salem, NY |
| | |
| **ROGERS** Henry of Union Village, NY | October 13, 1846 |
| **STEWART** Fannie of Argyle, NY | Greenwich, NY |
| | |
| **BOYD** John H. | October 15, 1846 |
| **BUNCE** Catherine | Whitehall, NY |
| | |
| **STOUGHTON** Halsey W. of Ft. Edward, NY | October 15, 1846 |
| **PAYNE** Loüiza M. of Hoosick, NY | Hoosick, NY |
| | |
| **BULLIONS** Alex B. of E. Hampton, Long Island, NY | November 13, 1846 |
| **SHILAND** Margaret dau of John of Cambridge, NY | Cambridge, NY |
| | |
| **CORLISS** Columbus of Glens Falls, NY | November 11, 1846 |
| **ROGERS** Mercy of Union Village, NY | Union Village, NY |
| | |
| **GILLETTE** Ralph C. of New York City | October 8, 1846 |
| **MC LEAN** Sarah of Jackson, NY | Jackson, NY |

HALL Joseph of Galesville, NY
RUSSELL Jane of Easton, NY

November 26, 1846
Easton, NY

COMSTOCK Allen of Port Kent
DAYTON Mary E. of Whitehall, NY

November 30, 1846
Whitehall, NY

SPICER Henry of Port Henry
FOSDICK Louisa of Whitehall, NY

November 30, 1846
Whitehall, NY

STONE Horace P. of Jackson, NY
BEEBE Sophia of Salem, NY
NY

December 22, 1846
N. White Creek,

DURHAM Anson
HALL Mary Antoinette

December 24, 1846
Greenwich, NY

FISHER William of Greenwich, NY
HANES Philenda of Greenwich, NY

December 16, 1846
Greenwich, NY

BURT George of Greenwich, NY
SCHEYVER Catherine N. of Greenwich, NY

December 29, 1846
Greenwich, NY

MACK Charles of Argyle, NY
CLARK Caroline of W. Rupert, Vt.

December 23, 1846
Salem, NY

LEE William of Cambridge, NY
GAMBLE Minerva of Cambridge, NY

December 24, 1846
Cambridge, NY

LYON Mr. of Ogdensburg, NY
SHILAND Eliza of Cambridge, NY

January 1, 1847
Cambridge, NY

ARCHER John of Jackson, NY
FERRIS Elizabeth of Greenwich, NY

December 30, 1846
Greenwich, NY

BENNETT A. G. of Schuylerville, NY
WROATH Maria of Schuylerville, NY

December 31, 1846
Schuylerville, NY

STONE Henry E. of Greenwich, NY
WHITE Margaret H. of Greenwich, NY

January 7, 1847
Greenwich, NY

HARRIS William
BARBER Orpah Maria of Hebron, NY

December 31, 1846
Salem, NY

SANBORN J. B. of Albion, NY
FLOWERS C. M. of W. Rupert, Vt.

January 7, 1847

MC KINNEY Sabin of E. Poultney, Vt.
CORLISS Elizabeth S. dau of Dr. Hiram Corliss

January 27, 1847
Greenwich, NY

| | |
|---|---|
| FRENCH William of Easton, NY | January 23, 1847 |
| LANGWORTHY Betsey of Easton, NY | Easton, NY |
| | |
| COOK Thomas W. of Greenwich, NY | January 24, 1847 |
| CLEMENTS Sophia C. of Saratoga, NY | Saratoga, NY |
| | |
| PEARCE Mason of Hampton, NY | January 25, 1847 |
| BLOSSOM Amanda of Salem, NY | Salem, NY |
| | |
| SAFFORD Nathaniel of Salem, NY | January 13, 1847 |
| VANDENBURGH Rachel of Easton, NY | Hebron, NY |
| | |
| DICKINSON E. C. | December 28, 1846 |
| GIBBS Sarah R. dau of Leonard of Greenwich, NY | Janesville, Wis. |
| | |
| YOUNGLOVE John of Greenwich, NY | February 3, 1847 |
| GEER Elizabeth V. B. of Glens Falls, NY | Glens Falls, NY |
| | |
| BOYD James | January 27, 1847 |
| GRAY Mary | Salem, NY |
| | |
| CLEVELAND Benjamin | January 28, 1847 |
| ATWOOD Mary | |
| | |
| BUCK David M. of White Creek, NY | February 7, 1847 |
| DILLINGHAM Jane E. of White Creek, NY | White Creek, NY |
| | |
| MC INTOSH Hiram of Princeton, NY | February 9, 1847 |
| KERR Helen E. | Jackson, NY |
| | |
| GILCHRIST James of Argyle, NY | February 10, 1847 |
| DEAN Laura of White Creek, NY | White Creek, NY |
| | |
| HUNTER W. G. of Dorset, Vt. | February 11, 1847 |
| WOOD Christianna E. of Hartford, NY | Hartford, NY |
| | |
| EDIE William J. of Jackson, NY | February 25, 1847 |
| WRIGHT Maria of Jackson, NY | Jackson, NY |
| | |
| KENYON Asa of Onondaga Co. NY | February 11, 1847 |
| TEFFT Dorcas A. of Easton, NY | Easton, NY |
| | |
| DE FOREST John of Sandy Hill, NY | March 3, 1847 |
| SYLVA Maria of Greenwich, NY | Greenwich, NY |
| | |
| BURKE Joseph A. of Salem, NY | March 11, 1847 |
| AMIDON Jane E. of Hebron, NY | Greenwich, NY |
| | |
| BRADLEY Charles of Greenwich, NY | March 25, 1847 |
| FENTON Clarinda of Greenwich, NY | Greenwich, NY |

| | |
|---|---|
| **NEWBURY** James R. of Greenwich, NY | March 25, 1847 |
| **REMINGTON** Jane E. of Greenwich, NY | Greenwich, NY |
| | |
| **COLLAMER** Foster W. of Easton, NY | March 30, 1847 |
| **ADAMS** Sarah Jane of Greenwich, NY | Greenwich, NY |
| | |
| **CAMPBELL** Archibald | April 3, 1847 |
| **FULLER** Sally | Lakeville, NY |
| | |
| **SAFFORD** Thomas D. | March 17, 1847 |
| **COON** Elizabeth | Salem, NY |
| | |
| **HULL** John H. | April 12, 1847 |
| **WILCOX** Matilda M. of Easton, NY | Easton, NY |
| | |
| **FOSTER** William of Jackson, NY | April 8, 1847 |
| **BILLINGS** Laura of Jackson, NY | Jackson, NY |
| | |
| **TEFFT** John P. of Greenwich, NY | April 14, 1847 |
| **TURNER** Mary of Saratoga, NY | Greenwich, NY |
| | |
| **WARNER** John E. of Jackson, NY | April 21, 1847 |
| **BARTON** Mary of Jackson, NY | Jackson, NY |
| | |
| **HUBBARD** Martin D. of Hartford, NY | May 10, 1847 |
| **RICE** Sophia B. dau of Thomas of White Creek, NY | White Creek, NY |
| | |
| **LIVINGSTON** William of Cambridge, NY | May 20, 1847 |
| **WELLS** Miriam of Cambridge, NY | Cambridge, NY |
| | |
| **CORBIN** P. M. of Lansingburgh, NY | May 24, 1847 |
| **BLATCHFORD** Jane | Lansingburgh, NY |
| | |
| **TEFFT** Benjamin T. of Greenwich, NY | May 20, 1847 |
| **DWELLIE** Caroline L. of Greenwich, NY | Greenwich, NY |
| | |
| **CHAPIN** John of Wisconsin | June 15, 1847 |
| **WILLIAMS** Elizabeth Ann of Easton, NY | Easton, NY |
| | |
| **BURDICK** Worden of Granville, NY | June 16, 1847 |
| **WILSON** Phebe of Hampton, NY | Hampton, NY |
| | |
| **MC KIE** William of Salem, NY | June 16, 1847 |
| **SMITH** Julia of Orwell, Vt. | Orwell, Vt. |
| | |
| **BULL** Isaac of Covington, Kentucky son of H. of Hebron | June 19, 1847 |
| **WALLDRADT** Gertrude A. of Cohoes, NY | Cohoes, NY |

| | |
|---|---|
| **CLEMENTS** Albert C. | June 28, 1847 |
| **BAKER** Mrs. Mary E. widow of D. C. of Whitesboro, NY | |
| dau of Sidney **WELLS** of Cambridge, NY | |
| | |
| **WING** Lorenzo P. of Salem, NY | June 9, 1847 |
| **WASHBURN** Lydia Ann of W. Exeter, NY | W. Exeter, NY |
| | |
| **MOORE** John of Jackson, NY | July 22, 1847 |
| **GRAHAM** Harriet of Jackson, NY | Jackson, NY |
| | |
| **KNIGHT** Elam C. of Providence, RI | August 30, 1847 |
| **CROSS** Mary Jane | Greenwich, NY |
| | |
| **COLE** James R. age 17yrs of Nassau, NY | August 28, 1847 |
| **WHEELER** Lydia J. age 45yrs of Nassau, NY | E. Greenbush, NY |
| | |
| **HANOR** Henry P. age 72yrs of Sand Lake, NY | September 4, 1847 |
| **YORKEE** Phebe age 70yrs of Schodeck, NY | Schodack, NY |
| | |
| **HANES** Isaac | September 7, 1847 |
| **HUTCHINS** Susannah | Greenwich, NY |
| | |
| **BROWN** William of Greenwich, NY | September 8, 1847 |
| **HANKS** Lois of Greenwich, NY | Greenwich, NY |
| | |
| **MOORE** Andrew of Hebron, NY | August 31, 1847 |
| **SIMPSON** Elizabeth of Jackson, NY | Jackson, NY |
| | |
| **MEEKER** Erastus of Schodac, NY | September 15, 1847 |
| **DU BOIS** Charlotte B. of Easton, NY | Easton, NY |
| | |
| **MOSCRIP** Robert of Greenwich, NY | September 20, 1847 |
| **WEAVER** Mary Abby of Greenwich, NY | Greenwich, NY |
| | |
| **SWEET** Charles A. of W. Granville, NY | September 15, 1847 |
| **SLOCUM** Elizabeth A. of Easton, NY | Easton, NY |
| | |
| **SMITH** H. L. of Rook Co. Wis. | September 15, 1847 |
| **GIFFORD** Amy Jane of Easton, NY | Easton, NY |
| | |
| **HAXTON** Andrew K. of Cambridge, NY | September 15, 1847 |
| **DARROW** Martha of Cambridge, NY | Cambridge, NY |
| | |
| **WALKER** George G. of Salem, NY | October 6, 1847 |
| **LAPHAM** Emily E. of Danby, Vt. | Damby, Vt. |
| | |
| **BUMSTEAD** Mr. ____ of New Jersey | October 7. 1847 |
| **MC CADMUS** Margaret of N. White Creek, NY NY | N. White Creek, |

| | |
|---|---|
| CALVERT John of Ft. Edward, NY<br>LANG Mary of Argyle, NY | October 11, 1847<br>Argyle, NY |
| PIERCE Juline formerly of Hamilton, NY<br>GRUMLEY Parnel M. of Argyle, NY | October 14, 1847<br>Argyle, NY |
| ANDREWS Norman T. of Greenwich, NY<br>MORSE Jane E. of Brockport, NY | October 26, 1847<br>Brockport, NY |
| SMITH Archibald of Troy, NY<br>WILLIS Frances of Easton, NY | November 17, 1847<br>Easton, NY |
| CLARK Lorenzo B. of Lakeville, NY<br>BARBER Samantha P. of N. Greenwich, NY | November 25, 1847<br>N. Greenwich, NY |
| NAYLOR Peter of Salem, NY<br>BRUCE Margaret M. of Salem, NY | November 25, 1847<br>Salem, NY |
| HEATH Hiram A. of Salem, NY<br>CORCORAN Helen M. of Albany, NY | November 8, 1847<br>Salem, NY |
| QUA Charles<br>CURTIS Ann dau of E. M.<br>NY | December 2, 1847<br>N. White Creek, |
| CAULKINS James of Ft. Edward, NY<br>CRAIG Mary of Ft. Edward, NY | December 9, 1847<br>Albany, NY |
| EDMONDS John G. of Saratoga, NY<br>MILLER Amanda M. of Bellville, Mi. | November 11, 1847<br>Racine |
| PHINNEY G. W. of New York City<br>VAN BUREN Jane of Albany, NY | December 12, 1847<br>Albany, NY |
| ROBINSON John A. of Easton, NY<br>TURNER Margaret E. of Lansingburgh, NY | December 1, 1847<br>Pittstown, NY |
| TAYLOR Sylvester of New York City<br>TRACY Augusta of Sand Lake, NY | December 1, 1847<br>Sand Lake, NY |
| FOSTER Asel of Greenwich, NY<br>ROBERSON Miss of Greenwich, NY | December 23, 1847<br>Greenwich, NY |
| PRATT John L.<br>BOWEN Mary A. dau of Sylvester | December 23, 1847<br>Cambridge, NY |
| MASON Rev. Jerome of Galesville, NY<br>GREEN Dianna L. of Greenwich, NY | January 10, 1848<br>Greenwich, NY |

WAWFORD William K.                                    December 1, 1847
BULKLEY Frances A.

FULLER Robert                                         January 12, 1848
PETTIT Mary                                           Northumberland,
NY

CAW William of Cohoes, NY                             January 12, 1848
ARTHUR Regina of Lansingburgh, NY                     Lansingburgh, NY

ROBERTSON Martin F. of Greenwich, NY                  January 5, 1848
COOK Sarah Jane of Greenwich, NY                      Greenwich, NY

SEAMAN George W.                                      January 5, 1848
CLARK Eliza                                           Greenwich, NY

NORTON Alexander formerly of Greenwich, NY            January 30, 1848
COTTRELL Martha                                       Albany, NY

MC WHORTER James of Hebron, NY                        January 27, 1848
FERGUSON Agnes of Jackson, NY                         Jackson, NY

RICHARDS Horace G. of Greenwich, NY                   January 8, 1848
ALLEN Sarah F. of Greenwich, NY                       Ft. Miller, NY

HANES Harvey of Greenwich, NY                         January 27, 1848
STEWART Sarah of Greenwich, NY                        Lake, NY

ROBERTSON Thomas of Cambridge, NY                     January 19, 1848
PALMER Mary Maria of Cambridge, NY                    Cambridge, NY

GREEN David of Greenwich, NY                          February 19, 1848
GREEN Caroline of Greenwich, NY                       Argyle, NY

DUTCHER Peter L.                                      March 2, 1848
POTTER Sarah Miranda                                  Easton, NY

HAWLEY David of Salem, NY                             February 16, 1848
MATHER Lydia Jane dau of Col. B.                      Schaghticoke, NY

KERR Henry of Argyle, NY                              February 24, 1848
KERR Jane of Argyle, NY                               Argyle, NY

CORLISS Hiram Md. of Greenwich, NY                    March 11, 1848
SAMPSON Mrs. Almy (HOWLAND) of New Bedford, Mass.     New York City

SERVICE Charles H.                                    March 18, 1848
WHEELER Mrs. Nancy A.                                 Northumberland,
NY

| | |
|---|---|
| **CRANDALL** Asa of Easton, NY | March 23, 1848 |
| **REMINGTON** Jane of Easton, NY | Easton, NY |
| | |
| **MC NEIL** Peter of Argyle, NY | March 14, 1848 |
| **WELSH** Ann E. of Galway, NY | Saratoga Springs, |
| NY | |
| | |
| **CULVER** Col. Henry of Jackson, NY | April 15, 1848 |
| **STORY** Sarah of Jackson, NY | New York City |
| | |
| **BROWNING** J. E. | April 15, 1848 |
| **STRAW** Mary A. | Buffalo, NY |
| | |
| **LANGWORTHY** Robert of Greenwich, NY | April 7, 1848 |
| **GREEN** Mary of Easton, NY | Easton, NY |
| | |
| **WILLIAMSON** Elias of Argyle, NY | April 11, 1848 |
| **WATSON** Nancy of Greenwich, NY | Greenwich, NY |
| | |
| **HURD** Samuel A. of Greenwich, NY | May 28, 1848 |
| **CANNON** Almira of Greenwich, NY | Galesville, NY |
| | |
| **MOFFITT** Martin of Greenwich, NY | June 28, 1848 |
| **HILLIGAN** Catherine of Greenwich, NY | Greenwich, NY |
| | |
| **MUNSON** A. G. of Hebron, NY | July 4, 1848 |
| **HARD** Ann of Rupert, Vt. | Greenwich, NY |
| | |
| **BARDEN** John T. of Pawlet, Vt. | July 5, 1848 |
| **MC CALL** Mary L. of Pawlet, Vt. | Saratoga Springs, |
| NY | |
| | |
| **MEAD** Abner of Easton, NY | August 3, 1848 |
| **OWEN** Jerusha of Easton, NY | |
| | |
| **JACKSON** Bradford | August 29, 1848 |
| **EDMONSTON** Helen Jane dau of E. D. of S. Troy, NY | Troy, NY |
| | |
| **WOLFE** William of Schaghticoke, NY | September 17, 1848 |
| **STOVER** Maria of Greenwich, NY | Greenwich, NY |
| | |
| **MC DOUGAL** Duncan of Springfield, Mass. | October 3, 1848 |
| **DYER** Delany of Greenwich, NY | Greenwich, NY |
| | |
| **COON** Leonard of Stillwater, NY | October 3, 1848 |
| **LUTTON** Sarah | |
| | |
| **FISH** James L. of Cambridge, NY | October 11, 1848 |
| **ROGERS** Melinda of Greenwich, NY | Greenwich, NY |

| | |
|---|---|
| REYNOLDS William A.<br>SHAW Sarah C. | October 15, 1848<br>Galesville, NY |
| REID Joseph of Allegany City, Pa.<br>HAY Eliza J. of Granville, NY | October 3, 1848<br>Washington, Pa. |
| THOMPSON Capt. James M. of Salem, NY<br>BEATY Mary of Salem, NY | October 25, 1848<br>Schuylerville, NY |
| HARWOOD Isaac F. of Bennington, Vt.<br>HARWOOD Mrs. Sophrona of Stillwater, NY | November 10, 1848<br>Greenwich, NY |
| BUCK Elijah of Arlington, Vt.<br>WHITE Elizabeth of Greenwich, NY | November 1, 1848<br>Greenwich, NY |
| VAN BUREN James H. of Easton, NY<br>TUCKER Martha of Greenwich, NY | November 15, 1848<br>Greenwich, NY |
| CHERRY Alex of Greenwich, NY<br>ALEXANDER Barbary of Jackson, NY | November 14, 1848<br>Jackson, NY |
| SKIFF Samuel of Cambridge, NY<br>CRANDALL Phebe Ann of Easton, NY | November 15, 1848 |
| ROBERTSON Joel of Cambridge, NY<br>MILLIMAN Angeline of Galesville, NY | November 21, 1848<br>Galesville, NY |
| HILLMAN Isaac of Jackson, NY<br>HILLMAN Sarah A. of Jackson, NY | November 30, 1848 |
| MOORE Charles H. of Greenwich, NY<br>HILL Martha of Cambridge, NY | December 14, 1848<br>Cambridge, NY |
| WOOD Samuel N. of N. White Creek, NY<br>PENDLETON Alice Ann of Easton, NY | December 18, 1848 |
| VANDERWERCKER James of Ft. Miller, NY<br>WALLER Charlotte of Greenwich, NY | January 3, 1849<br>Greenwich, NY |
| FOSTER Frederick of Easton, NY<br>CRANDALL Mary of Jackson, NY | November 30, 1848<br>Jackson, NY |
| GORHAM Josiah of Easton, NY<br>KENYON Caroline of Greenwich, NY | December 27, 1848<br>Greenwich, NY |
| WILCOX Jason of Schuylerville, NY<br>COON Mary of Lakeville, NY | January 1, 1849<br>Lakeville, NY |
| STRONG Alexander of Argyle, NY<br>CUMMINGS Caroline of Argyle, NY | October 19, 1848 |

AUSTIN Elijah of Arlington, Vt.
TRIPP Jane of Cambridge, NY

January 1, 1849
Cambridge, NY

PRENTISS John H. of Greenwich, NY
GEDDES Mary of Schaghticoke Point, NY
NY

January 11, 1849
Schaghticoke Pt.

VAN ESS James H. of Greenwich, NY
TRAVIS Frances M. of Greenwich, NY

January 11, 1849

STILLMAN Rev. S. L. of M. E. Church in Greenwich, NY
EGGLESTON Mrs. Lucretia M. of Troy, NY

January 6, 1849

ROGERS Archibald of Easton, NY
MOSHER Charlotte of Easton, NY

January 31, 1849
Easton, NY

SYLVA Franklin of Greenwich, NY
WATSON Mary of Greenwich, NY

February 1, 1849
Greenwich, NY

BARKLEY John D. of Argyle, NY
HALL Margaret J. of Argyle, NY

February 1, 1849
Argyle, NY

MARTIN Daniel M. of Argyle, NY
PIKE Caroline E. of Ft. Edward, NY

February 1, 1849
Greenwich, NY

VANCE William of Cambridge, NY
DUNCAN Eliza of Cambridge, NY

February 22, 1849

COOLEY Mr. ____ of Galesville, NY
TEFFT Jane of Galesville, NY

February 22, 1849
Galesville, NY

SEYBRANT Harvey B. of Argyle, NY
PRINDLE Martha A. of Argyle, NY

February 28, 1849
Argyle, NY

YOUNG Arnold of Greenwich, NY
TEFFT Mary Jane of Greenwich, NY

March 7, 1849

CLARK Thomas of Jackson, NY
BROWN Jane M. of Jackson, NY

March 15, 1849
Greenwich, NY

VAN SCHAICK C. M. of Easton, NY
LEONARD Catherine C. dau of Rev. Jacob Leonard

March 8, 1849
Cohoes, NY

ESTES Richard of N. Adams, Mass.
MC INTYRE Sarah C. of Argyle, NY

April 3, 1849
Greenwich, NY

DUNN William M. of Greenwich, NY
WASHBURN Roxie of Greenwich, NY

April 4, 1849

**BAGG** Edward of Utica, NY                                              April 11, 1849
**HUNT** Cornelia dau of late Montgomery Hunt                            Salem, NY

**VAN STEENBURG** Mathew of Greenwich, NY                                May 1, 1849
**SMITH** Eliza of Greenwich, NY                                         Greenwich, NY

**CUNDALL** James W. of Easton, NY                                       May 23, 1849
**BECKER** Caroline M. of Easton, NY                                     Easton, NY

**COLLINS** Thomas                                                       May 11, 1849
**VALANCE** Elizabeth recently of Glasgow, Scotland                      Cambridge, NY

**MC LEAN** William D. W. of Greenwich, NY                               June 5, 1849
**HOLMES** Mary E. dau of Dr. Cornelius Holmes                           Greenwich, NY

**SPAULDING** Henry R. of Warwick, RI                                    June 5, 1849
**CHAPMAN** Anna Maria dau of Henry of Greenwich, NY                     Greenwich, NY

**SMALL** James E. of Cambridge, NY                                      June 28, 1849
**STEVENSON** Ellen L. of Cambridge, NY                                  Cambridge, NY

**CURTIS** Benjamin of E. Greenwich, NY                                  July 3, 1849
**KAPPLE** Esther of Arlington, Vt.                                      Cambridge, NY

**WOODARD** Daniel of Ft. Edward, NY    (newspaper date)                 July 19, 1849
**GUNN** Delight of Ft. Edward, NY                                       Ft. Edward, NY

**COZZENS** William L. of N. Granville, NY                               August 23, 1849
**RHODES** Juliaette R. of N. Granville, NY

**CONLEE** Monroe of Greenwich, NY                                       September 4, 1849
**MARSHALL** Elizabeth of Cambridge, NY                                  Cambridge, NY

**WILCOX** Harvey of Easton, NY                                          September 23, 1849
**DURHAM** Ann Sophia of Easton, NY                                      Greenwich, NY

**STEWART** G. D. of Greenwich, NY                                       September 25, 1849
**STEWART** Mary J. of Argyle, NY                                        Coventry, NY

**WELLS** Albert of Greenwich, NY                                        September 20, 1849
**ACKLEY** Julia P. of Jackson, NY                                       Jackson, NY

**FOSTER** Albert of Greenwich, NY                                       October 3, 1849
**BLOWERS** Lydia H. of Easton, NY                                       Greenwich, NY

**LEWIS** Holden K. of Greenwich, NY                                     October 7, 1849
**REMINGTON** Anna of Greenwich, NY                                      Greenwich, NY

**TEFFT** Allen F. of Greenwich, NY                                      September 30, 1849
**WESTCOTT** Mary A. dau of Isaac of Stillwater, NY                      Stillwater, NY

| | |
|---|---|
| **EDDY** Walden of Greenwich, NY | October 9, 1849 |
| **BUDD** Catherine of Fishkill, NY | Fishkill, NY |
| | |
| **KENYON** James of Cambridge, NY | October 2, 1849 |
| **BARNES** F. Sophia dau of G. I. Barnes of Smithfield, RI | Smithfield, RI |
| | |
| **DEUEL** Joseph B. of Greenwich, NY | November 12, 1849 |
| **CARPENTER** Angeline B. of Greenfield, NY | Greenfield, NY |
| | |
| **BRADLEY** Hull of Ft. Edward, NY | January 7, 1850 |
| **HINDS** Emeline C. of Greenwich, NY | Greenwich, NY |
| | |
| **BRUCE** Hollis | January 23, 1850 |
| **LARKIN** Charlotte | Salem, NY |
| | |
| **NORTON** Leroy of Greenwich, NY | February 17, 1850 |
| **BURCH** Sophronia of Easton, NY | Greenwich, NY |
| | |
| **BOWEN** William of Hartford, NY | February 14, 1850 |
| **WRIGHT** Elizabeth A. | Jackson, NY |
| | |
| **CRYSLER** Martin of Oswego Co. NY | January 22, 1850 |
| **FOLGER** Rachel S. of Cambridge, NY | Cambridge, NY |
| | |
| **TEFFT** Lewis of Galesville, NY | February 21, 1850 |
| **WELLWOOD** Margaret of Galesville, NY | Galesville, NY |
| | |
| **ORELUP** Azor son of Rev. H. Orelup of Rochester, NY | January 17, 1850 |
| **LEONARD** Mary C. dau of Rev. J. Leonard of Cohoes, NY | Cohoes, NY |
| | |
| **MILLER** John S. of Troy, NY | March 11, 1850 |
| **COZZENS** Hannah P. of Easton, NY | Easton, NY |
| | |
| **BLAWIS** Erastus fo Union Village, NY | March 19, 1850 |
| **BENTLEY** Martha of Union Village, NY | Greenwich, NY |
| | |
| **O'DELL** D. M. of Ft. Miller, NY | March 14, 1850 |
| **BRISTOL** Cornelia of Ft. Miller, NY | Ft. Miller, NY |
| | |
| **THOMPSON** John R. of Salem, NY | April 3, 1850 |
| **CLARK** Margaret of Salem, NY | Salem, NY |
| | |
| **CRAWFORD** James M. of Salem, NY | April 4, 1850 |
| **THOMPSON** Ellen of Salem, NY | Salem, NY |
| | |
| **MC INTYRE** John of Bennington, Vt. | April 22, 1850 |
| **BERRY** Jane E. of Hoosick Falls, NY | |
| | |
| **ANDREWS** Lorenzo B. of Union Village, NY | April 29, 1850 |

COOLEY Betsey M. of Victory, NY

| | |
|---|---|
| SARGENT Byron of Rutland, Vt.<br>DAMON Martha H. of Schuylerville, NY | April 29, 1850 |
| ROGERS William C. of Brandon, Vt.<br>ELLIS Harriet C. dau of E. Ellis of Glens Falls, NY | April 30, 1850<br>Glens Falls, NY |
| EVERINGHAM Francis of Greenwich, NY<br>THOMPSON Mary of Greenwich, NY | May 15, 1850<br>Greenwich, NY |
| LA POINTE Vital of Greenwich, NY<br>LAMPIERE Rachel of Greenwich, NY | May 25, 1850 |
| CUTTING Shepherd S. of Greenwich, NY<br>PULLMAN Mary of Greenwich, NY | June 18, 1850<br>Greenwich, NY |
| CARPENTER John M. of Greenwich, NY<br>BILLINGS Frances M. of Greenwich, NY | June 20, 1850<br>Greenwich, NY |
| RANDLES Samuel of Greenwich, NY<br>PETTIS Sara A. of Eaton, NY | June 2, 1850<br>Eaton, NY |
| WILCOX Hiram K. of Easton, NY<br>VANDENBURGH Frances of Easton, NY | July 17, 1850<br>Easton, NY |
| TOMLINSON Albert of Castleton, Vt.<br>RICE Sarah Elizabeth of Jackson, NY | September 11, 1850<br>Jackson, NY |
| FIELDING Henry of Greenwich, NY<br>WALKER Mary Jane of Manchester, Vt. | September 18, 1850<br>Manchester, Vt. |
| PERO John of Greenwich, NY<br>BREWER Mary Jane of Greenwich, NY | September 27, 1850<br>Greenwich, NY |
| ANDREWS Loring of Jackson, NY<br>FITCH Emily of Salem, NY | September 26, 1850<br>Salem, NY |
| HYDE James T. of Hydesville, NY<br>ALLEN Frances E. dau of Cornelius of Salem, NY | September 18, 1850<br>Salem, NY |
| HOWARD Archibald of Greenwich, NY<br>RUGG Mary of Milton, NY | October 26, 1850 |
| FRENCH Charles of Manchester, Vt.<br>UTLEY Emily of Manchester, Vt. | September 26, 1850<br>Manchester, Vt. |
| SPAULDING William H. of Plainfield, NH<br>EDDY Sarah Ann of Manchester, Vt. | August 19, 1850<br>Manchester, Vt. |

KING Lemuel G. of Sunderland, Vt.          July 3, 1850
HICKS Betsey A. of Manchester, Vt.         Manchester, Vt.

CURTIS Benjamin F.                         October __, 1850
BUDLONG Hannah J.                          Marshall, Mi.

CHAMBERS Thomas of Greenwich, NY           November 29, 1850
HOWE Hannah of Easton, NY

CRONNIN Timothy of Salem, NY               December 3, 1850
LARKIN Helen of Salem, NY                  N. White Creek,
NY


## WASHINGTON COUNTY NEWS (Whitehall, NY)
### March 25, 1871 - September 17,1871

LILLIE Capt. David of Centerville, NY              March 18, 1871
STUFFLEBEAN Mary Ann of Whitehall, NY              Whitehall, NY

SUTHERLAND William formerly of Troy, NY            March 24, 1871
GILLETTE Allie W. of Whitehall, NY                 Whitehall, NY

COOK Eugene B. of Granville, NY                     March 22, 1871
RUGGLES Caroline S. of Granville, NY               Granville, NY

WARD M. E. of N. Granville, NY                      March 2, 1871
RICE Mary E. of Ft. Ann, NY                         Ft. Edward, NY

TUFTS A. F.                    (newspaper date)     September 9, 1871
WHITE Georgianna                                    Whitehall, NY


## WASHINGTON COUNTY PEOPLE'S JOURNAL
### January 5, 1854 - December 30, 1879

BRYAN George of Wallingford, Vt.                   January 1, 1854
WALSH Eliza Jane of Battenville, NY                Battenville, NY

STRANG Gabriel of Stillwater, NY                   December 27, 1853
FERGUSON Sarah E. of Easton, NY                    Stillwater, NY

BRUNDAGE Jesse E.                                  December 22, 1853
SHERMAN Lorena of Pittstown, NY

WILLIAMS George H. of Pittstown, NY                December 28, 1853
WALLACE Sarah E. of Hoosick, NY

STOVER Jacob of Schaghticoke, NY                   December 22, 1853

| | |
|---|---|
| HANER Catherine of Schaghticoke, NY | Schaghticoke, NY |
| SOPER Kingsley of Galesville, NY<br>MC CUMBER Sarah E. of Galesville, NY | December 21, 1853<br>Galesville, NY |
| MASON F. P. Md.<br>BRYANT Elizabeth W. | December 28, 1853<br>Galesville, NY |
| AUSTIN David L. of N. White Creek, NY<br>SEELEY Emily of Jackson, NY | January 4, 1854<br>Salem, NY |
| LIVERMORE Edgar of Northumberland, NY<br>FULLER Frances of Northumberland, NY | December 21, 1853<br>Northumberland, NY |
| SHEFFIELD George of Greenwich, NY<br>CHAPIN Sarah of Greenwich, NY | January 12, 1854<br>Greenwich, NY |
| HILL Jesse B. of Cambridge, NY<br>SLOCUM Rhoda A. of Wilton, NY | January 24, 1854<br>Wilton, NY |
| MURPHY Thomas of Demark, Me.<br>MC CHESNEY Orinthia of Schaghticoke, NY | January 19, 1854 |
| BRISTOL Erastus of Ft. Edward, NY<br>CARSWELL Betsey Ann of Greenwich, NY | February 1, 1854<br>Greenwich, NY |
| HOAG Jonathan E. of Easton, NY<br>WILCOX Mary M. of Easton, NY | February 7, 1854<br>Easton, NY |
| WILCOX Orrin L. of Greenwich, NY<br>LA PLANT Anna of Greenwich, NY | February 2, 1854<br>Greenwich, NY |
| GREEN John J. of Jackson, NY<br>WOODS Eliza Ann of Cambridge, NY | January 26, 1854<br>Cambridge, NY |
| LAW George of Anaquasicoke, NY<br>SCRIMIGER Margaret of Cambridge, NY | February 1, 1854<br>Cambridge, NY |
| ROBERSON Alfred of Greenwich, NY<br>WRIGHT M. of Greenwich, NY | February 8, 1854<br>Greenwich, NY |
| PRATT William of Lakeville, NY<br>WRIGHT Anna M. of N. Greenwich, NY | February 23, 1854<br>N. Greenwich, NY |
| DU BOIS Alonzo M. of Jackson, NY<br>STONE Mary A. of Jackson, NY | March 1, 1854<br>Jackson, NY |
| HOOD Daniel M. of N. Greenwich, NY<br>BRECKENRIDGE Charlotte dau of Col. Francis | February 22, 1854<br>N. Bennington, Vt. |

WILLIAMS Alanson of Ft. Edward, NY
DURKEE Delia of Ft. Edward, NY

March 8, 1854
Greenwich, NY

ROOD Samuel J. of Greenwich, NY
FROST Sarah A. of N. Bennington, Vt.

March 13, 1854
Lansingburgh, NY

MAXWELL James of Jackson, NY
GREEN Sarah of Cambridge, NY

March 8, 1854
Cambridge, NY

WHITE John of Salem, NY
MUNSON Dorcas J. of Hebron, NY

March 23, 1854
White Creek, NY

LIDDLE George of Greenwich, NY
CARUTHERS Mary Jane of Whitehall, NY

March 7, 1854
Pawlet, Vt.

SMITH William C. of White Creek, NY
ROBERTSON Agnes dau of J. B. of White Creek, NY

March 9, 1854
White Creek, NY

MC NEELEY James of Bennington, Vt.
MAXWELL Ann of Bennington, Vt.

March 16, 1854
White Creek, NY

SISSON Harvey of Cambridge, NY
SMITH Lodema of Cambridge, NY

April 4, 1854
Greenwich, NY

GIFFORD Royal C. of Easton, NY
WARREN Martha of Pittstown, NY

April 3, 1854

COWEN Benjamin of Worcester, Mass.
WILLIAMS Mary S. of Greenwich, NY

March 2, 1854
Greenwich, NY

PAXTON Thomas of Victory, NY
MC CALL Mrs. Delia D. of Greenwich, NY

March 2, 1854
Greenwich, NY

TURNER Stephen P. of Lansingburgh, NY
HOAG Harriet of Pittstown, NY

April 9, 1854
Greenwich, NY

ADAMS Elijah Jr. of E. Brookfield, Mass.
WILBUR Deborah M. of N. Easton, NY

April 5, 1854
Easton, NY

HASKELL D. D. of Troy, NY
MOWRY J. E. dau of late William H. of Greenwich, NY

April 18, 1854
Greenwich, NY

JOHNSTON Samuel of Cleveland, Ohio
PRATT Jane M. of Lakeville, NY

March 29, 1854
Lakeville, NY

WHITTAKER Seth H. of Greenwich, NY
TEFFT Lucina F. of Greenwich, NY

April 19, 1854
Greenwich, NY

MAYNARD John R. of Greenwich, NY

April 20, 1854

168 *Marriage Notices*

WANTON Cornelia A. of Greenwich, NY — Greenwich, NY

TEFFT James C. of Greenwich, NY — April 16, 1854
TABER Betsey of Greenwich, NY — Galesville, NY

MC NEIL J. S. Md. of New York City — May 4, 1854
BURLINGAME Sarah P. of Saratoga Springs, NY — Saratoga Spr., NY

BURGESS Amos — May 7, 1854
PHILLIPS Mehetable — Greenwich, NY

CRAMER Boardman J. of Saratoga, NY — May 20, 1854
WRIGHT Mary F. of Greenwich, NY — Greenwich, NY

ROGERS B. P. of Troy, NY — May 16, 1854
SPRAGUE Minnie E. dau of Horace of Kingsbury, NY — Kingsbury, NY

PINCKNEY J. Hoyt of Stark, NY — June 12, 1854
WILMARTH Julia F. dau of Enoch of Greenwich, NY — Greenwich, NY

PITCHER William of S. Branch, NJ — June 7, 1854
MC LEAN Mary Ann dau of Thomas of Jackson, NY

MARTIN James E. of Glens Falls, NY — June 1, 1854
CLARK Mary S. dau of Loraness of Sandy Hill, NY — Sandy Hill, NY

DEWEY Thomas of Poultney, Vt. — July 12, 1854
POTTER Caroline of Greenwich, NY — Greenwich, NY

CORNELL Richard of Greenwich, NY — August 23, 1854
DAWLEY Eliza of Greenwich, NY — Saratoga Spr., NY

COMBS Rev. N. of Jamesville, Saratoga Co. NY — July 13, 1854
SPRAGUE Delia of Glens Falls, NY — Milton, NY

LEGGETT Edwin F. of Saratoga, NY — August 17, 1854
BROUGHTON Philenda of Bald Mountain, NY — Bald Mountain, NY

REMINGTON George of Easton, NY — August 25, 1854
CLARK Mary dau of Thomas of Rose Common, Ire. — Easton, NY

PARTRIDGE A. N. of Clintonville, NY — September 21, 1854
PEGG Eliza dau of Rev. John Pegg — Easton, NY

DINGS John of Argyle, NY — September 19, 1854
MC FADDEN Margaret Jane of Ft. Edward, NY — Argyle, NY

BARKER William J. of Hebron, NY — September 20, 1854
MC DOUGAL Margaret Jane of Argyle, NY — Argyle, NY

NORTON Edgar of Greenwich, NY
WELLING J. A. of Easton, NY

September 27, 1854
Easton, NY

SCOFIELD R. H. of New Canaan, Conn.
PRINDLE Caroline E. of Argyle, NY

October 3, 1854
Argyle, NY

PRATT William of Greenwich, NY
SOMES Mary dau of Jonas of Argyle, NY

October 3, 1854
Argyle, NY

BURNHAM Noadiah of Greenwich, NY
VAN BENTHUYSEN Laura of Schuylerville, NY

October 3, 1854
Schuylerville, NY

HAYNESWORTH H. K. of S. Carolina
ARTHUR Malvina A.

October 2, 1854
W. Troy, NY

MASTEN James H. of Cohoes, NY
ARTHUR Almeda M. dau of John formerly of Greenwich

October 2, 1854
W. Troy, NY

BELL Sidney of Sandy Hill, NY
FISH Martha dau of Joseph of Sandy Hill, NY

September 28, 1854
Sandy Hill, NY

QUACKENBUSH T. W. of Easton, NY
GILCHRIST S. J. of Argyle, NY

October 2, 1854
S. Argyle, NY

FOSTER Asel of Greenwich, NY
JACKSON Phebe Jane of Greenwich, NY

October 25, 1854
Centre Falls, NY

BROWN John of Easton, NY
ROGERS Huldah of Battenville, NY

October 19, 1854
Battenville, NY

CAMPBELL Thomas of Cambridge, NY
CAMPBELL Ellen of New York City

October 21, 1854
Greenwich, NY

BURKE Samuel M. of Galesville, NY
TYLER Margiana S. dau of Phineas of New York City

October 15, 1854
New York City

HEMSTREET Alonzo of Easton, NY
WHITTAKER Elizabeth M. of Greenwich, NY

November 5, 1854
Greenwich, NY

HILL Lyman B. of Buffalo, NY
JOHNSON Martha B. of Easton, NY

November 2/9, 1854
Easton, NY

BALDWIN William C. of Saratoga Springs, NY
COREY Helen F. dau of Allen of Saratoga Springs, NY

November 1, 1854
Saratoga Spr., NY

TABOR L. T. of Easton, NY
BELL Esther Ann of Grenwich, NY

December 26, 1854
Greenwich, NY

MC CLELLAN John R. of Hebron, NY

December 20, 1854

**WHITE** Mary Jane of Hebron, NY

**COTTRELL** Charles H. of Easton, NY
**WRIGHT** Delia dau of John F. of Greenwich, NY
December 28, 1854
Greenwich, NY

**BUCKLEY** Dr. M. of Easton, NY
**TILFORD** Elizabeth dau of Robert of Jackson, NY
November 15, 1854

**MAXWELL** George of Jackson, NY
**TILFORD** Margaret of Jackson, NY
December 27, 1854

**ARNOTT** Morrison of Jackson, NY
**TILFORD** Jennett dau of Robert of Jackson, NY
December 27, 1854

**MC FARLAND** William of Jackson, NY
**BENNETT** Electa M. of Manchester, Vt.
January 25, 1855
Manchester, Vt.

**KENERSON** George of Bald Mountain, NY
**JOYNER** Eliza of Troy, NY
January 22, 1855
Galesville, NY

**WENDELL** Clarence L. of Greenwich, NY
**WATSON** Molvina of Greenwich, NY
January 25, 1855

**MAXWELL** Walter D. of Jackson, NY
**MC MILLAN** Hannah of Salem, NY
January 10, 1855
Salem, NY

**ROBERSON** Morgan of Greenwich, NY
**BARBER** Susan M. of Greenwich, NY
February 8, 1855
Greenwich, NY

**BECKER** Joseph H. of Easton, NY
**BUCKLEY** Maria of Schaghticoke, NY
February 14, 1855
Schaghticoke, NY

**MOWRY** William L. of Greenwich, NY
**COTTRELL** Mary E. of Easton, NY
February 22, 1855
Easton, NY

**ARMSTRONG** Archibald of Argyle, NY
**REID** Mary L. of Greenwich, NY
February 22, 1855
Greenwich, NY

**REYNOLDS** A. P. of Greenwich, NY
**SHERMAN** M. E. of Easton, NY
March 6, 1855
Easton, NY

**FIELD** Thomas F. Jr. of Brooklyn, NY
**EGGLESTON** Sarah E. of Brooklyn, NY
March 8, 1855
Pilgrim's Vale

**HALL** Lyman of Hartford, NY
**BURCH** Louisa M. of Easton, NY
March 22, 1855
Easton, NY

**REYNOLDS** A. D. of Greenwich, NY
**DOBBIN** Martha of Greenwich, NY
March 21, 1855
Greenwich, NY

WILLIAMS Charles H. C. of Providence, RI     January 23, 1855
LEE Matilda M. of Greenwich, NY     Hebron, NY

WILLIAMS Melancton B. of Brooklyn, NY     March 22, 1855
BINNINGER Nancy of Camden Valley, NY     Salem, NY

WILCOX Seymour of Lanesboro, Mass.     April 16, 1855
HENRY Mrs. M. dau of John BARNARD of Greenwich, NY     Sand Lake, NY

WESTON Theodore R. of Salem, NY     April 12, 1855
ATWOOD Jane A. of Salem, NY     Salem, NY

STOVER Rowland M. of Troy, NY     April 17, 1855
HOWARD Carrie F. dau of N. of New York City     New York City

DURKEE R. J. of Ft. Edward, NY     May 9, 1855
POTTER Eliza of Ft. Edward, NY     Greenwich, NY

THOMPSON John A. of Pine Plains, NY     May 9, 1855
VIELE Lucy Ann dau of Stephen L. of Ft. Miller, NY     Ft. Miller, NY

MONTGOMERY William of Galesville, NY     May 4, 1855
CLARK Elizabeth of Northumberland, NY     Northumberland, NY

MILLER David of Greenwich, NY     June 7, 1855
TEFFT Sarah of Greenwich, NY     Greenwich, NY

ANTHONY William of Greenwich, NY     June 12, 1855
FIELD Mary Jane of Greenwich, NY     Greenwich, NY

CROSSETT John M. of Glens Falls, NY     June 19, 1855
MUSHATT Mary Jane of Ft. Edward, NY     Greenwich, NY

SPICER Horace W. of Hoosick, NY     June 21, 1855
SISSON Cordelia M. of Hoosick, NY     Greenwich, NY

SMITH John T. of Easton, NY     June 23, 1855
FLACK Sarah Ann of Hartford, NY     Greenwich, NY

CHANDLER John D.     June 3, 1855
FULLER A. M. formerly of Greenwich, NY     Arlington, Mi.

BENNETT Benjamin B. of Greenwich, NY     July 5, 1855
CHAPIN Laura M. of Greenwich, NY     Greenwich, NY

VANDERWALKER John B. of Northumberland, NY     July 4, 1855
TIMMERMAN Elizabeth of S. Argyle, NY     S. Argyle, NY

WILLIAMS George F. of Jackson, NY     September 7, 1855

BURCH Marina E. of Greenwich, NY              Greenwich, NY

STRUBLE Daniel of Prairie Ronde              August 30, 1855
ROWLEY Jane C. of Schoolcraft, Mi.

TILTON Harvey H. of Schuylerville, NY         October 1, 1855
DAVIS Eveline of Schuylerville, NY            Granville, NY

NEWCOMB J. E. of Whitehall, NY                September 24, 1855
COOK Fanny of Whitehall, NY                   Whitehall, NY

BERRY John of Easton, NY                      October 13, 1855
CLARK Cartherine of Greenwich, NY             Greenwich, NY

DICKSON William G. of Savannah, Ga.           October 11, 1855
WILSON Miss dau of Nathan W. of Salem, NY     Salem, NY

ALLEN Edward C. of Troy, NY                   November 1, 1855
GIFFORD Louisa J. of Easton, NY               Easton, NY

CHARTIER Pierre of Sandy Hill, NY             November 7, 1855
BAIL Rozella of Glens Falls, NY               Glens Falls, NY

CULVER James S. of E. Greenwich, NY           October 30, 1855
HASTINGS Elsa Maria of Salem, NY              Salem, NY

RALSTON V. Y. of Quincey, Ill.                November 5, 1855
TAYLOR Lottie M. dau of William of Cambridge, NY   Cambridge, NY

ROCKWELL Harmon of Hadley                     November 14, 1855
TERHUME Mariette dau of late John of Northumberland, NY  Northumberland, NY

KENYON Clark H. of Greenwich, NY              November 21, 1855
COFFIN Ann H. of Easton, NY                   Greenwich, NY

HOLLEY Jeremiah of Batavia, NY                November 24, 1855
HERRINGTON Mary E. of Easton, NY              Easton, NY

RUSSELL D. C. of Salem, NY                    December 20, 1855
PEMBERTON Hattie A. dau of Henry C. of Albany, NY

BENNETT Jabez of Greenwich, NY                January 14, 1856
BROWN Catherine J. of Greenwich, NY           Greenwich, NY

MC CALL James of Argyle, NY                   January 1, 1856
STEWART Elizabeth of Ft. Edward, NY           Ft. Edward, NY

BAKER Richard N. of Troy, NY                  December 31, 1855
FILES Lucinda of Easton, NY                   Easton, NY

SERVICE Joshua  
LASHER Mary J.  

December 31, 1855  
Saratoga, NY

BAILEY Jerry of Greenwich, NY  
SERVICE Freelove C. of Greenwich, NY  

December 31, 1855  
Saratoga, NY

MESERVE Joseph of Illinois  
WOODS Elizabeth A. of Battenville, NY  

January 13, 1856  
Greenwich, NY

COREY Allen of New York City  
DEAN Mary E. of Greenwich, NY  

January 31, 1856  
Greenwich, NY

CLARK Jefferson of Easton, NY  
ENGLISH Mrs. Judith of Easton, NY  

January 27, 1856  
Easton, NY

MC FARLAND Joseph of Greenwich, NY  
ARMSTRONG Christiana of Argyle, NY  

January 31, 1856  
Argyle, NY

OATLEY Samuel of Brooklyn, NY  
PEMBERTON Mrs. Mary (TROWBRIDGE) of Brooklyn  

January 20, 1856  
New Haven, Conn.

POLLOCK Aaron of Argyle, NY  
MC NEIL Catherine Ann of Argyle, NY  

January 31, 1856  
Argyle, NY

PAUL Franc M.  
COLE Amanda M. dau of Curtis of Jackson, NY  

January 23, 1856  
Aberdeen, Miss.

FOWLER Alonzo G. of Aurora, Ill.  
DEUEL Nancy S. of Cambridge, NY  

February 19, 1856  
Cambridge, NY

SWEET Samuel M. of Moreau, NY  
THOMPSON Hannah M. of Moreau, NY  

February 23, 1856  
Greenwich, NY

RAMSEY John  
NEWMAN Mary Eleanor Delia dau of R. B. of Easton  

January 30, 1856  
New York City

BANKER Isaac A. of St. Paul, Minn.  
BAUCUS M. L. of Waterford, NY  

January 30, 1856  
St. Paul, Minn.

PARKER Frederick A. of Greenwich, NY  
GAYETTE Ann Sophia of Greenwich, NY  

March 6, 1856  
Greenwich, NY

FURSMAN E. L. of Schuylerville, NY  
LINDLEY Gertrude dau of J. H. of Albany, NY  

February 28, 1856  
Albany, NY

SAFFORD Joseph of Greenwich, NY  
GRAHAM Mary Jane of Greenwich, NY  

March 12, 1856  
Greenwich, NY

GREEN David of Easton, NY  

March 19, 1856

ENGLISH Rhoba M. of Easton, NY — Easton, NY

CHAPMAN Samuel of Philadelphia, Pa. — February 26, 1856
HOPKINS Libbie of Argyle, NY — Argyle, NY

FAXON Walter S. of Plano, Ill. — April 2, 1856
VOLENTINE Zelia M. of Bald Mountain, NY — Bald Mountain, NY

HASTINGS David Henry of Salem, NY — April 22, 1856
CULVER Sarah Jane of Jackson, NY — Jackson, NY

PATTISON John of Greenwich, NY — April 9, 1856
STORMONT Elizabeth of Jackson, NY — Albany, NY

MC MILLAN Harvey of Shushan, NY — April 15, 1856
HARNEY Mary A. of Shushan, NY

HILLMAN Hiram M. of Jackson, NY — July 28, 1856
RAYMOND Jane of Warrensburgh, NY — Coila, NY

MC FARLAND Murray of Salem, NY — May 8, 1856
FITCH Sarah S. dau of William of Salem, NY — Salem, NY

GIFFORD Gerritt of Easton, NY — May 17, 1856
HOAG Sarah of Easton, NY — N. Bennington, Vt.

CULVER Perry of Cambridge, NY — June 4, 1856
MC FARLAND Mary Ann dau of John of Salem, NY — Salem, NY

HANNA John E. of White Creek, NY — June 4, 1856
FISHER Cornelia M. dau of David of White Creek, NY — Ashgrove, NY

MC CHESNEY William N. of Greenwich, NY — June 17,1856
MILLER Mary S. dau of David of Greenwich, NY — Greenwich, NY

GIBBS Dr. Theron G. of Granville, NY — June 12, 1856
SMITH Harriet A. of Granville, NY

TUTTLE E. R. of Chicago, Ill. — June 15, 1856
SHERWOOD Mary E. formerly of Greenwich, NY — Cherry Valley, Ill.

THOMPSON James of N. White Creek, NY — June 16, 1856
BOYD Louisa M. dau of John L. of Taylor, NY — Taylor, NY

WOLFE David — June 20, 1856
LAMB Sarah — Peilla, Iowa

ROBINSON George I. — July 3, 1856
WRIGHT Elizabeth — Bald Mountain, NY

| | |
|---|---|
| WAIT Job S. of Cambridge, NY<br>WILSON Elizabeth of Greenwich, NY | July 5, 1856<br>Galesville, NY |
| WALDRON C. A. of Waterford, NY<br>WAIT Caroline M. of White Creek, NY | June 25, 1856<br>White Creek, NY |
| VAN BUREN Paul E. of Easton, NY<br>BULSON Julia E. of Easton, NY | July 12, 1856<br>Schaghticoke, NY |
| CAMPBELL C. D. recently of Clinton Co. Iowa<br>WILBUR Phebe T. of N. Easton, NY | July 11, 1856<br>Groton, NY |
| BROWNELL William T. S. of Cambridge, NY<br>KENNISON Charlotte of Easton, NY | August 3, 1856<br>Easton, NY |
| BUELL James of Troy, NY<br>KELLOGG Electa B. dau of Orrin of Cambridge, NY | August 4, 1856<br>Cambridge, NY |
| WILMARTH Alfred ot Greenwich, NY<br>BAUMES Catherine of Galesville, NY | August 17, 1856<br>Galesville, NY |
| SHAW Rufus of Hebron, NY<br>DURLING Isabel J. of Greenwich, NY | August 19, 1856<br>Greenwich, NY |
| SMITH John of Vermont<br>STOVER Almira of Greenwich, NY | September 2, 1856<br>Greenwich, NY |
| CALHOUN David H. of Greenwich, NY<br>COLLINS Elizabeth of Greenwich, NY | September 15, 1856<br>Troy, NY |
| WHELDON Francis James of Easton, NY<br>MARSHALL Mary of Cambridge, NY | September 23, 1856<br>Cambridge, NY |
| MC CREEDY George of Schuylerville, NY<br>FISHER Eveline of Easton, NY | September 17, 1856<br>Easton, NY |
| FISHER David W. of Easton, NY<br>GRAY Eliza A. of Schuylerville, NY | September 17, 1856<br>Easton, NY |
| FISHER Alfred of Easton, NY<br>GRAY Esther M. | September 17, 1856<br>Easton, NY |
| COWAN Charles H. of Buffalo, NY<br>MC ALLISTER Ann E. dau of late Dr. A. of Salem, NY | September 16, 1856<br>Salem, NY |
| JILLSON Harvey of Greenwich, NY<br>JAMES Eliza R. of Greenwich, NY | September 24, 1856<br>Greenwich, NY |
| KENYON Amasa C. of Michigan | September 24, 1856 |

| | |
|---|---|
| **TAYLOR** Elizabeth dau of late L. G. of Ft. Edward, NY | Ft. Edward, NY |
| **TAYLOR** D. W. of Ft. Edward, NY | October 8, 1856 |
| **WHIPPLE** Della E. of Greenwich, NY | Greenwich, NY |
| **RANDLES** Alexander of Argyle, NY | October 7, 1856 |
| **WHYTE** Sarah A. of Argyle, NY | Argyle, NY |
| **LAWRENCE** Phillip formerly of Greenwich, NY | July 13, 1856 |
| **CROSBEE** Helen M. of Hoosick, NY | White Creek, NY |
| **OSBORN** Richard Jr. of Sandy Creek, NY | October 14, 1856 |
| **GUNN** Diantha E. dau of C. J. of Greenwich, NY | Albany, NY |
| **SIBLEY** Samuel C. of Conneaut, Ohio | October 19, 1856 |
| **MORSE** Julia S. of Greenwich, NY | Greenwich, NY |
| **ALLEN** William C. of Greenwich, NY | October 14, 1856 |
| **BLAKELEY** Jennette of Lansingburgh, NY | Lansingburgh, NY |
| **STEWART** William H. | October 20, 1856 |
| **BOARDMAN** Mary of Bennington, Vt. | Union Village, NY |
| **PETTEYS** Horace of Cambridge, NY | October 20, 1856 |
| **CLARK** Phebe E. dau of Charles formerly of Washington Co. | Mina, NY |
| **PHELPS** Lewis H. of Cambridge, NY | November 5, 1856 |
| **BURCH** Thankful of Easton, NY | Easton, NY |
| **GOW** David of Argyle, NY | October 28, 1856 |
| **GILLIS** Margaret E. of Argyle, NY | Argyle, NY |
| **STEVENS** Henry of Easton, NY | October 23, 1856 |
| **BARKER** Cornelia of Easton, NY | Easton, NY |
| **HUGHSON** Wesley P. of Stillwater, NY | October 25, 1856 |
| **PERKINS** Lucy A. of Stillwater, NY | Stillwater, NY |
| **COLE** Andrew of Jackson, NY | October 23, 1856 |
| **HITCHCOCK** Miriam M. of Westhaven, Vt. | Westhaven, Vt. |
| **COPELAND** Leonard P. of Galesburg, Ill. | October 23, 1856 |
| **BOUGHTON** Mary Jane adopted dau of A. **JOHNSON** | W. Hebron, NY |
| **PERRINE** M. Billings of Canada West | November 10, 1856 |
| **BAILEY** Sarah Ann of Greenwich, NY | Greenwich, NY |
| **NEWMAN** Jacob | November 5, 1856 |
| **TALLMAN** Josephine of Victoryville, NY | Greenwich, NY |

COLE D. B. of Salem, NY
BROWN Maria S. adopted dau of David of Rupert, Vt.

November 6, 1856
Rupert, Vt.

PARKER Charles of W. Rupert, Vt.
WRIGHT Ellen R. dau of Caleb of Keene, NH

November 2, 1856
New York City

TOBEY Henry M. of Galesville, NY
MOORE Kate of Greenwich, NY

November 14, 1856
Greenwich, NY

SAFFORD Job S. of Jackson, NY
CONKLIN Eliza of Jackson, NY

November 12, 1856
Jackson, NY

ARCHER Joseph of Greenwich, NY
ALLEN Jane of Greenwich, NY

November 12, 1856
Greenwich, NY

DARROW Charles W. of Cambridge, NY
FORT Almira dau of Gerritt of Cambridge, NY

November 18, 1856

ALLEN U. C. of Sandy Hill, NY
STOVER Elizabeth dau of late Peter of Pittstown, NY

November 6, 1856
Pittstown, NY

MACUMBER James C. of Galesville, NY
CRAW Clarinda of Galesville, NY

November 6, 1856

WHITE George Jr. of Hebron, NY
BEATTIE Maria W. of Hebron, NY

November 25, 1856
Hebron, NY

FARRAR George W. of Galesville, NY
MACUMBER Caroline M. of Galesville, NY

November 23, 1856
Ft. Miller, NY

SALISBURY Mortimer of N. Greenwich, NY
SLADE Jennie Frances dau of Benjamin

November 18, 1856
Waldren, NY

COLLINS John of Greenwich, NY
NEELY Mary Ann of Greenwich, NY

December 15, 1856
Greenwich, NY

PARTRIDGE James O. of Salem, NY
DAVIS Mary L. of Salem, NY

December 11, 1856
Salem, NY

MC CLELLAN Robert of N. White Creek, NY
ARNOLD Margaret A. of N. White Creek, NY

December 11, 1856
White Creek, NY

MULKS William of Whitewater, Wis.     (newspaper date)
CROSS Laurietta formerly of Greenwich, NY

December 18, 1856

MILLOY William of Easton, NY
CAREY Mary Ann of Greenwich, NY

December 20, 1856
Jackson, NY

NORTON Aaron of Hartford, NY

December 22, 1856

| | |
|---|---|
| **BARON** Anna P. of Greenwich, NY | Greenwich, NY |
| **WILBUR** George of Easton, NY | December 12, 1856 |
| **ROBINSON** Huldah Jane of Easton, NY | Greenwich, NY |
| **DEAN** B. C. of Detroit, Mi. | December 22, 1856 |
| **WELLS** Frances E. step dau of Reuben **STONE** of Greenwich | Greenwich, NY |
| **MILLIMAN** Henry S. | December 18, 1856 |
| **STANTON** Mary L. | White Creek, NY |
| **WRIGHT** Charles F. of Ft. Miller, NY | December 11, 1856 |
| **LEWIS** Ann E. of Schuylerville, NY | Schuylerville, NY |
| **LACCA** Benjamin of Whitehall, NY | December 9, 1856 |
| **BRAYTON** Cynthia of Hartford, NY | Hartford, NY |
| **DURKEE** Merritt of Ft. Edward, NY | December 17, 1856 |
| **DURKEE** Maryette of Ft. Edward, NY | |
| **NEWBURY** Henry C. of Galesville, NY | December 24, 1856 |
| **SHERMAN** Emma E. of Galesville, NY | Galesville, NY |
| **FULLERTON** William Henry of W. Hebron, NY | December 24, 1856 |
| **AVERY** Janette of W. Granville, NY | W. Granville, NY |
| **FLYNN** James of Greenwich, NY | December 26, 1856 |
| **HEWITT** Bridget of Greenwich, NY | Greenwich, NY |
| **HONIBOOK** John of Victory Mills, NY | January 1, 1857 |
| **GOODWIN** Sarah Melissa of Victory Mills, NY | |
| **VANCE** William of Utica, NY | January 6, 1857 |
| **DUTCHER** Sarah of Easton, NY | |
| **GREEN** Russell of Cambridge, NY | December 23, 1856 |
| **COLE** M. of S. Easton, NY | S. Easton, NY |
| **WHIPPLE** Henry of Greenwich, NY | January 12, 1857 |
| **TAYLOR** Mary W. dau of L. G. of Ft. Edward, NY | Ft. Edward, NY |
| **VANDERWALKER** James of Ft. Miller, NY | December 10, 1856 |
| **WHEELER** Frances Mary of Forteville, NY | Northumberland, NY |
| **REYNOLDS** Edward P. | December 30, 1856 |
| **BENJAMIN** Marion | Northumberland, NY |
| **WALKER** T. H. of Salem, NY | January 13, 1857 |
| **MC NITT** Mary J. dau of B. F. of N. White Creek, NY | White Creek, NY |

| | |
|---|---|
| **PRINDLE** E. Webster of Ft. Dodge, Iowa | January 6, 1857 |
| **HURD** Lucy M. of Sandgate, Vt. | Salem, NY |
| **WADE** Willard of Sandgate, Vt. | January 10, 1857 |
| **MOFFITT** Maryette of Sandgate, Vt. | Sandgate, Vt. |
| **MOFFITT** Franklin of Sandgate, Vt. | January 10, 1857 |
| **MOREY** Joanna of Sandgate, Vt. | Sandgate, Vt. |
| **HOLLISTER** Ashbel W. of Pawlet, Vt. | January 15, 1857 |
| **WILLIAMS** Lucina of Pawlet, Vt. | Granville, NY |
| **SPENCER** David of Greenwich, NY | January 22, 1857 |
| **CLARK** Fannie H. dau of Daniel of Bennington Vt. | Bennington, Vt. |
| **MC MILLAN** Joseph of Salem, NY | January 21, 1857 |
| **WRIGHT** Delana P. of Jackson, NY | Jackson, NY |
| **GILCHRIST** Duncan of Argyle, NY | January 21, 1857 |
| **MARTIN** Sarah of Argyle, NY | Salem, NY |
| **GARY** Holden H. | January 19, 1857 |
| **SHERWIN** Mrs. Elizbeth dau of Henry **NICHOLS** | Troy, NY |
| **WEIR** Archibald H. of Easton, NY | January 22, 1857 |
| **REYNOLDS** Caroline A. of Easton, NY | Easton, NY |
| **HARRISON** William J. of Greenwich, NY | January 14, 1857 |
| **CHALLES** Louisa of Troy, NY | Troy, NY |
| **PRATT** John of Elmira, NY | February 4, 1857 |
| **PARKER** Margaret R. of Greenwich, NY | Greenwich, NY |
| **HAMILTON** William H. of Greenwich, NY | January 17, 1857 |
| **WALLER** Julia of Greenwich, NY | Schaghticoke, NY |
| **CULVER** Thomas of Cambridge, NY | January 27, 1857 |
| **GREEN** Sarah M. of Cambridge, NY | Cambridge, NY |
| **MC CLELLAN** George of Hebron, NY | January 28, 1857 |
| **LIDDLE** Margaret of Salem, NY | Salem, NY |
| **PARISH** Henry H. | January 29, 1857 |
| **PARISH** Mary dau of Leonard of Hebron, NY | Hebron, NY |
| **INGALLS** Thomas S. of Hartford, NY | February 4, 1857 |
| **NORTON** S. Adeline dau of Col. John Norton of Hartford | Hartford, NY |
| **DE COURCEY** Henry | February 12, 1857 |

LEONARD Jane                                    Salem, NY

BEECHER Edward of Granville, NY                 January 11, 1857
HARTWELL Mary A. of Granville, NY               Granville, NY

BEVERIDGE William of Hebron, NY                 February 11, 1857
REID Jane of Argyle, NY                         Argyle, NY

GREEN John of Cambridge, NY                     February 12, 1857
BECKER Louisa of Cambridge, NY                  Cambridge, NY

HILL Polaski of Hoosick, NY                     February 25, 1857
TRIPP Mary of Cambridge, NY                     Greenwich, NY

HUTTON P. W.                                    February 18, 1857
MICKLEJOHN Mary Jane                            Putnam, NY

KNAPP Francis S. of Greenwich, NY               March 12, 1857
PALMER Susannah of Greenwich, NY                Greenwich, NY

IVES P. C. of N. Granville, NY                  March 11, 1857
BUTLER Annis of Middletown, Vt.                 N. Granville, NY

ENGLISH Sanford of Easton, NY                   March 18, 1857
BURROUGHS Mary A. of Cambridge, NY              Cambridge, NY

YOUNG Hilan of Easton, NY                       March 19, 1857
BUNCE Catherine A. of Stillwater, NY            Stillwater, NY

PRATT H. G. of Waterford, Pa.                   March 6, 1857
VAUGHN Caroline E. formerly of Plattsburg, NY   Dixon, Ill.

MORSE Morgan of Duplain, Mi.                    March 29, 1857
GORHAM Mary S. of Easton, NY                    Greenwich, NY

POTTER Timothy of Greenwich, NY                 March 25, 1857
TABER Helen M. of Cambridge, NY                 Northumberland, NY

FAIRLEY William D. of Salem, NY                 March 19, 1857
MC KERRACHER Kate of Salem, NY                  Salem, NY

MC MILLAN George A. of Salem, NY                March 19, 1857
BENNETT Eliza Ann of Salem, NY                  Salem, NY

MC CORMICK Robert of Greenwich, NY              April 11, 1857
PALMER Mary Ann of Greenwich, NY                Greenwich, NY

AKIN Benjamin C. of White Creek, NY             April 13, 1857
WILKINSON Eliza J. of Cambridge, NY             Greenwich, NY

WILLIAMS Milton of Jackson, NY                         April 9, 1857
STEWART Sarah Jane dau of Phineas of Jackson, NY       Jackson, NY

SMITH Benjamin                                         April 10, 1857
ANGUS Jennette                                         Ft. Edward, NY

MARTIN Marcus M. of Troy, NY                           April 30, 1857
KING Caroline M. of Argyle, NY                         Argyle, NY

STEVENS John of Easton, NY                             May 9, 1857
BEADLE Mary Ann of Easton, NY                          Greenwich, NY

ANDERSON Andrew Jr. formerly of Salem, NY              May 4, 1857
CHAPIN Mary E. of S. Bend, Ind.                        S. Bend, Ind.

RUSSELL Dwight of Caldwell, NY                         May 26, 1857
GLEASON Almira of Sandy Hill, NY                       Greenwich, NY

DOOLITTLE Kimball W. of Saratoga, NY                   June 4, 1857
SMITH Mary P. of Saratoga, NY                          Greenwich, NY

EDDY Jeremiah A.                                       May 20, 1857
DIBBLE Ruth A. dau of Chauncey of Farmington, Iowa     Farmington, Iowa

DEVOE Charles of Easton, NY                            June 7, 1857
NORTON Hannah B. of Saratoga, NY                       Galesville, NY

LEWIS William A. of Easton, NY                         June 14, 1857
HALL Sarah E. of Galesville, NY                        Galesville, NY

NORTON Albert A. of Greenwich, NY                      June 23, 1857
WHEELOCK Ella M. of Greenwich, NY                      Greenwich, NY

BIGELOW George of Springfield, Mass.                   June 20, 1857
FULLER Anna Maria of Greenwich, NY                     Greenwich, NY

FORT J. W. of Easton, NY                               July 1, 1857
GIFFORD Eliza of Cambridge, NY                         Cambridge, NY

FLETCHER James of Greenwich, NY                        July 4, 1857
WOOD Catherine D. of Easton, NY                        Greenwich, NY

JAQUITH Ebenezer of Schuylerville, NY                  July 17, 1857
CHAPMAN Sarah E. of Easton, NY                         Galesville, NY

PROUTY George of Galesville, NY                        August 16, 1857
BUMP Ann E. of Galesville, NY                          Northumberland, NY

LANSING Uriah J. of Easton, NY                         September 1, 1857

WISWELL Lucinda A. of Easton, NY

MC DOUGAL William of Argyle, NY
MC CURDY Elizabeth D. S. of Salem, NY

EDDY Richard S. of Rutland, Vt.
ABEEL Matilda F. of Easton, NY

GOWRAN James of Ft. Ann, NY
STEVENS Mary A. of Kingsbury, NY

HALSTED Dewitt C. of Pittstown, NY
STOVER Harriet A. of Pittstown, NY

CRANDALL Warren of Easton, NY
MC FADDEN Jane Ann of Argyle, NY

SHERMAN Charles of Pittstown, NY
TABER Mary Elizabeth of Greenwich, NY

DOBBIN Andrew S. of Semonauk, Ill.
FULLERTON Anna M. dau of John of Charlotte, NY

ELDRIDGE Hiram of Ft. Edward, NY
CARSWELL Jane of Ft. Edward, NY

VAN KIRK Norman of Greenwich, NY      (newspaper date)
CONANT Kate of St Albans, Vt.

DUDLEY George H. of Rutland, Vt.
FOSTER Mina L. of Rutland, Vt.

WYLIE James of Greenwich, NY
DUDLEY Margaret of Greenwich, NY

STEWART William I. of Monticello, NY
TEFFT Nancy of N. Greenwich, NY

BARRETT David of Dresden, NY
LYON Sarah of Whitehall, NY

HOOFMAN George W. of Easton, NY
MORSE Sarah G. of Easton, NY

HATCH Gideon G. of Jackson, NY
CRANDALL Catherine of Easton, NY

RICHARDS Andrew D. of Greenwich, NY
KENYON Mary E. of Greenwich, NY

Greenwich, NY

August 27, 1857
Reids Corners, NY

September 9, 1857
Easton, NY

September 11, 1857

September 9, 1857
Pittstown, NY

September 22, 1857
Saratoga Spr., NY

October 5, 1857
Greenwich, NY

October 1, 1857
W. Charlotte, NY

October 11, 1857
Greenwich, NY

October 15, 1857
St. Albans, Vt.

September 5, 1857
Rutland, Vt.

October 19, 1857
Schuylerville, NY

October 14, 1857
N. Greenwich, NY

October 20, 1857
Whitehall, NY

October 20, 1857
Galesville, NY

December 2, 1857
Easton, NY

November 28, 1857
Greenwich, NY

| | |
|---|---|
| **CAMPBELL** Charles of Greenwich, NY | November 29, 1857 |
| **CUMMINGS** Mary of Greenwich, NY | Schuylerville, NY |
| | |
| **JAMES** Anson of Galesville, NY | November 12, 1857 |
| **DUEL** Agnes M. of Hebron, NY | Galesville, NY |
| | |
| **KENYON** Andrew of Greenwich, NY | December 2, 1857 |
| **FULLER** Jane Ann of Greenwich, NY | |
| | |
| **COFFIN** Alexander A. of Greenwich, NY | December 9, 1857 |
| **ALLEN** Mary C. of Cambridge, NY | Greenwich, NY |
| | |
| **SPARHAWK** Rufus S. of Greenwich, NY | December 17, 1857 |
| **WILDER** Mary E. of Dixmont, Me. | Greenwich, NY |
| | |
| **BOVIE** Sanford of Hoosick, NY | December 16, 1857 |
| **STOVER** Jane C. of Pittstown, NY | Pittstown, NY |
| | |
| **SMITH** Drew J. of Bald Mountain, NY | January 5, 1858 |
| **ENSIGN** Emily of Mechanicsville, NY | |
| | |
| **ALLEN** Joseph of Troy, NY | January 7, 1858 |
| **QUEEN** Christianna of Peekskill, NY | Greenwich, NY |
| | |
| **WYATT** Theodore F. of Sandgate, Vt. | January 6, 1858 |
| **HANSON** Annis of Salem, NY | Salem, NY |
| | |
| **BEATTIE** Ebenezer | December 29, 1857 |
| **BOYD** Sarah Elizabeth dau of late John Boyd | |
| | |
| **CLEVELAND** John of Salem, NY | January 5, 1858 |
| **BEATTIE** Sarah dau of late John W. | |
| | |
| **MC NEIL** James A. of Argyle, NY | January 7, 1858 |
| **LANT** Grace H. of Argyle, NY | |
| | |
| **MAIRS** James W. of Schenectady, NY | January 20, 1858 |
| **DYER** Amelia A. of Albany, NY | |
| | |
| **WILLIAMS** Oliver of Detroit, Mi. | January 28, 1858 |
| **WALKER** Mary dau of Hiram of Salem, NY | Salem, NY |
| | |
| **BUCK** Ezra H. of Arlington, Vt. | February 4, 1858 |
| **WOODWARD** Alice of Sandgate, Vt. | |
| | |
| **WILCOX** Thomas H. L. of Saratoga, NY | February 7, 1858 |
| **SERVICE** Lydia J. of Saratoga, NY | Saratoga, NY |
| | |
| **CRANDALL** George D. of Monmouth, Ill. | February 7, 1858 |

| | |
|---|---|
| RICHARDSON Elizabeth B. of Greenwich, NY | Greenwich, NY |
| MOTT John W.<br>HOUGHTON Almira L. dau of T. Houghton | February 3, 1858<br>Ft. Edward, NY |
| SCOTT John L.<br>VAUGHN Caroline P. | February 9, 1858<br>Putnam, NY |
| SHELDON Samuel of Easton, NY<br>DE RIDDER Mary of Salem, NY | February 16, 1858<br>Salem, NY |
| FAIRLEY John of Salem, NY<br>BEATY Mary of Salem, NY | February 9, 1858<br>Salem, NY |
| RICH Daniel S. of Salem, NY<br>DEUEL Mary E. of Greenfield, NY | February 9, 1858<br>Greenfield, NY |
| MC EACHRON James R.<br>GOURLEY Maggie | February 10, 1858<br>Hebron, NY |
| PITNEY J. H.<br>VAN VECHTEN Helen E. | February 4, 1858<br>White Creek, NY |
| PRIEST John of Greenwich, NY<br>HERRINGTON Charlotte of Greenwich, NY | November 4, 1857<br>White Creek, NY |
| CLARK Consider H. of Greenwich, NY<br>RUSSELL Amelia A. of Greenwich, NY | February 23, 1858<br>Greenwich, NY |
| FILLMORE Millard ex president of the US<br>MC INTOSH Mrs. Caroline E. of Albany, NY | February 10, 1858<br>Albany, NY |
| WILLIAMSON Daniel Russell<br>PATTERSON Margaret dau of R. Patterson | February 16, 1858<br>Putnam, NY |
| ROGERS Harvey J. of Galesville, NY<br>CORLISS Sarah of Easton, NY | February 25, 1858<br>Easton, NY |
| KENYON Harper of Greenwich, NY<br>CLOSSON Sarah Ann of Greenwich, NY | February 10, 1858<br>Salem, NY |
| LENDRUM John<br>WHYTE Charity A. | February 22, 1858<br>Argyle, NY |
| MARSHALL Alexander of Cambridge, NY<br>LEWIS Fanny M. of Jackson, NY | March 16, 1858<br>Jackson, NY |
| HARD Seymour of Arlington, Vt.<br>AYLSWORTH Sarah Elizabeth of Arlington, Vt. | March 16, 1858<br>Arlington, Vt. |

| | |
|---|---|
| **DENNIS** Deranzel D. of Greenwich, NY | March 17, 1858 |
| **HILL** Sarah of Greenwich, NY | Greenwich, NY |
| | |
| **TEFFT** Caleb of Moreau, NY | March 18, 1858 |
| **TEFFT** Lydia of Greenwich, NY | Greenwich, NY |
| | |
| **GREENE** William C. of Greenwich, NY | March 25, 1858 |
| **HERRINGTON** Ruth R. of Easton, NY | Greenwich, NY |
| | |
| **CAMPBELL** Brown of Cambridge, NY | March 25, 1858 |
| **CHAMBERS** Mary of Cambridge, NY | Greenwich, NY |
| | |
| **WRIGHT** John of Greenwich, NY | April 18, 1858 |
| **DAWLEY** Mrs. Sarah Ann of Greenwich, NY | Greenwich, NY |
| | |
| **DAWLEY** Morgan of Easton, NY | April 24, 1858 |
| **HILL** Ellen of Easton, NY | Easton, NY |
| | |
| **POTTER** Albert of Easton, NY | April 24, 1858 |
| **AMES** Amanda C. of Greenwich, NY | Easton, NY |
| | |
| **STOVER** John A. of Lansingville, NY | April 27, 1858 |
| **COTTRELL** Josephine E. of Troy, NY | Troy, NY |
| | |
| **NIXON** Rev. J. H. | April 21, 1858 |
| **JEWELL** Flora H. | Washington DC |
| | |
| **COOK** Cortland C. of Greenwich, NY | May 20, 1858 |
| **BUCKLEY** Naomi K. of Schaghticoke, NY | Schaghticoke, NY |
| | |
| **KNAPP** George T. H. of Brooklyn, NY | June 17, 1858 |
| **BURNHAM** Sarah Y. dau of William E. of Greenwich, NY | Greenwich, NY |
| | |
| **DYER** Martin D. of Greenwich, NY | June 1, 1858 |
| **ALLEN** Cornelia of Fairhaven, Vt. | Fairhaven, Vt. |
| | |
| **CAULKINS** James N. of Greenwich, NY | June 27, 1858 |
| **HILL** Maria of Greenwich, NY | |
| | |
| **TOWNSEND** Martin I. of Troy, NY | June 24, 1858 |
| **BAXTER** Marietta of Lansingburgh, NY | Lansingburgh, NY |
| | |
| **ROSS** John of Greenwich, NY | August 16, 1858 |
| **ROBINSON** Mary of Greenwich, NY | Greenwich, NY |
| | |
| **NEWTON** Lorenzo of Ft. Edward, NY | August 11, 1858 |
| **WASHBURN** Adelia of Galesville, NY | Galesville, NY |
| | |
| **GIBSON** Allen of Rockford, Ill. | August 16, 1858 |

| | |
|---|---|
| **STEWART** Eliza J. of Argyle, NY | Argyle, NY |
| **WILCOX** Oliver of Easton, NY | September 6, 1858 |
| **BURDICK** Calista of Greenwich, NY | Greenwich, NY |
| **WRIGHT** Daniel V. of Bald Mountain, NY | September 2, 1858 |
| **HOUSEWORTH** Mary Jane of Northumberland, NY | Northumberland, NY |
| **TOWLE** Robert H. | July 8, 1858 |
| **PENFIELD** Cornelia M. formerly of Greenwich, NY | Columbia, Cal. |
| **CARSWELL** John of Greenwich, NY | August 23, 1858 |
| **HAY** Abigail of Greenwich, NY | Greenwich, NY |
| **WILLIAMS** Julius of Easton, NY | September 21, 1858 |
| **SEELYE** Sarah E. of Schuylerville, NY | Schuylerville, NY |
| **PULLMAN** Henry of Greenwich, NY | August 30, 1858 |
| **REYNOLDS** Caroline A. of Greenwich, NY | Greenwich, NY |
| **ROBINSON** Edwin B. of Galesville, NY | October 4, 1858 |
| **THORNE** Frances C. of Bald Mountain, NY | Bald Mountain, NY |
| **DAY** Isreal of Bald Mountain, NY | October 6, 1858 |
| **POTTER** Harriet of Bald Mountain, NY | Bald Mountain, NY |
| **POTTER** George H. of Bald Mountain, NY | October 7, 1858 |
| **CLARK** Amanda C. of Bald Mountain, NY | Bald Mountain, NY |
| **HILL** Amasa P. of Easton, NY | November 10, 1858 |
| **CRANDALL** Mary L. of Easton, NY | Easton, NY |
| **BAKER** John E. of Schaghticoke, NY | November 17, 1858 |
| **STEVENS** Caroline W. dau of Ira C. of Greenwich, NY | Greenwich, NY |
| **KENYON** Peter of Cambridge, NY | November 24, 1858 |
| **BURROUGHS** Clementine of Cambridge, NY | Cambridge, NY |
| **SEARS** Daniel W. of Greenwich, NY | December 11, 1858 |
| **MILLIS** Harriet of Greenwich, NY | Greenwich, NY |
| **SHERMAN** Job S. of Greenwich, NY | December 15, 1858 |
| **WHIPPLE** Carrie A. dau of W. W. of Troy, NY | Troy, NY |
| **BEEBE** George of Salem, NY | December 9, 1858 |
| **MONTGOMERY** Maria of Salem, NY | Salem, NY |
| **CARTER** Calvin B. of Jackson, NY | December 23, 1858 |
| **LANGWORTHY** Hattie A. dau of Robert of Greenwich, NY | Greenwich, NY |

CAMPBELL Charles of Greenwich, NY                                      December 24, 1858
HARRISON Harriet of Greenwich, NY                                      Greenwich, NY

HOWE John A. of Albany, NY                                             December 28, 1858
RICE Delia dau of Daniel of Easton, NY                                 Easton, NY

MC FADDEN Michael of Hebron, NY                                        December 22, 1858
MC CLELLAN Margaret A. of Hebron, NY                                   Salem, NY

BRADFORD Alonzo of Hebron, NY                                          December 23, 1858
SMITH Jane E. of Argyle, NY                                            Argyle, NY

SIMPSON Andrew J. of Omaha, Neb.                                       December 23, 1858
FERRIS Mary A. of Ft. Edward, NY                                       Ft. Edward, NY

AYREY Thomas                                                           December 9, 1858
CRANDALL Susan W. formerly of Greenwich, NY                            Lawrence, Mass.

TEFFT Harvey of Greenwich, NY                                          January 3, 1859
LANGWORTHY Mary of Greenwich, NY                                       Greenwich, NY

PIKE George of Ft. Edward, NY                                          December 31, 1858
CLARK Sarah of Hebron, NY                                              Salem, NY

COVEY J. M. of Sandgate, Vt.                                           December 30, 1858
SNOW Lucy M. of Sandgate, Vt.                                          Sandgate, Vt.

LAING Giles P. of Schuylerville, NY                                    December 29, 1858
POND Bell dau of Mayo Pond of Schuylerville, NY                        Schuylerville, NY

CORNELL Charles A. of Easton, NY                                       December 30, 1858
SLOCUM Emeline M. of Easton, NY                                        Schaghticoke, NY

CAMPBELL Charles of Greenwich, NY                                      December 25, 1858
RAND Harriet Isabella of Greenwich, NY                                 Greenwich, NY

BRADFORD Alonzo of Hebron, NY                                          December 23, 1858
SMITH Jane E. of Argyle, NY                                            Argyle, NY

CULVER Charles D.                                                      December 28, 1858
BELLAMY Louisa A. dau of late Julius of Sandy Hill, NY                 Sandy Hill, NY

CRANDALL Henry of Glens Falls, NY                                      December 28, 1858
WATERS Betsey P. of Warrensburgh, NY                                   Warrensburgh, NY

CHAMBERLAIN Henry M. of Cambridge, Mass.                               November 20, 1858
DE PEU Harriet formerly of Salem, NY                                   Grand Rapids, Mi.

MUNSON William O. of Hebron, NY                                        January 11, 1859

PATRICK Harriet O. of Hebron, NY — Hebron, NY

PALMER E. W. of Cleveland, Ohio — January 11, 1859
KINGSLEY Julia M. dau of Warren of Ft. Edward, NY — Ft. Edward, NY

PRATT Cyrus W. of Cambridge, NY — January 5, 1859
HUNT Helen C. of Argyle, NY — Argyle, NY

INFIELD Edwin of Ft. Ann, NY — January 1, 1859
SWEET Betsey of Ft. Edward, NY — Ft. Edward, NY

VANCE Charles of Utica, NY — February 7, 1859
POTTER Harriet of Greenwich, NY

WINNIE George (newspaper date) — February 10, 1859
NICHOLS Martha A. dau of Henry of Troy, NY — Waterford, NY

WAUGH Joseph W. of Rockford, Ill. (newspaper date) — February 10, 1859
MARTIN Sarah J. formerly of Salem, NY — Rockford, Ill.

MAIN Parley of Easton, NY — February 22, 1859
WARNER N. E. of Easton, NY — Greenwich, NY

BENNETT Leroy A. of Greenwich, NY — February 26, 1859
OATLEY Mary E. of Greenwich, NY — Greenwich, NY

BAIN Jesse L. of Argyle, NY — February 23, 1859
KILMER Christianna of Providence, NY — Argyle, NY

BRADLEY Samuel of Ft. Edward, NY — February 23, 1859
GILLIS Jane Amelia of Argyle, NY — Argyle, NY

REID David W. of Argyle, NY — February 23, 1859
MILLER Marrion E. of Ft. Edward, NY — Ft. Edward, NY

STOUGHTON H. W. of Ft. Edward, NY — February 16, 1859
PAYNE E. A. of Cambridge, NY — Cambridge, NY

NICHOLS J. B. of Trinity, Cal. — February 10, 1859
BOYCE Sarah A. of Danby, Vt. — Danby, Vt.

HERRINGTON Bentley E. of Greenwich, NY — March 13, 1859
LEWIS Mary Ann of Greenwich, NY — Greenwich, NY

SAFFORD Joseph of Salem, NY — March 8, 1859
MORROW Helen of Greenwich, NY — Greenwich, NY

BARNARD John H. of Greenwich, NY — March 22, 1859
KENYON Caroline of Jackson, NY — Jackson, NY

GRIFFIN B. H. of Keene, NH                          March 16, 1859
HICKOK Esther L. of Ft. Edward, NY                  Ft. Edward, NY

KILMER James H. of Argyle, NY                       March 22, 1859
ANDERSON Sarah M. of Argyle, NY                     Argyle, NY

PARKER Henry of Greenwich, NY                       March 31, 1859
TULL Sarah of Greenwich, NY                         Greenwich, NY

FORD James of Argyle, NY                            March 30, 1859
MC DOUGAL Mary A. of Argyle, NY                     Argyle, NY

ALMY Egbert C. of Greenwich, NY                     April 6, 1859
HINCHMAN Sarah C. of Greenwich, NY                  Greenwich, NY

WYLIE James of Greenwich, NY                        April 8, 1859
PORTER Mary A. of Centre Falls, NY                  Greenwich, NY

HYATT Aaron of Battenville, NY                      April 6, 1859
GREEN Fanny M. of Easton, NY                        Easton, NY

LA POINTE Joseph C. of Greenwich, NY                April 9, 1859
DAWLEY Melissa M. of Greenwich, NY

MILLER David of Argyle, NY                          March 29, 1859
SKINNER Jane E. of Argyle, NY                       Schuyleville, NY

PELLITIER Peter of Ft. Edward, NY                   April 6, 1859
SWEET Mary of Ft. Edward, NY                        Ft. Edward, NY

LOWBER John of Bald Mountain, NY                    April 27, 1859
STROVER Prescilla of Schuylerville, NY              Schuylerville, NY

EGGLESTON James A. formerly of Greenwich, NY        April 14, 1859
GURDON Grace dau of Charles of Perry, Ill.          Perry, Ill.

LEE A. A. of Troy, NY                               May 5, 1859
ANDREWS J. E. of Stillwater, NY                     Stillwater, NY

HOLLAND Leonard C. of Greenwich, NY                 May 26, 1859
RIVERS Hattie C. of Greenwich, NY                   Greenwich, NY

SIPPERLEY John Md. of Greenwich, NY                 May 30, 1859
HEGEMAN Selina M. of Greenwich, NY

KNAPP Francis Z. of Greenwich, NY                   July 1, 1859
BENNETT Prudence of Greenwich, NY                   Greenwich, NY

BINNINGER Jacob of Camden, NY                       July 5, 1859

EASTMAN Livinia of Sardinia, Erie Co. NY      Fairhaven, Vt.

PINKERTON Samuel of Salem, NY      June 29, 1859
MC COLLISTER of Greenwich, NY      Salem, NY

WHITE James W. of Salem, NY      July 2, 1859
HOVER P. of Jackson, NY

FISH James L. of Cambridge, NY      July 13, 1859
MC CULLOCK Maria of Pittstown, NY      Pittstown, NY

LEE James of Greenwich, NY      August 20, 1859
WOODCOCK Mary Ann of Greenwich, NY      Schuylerville, NY

CLARK Moses E. of New York City      August 18, 1859
TANNER Emily M. of Greenwich, NY      Bolton, NY

BROWN George (or Simeon) of Waterford, NY      August 28, 1859
CRAMER Adelia of Greenwich, NY      Greenwich, NY
    (one issue names George, next issue names Simeon)

REYNOLDS Franklin of Easton, NY      August 31, 1859
TEFFT Caroline D. of Greenwich, NY      Greenwich, NY

AMES Chauncey P. of Greenwich, NY      September 12, 1859
JOHNSON Amelia of Greenwich, NY      Greenwich, NY

BRIGGS William H. of Schaghticoke, NY      September 23, 1859
BACON Sarah of Schaghticoke, NY

BAYLE Luke of Greenwich, NY      September 26, 1859
LEE Adeline of Bald Mountain, NY      Ft. Miller, NY

LA POINTE Ira of Greenwich, NY      September 26, 1859
LEE Zoa of Ft. Miller, NY      Ft. Miller, NY

CLARK Henry T. of Bellevue, Neb.      September 28, 1859
FIELDING Martha A. of Greenwich, NY      Greenwich, NY

WHITE Darwin W. of Greenwich, NY      September 28, 1859
ROBERSON Emeline of Greenwich, NY      Greenwich, NY

MC NEIL David of S. Argyle, NY      September 29, 1859
REID Catherine of S. Argyle, NY      S. Argyle, NY

GLEASON S. O. of Troy, NY      October 11, 1859
BURDICK Mary of Greenwich, NY      Greenwich, NY

PEARSON Edward      October 5, 1859
FULLER Phebe of Glens Falls, NY      Greenwich, NY

WOODARD James of Jackson, NY                           September 27, 1859
COLLINS Sarah of Jackson, NY                           Jackson, NY

GROVES James E. of Albany, NY                          October 4, 1859
RODGERS Elizabeth G. of Albany, NY                     Albany, NY

BIGELOW Charles H. of Troy, NY                         October 5, 1859
LYMAN Alida N. of Madison, Ohio                        Madison, Ohio

HOLLISTER Henry J. of N. Granville, NY                 October 13, 1859
MARTLING Susan C. of E. Whitehall, NY                  N. Granville, NY

BOYD William of Granville, NY                          October 3, 1859
CONGDON Dorcas of Hartford, NY                         Hartford, NY

BRYAN Stoughton H. of Easton, NY                       October 20, 1859
STOVER Louisa A. of Pittstown, NY                      Pittstown, NY

SHATTUCK Calvin S. of Greenwich, NY                    November 2, 1859
BRADSHAW Antoinette of Newark, NJ                      Newark, NJ

KEE James of Argyle, NY                                November 9, 1859
BITELEY Elizabeth of Ft. Edward, NY                    Greenwich, NY

BAXTER Edgar F. of Rockford, Ill.                      November 7, 1859
PRINDLE Maggie I. dau of Glover of Argyle, NY          Argyle, NY

CAMERON John P. formerly of Greenwich, NY              November 22, 1859
CLEMENT Susan E. of Canadear, NY                       Canadear, NY

SIPPERLEY A. M. of Schaghticoke, NY                    November 24, 1859
DUNCOMB Amanda of Schuylerville, NY                    Schuylerville, NY

TILLOTSON J. S. of Lanesboro, Mass.                    December 14, 1859
BARNARD Eunice H. of Greenwich, NY                     Greenwich, NY

CROSIER John of Hebron, NY                             December 13, 1859
OATMAN Mary J. of Saratoga, NY

HILL Francis of Cambridge, NY                          November 29, 1859
HILL Sarah of Jackson, NY                              Jackson, NY

HAYNES James H. of Granville, NY                       December 20, 1859
DORNS Margaret of Granville, NY                        Granville, NY

WEAVER Kendrick of Ft. Ann, NY                         December 28, 1859
HALL Margaret dau of Seneca of Sandy Hill, NY          Sandy Hill, NY

REYNOLDS Job of Montreal, Can. formerly of Hartford, NY January 2, 1860

| | |
|---|---|
| **MERRILL** Sally C. dau of J. S. of St. Albans, Vt. | St. Albans, Vt. |
| **BISHOP** Merritt of Jackson, NY<br>**STEVENS** Annie W. of Jackson, NY | January 31, 1860<br>Jackson, NY |
| **PRATT** Henry of Ft. Ann, NY<br>**REID** Kate of Greenwich, NY | January 4, 1860<br>Lakeville, NY |
| **VIELE** Herman of Saratoga, NY<br>**VANDENBURGH** Eve Alida of Easton, NY | February 2, 1860<br>Easton, NY |
| **MILLER** David of Argyle, NY<br>**EATON** Alvira of Queensbury, NY | February 11, 1860<br>Sandy Hill, NY |
| **WENTWORTH** Harry of Granville, NY<br>**O'BRIEN** Mrs. Martha of Granville, NY | February 3, 1860<br>Granville, NY |
| **NICHOLS** E. C.<br>**ROWAN** Sarah J. formerly of Washington Co. NY | January 31, 1860<br>Battle Creek, Mi. |
| **SLADE** Austin J. of Easton, NY<br>**DE RIDDER** Catlena S. of Easton, NY | January 31, 1860 |
| **SCOTT** James G.<br>**CRAMER** Lucretia A. of Northumberland, NY | February 9, 1860<br>Ft. Edward, NY |
| **JOHNSON** C. P. of Greenwich, NY<br>**BELL** Clara J. of Greenwich, NY | February 28, 1860<br>Greenwich, NY |
| **WRIGHT** Alva of Salem, NY<br>**FAIRLEY** Mary of Salem, NY | February 22, 1860<br>Salem, NY |
| **GETTY** John H. of Hebron, NY<br>**MILLER** Emma of Glens Falls, NY | February 13, 1860 |
| **RUSSELL** William A. of Salem, NY<br>**CALDWELL** Ada of Westchester, Co. NY | February 27, 1860<br>Salem, NY |
| **MINTURN** Charles A of Moravia, NY<br>**LEWIS** Phebe of Jackson, NY | March 7, 1860<br>Jackson, NY |
| **WILCOX** Edson G. of Greenwich, NY<br>**BURROUGHS** Sarah Jane of Cambridge, NY | March 6, 1860<br>Cambridge, NY |
| **MASON** Coomer<br>**DERBY** Betsey F. | March 5, 1860<br>N. Granville, NY |
| **JACKSON** A. W. of Whitehall, NY<br>**STODDARD** Eliza M. | January 29, 1860 |

SALISBURY John B. of Saratoga, NY                               March 14, 1860
STOVER Mary E. of N. Greenwich, NY                              N. Greenwich, NY

TEFFT William H. of New York City                              March 14, 1860
COOK Sarah dau of W. W. of Whitehall, NY

WRIGHT John of Salem, NY                                        March 13, 1860
HAYNER Melissa of Salem, NY                                     Salem, NY

WRIGHT John L. of Greenwich, NY                                 March 20, 1860
REMINGTON Joanna of Greenwich, NY                               Greenwich, NY

RICHARDS Albert of Greenwich, NY                                April 22, 1860
BENNETT Sarah Ann of Greenwich, NY                              Greenwich, NY

WALLER W. J. of Hartford, NY                                    April 11, 1860
DAICY Mary E. of Hartford, NY                                   Hartford, NY

HASTINGS Willis W. or Troy, NY                                  April 24, 1860
BARBER Helen C. dau of Charles P. of W. Troy, NY                W. Troy, NY

CARPENTER Ashur of Greenwich, NY                                May 8, 1860
HAYES Mary of Greenwich, NY                                     Greenwich, NY

GILBERT John A. of Muncie, Iowa                                 April 12, 1860
POTTER Mrs. Phebe of Galesville, NY                             Galesville, NY

LIDDELL William of Brooklyn, NY                                 May 15, 1860
HILL Eliza A. of Easton, NY                                     Easton, NY

BRADY Robert of Argyle, NY                                      April 5, 1860
CARSON M J. of Jackson, NY                                      Jackson, NY

CRUIKSHANK Robert of Salem, NY                                  April 16, 1860
WELLS M. E. of Salem, NY

BULSTON Moses of Easton, NY                                     May 8, 1860
NEWELL Helen of Greenwich, NY                                   Greenwich, NY

PETTEYS Ephraim B. of Greenwich, NY                             June 2, 1860
MC DONALD Mrs. Jane of Greenwich, NY                            Lakeville, NY

FURSMAN Edgar L. of Schuylerville, NY                           June 13, 1860
CRAMER Minerva of Schuylerville, NY                             Schuylerville, NY

NORTON Frederick of Troy, NY                                    June 7, 1860
PATTEN Maria of Troy, NY                                        Troy, NY

LANSING Wendell of Keeseville, NY formerly Greenwich            June 26, 1860

MACE Almira M. dau of John of Ausable, NY

| | |
|---|---|
| PIERSON William H. of Sandy Hill, NY | June 22, 1860 |
| MOORE Frank C. of Sandy Hill, NY | Sandy Hill, NY |
| | |
| MURCH Richard Jr. of Greenwich, NY | July 4, 1860 |
| DAWLEY Elizabeth of Greenwich, NY | Greenwich, NT |
| | |
| ROOT George W. of Schuylerville, NY | July 9, 1860 |
| HILL Harriet of Victory Mills, NY | Saratoga Spr., NY |
| | |
| GRAY George W. of N. White Creek, NY | July 3, 1860 |
| STEPHENSON Charlotte A. | Arlington, Vt. |
| | |
| WARNER James formerly of Cambridge, NY | July 4, 1860 |
| TOWNSEND Lottie of Sandwich, Ill. | Sandwich, Ill. |
| | |
| RHODES Richard A. | July 4, 1860 |
| MOORE Jane dau of P. D. of Jackson, NY | Reynoldsburg, Ohio |
| | |
| BAIN Peter E. of Argyle, NY | August 7, 1860 |
| PRINDLE Ellen Maria of Argyle, NY | Argyle, NY |
| | |
| BARBER Russell of Greenwich, NY | August 27, 1860 |
| MC CULLER Caroline of Greenwich, NY | |
| | |
| REYNOLDS William Harrison of Galesville, NY | August 26, 1860 |
| SHERMAN Mary Augusta of Galesville, NY | Galesville, NY |
| | |
| UPSON Anson J. of Clinton, NY | August 22, 1860 |
| WESTON Lydia dau of late Rev. J. W. FARLAN | Sandy Hill, NY |
| | |
| MILLER Richard N. of Minerva, NY | September 2, 1860 |
| KELLOGG Eliza L. of Minerva, NY | Minerva, NY |
| | |
| MANDELL D. W. of Middlebury, Vt. | September 12, 1860 |
| HOLMES Mattie B. of Greenwich, NY | Greenwich, NY |
| | |
| SELDEN Thomas of Rome, NY | September 5, 1860 |
| LEGGETT Rebecca S. of Saratoga, NY | Saratoga, NY |
| | |
| WOODARD Webster of Greenwich, NY | September 11, 1860 |
| LANGWORTHY Clementine of Greenwich, NY | Greenwich, NY |
| | |
| BRISBIN D. C. of Saratoga, NY | September 19, 1860 |
| TAYLOR Martha W. dau of Lansing G. of Ft. Edward, NY | Ft. Edward, NY |
| | |
| ALLEN Joseph B. | September 19, 1860 |
| BRIGGS Mrs. Cordelia dau of Van Schaick BECKER | Easton, NY |

**WRIGHT** Earl P. of Jackson, NY
**SKELLIE** Mary J. of Jackson, NY

September 18, 1860
Jackson, NY

**COMSTOCK** Edward of Glens Falls, NY
**DERBY** Eliza of Glens Falls, NY

September 20, 1860
Ft. Edward, NY

**YOUNG** Ira H. of Ft. Edward, NY
**MASON** Lucy W. of Castleton, Vt.

September 19, 1860
Castleton, Vt.

**KETCHUM** James of Greenwich, NY
**TEFFT** Mary of Greenwich, NY

September 25, 1860
Greenwich, NY

**STEWART** Kenyon of Jackson, NY
**NEWCOMB** Sarah P. of Easton, NY

September 26, 1860
Easton, NY

**LOWE** Frank S. of Richland, NY
**FIFIELD** Helen H. of Salem, NY

October 10, 1860
Salem, NY

**BARDWELL** Wayne of W. Pawlet, Vt.    (newspaper date)
**WILSON** Maggie of W. Hebron, NY

November 1, 1860

**SISSON** Oscar of S. Hoosick, NY
**HOYT** Mary Elizabeth of Pittstown, NY

Sept./Oct. 30, 1860
Greenwich, NY

**POTTER** Erastus of Greenwich, NY
**REED** Jane of Greenwich, NY

November 12, 1860
Northumberland, NY

**ROGERS** Henry of Salem, NY
**WARWICK** Mary J. of Salem, NY

November 20, 1860
Salem, NY

**ROGERS** Joshua J. of Hebron, NY
**THOMPSON** Maggie M. of Oswego Co. NY

November 7, 1860
Salem, NY

**PORTER** William D. of Salem, NY
**DILL** Elizabeth C. of Salem, NY

November 13, 1860
Salem, NY

**CARSWELL** D. B. of Ft. Edward, NY
**DONALDSON** Mary of Argyle, NY

November 14, 1860

**WILLETT** John R. of Argyle, NY
**HARSHAW** Nancy W. of Argyle, NY

November 13, 1860
Argyle, NY

**ANDERSON** Rev. A. R. of Venice, Washington Co. Pa.
**SHAW** Jennie N. of Greenwich, NY

October 11, 1860*

**DOBBIN** John
**WELLS** Anna M. dau of H. M.

November 22, 1860
Salem, NY

**RICE** Charles of N. White Creek, NY

October 24, 1860

HANCOCK Sarah J. of Granby, NY

| | |
|---|---|
| VAN BUREN J. H. of Easton, NY<br>ODEKIRK Susan of Cambridge, NY | December 25, 1860<br>Greenwich, NY |
| HOAG Jonathan of Easton, NY<br>ROBERSON Betsey dau of Jeremiah of Greenwich, NY | December 20, 1860<br>Greenwich, NY |
| REID Harvey J. of N. Greenwich, NY<br>PRINDLE Hattie S. dau of L. G. | December 31, 1860<br>Argyle, NY |
| GREEN F. Russell<br>RUSSELL Julia M. | December 25, 1860<br>St. Johnsville, NY |
| MANN Hosea of Greenwich, NY<br>STOVER Caroline of Greenwich, NY | December 28, 1860<br>Schuylerville, NY |
| FINCH John J. of Greenwich, NY<br>ALLEN Semantha of Greenwich, NY | January 1, 1861<br>Schuylerville, NY |
| WELCH John of Greenwich, NY<br>O'KEEFE Mary of Greenwich, NY | January 6, 1861<br>Saratoga Spr., NY |
| KNAPP Ira of Hoosick Four Corners, NY<br>GOODING Lucy Jane of N. Hoosick, NY | January 22, 1861<br>Greenwich, NY |
| WRIGHT Caleb of Greenwich, NY<br>KENYON Lucy of Greenwich, NY | January 23, 1861<br>Greenwich, NY |
| CROOKS Richard of Argyle, NY<br>DENNIS Libbie of Argyle, NY | January 20, 1861<br>Greenwich, NY |
| BASSETT Pardon of Greenwich, NY<br>MILLER Sarah of Greenwich, NY | February 6, 1861<br>Greenwich, NY |
| JOHNSON Alonzo of Greenwich, NY<br>STEWART Anna Maria of Greenwich, NY | February 8, 1861<br>Greenwich, NY |
| CORNELL Charles A. of Easton, NY<br>WRIGHT Margaret M. of Easton, NY | February 6, 1861<br>Easton, NY |
| PRATT Nelson<br>CLOUGH Mary E. | January 23, 1861<br>Greenwich, NY |
| MILLER J. E.<br>FERRIS Harrietta | January 24, 1861<br>Sandy Hill, NY |
| BROWN Loren of Schuylerville, NY<br>TAYLOR Clara of Schuylerville, NY | February 12, 1861<br>Schuylerville, NY |

HARDING William C. of Greenwich, NY — February 19, 1861 — Schuylerville, NY
STOVER Mary of Greenwich, NY

SLOCUM William Jr. of Ft. Miller, NY — February 20, 1861 — Schuylerville, NY
CLUTE Julia M. of Ft. Miller, NY

ALLEN William of N. Hoosick, NY — February 9, 1861 — N. Bennington, Vt.
MC ADOO Margaret of N. Bennington, Vt.

COOK Charles of Greenwich, NY — March 6, 1861 — Greenwich, NY
SPARHAWK Mary L. of Greenwich, NY

JORDAN E. C. of Jackson, NY — February 27, 1861 — Greenwich, NY
MELBY Harriet of Jackson, NY

WADE Charles H. of Easton, NY — March 23, 1861 — Greenwich, NY
MEADER Lydia Jane of Easton, NY

BURCH John of Cambridge, NY — March 20, 1861 — Greenwich, NY
BREWER Olive of Greenwich, NY

REMINGTON William of Galesville, NY — March 20, 1861 — Ft. Miller, NY
WEAVER Sarah Elizabeth of Ft. Miller, NY

HOUGHTON William A. — March 14, 1861 — Buskirks Bridge, NY
GROESBECK Maggie of Cambridge, NY

SCOTT William — March 19, 1861 — Cambridge, NY
HOVER Charlotte

GRANT Charles H. of Andover, NY — March 12, 1861 — Sandy Hill, NY
HILAND Margaret Ann of Ft. Edward, NY

PERKINS Mortimer — March 6, 1861 — Saratoga, NY
WRIGHT Terissa dau of Losee B.

HAMMOND Edward of Northumberland, NY — March 23, 1861 — Northumberland, NY
WILDY Mary of Northumberland, NY

LANE W. M. of Ft. Edward, NY — March 20, 1861 — Ballston Spa, NY
CONERY Eliza of Ballston Spa, NY

NUTTING D. W. formerly of Easton, NY — March 7, 1861 — Churchville, Iowa
GRAY Ellen M. formerly of Schaghticoke, NY

HILL Frederick E. of Cambridge, NY — April 13, 1861 — Greenwich, NY
RUNDELL Sarah A. of Cambridge, NY

CRANDALL Josiah of Warrensburgh, NY — April 10, 1861

| | |
|---|---|
| **FERRIS** Ann of Warrensburgh, NY | Warrensburgh, NY |
| **MAYNARD** W. H. of Cohoes, NY | April 22, 1861 |
| **PAYNE** Sarah J. of N. Easton, NY | N. Easton, NY |
| **DICKINSON** John of Alliance, Ohio | April 25, 1861 |
| **SMITH** Josie of Salem, NY | Salem, NY |
| **CORLISS** Hiram Md. of Greenwich, NY | May 14, 1861 |
| **COWEN** Maria of Greenwich, NY | Greenwich, NY |
| **HURD** Addison T. of Rupert, Vt. | May 2, 1861 |
| **HAY** Sarah of Rupert, Vt. | W. Rupert, Vt. |
| **HOVER** John of Cambridge, NY | May 23, 1861 |
| **SMITH** Cornelia A. of Cambridge, NY | |
| **STEVENS** Franklin of Salem, NY | June 6, 1861 |
| **BUSH** Esther of Orwell, Vt. | |
| **FOSTER** J. C. of Salem, NY | May 28, 1861 |
| **HILL** Mary A. of Salem, NY | Salem, NY |
| **HOLBROOK** Peter of Sandy Hill, NY | June 6, 1861 |
| **SLADE** Sarah M. of Hartford, NY | Hartford, NY |
| **REYNOLDS** Alexander C. of the Vt. Conference | June 18, 1861 |
| **STREEVER** Amanda of Argyle, NY | Argyle, NY |
| **COOPER** Edmond D. of Sharon Springs, NY | June 20, 1861 |
| **MC LEAN** Susanna dau of late John Mc Lean of Salem, NY | Essex, NY |
| (adopted dau of Henry H. **ROSS** of Essex, NY) | |
| **MC LEAN** Rev. John K. | June 26, 1861 |
| **HAWLEY** Sarah M. dau of David of Salem, NY | Salem, NY |
| **NELSON** Robert C. of Hebron, NY | July 4, 1861 |
| **CHAMBERLAIN** Sarah M. of Hebron, NY | Argyle, NY |
| **THOMPSON** Daniel J. of Argyle, NY | August 7, 1861 |
| **SMITH** Catherine C. of Sandy Hill, NY | Sandy Hill, NY |
| **PIERSON** Charles of Sandy Hill, NY | August 4, 1861 |
| **HUNTLEY** Lourie of Ft. Edward, NY | Sandy Hill, NY |
| **SPEIDLEBURG** Henry of Easton, NY | August 10, 1861 |
| **SHEARER** Elizabeth of Easton, NY | Galesville, NY |
| **BURROUGHS** Allen H. of Cambridge, NY | August 15, 1861 |
| **ALLEN** Antoinette of Cambridge, NY | Greenwich, NY |

BREWER Horace of Greenwich, NY
FISH Mary Ellen of Greenwich, NY

August 13, 1861
Greenwich, NY

GRANGER Joseph E. of Greenwich, NY
CARPENTER Mary E. of Greenwich, NY

September 18, 1861
Greenwich, NY

MACUMBER William of Galesville, NY
FERRIS Elizabeth D. of Easton, NY

September 15, 1861
Schuylerville, NY

BRADT Aurelius W. of Davenport, Iowa
TANNER Helen A. of Jackson, NY

September 25, 1861
Jackson, NY

WILLIAMS John Martin
SHRIVER Frances Anna dau of late Daniel

September 24, 1861
York, Pa.

SMITH N. H. of Somerset, NY
SPARHAWK Clementina of Greenwich, NY

October 8, 1861
Greenwich, NY

NESBIT Archibald M. of Macedonia, Ohio
PRATT Emma of Greenwich, NY

October 10, 1861
Greenwich, NY

HASTINGS Abraham B. of E. Salem, NY
THOMPSON Avalina of Greenwich, NY

October 16, 1861

BURGESS Henry of Argyle, NY
BAKER Mary Ann of Greenwich, NY

October 29, 1861
Greenwich, NY

WHYTE Joseph R. of Argyle, NY
LYTLE Emma of Albany, NY

October 31, 1861

JONES John B. of Salem, NY
WHEELOCK Adaliza dau of Lysander of Salem, NY

November 6, 1861
Salem, NY

WATSON William G. of Co. C. 77th Reg. NY Vol.
KENYON Josephine A. of Greenwich, NY

November 10, 1861

WINNEY James B. of Saratoga, NY
WILCOX Sarah S. of Easton, NY

November 18, 1861
Greenwich, NY

FRAATS Joseph of Schoharie Co. NY
TINGUE Delia Eliza of Cambridge, NY

November 13, 1861
Cambridge, NY

HITCHCOCK Charles F. formerly of Salem, NY
PEASE Mary E. of Aurora, Ill.

October 25, 1861
Aurora, Ill.

SPRAGUE Gibson W. of Greenwich, NY
ANTHONY Susan of Greenwich, NY

November 20, 1861
Greenwich, NY

BARDWELL Henry C. of Shelburn Falls, Mass.

November 12, 1861

SMITH Celestia M. of Hebron, NY                                    Salem, NY

BARDWELL George E. of Shelburn Falls, Mass.                        November 12, 1861
SMITH Claminda J. of Hebron, NY                                    Salem, NY

WHIPPLE David of Easton, NY                                        November 27, 1861
SPRINGER Sarah of Easton, NY                                       Schuylerville, NY

ROGERS Davenport of Ohio                                           December 12, 1861
TUCKER Louisa of Greenwich, NY                                     Greenwich, NY

VAIL Tideman age 68yrs of Saratoga Co. NY                          December 5, 1861
HOAG Anna age 69yrs of Wells, Vt.                                  Granville, NY

HART Charles M. of Easton, NY                                      December 18, 1861
MEAD Artie M. of Easton, NY                                        Greenwich, NY

CRANDALL John of Greenwich, NY                                     December 24, 1861
SHERMAN Mary Elizabeth dau of M. L. of Greenwich, NY    Greenwich, NY

MILLER Martin A. of Kingsbury, NY                                  December 25, 1861
WILCOX Mary Elizabeth of Greenwich, NY                             Greenwich, NY

HAWLEY A. G. of Glens Falls, NY                                    December 26, 1861
TAYLOR Harriet dau of Lansing of Ft. Edward, NY                    Ft. Edward, NY

WILCOX Orrin S. of Greenwich, NY                                   December 23, 1861
MILLER Minnie M. of Kingsbury, NY                                  Ft. Edward, NY

MOTT Thomas H. of Moreau, NY                                       January 1, 1862
ROBERSON Hattie of Greenwich, NY                                   Greenwich, NY

WRIGHT Daniel V. of Northumberland, NY                             January 8, 1862
WISWELL Frances H. of Greenwich, NY                                Greenwich, NY

TABER George                                                       January 11, 1862
POTTER Mary Jane                                                   Greenwich, NY

HOLBROOK Urbane A. of Greenwich, NY                                March 1, 1862
PLATT Catherine of Greenwich, NY                                   Greenwich, NY

EVERTS Orville                                                     February 29, 1862
WILSON L. Augusta dau of David                                     Elbridge, NY

TAYLOR Benjamin H. of Greenwich, NY                                March 18, 1862
SHORTT Fanny of Greenwich, NY                                      Greenwich, NY

WOODARD Clark E. of Greenwich, NY                                  March 12, 1862
REYNOLDS Margaret A. of Greenwich, NY                              Greenwich, NY

ARMSTRONG Edward of Hartford, NY                    March 10, 1862
DUNHAM Susan of Argyle, NY                          Argyle, NY

CROWL Edmond G. of Salem, NY                        March 12, 1862
POLLOCK Margaret of Argyle, NY                      Argyle, NY

BECKER Erastus of Cambridge, NY                     March 19, 1862
HILL Lydia Ann of Cambridge, NY                     Greenwich, NY

PARKER Charles of Greenwich, NY                     March 20, 1862
STOVER Christina dau of George of Greenwich, NY     Greenwich, NY

GREENE Isaac L. of Kinderhook, NY                   March 9, 1862
KENYON Phiseria dau of late Stephen formerly of Greenwich, NY

DE GARMO Chauncey of Northumberland, NY             February 20, 1862
SPICER Jennie E. dau of Eber of Moreau, NY          Moreau, NY

TAYLOR Daniel W. son of late Lansing of Ft. Edward, NY   March 13, 1862
MORGAN Melissa of Barkers Grove, NY                 Barkers Grove, NY

ESMOND Ira D. of Quaker Springs, NY                 March 13, 1862
BRISBIN Helen dau of William C.                     Barkers Grove, NY

DIMMICK Schuyler of Quaker Springs, NY              March 15, 1862
HILL Libbie of Easton, NY                           N. Easton, NY

CLARK John W. of Greenwich, NY                      March 26, 1862
CRANDALL Elizabeth W. of Easton, NY                 Easton, NY

CROSIER John of Jackson, NY                         March 26, 1862
WATSON Susanna of Greenwich, NY                     Greenwich, NY

CRANDALL John K. of Greenwich, NY                   March 30, 1862
LUTHER Nancy of Greenwich, NY                       Greenwich, NY

WINSLOW Morris of Watertown, NY                     April 16, 1862
EDDY Julia dau of Walden of Greenwich, NY           Greenwich, NY

GREEN Leroy J. of Greenwich, NY                     May 14, 1862
MUNN Frances of Greenwich, NY                       Greenwich, NY

BENNETT or (BARNETT) John M. of Ft. Ann, NY         June 4, 1862
RICHMOND Lucy dau of Volney of Hoosick Falls, NY    Hoosick Falls, NY

TEFFT Henry of Sandy Hill, NY                       May 10, 1862
WAIT Martha Hartford, NY                            Hartford, NY

WALKER William of E. Greenwich, NY                  May 22, 1862

| | |
|---|---|
| OATMAN Mary H. of Salem, NY | E. Greenwich, NY |
| CRANDALL David of Greenwich, NY<br>WOLFE Eliza of Greenwich, NY | June 29, 1862<br>Greenwich, NY |
| BARNES Chauncey M. of Salem, NY<br>HILLMAN Hattie of Greenwich, NY | July 3, 1862<br>Greenwich, NY |
| LARABEE Merritt W. of Pittstown, NY<br>WHITLEY Mary A. of Pittstown, NY | July 4, 1862<br>Greenwich, NY |
| LAMBERT Alexander of Union Village, NY<br>FENTON Mary L. of Schuylerville, NY | July 12, 1862<br>Saratoga Spr., NY |
| RUSSELL Alvin of Salem, NY<br>MALONEY Julia of Salem, NY | July 22, 1862 |
| CLARK Ransom of Hartford, NY<br>CHASE Sophia of Hartford, NY | July 21, 1862<br>Hartford, NY |
| HORNBROOK John of Greenwich, NY<br>LAMBERT Mary E. of Greenwich, NY | August 10, 1862<br>Schuylerville, NY |
| BLAWIS J. P. Md. of Ft. Miller, NY<br>CARSWELL Esther of Ft. Edward, NY | August 14, 1862<br>Ft. Edward, NY |
| BENNETT Martin of Greenwich, NY<br>STEWART Eliza of Sandgate, Vt. | August 24, 1862<br>Greenwich, NY |
| WAIT Wayland W. of Chicago, Ill.<br>GORDON Emma of Schaghticoke, NY | September 16, 1862<br>Fairhaven, Conn. |
| BURDICK Albert L. of Easton, NY<br>CHUBB Elizabeth M. of Greenwich, NY | September 29, 1862<br>Greenwich, NY |
| SALISBURY Amos M. of Greenwich, NY<br>WELCH Lucinda dau of Major A. Welch of Greenwich, NY | September 12, 1862<br>Schuylerville, NY |
| HOLLISTER Edward P. of New York City<br>GRISWOLD Agnes W. of Greenwich, NY | October 2, 1862<br>Greenwich, NY |
| FISHER Mr. ____ of Ohio<br>LENDRUM Christianna of Argyle, NY | October 1, 1862<br>Argyle, NY |
| MC COLLUM William of Argyle, NY<br>STEWART Maggie J. dau of John M. Stewart | September 23, 1862 |
| NORTON William S. of Salem, NY<br>SAFFORD Katie J. of Salem, NY | October 4, 1862<br>Ft. Edward, NY |

CLAPP B. D. of Ft. Edward, NY — September 23, 1862
WOOD Hannah A. of Ft. Edward, NY — Ft. Edward, NY

MC EACHRON Frank of Argyle, NY — October 9, 1862
FERGUSON Maggie of Argyle, NY — Argyle, NY

WILCOX Edson D. of Greenwich, NY — November 4, 1862
KENYON Phebe of Jackson, NY — Jackson, NY

HOPKINS Fayette W. of W. Rupert, Vt. — October 8, 1862
WHITE Frances M. of Hebron, NY — Hebron, NY

GRAY M. D. of Salem, NY — August 5, 1862
HARRIS Ruth — Kingsbury, NY

CROCKER E. A. of Sandy Hill, NY — October 22, 1862
PARRY Elizabeth dau of late Ransom STILES — Ft. Edward, NY

WILBUR Daniel of Jackson, NY — November 13, 1862
BLANCHARD Caroline of Jackson, NY

HAYDEN Rev. A. V. L. of W. Rupert, Vt. — October 28, 1862
SHERMAN Anna dau of Grandison of Salem, NY — Salem, NY

LARKIN William N. of E. Greenwich, NY — October 24, 1862
RAINEY Anna M. of E. Greenwich, NY — Ft. Edward, NY

ROGERS A. F. of Hebron, NY — October 22, 1862
WILLIAMSON C. A. of Argyle, NY — Argyle, NY

KENYON John C. of Greenwich, NY — December 7, 1862
LEWIS Kate D. of Waterford, NY — Greenwich, NY

BROWN Edward A. of Troy, NY — December 7, 1862
TEFFT Jennie A. of Greenwich, NY — Greenwich, NY

REYNOLDS Frederick A. of Greenwich, NY — December 1, 1862
KINCAID Mary B. of Kingsbury, NY — Kingsbury, NY

RUSSELL B. W. of Hartford, NY — December 4, 1862
BRAYTON Sylvia of Hartford, NY — Hartford, NY

DECKER Abram of Greenwich, NY — December 31, 1862
FOMES Mary E. of Greenwich, NY — Greenwich, NY

BAKER Henry E. of Sandy Hill, NY — December 24, 1862
MC FARLAND Livona dau of Joseph of Sandy Hill, NY — Sandy Hill, NY

RICHARDS Ralph of Sandy Hill, NY — December 25, 1862

HARDEN Fanny of Sandy Hill, NY                                         Sandy Hill, NY

MOORE William W. of Greenwich, NY                              January 14, 1863
NEWBURY Anna E. of Greenwich, NY                               Galesville, NY

JONES James Jr. of Stranraer, Scotland                             January 5, 1863
GETTY Sarah E. dau of Isaac R.                                        W. Troy, NY

COLLINS James E. of Jackson, NY                                   January 22, 1863
STEWART Julia of Greenwich, NY                                    Greenwich, NY

CANNAIN Morris of Greenwich, NY                                January 22, 1863
SPRINGER Eliza Jane of Greenwich, NY                          Greenwich, NY

PALMER Rev. C. W. of Cambridge, NY                            January 21, 1863
DAVIES Anna J. of Brooklyn, NY                                     Brooklyn, NY

BALL Sylvanus of Cambridge, NY                                     February 4, 1863
BREWER Melissa J. of Greenwich, NY

FIELDING David C. of Salem, NY                                     February 4, 1863
ROGERS Julia E. of Salem, NY

GAVETTE John W. of Greenwich, NY                              February 12, 1863
WELLS Julia M. of Greenwich, NY                                  Greenwich, NY

FLANDERS Moses of Ilion, NY                                        February 25, 1863
BROOKS Addie of Greenwich, NY

WHITE Walter S. of Hebron, NY                                      February 15, 1863
PARISH Juliette dau of Daniel of Hebron, NY

WILLIAMSON Frederick J. of 123rd Reg. NY Vol.           February 21, 1863
THOMPSON Mary J. dau of David B. of Salem, NY

WINNING John of E. Hebron, NY                                    March 10, 1863
CARSON Matilda of E. Greenwich, NY                            Greenwich, NY

SHARPE H. K. of White Creek, NY                                 March 4, 1863
SMITH Catèlena dau of Capt. Ezra Smith of White Creek    White Creek, NY

SHEPHERD Juline P. of Greenwich, NY                         March 25, 1863
CARPENTER Jennie E. of Greenwich, NY                       Greenwich, NY

DOOLITTLE George M. of Winchester, NH                     March 25, 1863
SHEPHERD Sarah A. of Greenwich, NY                         Greenwich, NY

HEDGES Henry of Jackson, NY                                        March 12, 1863
BURT Aseneth of Shushan, NY                                         Jackson, NY

| | |
|---|---|
| **NORTHUP** George E. of Greenwich, NY | April 23, 1863 |
| **FITCH** Sarah A. of Cambridge, NY | Cambridge, NY |
| | |
| **KING** John of Salem, NY | June 2, 1863 |
| **SHEPARD** Elizabeth of Norfolk, NY | Saratoga Spr., NY |
| | |
| **BURROUGHS** Lewis Z. of Cambridge, NY | June 2, 1863 |
| **EDIE** Annie L. of Cambridge, NY | Greenwich, NY |
| | |
| **BENNETT** Sidney of Easton, NY | May 31, 1863 |
| **TABER** Sarah E. of Easton, NY | Schuylerville, NY |
| | |
| **HERMANCE** Dr. C. W. of Saratoga Springs, NY | June 2, 1863 |
| **MOTT** Lydia W. of Ft. Edward, NY | Ft. Edward, NY |
| | |
| **MC MASTERS** Alvin J. of E. Albany, NY | June 21, 1863 |
| **BENNETT** Charlotte of Greenwich, NY | Greenwich, NY |
| | |
| **DECKER** Peter of Battenville, NY | July 4, 1863 |
| **BARDEN** Rachael of Battenville, NY | Battenville, NY |
| | |
| **WOLFE** Martin formerly of Greenwich, NY | June 19, 1863 |
| **PARTELO** Aseneth of St. Louis, Mi. | St. Louis, Mi. |
| | |
| **SHERMAN** Sterling of W. Rupert, Vt. | June 23, 1863 |
| **DE MERRITT** Elizabeth J. of Dover, NH | Salem, NY |
| | |
| **BENNETT** Exodus Jr. of Union Village, NY | July 11, 1863 |
| **DURLING** Mary Elizabeth of Greenwich, NY | Greenwich, NY |
| | |
| **DAVIS** Everett of N. Adams, Mass. | July 18, 1863 |
| **BENNETT** Ellen of Greenwich, NY | Greenwich, NY |
| | |
| **BAKER** H. of Northumberland, NY | July 4, 1863 |
| **JOHNSON** Mary of Northumberland, NY | Northumberland, NY |
| | |
| **CURTIS** John Williams | August 27, 1863 |
| **WHITE** Bethiah Hawley of Union village, NY | Union Village, NY |
| | |
| **ALEXANDER** Joseph H. Div Quartermaster, Newborn, NC | August 30, 1863 |
| **MAXWELL** Kate D. of Jackson, NY | |
| | |
| **BROWNELL** Gideon B. of Cambridge, NY | September 1, 1863 |
| **WOOD** Laura C. of N. White Creek, NY | Greenwich, NY |
| | |
| **SEVERN** William of Greenwich, NY | September 8, 1863 |
| **EDIE** Sarah of Greenwich, NY | |
| | |
| **MORTON** Robert of New York City | September 17, 1863 |

WOODS Sarah M. of Coila, NY

| | |
|---|---|
| HILL Henry H. of Easton, NY | October 1, 1863 |
| HERRINGTON Elisabeth L. of Easton, NY | Greenwich, NY |
| | |
| AMES Almon A. of Greenwich, NY | September 26, 1863 |
| JOHNSON Caroline of Greenwich, NY | Greenwich, NY |
| | |
| HOYSRADT William H. of Ft. Edward, NY | October 13, 1863 |
| COOK Emeline of Ft. Edward, NY | Greenwich, NY |
| | |
| EDMONDSON James of Greenwich, NY | October 21, 1863 |
| SIXBY Jane E. of Seward, NY | Greenwich, NY |
| | |
| POTTER Lewis of Easton, NY | October 27, 1863 |
| ELDRIDGE Anna of Easton, NY | Easton, NY |
| | |
| BISHOP Joseph of Northumberland, NY | November 11, 1863 |
| STEWART Margaret of Ft. Miller, NY | Ft. Miller, NY |
| | |
| POTTER Albert of Glens Falls, NY | October 23, 1863 |
| BURDICK Carrie of Glens Falls, NY | Ft. Edward, NY |
| | |
| KNAPP Gilbert H. of E. Greenwich, NY | December 27, 1863 |
| MORRIS Mary H. of Greenwich, NY | Schuylerville, NY |
| | |
| BECKER Daniel of Cambridge, NY | January 24, 1864 |
| HILLMAN Chloe A. dau of John Hillman | Greenwich, NY |
| | |
| KENYON Henry L. of Dorset, Vt. | January 20, 1864 |
| HILL Mary E. of Arlington, Vt. | Cambridge, NY |
| | |
| CRANDALL Thomas of Easton, NY | February 8, 1864 |
| LEWIS Sarah of Jackson, NY | Jackson, NY |
| | |
| MC CLELLAN William P. of Mentor, Ohio | February 8, 1864 |
| SOMES Anna of Greenwich, NY | Lakeville, NY |
| (at her brother-in-law's William PRATT) | |
| | |
| CONNOR Henry of Salem, NY     (newspaper date) | February 18, 1864 |
| HOLDEN Eva of Chester, Vt. | |
| | |
| ENGLISH Charles W. of Cambridge, NY | January 13, 1864 |
| HILLMAN Harriet Jane of Cambridge, NY | Cambridge, NY |
| | |
| TAYLOR Henry of Easton, NY | February 18, 1864 |
| CHAPIN Delia A. of Greenwich, NY | Greenwich, NY |
| | |
| ARMINGTON Hiram of Albany, NY | February 18, 1864 |
| WILLARD Emma of Battenville, NY | Battenville, NY |

RUNDELL Francis of Greenwich, NY
AUSTIN Lavinna of Greenwich, NY

February 18, 1864
Greenwich, NY

SEELYE George E. of Geneva, NY
COLEMAN Evelyn dau of Col. William Coleman

February 17, 1864
Sandy Hill, NY

DOYLE Joseph M. of Norwich, Conn.
WARREN Mary E. of Easton, NY

March 4, 1864
Greenwich, NY

LANDERS Octavus of Northumberland, NY
GRAY Mary E. of Greenwich, NY

March 1, 1864

BREWER William of Greenwich, NY
DODD Eliza of Cambridge, NY

March 20, 1864
Schaghticoke, NY

GREEN Rodney of Greenwich, NY
WOLFE Catherine E. of Greenwich, NY

April 3, 1864
Greenwich, NY

MASON Capt. A. T. of 123rd Reg. NY Vol.
HEATH Julia M. of Greenwich, NY

April 6, 1864
Greenwich, NY

ELDRIDGE John H. of Easton, NY
SLADE Sarah E. of Easton, NY

April 13, 1864
Easton, NY

KNAPP Jabez age 83yrs of Shaftsbury, Vt.
WELLMAN Thankful age 81yrs of Shaftsbury, Vt.

April 26, 1864
White Creek, NY

TURNER Henry H. of Danamora, NY
REED Maggie A. of Greenwich, NY

May 10, 1864
Greenwich, NY

CARPENTER David W. of Greenwich, NY
POTTER Hannah of Greenwich, NY

May 22, 1864
Greenwich, NY

MAXSON Charles B. of 12th Reg. Vet. Reserves
LEWIS Mary J. of Galesville, NY

May 23, 1864
Galesville, NY

SMITH Joseph T. of Schuylerville, NY
HUGHES Catie of Greenwich, NY

May 24, 1864
Greenwich, NY

CLARK Palmer E. of Greenwich, NY
MC DONALD Elisabeth of Greenwich, NY

May 28, 1864
Greenwich, NY

CHASE John B. of Greenwich, NY
HAY Ann of Greenwich, NY

May 12, 1864
Lakeville, NY

MC EACHRON William of Argyle, NY
GALUSHA Lydia of Ft. Edward, NY

June 1, 1864
Ft. Edward, NY

HILL Thomas W. of N. Cambridge, NY

June 7, 1864

**EDIE** Mary of N. Cambridge, NY — Greenwich, NY

**MEREDITH** Robert R. of the Troy Conference — May 31, 1864
**THOMPSON** Carrie A. of Greenfield, NY — Greenfield, NY

**MC MASTERS** William S. of Lockport, NY — June 8, 1864
**REYNOLDS** Mary dau of Porter of Galesville, NY — Galesville, NY

**EDWARDS** John M. of Ft. Edward, NY — June 9, 1864
**WARD** Henrietta dau of D. O. of Pleasant Valley, NY — Pleasant Valley, NY

**KENYON** Lewis of Easton, NY — August 2, 1864
**WILLIAMS** Polly of Easton, NY — Easton, NY

**ATWOOD** A. G. of Salem, NY — July 18, 1864
**PIKE** Jane of Salem, NY — Salem, NY

**MC NULTY** James of Greenwich, NY — August 28, 1864
**MC CUE** Bridget of Greenwich, NY — Greenwich, NY

**GRANGER** Ezra — August 13, 1864
**SMITH** Mary Jane — Schuylerville, NY

**DENNIS** Deranzel D. of Greenwich, NY — September 22, 1864
**SPENCER** Martha A. of Greenwich, NY — Greenwich, NY

**ERVIN** Saunnie B. Md. of Lake, NY — October 12, 1864
**STEWART** Anna M. of Lake, NY — E. Greenwich, NY

**LUTHER** Almon of Greenwich, NY — October 20, 1864
**SEELYE** Mary F. of Schuylerville, NY — Schuylerville, NY

**SEELYE** Nelson I. of Schuylerville, NY — October 19, 1864
**MORRIS** Nancy E. of Schoharie, NY — Schoharie, NY

**ENGLISH** Alexander L. of Easton, NY — October 25, 1864
**HILL** Lois of Cambridge, NY — Cambridge, NY

**CRANDALL** John H. of Lake George, NY — October 13, 1864
**BOYNTON** S. Araminta of Peterborough, NH

**DUPY** Joshua of Greenwich, NY — November 1, 1864
**KENYON** Caroline of Greenwich, NY

**SEARLES** Royal E. of Easton, NY — December 18, 1864
**MABB** Maria of Easton, NY — Greenwich, NY

**COULTER** George of Arlington, Vt. — December 23, 1864
**STONE** Mary of Arlington, Vt. — Cambridge, NY

| | |
|---|---|
| ROBERTSON James E. of Coila, NY | December 29, 1864 |
| REID Mary Jane of N. Greenwich, NY | Greenwich, NY |
| | |
| ALLEN Joel of Cambridge, NY | December 31, 1864 |
| STARR Mattie of Cambridge, NY | White Creek, NY |
| | |
| WHIPPLE William of Easton, NY | January 15, 1865 |
| WHEELER Abbie H. of Stratford, Conn. | Greenwich, NY |
| | |
| KENYON Perry M. of Cambridge, NY | January 17, 1865 |
| WEIR Amanda J. of Jackson, NY | Jackson, NY |
| | |
| OWEN Henry B. of Greenwich, NY | January 25, 1865 |
| HILL Jane of Greenwich, NY | Schuylerville, NY |
| | |
| DWELLIE Horace of formerly of Northwood | December 26, 1864 |
| HINMAN Helen E. of Bristol(both of Worth Co. Iowa) | |
| | |
| TUCKER John D. W. of Greenwich, NY | February 1, 1865 |
| DICKINSON Harriet of Queensbury, NY | Ft. Ann, NY |
| | |
| WILSON John S. of Greenwich, NY | March 11, 1865 |
| LAMPMAN Mary L. of Greenwich, NY | Greenwich, NY |
| | |
| KENYON Otis L. of Greenwich, NY | March 14, 1865 |
| EDIE Christiana of Greenwich, NY | Greenwich, NY |
| | |
| SMITH Reuben of Jackson, NY | March 14, 1865 |
| COLBY Martha W. of Jackson, NY | |
| | |
| TALLMADGE Eli H. of Saratoga, NY | March 29, 1865 |
| PRINDLE Amanda M. of Greenwich, NY | Greenwich, NY |
| | |
| WILCOX K. N. of Greenwich, NY | March 30, 1865 |
| KENYON Paulina D. of Greenwich, NY | Greenwich, NY |
| | |
| HAY Alexander of Greenwich, NY | April 5, 1865 |
| BURDICK Mary Eliza of Greenwich, NY | Centre Falls, NY |
| | |
| RICE Robert W. of Greenwich, NY | April 12, 1865 |
| POND Martha of Schuylerville, NY | Schuylerville, NY |
| | |
| SLADE Israel of Easton, NY | April 11, 1865 |
| FREEMAN Hattie of Easton, NY | |
| | |
| GROOME John of Greenwich, NY | April 25, 1865 |
| MC DONALD Angie of Greenwich, NY | Greenwich, NY |
| | |
| MARTIN John W. of Cambridge, NY | May 4, 1865 |

| | |
|---|---|
| **SAXBURY** Sarah M. of White Creek, NY | White Creek, NY |
| **TUTTLE** Frank M. of Geneva, NY<br>**BARKER** Eunice J. of Geneva, NY | May 10, 1865<br>Easton, NY |
| **BIXBY** Adolphus of New Hampshire<br>**JONES** Lydia of Coila, NY | May 25, 1865 |
| **MC CLELLAN** James M. of W. Hebron, NY<br>**DONELSON** Maria of W. Hebron, NY | May 16, 1865<br>Argyle, NY |
| **RICHARDS** Albert W. of Argyle, NY<br>**ROBINSON** Anna Elizabeth of Argyle, NY | June 20, 1865<br>Argyle, NY |
| **MOWRY** Charles T. of Greenwich, NY<br>**BLANCHARD** Hattie M. dau of Anthony of Salem, NY | June 14, 1865<br>Salem, NY |
| **HOAG** J. E.<br>**DWELLIE** Lydia M. | June 28, 1865<br>Greenwich, NY |
| **BEEBE** Andrew of Shushan, NY<br>**CURTIS** Dora Arlington, Vt. | July 4, 1865<br>Shushan, NY |
| **COLE** Lewis of Jackson, NY<br>**COWAN** Agnes of Jackson, NY | July 6, 1865 |
| **KING** James M. of Ft. Edward, NY<br>**MC FARLAND** Mary H. of Ft. Edward, NY | July 11, 1865<br>Cambridge, NY |
| **VROOMAN** John of Essex, NY<br>**GALLETT** Henrietta of Schuylerville, NY | July 18, 1865<br>Schuylerville, NY |
| **BREWER** Lewis L. of Greenwich, NY<br>**RICHARDS** Susan M. of Greenwich, NY | July 30, 1865<br>Kingsbury, NY |
| **SPENCER** Will H. of Greenwich, NY<br>**NEWBERRY** Emma C. dau of Stephen | August 13, 1865<br>Greenwich, NY |
| **WILLIAMS** Albert of Ft. Edward, NY<br>**MC MURRAY** Julia E. of Ft. Edward, NY | August 17, 1865<br>Greenwich, NY |
| **LANSING** G. Y. of Greenwich, NY<br>**WRIGHT** Sarah A. of Greenwich, NY | September 5, 1865<br>Bald Mountain, NY |
| **WRIGHT** William H. of Greenwich, NY<br>**FOSTER** Julia E. dau of Allen of Greenwich, NY | September 6, 1865<br>Greenwich, NY |
| **FOLLETT** Joseph L. of St. Louis, Missouri<br>**BARNARD** Emily F. of Greenwich, NY | September 8, 1865<br>Greenwich, NY |

| | |
|---|---|
| **BRADT** Abram G. of Burnt Hills, NY | September 12, 1865 |
| **STOVER** Harriet A. of N. Greenwich, NY | N. Greenwich, NY |
| | |
| **STEWART** Robert | September 26, 1865 |
| **SHAW** Jennie dau of Archibald | Greenwich, NY |
| | |
| **WEATHERHEAD** Charles E. of Chester, NY | October 5, 1865 |
| **FERRIS** Deborah J. of Easton, NY | Greenwich, NY |
| | |
| **GRIFFIN** Amos B. of Easton, NY | October 11, 1865 |
| **FROST** Hattie A. of Greenwich, NY | Greenwich, NY |
| | |
| **BOSWORTH** Harvey M. of Greenwich, NY | November 9, 1865 |
| **WHITE** Nicie J. of Greenwich, NY | |
| | |
| **BOOTIER** Nelson of Greenwich, NY | November 11, 1865 |
| **YOUNG** Ellen of Greenwich, NY | Greenwich, NY |
| | |
| **GUNN** Charles J. of Greenwich, NY | November 12, 1865 |
| **WHIPPLE** Ada of Greenwich, NY | Greenwich, NY |
| | |
| **GREEN** Rensalaer C. of Galesville, NY | November 5, 1865 |
| **DAWLEY** Alzina of Greenwich, NY | Greenwich, NY |
| | |
| **HALL** P. M. of Hebron, NY | November 21, 1865 |
| **WRIGHT** Harriet of Greenwich, NY | |
| | |
| **HOPKINS** John of Argyle, NY | November 29, 1865 |
| **STOWE** Elizabeth J. of Argyle, NY | Greenwich, NY |
| | |
| **YOUNG** Alonzo of Easton, NY | November 29, 1865 |
| **CRANDALL** Annie Adelia of Greenwich, NY | Greenwich, NY |
| | |
| **DURLING** Alfred of Greenwich, NY | December 4, 1865 |
| **DAWLEY** Julia of Greenwich, NY | Greenwich, NY |
| | |
| **MC MILLAN** Johnie of Argyle, NY | November 30, 1865 |
| **FORD** Mary E. of Ft. Edward, NY | |
| | |
| **GIBBS** Jay of Rupert, Vt. | November 22, 1865 |
| **JENKINS** Ellen of Rupert, Vt. | W. Rupert, Vt. |
| | |
| **CARPENTER** Newlon of Greenwich, NY | December 6, 1865 |
| **TEFFT** Harriet C. of Greenwich, NY | Greenwich, NY |
| | |
| **COWAN** George L. of Jackson, NY | December 6, 1865 |
| **WILSON** Mary J. of Cambridge, NY | |
| | |
| **BROWNELL** Spencer of Cambridge, NY | December 7, 1865 |

**KENYON** Jane M. of Cambridge, NY

**KIPP** Z. Taylor of Easton, NY                    December 9, 1865
**RANDALL** Marion A. of Easton, NY

**RUSSELL** William A. of Salem, NY                 November 15, 1865
**FOX** Mattie dau of A. Fox late of Fitchburg, Mass.    New Ipswich, NH

**WRIGHT** Horace V. of Greenwich, NY               December 25, 1865
**FULLER** Emma of Greenwich, NY                    Greenwich, NY

**FORBES** Charles H. of Ft. Edward, NY             December 20, 1865
**DEWITT** Eliza of Ft. Edward, NY

**BURCH** Joel of Easton, NY                        December 24, 1865
**HOFFMAN** Lucinda of Greenwich, NY

**TULL** Job of Greenwich, NY                       January 3, 1866
**SALISBURY** Loeza M. dau of Orson                 Greenwich, NY

**HATCH** Forest R. of Jackson, NY                  December 28, 1865
**RAY** Charliphene A. of Battenville, NY           Greenwich, NY

**DURLING** Edward W. of Greenwich, NY              January 1, 1866
**AUSTIN** Lucinda of Greenwich, NY                 Greenwich, NY

**CONNOR** Thomas of Roswell, Pa.                   December 30, 1865
**SHRIVER** Elizabeth B. of Green Island            Green Island

**GREEN** Andrew of Ft. Edward, NY                  January 4, 1866
**DURKEE** Cynthia M. of Ft. Edward, NY             Greenwich, NY

**REYNOLDS** W. P. of Galesville, NY                January 2, 1866
**PRESTON** Harriet dau of J. R. of Schuylerville, NY    Schuylerville, NY

**RANDALL** Edward E. of Easton, NY                 January 1, 1866
**KIPP** Catherine of Easton, NY

**LAMPMAN** John of Easton, NY                      January 7, 1866
**KNAPP** Elvera of Easton, NY

**MAHAFFY** Thomas of Hebron, NY                    January 4, 1866
**MC KNIGHT** Maretta J. of Hebron, NY             Hebron, NY

**HENRY** Carr (or **CARR** Henry) of Argyle, NY    December 28, 1866
**SKELLIE** Martha of Argyle, NY                    Argyle, NY

**CRANDALL** Nathan R. of Greenwich, NY             January 17, 1866
**ROGERS** Mary of Greenwich, NY                    Greenwich, NY

RUSSELL Richard B. of Greenwich, NY      January 17, 1866
BRIGGS Hannah A. of Greenwich, NY      Greenwich, NY

WEST O. C. of Tolland, Conn.      January 18, 1866
WALLER Amanda C. dau of Sidney of Greenwich, NY      Greenwich, NY

CORNELL Hiram K. of Greenwich, NY      January 24, 1866
STILLMAN Mary of Greenwich, NY      Greenwich, NY

JILLSON H. of Argyle, NY      January 3, 1866
MC FADDEN Elizabeth A. of Sandy Hill, NY      Sandy Hill, NY

STEVENS Edward R. of Greenwich, NY      January 24, 1866
TEFFT Ruth S. dau of Asa C. of Ft. Miller, NY      Ft. Miller, NY

OBERN John of Easton, NY      February 1, 1866
HERRINGTON Harriet Ann of Easton, NY      Greenwich, NY

THOMAS George W. of Easton, NY    (newspaper date)      February 8, 1866
WILBUR Celia J. of Girard, Mi.      Girard, Mi.

TAYLOR Charles W. of Argyle, NY      January 30, 1866
HAWKINS E. Orra of Argyle, NY      Argyle, NY

DOBBIN Jamea J. of Somonauk, Ill.      February 28, 1866
TEFFT Nancy M. of Argyle, NY      Argyle, NY

GALE Fred A. of Greenwich, NY      February 28, 1866
BARNARD Phebe A. of Greenwich, NY      Greenwich, NY

BAIN William A. of Argyle, NY      March 13, 1866
MOREHOUSE Phebe Ann of Hebron, NY      Salem, NY

WHYTE Charles of Argyle, NY      February 13, 1866
BEATTIE Sarah E. dau of late Thomas of Argyle, NY      Argyle, NY

MAXWELL James of Jackson, NY      March 14, 1866
ROBERTSON Eliza of Jackson, NY      Jackson, NY

MUNN Nathan of Schuylerville, NY      March 22, 1866
SUTFIN Elizabeth of Victory Mills, NY

TUCKER Augustus of Lakeville, NY      March 21, 1866
MC KALLOR Julia of S. Argyle, NY      Cambridge, NY

HILL William of Eagle Bridge, NY      March 22, 1866
ROCK Lydia of Eagle Bridge, NY      Eagle Bridge, NY

SHELDON Edgar of Constantine, Mi.      March 20, 1866

**SHELDON** Mary A. of Rupert, Vt.

| | |
|---|---|
| **MC NAUGHTON** J. of Cambridge, NY | March 28, 1866 |
| **HARSHA** Maria H. of Cambridge, NY | White Creek, NY |
| | |
| **REYNOLDS** John C. of Newburgh, NY | March 27, 1866 |
| **MC DOUGAL** Nancy of Argyle, NY | Belcher, NY |
| | |
| **PARK** Pliny E. of Salem, NY | March 21, 1866 |
| **HULL** Kate of Orwell, Vt. | Orwell, Vt. |
| | |
| **HOLLINGSWORTH** Levi of N. Lewisburg, Ohio | April 5, 1866 |
| **ALLEN** Eliza of Union Village, NY | Columbus, Ohio |
| | |
| **GIFFORD** John I. of Albany, NY | April 26, 1866 |
| **WHISH** Mary I. of Albany, NY | Albany, NY |
| | |
| **ENGLISH** David of Cambridge, NY | April 23, 1866 |
| **RICE** Jane Ann of Salem, NY | Salem, NY |
| | |
| **LANDON** Cassius D. of Whitehall, NY | May 1, 1866 |
| **BENJAMIN** Josie A. of Whitehall, NY | Whitehall, NY |
| | |
| **HULL** James M. of Argyle, NY | May 8, 1866 |
| **WOODARD** Kate M. dau of Lyman | Whitehall, NY |
| | |
| **MASTERS** N. M. of New York son of J. T. of Greenwich | June 6, 1866 |
| **HERVIE** Mollie of Cincinnati, Ohio | |
| | |
| **ATWATER** Albert C. of Addison, NY | June 4, 1866 |
| **CARSWELL** Magaret B. of Salem, NY | Salem, NY |
| | |
| **FOWLER** Franklin of Cambridge, NY | June 2, 1866 |
| **SHAW** Addie J. of Cambridge, NY | Cambridge, NY |
| | |
| **BLAKEMAN** John of Sandy Hill, NY | June 7, 1866 |
| **BEATTIE** Mary J. of Coila, NY | Coila, NY |
| | |
| **MC GINN** John of Sandy Hill, NY | May 30, 1866 |
| **WARREN** Rachel A. of Sandy Hill, NY | Sandy Hill, NY |
| | |
| **WELLING** N. B. of Saratoga Springs, NY   (newspaper date) | June 21, 1866 |
| **ENSIGN** Mary A. of Easton, NY | Easton, NY |
| | |
| **MICKLEJOHN** Andrew G. of Putnam, NY | May 29, 1866 |
| **LEDGERWOOD** Elizabeth E. of Putnam, NY | Putnam, NY |
| | |
| **SAWYER** James W. of Chicago, Ill.      (newspaper date) | June 21, 1866 |
| **FISHER** Ruth D. formerly of White Creek, NY | Palatine, NY |

| | |
|---|---|
| **DAVIDSON** John | June 7, 1866 |
| **HUTTON** Elizabeth | Putnam, NY |
| | |
| **LANSING** Abram W. formerly of Greenwich, NY | June 19, 1866 |
| **STRAIGHT** Hannah of Plattsburgh, NY | Plattsburgh, NY |
| | |
| **BROUGHTON** Albert K. of Salem, NY | June 18, 1866 |
| **DAVIS** Laura E. dau of Rev. H. M. Davis of Salem, NY | Salem, NY |
| | |
| **CRANDALL** George W. of Greenwich, NY | June 27, 1866 |
| **LOVEJOY** Frank C. of N. White Creek, NY | White Creek, NY |
| | |
| **BAKER** Gideon of Greenwich, NY | July 5, 1866 |
| **NEILSON** Ann Aurelia dau of Charles of Bemis Heights, NY | Bemis Heights, NY |
| | |
| **FREEMAN** Romeyn of Watertown, NY | July 10, 1866 |
| **EDDY** Mandy M. dau of Walden of Greenwich, NY | Greenwich, NY |
| | |
| **LAMB** David 2nd of Granville, NY | June 5, 1866 |
| **BAKER** Frances dau of Ransom O. of Stillwater, NY | Stillwater, NY |
| | |
| **MILLIS** John of Schuylerville, NY | July 10, 1866 |
| **FERRIS** Nancy M. of Greenwich, NY | Greenwich, NY |
| | |
| **CAMPBELL** Jerome M. of Poultney, Vt. | July 10, 1866 |
| **POTTER** Susanna R. | Easton, NY |
| | |
| **WHEELOCK** Edgar L. of Cambridge, NY | July 11, 1866 |
| **MARSH** Ermina A. of Boston, Mass. | Cambridge, NY |
| | |
| **BEATTIE** David H. of Salem, NY | July 11, 1866 |
| **WHITE** Elizabeth of Hebron, NY | W. Hebron, NY |
| | |
| **DELAVERGNE** Joseph of Easton, NY | July 22, 1866 |
| **TAYLOR** Maria of Easton, NY | Easton, NY |
| | |
| **DE RIDDER** Simon of Schuylerville, NY | July 29, 1866 |
| **PETTIT** Sarah E. of Saratoga, NY | Easton, NY |
| | |
| **LYONS** H. E. of Shushan, NY (newspaper date) | August 2, 1866 |
| **MC CARTY** Libbie of Esperance, NY | Albany, NY |
| | |
| **NICHOLS** Alfred F. of Ft. Miller, NY | July 26, 1866 |
| **CANNAIN** Eliza J. of Battenville, NY | Battenville, NY |
| | |
| **PARKS** James G. of Montreal, Canada | August 8, 1866 |
| **SPARHAWK** Martha A. of Greenwich, NY | Greenwich, NY |
| | |
| **HEADDINGS** William of Cohoes, NY | August 22, 1866 |

| | |
|---|---|
| GRANGER Margaret of Battenville, NY | Battenville, NY |
| TORENTO Lewis of Cohoes, NY<br>CANNAIN Eliza J. of Battenville, NY | August 12, 1866<br>Battenville, NY |
| BORDEN Isaac<br>WRIGHT Maggie dau of Edward | September 5, 1866<br>Easton, NY |
| FROST Stephen R. of Greenwich, NY<br>BEEBE Juliette M. of Greenwich, NY | September 12, 1866<br>Greenwich, NY |
| PIERCE Hosea A. of White Creek, NY<br>WHITE Cornna F. of White Creek, NY | September 9, 1866<br>Cambridge, NY |
| MC KINNEY Alex of Salem, NY<br>FERGUSON Maggie of Cambridge, NY | September 13, 1866 |
| ROBERTSON J. W. of Cambridge, NY<br>RICE Kate dau of Harvey of Anaquasicoke, NY | September 12, 1866 |
| SMITH William C. of Easton, NY<br>HILL Mercia A. of Easton, NY | September 25, 1866<br>Greenwich, NY |
| HUTCHINS Horace of Union Village, NY<br>BARR Jane of Cambridge, NY | September 18, 1866<br>Cambridge, NY |
| DEAN Joel B. of Creek Center, NY<br>DAYTON Christy Ann of Greenwich, NY | October 16, 1866<br>Centre falls, NY |
| COOK Joseph L. of Wallingford, Vt.<br>GRIFFIN Emily A. of Hartford, NY | October 8, 1866<br>Hartford, NY |
| MOWRY Merritt of Greenwich, NY<br>SEABURY Mary A. of Saratoga Springs, NY | October 23, 1866<br>Greenwich, NY |
| WILDER Abel of Greenwich, NY<br>MOSHER Emily of Greenwich, NY | October 24, 1866<br>Niagara City, NY |
| WEIR Sydney B. of Hartford, NY    (newspaper date)<br>STALKER Marion D. of Argyle, NY | November 8, 1866<br>Greenwich, NY |
| SKELLIE Lavinus of Cambridge, NY<br>KENDALL Isabella of Cambridge, NY | November 8, 1866<br>Cambridge, NY |
| WHELDON J. O. of Greenwich, NY<br>STEWART Ella C. of Greenwich, NY | November 14, 1866<br>Greenwich, NY |
| WHITE Willard W. of Jackson, NY<br>WILSON Ann Eliza of Jackson, NY | November 15, 1866<br>Greenwich, NY |

**NOBLE** Rev. J. H. of Schaghticoke, NY   (newspaper date)     November 22, 1866
**CHAMBERLAIN** Caroline W. of Aurora, Ind.     Aurora, Ind.

**HAYES** Joseph H. of Washington DC     November 15, 1866
**WOODARD** Emma E. dau of Daniel of Salem, NY     Salem, NY

**REYNOLDS** George C. of Greenwich, NY     December 10, 1866
**BARREN** Lucelia A. of Greenwich, NY     Greenwich, NY

**LANSING** Uriah J. of Greenwich, NY     December 4, 1866
**SPENCER** Arsabinda A. of Greenwich, NY     Greenwich, NY

**HUGHES** A. K. of the US Navy     December 12, 1866
**WHELDON** Marion dau of Darius of Easton, NY     Easton, NY

**MC ELHINNEY** Samuel of Henderson, Ill.     December 11, 1866
**STEWART** C. Eliza of Jackson, NY     Jackson, NY

**HEWITT** A. E. of Albany, NY     December 11, 1866
**HARREL** Minerva of Cambridge, NY     Cambridge, NY

**PETTEYS** Edgar M. of Easton, NY     December 20, 1866
**SLADE** Elsie of Easton, NY     Easton, NY

**KENYON** Freeman of Jackson, NY     December 25, 1866
**ANTHONY** Nancy M. of Cambridge, NY     Cambridge, NY

**ALEXANDER** Robert of Jackson, NY     December 26, 1866
**SHELDON** Christinnaet dau of William of Shenevanes, NY     E. Greenwich, NY

**MC COLLUM** John of S. Argyle, NY     December 19, 1866
**ARMSTRONG** Maggie of S. Argyle, NY     S. Argyle, NY

**BENTLEY** Elias J. of Manchester, Vt.     December 11, 1866
**MARSH** Emily J. of Arlington, Vt.     Cambridge, NY

**WOOD** Henry C. of White Creek, NY     December 12, 1866
**CLOSSON** Lydia of White Creek, NY     Cambridge, NY

**BROWNELL** Simeon of Cambridge, NY     December 25, 1866
**DILLINGHAM** Sarah B. of Cambridge, NY     Cambridge, NY

**EDIE** Peter of Cambridge, NY     December 27, 1866
**MEAD** Sarah of Easton, NY     Cambridge, NY

**HASTINGS** Jonathan of Milwaukee, Wis.     January 3, 1867
**HARMON** Elsie of Greenwich, NY     Greenwich, NY

**BATTY** Orlando D. of Greenwich, NY     January 5, 1867

DENNIS Electa S. of Greenwich, NY

Greenwich, NY

SPARHAWK Oscar F. of Greenwich, NY
SHELDON Sarah Jane of Ft. Edward, NY

January 2, 1867
Ft. Edward, NY

TEFFT Franklin G. of Greenwich, NY
ADAMS Maria Ann of Easton, NY

January 1, 1867
Easton, NY

ROBINSON Henry Joseph of Greenwich, NY
STOVER Sarah Matilda of Greenwich, NY

November 23, 1866

CLUM Charles E. of Troy, NY
TEFFT Lydia Augusta of Greenwich, NY

January 17, 1867
Greenwich, NY

SMITH William of Jackson, NY
BARBER Lucie of Jackson, NY

January 22, 1867
Jackson, NY

THOMAS Edwin A. of Easton, NY
LENT Mary L. of Easton, NY

January 24, 1867
Greenwich, NY

SMITH Charles A. of Troy, NY
FENTON Minnie J. dau of Calvin of Greenwich, NY

January 29, 1867
Greenwich, NY

SMITH Daniel C. of Danby, Vt.
WILBUR Louis C. dau of Henry of Danby, Vt.

January 24, 1867
Danby, Vt.

BENNETT Harvey of Greenwich, NY
GRIFFIN Ellenor of Greenwich, NY

February 1, 1867
Greenwich, NY

MAXWELL Robert of Greenwich, NY
ROBERTSON Barbara

January 8, 1867
E. Greenwich, NY

MC CLELLAN James of Cambridge, NY
BAIN Annie M. of Argyle, NY

January 16, 1867
Argyle, NY

RICE Harvey of Jackson, NY
CAMPBELL Lucy M. of Jackson, NY

January 16, 1867
Cambridge, NY

SWERTFIGER Dan of Saratoga Springs, NY
BONNY Angelica of Saratoga Springs, NY

February 9, 1867
Greenwich, NY

WENTWORTH Havaland H. of Jackson, NY
REMINGTON Ella M. of Greenwich, NY

February 11, 1867
Union Village, NY

BARBER Horton A. of Greenwich, NY
MAXWELL Jennie of Jackson, NY

February 20, 1867
Jackson, NY

GARDNER William G. of Galesville, NY
BABCOCK Mrs. Laura F. of Galesville, NY

March 3, 1867

COULTER Lewis S. of Jackson, NY                       January 24, 1867
NICHOLSON Caroline L. of White Creek, NY         Cambridge, NY

GIFFORD Orlon C. of Easton, NY                           March 6, 1867
GILBERT Hattie E. of Jackson, NY                   Cambridge, NY

CARR Munroe W. of Jewett, NY                       February 28, 1867
WARD Eliza M. of Chester, NY                        Chester, NY
(He lost both eyes at Ft. Hudson, 90th NY Vol.)

SAFFORD R. S.             (newspaper date)    March 21, 1867
RUSTE Helen M. dau of Samuel formerly of Cambridge, NY  Aurora, Ill.

STEVENSON John A. of Coila, NY                   March 21, 1867
SHILAND Libbie of Jackson, NY                  Jackson, NY

THORPE John of Greenwich, NY                   March 10, 1867
BASSETT Mrs. Sarah A of Greenwich, NY         Greenwich, NY

TEFFT Caleb B. of Argyle, NY                    March 18, 1867
NICHOLS Helen A. of Ft. Miller, NY            Ft. Miller, NY

BOWKER Martin of Greenwich, NY               March 18, 1867
FAIRBANKS Melissa of Greenwich, NY         Greenwich, NY

LAMBERT Dr. of Hoosick Falls, NY             April 2, 1867
RUSSELL Helen E. dau of David of Salem, NY     Salem, NY

HOOK Charles                                 April 9, 1867
TEFFT Caroline W. dau of S. B. formerly of Greenwich, NY  Monroe, Iowa

COON James S. of Argyle, NY                    May 5, 1867
CRAWFORD Mrs. May H. of Argyle, NY         Greenwich, NY

MILLER J. F. of Sandy hill, NY                   May 5, 1867
LAMPHIER Almira of Galesville, NY            Galesville, NY

BRITT A. J. of Greenwich, NY                    May 29, 1867
EVANS Lucy A. of Greenwich, NY             Greenwich, NY

DUDLEY Martin                            July 1, 1867
SCHOULTZ Zephrin dau of E. N. of Greenwich, NY    Schuylerville, NY

DUDLEY Julian                             July 1, 1867
SCHULTZ Alberna dau of E. N. of Greenwich, NY     Schuylerville, NY

BISBEE Capt. Wright of Boston, Mass.            July 4, 1867
LAMB Georgia A. dau of R. A. of Greenwich, NY    Greenwich, NY

**BROWN** Philander of Easton, NY
**ENGLISH** Ruby of Easton, NY

July 4, 1867
Greenwich, NY

**PIERCE** Arthur G. of Greenwich, NY
**BREWER** Sarah E. of Battenville, NY

July 31, 1867
Battenville, NY

**TOWNE** Edward of Granville, NY
**SNOW** Fannie of Granville, NY

July 25, 1867
Granville, NY

**PARISH** Newton of Hebron, NY
**WOODARD** Marie of Salem, NY

April 25, 1867
Cambridge, NY

**HUGGINS** John of Salem, NY
**MARSHALL** P. Hattie of Salem, NY

August 28, 1867
Cambridge, NY

**MC NEAR** Josiah F. of Columbus City, Ind.
**TUCKER** Antoinette A. dau of Alanson of Etna, Ind.

September 5, 1867
Etna, Ind.

**MAXWELL** Robert A. of Chicago, Ill.
**MC LEAN** Mary dau of late Henry

September 17, 1867
Jackson, NY

**MONCRIEF** William T. of Rupert, Vt.
**LANG** Zulia M. of Hebron, NY

September 12, 1867
Salem, NY

**JOHNSTON** James of Hebron, NY
**MC GILL** Sarah J. of Hebron, NY

September 11, 1867
Coila, NY

**FLEMING** Andrew J. of Salem, NY
**CHANDLER** Eva M. of Salem, NY

September 12, 1867
Salem, NY

**JONES** Rollin B. of Rutland, Vt.
**RUGGLES** Augusta A. dau of Reul of Ft. Edward, NY

September 18, 1867
Ft. Edward, NY

**KINGSLEY** Horace of Ft. Edward, NY
**USHER** Maria C. of Ft. Edward, NY

September 18, 1867
Ft. Edward, NY

**LOWRY** Charles of Greenwich, NY
**MAXSON** Elizabeth of Glens Falls, NY

October 9, 1867
Glens Falls, NY

**FOWLER** Freeman of Easton, NY
**BOWEN** Amelia A. of Cambridge, NY

October 9, 1867
Cambridge, NY

**HAMMOND** Fay of Pawlet, Vt.
**WELLS** Emma L. of Hunter, NY

October 1, 1867
Pawlet, Vt.

**TOUSLEY** Charles B. of Ft. Edward, NY
**ALLEN** Libbie of Ft. Edward, NY

October 1, 1867
Troy, NY

**SWARTWOOD** Loren
**MC CREEDY** Mary

September 24, 1867
Schuylerville, NY

BUCK Edward G. of Ft. Edward, NY
DEWEY Eliza J. of Ft. Edward, NY

October 17, 1867
Ft. Edward, NY

CULVER Jonathan L. of Cambridge, NY
MITCHELL Isabella of Cambridge, NY

September 16, 1867
Salem, NY

COWLES Benjamin F. Jr.
FAXON Hattie A. dau of W. A. of Glens Falls, NY

October 17, 1867
Glens Falls, NY

SLOCUM Frederick R. of Barkers Grove, NY
ALLEN Celestie M. dau of William of Barkers Grove, NY

October 30, 1867
Easton, NY

WHITTAKER Leroy
KENYON Kate D. of Greenwich, NY

October 31, 1867
Galesville, NY

VAN SCHAICK Levi of E. Greenwich, NY
TRIPP Sarah of Chester, Vt.

October 27, 1867
Battenville, NY

ESTEY Julius J. of Brattleboro, Vt.
GRAY Florence C. dau of Dr. Henry C. Gray of Cambridge
(date given was November 29, 1867, date of issue November 7, 1867)

November 29, 1867
Cambridge, NY

TEFFT Oscar of Greenwich, NY
ROBINSON Julia A. of Greenwich, NY

November 6, 1867
Galesville, NY

OSBORN Richard of Green Island
BAKER Charlotte E. of Northumberland, NY

October 17, 1867
Saratoga Spr., NY

VANDENBURGH Solon of Schuylerville, NY
ROBERSON Maria L. of Greenwich, NY

November 7, 1867
Greenwich, NY

RUSSELL George J. of Greenwich, NY
TEFFT Lydia W. of Greenwich, NY

November 19, 1867
Greenwich, NY

JOSLIN J. L. of Cambridge, NY
ALLEN Lottie P. of Cambridge, NY

November 12, 1867
Cambridge, NY

DAVIS Edwin M. of Greenwich, NY
MC ERVING Mary Elizabeth of Greenwich, NY

November 24, 1867
Greenwich, NY

MC LAREN Prof. William of Sandy Hill, NY
BARKLEY Carrie M. dau of Alexander of Argyle, NY

November 14, 1867
Argyle, NY

TUCKER James R. of Greenwich, NY
TANNER Julia E. dau of William S. of Greenwich, NY

November 6, 1867
Greenwich, NY

RICHARDS John W. of Greenwich, NY
ROOD Altie M. of Greenwich, NY

November 27, 1867
Greenwich, NY

| | |
|---|---|
| **CAMPBELL** M. Charles of Greenwich, NY<br>**LING** Mary of Greenwich, NY | November 28, 1867<br>Greenwich, NY |
| **MC MURRAY** Sylvester S.<br>**MC INTYRE** Ann Lavina | January 16, 1868<br>S. Argyle, NY |
| **SCOTT** Walter<br>**BROWN** Maggie | January 14, 1868<br>S. Argyle, NY |
| **SELFRIDGE** Richard S.<br>**RICHMOND** Augusta L. of Galesville, NY | January 24, 1868<br>Galesville, NY |
| **REYNOLDS** Andrew<br>**BARKLEY** Esther Mary | January 22, 1868 |
| **CARSON** Burton of Hebron, NY<br>**BRADY** Isabella of Hebron, NY | January 31, 1868<br>Greenwich, NY |
| **CRAMER** David T. of Saratoga, NY<br>**BURCH** Rosa of Saratoga Springs, NY | February 4, 1868<br>Greenwich, NY |
| **HUTCHINGS** William H.<br>**SCOTT** Mary M. | January 21, 1868<br>Argyle, NY |
| **HOPKINS** George M.<br>**LINDSAY** Mary | January 21, 1868 |
| **LESTER** Samuel<br>**RANDLES** Maggie | January 23, 1868 |
| **MC DOUGAL** James<br>**MC DOUGAL** Jennie | January 23, 1868 |
| **MC CORMICK** Thomas of Greenwich, NY<br>**SPRINGER** Caroline of Greenwich, NY | February 11, 1868<br>Greenwich, NY |
| **MC DOUGAL** John W.<br>**STALKER** Agnes | February 6, 1868<br>N. Argyle, NY |
| **KING** Daniel of Argyle, NY<br>**HANDY** Sara of Saratoga Springs, NY | February 12, 1868<br>Ft. Edward, NY |
| **WESTINGHOUSE** George of Greenwich, NY<br>**OWEN** Deborah F. of Greenwich, NY | February 19, 1868<br>Greenwich, NY |
| **COPELAND** W. A. (or J. W.)<br>**BROWN** Libbie | February 19, 1868<br>N. Argyle, NY |
| **REYNOLDS** George H. of Greenwich, NY<br>**CONKLIN** Mary E. of Greenwich, NY | February 23, 1868<br>Greenwich, NY |

KRUM Hobart of Schoharie, NY
WASHBURN Frank H. of Ft. Edward, NY

February 26, 1868
Ft. Edward, NY

TRAVER Andrew
FINN Kate

March 4, 1868
Ft. Edward, NY

WILLIAMS John of Salem, NY
WILSON Rebecca of Salem, NY

March 4, 1868
N. Argyle, NY

GAVETTE Asahel of Argyle, NY
FISHER Fanny of White Creek, NY

March 4, 1868
White Creek, NY

DE RIDDER John H. of Schuylerville, NY
HANNUM Maria T. of Huntington, Mass.

February 26, 1868
Huntington, Mass.

CALHOUN James of Greenwich, NY
RIDDLE Margaret of S. Argyle, NY

February 25, 1868
N. Argyle, NY

PAGE Bishop E. of Saratoga Springs, NY
VIALL Olive E. of Schaghticoke, NY

March 30, 1868
Schaghticoke, NY

NORTON David S. of Hartford, NY
SHANNON Augusta of Argyle, NY

April 8, 1868
Argyle, NY

CONLEE Cortland M. of Kingsbury, NY
ALSTON Addie M. of Greenwich, NY

April 19, 1868
Greenwich, NY

ROBERTSON Edward B. of Greenwich, NY
CONKLIN Sarah of Easton, NY

May 13, 1868
Easton, NY

HALL William D. of Argyle, NY
MC ELWAIN Jane of Ft. Covington, NY

April 27, 1868
Ft. Covington, NY

DEMITH Benjamin F. of Greenwich, NY
WILDER Harriet M. of Greenwich, NY

May 30, 1868
Greenwich, NY

SPRINGER Joseph A. of Greenwich, NY
STACY Delinda Jane of Greenwich, NY

July 3, 1868
Greenwich, NY

RICE John L. of Shushan, NY
BREWER Lottie of Greenwich, NY

July 2, 1868
Greenwich, NY

HOFFMAN Joseph of Greenwich, NY
FILES Mahabie of Easton, NY

July 3, 1868
Easton, NY

SMITH Thomas M. of Troy, NY
MOWRY Lydia A. of Greenwich, NY

August 24, 1868
Greenwich, NY

STEVENS J. C. of Greenwich, NY

September __, 1868

**BROWN** May Helen dau of Charles of Castleton, Vt.     Castleton, Vt.

**FROST** James W. of New York City                      September 15, 1868
**MOORE** Kate of Greenwich, NY                          Greenwich, NY

**HAYNER** Addison G. of Cambridge, NY                   September 10, 1868
**WATERS** Ruth A. of Hoosick, NY                        Cambridge, NY

**LOUP** William H. of Luzerne, NY                       October 7, 1868
**STOVER** Josephine E. of Greenwich, NY                 Greenwich, NY

**ADAMS** Thomas L. of Greenwich, NY                     October 8, 1868
**CLOSSON** Mary H. of Victory, NY                       Victory, NY

**REMINGTON** Thomas of Greenwich, NY                    October 8, 1868
**ADAMS** Maria of Greenwich, NY                         Greenwich, NY

**LAMB** Henry F. of N. Bennington, Vt.                  October 8, 1868
**LOURIE** Jennie of Greenwich, NY                       Greenwich, NY

**STILLMAN** S. L. Jr. of Greenwich, NY                  October 20, 1868
**MC GOWAN** Ruth of Rose Valley, NY                     Rose Valley, NY

**NORTHUP** Joseph Henry of Easton, NY                   October 23, 1868
**GIFFORD** Phebe Jane of Easton, NY                     Easton, NY

**CARPENTER** Alvin L. of Glens Falls, NY                October 21, 1868
**MAYHEW** Alida C. dau of C. W. of Schuylerville, NY    Schuylerville, NY

**DERRY** George of Battenville, NY                      October 22, 1868
**BLANCHARD** Delia of Battenville, NY                   Battenville, NY

**KENYON** Alfred F. of Greenwich, NY                    October 28, 1868
**CRANDALL** Mary A. of Ft. Edward, NY                   Ft. Edward, NY

**GIBBS** James of Greenwich, NY                         November 7, 1868
**GREEN** Julia A. of Greenwich, NY                      Greenwich, NY

**BENNETT** Hiram M. of Greenwich, NY                    November 12, 1868
**DINGS** Emma F. of Greenwich, NY                       Greenwich, NY

**ALLEN** Joshua of Easton, NY                           November 23, 1868
**WILBUR** Ellen A. of Easton, NY                        Easton, NY

**STEWART** James H. of Greenwich, NY                    December 2, 1868
**MOORE** Mary R. of Greenwich, NY                       Greenwich, NY

**HALL** William of Springfield, Vt.                     November 25, 1868
**WEIR** Mary E. of Jackson, NY                          Greenwich, NY

GREENE Hiram G. of Cambridge, NY
FULLER Achasah of Easton, NY

November 28, 1868
Greenwich, NY

WILSON Gilbert formerly of Greenwich, NY
BROWNLEE Maggie of Marion, Ind.

November 12, 1868
Marion, Ind.

WEIR John of Cambridge, NY
KERNAGHAN Margaret J. of Greenwich, NY

December 4, 1868
Greenwich, NY

DARROW Christopher of Easton, NY
PRATT Jerusha of Easton, NY

December 8, 1868
Easton, NY

REID John Mc A. of S. Argyle, NY
LENDRUM Annie of S. Argyle, NY

December 15, 1868
S. Argyle, NY

TAYLOR Albert G.
POTTER Fanny A.

December 16, 1868
Ft. Edward, NY

(missing issues 1869 - 1874)

SPRAGUE William L. of Greenwich, NY
RATHBUN Jennie dau of Hiram

January 3, 1875
Greenwich, NY

BROWN James of Salem, NY
BELL Mary A. of W. Hebron, NY

December 24, 1874
W. Hebron, NY

FLEMING William of N. Hebron, NY
GETTY Sarah dau of Chester of N. Hebron, NY

December 24, 1874
W. Hebron, NY

BABCOCK Osmer A. of Easton, NY
BURCH Frances Adelaide of Hebron, NY

December 24, 1874
W. Hebron, NY

PARSONS Chapin
PENFIELD Susannah

December 24, 1874

WILSON Dr. ____
GUY Julia

December 30, 1874
Ft. Miller, NY

CORNELL Charles P. of Greenwich, NY
BROWN Anna E. of Troy, NY

December 6, 1874
Troy, NY

ROBERTSON Robert Alexander of Lakeville, NY
CLARK Clara A. of Lakeville, NY

January 13, 1875
Lakeville, NY

SIMPSON Stephen L. of Easton, NY
REYNOLDS Evelyn L. of Easton, NY

January 14, 1875
Easton, NY

PALMER Robert C. of W. Pawlet, Vt.
MAHAFFY Mary E. of Salem, NY

December 31, 1874
Salem, NY

| | |
|---|---|
| **HAWKS** Frederick of Hartford, NY<br>**BURTON** Miss E. of Hartford, NY | January 6, 1875<br>Sandy Hill, NY |
| **CLEMMONS** Rollin of Dresden, NY<br>**BAILEY** Martha Emeline of S. Hartford, NY | December 31, 1874<br>Glens Falls, NY |
| **MIX** Alonzo L. of Long Lake, NY<br>**SOMERVILLE** Maggie E. dau of E. W. of Johnsburg, NY | December 30, 1874<br>Johnsburg, NY |
| **FISH** William H. of Ft. Edward, NY<br>**TRAVER** Georgia A. of Ft. Edward, NY | January 6, 1875<br>Caldwell, NY |
| **CLUTE** John of Whitehall, NY<br>**HULETT** Maria A. of Putnam, NY | January 7, 1875<br>Putnam, NY |
| **LAING** William D. of Northumberland, NY<br>**PALMER** Helen M. of Northumberland, NY | December 24, 1874<br>Northumberland, NY |
| **UNDERWOOD** C. W. of Ft. Edward, NY<br>**SMITH** Mary of Mechanicsville, NY | January 21, 1875<br>Mechanicsville, NY |
| **CLARK** James E. of Kingsbury, NY<br>**TENNOT** Flora E. of Sandy Hill, NY | January 16, 1875<br>Sandy Hill, NY |
| **JONES** Augustus F. of Poultney, Vt.<br>**TRIPP** Sarah E. of Ft. Ann, NY | January 18, 1875<br>Hartford, NY |
| **WILSON** Lyman G. of Glens Falls, NY<br>**PARKS** Ella K. of Glens Falls, NY | January 13, 1875<br>Glens Fall, NY |
| **HUDSON** John<br>**WADE** Amanda | December 25, 1874<br>Easton, NY |
| **GARRICK** Melancton W. of Granville, NY<br>**BEDELL** Emma A. of Granville, NY | January 20, 1875<br>Granville, NY |
| **CENTER** Charles of Whitehall, NY<br>**CLANCY** Eliza of Whitehall, NY | January 19, 1875<br>Whitehall, NY |
| **SANTERS** Joseph of Sandgate, Vt.<br>**FOSTER** Mina of Shushan, NY | January 1, 1875<br>Cambridge, NY |
| **ELDRIDGE** Ahira Jr. of Cambridge, NY<br>**WOODWARD** Carrie M. dau of late J. D. of Castleton, Vt. | January 26, 1875<br>Ft. Edward, NY |
| **KING** Walter of Cambridge, NY<br>**BAKER** Mary L. of Hoosick, NY | January 28, 1875<br>Hoosick Falls, NY |
| **ROGERS** Gen. J. C. of Sandy Hill, NY<br>**COLEMAN** Lizzie M. of Sandy Hill, NY | January 26, 1875<br>Sandy Hill, NY |

LEE Napoleon L.
YARTER Hattie

January 11, 1875
Glens Falls, NY

BLAKE William J. of Ft. Edward, NY
METCALF Jennie E. of Ft. Edward, NY

January 20, 1875
Ft. Edward, NY

NELSON Silas M.
DENNISON Libbie A.

January 20, 1875
S. Granville, NY

KELLEHER William of Ft. Edward, NY
DAVEN Hannah of Ft. Edward, NY

January 26, 1875
Ft. Edward, NY

SHELDON F. G. of Ft. Ann, NY
MC FADDEN Julia E. of W. Chazy, NY

January 19, 1875
W. Chazy, NY

WING Levi H.
BALDWIN Louisa

January 28, 1875
Glens Falls, NY

STONE E. of Argyle, NY
MATHEWS Carrie of Argyle, NY

January 27, 1875
Argyle, NY

TOMB J. S.
STEELE Emma J.

January 27, 1875
Salem, NY

MULLEN Mathew of Hebron, NY
CONNELLY Margaret of Hebron, NY

January 25, 1875

BECKER James E. of Easton, NY
BROWNELL Hannah D. of Easton, NY

February 10, 1875
Easton, NY

GIFFORD George of Easton, NY
BUCKLEY Estella of Schaghticoke, NY

February 10, 1875
Schaghticoke, NY

JAMES Sylvester B. of Hoosick, NY
BOSWORTH Julia H. of Buskirks Bridge, NY

February 9, 1875
Buskirks Bridge, NY

CRANSTON John H. of Shaftsbury, NY
HILL Martha E. of Bennington, Vt.

February 5, 1875
White Creek, NY

COMERFORD Peter of Salem, NY
MARTIN Agnes of Ft. Edward, NY

February 9, 1875
Ft. Edward, NY

POOR W. C.
BENTLEY Mrs. Laura A.

January 14, 1875
Salem, NY

CRANDALL John L.
BUCKLEY Edna A.

February 24, 1875
Easton, NY

WOODWORTH George

January 30, 1875

*Marriage Notices*

**WENDELL** Mrs. Anna

Greenwich, NY

**HURTUBIS** Trufley of Whitehall, NY
**GOODOUT** Celia of Whitehall, NY

February 8, 1875
Whitehall, NY

**DEVINE** William G. of Kingsbury, NY
**FREEMAN** Alice of Kingsbury, NY

February 16, 1875
Kingsbury, NY

**HARKNESS** Brainard T. of Cambridge, NY (newspaper date)
**TEFFT** Effie B. of Jamestown, NY

February 25, 1875
Jamestown, NY

**WELLS** John J. of Sandy Hill, NY
**TAYLOR** Ella of Sandy Hill, NY

February 13, 1875
Glens Falls, NY

**MC MILLAN** William C. of Jackson, NY
**WEIR** Ella R. of Cambridge, NY

February 24, 1875
Cambridge, NY

**WATTS** I. H. of Whitehall, NY
**DOUGLAS** Emma

February 8, 1875
N. Granville, NY

**MAXWELL** George of Whitehall, NY
**SPELLING** Kate of Whitehall, NY

February 21, 1875
Whitehall, NY

**MC COLLUM** James of Argyle, NY
**IRVING** Mary J. of Argyle, NY

February 28, 1875
Argyle, NY

**CELSIS** Frank of Cambridge, NY
**CROWDER** Phebe of Cambridge, NY

February 22, 1875
Cambridge, NY

**JONES** Nathan
**DE KALB** Ida L.

February 24, 1875
Granville, NY

**BAKER** George F.
**WILEY** Alzina L.

February 27, 1875
Granville, NY

**MAHAFFY** Norman
**MC GEOCH** Ruth

February 24, 1875
Argyle, NY

**SWAN** Henry A. of Glens Falls, NY
**BULLARD** Emma A. of Glens Falls, NY

February 25, 1875
Glens Falls, NY

**MOTT** Dr. O. H. of Ft. Ann, NY
**MOORE** Mary E.

February 16, 1875
Glens Falls, NY

**DE KALB** Edward S. of Granville, NY
**BARTLETT** Mary E. dau of Edward S. of Granville, NY

March 10, 1875
Granville, NY

**POTTER** Warren J. of Queensbury, NY
**GRAVES** Mary Lavina of Glens Falls, NY

March 4, 1875
Glens Falls, NY

CORNELL Stephen W. of Indian River, NY     March 8, 1875
SAGE Ida L. of Stony Crek, NY

BARTON Joel of Ft. Edward, NY     March 10, 1875
KINNE Lilly of Canaan, NY     Canaan, NY

SHIELDS William P. of Luzerne, NY     March 10, 1875
HOGLE Frances C. of Luzerne, NY     Warrensburgh, NY

VIETS Martin H. of Eagle Bridge, NY     March 3, 1875
SLADE Miss ____ of Saratoga Springs, NY     White Creek, NY

KENYON Elmer of Buskirks Bridge, NY     March 4, 1875
TURNER Ruth B. of Schaghticoke, NY     Schaghticoke, NY

WASHBURN Earle/Isaac of Northumberland, NY     March 11, 1875
KINGSLEY Ella dau of George     Whitehall, NY

MC NEIL George formerly of Argyle, NY     March 10, 1875
GEDNEY Josephine dau of late Dr. I. Roosevelt     New York City

BROMLEY Orson of Shaftsbury, Vt.     March 20, 1875
FOX Emma of Shaftsbury, Vt.     White Creek, NY

SMITH Stephen H. of Hebron, NY     (newspaper date)     April 1, 1875
CLARK Eliza J. of Fredonia, NY     Fredonia, NY

MC ALLISTER Solomon H. of Greenwich, NY     March 13, 1875
MACKIN Katie of Troy, NY     Greenwich, NY

SWEENEY James of Salem, NY     March 30, 1875
SLATTERY Maggie of Salem, NY     Salem, NY

ROBINSON William of Glens Falls, NY     March 28, 1875
COWAN Phebe Ann of S. Granville, NY     N. Hebron, NY

MOSHER Bonaparte of Sandy Hill, NY     March 31, 1875
COTY Addie     Ft. Edward, NY

BENEDICT Luther of Clifton Park, NY     March 25, 1875
BROWN Caroline P. of Half Moon, NY     Glens Falls, NY

NOXON Amos J. of Ft. Ann, NY     March 31, 1875
CARLTON Ruth M. of Granville, NY     Granville, NY

SWEET Daniel V. of E. Pawlet, Vt.     March 30, 1875
VAIL Ella J. of E. Pawlet, Vt.     Granville, NY

HOWES O. G.     March 28, 1875

**REAMER** Mrs. Sarah M.                                    Ft. Ann, NY

**MONAHAN** James of Ft. Ann, NY                            April 4, 1875
**GORMAN** Mary of Ft. Ann, NY                              Sandy Hill, NY

**MAXAM** James of Warrensburgh, NY                         April 6, 1875
**WILLIAMS** Orcelia of Sandy Hill, NY                      Sandy Hill, NY

**MC MULLEN** James of Argyle, NY                           April 6, 1875
**DOBBIN** Jane of Salem, NY                                Salem, NY

**REYNOLDS** Charles O. of Greenwich, NY                    April 1, 1875
**FARRER** Hattie L. of Schuylerville, NY                   Schuylerville, NY

**HAINES** Charles D. of Boston, Mass.                      April 14, 1875
**KINGSLEY** Lida of Sandy Hill, NY                         Sandy Hill, NY

**LAKE** Stephen D. of Boston, Mass.                        April 14, 1875
**KINGSLEY** Frankie of Sandy Hill, NY                      Sandy Hill, NY

**KING** George of Easton, NY                               March 31, 1875
**CORNELL** Jennette of Easton, NY

**STEVENS** Melvin S. of Salem, NY                          April 15, 1875
**FAIRLEY** Kate M. of Salem, NY                            Rupert, Vt.

**FEELEY** Martin                                           April 21, 1875
**HEYSETT** Maggie                                          Whitehall, NY

**MC GURTY** John                                           May 3, 1875
**MOONEY** Maggie                                           Whitehall, NY

**GULLY** Martin                                            May 3, 1875
**MC GURTY** Kate                                           Whitehall, NY

**GRAVES** William of Whitehall, NY                         May 6, 1875
**CARVER** Tamsen B. of Whitehall, NY                       Whitehall, NY

**FULLER** J. R. of Ft. Miller, NY                          May 6, 1875
**SHEPPARD** Mary of Ft. Miller, NY                         Bacon Hill, NY

**MOTT** Dr. Albert of Stillwater, NY formerly Sandy Hill, NY May 6, 1875
**NORTHUP** Mary L. of Troy, NY                             Troy, NY

**WAKEVILLE** Charles E. of Burlington, Vt.                 May 12, 1875
**BUSH** Florence E.                                        S. Glens Falls, NY

**MILLER** Joseph of Greenwich, NY                          May 26, 1875
**SILK** Ann of N. Adams, NY                                Schuylerville, NY

BROWNE A. G. of Middlebury, Vt.
WILKINS Mary E. of Salem, NY

May 20, 1875
Salem, NY

SMITH Thomas of Whitehall, NY
WATERS Maggie of Whitehall, NY

May 27, 1875
Whitehall, NY

BAIN John Henry of S. Argyle, NY
SMITH Nancy Isabel of Kirkwood, Ill.

May 25, 1875
N. Argyle, NY

BROOKS Levi D. of Sandy Hill, NY
DEMPSEY Mary Ann of Sandy Hill, NY

June 6, 1875
Sandy Hill, NY

HAMILTON William of Mooers, NY
MERRILL Nellie of Sandy Hill, NY

June 6, 1875
Sandy Hill, NY

REED Henry of Edinburgh, Pa.
ROBINSON Alice M. of Sandy Hill, NY

June 23, 1875
Sandy Hill, NY

BENWAY Charles H. of Sandy Hill, NY
HENRY Sarah J. of Sandy Hill, NY

June 10, 1875
Sandy Hill, NY

CAMPBELL Charles G. of Greenwich, NY
PILLING Sarah of Greenwich, NY

May 9, 1875
Stillwater, NY

LAING Myron E. of Greenwich, NY
TAYLOR Fannie

July 14, 1875
Northumberland, NY

TAYLOR William of Cambridge, NY
FAIRBROTHER Celia of Eagle Bridge, NY

July 2, 1875

LEWIS Frank B. of N. Bennington, Vt.
KENT Mary F. of N. Bennington, Vt.

July 24, 1875
Greenwich, NY

DONALDSON Richard of Hartford, NY
DUNN Katie of Hartford, NY

July 25, 1875
Greenwich, NY

TAYLOR James W. of Argyle, NY
BAIN Jennie of Argyle, NY

July 27, 1875
Argyle, NY

PREFOUNTAIN George of Whitehall, NY
LORTIE Emma C. of Whitehall, NY

August 4, 1875
Whitehall, NY

STEWART Dr. D. A. of Winona, Minn.
HALL Minnie A. of Greenwich, NY

August 24, 1875
Whitehall, NY

SEVERANCE Stephen of Greenwich, NY
TAGGET Margaret of Greenwich, NY

August 14, 1875
Greenwich, NY

COOKINGHAM J. Mortimer of Newburgh, NY

June 23, 1875

**CHASE** Libbie dau of Samuel of Easton, NY — Newburgh, NY

**BURDICK** William M. of Hydesville, Vt.
**WRIGHT** M. C. of Hebron, NY — August 17, 1875 / Cambridge, NY

**FOSTER** Charles E. of Shushan, NY
**SAYLES** Anna R. of Shushan, NY — September 1, 1875 / Cambridge, NY

**BOWEN** Orley M. of Hartford, NY
**KINCAID** Ida M. of Smiths Basin, NY — September 1, 1875 / Smiths Basin, NY

**SEARLES** Hiram M. of Salem, NY
**SHIPLEY** Mrs. Martha M. of Salem, NY — September 2, 1875 / Salem, NY

**MC ENERY** Michael
**CARNEY** Honora — August 26, 1875 / Cambridge, NY

**GRAY** Thomas of Stony Creek, NY
**RHODES** Mary M. of Stony Creek, NY — August 15, 1875 / Stony Creek, NY

**JORDAN** Thomas Leroy of Cambridge, NY
**CAVANAUGH** Mary of Cambridge, NY — September 5, 1875 / Salem, NY

**MC MILLAN** Abraham of Salem, NY
**PARISH** Helen M. of Salem, NY — September 8, 1875 / Salem, NY

**FAXON** Walter S. of Hartford, NY
**RATHBUN** Addie J. of Whitehall, NY — September 1, 1875 / N. Granville, NY

**ATWELL** Frank
**HOPSON** Lillie E. — September 14, 1875 / Whitehall, NY

**HUGHES** Bernard M. of Hartford, NY   (newspaper date)
**SMITH** Mary E. — September 23, 1875 / Fairhaven, Vt.

**WAIT** Cassius G. of Granville, NY
**RYDER** Ella J. of Granville, NY — September 1, 1875 / N. Granville, NY

**ORCUTT** George H. of Jackson, NY
**HALL** Mary E. of E. Greenwich, NY — September 15, 1875 / Salem, NY

**HILL** W. W. of Salem, NY
**BROWN** Mary of Salem, NY — September 15, 1875 / Salem, NY

**GOULD** Abram of San Francisco, Cal.
**KEGLER** Sophia of Salem, NY — September 14, 1875 / Salem, NY

**LAMB** Henry F. of N. Bennington, Vt.
**SIMMONS** Carrie M. dau of George W. and Abigail P. — September 15, 1875 / N. Bennington, Vt.

SULLIVAN Calvin of Quaker Springs, NY
ABEEL Annie of Easton, NY

September 9, 1875
Ft. Edward, NY

WILLETT Addison of N. Granville, NY
SHUMWAY Eliza of N. Granville, NY

September 7, 1875
N. Granville, NY

NYE James H. of Cayutaville, NY
WHITNEY Florence C. of Syracuse, NY
(sister of Leroy Whitney of Sandy Hill, NY)

September 16, 1875
Sandy Hill, NY

PARISH John H. of Ft. Edward, NY
BRIGGS Almira L. of Appleton, Wis.

September 8, 1875
Appleton, Wis.

PETERS James W. of Ft. Edward, NY
DOWNER Helen G. of Ft. Edward, NY

September 12, 1875
Ft. Edward, NY

SANDERSON B. H. of Cambridge, NY
HILLS Charlotte of N. Granville, NY

September 8, 1875
N. Granville, NY

STAFFORD Thomas of Cambridge, NY
HILLMAN Sophia of Cambridge, NY

September 11, 1875
Cambridge, NY

COLEMAN Richard T. of Sandy Hill, NY
BAILEY Addie D. dau of Franklin of Ft. Ann, NY

September 28, 1875
Ft. Ann, NY

CAMP Norman D. of Glens Falls, NY
LANIFIER Sarah L. of Chester, NY

September 22, 1875
Sandy Hill, NY

EMOND Augustus of Sandy Hill, NY    (newspaper date)
LONGTAINE Marie Rose of Sandy Hill, NY

October 7, 1875
Sandy Hill, NY

CURTIS Walter of Sandy Hill, NY    (newspaper date)
FOSTER Emma D. of Sandy Hill, NY

October 7, 1875
Sandy Hill, NY

EDWARDS Thomas W. of Whitehall, NY
REED Hattie E. of Whitehall, NY

September 21, 1875
Whitehall, NY

SINCLAIR Joseph of Whitehall, NY
FISH Helen M. of Whitehall, NY

September 19, 1875
E. Whitehall, NY

HASWELL Sherwood son of Hiram M. of White Creek, NY
PERCY Ella R. dau of William of Hoosick, NY

September 29, 1875
Hoosick, NY

DONAHUE David E.
LAMPMAN Harriet L.

October 2, 1875
Galesville, NY

ROSS Perry T.
LOSEE Emma

September 30, 1875
Gansevort, NY

**GOW** Frank F. Md.  
**COCRANE** Mary E. T.  
October 6, 1875  
Galesville, NY

**BAKER** Charles of Comstocks, NY  
**DAVIS** Minnie E. dau of Rev. E. E. of Whitehall, NY  
September 30, 1875  
Whitehall, NY

**MC INTOSH** Frederick W. Ft. Edward, NY  
**SANDERS** Lucy F. of Sandy Hill, NY  
October 3, 1875  
Sandy Hill, NY

**VIELE** Harlam P. of Glens Falls, NY  
**HAMILTON** Ella J. of Moreau, NY  
September 23, 1875  
Sandy Hill, NY

**JOHNSON** Joseph R. of Ft. Edward, NY  
**BRAZIER** Mary E. of Bolton, NY  
September 25, 1875  
Bolton, NY

**EDWARDS** Daniel of Greenwich, NY  
**LANDERS** Ellen D. of French Mountain, NY  
September 24, 1875  
French Mtn., NY

**STEARNS** Jerome M. of Hoosick, NY  
**SANDERS** Carrie M. of Bennington, Vt.  
September 29, 1875  
Cambridge, NY

**BAKER** Samuel D. of Ft. Miller, NY  
**NEWBURY** Hattie of Greenwich, NY  
October 20, 1875  
Greenwich, NY

**HOWE** Wiliam H. of Sandy Hill, NY  
**GILMAN** Emma F. of Sandy Hill, NY  
October 13, 1875  
Sandy Hill, NY

**HILL** Truman T. of Sandy Hill, NY  
**MEAD** Cynthia of Johnsburgh, NY  
October 13, 1875  
Sandy Hill, NY

**WICKHAM** Warren of Chester, NY  
**BURDICK** Mrs. Thea of Glens Falls, NY  
October 7, 1875  
Glens Falls, NY

**SNALLON** Wesley J. of Middletown, Vt. (newspaper date)  
**DICKERSON** Laura of Middletown, Vt.  
October 21, 1875  
Granville, NY

**LEONARD** William Henry of Hampton, NY  
**BELDEN** Emma A. of Whitehall, NY  
October 6, 1875  
Whitehall, NY

**GRAVES** William of Malone, NY  
**ALLORD** Mary of Hampton, NY  
October 7, 1875  
Whitehall, NY

**LOOMIS** Amos of Whitehall, NY  
**TRUFFREY** Hattie of Granville, NY  
October 8, 1875  
Whitehall, NY

**WAGMAN** John of Ft. Miller, NY  
**BENNETT** Ida of Old Saratoga, NY  
October 6, 1875  
Old Saratoga, NY

**STEELE** Thomas B. of Cherokee, Iowa formerly Salem, NY  
**WASHBURN** Celia M. of Waverly, Iowa  
August 25, 1875  
Waverly, Iowa

COLE Frederick of Arlington, Vt.
ANDREWS Frances V. of Arlington, Vt.

October 3, 1875
White Creek, NY

CARTER William N. of Greenwich, NY
JOHNSON Sarah E. of Greenwich, NY

October 20, 1875
Greenwich, NY

GRAY Albert W. of Middletown, Vt.
HOLBROOK Martha M. of Sandy Hill, NY

October 20, 1875
Sandy Hill, NY

RICH Leonard of Whitehall, NY
GREEN Sarah J. of Whitehall, NY

October 20, 1875
Whitehall, NY

OWEN David of Eagle Bridge, NY
BENTLEY Alice of Cambridge, NY

October 16, 1875
Cambridge, NY

HOWARD Marshall E. of Hebron, NY
NELSON H. Dora of Rupert, Vt.

October 10, 1875
Rupert, Vt.

HARRINGTON Joseph of Shaftsbury, Vt.
ELWELL Marion of Shaftsbury, Vt.

October 13, 1875
White Creek, NY

RICHARDS Eugene H. of Hampton, NY
SINCLAIR Edna L. of Poultney, Vt.

October 19, 1875
Poultney, Vt.

STEARNS Henry of N. Granville, NY
HALL Lucinda of Wells, Vt.

October 17, 1875
Granville, NY

CHASE Clarence of Easton, NY
KENYON Anna of Easton, NY

October 13, 1875
Easton, NY

SPENCER James of Whitehall, NY
JOHNSON Elizabeth of Whitehall, NY

October 21, 1875
Whitehall, NY

CHAUBIN Leander of N. Granville, NY
GOODRICH Sarah of N. Granville, NY

October 21, 1875
N. Granville, NY

HALL Edward of Ft. Ann, NY          (newspaper date)
MERWIN Frances Ida of Orwell, Vt.

November 4, 1875
Orwell, Vt.

MARSH John H. of Sandgate, Vt.          (newspaper date)
TURNER Virginia of Sandgate, Vt.

November 4, 1875
Sandgate, Vt.

DALTON Michael of Whitehall, NY
LAVEY Kate of Whitehall, NY

October 13, 1875
Whitehall, NY

WHEELOCK Samuel B. of Greenwich, NY
MILLER Mary Louise of Greenwich, NY

November 4, 1875
Greenwich, NY

JUBERT Albert of Gansevort, NY

October 6, 1875

**CHUBB** Ida of Gansevort, NY — Greenwich, NY

**MANUEL** John of Salem, NY — November 3, 1875
**HARRIS** Elizabeth E. of Salem, NY — Greenwich, NY

**MORRISON** John of Sandy Hill, NY — October 31, 1875
**OWENS** Mary of Sandy Hill, NY — Sandy Hill, NY

**PALMITEER** Samuel K. of Glens Falls, NY — November 3, 1875
**HOUSE** Rhoda J. of Sandy Hill, NY — Sandy Hill, NY

**BEST** George of Putnam, NY — October 21, 1875
**PETERS** Lucy of Putnam, NY — Putnam, NY

**BENNETT** James E. of Pittsfield, Mass. — October 28, 1875
**HARRISON** Jane E. of Ft. Edward, NY — Ft. Edward, NY

**BARKER** Frank G. of N. Argyle, NY — November 2, 1875
**LAUGHLIN** Etta

**MADISON** Noah of Glastonbury, Vt. — November 1, 1875
**JONES** Aurilla of Sunderland, Vt. — Jackson, NY

**BUTCHER** William H. of Gansevort, NY — October 28, 1875
**BRADFORD** Agnes W. of Cambridge, NY — Cambridge, NY

**CARLTON** Frank D. of Sandy Hill, NY — October 27, 1875
**GAMBLE** Ella of Sandy Hill, NY — Sandy Hill, NY

**GILLETTE** M. of Hebron, NY — November 10, 1875
**EAGER** J. E. of Salem, NY — Salem, NY

**SMITH** E. R. of Salem, NY — November 10, 1875
**ROWLES** Annie E. of Plattsburgh, NY — Plattsburgh, NY

**MC LINE** John of S. Argyle, NY — November 3, 1875
**HUGHES** Mrs. Anna of S. Argyle, NY — S. Argyle, NY

**SAFFORD** Myron C. of Salem, NY — October 28, 1875
**YOUNG** Ella M. of Jackson, NY — Jackson, NY

**HARRINGTON** Joseph C. of Easton, NY — October 28, 1875
**HILL** Ella A. of Cambridge, NY — Easton, NY

**PRATT** Edwin of Easton, NY — November 10, 1875
**SHERMAN** Mary C. of Pittstown, NY — Pittstown, NY

**DAVIS** William H. of Battenville, NY — November 15, 1875
**LACKEY** Mary of Barnumville, NY — Dorset, Vt.

WRIGHT T. A. of New York City
GIBSON Mary dau of James of Salem, NY

November 18, 1875
Salem, NY

STEVENS William of Hoosick, NY
STEWART Clara L. of Cambridge, NY

November 13, 1875
Cambridge, NY

SCOVILLE George R. of Luzerne, NY
STARRETT Minnie F. of Sandy Hill, NY

November 3, 1875
Sandy Hill, NY

SMITH George of Ft. Edward, NY
DEYOE Nancy E. of Ft. Edward, NY

November 8, 1875
Sandy Hill, NY

PARKER Frank G. of N. Argyle, NY
LAUGHLIN Etta of E. Hartford, NY

November 2, 1875

LARKIN M. of Middle Falls, NY
LARKIN Ida of W. Hebron, NY

November 24, 1875
Salem, NY

SENTON Dr. B. C. of Glens Falls, NY
LONG Jennie of Whitehall, NY

November 19, 1875
Whitehall, NY

CURTIS Willie J. of Schaghticoke, NY
BURCH Stella G. of S. Cambridge, NY

November 18, 1875
S. Cambridge, NY

JENKINS N. L. of Greenwich, NY
HILL Elizabeth of Greenwich, NY

November 24, 1875
Coila, NY

CONE Harlan P. of Ft. Ann, NY
VAUGHN Sarah Elizabeth of Ft. Ann, NY

November 21, 1875
Ft. Ann, NY

RUSSELL William Luther
WEIR Rilla R. dau of Abram of White Creek, NY

December 8, 1875
Centre Fall, NY

LINK Charles H. of Cambridge, NY
WEIR Emma J. of Jackson, NY

December 8, 1875
Jackson, NY

BEATTIE John of Salem, NY
AUSTIN Louise of Salem, NY

December 3, 1875
Salem, NY

DURKEE Wellington
HILTON Mrs. Phebe

November 17, 1875
Ft. Edward, NY

PERRY J. of Argyle, NY                    (newspaper date)
MC COLLOUGH May T. of Argyle, NY

December 9, 1875
Glens Falls, NY

TEFFT H. B. of Greenwich, NY
SMITH Sarah of Troy, NY

December 16, 1875
Troy, NY

FINCH Lewis Henry of Greenwich, NY

December 5, 1875

BABCOCK Mattie of Greenwich, NY

PERRY Clark of Warrensburgh, NY
DURKEE Lida of Ft. Edward, NY

SLOCUM Lewis of Easton, NY
BAKER Augusta of Saratoga Springs, NY

MANNING William
RICE Julia

SANBORN Lansing G.
ROBINSON Eliza

DUEL C. H. of S. Granville, NY
PARSONS Carrie E. of S. Granville, NY

PECK George T. of Camden, NY
OLIVER Lottie W. of Camden, NY

BORDEN Elias of Easton, NY
GIFFORD Mary dau of Alexander of Argyle, NY

MC MULLEN James of Nevada
GIFFORD Matilda dau of Alexander of Argyle, NY

GOODRICH William H.
MULHOLLAND Julia

LOURIE William of Greenwich, NY
BURNETT Laura E. of Salem, NY

COOK Northrup E.
PARISH Abigail E. of Ft. Edward, NY

LEONARD Dewitt of Brattleboro, Vt.
BAKER Cora G. of Brattleboro, Vt.

GUY George W. of Northumberland, NY
HOLBROOK Mary E. of Sandy Hill, NY

MC CLAUGHRY E. Morrison of Edinboro, Pa.
MC FARLAND Mrs. C. L. formerly of Greenwich, NY

TEFFT Frederick J. of Greenwich, NY
FOSTER Emma G.

HASTINGS Joseph W.
VAUGHN Maria G.

Salem, NY

November 28, 1875
Ft. Edward, NY

December 9, 1875
Saratoga, NY

December 15, 1875
N. Argyle, NY

December 4, 1875
Shushan, NY

December 9, 1875
N. Heborn, NY

December 11, 1875
E. Salem, NY

December 15, 1875
Argyle, NY

December 15, 1875
Argyle, NY

December 5, 1875
Whitehall, NY

December 23, 1875
Salem, NY

December 23, 1875
Ft. Edward, NY

July 15, 1876
Hampton, NY

July 23, 1876
Sandy Hill, NY

July 28, 1876
Milford, NY

July 1, 1876
Stillwater, NY

August 5, 1876
Ft. Ann, NY

JOLY Napoleon of Whitehall, NY
PROVOST Mary of Whitehall, NY

August 15, 1876
Whitehall, NY

CAHART Henry S.
SOULE Nellie M. formerly of Greenwich, NY

August 30, 1876
Sing Sing, NY

SMITH Frank W. of Middle Falls, NY
CLEMENT Nancy E. of Middle Falls, NY

September 5, 1876
Middle Falls, NY

MC CLELLAN John of Greenwich, NY
COLE Mrs. L. A. of Greenwich, NY

September 7, 1876
Greenwich, NY

DAVIS Thomas of Hartford, NY
BRANDWICK Kate of Hartford, NY

September 5, 1876
Sandy Hill, NY

SMITH S. C. formerly of Greenwich, NY
CRANDALL Ella D. formerly of Greenwich, NY

August 10, 1876
Cascade Portage Br.

FOLGER Merritt C. of Granville, NY
BAKER Alice A. of Granville, NY

September 13, 1876
Granville, NY

PETTEYS Edgar M. of Easton, NY
DAVISON M. Frank dau of James of Greenwich, NY

September 27, 1876
Greenwich, NY

GIMBLE Gilbert S. of Greenwich, NY
HOLBROOK Mrs. Catherine of Greenwich, NY

September 9, 1876
Greenwich, NY

INGALSBEE Grenville M.
GROESBECK Franc E. dau of Amasa HOWLAND

September 20, 1876
Ft. Edward, NY

HARVEY Charles E. of Granville, NY
CARLTON Sarah E. of Granville, NY

September 12, 1876
Granville, NY

MC DONALD James S. of Salem, NY
MARTIN Sophia C. dau of Jarvis of Greenwich, NY

October 4, 1876
Greenwich, NY

MC MURRAY John A. of Jackson, NY
SELFRIDGE S. Maggie of Jackson, NY

October 2, 1876

FENTON George E. of Hoosick Falls, NY
ANDREWS Ellen of Salem, NY

October 18, 1876
Greenwich, NY

BEATTIE Robert son of John C. of Salem, NY
SHERMAN Frank

October 11, 1876
E. Salem, NY

KENYON Hamper of Greenwich, NY
WILLIAMS Elizabeth F. of Defriestville, NY

October 11, 1876
Bath on the Hudson

ROGERS Newton

October 18, 1876

**MUNSON** Carrie                                   Hebron, NY

**MOORE** John A. of Schuylerville, NY              November 1, 1876
**ROURK** Rose of Hebron, NY                        Salem, NY

**TYREL** William A. of S. Dorset, Vt.             November 1, 1876
**BRYANT** Emma E. of Manchester, Vt.               Shushan, NY

**WILLIAMS** Gilbert S.                             November 21, 1876
**RANDALL** Ida J. of Eagle Bridge, NY              Salem, NY

**WALLACE** Gideon S. of White Creek, NY            December 11, 1876
**SISSON** Julia A. of White Creek, NY              Cambridge, NY

**BURCH** William R. of Greenwich, NY               December 23, 1876
**PLATT** Clarissa of Greenwich, NY                 Greenwich, NY

**STEVENS** Royal B. of Ft. Ann, NY                 December 13, 1876
**BURGESS** Rena of Ft. Ann, NY                     South Bay, NY

**PATTEE** Nelson J. of Ft. Edward, NY              December 20, 1876
**HOWE** Mary Alice of Ft. Edward, NY               Sandy Hill, NY

**JENKINS** Zerah of Quaker St., NY                 December 20, 1876
**SWEET** Nellie of White Creek, NY                 White Creek, NY

**WHITE** H. of Whitehall, NY                       December 20, 1876
**MC FARLAND** Mrs. ____ of Salem, NY               Salem, NY

**STEVENSON** T. J. of Cortland, NY                 December 20, 1876
**BEEBE** Laura of Salem, NY                        Salem, NY

**TEFFT** John                                      December 20, 1876
**DILLON** Addie                                    Salem, NY

**GUARDEPHE** Eugene of Galesville, NY              November 4, 1876
**HOFFMAN** Laura of Galesville, NY                 Galesville, NY

**MC INTYRE** John of Columbia Co. NY               November 30, 1876
**PLINY** Jennie of Washington Co. NY               Galesville, NY

**COTTRELL** Henry C. of White Creek, NY            December 27, 1876
**CARPENTER** Lucinda E. of White Creek, NY         Eagle Bridge, NY

**WHIPPLE** Seneca of Summit, NY                    December 27, 1876
**BAKER** Arena of Pittstown, NY

**HILL** George of Bennington, Vt.                  December 23, 1876
**WARN** Ida of Bennington, Vt.                     White Creek, NY

| | |
|---|---|
| MOSHER Ira A. of Eagle Bridge, NY<br>CORNELL Ella F. of White Creek, NY | December 8, 1876 |
| MONROE Charles E.<br>BURCH Leonora | December 26, 1876<br>Granville, NY |
| PALMER Almond E. of S. Granville, NY<br>RAY Mary I. of N. Hebron, NY | December 24, 1876<br>Lake, NY |
| ARCHIBALD Andrew J. of Ft. Edward, NY<br>PHILLIPS Lizzie of Adams, NY | December 26, 1876<br>Adams, NY |
| BAUDOIN Frank of Ft. Ann, NY<br>DEAN Abby of Ft. Ann, NY | December 25, 1876<br>Ft. Ann, NY |
| RUNDELL Eugene of S. Cambridge, NY<br>CASS Ada of S. Cambridge, NY | January 1, 1877<br>S. Cambridge, NY |
| MC QUARRIE Daniel Jr. of Argyle, NY<br>OLDS Jennie of Argyle, NY | December 27, 1876<br>Ft. Edward, NY |
| HALL Barnes<br>KETCHUM Dilly | January 1, 1877<br>Argyle, NY |
| WILLETT John A. of Granville, NY<br>WILEY F. Allene of Granville, NY | December 20, 1876<br>N. Granville, NY |
| GRAHAM Oscar F. of Ft. Ann, NY<br>PARISH Roxanna M. of Ft. Ann, NY | January 1, 1877<br>Granville, NY |
| TRUMBULL John of Bald Mountain, NY<br>DYRON Katie of Bald Mountain, NY | January 21, 1877<br>Greenwich, NY |
| LOCKWOOD J. W.<br>BLANCHARD Anna Eliza formerly of Salem, NY | January 9, 1877<br>Saratoga, NY |
| KINNER Anthony of Whitehall, NY<br>HACKETT Maggie of Sandy Hill, NY | January 24, 1877<br>Sandy Hill, NY |
| STRAY Sidney M. of E. Lake George, NY<br>SEELYE Cynthia of Queensbury, NY | January 15, 1877<br>Queensbury, NY |
| CODNER Merritt of Queensbury, NY<br>WILKIE Helen L. of Queensbury, NY | January 17, 1877<br>Queensbury, NY |
| SKEELS James of Whitehall, NY<br>CULL Emma of Whitehall, NY | January 30, 1877<br>Whitehall, NY |
| SANBORN Charles C. of Schuylerville, NY | February 6, 1877 |

**REYNOLDS** S. Elizabeth of Greenwich, NY — Greenwich, NY

**BULL** Charles E.
**WILLIAMS** Abbie J.
January 31, 1877
Argyle, NY

**BENNETT** James
**SIMMONS** Mrs. May
January 28, 1877
Salem, NY

**KEYES** Hugh
**DENNISON** Maggie J. of W. Hebron, NY
January 24, 1877
W. Hebron, NY

**MONTEITH** John of Hebron, NY
**CONATY** Mary of Hebron, NY
January 19, 1877
S. Argyle, NY

**ROSE** Ebenezer of Shaftsbury, Vt.
**FRINK** Anna Eliza of N. Bennington, Vt.
January 22, 1877
Cambridge, NY

**O'CONNOR** Eugene of Sandy Hill, NY
**COX** Celia of Sandy Hill, NY
February 7, 1877
Sandy Hill, NY

**BEEBE** Norman
**STANLEY** Lena
February 6, 1877
Shushan, NY

**BEEBE** Thomas
**STANLEY** Nellie
February 6, 1877
Shushan, NY

**BULSON** Moses of Easton, NY (newspaper date)
**CRANDALL** Clementine E. of Greenwich, NY
February 22, 1877
Greenwich, NY

**ARNOLD** Alexander of Greenwich, NY
**SPENCER** Mrs. Emma of Greenwich, NY
February 21, 1877
Greenwich, NY

**RAINEY** Charles of Greenwich, NY
**DELAVERGNE** Mrs. Maria of Greenwich, NY
February 21, 1877
Greenwich, NY

**STEWART** David T. of Greenwich, NY
**REYNOLDS** Sarah A. of Greenwich, NY
February 22, 1877
Greenwich, NY

**BLAIR** James of Greenwich, NY
**GARDNER** Frank M. of Greenwich, NY
February 1, 1877
Greenwich, NY

**GREEN** David V. of Greenwich, NY
**STOVER** Eliza of Greenwich, NY
February 11, 1877
Greenwich, NY

**ORTON** Benjamin of Easton, NY
**VANDECAR** Eliza of Troy, NY
February 14, 1877

**LONG** Lucius L. of Greenwich, NY
**DEAN** Sarah F. of Ft. Ewell ?
December 17, 1876

LONG Thadeus of Greenwich, NY  
STOVER Lottie of Saratoga Springs, NY  
January 24, 1877  
Saratoga Spr., NY

HILL Wallace B. of Salem, NY  
EYERS E. of Saratoga, NY  
January 24, 1877  
Saratoga Spr., NY

BUCKLEY Franklin B. of Easton, NY  
GIFFORD Helen of Easton, NY  
February 14, 1877  
Easton, NY

LESTER Alfred of Sandy Hill, NY  
CLARK Florence of Sandy Hill, NY  
February 6, 1877  
Sandy Hill, NY

GOODSPEED Jerome B. of Wells, Vt.  
LAMB Adelia of Wells, Vt.  
February 13, 1877  
Wells, Vt.

HULLETT Rollin S. of Pawlet, Vt.  
CROSLEY Julia M. of Pawlet, Vt.  
February 14, 1877  
N. Granville, NY

MARTIN William L.  
OATMAN Lucy  
February 21, 1877  
Belcher, NY

ARCHIBALD S. Henry of Wallingford, Vt. (newspaper date) March 1, 1877  
NELSON Esther A. of W. Pawlet, Vt.  
W. Pawlet, Vt.

PHULSIPHER John A. of Cyuga, NY  
GRAHAM Catherine M. of Hartford, NY  
February 14, 1877  
Sandy Hill, NY

PARSONS William of Albany, NY  
LANDING Susie of Greenwich, NY  
February 13, 1877  
Easton, NY

BALL Wilson A. of Jackson, NY  
GOODRICH Lottie A. of Jackson, NY  
March 30, 1877  
Greenwich, NY

MOORE John A. of Salem, NY  
WEYMON Harriet C. of Salem, NY  
March 28, 1877  
Salem, NY

BAIN Alvin of Copake, NY  
DEVOE Lizzie of Valatie, NY  
March 19, 1877  
Valatie, NY

STRAIN Robert of Darien, Ga.  
WILDE Lizzie A. dau of Theodore  
March 21, 1877  
Valatie, NY

GILCHRIST Andrew  
ROOT Phebe M.  
March 29, 1877  
N. Argyle, NY

WEIR Sherman of Jackson, NY  
SHIELDS Maggie of Argyle, NY  
March 28, 1877  
Argyle, NY

SISSON George H. of White Creek, NY  
March 21, 1877

| | |
|---|---|
| **PALMER** Lottie P. of Cambridge, NY | Cambridge, NY |
| **LEDGERWOOD** Edgar of Putnam, NY<br>**LAW** Agnes Jennette of Albany, NY | April 5, 1877<br>Albany, NY |
| **BERNUM** Walter of Pittstown, NY<br>**BENTLEY** Cora M. of Cambridge, NY | April 10, 1877<br>Jackson, NY |
| **GRAW** John M.<br>**WELCH** Kate | April 24, 1877<br>Greenwich, NY |
| **GIBBS** George of Putnam, NY<br>**HALE** Marion of Putnam, NY | April 25, 1877<br>Putnam, NY |
| **BOWEN** Albert of Columbia Co. NY<br>**BARRELL** Mrs. Cyrus of S. Hartford, NY | April 26, 1877<br>S. Hartford, NY |
| **BROOKS** Melvin M. of Ft. Edward, NY<br>**MORGAN** Katherine J. of Ft. Edward, NY | May 7, 1877<br>Ft. Edward, NY |
| **CALHOUN** James H. of Greenwich, NY<br>**RICHARDS** Mary E. of Greenwich, NY | May 19, 1877<br>Greenwich, NY |
| **BALDWIN** Charles<br>**BARRY** Sarah M. formerly of Greenwich, NY | May 3, 1877<br>Chicago, Ill. |
| **MC BREEN** James of Wells, Vt.<br>**LEWIS** Edna of Wells, Vt. | May 13, 1877<br>Granville, NY |
| **BEECHER** John J. of S. Granville, NY<br>**LEE** Mary M. of S. Granville, NY | May 16, 1877<br>Granville, NY |
| **WHITNEY** Oliver H. of Maquoketa, Iowa<br>**TOOMEY** Frances C. of Greenwich, NY | June 6, 1877<br>Greenwich, NY |
| **OLMSTEAD** Rev. C. T. of Morley, NY<br>**DEUEL** Mary M. dau of George<br>(granddaughter of Walter **ROGERS** of Ft. Edward, NY) | May 24, 1877<br>Ft. Edward, NY |
| **HARPER** Frank of Ft. Edward, NY<br>**SHERWOOD** Lizzie | May 12, 1877<br>Milton, NY |
| **SAFFORD** John      (newspaper date)<br>**MOORE** Mary L. | June 7, 1877<br>N. Argyle, NY |
| **BULL** Zilphia D. of Ft. Edward, NY<br>**GREGORY** Addie L. of Ft. Edward, NY | May 28, 1877<br>Ft. Edward, NY |
| **INMAN** Eugene of Argyle, NY<br>**BURGESS** Ruth E. | June 2, 1877<br>Argyle, NY |

**JOHNSON** Milo D. of Whitehall, NY
**BROWN** Jennie M. of Whitehall, NY

June 10, 1877
Whitehall, NY

**MURCH** Nelson of Greenwich, NY
**BLAIR** Maggie of Greenwich, NY

July 7, 1877
Greenwich, NY

**CUTLER** Robert of Ft. Ann, NY
**CARTER** Minerva R. of Ft. Edward, NY

July 4, 1877
Argyle, NY

**CAMPBELL** William D.
**DEYOE** Mary J.

November 26, 1874
Cambridge, NY

**BARBER** W. E. of Schuylerville, NY
**LEWIS** Gertrude M. of Schuylerville, NY

July 16, 1877
N. Easton, NY

**ROBINSON** George H. of White Creek, NY
**PRATT** Emma of White Creek, NY

July 31, 1877
Cambridge, NY

**WILKINS** Clark N. of Dorset, Vt.
**MASON** Colinda of Dorset, Vt.

August 12, 1877
Salem, NY

**THOMPSON** W. B. of Cambridge, NY
**PARISH** Hettie of Ft. Edward, NY

August 18, 1877
Whitehall, NY

**KNAPP** Ephraim of E. Bennington, Vt.
**LYON** Mary Ann of E. Bennington, Vt.

August 21, 1877
Cambridge, NY

**RICE** John C. of Cambridge, NY
**WALKER** Libbie J. of Cambridge, NY

August 16, 1877
White Creek, NY

**MC LENITHEN** Charles of Woodford, Vt.
**EDDY** Cora of Woodford, Vt.

August 19, 1877
White Creek, NY

**COON** F. P. of Schuylerville, NY
**ROBBINS** Hattie A. of Stillwater, NY

August 22, 1877
Stillwater, NY

**LESTER** J. J. of Moses Kill, NY
**WILSON** Fannie of Sandy Hill, NY

August 18, 1877
Ft. Edward, NY

**CURTIS** Daniel A. of Schaghticoke, NY
**AUSTIN** Mary E. of Cambridge, NY

September 6, 1877
Greenwich, NY

**HAY** James of Greenwich, NY
**WOOD** Julia A. of Cambridge, NY

September 4, 1877
Cambridge, NY

**WRIGHT** Horace of Greenwich, NY
**HAY** Lota A. of Greenwich, NY

August 29, 1877
Salem, NY

**ESTES** William M. of Bennington, Vt.

August 27, 1877

**GREEN** Irene of Hoosick Falls, NY — White Creek, NY

**ABELL** Edrick S. of Greenwich, NY
**CUBIT** Annie A. of Greenwich, NY — September 13, 1877 Greenwich, NY

**SKELLIE** James E.
**MC CLELLAN** Hattie — September 11, 1877 Cambridge, NY

**BARNARD** Charles G. of Pittsford, Vt.
**COATS** Belle of Whitehall, NY — September 5, 1877 Whitehall, NY

**INGALLS** George of Whitehall, NY
**WELLS** Dollie of Whitehall, NY — September 7, 1877 Whitehall, NY

**ACKINS** William J.
**BARTHOLOMEW** Emma J. — September 5, 1877 Whitehall, NY

**BROWN** Lewis
**AMMOND** Eliza — September 1, 1877 Whitehall, NY

**SALMON** Lewis of Conklingville, NY
**DOW** Nettie of Thurman, NY — September 4, 1877 Sandy Hill, NY

**PRYOR** John G. of Easton, NY
**GAVETT** Mary Frances of Greenwich, NY — September 20, 1877 Greenwich, NY

**CROSBY** William H.
**NORTON** Etta B. of Granville, NY — September 13, 1877 Granville, NY

**BALDWIN** Hiram of Jackson, NY
**BAKER** Lucy of Jackson, NY — July 4, 1877 Albany, NY

**O'HERON** Michael
**DELANEY** Kate — September 12, 1877 Cambridge, NY

**BLAKEMAN** Merritt of Kingsbury, NY
**BECK** Janie of Ft. Edward, NY — September 12, 1877 Ft. Edward, NY

**MC KEE** Charles H. of Albany, NY
**ADAMS** Sarah L. of Whitehall, NY — September 12, 1877 Whitehall, NY

**STATIA** John J. of Sandy Hill, NY
**STEVENS** Kittie of Ft. Ann, NY — September 6, 1877 Ft. Ann, NY

**STEINSBY** Edward of Sandy Hill, NY
**HILL** Maggie E. of Sandy Hill, NY — September 14, 1877 Sandy Hill, NY

**HAMLIN** Lewis W. of Queensbury, NY
**HAMLIN** May E. of Glens Falls, NY — September 13, 1877 Sandy Hill, NY

DORSEY John S. of Hartford, NY
BAILEY May A. of Hartford, NY

September 18, 1877
Sandy Hill, NY

GOWER Charles J. of Glens Falls, NY
FISH Amy F. of Glens Falls, NY

September 16, 1877
Sandy Hill, NY

STEVENS Jerome of Ft. Ann, NY
LYNES Martha B. of Ft. Ann, NY

September 12, 1877
Ft. Ann, NY

HOGAN Michael of Poultney, Vt.
CAMPBELL Charlotte of Poultney, Vt.

September 20, 1877
Granville, NY

PIKE Franklin of Ft. Edward, NY
MORGAN Ella of Argyle, NY

Sept. 16/18, 1877

SPENCER Lyman J. of Easton, NY
HENRY Mary L. of Greenwich, NY

August 30, 1877

RAY Evans of Pittstown, NY
WHITE Emma of Pittstown, NY

August 29, 1877
Buskirks Br., NY

SHAW Charles of White Creek, NY
GOODELL Angelina of White Creek, NY

September 13, 1877
Buskirks Br., NY

BROWNELL Isaac W. of White Creek, NY
GIFFORD Hattie of Racine, Wis.

September 13, 1877
Racine, Wis.

HAGGART A. J. of Salem, NY
LANSING Jennie A. of Greenwich, NY

October 4, 1877
Greenwich, NY

DWIGHT Lyman of Whitehall, NY
ADAMS Mrs. Nancy of Carson City, Nev.

September 30, 1877
S. Hero, Vt.

REED Charles son of L. S. of Valley Falls, NY
RAY Ada of Tomhannock, NY

September 26, 1877
Tomhannock, NY

PRIEST William W. of Camden, NY
LE BARRON Jennie of Shushan, NY

September 27, 1877
Cambridge, NY

FOSTER Thomas
MC CLINTOCK Ellen

September 24, 1877
Salem, NY

SAFFORD Charles
WILLARD Mrs. Eunice A.

September 20, 1877

KIPP Charles E. of Easton, NY
HEWITT Martha of Moores Forks, NY

September 29, 1877
Greenwich, NY

DENNIS Henry E. of Shushan, NY

October 2, 1877

**WAIT** Mrs. Mary A. of Shushan, NY

Greenwich, NY

**BARBER** Joseph W.
**FISHER** Julia E.

October 10, 1877
Greenwich, NY

**WILTSEY** Myron
**SLOCUM** Hattie

October 10, 1877

**BRADLEY** John C. of Ft. Edward, NY
**BAKER** Fannie of Ft. Edward, NY

October 11, 1877
Cambridge, NY

**KEECH** Ortie C. of Ft. Ann, NY
**KEECH** Nonie of Ft. Ann, NY

October 10, 1877
Sandy Hill, NY

**PECK** Henry J. of Hampton, NY
**SMITH** Hattie L. of Sandgate, Vt.

October 3, 1877
Sandgate, Vt.

**WEIR** Delevan B. of Greenwich, NY
**RICKERT** Maggie A. of Easton, NY

October 17, 1877
Greenwich, NY

**MC MILLAN** Robert A. of Argyle, NY
**MC EACHRON** Maggie Bell of Argyle, NY

October 23, 1877
Argyle, NY

**MEADER** Robert of Easton, NY
**KING** Charlotte Jane of White Creek, NY

September 1, 1877
Shushan, NY

**MORSE** George A. of Granville, NY
**HEATH** Sarah A. of Granville, NY

October 14, 1877
N. Granville, NY

**MARVIN** Henry of W. Hebron, NY
**GILLETTE** Frances A. of W. Hebron, NY

October 17, 1877
Belcher, NY

**LLOYD** F. of Schuylerville, NY
**MAYERS** Flora of Schuylerville, NY

October 10, 1877
Easton, NY

**GROFF** F. G. of Tonowanda, NY
**SPOONER** Flora of Whitehall, NY

October 22, 1877
Whitehall, NY

**NORTON** Reuben F.
**TENSE** Carrie

October 29, 1877
Whitehall, NY

**MACKENZIE** O. of Albany, NY
**EDSON** Lillie S. of Greenwich, NY

July 3, 1877
Troy, NY

**OWENS** John of California
**GRIFFIN** Eleanor of Easton, NY

October 24, 1877
Easton, NY

**WEAVER** Eugene A. of Bolton, NY
**CLARK** Martha F. of Ft. Ann, NY

October 28, 1877
Ft. Ann, NY

**LAVANA** Arthur of Jackson, NY
**PRATT** Rosa of White Creek, NY

October 28, 1877
Jackson, NY

**BRIGGS** Eugene of California
**WRIGHT** Frankie of Easton, NY

November 7, 1877
Easton, NY

**WITBECK** Harvey of Minnesota
**STRAIGHT** Lydia of Hartford, NY

November 14, 1877
Hartford, NY

**HAY** James of Lake, NY
**BROWN** Sarah of Lake, NY

November 14, 1877
Lake, NY

**AUSTIN** Ebenezer          (newspaper date)
**JENKINS** Flora L.

November 29, 1877
Cambridge, NY

**EDWARDS** John W. of Granville, NY
**DAVIS** Jane of M. Granville, NY

November 8, 1877
M. Granville, NY

**SHILAND** Wallace J. of Youngstown, Oh. formerly Coila
**KENNEDY** Jessie of Youngstown, Ohio

November 15, 1877
Youngstown, Ohio

**CARR** Frederick of Greenbush, NY
**RIFENBURG** Fannie of Sandy Hill, NY

November 8, 1877
Sandy Hill, NY

**DUFFY** Charles
**GLYNN** Sabina

November 28, 1877
Whitehall, NY

**MC LACKLIN** James
**DUFFY** Jennie

November 29, 1877
Whitehall, NY

**SMITH** Albert of Sandy Hill, NY
**STARRETT** Mary J. of Sandy Hill, NY

November 21, 1877
Glens Falls, NY

**WHITTAKER** Phillip A. of the Glen, NY
**JACKSON** Martha of Moreau, NY

November 22, 1877
Moreau, NY

**WELCH** Frederick
**HUDSON** Caroline

November 25, 1877
Ft. Miller, NY

**PATTEN** Oscar of Ft. Ann, NY
**MOSIER** Fanny P. of Whitehall, NY

December 3, 1877
Argyle, NY

**GROAT** Ally of Auburn, NY
**COTTRELL** Frank of Greenwich, NY

December 12, 1877
Greenwich, NY

**BARR** H. H. of Dresden, NY
**SHANNON** Lenora of Argyle, NY

November 30, 1877
Louisville, Ky.

**EYCLESHYMER** Herbert

October 24, 1877

**HENRY** Alida M.     Eagle Bridge, NY

**CULVER** John S. of Greenwich, NY     December 10, 1877
**ROBINSON** Emma of Galesville, NY     Greenwich, NY

**HERRINGTON** Russell     December 12, 1877
**BOSWORTH** Jennie F. of Pittstown, NY     Pittstown, NY

**LOWSEN** Frank A. of Hoosick, NY     November 29, 1877
**HAVILAND** Emma of Pittstown, NY     Pittstown, NY

**MINCKLER** John W. of Grand Isle, Vt.     December 10, 1877
**MURPHY** Anna E. of Sandy Hill, NY     Sandy Hill, NY

**COOPER** Henry S.     December 8, 1877
**KIRKHAM** Ellen     Sandy Hill, NY

**HURD** Nathan H. of Gansevort, NY     December 2, 1877
**SMITH** Lila of Gansevort, NY     Sandy Hill, NY

**BARDEN** Asahel of Argyle, NY    (newspaper date)    December 27, 1877
**CUTLER** A. M.     Ghent, NY

**BEATTIE** John J.     December 19, 1877
**TOWNSEND** Eva     Salem, NY

**DORVAL** Alphonzo Md. of Whitehall, NY     December 17, 1877
**SMITH** Estella M. of Whitehall, NY     Whitehall, NY

**JOHNSON** Allen E. of Greenwich, NY     January 1, 1878
**GIFFORD** H. Louise of Easton, NY     Easton, NY

**MARTIN** Frank of N. Hoosick, NY     December 25, 1877
**SMITH** Elizabeth of Hoosick Falls, NY     Cambridge, NY

**WORDEN** Benjamin A. of Hoosick Falls, NY     December 25, 1877
**HALE** Ida J. of Hoosick Falls, NY     Cambridge, NY

**GALUSHA** Reuben H. of Ft. Miller, NY     December 26, 1877
**WEAVER** Helen M. of Schuylerville, NY     Schuylerville, NY

**THOMPSON** George B. of Bacon Hill, NY     December 13, 1877
**HENRY** Sarah E. Delle

**GERMAIN** Bony of Ft. Miller, NY     January 1, 1878
**GALUSHA** Allie of Ft. Miller, NY     Ft. Miller, NY

**FULLER** Mr. \_\_\_\_ of Gansevort, NY     December 25, 1877
**FLYNN** Nellie of Ft. Ann, NY     Ft. Ann, NY

| | |
|---|---|
| **WOOD** Albert | December 24, 1877 |
| **NUTTING** Jennie | Cambridge, NY |
| | |
| **SHELDON** George L. G. of Easton, NY | December 25, 1877 |
| **CRANDALL** Ella of Easton, NY | |
| | |
| **CORLISS** A. T. of Easton, NY | January 1, 1878 |
| **COLLAMER** Hettie E. of Easton, NY | Easton, NY |
| | |
| **JOSLIN** Edward A. of Hoosick, NY | January 1, 1878 |
| **KIPP** Minerva A. of Pittstown, NY | Pittstown, NY |
| | |
| **WILLIAMSON** Thomas F. of Greenwich, NY | January 16, 1878 |
| **REYNOLDS** Hattie N. of Greenwich, NY | Greenwich, NY |
| | |
| **WELCH** Charles of Schuylerville, NY | January 1, 1878 |
| **SULLIVAN** Anna of Schuylerville, NY | Greenwich, NY |
| | |
| **MC ARTHUR** James L. of Granville, NY | January 15, 1878 |
| **LEWIS** Anna of Granville, NY | Granville, NY |
| | |
| **NICHOLSON** Stephen of Forteville, NY | December 31, 1877 |
| **BACHELOR** Jennie of W. Ft. Ann, NY | W. Ft. Ann, NY |
| | |
| **WELLS** Harris A. of Wilton, NY | January 3, 1878 |
| **IDE** Hettie E. of Wilton, NY | Wilton, NY |
| | |
| **HURD** Charles | December 31, 1877 |
| **LUNDIGRUN** Nellie | Granville, NY |
| | |
| **COOPER** James | January 1, 1878 |
| **HORTON** Esther | N. Granville, NY |
| | |
| **DENNISON** Andrew Jr. of Hebron, NY | January 1, 1878 |
| **DICKSON** Loretta of Hebron, NY | Hebron, NY |
| | |
| **HEATH** Eugene B. of Shushan, NY | January 12, 1878 |
| **CLARK** Anna of Shushan, NY | Shushan, NY |
| | |
| **BEVERIDGE** James A. | December 20, 1877 |
| **SANDERS** Frances E. | S. Argyle, NY |
| | |
| **HARRINGTON** Clarence of Easton, NY | January 27, 1878 |
| **TEFFT** Sarah A. of Easton, NY | Greenwich, NY |
| | |
| **LANSING** G. V. P. | January 30, 1878 |
| **LANSING** Caroline M. | Greenwich, NY |
| | |
| **WILLIAMSON** Elias of Greenwich, NY | February 6, 1878 |

PETTEYS Helen J. of Greenwich, NY                                      Greenwich, NY

SPENCE David                    (newspaper date)      February 7, 1878
ALLEN Mary Ann                                        N. Argyle, NY

COPELAND James                                        January 16, 1878
MC DOUGAL Mary Frances                                N. Argyle, NY

BURTON Willard E.                                     January 17, 1878
PARKERSON Ida E.                                      N. Argyle, NY

RICHARDS James of Whitehall, NY                       January 24, 1878
COATS Mary of Whitehall, NY                           Whitehall, NY

HARWOOD James of Washington, Iowa                     January 25, 1878
FISHER Elizabeth of Greenwich, NY                     Greenwich, NY

BACHELDER A. G. of W. Ft. Ann, NY                     January 16, 1878
PATTERSON Alice M. of W. Ft. Ann, NY                  Pattens Mills, NY

SHAW Robert of Salem, NY                              January 22, 1878
STEWART Sarah M. of Argyle, NY                        Argyle, NY

FOSTER Frank P. of Greenwich, NY                      January 24, 1878
RALSTON Mary A. of Greenwich, NY                      Salem, NY

BARBER Leverett of Dresden, NY                        January 22, 1878
BARTLETT Sarah of Dresden, NY                         Dresden, NY

HERBERT George H. of Albany, NY                       January 31, 1878
PARKS Mrs. Mary M. of E. Whitehall, NY                E. Whitehall, NY

HAXTON H. F. of E. Cambridge, NY                      February 6, 1878
WEATHERWAX Mary F. of Cambridge, NY                   Cambridge, NY

JOHNSON E. P. of Sandy Hill, NY                       January 23, 1878
BROWNELL Clara of Troy, NY                            Troy, NY

BABCOCK Benjamin of Easton, NY                        January 1, 1878
HILL Priscilla J. L. of Schuylerville, NY             Schuylerville, NY

HOPKINS Joseph H.                                     February 20, 1878
DURKEE Mrs. Nettie                                    Durkeetown, NY

KELLEY Adelbert H. of Westhaven, Vt.                  February 13, 1878
BARTHOLOMEW Laura A. of Whitehall, NY                 Granville, NY

BETTS Howard H. of Brooklyn, NY                       January 30, 1878
VANDERWALKER Clara formerly of Whitehall, NY          Elizabethtown, NJ

STEVENS Abner of South Bay, NY  February 10, 1878
WASHBURN Francella of Welch Hollow, NY  Ft. Ann, NY

BAIN James W. of Argyle, NY  February 14, 1878
MULLEN Maggie of Argyle, NY  Greenwich, NY

WHELDON John H. of Easton, NY  February 26, 1878
WILCOX Jennie E. of Greenwich, NY  Greenwich, NY

DE LONG Miles H.  February 21, 1878
DE LONG Harriet O.  Greenwich, NY

CONWAY John of Greenwich, NY  March 5, 1878
KENNEDY Jennie of Greenwich, NY  Greenwich, NY

CENTER B. E.  March 6, 1878
MILKS Anna  Valley Falls, NY

REDFERN M. of Ft. Edward, NY  November 7, 1877
HILLMAN Ella J. of Troy, NY  Glen's Falls, NY

HOPE Joseph of Whitehall, NY  February 24, 1878
CASE Zozia of Whitehall, NY  Whitehall, NY

YARTER Imville of Sandy Hill, NY  February 20, 1878
BARKER Ida May of Ft. Ann, NY  Ft. Ann, NY

INGALLS Charles of Westhaven, Vt.  February 20, 1878
BENJAMIN Mary F. of Dresden, NY  Dresden, NY

FAYHEY Thomas  February 26, 1878
HUGHES Bridget of Cambridge, NY  Cambridge, NY

AYRES George J. of Hebron, NY  February 17, 1878
WOODWARD Ida May of Pottersville, NY  Chester, NY

MC DONNELL Patrick of Cambridge, NY  February 19, 1878
KEARNS Mary of Boston, Mass.  Boston, Mass.

ORTON Fred of Williamstown, Mass.  March 2, 1878
BAIN Emma E. of Greenwich, NY  Lake, NY

TUBBS Albert A. of Ft. Miller, NY  March 7, 1878
MOSNIER Alice E. of Greenwich, NY  Lake, NY

REDDING Frank H. of Poultney, Vt.  February 20, 1878
MORRISON Emma L. of N. Granville, NY  N. Granville, NY

LADUE Patrick  March 4, 1878

| | |
|---|---|
| **DALTON** Mary | M. Granville, NY |
| | |
| **BETTS** Morgan of Easton, NY | February 2_, 1878 |
| **DARROW** Mary J. of Easton, NY | N. Easton, NY |
| | |
| **GREGORY** Edward of Dresden, NY | March 3, 1878 |
| **GRANGER** Phebe Jane of Ft. Ann, NY | Dresden, NY |
| | |
| **WILCOX** Enos of Greenwich, NY | March 18, 1878 |
| **NEIL** Kate formerly of Easton, NY | Warsaw, NY |
| | |
| **MASON** George A. of Cambridge, NY | March 4, 1878 |
| **CARR** Lula M. of Washington DC | Washington DC |
| | |
| **FLAGLER** Fred of Hartford, NY | February 20, 1878 |
| **DUERS** Esther of Queensbury, NY | Sandy Hill, NY |
| | |
| **BREEN** Patrick of Glens Falls, NY | February 26, 1878 |
| **GENERIN?** Nora of Smiths Basin, NY | Sandy Hill, NY |
| | |
| **RODGERS** George H. of Argyle, NY | March 6, 1878 |
| **DOWNS** Sarah L. of Ft. Edward, NY | Ft. Edward, NY |
| | |
| **KELLOGG** Eben of Jackson, NY | February 28, 1878 |
| **WASHBURN** Eudora of Jackson, NY | Jackson, NY |
| | |
| **STEELE** Daniel T. | March 13, 1878 |
| **BROWN** Georgia B. dau of Rev. Hugh Brown | Shushan, NY |
| | |
| **RICE** R. N. of Cambridge, NY | March 12, 1878 |
| **MOTSIFF** Mary A. of Cambridge, NY | Cambridge, NY |
| | |
| **TRACY** Nathan J. of Dresden, NY (newspaper date) | March 21, 1878 |
| **SLOAN** Hattie J. of Ft. Ann, NY | Ft. Ann, NY |
| | |
| **BYINGTON** J. Storrs of Galveston Tx. | March 12, 1878 |
| **NORTHUP** Mattie E. of Sandy Hill, NY | New York City |
| | |
| **DINNE** Charles | March 18, 1878 |
| **MINELE** Ellen | Whitehall, NY |
| | |
| **HARVEY** Joel of Ft. Ann, NY | March 13, 1878 |
| **WILLIAMS** Sarah of Ausable Forks, NY | N. Granville, NY |
| | |
| **TABER** Charles E. of Easton, NY | April 3, 1878 |
| **JOHNSTON** Sarah E. of Greenwich, NY | Greenwich, NY |
| | |
| **STARKS** Charles of Comstock, NY | March 18, 1878 |
| **HALL** Carrie of Ft. Ann, NY | Comstock, NY |

PARKER George of Granville, NY
DAY Abbie of Granville, NY

March 16, 1878
Hartford, NY

HARRINGTON Warren W. of Ft. Edward, NY
GOODFELLOW Hattie E. of Ft. Edward, NY

March 26, 1878
Ft. Edward, NY

CAMPBELL William of W. Ft. Ann, NY
BAILEY Minnie of W. Ft. Ann, NY

March 27, 1878
W. Ft. Ann, NY

WYMAN William of Kanes Falls, NY
BAIN Ella of Kanes Falls, NY

March 30, 1878
Ft. Ann, NY

WHITE James of Greenwich, NY
DOUGHTY Mary of Schuylerville, NY

April 9, 1878
Saratoga Spr., NY

WOOD Charles F. of Whitehall, NY
REED Irena D. of Whitehall, NY

March 27, 1878
Whitehall, NY

ROBERTSON Alvin
QUA Maggie A. of Cambridge, NY

March 4, 1878
Cambridge, NY

ARNOTT Robert of Jackson, NY
CRANDALL Frankie Cornelia of Bellport, NY

March 28, 1878
Coila, NY

ROBINSON Thomas                    (newspaper date)
MILLER Aurie

April 18, 1878
Ft. Ann, NY

CULVER Seth E. of Pawlet, Vt.
FAXON Kittie A. of Hartford, NY .

April 8, 1878
Sandy Hill, NY

GRIFFIN Orlon
WILTSEY Sarah of Adamsville, NY

March 25, 1878
Hartford, NY

MC MILLAN William
LIVINGSTON Sarah A.

April 4, 1878
Argyle, NY

WILSON George of Cambridge, NY
WINN Anna of Cambridge, NY

April 17, 1878
Cambridge, NY

CAREY Millard of Schuylerville, NY
SHELDON Katie C. of Easton, NY

March 3, 1878
Easton, NY

RUSSELL Michael M. of Ft. Edward, NY
BUSENO Angie

April 22, 1878
Sandy Hill, NY

TEFFT John of Ft. Edward, NY
SULLIVAN Maggie of Ft. Edward, NY

April 23, 1878
Ft. Edward, NY

DONALDSON Samuel H.

April 21, 1878

**BECKWITH** Lois                                              Whitehall, NY

**WATERS** William                                            April 24, 1878
**BISHOP** Hattie F.                                          Cambridge, NY

**CLARK** Edward E.                                           April 25, 1878
**MARTIN** Lizzie dau of James E. of St. Paul, Minn.          Sandy Hill, NY

**HOWK** Horace P. of Comstocks, NY                           April 21, 1878
**MILLER** Melissa A. of Comstocks, NY                        Sandy Hill, NY

**MOORE** William of Schuylerville, NY                        April 23, 1878
**CLARK** Martha of Victory Mills, NY                         Victory Mills, NY

**PRATT** Frank L.                                            April 21, 1878
**BENSON** Julia                                              N. Easton, NY

**GLEASON** Alonzo of Greenwich, NY                           May 13, 1878
**ROBINSON** Abbie of Greenwich, NY                           Greenwich, NY

**STEVES** Robert of Ft. Ann, NY                              April 24, 1878
**PINE** Ann of Ft. Ann, NY                                   Ft. Ann, NY

**RYAN** John of Saratoga Springs, NY                         May 3, 1878
**BRAYTON** Mrs. Harriet A. of Saratoga Springs, NY           Ft. Edward, NY

**GUARDEPHE** Modesta of Glens Falls, NY                      April 25, 1878
**KNAPP** Alma A. of Moreau, NY                               Moreau, NY

**LOVETT** Frank of Saratoga, NY                              April 26, 1878
**BEEBE** Ada of Easton, NY

**CONGDON** Willard of Hartford, NY                           May 14, 1878
**WELCH** Ellen of Hartford, NY                               Ft. Edward, NY

**STRATTON** Asille of Bennington, Vt.                        May 7, 1878
**WOODARD** Alida of Shaftsbury, Vt.                          White Creek, NY

**BROWNELL** John H. of Easton, NY                            May 16, 1878
**BAILEY** Mrs. Amy A. of S. Cambridge, NY                    N. Easton, NY

**SCOTT** William E. of Granville, NY                         May 18, 1878
**TAYLOR** Carrie of Granville, NY                            Granville, NY

**WOODARD** George W. of Dorset, Vt.                          May 21, 1878
**TOBIN** Lamira of Dorset, Vt.                               Granville, NY

**THOMPSON** James A. of Greenwich, NY    (newspaper date) May 30, 1878
**HENDERSON** Mary E. of Greenwich, NY

| | |
|---|---|
| **THOMPSON** O. F. | May 18, 1878 |
| **AMIDON** Sarah A. | Granville, NY |
| | |
| **MC DOUGAL** William of Gloversville, NY | May 2, 1878 |
| **DURKEE** Nellie of Gloversville, NY | Gloversville, NY |
| | |
| **WILLARD** A. Irving of Cambridge, NY | May 22, 1878 |
| **BLANCHARD** Julia A. of Jackson, NY | Jackson, NY |
| | |
| **GREEN** Sanford | May 1, 1878 |
| **WILCOX** Mary A. formerly of Greenwich, NY | Fox Lake, Wis. |
| | |
| **DURKEE** Charles | May 25, 1878 |
| **PIKE** Eunice | Sandy Hill, NY |
| | |
| **SMITH** John B. of Pownal, Vt. | June 1, 1878 |
| **AMES** Louisa of Pownal, Vt. | Pownal, Vt. |
| | |
| **REED** Edward of Glens Falls, NY | June 1, 1878 |
| **NORTON** M. Emma of Glens Falls, NY | Glens Falls, NY |
| | |
| **JULIUS** Joseph of Hampton, NY | May 30, 1878 |
| **OSMORE** Helen Madora of Fairhaven, Vt. | Putnam, NY |
| | |
| **BACHELDER** Nathan of Hampton, NY (newspaper date) | June 20, 1878 |
| **BOSWORTH** Myra L. of Fairhaven, Vt. | Albany, NY |
| | |
| **HALYARD** William A. of Greenwich, NY | June 11, 1878 |
| **ST PAUL** Anna M. of Red Hook, NY | Red Hook, NY |
| | |
| **DURYEA** A. of Rochester, Minn. | June 13, 1878 |
| **HILLMAN** Alice formerly of Jackson, NY | Rochester, Minn. |
| | |
| **BROWN** John A. of Columbus, Ohio (newspaper date) | June 27, 1878 |
| **GRISWOLD** Mary J. of Whitehall, NY | Whitehall, NY |
| | |
| **HAY** Merritt C. | June 14, 1878 |
| **WILLIAMS** Catherine of M. Granville, NY | M. Granville, NY |
| | |
| **HURNISTANE** C. A. of Westhaven, Vt. | June 19, 1878 |
| **ROWE** Mary of Fairhaven, Vt. | Granville, NY |
| | |
| **STEVENS** D. of Glens Falls, NY | June 23, 1878 |
| **WALES** Ida of Glens Falls, NY | Sandy Hill, NY |
| | |
| **VENDEE** H. L. of Rutland, Vt. | June 26, 1878 |
| **BRIEN** Nellie of Hydesville, NY | Hydesville, NY |
| | |
| **BROWNELL** Preserved of Easton, NY | July 14, 1878 |

**WHIPPLE** Mary E. of Easton, NY

N. Easton, NY

**HOPE** James Douglas of Watkins, NY
**AKESTER** Emma Jane of Roxham, Quebec

July 11, 1878
Troy, NY

**LADEAUX** George of Sandy Hill, NY
**PATNODE** Mary A. of Sandy Hill, NY

July 8, 1878
Sandy Hill, NY

**WESTCOTT** Clark H. of Ft. Ann, NY
**MAYFIELD** Aseneth J. of Ft. Ann, NY

June 9, 1878

**POST** David E. of N. Granville, NY
**OSBORN** Hattie M. of Hamilton ?

July 3, 1878
Hamilton ?

**DE RIDDER** B. S. of Schuylerville, NY
**COLE** Martha A. of Troy, NY

July 10, 1878
Schuylerville, NY

**GATES** Charles of White Creek, NY
**BEAGLE** Edith of Bennington, Vt.

July 18, 1878
White Creek, NY

**JOHNSON** S. E. of Ft. Edward, NY
**SMITH** Maggie A. of Ft. Edward, NY

July 23, 1878
Ft. Edward, NY

**SIMMONS** Joseph E. of Ft. Edward, NY
**STODDARD** Lizzie of Boston, Mass.

July 17, 1878
Arlington Heights

**CARPENTER** B. L. of Tinmouth, Vt.
**WING** M. A. of Clarendon Springs, Vt.

July 16, 1878
Granville, NY

**INGALLS** Fred H. of Crown Point, NY
**MC GHEE** Minnie O. of Whitehall, NY

July 28, 1878
Whitehall, NY

**KEECH** Bony of Ft. Ann, NY          (newspaper date)
**HOAG** Julia A. of Ft. Ann, NY

August 8, 1878
W. Ft. Ann, NY

**SMITH** C. E. of Cambridge, NY
**SHORTT** M. Alma of Cambridge, NY

August 1, 1878
Cambridge, NY

**PHOENIX** William of Whitehall, NY
**ROUSE** Emelia of Whitehall, NY

August 11, 1878
Whitehall, NY

**FOURNIER** Hourniadas of Whitehall, NY
**SAWYER** Suzanne of Whitehall, NY

August 10, 1878
Whitehall, NY

**PALMER** Earl of W. Ft. Ann, NY
**RIPLEY** Louise of W. Ft. Ann, NY

August 15, 1878
Ft. Edward, NY

**MAXFIELD** George of Ft. Ann, NY
**STEVENS** Fanny J. of Ft. Ann, NY

August 4, 1878
Lake George, NY

WINEHALL Jenks L. of New York City
FISH Elizabeth May dau of Chauncey of Fairhaven Vt.
August 15, 1878
Fairhaven, Vt.

PORTER Geraldo of Danby, Vt.
HEWLETT Addie of Danby, Vt.
August 21, 1878
Granville, NY

GURLEY Lewis E. of Troy, NY
BROWN Louisa A. dau of William formerly of Ft. Edward
August 21, 1878
Newport, NY

WHITNEY Judson of Owego, NY
HOAG Frank A. of S. Easton, NY
September 3, 1878
S. Easton, NY

HASKELL William of Lansingburgh, NY
FERGUSON Mattie H. of S. Argyle, NY
September 4, 1878
S. Argyle, NY

COMISKEE James of Bacon Hill, NY
MULQUEEN Mary of Schuylerville, NY
August 22, 1878
Schuylerville, NY

CARTER Robert
ROBINSON Matildy
August 22, 1878
Argyle, NY

SOPER Kingsley of Ft. Edward, NY
PARTRIDGE Martha of Ft. Edward, NY
August 8, 1878
Ft. Ann, NY

GILCHRIST A. W. of Hartford, NY
WARD Martha of M. Granville, NY
September 5, 1878
M. Granville, NY

LOBDELL Charles E. of W. Troy, NY
HASKELL Lena M. of Greenwich, NY
September 18, 1878
Greenwich, NY

LADUSCO Alfred
OGDEN Elizabeth of Victory Mills, NY
September 13, 1878
Greenwich, NY

MEADER Lorenzo
DUNIVAN Cornelia of Easton, NY
September 18, 1878
Greenwich, NY

BILLINGS Edward of Montana
FOSTER Mary of Whitehall, NY
September 17, 1878
Whitehall, NY

COLLINS E. A. of Whitehall, NY
HALL Anna of Whitehall, NY
September 11, 1878
Whitehall, NY

COCAKLY James of Victory Mills, NY
ROGERS Emma of Schuylerville, NY
September 11, 1878
Schuylerville, NY

KENDRICK Frederick E. of Troy, NY
GIFFORD Annie of Johnsonville, NY
September 4, 1878
Johnsonville, NY

ATWOOD Arthur G. of Hoosick Falls, NY
September 11, 1878

NORTON Edna of Cambridge, NY	Cambridge, NY

HOWLAND Stephen of Ft. Edward, NY	August 14, 1878
WORFOLK Minnie of Cleveland, Ohio	Cleveland, Ohio

HALL Roswell of Glens Falls, NY	(newspaper date)	September 19, 1878
SHERRILL Annie of Sandy Hill, NY	Sandy Hill, NY

MOSHER Edwin of Schaghticoke, NY	September 24, 1878
HUTTON Josephine of Easton, NY	Easton, NY

TREMBLY John of Victory, NY	September 2, 1878
JOHNSON Emma of Schuylerville, NY	Easton, NY

WILLIAMS John H. of Saratoga Springs, NY	September 2, 1878
CAREY Alice of Schuylerville, NY	Easton, NY

ALLEN Henry C.	September 11, 1878
HUTCHINGS Leah J.	White Creek, NY

GILBERT George J. of Salem, NY	September 5, 1878
ROBERTS Julia Ann dau of Dexter of Manchester, Vt.	Manchester, Vt.

MANVILLE John J. of Whitehall, NY	(newspaper date)	October 3, 1878
HOYT Ida E. dau of James A. of Saratoga Springs, NY	Saratoga Spr., NY

NICHOLS George J. of Hoosick Falls, NY	October 9, 1878
SMITH Emma of Greenwich, NY	Greenwich, NY

GOODRO Frederick of Whitehall, NY	October 3, 1878
VARICY Addie of Whitehall, NY	Whitehall, NY

NEWTON Warren of Kingsbury, NY	October 3, 1878
FAXON Helen of Kingsbury, NY

KNAPP Fred of Ft. Edward, NY	September 2, 1878
HAMMOND Jennie of Ft. Edward, NY	Ft. Edward, NY

BARRY Patrick of Whitehall, NY	October 1, 1878
COLLINS Anna of Whitehall, NY	Whitehall, NY

BROWN C. J. of Castleton, Vt.	September 29, 1878
DAVIS Addie of Castleton, Vt.	Hampton, NY

ALLEN Rhodes F. of Vly Summit, NY	October 1, 1878
BADGER Mary F. of W. Cambridge, NY	Coila, NY

ELTZROTH W. F. of Lebanon, Ohio	September 24, 1878
WILSON Nellie F. of Sandy Hill, NY	Sandy Hill, NY

**BARRINGTON** Sylvester of Troy, NY
**COTTER** Mary E. of Ft. Ann, NY

October 13, 1878
Ft. Ann, NY

**BLANCHARD** John of Whitehall, NY
**SAWYER** Julia of Whitehall, NY

October 7, 1878
Whitehall, NY

**ABEEL** E. S.
**BARTLETT** Frances dau of Joseph of Greenwich, NY

October 23, 1878
Greenwich, NY

**ROSE** Charles of Ft. Ann, NY
**MEAD** Ella of Ft. Ann, NY

October 15, 1878
Ft. Ann, NY

**RICE** Charles Eddy formerly of Cambridge, NY
**BISSELL** Jennie of Stockton, Cal.

September 10, 1878
Stockton, Cal.

**SMITH** Henry of Cape Vincent, NY
**HYDE** Addie of Sandy Hill, NY

October 5, 1878
Sandy Hill, NY

**ASHLEY** William A. of Ft. Edward, NY
**LEWIS** Mrs C. of Ft. Edward, NY

October 9, 1878
Ft. Edward, NY

**ELLIS** William E. of Argyle, NY
**BELL** Lydia A. of Ft. Edward, NY

October 8, 1878
Ft. Edward, NY

**HODGE** A. of S. Hartford, NY
**SANDERSON** Hattie M. of Chaumont, NY

September 9, 1878
Chaumont, NY

**MARCH** Daniel Jr. of Pittsburg, Pa.
**STEVENSON** Jennie H. of Cambridge, NY

October 3, 1878
Pittsfield, Mass.

**MC KENNA** Daniel of Victory Mills, NY
**MULLEN** Ann of Victory Mills, NY

October 12, 1878

**DUMAS** Lewis of Victory Mills, NY
**RIVETT** Lena of Victory Mills, NY

October 3, 1878
Schuylerville, NY

**PRINDLE** John of Victory Mills, NY
**PRINTER** Maggie of Schuylerville, NY

October 10, 1878
Schuylerville, NY

**BILLINGS** William of Westhaven, Vt.
**MANCHESTER** Lydia E. dau of L.

October 23, 1878
Hampton, NY

**BROWN** Luther of Benson, Vt.
**GRINNELL** Mary E. of Benson, Vt.

October 30, 1878
Ft. Edward, NY

**TEMPLE** Orris
**WARREN** Angie

October 23, 1878
Granville, NY

**KINGSLEY** Freeland of Comstocks, NY

October 23, 1878

**HAYES** Mary E. of Peru, NY

N. Granville, NY

**MAYO** Jerry of Pawlet, Vt.
**COOK** Emma J. of N. Hebron, NY

October 22, 1878
Salem, NY

**CHAPMAN** Charles of Northumberland, NY
**BURT** Addie dau of Stephen J. of Northumberland, NY

October 16, 1878

**NORSE** Melvin H. of Winhall, Vt.
**SHATTUCK** Jane E. of Winhall, Vt.

November 6, 1878
Cambridge, NY

**CALVIN** Ervin of Smiths Basin, NY
**LOVELACE** Addie of Glens Falls, NY

November 8, 1878
N. Granville, NY

**SISSON** Walter M. of White Creek, NY
**WAIT** Mary L. of Easton, NY

November 20, 1878
Easton, NY

**REA** Robert T. of Brooklyn, NY
**MC NULTY** Sarah J. formerly of Ft. Ann, NY

November 11, 1878
Brooklyn, NY

**SMITH** James F. of S. Hartford, NY
**HARVEY** Minnie E. dau of Capt. T. D. Harvey

November 13, 1878
Ticonderoga, NY

**ALMY** Andrew of Easton, NY
**THOMPSON** Nora of Easton, NY

November 27, 1878
Easton, NY

**KELLIE** Charles
**HEWITT** Hattie of N. Greenwich, NY

November 10, 1878
Schuylerville, NY

**DOTY** Byron L. of Glens Falls, NY
**WEBSTER** Jennie of Catskill, NY

November 26, 1878
Ft. Edward, NY

**SHAW** Benjamin F. of Glens Falls, NY
**PEARSON** Cora A. of Ft. Edward, NY

November 28, 1878
Ft. Edward, NY

**WELCH** Edward C. of N. Chatham, NY
**HEART** Lillie E. of Schuylerville, NY

November 27, 1878
Schuylerville, NY

**DAY** Finton W. of Sandy Hill, NY
**KILLIAN** Dora of Sandy Hill, NY

November 27, 1878
Sandy Hill, NY

**CARNEY** Patrick
**SHEVLIN** Rose

November 27, 1878
Sandy Hill, NY

**WRIGHT** Charles T. of Kingsbury, NY
**WALLER** Lydia A. of Hartford, NY

November 20, 1878
Hartford, NY

**DURLING** John H. of Middle Falls, NY
**STOVER** Ida May of Cambridge, NY

December 6, 1878
Cambridge, NY

DAVIS Francis B.
UNDERWOOD Julia
December 5, 1878
Ft. Edward, NY

DAVISON Robert J.
HALL Maggie J.
December 2, 1878
French Mtn., NY

FULLER George E. of Amherst, Mass.    (newspaper date)
WALSH Jennie of Cambridge, NY
December 12, 1878

HARDING C. W. of Whitehall, NY
BOYD Kate L. dau of John H. of Whitehall, NY
December 5, 1878
Whitehall, NY

WELLS Sidney of Knox, NY
BARBER Alma F. of W. Bernet, NY
December 5, 1878
Whitehall, NY

HILL H. D. W. of Whitehall, NY
WHEELER Mrs. A. J. of Sudbury, Vt.
December 22, 1878
Sandy Hill, NY

SPROAT Augustus
BEACH Mari
December 25, 1878
Valley Falls, NY

TAYLOR R. W. of Albany, NY
BRIGGS Fannie M. formerly of W. Hartford, NY
November 27, 1878
Rochester, NY

MINTON Andrew of Kingsbury, NY
WAIT Evie E. of Ft. Ann, NY
December 17, 1878
Ft. Ann, NY

MC ARTHUR John R. of Jackson, NY
TILFORD Sarah of Jackson, NY
December 11, 1878
Salem, NY

DUEL Pardon of Quaker Springs, NY
ABELL Sarah E. of Ketchums Corners, NY
November 28, 1878
Schuylerville, NY

CRANDALL Jerome of Greenwich, NY
MC MURRAY Lizzie of Schuylerville, NY
December 27, 1878
Schuylerville, NY

DAVISON Robert/William of Hartford, NY
ST MARY Jennie A. of Easton, NY
December 24, 1878
Easton, NY

NORTON Enoch B.
WARD Hattie
November 23, 1878
Hartford, NY

BROOKS Frank
HERSAY Mary
December 10, 1878
Hartford, NY

SINNOTT William
MC NEELEY Mary
December 26, 1878
Whitehall, NY

NADEAU Joseph of Crown Point, NY
December 24, 1878

**GRAY** Carrie of Fairhaven, Vt.

Fairhaven, Vt.

**HATCH** Norman J. of Hartford, NY
**DEAN** Laura A. of Hartford, NY

December 25, 1878
Ft. Edward, NY

**WRIGHT** John G. of Greenwich, NY
**EGGLESTON** Lydia M. of Lake, NY

November 19, 1878
Greenwich, NY

**WATERS** Barber F. of Easton, NY
**HERRINGTON** Cynthia J. of Cambridge, NY

January 1, 1879
Greenwich, NY

**MOSIER** Montgomery of Easton, NY
**EDDY** Mrs. Matilda of Easton, NY

January 1, 1879
Easton, NY

**MASON** Lyman of Sandy Hill, NY
**ELDRIDGE** Emma A. of Sandy Hill, NY

December 18, 1878
Sandy Hill, NY

**ATWOOD** C. W. of Cambridge, NY
**HALL** Martha of M. Granville, NY

January 1, 1879
M. Granville, NY

**WILLIAMS** Benjamin of Hoosick Falls, NY
**BULL** Lida

January 1, 1879
M. Granville, NY

**HARLOW** Judson R. of Whitehall, NY
**MILLER** Susan of Troy, NY

December 28, 1878
Troy, NY

**MOSES** Fayette of Ft. Miller, NY
**GALUSHA** Sophia of Ft. Miller, NY

December 4, 1878
Ft. Miller, NY

**CLUFF** Charles of Comstocks, NY
**GIBBS** Alice of N. Granville, NY

December 18, 1878
N. Granville, NY

**JUCKET** Marcellus          (newspaper date)
**RICHARDSON** Betty

January 9, 1879
N. Granville, NY

**WINTERS** Henry of Boston, Mass.
**NELSON** Libbie of Ft. Ann, NY

December 26, 1878
Ft. Ann, NY

**HILL** Charles A. of Michigan
**HERBERT** Emily J. of Whitehall, NY

January 1, 1879
N. Granville, NY

**DUNCAN** Paul of Whitehall, NY
**LOROIN** Susan of Whitehall, NY

January 2, 1879
Whitehall, NY

**NORMARDAIN** Zephyr
**ST HILAIRE** Eugenie

December 26, 1878
Whitehall, NY

**BRAYMAN** William of Ft. Edward, NY
**GATES** Belle of Ft. Edward, NY

December 31, 1878
Sandy Hill, NY

| | |
|---|---|
| **MATTISON** Andrew H. | January 1, 1879 |
| **WILKINS** Nellie E. | Sandy Hill, NY |
| | |
| **WAIT** William F. | January 9, 1878 |
| **BRYAN** Lydia a | Schaghticoke, NY |
| | |
| **FRY** John W. of Clinton Park, NY | January 15, 1879 |
| **BAUCUS** Elva of Schaghticoke, NY | Schaghticoke, NY |
| | |
| **HATCH** George of Hartford, NY | January 9, 1879 |
| **NORTON** Lottie A. of Hartford, NY | Hartford, NY |
| | |
| **SEARCH** E. N. M. of Philadelphia, Pa. | January 16, 1879 |
| **WARREN** Ella of Cambridge, NY | Cambridge, NY |
| | |
| **YOUNG** J. Hall Missionary at Ft. Wrangel | December 15, 1878 |
| **KELLOGG** Fannie E. dau of Rev. L. of N. Granville, NY | Sitka, Alaska |
| | |
| **WINCHELL** Harvey of Poultney, Vt. | January 13, 1879 |
| **HICKEY** Della T. of Poultney, Vt. | N. Granville, NY |
| | |
| **BASCOM** Benjamin H. of Lake City, Col. | January 28, 1879 |
| **GRISWOLD** Libbie dau of A. H. of Whitehall, NY | Whitehall, NY |
| | |
| **WRIGHT** Lyman of Smiths Basin, NY | January 22, 1879 |
| **NICHOLSON** Emma of Ft. Ann, NY | Ft. Ann, NY |
| | |
| **DEVINE** George H. of Kingsbury, NY | January 22, 1879 |
| **BRAYTON** Althea of Kingsbury, NY | Kingsbury, NY |
| | |
| **FLEMING** Paul of Sandy Hill, NY | January 21, 1879 |
| **DEUERS** Eliza Jane of Sandy Hill, NY | Sandy Hill, NY |
| | |
| **MILLER** Nelson of Kingsbury, NY | January 21, 1879 |
| **SEWARD** Lucretia of Hartford, NY | S. Hartford, NY |
| | |
| **ADAMS** Martin H. of Ft. Ann, NY | January 8, 1879 |
| **GREEN** Sarah M. of Jackson, NY | Cambridge, NY |
| | |
| **BABCOCK** Dewitt of Ft. Ann, NY | January 16, 1879 |
| **SKINNER** Ida of Poultney, Vt. | Poultney, Vt. |
| | |
| **DUNN** William of Sudbury, Vt. | December 31, 1878 |
| **MARTIN** Nettie of Sudbury, Vt. | Hampton, NY |
| | |
| **WEIR** Hamilton L. of E. Hartford, NY | December 24, 1878 |
| **KING** Emma of E. Hartford, NY | N. Argyle, NY |
| | |
| **GILMORE** David W. of Summit, NY | January 29, 1879 |

**HERRINGTON** Calista M. of Summit, NY

| | |
|---|---|
| **WESTCOTT** Charles of Ft. Ann, NY | January 26, 1879 |
| **HUSTIS** Libbie of W. Ft. Ann, NY | W. Ft. Ann, NY |
| | |
| **TILFORD** George E. of Ft. Edward, NY | January 29, 1879 |
| **FINLAY** Julia F. of Ft. Edward, NY | Glens Falls, NY |
| | |
| **POLLOCK** David of Argyle, NY | January 29, 1879 |
| **VANDENBURGH** Catherine of Northumberland, NY | Northumberland, NY |
| | |
| **CLEMENTS** Orson A. formerly of Ft. Ann, NY | January 23, 1879 |
| **JUDGE** Mrs. Alma L. of W. Troy, NY | W. Troy, NY |
| | |
| **BIXBY** Edwin M. of Poultney, Vt. | February 6, 1879 |
| **WILCOX** Carrie E. of Wells, Vt. | Wells, Vt. |
| | |
| **VAN BUREN** Edward C. of Easton, NY | February 6, 1879 |
| **SWAN** Stella E. of Easton, NY | |
| | |
| **ARMSTRONG** William of Schuylerville, NY | February 4, 1879 |
| **MC AULIFF** Helen of Schuylerville, NY | Saratoga Spr., NY |
| | |
| **STILLMAN** Noyes G. of S. Brunswick, NJ (newspaper date) | February 20, 1879 |
| **PARKS** Pliney F. formerly of Salem, NY | New Brunswick, NJ |
| | |
| **MAYNARD** Levi G. of Hartford, NY | February 5, 1879 |
| **SPRING** Emma dau of Roswell of S. Granville, NY | S. Granville, NY |
| | |
| **CARPENTER** Charles of S. Granville, NY | February 11, 1879 |
| **BROWN** Jennie of N. Hebron, NY | N. Hebron, NY |
| | |
| **SULLIVAN** Andrew of Easton, NY | February 5, 1879 |
| **MC DURPHEE** Mary of Greenwich, NY | Schuylerville, NY |
| | |
| **HALL** Richard D. of Clarks Mills, NY | February 8, 1879 |
| **HENSEY** Carrie of Clarks Mills, NY | Clarks Mills, NY |
| | |
| **WOOD** Isaac of Whitehall, NY | February 26, 1879 |
| **KIDDER** Katie P. of Fairhaven, Vt. | Fairhaven, Vt. |
| | |
| **WEATHERWAX** John P. Ballston Spa, NY | February 14, 1879 |
| **HILL** Emily S. of Sandy Hill, NY | Sandy Hill, NY |
| | |
| **WAIT** Reuben of Ft. Miller, NY | February 26, 1879 |
| **GREEN** Abbie of Argyle, NY | Argyle, NY |
| | |
| **MURRAY** George O. of Hampton, NY | February 20, 1879 |
| **WHITE** Fannie E. of Westhaven, Vt. | Ft. Ann, NY |

TRAPHAGENOT Edward of Glens Falls, NY     March 2, 1879
GILCHRIST Annie Q. of Warrensburgh, NY     Sandy Hill, NY

MIDDLETON Charles M. of Hartford, NY (newspaper date) March 20, 1879
HILLS Mary J. of Hartford, NY     Sandy Hill, NY

STICKNEY Frank D.     March 13, 1879
VAN SCHAICK Mary     Sandy Hill, NY

STODDARD Abijah of Coila, NY     March 17, 1879
DONALDSON Lydia R.     Hartford, NY

DAVIS Edward of Hartford, NY     March 19, 1879
MASON Anna of N. Granville, NY     N. Granville, NY

BARBER Ralph     March 18, 1879
KILBOURN Julia     Fairhaven, Vt.

DURKEE Halsey of Ft. Edward, NY     March 26, 1879
GIFFORD Melissa of Kingsbury, NY     Sandy Hill, NY

DUNN George J. of Ticonderoga, NY     March 20, 1879
BARRETT L. Florence of Ft. Ann, NY     Ft. Ann, NY

CUMMINGS Eugene of W. Ft. Ann, NY     March 20, 1879
CORLEW Sarah of W. Ft. Ann, NY     W. Ft. Ann, NY

CRONK Rev. Delos of Hartford, NY     March 20, 1879
DAICY Isabella of Hartford, NY     Hartford, NY

RAY J. L. of Middleton, Vt.     March 18, 1879
GATES Maggie of Middleton, Vt.     Hampton, NY

POPE Harris of Castleton, Vt.     March 19, 1879
FISH Frances of Castleton, Vt.     Hampton, NY

WOODCOCK Loren of Kansas     March 18, 1879
MEARS Mary A. of Manchester, Vt.     Shushan, NY

HAYES Minard R. of Warrensburgh, NY     March 23, 1879
PERRY Hattie Belle     Raceville, NY

VAUGHN Milbern of Kingsbury, NY     March 27, 1879
TAYLOR Corey R. of Kingsbury, NY     Kingsbury St., NY

GREEN George of Queensbury, NY     March 27, 1879
HOLCOMB Lucy of Brooklyn, NY     Kingsbury St., NY

SOPER Arthur L. of Bolton, NY     March 20, 1879

CARPENTER Alice of Warrensburgh, NY

Warrensburgh, NY

COGSHALL William of Syracuse, NY
BRIGGS Nettie of Easton, NY

April 10, 1879
Easton, NY

MC CALL Thomas of S. Hartford, NY   (newspaper date)
BROWN Stella of Granville, NY

April 17, 1879

KETCHUM Henry C. of Bennington, Vt.
BRUCE Elsie J. of Bennington, Vt.

April 6, 1879
White Creek, NY

HALE William
SMITH Delia

April 1, 1879
Argyle, NY

COATS Alexander of Whitehall, NY
KINNEY Mrs. F. L. of Whitehall, NY

April 13, 1879
Whitehall, NY

WRIGHT Charles of Charlton, NY
CAPEN Carrie of Granville, NY

April 8, 1879
Granville, NY

DWYER Thomas of Sandy Hill, NY
MULANE Mary of Sandy Hill, NY

April 16, 1879
Sandy Hill, NY

FENTON Frank W. of Sandy Hill, NY
HAWKS Hattie of Sandy Hill, NY

April 17, 1879
Sandy Hill, NY

PROVOST Joseph
STEWART Matilda M.

April 13, 1879
Whitehall, NY

BREASON William of Argyle, NY
PARKER Cornelia of Sandy Hill, NY

April 19, 1879
Sandy Hill, NY

HULETT Oliver of Smiths Basin, NY
SMALLEY Minerva E. of Smiths Basin, NY

April 17, 1879
Smiths Basin, NY

HARVEY Edwin W. of Ferrisburgh, Vt.
AUSTIN Harriet V. of Bennington, Vt.

March 30, 1879
White Creek, NY

DEUEL George of Easton, NY
GORHAM Lydia S. of Easton, NY

May 13, 1879
Schuylerville, NY

JOHNSON E. R. of Ft. Edward, NY
PEARL Mrs. Cornelia of Ft. Edward, NY

May 3, 1879
Glen's Falls, NY

WILLIAMS David M. of Hampton, NY
STEENBURG Alida of Hampton, NY

May 20, 1879
Whitehall, NY

PAINE John A. of Hubbarton, Vt.
SLASUM Miss ____ of Hubbarton, Vt.

May 18, 1879
Hampton, NY

FISH Preserved of Whitehall, NY
TERRY Emma of Whitehall, NY

May 28, 1879
Whitehall, NY

BEAULAC Frank of Sandy Hill, NY
RABILLARD Mary of Sandy Hill, NY

May 27, 1879
Glens Falls, NY

NASH George M.
VANDENBURGH Fannie M.

June 3, 1879
Sandy Hill, NY

WRIGHT Isaac of Bald Mountain, NY
SILVEY Carrie of Easton, NY

July 8, 1879
Easton, NY

ALLEN J. M. of Sandy Hill, NY
LEMM Armenia C. of Ft Edward, NY

June 1, 1879
Sandy Hill, NY

CANFIELD James
CALLAHAN Katie

June 4, 1879
Sandy Hill, NY

DOYLE Joseph
MULLEN Ellen

June 4, 1879
Sandy Hill, NY

MOON George A. of Shaftsbury, Vt.
NOYES Mary L. of N. Bennington, Vt.

May 25, 1879
White Creek, NY

BEACH Charles T. of Sandy Hill, NY
JUDSON Alexina of Sandy Hill, NY

June 5, 1879
Sandy Hill, NY

GILCHRIST Alexander of Harvard, Neb.
TAYLOR Nellie P. of Sandy Hill, NY

June 9, 1879
Sandy Hill, NY

MITCHELL F. A. of Little Falls, NY
FAIRBANKS Ophelia of Greenwich, NY

June 25, 1879
Greenwich, NY

ROBINSON George H. of Hoosick Falls, NY
SPENCER Lucy A. of Hoosick Falls, NY

May 31, 1879
Greenwich, NY

BULL R. C. of Troy, NY
HENRY Helen Libbie of Cambridge, NY

June 12, 1879
Cambridge, NY

POTVIN Louis of Sandy Hill, NY
COUTER Jennie of Sandy Hill, NY

June 15, 1879
Sandy Hill, NY

CHASE D. M. of Rutland, Vt.
LOGAN Margaret of Ira, Vt.

July 3, 1879
Hampton, NY

CAMPBELL E. L. of Rutland, Vt.
HEATH Etta V. of Rutland, NY

July 4, 1879
Hampton, NY

GREEN James

June 23, 1879

TATRO Lucy

W. Rupert, Vt.

MANCHESTER Hiram L. of Whitehall, NY
BARTHOLOMEW Flora L. of Poultney, Vt.

July 8, 1879
Ft. Edward, NY

LA BARGE Samuel of Whitehall, NY
CAMPBELL Mary of Whitehall, NY

July 12, 1879
Whitehall, NY

PINNSENAULT Adolphe of Sandy Hill, NY
BELGARD Mary of Whitehall, NY

July 12, 1879
Whitehall, NY

RICHARDS Alfred of Whitehall, NY
GRAY Mary Johanna of Whitehall, NY

July 13, 1879
Whitehall, NY

BENNETT George H.
GALUSHA Etta of Wilton, NY

July 21, 1879
Bald Mountain, NY

MC CLAUGHRY Charles M. of Salem, NY
HANKS Mary J.

July 16, 1879
Lakeville, NY

WEST Truman F. of W. Ft. Ann, NY
PALMER Clara C. of W. Ft. Ann, NY

July 20, 1879
Sanfords Ridge, NY

HAXTON Baxter of Ft. Edward, NY
CARSWELL Helen E. of Ft. Miller, NY

July 30, 1879
Ft. Miller, NY

WILLIAMS Asa of Pawlet, Vt.
HINTON Mary E. of Pawlet, Vt.

August 2, 1879
M. Granville, NY

DAY John C.
WEEKS Emma

August 15, 1879
Pawlet, Vt.

WESTCOTT Thomas C. of Moreau, NY
BROMLEY Mary E. of Sandy Hill, NY

August 20, 1879
Sandy Hill, NY

MOODY John of Poultney, Vt.
VAN STEENBURG Mary of Hampton, NY

August 9, 1879
Hampton, NY

ELMS Elisha
CHASE Emma of Hartford, NY

August 14, 1879
Ft. Edward, NY

HOYT F. M. of Arlington, Vt.
CROFOOT Alice M. of Arlington, Vt.

August 20, 1879
Cambridge, NY

THURMAN George L. of Sandy Hill, NY
WINSLOW Lavinia of Stony Creek, NY

August 23, 1879
Sandy Hill, NY

TOLEMAN William of Hartford, NY
INGALSBEE Mary of Hartford, NY

September 1, 1879
Hartford, NY

MC GIVER Charles of Bennington, Vt.  
BROOKS Lucy Jane of Bennington, Vt.  
August 16, 1879  
White Creek, NY

CARPENTER Asahel of Moreau, NY  
BROWN Sarah M. of Sandy Hill, NY  
August 21, 1879  
Sandy Hill, NY

FAIRLEY Edson J. of Ft. Ann, NY  
VAUGHN Mary J. of Ft. Ann, NY  
September 9, 1879  
Ft. Ann, NY

BECKER John  
HILLMAN Ella  
September 18, 1879  
Easton, NY

BAKER Mathew  
SHAUGNESSEY Mrs. Margaret  
October 1, 1879  
Granville, NY

KIBLIN Charles of Granville, NY  
GRAY Eliza dau of J. Warren Gray of Granville, NY  
October 6, 1879  
Granville, NY

SAFFORD J. R. of Granville, NY  
GORHAM Elizabeth of Poultney, Vt.  
September 27, 1879  
Hampton, NY

HEATH W. D. of Mendon, Vt.  
CARRUTH Mary of Mendon, Vt.  
September 30, 1879  
Hampton, NY

HERRINGTON John of Factory Point, Vt.  
MINER Mrs. Frances of Hotchkissville, Conn.  
September 28, 1879  
Shushan, NY

POST Thomas  
ALDOUS Hannah  
September 20, 1879  
N. Greenwich, NY

ROZZELL George E. of Ft. Edward, NY  
HAWLEY Nellie of Moreau, NY  
October 2, 1879  
Moreau, NY

PERRY Henry R. of White Creek, NY  
COTTRELL Agnes L. of White Creek, NY  
October 8, 1879  
White Creek, NY

HASTINGS Charles L. of Shaftsbury, Vt.  
MONTGOMERY Emma L. of Shaftsbury, Vt.  
October 5, 1879  
White Creek, NY

HILL Henry C. of Hoosick Falls, NY  
HODGE Helen Mc Farland of Whitehall, NY  
October 15, 1879  
Ash Grove, NY

WILLIAMS Charles of Sandy Hill, NY  
PRESCOTT Mary of Sandy Hill, NY  
October 16, 1879  
Sandy Hill, NY

SLADE John A. of Pittstown, NY  
EDDY Belle of Pittstown, NY  
October 8, 1879  
Pittstown, NY

ELLIS Horace D. son of Z. C. of Fairhaven, Vt.  
October 15, 1879

**ADAMS** Alice A. dau of A. N. of Fairhaven, Vt.      Fairhaven, Vt.

**CLARK** Theodore L. of Poultney, Vt.      October 22, 1879
**DOWNS** Carrie D. of Hampton, NY      Hampton, NY

**SHERMAN** Frank of Clarks Mills, NY      November 6, 1879
**JOHNSON** Elizabeth A. of Clarks Mills, NY      Greenwich, NY

**WALSH** Charles P. of Sutherland, Vt.      October 12, 1879
**PENNIMAN** Emma of Greenwich, NY      Greenwich, NY

**PERT** John of Luzerne, NY      November 10, 1879
**GUYART** Julia of Luzerne, NY      Sandy Hill, NY

**CONKLIN** Byron of Sandy Hill, NY      September 30, 1879
**KNAPP** Effie of Sandy Hill, NY      Sandy Hill, NY

**EFNER** Charles A. of Glens Falls, NY      November 1, 1879
**JOHNSON** Mary E. of Ft. Edward, NY      Ft. Edward, NY

**MOSHER** William E.      November 5, 1879
**ADAMS** Hattie J.      Sandy Hill, NY

**MOSHER** M. N.      October 29, 1879
**PATTEN** M. L.      N. Argyle, NY

**WEIR** James D. of Cambridge, NY      November 5, 1879
**GIFFORD** Mattie of Cambridge, NY      Cambridge, NY

**LLOYD** John A. of Granville, NY      October 29, 1879
**RHODES** Irena of N. Granville, NY      Granville, NY

**FOOTE** Frederick S. of Whitehall, NY      November 5, 1879
**CARTER** Fannie f. of Ft. Ann, NY      Ft. Ann, NY

**HERRON** Michael of Greenwich, NY      November 26, 1879
**BRADY** Bridget of Greenwich, NY      Greenwich, NY

**INGALLS** Fred of Lynn, Mass.      November 20, 1879
**GUNN** Emma F. dau of W. F. & R. F. of Ft. Edward, NY      Ft. Edward, NY

**NILES** William of Ft. Edward, NY      November 18, 1879
**YOUNG** Anna of Ft. Edward, NY      Ft. Edward, NY

**SMITH** Arthur P. of Ticonderoga, NY      November 26, 1879
**FRENCH** Amy of Sandy Hill, NY      Sandy Hill, NY

**TARBELL** William of Danby, Vt.      November 19, 1879
**BROWN** Helen L. of Danby, Vt.      Granville, NY

LOOMIS Amos L. of Granville, NY
REED Mary E. of Granville, NY

November 26, 1879
Whitehall, NY

MORRISON E. P. of Sandy Hill, NY
CALLAHAN Julia of Sandy Hill, NY

October 28, 1879
Sandy Hill, NY

WAIT Oscar of Ft. Miller, NY
PLUNKETT Mary of Ft. Miller, NY

November 18, 1879
Ft. Miller, NY

HAYNER Schuyler of E. Galway, NY
MILLER Gussie of Harts Falls, NY

November 24, 1879
Harts Falls, NY

TUCKER Franklin of N. Greenwich, NY
GRIFFIN Mrs. Mary Jane of Greenwich, NY

November 4, 1879

CHASE Norman of Bennington, Vt.
ELWELL Rhoda of Bennington, NY

November 26, 1879
White Creek, NY

JOHNSON M. L. of Cambridge, NY
FOWLER Jennie M. of Cambridge, NY

November 26, 1879
Cambridge, NY

MERWIN Tyler
BARKER Fannie L. of S. Hartford, NY

November 24, 1879
S. Hartford, NY

HYATT John of Battenville, NY
FRENCH Annie M. of Battenville, NY

November 24, 1879
Bald Mountain, NY

CARSWELL Charles of Argyle, NY
GREEN Eva dau of Seth of N. Greenwich, NY

December 10, 1879
N. Greenwich, NY

GILSON Henry of Monroe, NY
BATES Ella M. of Queensbury, NY

December 2, 1879
Monroe, NY

TAYLOR John Andrew
POLLOCK Amanda

December 10, 1879
N. Argyle, NY

JUDD C. H. of Whitehall, NY
BLATCHLEY Mary J. of Whitehall, NY

December 6, 1879
Whitehall, NY

PARKER Richard of New York City
ANDERSON Mattie of Putnam, NY

December 9, 1879
Putnam, NY

HARRIGAN Edward W. of Comstocks, NY
WHITE Minnie L. dau of George C. of Granville, NY
      (grand dau of late Peter COMSTOCK of Port Kent, NY)

December 10, 1879
Granville, NY

KIPP Cornelius W. of Pittstown, NY
SHERMAN Angelia L. of Pittstown, NY

December 3, 1879
Pittstown, NY

WADE Amos M. of Easton, NY  
HUDSON Myraette R. of Rock City, NY  
December 5, 1879  
N. Easton, NY

RATHBUN Stephen M. of Easton, NY  
WALKER Sarah E. of Cambridge, NY  
December 17, 1879  
N. Easton, NY

MC EACHRON Andrew S. of Schuylerville, NY  
PHILLIPS Mary E. of Schuylerville, NY  
December 3, 1879  
Schuylerville, NY

NACY John J. of Schuylerville, NY  
GATES Ada of Sandy Hill, NY  
December 15, 1879  
Ft. Edward, NY

DOWNING Edward of Pittstown, NY  
HALL Lottie of Pittstown, NY  
December 10, 1879

WISWELL James J. of Fairhaven, Vt.  
DUNNING Alice of Fairhaven, Vt.  
December 3, 1879  
Fairhaven, Vt.

WILEY Allen J.  
KING Nettie  
December 17, 1879  
Johnsonville, NY

PARSONS W. of Castleton, Vt.  
MANDERS Gussie of Castleton, Vt.  
December 17, 1879  
Fairhaven, Vt.

OAKUM George B. of Poultney, Vt.  
WESTCOTT Angie E. of Poultney, Vt.  
December 17, 1879  
Hampton, NY

EDWARDS Daniel of Greenwich, NY  
NORTON Carrie E. of Hartford, NY  
December 24, 1879  
Hartford, NY

COON Elverton of Middle Falls, NY  
LEE Annie of Lansingburgh, NY  
December 24, 1879  
Lansingburgh, NY

BARKER C. F. of Sandy Hill, NY  
TAYLOR Maggie F. of Sandy Hill, NY  
December 18, 1879  
Sandy Hill, NY

CANFIELD S. Rollo  
NICKERSON Libbie of Ft. Edward, NY  
December 17, 1879  
Ft. Edward, NY

SAFFORD Charles H.  
WELLING Mrs. Libbie B.  
December 21, 1879  
S. Cambridge, NY

HUNT T. Albert of Cambridge, NY  
CARPENTER Sarah of Eagle Bridge, NY  
December 24, 1879  
Eagle Bridge, NY

BENNETT D. H. of Cohoes, NY  
SOMERS Mrs. ____ of Sandy Hill, NY  
December 25, 1879  
Sandy Hill, NY

ATWATER C. W. of Clarendon, Vt.  
EASTMAN Mary A. of Clarendon, Vt.  
December 24, 1879  
Granville, NY

VANCE Robert
TEMPLE Carrie E.

December 31, 1879
Ft. Ann, NY

PATTERSON F. G. of N. Hebron, NY
HAY Julia E. of N. Hebron, NY

December 25, 1879
Hebron, NY

BOYCE Orlando of Ft. Ann, NY
MC CONNELL Libbie of Ft. Ann, NY

December 24, 1879
Ft. Ann, NY

MATTISON Albert of Ft. Ann, NY
KEECH Althea of Ft. Ann, NY

December 25, 1879
Ft. Ann, NY

PRITCHARD Owen
KENNEDY Ella

December 31, 1879
Granville, NY

VOSE Edward G.
TEMPLE Carrie E.

December 31, 1879
Ft. Ann, NY

## WASHINGTON COUNTY POST
### May 5, 1837 - December 26, 1879

THOMPSON David B. of Salem, NY
MC NAUGHTON Jane of Salem, NY

May 2, 1837
Salem, NY

SHEPARD George W. of Ogdensburg, NY
PROUDFIT Susannah Jane of Salem, NY

May 16, 1837
Salem, NY

VAN ALSTYNE Peter of Troy, NY
HARWOOD Mrs. Mary L.

May 10, 1837
Sandy Hill, NY

ROBERTSON Hiram of Union Village, NY
GRAVIN Mary Ann of Union Village, NY

May 18, 1837
Cambridge, NY

GILCHRIST James D.
PATTEN Hannah A.

May 18, 1837
Argyle, NY

ROBERTSON Alexander of Salem, NY
MC DOUGAL Jane S. of Greenwich, NY

June 21, 1837

CRONKHITE Hanmer P. of Fonda, NY
THOMAS Sarah S. day of John of Union Village, NY

June 15, 1837
Union Village, NY

HULETT Mason of Granville, NY
BROWN Eveline of Hartford, NY

June 15, 1837

NELSON James of Ft. Ann, NY
COLEMAN Marietta of Ft. Ann, NY

June 11, 1837

| | |
|---|---|
| COLLINS Julius of Jackson, NY | June 29, 1837 |
| WOODARD Ann of Jackson, NY | Jackson, NY |
| | |
| ALEXANDER Maxwell of Jackson, NY | July 4, 1837 |
| SMALL Ann of Jackson, NY | Jackson, NY |
| | |
| GRAHAM John I. of Putnam, NY | July 5, 1837 |
| WILLIAMSON Fanny of Putnam, NY | Putnam, NY |
| | |
| JONES Zebulon of Hancock, NH | August 28, 1837 |
| SHERMAN Elizabeth D. of Salem, NY | Salem, NY |
| | |
| HEWITT Henry H. of Troy, NY | July 29, 1837 |
| CLAPP Maria L. of Salem, NY | Salem, NY |
| | |
| BASSETT Thomas R. of Salem, NY | September 27, 1837 |
| ROWAN Mary of New York City | New York City |
| | |
| FORD Daniel of Salem, NY | September 5, 1837 |
| SAFFORD Lucy Ann of Salem, NY | Salem, NY |
| | |
| THAYER Edward of Granville, NY | September 16, 1837 |
| WHEELER Hannah of Granville, NY | Granville, NY |
| | |
| DECKER Jacob of Cambridge, NY | October 19, 1837 |
| HILL Mary Ann of Salem, NY | |
| | |
| BACON Ezra of Castleton, Vt. | October 10, 1837 |
| GOODRICH Adelia dau of Asa of Whitehall, NY | Castleton, Vt. |
| | |
| FOSTER Robert L. | October 17, 1837 |
| SIMSON Margaret V. T. dau of Anderson | Jackson, NY |
| | |
| SIMSON Nelson of Jackson, NY | October 18, 1837 |
| CROCKER Mary dau of Benjamin of White Creek, NY | White Creek, NY |
| | |
| BARTHOLOMEW Horace of Whitehall, NY(newspaper date) | November 9, 1837 |
| SKAATES Elizabeth of Hartford, Conn. | Hartford, Conn. |
| | |
| DEAN Hiram of Fosterville, Cayuga Co. NY | November 22, 1837 |
| MC CRACKEN Susan of Salem, NY | |
| | |
| CONKEY Nathaniel | November 17, 1837 |
| COVEL Charlotte | |
| | |
| GAYLORD Henry of Whitehall, NY | December 5, 1837 |
| EDDY Lydia of Whitehall, NY | Whitehall, NY |
| | |
| MARTIN Alvin | December 14, 1837 |
| JILLSON Laura Ann | Whitehall, NY |

**HERALD** James of Whitehall, NY  
**GOSS** Fanny of Whitehall, NY  
December 21, 1837  
Whitehall, NY

**PORTER** George W. of Hebron, NY  
**HOPKINS** Margaret Ann dau of Ervwin of Granville, NY  
October 26, 1837  
Granville, NY

**PORTER** Edward of Hebron, NY  
**INGERSOLL** Ruth of Hebron, NY  
November 22, 1837  
Hebron, NY

**PORTER** Robert B. of Michigan  
**BULL** Mary dau of Henry of Hebron, NY  
   (last three all sons of Judge Porter)  
December 13, 1837  
Hebron, NY

**PEETS** Dewitt C. of Granville, NY  
**CARPENTER** Mary Jane of Granville, NY  
January 4, 1838  
Granville, NY

**WARNER** Gerritt W. of Cambridge, NY  
**FENTON** Julia Ann dau of Erastus of Cambridge, NY  
January 4, 1838  
Cambridge, NY

**GREEN** John of Hoosick, NY  
**WRIGHT** Mrs. Elizabeth of Salem, NY  
January 2, 1838  
Salem, NY

**STEWART** Jared D. of Greenwich, NY  
**CAMPBELL** Jane of Greenwich, NY  
January 23, 1838

**HOPKINS** George  
**MC ALLISTER** Eliza Jane dau of Ebenezer of Salem, NY  
January 25, 1838

**JENKINS** Nelson of Hartford, NY  
**BRAYTON** Mary of Hartford, NY  
February 1, 1838  
Granville, NY

**WATKINS** Henry K.  
**HANES** Zina M.  
February 10, 183  
Salem, NY

**ROBERTSON** George of White Creek, NY (newspaper date)  
**WOODS** Nancy of Jackson, NY  
February 22, 1838  
Jackson, NY

**AVERY** John B. of Jackson, NY  
**BEEBE** Maria of Salem, NY  
February 21, 1838  
Salem, NY

**CLOUGH** Elijah of Salem, NY  
**CHAMBERLAIN** Ann Eliza dau of Andrew of Salem, NY  
February 27, 1838  
Salem, NY

**HARTWELL** Moses of Jackson, NY  
**STOUT** Harriet of Greenwich, NY  
February 21, 1838  
Greenwich, NY

**GRAVES** Horatio of Pawlet, Vt.    (newspaper date)  
**MASON** Betsey of Rupert, Vt.  
March 1, 1838  
Northumberland, NY

MYERS Michael of Whitehall, NY                          February 22, 1838
MYERS Mary of Whitehall, NY                             Whitehall, NY

SMITH William of Granville, NY                          February 27, 1838
SMITH Mrs. Maria of Granville, NY                       Granville, NY

WHITESIDE Henry of Cambridge, NY                        January 24, 1838
WHITESIDE Margaret dau of Mrs. Abby Whiteside           Cambridge, NY

NEWCOMB Wesley Md. of Albany, NY                        February 20, 1838
POST Helen of Palmyra, NY                               Palmyra, NY

BILLINGS Albert of Jackson, NY                          March 8, 1838
CLAPP Almira M. of Jackson, NY

ACKLEY Orrin of Cambridge, NY                           March 29, 1838
ARCHIBALD Elizabeth dau of Robert of Salem, NY          Salem, NY

COLLINS Anson of Jackson, NY                            April 5, 1838
COLE Caroline of Jackson, NY                            Jackson, NY

SAFFORD William of Salem, NY                            April 10, 1838
HANNA Mary dau of Robert of Salem, NY                   Salem, NY

DUERS John of Kingsbury, NY                             May 10, 1838
BEATTIE Jane of White Creek, NY                         White Creek, NY

MC INTYRE Safford of Salem, NY                          May 23, 1838
MC CLUSKEY Margaret of Salem, NY

CRUIKSHANK James M.                                     May 31, 1838
BASSETT Ann Eliza dau of Russell                        Salem, NY

GILLETTE Rev. P. D. of Union Village, NY                May 29, 1838
HOLLISTER Harriet dau of Reuben of Ballston, NY         Ballston, NY

BARBER Joshua                                           June 11, 1838
BILLINGS Mary Ann                                       Jackson, NY

BUEL Jonathan                                           June 7, 1838
CORNELL Delia                                           Easton, NY

HOPKINS Dwelle of Rupert, Vt.                           June 25, 1838
CLEVELAND Mary of Salem, NY                             Salem, NY

WEIR Thomas E. of Jackson, NY                           July 12, 1838
WATSON Hannah of Jackson, NY                            Salem, NY

PORTER William Jr. of Jordan, NY                        July 18, 1838
BLANCHARD Ellen Jane dau of Anthony I. of Salem, NY     Plattsburgh, NY

HANNA Robert Jr. of Salem, NY  
RAY Mary Ann of Hebron, NY  
July 31, 1838  
Hebron, NY

HEATON William C. of New York City  
WARFORD Maria D. dau of late Samuel formerly of Salem  
July 14, 1838  
New York City

CAMPBELL George of Jackson, NY  
WOODWORTH Charlotte dau of Ira of Salem, NY  
September 5, 1838

SKINNER Cortland of Cambridge, NY  
SHERMAN Rhoda of Cambridge, NY  
September 15, 1838  
Cambridge, NY

HARVEY Joseph G. of Jackson, NY  
BIGGS Rozillanor H. of Jackson, NY  
September 5, 1838  
Jackson, NY

LAMBERT David C. of White Creek, NY  
NELSON Ann Eliza of White Creek, NY  
September 11, 1838  
White Creek, NY

YATES Christopher Md. of New York City  
WILLARD Emma of Troy, NY  
September 17, 1838  
Troy, NY

RICE Silas of Jackson, NY  
CLAPP Jane Ann dau of Stephen of Salem, NY  
September 20, 1838

CRITTENDEN Alpheus C.  
SHARP Orra Cornelia  
September 19, 1838  
White Creek, NY

ROBERTSON Archibald Jr. of Bennington, Vt.  
KING Julia recently of Troy, NY  
September 27, 1838  
Salem, NY

COMSTOCK Thomas of Albany, NY      (newspaper date)  
FOWLER Phebe dau of Thomas of White Creek, NY  
October 4, 1838  
White Creek, NY

ALLEN Rev. Edward D. of Albany, NY     (newspaper date)  
GOODSELL Jane P. of Woodbridge, Conn.  
October 4, 1838  
White Creek, NY

LEE Nathaniel or Troy, NY  
CROWL Susanna of Salem, NY  
September 29, 1838

DANFORTH Jonathan E. of Salem, NY  
MARTIN Lucinda of Salem, NY  
October 4, 1838  
Salem, NY

VIELE Hiram of Rochester, NY  
MC FARLAND Abby M. dau of late William M. of Salem  
October 17, 1838  
Salem, NY

ARMITAGE William J. of Rochester, NY  
VAN DERLIP Elsey Ann of Troy, NY  
October 22, 1838  
Troy, NY

DICKINSON Sylvanus Jr. of Salem, NY  
October 17, 1838

**FOX** Eunice Lucy of Salem, NY — White Creek, NY

**COGSHALL** Thomas of Salem, NY — November 19, 1838
**BEATY** Harriet dau of Samuel of Salem, NY

**MC LAURY** Thomas of Kortright, NY — November 28, 1838
**SAVAGE** Eliza D. of Argyle, NY — Argyle, NY

**UPHAM** Joseph — December 20, 1838
**RICHARDS** Phebe Elizabeth — Troy, NY

**ERWIN** James of Lansingburgh, NY — January 8, 1839
**ACKLEY** Mary of Jackson, NY — Jackson, NY

**TAYLOR** Andrew of Argyle, NY — January 10, 1839
**TOMES** Ann Maria of Argyle, NY — Argyle, NY

**HOWARD** Isaac H. of Greenwich, NY — January 17, 1839
**HARDEN** Margaret of Greenwich, NY — Greenwich, NY

**TUCKER** Nathan of Greenwich, NY — January 1, 1839
**ROBINSON** Eleanor of Greenwich, NY — Lakeville, NY

**FULLER** Daniel of Jackson, NY — January 16, 1839
**MOORE** Charlotte of Jackson, NY — Jackson, NY

**WOODRUFF** John of Tinmouth, Vt. — January 10, 1839
**PERKINS** Mary Ann of Pawlet, Vt. — Shushan, NY

**WOODRUFF** George W. (twin brother of above) — January 10, 1839
**PERKINS** Margaret (twin sister of above) — Shushan, NY

**WORT** John of Granville, NY — February 3, 1839
**COLLINS** Clarissa of Granville, NY — Granville, NY

**HARRINGTON** C. M. of Arlington, Vt. — January 29, 1839
**COOK** Jerusha Jane dau of Samuel of Ft. Ann, NY — Ft. Ann, NY

**MOSHER** James C. of Greenwich, NY — January 31, 1839
**LEWIS** Almy of Easton, NY — White Creek, NY

**ROBINSON** Lewis of Easton, NY — January 31, 1839
**REYNOLDS** Jane Ann of Easton, NY — White Creek, NY

**PARKS** Marvin B. of Moreau, NY — February 6, 1839
**COOPER** Gertrude A. of Sandy Hill, NY — Sandy Hill, NY

**BARNES** William M. of Salem, NY — February 19, 1839
**WRIGHT** Mrs. Jane of Salem, NY — Jackson, NY

**FREEMAN** Lyman of Cambridge, NY
**FLANDERS** Eliza of Cambridge, NY

February 18, 1839
Union Village, NY

**SEARLES** Thomas of Hampton, NY
**PARMER** Louisa of Granville, NY

February 17, 1839
Granville, NY

**LEWIS** Amasa of Wells, Vt.
**JONES** Sarah Ann of Pawlet, Vt.

January 17, 1839

**WHITBECK** Henry of Easton, NY
**POTTER** Mehetible of Easton, NY

February 27, 1839
Easton, NY

**ENGLISH** Eser of Easton, NY
**WATERS** Miss ____ of Easton, NY

February 27, 1839
Easton, NY

**BURTIS** John of Hoosic, NY
**HANKS** Celinda of Salem, NY

March 2, 1839
Salem, NY

**SHERWIN** Marvin C. of Whitehall, NY
**MILLARD** Lydia Jane of Whitehall, NY

March 5, 1839
Whitehall, NY

**RUSSELL** John of Hebron, NY
**TOWNSEND** Laura Ann dau of Calvin of Hartford, NY

March 5, 1839
Hartford, NY

**UTLEY** Ralph of Landgrove, Vt.
**NOBLE** Laura of Whitehall, NY

March 6, 1839
Whitehall, NY

**STURDEVANT** G. A. of W. Troy, NY
**VIELE** Jane L. dau of S. L. of Ft. Miller, NY

March 6, 1839
Ft. Miller, NY

**GROESBECK** Nicolas
**HAYNES** Hersey

March 6, 1839
Pittstown, NY

**WHEADON** George of Hartford, NY
**LYTLE** Hannah A. of Argyle, NY

February 21, 1839
Argyle, NY

**HENRY** James of Union Village, NY
**CONLEY** Ruby of Centre Falls, NY

February 27, 1839
Centre Falls, NY

**SPUNNER** George of White Creek, NY    (newspaper date)
**YOUNG** Sarah of Salem, NY

March 21, 1839
Jackson, NY

**SHELDON** Tallmadge of Kingsbury, NY
**TEFFT** Betsey of Kingsbury, NY

March 5, 1839

**WINSHIP** Ransom J.
**SHEPHERD** Catherine

February 24, 1839

**SHEPHERD** Harris    (newspaper date)

March 21, 1839

**WINSHIP** Polly Ann

| | |
|---|---|
| **TAYLOR** Philander of Ft. Ann, NY <br> **BARKER** Harriet of Ft. Ann, NY | February 21, 1839 |
| **GARSON** Erastus of Ft. Ann, NY <br> **SHELDON** Caroline dau of Nathan of Ft. Ann, NY | March 5, 1839 |
| **FITCH** Samuel S. of Salem, NY <br> **OSBORN** Harriet of Easton, NY | March 21, 1839 <br> Easton, NY |
| **HORTON** J. H. of White Creek, NY <br> **GETTY** Jane Ann of Hebron, NY | March 26, 1839 <br> Hebron, NY |
| **CALHOUN** James <br> **HUTTON** Susanna | February 14, 1839 <br> Centre Falls, NY |
| **AUSTIN** Simeon of Cambridge, NY <br> **HERRINGTON** Ann of Cambridge, NY | April 4, 1839 <br> Cambridge, NY |
| **WILKINSON** George of Sandgate, Vt. <br> **WATERS** Jane of Sandgate, Vt. | April 21, 1839 <br> Sandgate, Vt. |
| **WEBSTER** David <br> **DUNHAM** Phebe | April 28, 1839 <br> Hartford, NY |
| **WHITTEMORE** John <br> **BRAYTON** Carlystin dau of Carn | May 9, 1839 <br> Hartford, NY |
| **MAYNARD** Amby <br> **GATES** Emily dau of Harvey | May 14, 1839 <br> Hartford, NY |
| **BARNETT** George of Hoosick, NY <br> **CHASE** Patience M. of Hoosick, NY | May 8, 1839 <br> N. Hoosick, NY |
| **CHASE** George of Hoosick, NY <br> **WELLS** Mary of White Creek, NY | April 21, 1839 <br> N. White Creek, NY |
| **NEWCOMB** William <br> **CHASE** Elizabeth of Pittstown, NY | May 5, 1839 <br> Pittstown, NY |
| **SHEPHERD** Charles of Ogdensburg, NY <br> **RIPLEY** Laura S. of Ogdensburg, NY | May 3, 1839 <br> Ogdensburg, NY |
| **LOVELAND** Jared of Salem, NY <br> **FORD** Eliza of Salem, NY | May 26, 1839 <br> Ft. Edward, NY |
| **GRAVES** Rufus of Granville, NY <br> **PAIGE** Happolonia of Rutland, Vt. | May 22, 1839 <br> Rutland, NY |

CROSBY Samuel W.
WOODWORTH Betsey

May 14, 1839
White Creek, NY

DOTY James B.
VAN BUREN Mariah dau of Daniel

May 21, 1839
Easton, NY

WYMAN Horace of Albany, NY
DAVISON Julia A. of Albany, NY

June 12, 1839

MILLER Gilbert
BANKER Maria dau of Timothy of Pittstown, NY

June 13, 1839
Pittstown, NY

MANHAM Ephraim of Middlebury, Vt.
NAYLOR Eliza A. of Bristol, NY

June 27, 1839
Bristol, NY

SPENCER Fayette L. of Granville, NY
RAHN Caroline E. dau of Charles of Philadelphia, Pa.

June 30, 1839
Granville, NY

STILES Samuel of Ft. Edward, NY
MC DONALD Mary of Ft. Edward, NY

July 14, 1839
Ft. Edward, NY

MILLER Albert of Constantine, Mi.
WELLS Emily of Mottville, Mi.

June 13, 1839
Mottville, Mi.

MURDOCK Stephen M.
SHERMAN Catherine J.

July 4, 1839
Rupert, Vt.

WALLER Rodney of Hartford, NY
ELKINS Lucretia of Hartford, NY

July 14, 1839
Hartford, NY

ROWAN Daniel
CLEVELAND Sarah dau of late Palmer

July 24, 1839

HUNTINGTON Rev. E. A.
VAN VECHTEN Anne E.

July 30, 1839
Schenectady, NY

SAVAGE Edwin of Union College
VAN VECHTEN Sarah

July 30, 1839
Schenectady, NY

BIDWELL John of Argyle, NY
MC FADDEN Sarah

August 7, 1839
Argyle, NY

MC LEAN Henry of Jackson, NY
FITCH Sophia dau of William of Salem, NY

September 17, 1839
Salem, NY

SHERRILL H. of New Hartford, NY
SHERRILL Mary E. dau of Darius of Sandy Hill, NY

September 4, 1839

CHURCH La Mott age 30 yrs

September 12, 1839

**WILBUR** Widow age 75 yrs                                    Greenwich, NY

**LIDDLE** John of Salem, NY                                   September 26, 1839
**MERRITT** Catherine of Salem, NY                             Salem, NY

**WARNER** Capt. Solomon Jr. of Jackson, NY                    September 26, 1839
**TEFFT** Eliza of Jackson, NY                                 Jackson, NY

**SAFFORD** Gideon of Argyle, NY                               August 27, 1839
**MATHEWS** Isabelle sister of Henry                           Troy, NY

**EARENESS** Henderson of Salem, NY                            October 2, 1839
**TIBBETS** Nancy M. of Salem, NY

**CROSBY** E. M. formerly of Granville, NY                     October 3, 1839
**PARKER** Caroline dau of W. H. of Whitehall, NY              Whitehall, NY

**PARRY** Rev. Joseph                                          September 24, 1839
**IVES** Mary dau of Maj. Oliver Ives                          Sandy Hill, NY

**HOWLAND** Gardner of Salem, NY                               September 18, 1839
**FORD** Elizabeth of Ballston Spa, NY                         Ballston Spa, NY

**ROOT** William of Carbondale, Pa.                            October 7, 1839
**MC KILLIP** Mrs. Ada of Salem, NY

**GIDDINGS** William B. of Poultney, Vt.    (newspaper date)   October 24, 1839
**GOODRICH** Sarah Ann of Granville, NY

**WELLS** Leonard of White Creek, NY                           October 16, 1839
**ALLEN** Eliza of White Creek, NY                             White Creek, NY

**WELLS** Leonard of White Creek, NY                           October 17, 1839
**BURT** Nora Jane of Northumberland, NY                       Northumberland, NY

**SIMPSON** Robert of Jackson, NY                              October 23, 1839
**SIMPSON** Hetty of Jackson, NY                               Jackson, NY

**MOWER** Samuel A. of Chittenango, NY                         October 30, 1839
**WRIGHT** Ellen M. of Sandy Hill, NY

**HOYLE** George V. of Champlain, NY                           November 12, 1839
**MOORE** Catherine A. dau of Allen R. of Granville, NY        M. Granville, NY

**HIBBARD** Elijah of Rupert, Vt.                              November 17, 1839
**BILLINGS** Almeda of Salem, NY                               Salem, NY

**BAILEY** Gilbert of Union Village, NY                        November 20, 1839
**WARD** Ann dau of John of Troy, NY                           Troy, NY

HATTORNE Ira of Salem, NY
GLEASON Labrina Mandana of Salem, NY

November 6, 1839
Salem, NY

MARTIN James S. of Salem, NY
HANKS Ann dau of Col. Joseph Hanks of Salem, NY

December 5, 1839
Salem, NY

WARNER Abner of Jackson, NY
RANDLES Martha E. of Hebron, NY

December 5, 1839
Hebron, NY

QUACKENBUSH John L. of Hoosick, NY
BROWNELL Mary E. of Pownal, Vt.

December 14, 1839
Cambridge, NY

RICE George G.
CAMPBELL Catherine dau of David

November 19, 1839
Jackson, NY

GRAVES Newcomb of Granville, NY
BISHOP Eliza Laura dau of late Isaac of Granville, NY

November 25, 1839
Granville, NY

FOX Rufus of Salem, NY
SCHIDMORE Emeline of Salem, NY

December 18, 1839
Salem, NY

EDDY William S. of Whitehall, NY
BILLINGS Martha S. dau of Jesse L. of Whitehall, NY

January 1, 1840
Whitehall, NY

LIVINGSTON Alexander of Jackson, NY
ROBERTSON Rebecca W. dau of James of Cambridge, NY

December 31, 1839
Cambridge, NY

STEVENS Cyrus of Albany, NY
MILLER Frances H. of Troy, NY

January 7, 1840
Troy, NY

WELLS Jonas H.
SMITH Sally Ann dau of Asa of White Creek, NY

January 1, 1840
Jackson, NY

GRAY Dr. Henry of White Creek, NY
NILES Mary W. of Shaftsbury, Vt.

January 2, 1840
Shaftsbury, Vt.

FOWLER David of White Creek, NY
FOWLER Sarah Ann of Cambridge, NY

January 9, 1840
Cambridge, NY

WAIT Manser K. of Granville, NY
HAILE Julia Ann dau of Samuel of Hartford, NY

January 16, 1840
Hartford, NY

CROTTY John of Cambridge, NY
MC MILLAN Agnes of Salem, NY

January 30, 1839
Salem, NY

STEWART Walter of Salem, NY
REID Eunice M. of Salem, NY

January 31, 1840

COREY Walter

February 9, 1840

CRANDALL Maraby of Grafton, NY — Salem, NY

GREEN Lemuel of Pittsfield — February 12, 1840
MC KAY Jane M. of Salem, NY — Salem, NY

ROGERS Lewis of Whitehall, NY — February 12, 1840
FULLER Marcia of Castleton, Vt. — Castleton, Vt.

INGRAHAM Anson of Cambridge, NY — February 12, 1840
MC MURRAY Margaret Ann of Cambridge, NY

JOSLIN George W. of Hebron, NY — February 5, 1840
GILMORE Elizabeth of Bennington, Vt. — Bennington, Vt.

HODGES Simeon of White Creek, NY — March 15, 1840
WILLIS Emela of Hoosick, NY — Cambridge, NY

PORTER Orson of Pawlet, Vt. — March 6, 1840
BEEBE Julia of Pawlet, Vt. — Salem, NY

BLOSSOM Zenas of Salem, NY — March 29, 1840
HUNT Mary Ann of Salem, NY — White Creek, NY

DILL Merrills of Whitehall, NY — April 16, 1840
HASTIN Caroline of Whitehall, NY — Whitehall, NY

RICE Roswell N. of Salem, NY — May 14, 1840
HODGES Elizabeth Ann of Salem, NY

WILLIAMSON William of Salem, NY — May 28, 1840
WILLIAMS Catherine of Salem, NY

PARKER William H. — May 26, 1840
WHEELER Mary Ann — Whitehall, NY

WHIPPLE Job T. of Union Village, NY — May 26, 1840
WILSON Maria of Centre Falls, NY

STUART John — May 30, 1840
ELDRIDGE Phebe Ann — White Creek, NY

CROSIER John R. of Jackson, NY — July 2, 1840
HETH Helen of Salem, NY — Salem, NY

VOLENTINE Joel 2nd of Salem, NY — July 1, 1840
HAMMOND Lydia of Jackson, NY — Jackson, NY

GRAY Anson of Troy, NY — July 14, 1840
BUCKINGHAM Elizabeth of Troy, NY — Troy, NY

**DYER** Dr. Martin of Union Village, NY
**SAFFORD** Harriet of Union Village, NY

July 19, 1840
Union Village, NY

**SKINNER** Reuben of M. Granville, NY  (newspaper date)
**PARKER** Mrs. ____ of M. Granville, NY

August 27, 1840

**NICHOLS** Russell of Whitehall, NY
**GRIGGS** Julia Ann of Whitehall, NY

August 24, 1840
Whitehall, NY

**GREEN** S. R. of Whitehall, NY
**SHADDOCK** Adelade of Whitehall, NY

August 26, 1840
Whitehall, NY

**THOMAS** Reuben of Sandgate, Vt.  (newspaper date)
**WELLER** Ellen of Salem, NY

September 10, 1840
Salem, NY

**POTTER** Richard of Pittstown, NY
**STILES** Christianna of Pittstown, NY

September 20, 1840
Jackson, NY

**MASTERS** John T of Schaghticoke, NY
**MOREY** Mary of Union Village, NY

September 16/23, 1840
Union Village, NY

**JONES** Lorenzo of Cornwall, Vt.
**SHERMAN** Thankful J. of Salem, NY

September 28, 1840
Salem, NY

**WHIPLEY** Simeon W. of Salem, NY
**WILLIAMS** Jane dau of Eli S. of Salem, NY

September 24, 1840

**THOMPSON** William of Jackson, NY
**BUCK** Aurelia of Arlington, Vt.

September 15, 1840
Arlington, Vt.

**MATHER** Ira N. of Benson, Vt.
**EASTON** Lucy of Benson, Vt.

September 21, 1840
Benson, Vt.

**WOOD** William of York, NY
**RUSSELL** Mary of Jackson, NY

October 1, 1840
Jackson, NY

**GRIFFIN** James W. of Oswego, NY  (newspaper date)
**RISING** Ann D. of Jackson, NY

October 22, 1840
Jackson, NY

**THOMPSON** Andrew Jr. of Jackson, NY
**STEVENS** Eliza of Jackson, NY

October 7, 1840

**MC COUN** Coles of Salem, NY
**STOCKWELL** Grace Ann of Salem, NY

October 20, 1840
Whitehall, NY

**HILL** Hiram H.
**POTTER** Caroline

October 4, 1840
Hampton, NY

**GOWEY** Solomon of St. Joseph, Mi.

October 13, 1840

**YOUNG** Mary Ann                Poultney, Vt.

**HURLBURT** Reuben of Dresden, NY       October 15, 1840
**TALLMADGE** Polly Ann of Dresden, NY     Dresden, NY

**JUCKET** Daniel of Whitehall, NY         October 18, 1840
**WHEADON** Rachel of Whitehall, NY      Whitehall, NY

**RICE** Volney of Putnam, NY             October 11, 1840
**TUCKER** Adeline L. of Putnam, NY       Dresden, NY

**SUDAM** R. V. of Hoosick, NY           November 2, 1840
**BEATY** Sarah of Salem, NY             Schaghticoke, NY

**GETTY** Andrew C. of Greenwich, NY      November 5, 1840
**HALL** Cornelia T. of Greenwich, NY      Greenwich, NY

**BLANCHARD** H. T. of Whitehall, NY      November 13, 1840
**CHALMERS** Julia A. of Plattsburgh, NY    Plattsburgh, NY

**GLINES** John of Whitehall, NY           November 12, 1840
**BERTO** Harriet of Hampton, NY         Hampton, NY

**BIDWELL** Darwin P. of Whitehall, NY     November 18, 1840
**OSGOOD** Margaret D. of Whitehall, NY    Whitehall, NY

**UPHAM** Alfred W. of Philadelphia, Pa.    (newspaper date)    December 3, 1840
**GRANGER** Mrs. Elizabeth R. dau of Dr. Leonard **GIBBS**    Granville, NY

**CULVER** Samuel of Jackson, NY          December 3, 1840
**BRUCE** Hannah of Salem, NY

**ARCHIBALD** James M. of Cambridge, NY    December 3, 1840
**MITCHELL** Jane of Cambridge, NY

**BAYLEY** Calvin E. of Manlius, NY        December 1, 1840
**FISHER** Ann T. of White Creek, NY       White Creek, NY

**ROBINSON** Benjamin F. of Salem, NY      February 17, 1841
**DODD** Catherine of Salem, NY           Salem, NY

**VOLENTINE** Daniel 2nd of Salem, NY      March 17, 1841
**RUSTE** Sarah Jane dau of Samuel of White Creek, NY    White Creek, NY

**RANDALL** Daniel of White Creek, NY      February 5, 1841
**DECKER** June of White Creek, NY       White Creek, NY

**WHITE** Rufus of Salem, NY             April 7, 1841
**DUNCAN** Lois of Salem, NY            Salem, NY

SIMPSON Simeon Dewitt of Jackson, NY
HAMMOND Penelope of Greenwich, NY

April 7, 1841
Greenwich, NY

WESTON Cornelius F. formerly of Salem, NY
ANDREWS Isabella

March 18, 1841
Granville, Ill.

BURNETT John of Salem, NY
TURNER Sarah of Salem, NY

May 6, 1841
Salem, NY

MARTIN Sidney of Salem, NY
HURD Mary Ann

May 6, 1841
Salem, NY

BAKER Reuben of Salem, NY
YOULEN Laura of Salem, NY

May 17, 1841
Salem, NY

LAKIN Rodney of Salem, NY
EGGLESTON Nancy of Hebron, NY

May 13, 1841
Hebron, NY

FITCH Josephus of Salem, NY
BEATY Jane dau of John of Salem, NY

May 26, 1841
Salem, NY

FOX Joseph Jr. of Lansingburgh, NY
CORBETT Martha W. of Jackson, NY

June 12, 1841
Jackson, NY

BACON Henry of Tecumseh, Mi.
CLEVELAND Elizabeth A. W. of Cambridge, NY

June 17, 1841
Cambridge, NY

LIVINGSTON William of Jackson, NY
SCOTT Jennette of Salem, MY

July 6, 1841
Cambridge, NY

COOK John of White Creek, NY
GILMORE Marie of Cambridge, NY

July 20, 1841
Cambridge, NY

BANARD Abner C. of Salem, NY
SAFFORD Lucy Jane of Salem, NY

July 21, 1841
Salem, NY

WHITCOMB Oliver of Salem, NY
SCOVILLE Eliza of Salem, NY

September 1, 1841

WILLARD Abel Jr. of Fairhaven, Vt.
DOANE Mary of Hartford, NY

September 1, 1841
Granville, NY

TEFFT E. N. of Jackson, NY
RICH Jane Amanda dau of Joel of White Creek, NY

September 20, 1841
White Creek, NY

STEVENS Thomas Jr. of Jackson, NY
MOORE Sarah Ann of Jackson, NY

September 14, 1841
Jackson, NY

CURTIS Frederick

September 15, 1841

**DUNHAM** Mary E. dau of James formerly of Jackson, NY      Ballston, NY

**WILCOX** Gerritt W. son of Robert    (newspaper date)      October 7, 1841
**BULL** Lydia Maria dau of Henry of Hebron, NY      Hebron, NY

**WOLCOTT** W. Grosvenor Md. of Chataugua Co. NY      October 20, 1841
**DUNHAM** Harriet A. of Whitehall, NY      Whitehall, NY

**CLAPP** Leonidas of Salem, NY      October 28, 1841
**CHAMBERLAIN** Jane dau of late Andrew of Salem, NY      Salem, NY

**CURTIS** Berlin of Sandgate, Vt.      November 10, 1841
**MC CLAUGHRY** Sarah T. dau of Thomas of Salem NY      Salem, NY

**SHERMAN** Henry Osman of W. Rupert, Vt.      December 30, 1841
**INGERSOLL** Huldah M. of Hebron, NY      Hebron, NY

**WALKER** Rufus E. of Salem, NY      January 1, 1842
**LARKIN** Harriet of Salem, NY      Salem, NY

**BASCOM** Oliver of Whitehall, NY      January 6, 1842
**TANNER** Almira of Whitehall, NY      Whitehall, NY

**LOWE** Samuel J. of Chicago, Ill.      December 30, 1841
**BEATTIE** Eliza J. of Chicago, Ill.      Chicago, Ill.

**MURDOCK** Samuel Jr. of Salem, NY      January 18, 1842
**GRAVES** Fidelia M. of Salem, NY      Salem, NY

**COLLINS** William Md. of Battenville, NY      January 24, 1842
**WOODARD** Sarah Maria of Jackson, NY      Jackson, NY

**GETTY** Thomas of Hebron, NY      January 26, 1842
**MARTIN** Lucy of Salem, NY      Salem, NY

**CARTER** James of Salem, NY      January 27, 1842
**STEWART** Jane of Salem, NY      Salem, NY

**COON** Thomas P. of Salem, NY      January 27, 1842
**MACK** Jane of Salem, NY      Salem, NY

**BEATY** John Jr. of Salem, NY      January 19, 1842
**GLAZIER** Zilpha of Greenwich, NY      Greenwich, NY

**GRAVES** Francis of Rupert, Vt.      January 11, 1842
**BOWE** Esther Ann of Wells, Vt.      Wells, Vt.

**WHITESIDE** William of Chautaugua Co. NY      March 2, 1842
**CORNELL** Maria Jennett of Cambridge, NY      Cambridge, NY

HARMON Josiah of W. Rupert, Vt.
SMITH Ann of W. Rupert, Vt.

March 9, 1842
W. Rupert, Vt.

MURRELL Stephen of Hartford, NY
NORTON Almira of Hartford, NY

March 23, 1842
Hartford, NY

PERKINS William of Sandgate, Vt.
THOMPSON Sarah Grace of Salem, NY

March 10, 1842
Salem, NY

SUTLIFF John of Fairhaven, Vt.
MC NISH Priscilla of Salem, NY

March 6, 1842
Salem, NY

MC ALLISTER Archibald W. of Salem, NY
ALLEN Sarah G. of S. Hartford, NY

March 24, 1842
S. Hartford, NY

WOODWORTH Charles G. of Salem, NY
PARKS Miss ____ of Salem, NY

March 31, 1842
Salem, NY

OVETT Samuel of Jackson, NY
HODGES Harriet of Salem, NY

April 25, 1842

HENRY William of Argyle, NY
ROBERTSON Mary L. of Argyle, NY

May 4, 1842
Argyle, NY

HILL James of Argyle, NY
MARTIN Agnes dau of Andrew of Salem, NY

May 19, 1842

ROBERTSON Abner C. of Greenwich, NY
WOODWORTH Eliza of Salem, NY

May 19, 1842

LARKIN Henry
HILL Allin of Granville, NY

May 25, 1842

WALKER Emery
HILL Delia of Granville, NY

May 25, 1842

SLADE Barton of Simpronia, NY
QUACKENBUSH Catherine of Salem, NY

June 20, 1842
Salem, NY

WELLS Joseph of Easton, NY
JOHNSON Ann Eliza of Salem, NY

June 14, 1842

MATTISON John W of White Creek, NY
WARN Maria of White Creek, NY

June 20, 1842
N. White Creek, NY

ORVIS Joseph U.
NAZRO Elizabeth dau of Henry

June 29, 1842
Troy, NY

PROUDFIT Alexander

June 28, 1842

**WILLIAMS** Delia of Newburgh, NY — Cambridge, NY

**BANARD** Abner C. of Salem, NY
**SAFFORD** Lucy Jane of Salem, NY — July 21, 1842 / Salem, NY

**FENTON** E. Pearl of Cambridge, NY
**COBB** Lucia M. of Cambridge, NY — September 4, 1842 / Cambridge, NY

**FISK** Thomas B. of Shushan, NY
**BARTLETT** Amorette of Jackson, NY — July 26, 1842 / Jackson, NY

**SMALLEY** Enos of Shushan, NY
**MEEKER** Mary D. of Sandgate, Vt. — August 17, 1842 / Sandgate, Vt.

**GROOT** John A. of Shushan, NY
**HEATH** Eliza Jane of Shushan, NY — August 25, 1842 / Shushan, NY

**DOBBIN** David of Jackson, NY
**KNOWLTON** Lucy of Shushan, NY — September 6, 1842 / Shushan, NY

**PIZAR** Martin of Pittstown, NY
**CHURCH** Mary E. of Shushan, NY — September 6, 1842 / Shushan, NY

**LAWRENCE** Samuel of Troy, NY
**LONG** Harriet dau of Edward of Cambridge, NY — September 8, 1842

**SHERMAN** Enoch S. of W. Rupert, Vt.
**HASELTINE** Abby E. of Pembroke, NH — October 6, 1842

**MC NISH** Ephraim of Salem, NY
**PERRY** Jane M. of Salem, NY — October 20, 1842 / Salem, NY

**PERRY** Hugh Jr. of Salem, NY
**BEERS** Margaret of Salem, NY — October 19, 1842

**ARMSTRONG** Asher of Cambridge, NY
**HARRIS** Adelia S. of Hoosick, NY — October 6, 1842 / Hartford, NY

**WINCHESTER** Fay R.    (newspaper date)
**HUGHES** Jane — November 2, 1842 / White Creek, NY

**NAYLOR** Thomas S. of Union Village, NY
**ROOD** Celinda of Union Village, NY — November 1, 1842 / Troy, NY

**TILFORD** James S. of New York City
**PERRY** Ruth G. of White Creek, NY — November 20, 1842 / Union Village, NY

**GUNNISON** James of Salem, NY
**WHISKEY** Mary A. of Hoosick, NY — November 24, 1842 / Hoosick, NY

**GERMAIN** James B. of Newburgh, NY
**RICE** Catherine Ann dau of Clark Rice of Jackson, NY

November 17, 1842
Jackson, NY

**PATTISON** John J. of Troy, NY
**STILES** Sarah M. of Argyle, NY

December 7, 1842
Argyle, NY

**PIERCE** Henry P. of New Sweden, NY
**WHITE** Olive Maria of Jackson, NY

December 12, 1842

**TINKEY** Stephen 2nd of Argyle, NY
**HENRY** Margaret of Argyle, NY

December 22, 1842
Argyle, NY

**ELDRICH** Ichabod of Cambridge, NY
**HARVEY** Pamelia of Troy, NY

December 21, 1842

**HULL** Dr. A. Dennison of Lansingburgh, NY
**ALVORD** Catherine dau of Elisha of Lansingburgh, NY

December 22, 1842
Lansingburgh, NY

**LACKEY** David of Hebron, NY
**SCOVILLE** Mary of Hebron, NY

December 8, 1842
Hebron, NY

**GRAY** John W. of Salem, NY
**COOPER** Caroline of Salem, NY

January 12, 1843
Salem, NY

**BARCLAY** Henry of Hebron, NY
**MC INTYRE** Elizabeth dau of John of Argyle, NY

January 17, 1843

**RICHMOND** Josiah of Hoosick, NY
**MILLIMAN** Lydia of Salem, NY

January 19, 1843
Salem, NY

**WISWELL** J. T. of Whitehall, NY
**VAUGHN** Helen M. of Whitehall, NY

January 24, 1843
Whitehall, NY

**LAW** David of Salem, NY
**ROBERTSON** Mary Ann of Argyle, NY

February 7, 1843

**MC SHERMAN** William of Rupert, Vt.
**LEWIS** Hannah of Rupert, Vt.

February 15, 1843
Rupert, Vt.

**BARNEY** Henry of E. Bennington, Vt.
**KEYES** Hester Ann of N. Bennington, Vt.
(Newspaper date was April 5, 1843, date of marriage could be March 29)

April 29, 1843
White Creek, NY

**DUNCAN** David of Salem, NY
**CARTER** Patience of Salem, NY

March 30, 1843
Salem, NY

**GETTY** William F. of Hebron, NY
**WHITE** Jane of Hebron, NY

April 6, 1843
Hebron, NY

**ROBERTSON** John F. of Argyle, NY      March 9, 1843
**ALEXANDER** Mary dau of Robert of Jackson, NY

**GRAVES** William A. of W. Granville, NY      April 4, 1843
**HALL** Caroline P. dau of Alexander of Hartford, NY      W. Granville, NY

**CARLEY** Newman B. of Whitingham, Vt.      April 27, 1843
**WILLIAMS** Mary Jane of Cambridge, NY      Cambridge, NY

**PATTERSON** Benjamin F. of Union Village, NY      April 27, 1843
**JACKSON** Eliza A. of Union village, NY      Battenville, NY

**ASHTON** William R. of Argyle, NY      April 27, 1843
**MILLS** Sarah A. of Argyle, NY      Argyle, NY

**SCOTT** James of Queensbury, NY      May 16, 1843
**SCOTT** Ann Stewart of Salem, NY

**SCOTT** William Jr. of Salem, NY      May 17, 1843
**LIVINGSTON** Mary Ann of Cambridge, NY

**BLANCHARD** Charles M. of Cambridge, NY      May 16, 1843
**SQUARES** Sarah of Argyle, NY

**PARKER** Thomas of Castleton, Vt.      May 4, 1843
**VIVIAN** Ann S. of Castleton, Vt.      Whitehall, NY

**ST CLAIR** Joseph      May 11, 1843
**NELSON** Betsey      Whitehall, NY

**PEASE** Calvin      May 4, 1843
**SWIFT** Sally      Whitehall, NY

**BLOSSOM** John of Salem, NY      June 7, 1843
**EGGLESTON** Margaret of Hebron, NY      Hebron, NY

**ROGERS** Wilson of Hebron, NY      July 4, 1843
**CLARK** Mary of Hebron, NY      Salem, NY

**BROUGHTON** Horace of Salem, NY      August 2, 1843
**STEVENS** Matilda of Hebron, NY      Hebron, NY

**TILFORD** George of Argyle, NY      August 3, 1843
**LISTER** Sarah M. of Argyle, NY      Argyle, NY

**SALISBURY** John of Jackson, NY      August 10, 1843
**COLLINS** Mrs. ____ widow of John      Jackson, NY

**CURTIS** William D. of Warren, Wis.      September 18, 1843
**THOMPSON** Mary Ann of Salem, NY      Salem, NY

BILLINGS Peter Perine of Jackson, NY
PORTER Abigail Towne of White Creek, NY

September 12, 1843
White Creek, NY

HURD Edwin F.
PARSONS Jane L.

September 4, 1843
White Creek, NY

LAW Edward
ROBINSON Jennett of Argyle, NY

September 12, 1843
Argyle, NY

GROVENGER Harmon S. of Schaghticoke, NY
LAMB Elizabeth A. of Battenville, NY

September 13, 1843
E. White Creek, NY

GROVENGER Jacob N. of Schaghticoke, NY
SMITH Eliza J. of Battenville, NY

September 13, 1843
E. White Creek, NY

BALEY Gilbert
BILLINGS M. A. of Jackson, NY

September 11, 1843
Jackson, NY

STEVENSON John M. of Cambridge, NY
NEWTON Seraph dau Rev. E. H.

September 20, 1843
White Creek, NY

COLE William H. of Jackson, NY
HERRINGTON Sarah of White Creek, NY

September 25, 1843
White Creek, NY

GRAY Mathew D. of Salem, NY
WILSON Martha J. of Troy, NY

October 3, 1843
Troy, NY

FOSTER Andrew B. of Dorchester, Mass.
COOLEY Jane C. of Amherst, Mass.

October 3, 1843
Salem, NY

FERRIS James of Sandy Hill, NY
FANCHER Jane adopted dau of Ira

October 19, 1843
Sandy Hill, NY

PATTEN William of Illinois
PRATT Elizabeth of Greenwich, NY

October 11, 1843
Greenwich, NY

MC CLEARY James of Cambridge, NY
BEEBE Julia of Jackson, NY

October 12, 1843
Jackson, NY

MURPHY Robert of Whitehall, NY
STEVENSON Jane of Whitehall, NY

October 16, 1843
Whitehall, NY

BARBER George of E. Whitehall, NY
MANCHESTER Maria of E. Whitehall, NY

September 28, 1843
E. Whitehall, NY

KILBURN Edson of E. Whitehall, NY
WRIGHT Martha of E. Whitehall, NY

October 12, 1843
E. Whitehall, NY

EGGLESTON Taylor of Galesville, NY

October 15, 1843

**ROGERS** Eliza of Galesville, NY

Galesville, NY

**WHELDON** William H. of Union Village, NY
**THOMAS** Charlotte of Union Village, NY

October 23, 1843
Union Village, NY

**HALL** Ebenezer C. of Union Village, NY
**GRANDY** Mary of Union Village, NY

October 23, 1843
Schuylerville, NY

**CHUBB** Simon M. of Union Village, NY
**NELSON** Lydia of Stillwater, NY

October 17, 1843
Stillwater, NY

**STEWART** John of Jackson, NY
**BROWNING** Clementine of Jackson, NY

October 17, 1843
Greenwich, NY

**SHATTUCK** Franklin B. of Greenwich, NY
**ROBINSON** Mary Ann of Greenwich, NY

October 25, 1843
Union Village, NY

**AUSTIN** Abner of Cambridge, NY
**SPRAGUE** Ann of Salem, NY

October 26, 1843
Salem, NY

**COLESTON** Charles
**BILLINGS** Amanda

October 2, 1843
Rutland, Vt.

**BARTO** Joseph of Fairhaven, Vt.
**GILMORE** Filena of Whitehall, NY

November 9, 1843
Whitehall, NY

**MONTGOMERY** William of Centre Falls, NY
**COOK** Jane of Battenville, NY

November 2, 1843
Battenville, NY

**BURCH** Abram of Easton, NY
**KENDRICK** Olive of Easton, NY

October 13, 1843
Easton, NY

**OTTERSON** Benjamin F. of Granville, NY
**RICHARDSON** Nancy of W. Poultney, Vt.

October 31, 1843
W. Poultney, Vt.

**ROGERS** John F. of Whitehall, NY
**SMITH** Sarah

November 14, 1843
Dover, NH

**HOVEY** Charles of Lowell
**SMITH** Catherine dau of Joseph of Dover, NH

November 14, 1843
Dover, NH

**RATHBORN** Elijah of Whitehall, NY
**RATHBORN** Abigail of Whitehall, NY

October 9, 1843
Whitehall, NY

**SHEARER** Volney
**ROGERS** Ann

November 1, 1843
Greenwich, NY

**BURKE** William of Union Village, NY
**DOLPH** Almira of Union Village, NY

November 14, 1843
Union Village, NY

**HUGHES** Hazen of Perington, NY
**HARD** Jane of Perington, NY

November 9, 1843
Jackson, NY

**GREEN** Emery B. of Waterford, NY
**CROSBY** Mary B. of White Creek, NY

November 16, 1843
White Creek, NY

**TANNER** Artemus of Ballston, NY
**CONLEE** Elsa of Centre Falls, NY

December 26, 1843
Centre Falls, NY

**ORCUTT** Nathan of Jackson, NY
**GRAHAM** Margaret dau of William of Jackson, NY

January 1, 1844
Jackson, NY

**MILLER** Lewis P. of Easton, NY
**BISHOP** Marinda J. of Easton, NY

January 11, 1844
Easton, NY

**SHERWIN** Andrew J.
**NICHOLS** Mary Jane

January 18, 1844
Salem, NY

**CORBETT** Elijah of White Creek, NY
**UNDERWOOD** Mrs. Myra of Hartford, Vt.

December 27, 1843
Hartford, Vt

**ORCUTT** Hugh of Jackson, NY
**CLAPP** Julia Ann

January 10, 1844
Jackson, NY

**PATTERSON** Robert of Putnam, NY
**BEVERAGE** Jennett of Hebron, NY

January 23, 1844
Hebron, NY

**FISHER** David of White Creek, NY
**TRUMBULL** Fanny of Rupert, Vt.

February 8, 1844
Rupert, Vt.

**CONKEY** Daniel of Salem, NY
**ACKLEY** Elizabeth of Salem, NY

February 9, 1844
Hebron, NY

**MYERS** M. J. of Whitehall, NY
**ALLEN** Mary dau of Dr. A. Allen of W. Granville, NY

January 30, 1844
W. Granville, NY

**NOYES** William of Poultney, Vt.
**PRINDLE** Lucy of Poultney, Vt.

January 30, 1844
Poultney, Vt.

**LAWRENCE** Capt. F. of Mass.
**MONCRIEF** Jane of Greenwich, NY

March 29, 1844
Greenwich, NY

**THOMPSON** Andrew L. of Salem, NY
**WRIGHT** Agnes of Salem, NY

April 10, 1844
Salem, NY

**BROCKWAY** William W. of Albany, NY
**GRAY** Hannah dau of Dr. Henry Gray of White Creek, NY

May 7, 1844
White Creek, NY

**BURRITT** Thomas Roland of N. White Creek, NY

May 14, 1844

WOODWORTH Angeline of N. White Creek, NY        N. White Creek, NY

FLACK John of Whitehall, NY                     May 23, 1844
PENFIELD Laura dau of John of Whitehall, NY     Whitehall, NY

GAVETT Horace of Argyle, NY                     May 9, 1844
ROUSE Emily of Argyle, NY                       Argyle, NY

CULBERTSON Rev. M. S. of Chambersburg, Pa.      May 16, 1844
DUNLAP Mary dau of Peter of Greenwich, NY       Salem, NY

WOODWORTH J. G. of Salem, NY                    May 29, 1844
CANFIELD Augusta of Arlington, Vt.              Arlington, Vt.

MACK R. H. of Salem, NY                         May 30, 1844
ABBOTT Mary D. of Whitehall, NY                 Whitehall, NY

HYDE A. W. of Castleton, Vt.                    June 4, 1844
RUSSELL Mary E. dau of Hon. D. Russell of Salem, NY    Salem, NY

SHARPE H. K. Atty. of Salem, NY                 June 6, 1844
MARTIN Jane B. dau of Andrew of Salem, NY

WHEELER A. of Salem, NY                         June 4, 1844
THOMPSON Grace dau of John of Salem, NY

BANCROFT B. F.                                  June 12, 1844
BULKLEY Mary Jane dau of Gen. Edward Bulkley    N. Granville, NY

NEWMAN John Henry of Troy, NY                   July 9, 1844
LOOMIS Sylvia Ann of Cambridge, NY              Cambridge, NY

WARREN H.                      (newspaper date) July 24, 1844
CURTIS Sarah Ann formerly of Salem, NY          Warren, Wis.

ALLEN E. D. of Troy, NY                         July 25, 1844
BARKER Mary C. dau of Aaron of Easton, NY       Easton, NY

HILL Moses of Salem, NY                         August 22, 1844
LONG Nancy M. of Salem, NY                      Salem, NY

FREEMAN Wallace W.                              September 9, 1844
RUSSELL Catherine dau of David                  Salem, NY

CUMMINGS Mr. Ethel of Granville, NY             August 18, 1844
DANIELS Mary of Granville, NY                   Granville, NY

COOK Adin V. of Granville, NY                   September 3, 1844
WOODELL Malissa S. of Granville, NY             Granville, NY

STEWART Dr. Joseph D. of White Creek, NY
WHITCOMB Eliza G. of White Creek, NY

August 29, 1844
White Creek, NY

DOBBIN Alexander of Greenwich, NY
MC LEAN Martha of Jackson, NY

September 3, 1844
Jackson, NY

THOMPSON James of Jackson, NY
WHITE Janett dau of Rev. James White of Salem, NY

September 3, 1844
Cambridge, NY

RICE James
SMITH Miss ____ dau of Allen

September 3, 1844
White Creek, NY

ALEXANDER William of Greenwich, NY
MC RALLER Amanda of Argyle, NY

September 3, 1844
Argyle, NY

HILL Wallace
LAKIN Susan

October 25, 1844
Salem, NY

STEELE Joshua of Salem, NY
BEATY Mary Ann of Salem, NY

October 8, 1844
Cambridge, NY

GROVER Charles of Bennington, Vt.
PRUYN Charlotte A. of Cambridge, NY

October 8, 1844
Cambridge, NY

HERRINGTON Charles 2nd of Easton, NY
WOODHOUSE Sarah of Jackson, NY

October 29, 1844
Salem, NY

MC CLELLAN James R. of Hebron, NY
WHEADON C. Maretta of Hebron, NY

October 18, 1844
Hebron, NY

WILDER A. H. Md. of Pittsfield, Mass
BARNUM Rosanna of N. White Creek, NY

November 26, 1844
N. White Creek, NY

CLOW Andrew of Hoosick, NY
ODEKIRK Martha of Hoosick, NY

January 6, 1845
White Creek, NY

PIERCE William W. of Troy, NY
WHELDON Sarah M. of Easton, NY

January 16, 1845
Easton, NY

GILBERT Mr. ____ of Cambridge, NY
SELEE Harriet A. of Jackson, NY

January 16, 1845
Cambridge, NY

DECKER Robert of White Creek, NY
WOOD Mary of Cambridge, NY

January 22, 1845

MATHEWS Sidney of Greenwich, NY
PRATT Sarah Maria of Greenwich, NY

February 12, 1845
Greenwich, NY

STEVENSON William of Argyle, NY

February 12, 1845

| | |
|---|---|
| **TERRY** Susan of Argyle, NY | Argyle, NY |
| **FILLMORE** Rev. Isaac O. of Cambridge, NY | March 5, 1845 |
| **PARMALEE** Julia of Lansingburgh, NY | Lansingburgh, NY |
| **FLACK** David H. of Lansingburgh, NY | March 25, 1845 |
| **NEWCOMB** Sarah of Pittstown, NY | Pittstown, NY |
| **FOSTER** Andrew of Hebron, NY | March 27, 1845 |
| **LYLE** Jane of Salem, NY | Hebron, NY |
| **BILLINGS** Philo of Salem, NY | March 27, 1845 |
| **JENKINS** Altana of Salem, NY | Salem, NY |
| **NELSON** Edwin of Rupert, Vt. | April 15, 1845 |
| **STEVENS** Ann P. of Rupert, Vt. | W. Rupert, Vt. |
| **BENNETT** Charles W. of Cambridge, NY | May 14, 1845 |
| **DEAN** Loura of Granville, NY | Granville, NY |
| **AUSTIN** James M. Md. | May 20, 1845 |
| **DUER** Catherine dau of late Hugh **PEEBLES** | Waterford, NY |
| **CHAPMAN** Washington of Argyle, NY | June 17, 1845 |
| **GOODWIN** Caroline A. of Pawlet, Vt. | Pawlet, Vt. |
| **MARTIN** George D. of Pawlet, Vt. | June 19, 1845 |
| **LOOMIS** Candace of Pawlet, Vt. | Pawlet, Vt. |
| **WALKER** John C. of Manchester Vt. | July 1, 1845 |
| **MC COLLISTER** Catherine dau of William of Salem, NY | Salem, NY |
| **DAY** W. G. of Granville, NY | July 3, 1845 |
| **SHAW** Ann Maria of Lake George, NY | Lake George, NY |
| **BEACH** Melville of Sandy Hill, NY | July 3, 1845 |
| **LEIGH** Louisa of Argyle, NY | Battenville, NY |
| **PATTERSON** Spencer G. of Salem, NY | July 17, 1845 |
| **SNYDER** Jane of Salem, NY | W. Hebron, NY |
| **BIGELOW** Abram of Buskirks Bridge, NY | May 23, 1845 |
| **CHURCH** Cynthia Ann of Shushan, NY | Shushan, NY |
| **AVERY** Charles A. of Jackson, NY | September 9, 1845 |
| **COOK** Eliza of Jackson, NY | Jackson, NY |
| **NORTHUP** Oscar F. of Hebron, NY | August 11, 1845 |
| **LYMAN** Lucia Ann of Shushan, NY | Salem, NY |

**TRUMBULL** George of Rupert, Vt.
**SHELDON** Mary of Rupert, Vt.

September 25, 1845
Rupert, Vt.

**NELSON** John of Hebron, NY
**DOBBIN** Mary of Jackson, NY

September 25, 1845
Jackson, NY

**JACKSON** Hollis of Newfane, Vt.
**GOULD** Sarah D. dau of Abraham of Salem, NY

October 5, 1845

**GRAY** David S. of Salem, NY
**BEATTIE** Margaret Ann of Salem, NY

October 7, 1845
Salem, NY

**REED** Rev. Villeroy D. of Lansingburgh, NY
**WILCOX** Emily

October 21, 1845
Orwell, Vt.

**POTTER** Joseph of Whitehall, NY
**BOYES** Catherine E. dau of Joseph of Union Village, NY

October 23, 1845
Union Village, NY

**WALLACE** Daniel of Greenwich, NY
**BURROUGHS** Jane of Greenwich, NY

October 11, 1845
Lakeville, NY

**WEBSTER** Joseph P. of Deergrove, Ill.
**STAPLES** Phebe Ann formerly of Pawlet, Vt.

January 26, 1849

**WRIGHT** Morris of Cambridge, NY
**RUSTE** Maria dau of Samuel

February 23, 1849
N. White Creek, NY

**GASTON** Ogden of Schaghticoke, NY
**SIMPSON** Elizabeth of Jackson, NY

March 1, 1849

**FOWLER** Dewitt Clinton of N. White Creek, NY
**PRATT** Henrietta E. dau of W. S. of N. White Creek, NY

March 8, 1849

**PEARSON** Joseph of White Creek, NY
**WELLS** Abby F. of Salem, NY

March 26, 1849

**YOUNG** Robert E.
**CLARK** Louenza

March 29, 1849
Jackson, NY

**BROWNELL** Humphrey K. of White Creek, NY
**OATMAN** Sarah of Sandgate, Vt.

May 1, 1849
Bennington, Vt.

**VOLENTINE** Thomas of Jackson, NY
**GILBERT** Miss of Shushan, NY

April 25, 1849
Jackson, NY

**SHILAND** Rev. Andrew of Habron, NY
**STARK** Mary

April 25, 1849
New York City

**MC HANG** William H. of Albany, NY

May 24, 1849

**HAMBLIN** Frances of Argyle, NY
Argyle, NY

**BARESE** Perry C. of Troy, NY
May 30, 1849
**ALLEN** Mrs. R. of Salem, NY
Salem, NY

**RATHBUN** Stephen of Easton, NY
June 6, 1849
**HILL** Jane of Cambridge, NY
White Creek, NY

**ESTEY** James T. of Leroy, NY
June 21, 1849
**TEFFT** Martha C. of White Creek, NY

**LEE** Hon. William L. formerly of Salem, NY
March 11, 1849
**NEWTON** Catherine E. dau of D. L. of Albany, NY
Honolulu

**HILL** Abner of Arlington, Vt.
July 11, 1849
**HILL** Carolina of N. White Creek, NY
Salem, NY

**SHELDON** Thadeus D. of Pawlet, Vt.
July 31, 1849
**UNDERHILL** Mary of Rupert, Vt.
Rupert, Vt.

**FISHER** H. K. of Ashgrove, NY
August 2, 1849
**DOW** Eliza M. of Shaftsbury, Vt.

**WRIGHT** Simeon of Salem, NY
August 12, 1849
**SHARP** Marilla of Jackson, NY
W. Arlington, Vt.

**PIERSON** E. C. of Glens Falls, NY
August 15, 1849
**JOHNSON** Ursala of Shushan, NY
Salem, NY

**WILSON** Lewis
August 16, 1849
**LEE** Nancy
Argyle, NY

**CHAMBERS** Robert of Cambridge, NY
August 19, 1849
**GRIFFITH** Elizabeth of Troy, NY
Troy, NY

**HILLMAN** Morgan H. of Jackson, NY
August 22, 1849
**HARWOOD** Ruth E. of Easton, NY
Easton, NY

**KING** William F. of Cambridge, NY
September 5, 1849
**BROWNELL** Phebe Ann of Easton, NY
Washington Co. Hall

**COLE** Morgan Md. of White Creek, NY
September 16, 1849
**HODGEMAN** L. A. of Pittstown, NY
Pittstown, NY

**OSBORN** Henry S. of Salem, MY
September 11, 1849
**MC ALLISTER** Caroline of Salem, NY
Salem, NY

**SEARLE** Samuel T. of Buskirks Bridge, NY
September 11, 1849
**SOUTHWORTH** Cornelia F. dau of Joseph of Union Village
Union Village, NY

LOURIS Alexander of Jackson, NY
BIGELOW Mary dau of Anson of Easton, NY

September 5, 1849
Easton, NY

CHASE J. Jr. of Hoosick, NY
BARKER Hannah E. of N. Hector, NY

September 18, 1849
N. Hector, NY

MC FARLAND John A. of Jackson, NY
HAWLEY Amanda H. of N. White Creek, NY

September 24, 1849
N. White Creek, NY

GIFFORD Ira of Cambridge, NY
BANKER Catherine E. of Pittstown, NY

September 13, 1849
Troy, NY

LESTER Charles S. Atty.
COOK Lucy E. of Saratoga, NY

September 20, 1849
Saratoga, NY

BIRMINGHAM Thomas of Troy, NY
COAN Lucinda of Sandgate, Vt.

September 27, 1849
Salem, NY

ADDAM Preston of Moriah, NY
SMITH Harriet C. dau of Elias

September 25, 1849
Moriah, NY

MC LAURY E. F. of Kortwright, NY
PARISH Susannah H. dau of Hiram of Jackson, NY

October 3, 1849
Jackson, NY

HARWOOD Thomas W. of Jackson, NY
DONAHUE Prudy of Cambridge, NY

October 2, 1849
Cambridge, NY

WAIT Benjamin F. of White Creek, NY
TAFT Clarinda of Shaftsbury, Vt.

October 23, 1849
Cambridge, NY

SCOVILLE James P. of Saratoga, NY
BEATTY Nancy of Salem, NY

October 8, 1849
Troy, NY

OATMAN Charles of Arlington, Vt.
MARTIN Mary of Salem, NY

October 31, 1849
Salem, NY

STONE George of Manchester, Vt.
HOLMES Sarah L. of Jackson, NY

November 1, 1849
Jackson, NY

GREEN Daniel of Cambridge, NY
DEWELL Mary of Cambridge, NY

November 1, 1849

TILTON T. E. of Dayton, Ohio
HALL Charlotte J. of Cambridge, NY

November 8, 1849
Cambridge, NY

MC KIE Edwin of Cambridge, NY
MOSHER Marie A. dau of late Dr. R. of Easton, NY

October 31, 1849
Easton, NY

LAWRENCE William

November 19, 1849

**BROWN** Mary Antoinette dau of Peter of Salem, NY — Salem, NY

**WELCH** John A. of Cambridge, NY
**MC MILLAN** Frances Ann of Easton, NY — November 14, 1849 / Schuylerville, NY

**ROBERTSON** Charles of Greenwich, NY
**AKIN** Eliza Ann — November 18, 1849 / Centre Falls, NY

**CRARY** Charles Atty.
**MATHEWS** Mary dau of late Henry — December 6, 1849 / Salem, NY

**FOSTER** Simeon B. of Salem, NY
**BARTLETT** Hulda Maria of Jackson, NY — December 5, 1849 / White Creek, NY

**MOORE** William A. of Jackson, NY
**DUNHAM** Sarah O. of Jackson, NY — December 4, 1849 / Jackson, NY

**CROSIER** John K. of Salem, NY
**HILL** Jane of Salem, NY — November 28, 1849 / Salem, NY

**DAILEY** John of Cambridge, NY
**NELSON** Margaret of Cambridge, NY — November 28, 1849 / White Creek, NY

**STEARNS** William of Hebron, NY
**SCOTT** Ann of Sandgate, Vt. — November 8, 1849 / Sandgate, Vt.

**HURD** John C. of Salem NY
**WILLIAMS** Mary Ann of Salem, NY — December 19, 1849 / Jackson, NY

**FULLER** Ira of Cambridge, NY
**CULVER** Clarissa B. of Cambridge, NY — January 3, 1850 / Cambridge, NY

**HEWITT** Anson B. of Manchester, Vt. formerly Saratoga
**KENYON** Charlotte dau of John of Shaftsbury, Vt. — January 2, 1850 / Cambridge, NY

**WAIT** Edmond C. of Cambridge, NY
**BEEDLE** Sarah of Easton, NY — January 3, 1850 / Easton, NY

**MYERS** Charles of Hoosick, NY
**FARNAM** Mary Ann of Hoosick, NY — January 5, 1850 / White Creek, NY

**BARRINGTON** Henry B. of Hartford, NY
**BROWNELL** Sally of White Creek, NY — January 6, 1850 / White Creek, NY

**WOODWORTH** John of Salem, NY
**HOLDEN** Anna M. of Arlington, Vt. — January 15, 1850 / Arlington, Vt.

**HEATH** Joshua C. of Warrensburgh, NY
**PETTIS** Mary E. of Warrensburgh, NY — January 10, 1850 / White Creek, NY

**HAY** James of Jackson, NY
**RANDALL** Jane Ann of Jackson, NY

January 18, 1850
White Creek, NY

**GILLIS** James Gideon of Salem, NY
**BOYD** Elizabeth of Salem, NY

January 16, 1850
Salem, NY

**GRAY** David of Salem NY
**HAWLEY** Charlotte of Troy, NY

January 17, 1850
Troy, NY

**WALLER** Nathan of Hartford, NY
**BOWEN** Lydia of Hartford, NY

January 24, 1850
Hartford, NY

**DEAN** Solomon of White Creek, NY
**ACKLEY** Maria of White Creek, NY

January 29, 1850
White Creek, NY

**CLEVELAND** Clark of Jackson, NY
**LYON** Minerva of Salem NY

January 23, 1850
Manchester, Vt.

**PRINDLE** Norman of Pawlet, Vt.
**LYON** Harriet of Manchester, Vt.

January 23, 1850
Manchester, Vt.

**BRUCE** Hollis of Salem, NY
**LARKIN** Charlotte of Salem, NY

January 23, 1850
Salem, NY

**CLARK** Robert of Salem, NY
**HUGGINS** Prudence of Jackson, NY

February 6, 1850
Jackson, NY

**GETTY** Charles A. of Hebron, NY
**THOMPSON** Mary E. of Salem, NY

January 29, 1850
Saratoga Springs, NY

**BLOWERS** James of White Creek, NY
**ANDREWS** Samantha of Shaftsbury, Vt.

February 6, 1850
Shaftsbury, Vt.

**GATES** H. H. of Castleton, Vt.
**GRAY** Sarah Jane of Arlington, Vt.

December 24, 1849
Castleton, Vt.

**LYTLE** John R. of Salem, NY
**MC NAUGHTON** Jane G. of Salem, NY

February 19, 1850
Salem, NY

**ROGERS** James of Poultney, Vt.
**STONE** Sarah E. of Jackson, NY

February 6, 1850

**NEHEE** P. H. of Stillwater, NY
**BULL** Jane of Hebron, NY

February 20, 1850
Hebron, NY

**KELLY** Patrick of White Creek, NY
**BOYDEN** Alice of White Creek, NY

February 23, 1850

**HOVER** Charles of Cambridge, NY

February 15, 1850

ARCHER Elizabeth of Cambridge, NY                                    Battenville, NY

MILLIS Daniel of Cambridge, NY                                       February 21, 1850
RANDALL Emma of N. White Creek, NY                                   Buskirks Bridge, NY

STANLEY David of Shaftsbury, Vt.                                     March 6, 1850
BURNETT Sarah Jane of Salem, NY                                      Jackson, NY

BECKER J. V. S. of Easton, NY                                        March 12, 1850
SMALL Sarah E. of Cambridge, NY                                      Cambridge, NY

PARK Derastus B. of Salem, NY                                        March 14, 1850
BARKER Sarah H. of Salem, NY                                         Salem, NY

LUSK Rev. H. K. of Cambridge, NY                                     March 13, 1850
WHYTE Margaret dau of late Rev. James Whyte                          Cambridge, NY

MC LEAN Henry K. Md. of Jackson, NY                                  March 20, 1850
ARMSTRONG T. Elizabeth dau of P. M. of Hoosick, NY                   Hoosick, NY

HANSON Seth T. of Salem, NY                                          March 13, 1850
MC WITHEY Eunice of Schuylerville, NY                                Schuylerville, NY

THAYER F. of Troy, NY                                                April 30, 1850
MC KIE Catherine dau of George of W. Cambridge, NY

BOWEN Erastus of White Creek, NY                                     June 10, 1850
DELAVERGNE Elizabeth B. of Easton, NY                                N. White Creek, NY

SHERMAN Josiah of Whitehall, NY                                      June 3, 1850
WILSON M. E. of Chester, NH                                          Chester, NH

YOUNG William of Pennsylvania                                        June 6, 1850
HAWLEY Susan of White Creek, NY                                      Arlington, Vt.

BARTHOLOMEW Birney of Whitehall, NY                                  June 15, 1850
FERRIN Aseneth M. of Whitehall, NY                                   Whitehall, NY

FAIRCHILD John of Ulysses, NY                                        July 21, 1850
CORNELL Maria of Ulysses, NY                                         White Creek, NY

WARN Orville                                                         July 4, 1850
CHASE Saber of Manchester, Vt.                                       Pawlet, Vt.

BISHOP Charles R. formerly of Kingsbury, NY                          August 4., 1850
PAUHL Bernice of Hololulu, Hawaii                                    Honolulu, Hawaii

HYDE James T. of Hydesville, Vt.                                     September 18, 1850
ALLEN Frances Elizabeth dau of Cornelius of Salem, NY                Salem, NY

WATERHOUSE Horace A. of Manchester, Vt.  September 24, 1850
PROUT Julia E. of Salem, NY  Salem, NY

FAIRLEY James A. of Lansingburgh, NY  September 18, 1850
SMART Mary of Waterford, NY  Salem, NY

TEFFT Hon. Henry A. formerly of Washington Co. NY  July 9, 1850
DANA Jenorita Eliza Josefa dau of William G.  Niperne, Cal.

EATON Loren of Salem, NY  September 26, 1850
FITCH Emily of Salem, NY  Salem, NY

WATERS Edwin S. of E. Greenwich, NY  October 1, 1850
JOHNSON Ellen M. of Union Village, NY  E. Greenwich, NY

GRANT Rev. James W. of White Creek, NY  October 17, 1850
LIVINGSTON E. C. of Whitehall, NY  Whitehall, NY

STAPLES Abram of N. White Creek, NY  November 6, 1850
HAVILAND Lydia of Glens Falls, NY  Glens Falls, NY

DURPHEE Isaac W. of Cambridge, NY  November 6, 1850
SISSON Sarah M. dau of Ira & Betsey of White Creek, NY  White Creek, NY

COPELAND Levi of Hebron, NY  October 23, 1850
FAIRLEY Mary Jane of Salem, NY  Salem, NY

HOONBECK Alexander of Rochester, Ulster Co. NY  November 20, 1850
CULVER Mary Ann of Cambridge, NY

ROOT William of Pawlet, Vt.  November 30, 1850
EASTMAN Caroline of Rupert, NY  Rupert, Vt.

FOSDICK George W.  November 27, 1850
HADAWAY Huldah E.  Moriah, NY

BEATTY Nicholson of Easton, NY  December 11, 1850
GORSLINE Janette of Schaghticoke, NY  Schaghticoke, NY

HARLOW Isaac 2nd of Whitehall, NY  November 26, 1850
FELTON A. F. of Parishville, NY  Ticonderoga, NY

GOULD John J. of Cambridge, NY  December 31, 1850
CARY Susannah of Hebron, NY

LIVINGSTON Thomas of Cambridge, NY  January 1, 1851
BARBER Julia of White Creek, NY

ALLEN William of Granville, NY  January 6, 1851

**GRIFFIN** Deborah of Easton, NY

**SCHRANTON** Dr. J. H. of Union Village, NY      January 8, 1851
**SLOCUM** Mary of Pittstown, NY      Pittstown, NY

**MC LEARY** Daniel of Salem, NY      January 14, 1851
**BOYD** Emily of Salem, NY      Salem, NY

**FAIRLY** William of Salem, NY      January 8, 1851
**SAFFORD** Mary of Salem, NY

**RICH** William of Salem, NY      January 21, 1851
**PARK** Sarah E. of Salem, NY

**WRIGHT** Robert C. of Salem,NY      January 30, 1851
**COLLINS** Mrs. Lucinda of Wisconsin

**WASHBURN** Thomas      January 29, 1851
**WOODELL** Matilda      Hartford, NY

**REYNOLDS** Samuel      January 30, 1851
**WASHBURN** Mary of Hartford, NY      Hartford, NY

**BROWNELL** Job W. of Easton, NY      February 15, 1851
**RATHBUN** Julia of Easton, NY      N. White Creek, NY

**DUNN** Henry of Greenwich, NY      February 19, 1851
**WATERS** Elizabeth of Greenwich, NY

**BEATTIE** David of Salem, NY      February 12, 1851
**GETTY** Nancy W. of W. Hebron, NY      Hebron, NY

**MC CLELLAN** William of Jackson, NY      February 27, 1851
**GAMBLE** Charlotte of Jackson, NY      Jackson, NY

**BENNETT** John formerly of White Creek, NY      February 11, 1851
**CURTIS** Cornelia A. of Maumenee, Ill      Maumenee, Ill.

**ROBERTSON** Duncan of Argyle, NY      February 27, 1851
**ARMSTRONG** Alice of Argyle, NY      Argyle, NY

**BAIN** Hugh G. of Argyle, NY      February 25, 1851
**MC INTYRE** Esther of Argyle, NY

**BARNES** Henry Jr.      March 18, 1851
**MC LEAN** Ellen      Jackson, NY

**MOSHER** John of Waterloo, Wis.      March 20, 1851
**CROSS** Charity L. of White Creek, NY      White Creek, NY

MC NAUGHT Jeremiah of Union Village, NY     April 3, 1851
WEST Julia of Union Village, NY     Union Village, NY

REYNOLDS Dudley H. of Lockport, NY     April 3, 1851
PARKER Harriet S. of Greenwich, NY     Union Village, NY

DOUBLEDAY Horace L. of Sandy Hill, NY     April 20, 1851
PLATT Catherine of Sandy Hill, NY     Sandy Hill, NY

LONG Col. Berry of Cambridge, NY     May 15, 1851
BAKER Margaret of White Creek, NY     White Creek, NY

CHAPIN Lyman of Easton, NY     May 24, 1851
MOORE Mary of Easton, NY     White Creek, NY

STEAD Henry Jr. of Greenwich, NY     May 14, 1851
REED Sarah E. dau of William of Easton, NY     Easton, NY

PERRINE Nicholson P. of Rennsalaer Co. NY     May 7, 1851
MAIRS Margaret dau of late Rev. George of Argyle, NY     Argyle, NY

TIPLADY John of Hebron, NY     May 21/27, 1851
HASTINGS Mrs. Sussetta of Lowell, Mass.     Lowell, Mass.

MC KIE Charles R. of Clinton Co. Mi.    (newspaper date)     May 29, 1851
VOLENTINE Mary A. dau of Daniel of Jackson, NY     Jackson, NY

GIFFORD Ira M. of Peoria, Ill.     May 31, 1851
STRATTON Martha B. of Lansingburgh, NY     Jackson, NY

COLBY Joseph K. of Troy, NY     June 17, 1851
ROBERTSON Jane of Troy, NY

THOMPSON B. M. of Glens Falls, NY     June 25, 1851
SHERMAN Abby G. of Glens Falls, NY

STODDARD Horace L. of Arlington, Vt.     July 4, 1851
COREY Clarinda D. of White Creek, NY     White Creek, NY

ANDREWS Justine E. of Jackson, NY     July 12, 1851
HAZLEM Mary A. of Jackson, NY     White Creek, NY

RATHBONE Paul of Easton, NY     July 3, 1851
GIFFORD Mary dau of Nathan of Cambridge, NY     Cambridge, NY

LUDLOW Jacob of Ballston Spa, NY     July 8, 1851
VAUGHN Mary of Kingsbury, NY

CARSON Thomas     June 25, 1851

**COLLIGAN** Ann of Rutland, Vt.                    Putnam, NY

**KNAPP** Henry J. of Union Village, NY             July 3, 1851
**SHERWOOD** Julia A.                               Union Village, NY

**AMIDON** Henry of Salem, NY                       July 15, 1851
**STEVENS** Adeline of Salem, NY                    Salem, NY

**WITHERELL** Jacob of Bennington, Vt.              August 2, 1851
**ROBERTSON** Emily                                 White Creek, MY

**WINDSOR** Joseph of Troy, NY                      January 1, 1854
**BENNETT** Susan C. of Cambridge, NY               Cambridge, NY

**MAWHINNEY** William of Cambridge, NY              December 29, 1853
**SWANZY** Eliza of Cambridge, NY

**PIKE** George E. of Eastport, Maine               January 3, 1854
**SANDS** Susan F. of Castleton, Vt.                Cambridge, NY

**BARTON** Eli Jr. of White Creek, NY               January 5, 1854
**SMITH** Charlotte of White Creek, NY

**BARKER** Slocum of White Creek, NY                December 28, 1853
**CROSS** Adelaide of Shaftsbury, Vt.

**WHITE** Joseph of Euelyd, Ohio                    January 3, 1854
**HUGHES** Sarah M. of Cambridge, NY                Bristol, Ind.

**HUNT** John P. of White Creek, NY                 January 19, 1854
**BURDICK** Nancy S. of White Creek, NY

**PATRELL** Cary of Arlington, Vt.                  January 25, 1854
**CLARK** Mary of Hoosick, NY                       White Creek, NY

**HAWTHORNE** Henry H.                              February 14, 1854
**GILL** Adelle of Hoosick Falls, NY                Cambridge, NY

**HERRINGTON** T. of Arlington, Vt.                 February 1, 1854
**WINLESS** Catherine of E. Salem, NY               E. Salem, NY

**AYLSWORTH** Myron of Shaftsbury, Vt.              February 14, 1854
**EDDY** Clarissa of Shaftsbury, Vt.                Shaftsbury, Vt.

**DU BOIS** Alonzo                                  March 1, 1854
**STONE** Mary A. dau of Col. A. Stone              Jackson, NY

**PHELPS** George R. of Brunswick, NY               February 20, 1854
**ASHLEY** Margaret A. of Brunswick, NY             Cambridge, NY

LEWIS James D. of Fabius, NY         (newspaper date)     April 7, 1854
SURDAM Jane Maria of White Creek, NY     White Creek, NY

GRAHAM James Mc Lean     March 30, 1854
JOHNSON Elizabeth dau of Leonard formerly of White Creek   Reynoldsburg, Oh.

BREESE John of Waterloo, Ohio     June 6, 1854
BLOWERS Harriet of White Creek, NY     White Creek, NY

DAY Henry C. of Albany, NY     June 1, 1854
FLOOD Laura E. of Brooklyn, NY     Brooklyn, NY

MONEYPENNY John Md. of New York City     June 22, 1854
MC CAULEY Margaret dau of Peter of Coila, NY

GRAY J. J. of San Francisco, Cal.     July 27, 1854
BOYD Mattie W. dau of late Hugh of N. White Creek, NY   N. White Creek, NY

BRACKETT Dr. of Alabama     August 4, 1854
BILLINGS Amanda dau of Elisha of Jackson, NY     Jackson, NY

LARMON John of Cambridge, NY     September 12, 1854
KING Frances L. dau of John of White Creek, NY     Eagle Bridge, NY

ANDRUS J. M. of Pawlet, Vt.     September 20, 1854
RUSTE Mary E. of White Creek, NY

MC DOUGAL Alexander of Cambridge, NY     September 10, 1854
MC KIEVER Ann of White Creek, NY     White Creek, NY

FENTON Walter L. of Cambridge, NY     September 27, 1854
HOUGHTON Sarah E. dau of Andrew of Buskirks Bridge   Buskirks Bridge, NY

COWAN John H. of Cambridge, NY     July 26, 1854
SKELLIE Rosilly of Cambridge, NY     White Creek, NY

SHERWOOD Lemuel of Hoosick, NY     August 14, 1854
HAYNES Mary E. of Hoosick, NY     White Creek, NY

RUSSELL Hudson A. of White Creek, NY     October 4, 1854
EDDY Mary Ann of Shaftsbury, Vt.

BRIGGS Christopher of Ft. Covington, NY     October 3, 1854
RUSSELL Sylvia formerly of White Creek, NY

ROBINSON George C. of Ft. Covington, NY     October 5, 1854
SPENCER Mrs. Clarissa of Ft. Covington, NY

GAGE William A. of Bedford, NH     October 16, 1854

**MERRILL** Mary Jane Nassau, NH                                    Jackson, NY

**BARBER** Alvin S. of Jackson, NY                                  October 12, 1854
**CLARK** Mary M. of Jackson, NY                                    Jackson, NY

**WHITE** John of Hebron, NY                                        October 25, 1854
**PARISH** Sarah of Jackson, NY

**TEFFT** James Cutler formerly of White Creek, NY                  October 31, 1854
**SEXTON** Louisa Rebecca                                           Leroy, NY

**ROBERTSON** James S. of Coila, NY                                 November 23, 1854
**WARNER** Elizabeth dau of William S. of White Creek, NY           White Creek, NY

**WILSON** S. Newton of Genesse, Id.                                December 26, 1854
**JOSLIN** Ann Eliza of Cambridge, NY

**MITCHELL** Joseph of Cambridge, NY                                December 27, 1854
**CULVER** Mary of Jackson, NY                                      Jackson, NY

**THOMAS** Samuel of Easton, NY                                     December 25, 1854
**SLOCUM** Mary E. of Granville, NY                                 White Creek, NY

**WILLETT** Franklin of Cambridge, NY                               January 1, 1855
**BROWNELL** Adelia of Easton, NY

**GARDNER** Alonzo of White Creek, NY                               January 3, 1855
**MONROE** Sarah of White Creek, NY

**SWEET** Aruna H. Jr.                                              January 2, 1855
**VAN VECHTEN** Martha A. dau of Cornelius of White Creek           Eagle Bridge, NY

**MC OMBER** Jeremiah M.                                            January 18, 1855
**RICE** Wealthy Ann                                                White Creek, NY

**GOODWIN** George of White Creek, NY                               January 24, 1855
**BENNETT** Eliza dau of late Rev. E. E. of White Creek, NY         White Creek, NY

**LOURIE** thomas B. of Cambridge, NY                               January 25, 1855
**STEVENSON** Sarah Jane dau of John of Cambridge, NY

**WILSON** Joseph W.                                                January 13, 1855
**MILLER** Elizabeth dau of late Rev. J. P. formerly Argyle         Salem, NY

**BEVERIDGE** Andrew of Greenwich, NY                               January 30, 1855
**MC ARTHUR** Jennett A. of E. Salem, NY                            E. Salem, NY

**FRENCH** Orrin of Salem, NY                                       December 17, 1854
**RANDALL** Betsey of Salem, NY                                     Shushan, NY

HARRINGTON Benjamin of Easton, NY       February 13, 1855
HARRINGTON Hannah of Easton, NY       White Creek, NY

TILLOTSON William       January 1, 1855
WALLACE L. M.       Shushan, NY

FENTON A. H. of Aurora, Ill.       January 25, 1855
WING Martha dau of Charles       Shushan, NY

PALMER J. H. formerly of N. White Creek, NY       March 1, 1855
FISHER Martha of Montgomery Co. Md.       Rockville, Md.

BUSHNELL Edward I. of Armenia, NY       March 20, 1855
SHERMAN Sarah Jane of Cambridge, NY       Cambridge, NY

HILL Alexander of Cambridge, NY       March 15, 1855
GLASS Lydia M. of Skeneatles, NY       Cambridge, NY

AMES Bernice D. pf Ft. Edward, NY       March 20, 1855
KING Sarah E. of Ft. Edward, NY       Ft. Edward, NY

QUA John A. of Ft. Covington, NY       March 17, 1855
STARKS Delight M. of Ft. Covington, NY       Ft. Covington, NY

SMITH A. of Waymart, Pa.       April 1, 1855
DORR Sarah M. formerly of White Creek, NY       Waymart, Pa.

WILLETT John of Cambridge, NY       March 7, 1855
WOOD Priscilla of Cambridge, NY       White Creek, NY

MICKEL James of Argyle, NY     (newspaper date)       April 13, 1855
POWELL Nancy of Hebron, NY       Hebron, NY

ROBERTSON William P. of N. White Creek, NY       April 24, 1855
HUBBARD Permelia F. of N. White Creek, NY       N. White Creek, NY

LAWRENCE R. O.       April 22, 1855
HEATH M. dau of J. D.       Shushan, NY

FOWLER James P. of Cambridge, NY       May 24, 1855
JOSLIN Harriet dau of late William of Cambridge, NY       Cambridge, NY

SMITH Guy of Sandgate, Vt.       June 5, 1855
MILLER Electa Maria dau of William S. of Hampton, NY       Low Hampton, NY

WATTLES Alden of New York City       May 20, 1855
BINNINGER Helen dau of A. M.       New York City

MC HENRY Rev. D. S. of Michigan       May 12, 1855

**BARBER** Margaret M. dau of David of White Creek, NY — White Creek, NY

**LIVINGSTON** John R. formerly of White Creek, NY — May 24, 1855
**GRAHAM** Margaret Jane of Reynoldsburg, Oh. — Reynoldsburg, Oh.

**CORNELL** Flavius T. of White Creek, NY — July 4, 1855
**DUEL** Mary Elizabeth of Cambridge, NY — Cambridge, NY

**FOWLER** William P. of White Creek, NY — August 1, 1855
**GOODING** Ellen of White Creek, NY — White Creek, NY

**POWELL** William Henry of Peoria, Ill. — August 7, 1855
**PRATT** Lucy H. dau of David of Cambridge, NY

**LOVELAND** E. W. of San Franciso, Cal. — August 15, 1855
**GRAY** Margaret of White Creek, NY

**CARROL** John W. of Sunderland, Vt. — August 16, 1855
**CLEARWATER** Harriet C. of Sunderland, NY — White Creek, NY

**SOUTHWICK** A. J. of Cambridge, NY (removed to Iowa) — October 2, 1855
**GRAY** Mary B. dau of Henry C. of Cambridge, NY — Cambridge, NY

**HOOKER** Samuel B. of Allegeny Co. Mi. — October 31, 1855
**WATKINS** Zina Maria of White Creek, NY — Cambridge, NY

**CHENEY** John of Londonderry, Vt. — October 30, 1855
**KNAPP** Armena of Waverly, NY — White Creek, NY

**WOODWORTH** Alfred of White Creek, NY — November 15, 1855
**WOOD** Martha A. of White Creek, NY

**PRATT** Adam C. of Cambridge, NY — November 19, 1855
**CRONKHITE** Amy Ann of Greenfield, NY

**BAKER** Fletcher of White Creek, NY — Thanksgiving Day
**WELLS** Ellen M. of White Creek, NY

**WAIT** A. D. of Ft. Edward, NY — December 11, 1855
**DARROW** Celina dau of Hiram — Cambridge, NY

**RUSSELL** Derick C. Atty. of Salem, NY — December 20, 1855
**PEMBERTON** Hattie A. dau of Henry of Albany, NY — Albany, NY

**BUDD** John J. of Chatham, Columbia Co. NY — December 19, 1855
**PALMER** Derinda of White Creek, NY — White Creek, NY

**HEATH** Bartlett — December 24, 1855
**WING** Hannah Maria — Shushan, NY

| | |
|---|---|
| **WING** Merritt F. | December 24, 1855 |
| **JACKSON** Sarah D. | Shushan, NY |
| | |
| **BARNES** Merritt formerly of W. Arlington, Vt. | December 9, 1855 |
| **CRAWFORD** Clarissa E. of Saratoga Springs, NY | Saratoga Springs, NY |
| | |
| **MANNING** John B. of Albany, NY | January 14, 1856 |
| **HOUSE** Elizabeth of White Creek, NY | White Creek, NY |
| | |
| **BLOWERS** William M. of White Creek, NY | January 17, 1856 |
| **HASOM** Caroline of Cambridge, NY | Cambridge, NY |
| | |
| **DARROW** J. C. of Cambridge, NY | January 22, 1856 |
| **KING** Mary A. of Cambridge, NY | Cambridge, NY |
| | |
| **ROUSE** Joseph of Argyle, NY | January 17, 1856 |
| **MAXWELL** Margaret Ann of Jackson, NY | Jackson, NY |
| | |
| **EDDY** Albert C. of Cambridge, NY | February 5, 1856 |
| **BARTON** Charlotte of Cambridge, NY | Cambridge, NY |
| | |
| **STEVENS** Martin P. of Shushan, NY | February 6, 1856 |
| **VOLENTINE** Elsie Sophia of Jackson, NY | Jackson, NY |
| | |
| **FOSTER** Daniel A. of Cambridge, NY | February 5, 1856 |
| **DANA** Caroline of Cambridge, NY | Cambridge, NY |
| | |
| **FOWLER** Alonzo G. of Aurora, Ill. | February 19, 1856 |
| **DEUEL** Nancy B. of Cambridge, NY | Cambridge, NY |
| | |
| **AUSTIN** William | February 21, 1856 |
| **HASTINGS** Fanny A. | Shushan, NY |
| | |
| **O'KEEFE** John O. of Jackson, NY | February 29, 1856 |
| **NORTON** Sarina of Jackson, NY | White Creek, NY |
| | |
| **FRENCH** Franklin of N. Hoosick, NY | March 2, 1856 |
| **MATTISON** Sally of White Creek, NY | White Creek, NY |
| | |
| **KING** G. H. of Ft. Plain, NY | March 5, 1856 |
| **TILLINGHAST** Teressa of Pittstown, NY | Pittstown, NY |
| | |
| **PELOR** John H. of Troy, NY | March 5, 1856 |
| **MURRELL** Louisa of White Creek, NY | White Creek, NY |
| | |
| **BARTON** Henry G. of White Creek, NY | October 20, 1855 |
| **MC ALL** Helen M. of White Creek, NY | White Creek, NY |
| | |
| **MASON** Nathan of Madison, Wis. | February 26, 1856 |

**GIFFORD** Elizabeth of Cambridge, NY                    White Creek, NY

**HARWOOD** John of Bennington, Vt.                    March 16, 1856
**CRAWFORD** Clarissa of Bennington, Vt.                    White Creek, NY

**HILL** Thomas W.                    March 26, 1856
**GREEN** Alviry                    White Creek, NY

**NICHOLSON** Rollin E. of White Creek, NY                    May 22, 1856
**HANNA** Mary E. of White Creek, NY                    White Creek, NY

**THATCHER** J. K. of Albany, NY                    June 3, 1856
**PUTNAM** Mary D. B. of White Creek, NY                    White Creek, NY

**CULVER** Henry of Cambridge, NY                    June 4, 1856
**MC FARLAND** Mary Jane dau of Col. John of Salem, NY                    Salem, NY

**BABCOCK** John                    June 10, 1856
**NELSON** Margaret of Coila, NY                    Coila, NY

**BEALS** Alden P. of Cambridge, NY                    June 14, 1856
**WAIT** Augusta dau of late Justin of Hatfield, Mass                    Hatfield, Mass.

**SAYLES** Francis O. of Shushan, NY                    June 15, 1856
**LAWRENCE** Sarah E. of Shushan, NY                    Buskirks Bridge, NY

**HANNA** Robert of Salem, NY                    June 19, 1856
**RUSTE** Amanda of White Creek, NY                    White Creek, NY

**JOSLIN** Martin of White Creek, NY                    July 2, 1856
**WELLS** Abiah of White Creek, NY                    Cambridge, NY

**LEPPERMAN** Abram                    July 20, 1856
**GROVER** Ruth Adelaide of N. Bennington, Vt.                    Buskirks Bridge, NY

**BROWNELL** William of Cambridge, NY                    August 3, 1856
**KENNISON** Charlotte of Easton, NY                    Cambridge, NY

**BUELL** James of Troy, NY                    (newspaper date)                    August 8, 1856
**KELLOGG** Electa B. dau of Orrin of Cambridge, NY                    Cambridge, NY

**MC FARLAND** Samuel of Cambridge, NY                    August 9, 1856
**CENTER** Caroline of White Creek, NY                    Pittstown, NY

**CRAIG** James of Hebron, NY                    September 9, 1856
**PARISH** Jane of Jackson, NY                    Jackson, NY

**MINOR** Clement S. Jr. of Rutland, Vt.                    September 15, 1856
**CLAPP** Mary C. dau of Col. E. W. of Jackson, NY                    Jackson, NY

| | |
|---|---|
| **WHELDON** Francis J. of Easton, NY | September 23, 1856 |
| **MARSHALL** Mary of Cambridge, NY | Cambridge, NY |
| | |
| **LAWRENCE** Phillip of Hoosick, NY | July 13, 1856 |
| **CROSBEE** Helen M. of Hoosick, NY | White Creek, NY |
| | |
| **SLADE** Nelson of Hoosick, NY | September 9, 1856 |
| **NICHOLS** Charlot of Pittstown, NY | White Creek, NY |
| | |
| **BOSWORTH** George of Union Village, NY | September 24, 1856 |
| **BLOOMINGDALE** Anna C. of Union Village, NY | |
| | |
| **BEATTIE** Samuel B. of Salem, NY | September 29, 1856 |
| **GOODWIN** Eliza M. of Pawlet, Vt. | Lake, NY |
| | |
| **HARPER** William of Jackson, NY | October 22, 1856 |
| **MAXWELL** Jennette Ann of Jackson, NY | |
| | |
| **SCOTT** Olin of Bennington, Vt. | October 30, 1856 |
| **GILBERT** Celestia E. dau of Samuel of Shushan, NY | Shushan, NY |
| | |
| **LAKE** Thomas H. of White Creek, NY | November 11, 1856 |
| **WYMAN** Lydia M. of White Creek, NY | White Creek, NY |
| | |
| **HARD** Thomas G. of W. Rupert, Vt. | November 16, 1856 |
| **HOWE** Bethiah of Wells, Vt. | W. Rupert, Vt. |
| | |
| **PRENTISS** Mason of White Creek, NY | October 15, 1856 |
| **ELLIS** Mary of White Creek, NY | N. White Creek, NY |
| | |
| **BARBER** Andrew of Pownal, Vt. | November 26, 1856 |
| **SHAW** Laura A. | N. White Creek, NY |
| | |
| **KENNEDY** Lysander W. of Cambridge, NY | November 26, 1856 |
| **STEVENSON** Anna May dau of William of Cambridge, NY | Cambridge, NY |
| | |
| **SCOTT** Rev. J. P. of Ohio | December 2, 1856 |
| **GIFFORD** M. Julia of Coila, NY | Coila, NY |
| | |
| **RAIDEN** John of Buskirks Bridge, NY | December 20, 1856 |
| **STAR** Mary Jane of Cambridge, NY | Cambridge, NY |
| | |
| **WESTCOTT** Oliver | December 16, 1856 |
| **LEE** Harriet M. | Trenton Falls |
| | |
| **RICH** Charles H. of White Creek, NY | December 23, 1856 |
| **MC CLELLAN** Sarah M. of Cambridge, NY | Cambridge, NY |
| | |
| **PRATT** Edward of White Creek, NY | December 26, 1856 |

| | |
|---|---|
| **POMEROY** Delia of Poultney, Vt. | Poultney, Vt. |
| | |
| **MASTEN** Cornelius S. of Beloit, Wis. | January 6, 1857 |
| **RUSSELL** Josephine M dau of George of E. Salem, NY | |
| | |
| **COON** Russell S. of Salem, NY | December 31, 1856 |
| **OVIATT** Margaret grand dau of John MC MILLAN | Salem, NY |
| | |
| **MC NEIL** Alexander of E. Greenwich, NY | December 30, 1856 |
| **MC ARTHUR** Elizabeth dau of Robert of Jackson, NY | Jackson, NY |
| | |
| **WHELDON** John M. of Pawlet, Vt. | January 1, 1857 |
| **PARKER** Mary Eliza dau of Col. Joseph of W. Rupert, Vt. | W. Rupert, Vt. |
| | |
| **CRUIKSHANK** James A. of Salem, NY | December 31, 1856 |
| **TIPLADY** Sarah E. dau of John of Hebron, NY | Hebron, NY |
| | |
| **MC FADDEN** Archibald of Ft. Edward, NY | January 6, 1857 |
| **TAYLOR** Deborah of Lakeville, NY | |
| | |
| **HAGER** Frederick M. of Cambridge, NY | January 1, 1857 |
| **BROWNELL** Sylva of Cambridge, NY | White Creek, NY |
| | |
| **OVIATT** Wilson of Salem, NY | February 5, 1857 |
| **HUBBARD** Margaret of White Creek, NY | White Creek, NY |
| | |
| **ASHTON** Dr. John | January 29/31, 1857 |
| **LOURIE** Jennette | |
| | |
| **TROWBRIDGE** George B. of New York City | February 12, 1857 |
| **FENTON** Adeline dau of Zalmon of Cambridge, NY | Cambridge, NY |
| | |
| **HALL** Fayette of Hartford, NY | January 20, 1857 |
| **COTTON** Cyntha of Hartford, NY | Hartford, NY |
| | |
| **LENDRUM** William of Argyle, NY | January 28, 1857 |
| **HARSHA** Mary of Argyle, NY | Argyle, NY |
| | |
| **GREEN** Morris | February 10, 1857 |
| **GILBERT** Harriet A. of Jackson, NY | |
| | |
| **ARNOTT** William of Jackson, NY | February 10, 1857 |
| **KERR** Mary of Jackson, NY | |
| | |
| **NILES** Harmon D. of Shaftsbury, Vt. | January 28, 1857 |
| **TINKHAM** Oceana G. of Shaftsbury, Vt. | White Creek, NY |
| | |
| **CAMPBELL** Niles of Onieda Co. NY | March 4, 1857 |
| **FULLER** Helen W. dau of Freeman of White Creek, NY | White Creek, NY |

FULLER Nathaniel of Shaftsbury, Vt.                                    March 12, 1857
FRENCH Mrs. Hannah Roxanna of Weston, Vt.                              White Creek, NY

BULLIONS David G. of W. Milton, NY                                     March 19, 1857
GREEN Julia A. of Cambridge, NY                                        Cambridge, NY

BAKER Benjamin of White Creek, NY                                      March 19, 1857
WITHERELL Eunice A. dau of Alanson of White Creek, NY  White Creek, NY

WITHERELL Lafayette of White Creek, NY                                 March 21, 1857
BAKER Sarah R. dau of Bennett of White Creek, NY

GREEN James Jr. of Cambridge, NY                                       February 13, 1857
GREEN Ruth H. dau of Thomas S. of Cambridge, NY

PRATT William J. of White Creek, NY                                    March 26, 1857
CENTER Iva J. of White Creek, NY                                       White Creek, NY

TINGUE Leonard of Cambridge, NY                                        April 19, 1857
CALLAHAN Margaret of Cambridge, NY                                     Schuylerville, NY

FARRELL Martin Edgar of Lansingburgh, NY                               March 25, 1857
ADAMS Delia of Lansingburgh, NY                                        Lansingburgh, NY

WALLIS Marvin of White Creek, NY                                       April 18, 1857
BARNHART Elisabeth of White Creek, NY                                  White Creek, NY

SMITH Daniel of New York City                                          April 12, 1857
GARRETT Mary Ann                                                       Johnsonville, NY

WEBB Martin of Cambridge, NY                                           April 30, 1857
MAYNARD Amanda of N. White Creek, NY                                   N. White Creek, NY

DAVIS Harvey J. of Springfield, Mi.                                    May 14, 1857
SIMPSON Maria A. of Springfield, Mi.

GRAY Clark of Penfield, NY                                             May 14, 1857
WATKINS Atlanta of N. White Creek, NY

HAWLEY Curtis R. of White Creek, NY                                    June 2, 1857
HAWLEY Julia E. of White Creek, NY                                     White Creek, NY

WATKINS John of White Creek, NY                                        June 25, 1857
FENTON Mary J. of White Creek, NY                                      Cambridge, NY

HOYT George P.                                                         June 24, 1857
TURNER E. M. of Sandgate, Vt.                                          Cambridge, NY

PERRY William H. of White Creek, NY  (newspaper date)                  July 3, 1857

**MOSHER** Mary D. dau of David of White Creek, NY — White Creek, NY

**FERGUSON** John of Salem, NY — July 4, 1857
**WILDER** Susan of Jackson, NY — Shushan, NY

**WALKLEY** W. E. of White Creek, NY — July 29, 1857
**HOGABOOM** Jennie E. of Claverack, NY — Claverack, NY

**CORNELL** Mc D. of Philadelphia, Pa. — July 25, 1857
**NOXON** Phebe Ann dau of James P. formerly White Creek — Philadelphia, Pa.

**WINNIE** Smith of White Creek, NY — August 5, 1857
**CHASE** Sharlot of White Creek, NY — White Creek, NY

**MILLER** James L. formerly of White Creek, NY — August 6, 1857
**CONNEL** Jennette M. Keokuk, Iowa — Keokuk, Iowa

**SMITH** James of White Creek, NY — August 16, 1857
**MILLIMAN** Lucy Ann of White Creek, NY — White Creek, NY

**WOODARD** Gibson of Shaftsbury, Vt. — August 15, 1857
**EDDY** Esther M. of White Creek, NY — White Creek, NY

**KILBOURN** Sylvanus of Sunderland, Vt. — August 18, 1857
**BENTLEY** Lydia of Sunderland, Vt. — White Creek, NY

**PETERS** Richard of Salem, NY — September 2, 1857
**WELCH** Catherine of Salem, NY — White Creek, NY

**NORTON** Warren of N. White Creek, NY — September 1, 1857
**BLIVEN** Lydia W. of Galesville, NY — Galesville, NY

**DUNN** Charles of Jackson, NY — September 2, 1857
**TILFORD** Mary J. of Jackson, NY — Jackson, NY

**HOUGHTON** J. S. of New York City — September 17, 1857
**HOUGHTON** Mrs. Alfred of Cambridge, NY — White Creek, NY

**BARTON** Mial P. of White Creek, NY — September 24, 1857
**WILSON** M. Antoinette of White Creek, NY — White Creek, NY

**PARRY** Joseph Jr. of Davenport, Iowa — September 22, 1857
**BECKER** Arminta C. of Easton, NY — Easton, NY

**WADSWORTH** George W. of Jackson, NY — September 28, 1857
**BURKE** Catherine of Jackson, NY

**MC VEAGH** Charles — August 12, 1857
**WARNER** Sarah M. formerly of Cambridge, NY — Mariposs, Cal.

BARRETT David of Dresden, NY     October 20, 1857
LYON Sarah of Whitehall, NY     Whitehall, NY

SANDERSON E. L. of Greenwich, NY     November 3, 1857
NASH Mary E. dau of Edwin B. of Ft. Edward, NY     Ft. Edward, NY

PRIEST Josiah of Greenwich, NY     November 4, 1857
HARRINGTON Charlotte of Greewich, NY     White Creek, NY

ARMSTRONG Archibald of Salem, NY     November 5, 1857
FOSTER Mary M. dau of Robert L. of Salem, NY

BUDD John C. of New York City     October 14, 1857
IVES Mary Azelia of S. Easton, NY     S. Easton, NY

KINNEY John of Shaftsbury, Vt.     November 15, 1857
FISHER Margaret of Shaftsbury, Vt.     White Creek, NY

RANNEY Evander W. Md. of New York City     December 9, 1857
QUA Ann C. of Brooklyn, NY     Brooklyn, NY

HILLMAN Lafayette of Jackson, NY     December 26/30, 1857
BARBER Olive of Jackson, NY     Union Village, NY

HUBBARD Edgar B. of Wauconda, Ill.     December 22, 1857
BROWN F. M. formerly of White Creek, NY     Wauconda, Ill.

BULL Gurdon of Troy, NY     January 13, 1858
FULLER Jane E. dau of F. A. of White Creek, NY     White Creek, NY

KING Valentine of Russelton, Canada     January 4, 1858
CLEMENT Martha A. of Ft. Edward, NY     Ft. Edward, NY

WHITFORD Daniel P. of Saratoga Springs, NY     January 13, 1858
CHURCHILL Adelia dau of David of Ft. Edward, NY     Ft. Edward, NY

STANNARD Waters A. of Clinton, Conn.     January 20, 1858
STEVENSON Sarah Mary of Cambridge, NY

BAKER Jehail of White Creek, NY     January 20, 1858
HALL Alvira L. dau of Orla of Salem, NY     Salem, NY

GADSON William Q. of Chicago, Ill.     January 26, 1858
RICH Margaret P. F. of White Creek, NY

ROBERTSON Edgerton J. of Cambridge, NY     January 27, 1858
RICE Minnie S. dau of Daniel of Easton, NY     Easton, NY

STOWELL Ebenezer W. of Windham, Vt.    (newspaper date) March 4, 1858

**WHITCOMB** Mariah J. of Windham, Vt.

**KING** William H. of White Creek, NY                    March 3, 1858
**AGAN** Mary C. of White Creek, NY

**HARRINGTON** Elisha                                     March 3, 1858
**AUSTIN** Rosanna M.                                     N. White Creek, NY

**ELDRICH** William of N. White Creek, NY                 March 16, 1858
**MAXWELL** Elizabeth of Jackson, NY

**LIVINGSTON** J. P.                                      March 27, 1858
**GREEN** Patience                                        Cambridge, NY

**MORSE** Horace of Greenwich, NY                         April 6, 1858
**HUTTON** Mary A. of Greenwich, NY                       Greenwich, NY

**NIXON** Rev. J. H.                                      April 21, 1858
**JEWELL** Flora H.                                       Washington DC

**PRATT** D. H. of White Creek, NY                        April 27, 1858
**CONANT** Charlotte of W. Pawlet, Vt.                    W. Pawlet, Vt.

**SLOAN** Rev. J. R. W. of New York City                  May 4, 1858
**MC CLAREN** Margaret C. dau of Rev. Donald Mc Claren    Geneva, NY

**MERRIAM** A. B. of Cincinnati, Ohio                     June 10, 1858
**BRACKETT** Amanda B. dau of Col. **BILLINGS** of E. Salem  E. Salem, NY

**BARBER** George M. formerly of White Creek, NY          June 2, 1858
**TAGGART** Jennie of Keokuk, Iowa                        Keokuk, Iowa

**NICHOLS** J. H. of White Creek, NY                      June 16, 1858
**WYLIE** Hattie dau of John W. of Pittsfield, Mass       Pittsfield, Mass.

**ARMSTRONG** D. H. Md. of Wayne Co. NY                   June 10, 1858
**FITCH** Mary W. of Salem, NY                            Salem, NY

**JENNINGS** John P. of Troy, NY                          June 21, 1858
**HILLMAN** Louise M. of Greenwich, NY                    Troy, NY

**CLAPP** George of Rupert, Vt.                           July 1, 1858
**PRATT** Deborah A. of Cambridge, NY                     Cambridge, NY

**YOUNG** James of Jackson, NY                            June 14, 1858
**HARPER** Mary Ann of Jackson, NY                        Jackson, NY

**DYER** Martin D.                                        July 1, 1858
**ALLEN** Cornelia                                        Fairhaven, Vt.

COON Parry of Hoosick Falls, NY
MC OMBER Susan of Hoosick Falls, NY

January 3, 1858

BALDWIN Samuel of Cambridge, NY
CRAMER Elizabeth of Cambridge, NY

June 24, 1858
White Creek, NY

SLOCUM Miron C. of White Creek, NY
CURTIS Emily of Shaftsbury, Vt.

July 2, 1858
White Creek, NY

MILLINGTON Solomon of N. Bennington, Vt.
HOGLE Sarah Jane of Ashtabula, Ohio

July 4, 1858
White Creek, NY

BUCK David of Shaftsbury, Vt.
OLIN Miriam S. of Shaftsbury, Vt.

July 14, 1858
White Creek, NY

WALLACE Robert B. of Waterford, NY
MAIN Mary C. of Easton, NY

June 29, 1858
Lansingburgh, NY

KING B. W. of Ft. Edward, NY
PALMER Eliza A. of Hartford, NY

August 9, 1858
Hartford, NY

WHITTAKER Horace of Greenwich, NY
BAIN Catherine A. of Greenwich, NY

August 12, 1858
Argyle, NY

BLAKELEY Warren of Union Village, NY
WILLIAMS Hannah M. of W. Troy, NY

August 11, 1858
W. Troy, NY

BAUMES Adam of Galesville, NY
SADLEY Lucinda of Easton, NY

August 5, 1858
Ft. Miller, NY

BULLIONS Alexander B. of Waukeshaw, Wis.
EDDY Lucy J. dau of Titus of Troy, NY

August 25, 1858
Troy, NY

SMART W. S. of Xenia, Ohio
CHIPMAN S. J.

September 8, 1858
Cheam Hill, Vt.

BRADFORD George W. of Bennington, Vt.
GOULD Sarah Jane of Bennington, Vt.

September 11, 1858
White Creek, NY

RIDER Isaac of Rider, Green Co. NY
COOPER Eveline of N. White Creek, NY

August 24, 1858
N. White Creek, NY

WRIGHT Clark of N. Hoosick, NY
BOWEN Harriet A. of N. Bennington, Vt.

September 15, 1858
Cambridge, NY

SHILAND Thomas E. of White Creek, NY
BLAKELEY Mary B. of White Creek, NY

September 22, 1858
White Creek, NY

HENRY J. J. of Granville, NY

September 15, 1858

FULLER Sarah J. dau of F. A. of White Creek, NY — White Creek, NY

ASHTON James W. of Ash Grove, NY — September 21, 1858
ARMSTRONG Sarah F. dau of George of Salem, NY — Salem, NY

CURTIS Horace B. of Sandgate, Vt. — September 1, 1858
HURD Adaline of Sandgate, Vt. — Cambridge, NY

ARNOLD Henry L. of N. White Creek, NY — October 21, 1858
LIVINGSTON Sarah Jane of N. White Creek, NY

BOYER Albert of E. Arlington, Vt. — October 2, 1858
ARMSTRONG Sarah of E. Arlington, Vt. — E. Arlington, Vt.

THOMAS William W. of Bennington, Vt. — November 11, 1858
FOWLER Henrietta of White Creek, NY

WILLARD H. Hubbell of Lexington, Mass. — November 11, 1858
HARRINGTON Mary A. of Cambridge, NY — Coila, NY

THOMAS David of Milport, NY — November 15, 1858
DEAN Sila M. of Cambridge, NY — White Creek, NY

GREEN Sullivan — October 14, 1858
DANFORTH Axy S. of Hoosick, NY — White Creek, NY

SNOW J. C. of Sandgate, Vt. — December 1, 1858
HURD Sylvia of Sandgate, Vt. — Cambridge, NY

SHAW Cornelius of Cohoes, NY — November 23, 1858
SPRAGUE Hellen M. of Salem, NY — Salem, NY

HOWARD Charles of Hebron, NY — November 16, 1858
BOSWORTH Eliza L. dau of Hezekiah of Hampton, NY — Hampton, NY

MASON Charles M. of Elkhorn, Wis. — November 25, 1858
BUCKLEY Ann Eliza dau of Ezra of Schaghticoke, NY

MC CLELLAN Robert H. of Galena, Ill. — December 1, 1858
SANFORD Carrie dau of Giles of Albany, NY — Framingham, Mass.

COGSHALL Peter of Easton, NY — November 25, 1858
BUCKLEY Sarah J. of Easton, NY — Easton, NY

GROESBECK William H. of Schaghticoke, NY — November 25, 1858
DURFEE Margaret S. of Cambridge, NY — Cambridge, NY

BURCH Henry S. — December 8, 1858
LEE Eliza M. — Cambridge, NY

**BRIGGS** Dennis of Shushan, NY
**BREWER** Amelia of Shushan, NY

December 12, 1858

**TINGUE** George A. of Cambridge, NY
**WOODWARD** Emila A. of Pawlet, Vt.

November 2, 1858

**HOVER** Henry of Jackson, NY
**HOVER** Flora of Jackson, NY

December 11, 1858
White Creek, NY

**NILES** Nathaniel M. of White Creek, NY
**SCRIVER** Irena of Troy, NY

December 16, 1858
Troy, NY

**BANCROFT** George D. of Ft. Edward, NY
**LADUE** Mattie of St. Edward, NY

December 15, 1858
Sandy Hill, NY

**HULSKAMP** Theodore of White Creek, NY
**ZOLLER** Sophia of Ft. Edward, NY

December 15, 1858
Sandy Hill, NY

**LANGWORTHY** Phineas B. of Greenwich, NY
**WEIR** Bersinet dau of David of Jackson, NY

December 22, 1858
Jackson, NY

**GRIFFIN** John A. of Sudbury, Vt.
**FOWLER** Helen Frances of Easton, NY

December 22, 1858
Easton, NY

**GREEN** Amos M.
**REID** Margaret A. of Greenwich, NY

December 11, 1858
Lakeville, NY

**BISHOP** John of Argyle, NY
**MC NEIL** Jane of Ft. Edward, NY

November 25, 1858

**GUTHRIE** Samuel of Hebron, NY
**DINGS** Rozelia of Argyle, NY

December 16, 1858

**SHELDON** Cornelius M. of Rupert, Vt.
**FOWLER** Julia A. of Rupert, Vt.

December 22, 1858
Rupert, Vt.

**HAWLEY** Edwin E. of Troy, NY
**PATTERSON** Carrie E. of Troy, NY

December 28, 1858
Troy, NY

**HILL** H. H. of Arlington, Vt.
**WAIT** Phebe of Shaftsbury, Vt.

January 5, 1859
Cambridge, NY

**LOVELL** Henry R. of Whitehall, NY
**HARRISON** Maria F. of Cambridge, NY

December 21, 1858
Westfield, Mass.

**HASTINGS** John of Jackson, NY
**WILDER** Betsey J. of Jackson, NY

January 4, 1859
Jackson, NY

**YOUNG** Alfred of Poultney, Vt.

January 6, 1859

**HOUGH** Lois of Poultney, Vt.                                  Eagle Bridge, NY

**HALL** John of Ft. Ann, NY                                     December 28, 1858
**HOPKINS** Nancy E. of Ft. Ann, NY

**MILLIMAN** George of Hoosick, NY                               January 2, 1859
**HOVER** Eliza Ann of Hoosick, NY                               N. Cambridge, NY

**HILL** Edwin                                                   January 13/19, 1859
**RICHARDSON** Mary D. C. dau of late A. E.                      Argyle, NY

**CROSBY** S. W. of White Creek, NY                              January 20, 1859
**COLLINS** Sarah M. of Jackson, NY                              Jackson, NY

**GOODING** Seymour of Hoosick, NY                               January 24, 1859
**MILLIMAN** Marcia of Hoosick, NY                               N. Hoosick, NY

**SHEDD** Gilford D. of White Creek, NY                          January 24, 1859
**GOODING** Mary E. of Hoosick, NY                               N. Hoosick, NY

**FULLER** Olney                                                 January 24, 1859
**MILLIMAN** Betsey                                              N. Hoosick, NY

**RICE** C. H. of Stockbridge, Vt.                               February 16, 1859
**TEFFT** Emily of Greenwich, NY                                 Greenwich, NY

**AUSTIN** Thomas C. of W. Arlington, Vt.                        February 9, 1859
**HARRINGTON** Angeline of Easton, NY                            Easton, NY

**BEVERIDGE** James of Greenwich, NY                             February 10, 1859
**ARMSTRONG** Mary of Argyle, NY                                 Argyle, NY

**RANDLES** William of Argyle, NY                                January 10, 1859
**MC COY** Sarah A. of Argyle, NY                                Argyle, NY

**ROGERS** Sidney                                                February 8, 1859
**CRAWFORD** Mrs. Sarah                                          Hebron, NY

**BEATTIE** James of Hebron, NY                                  February 9, 1859
**BEATTIE** Sarah M. of Hebron, NY                               Hebron, NY

**COX** Ralph of Hoosick, NY                                     February 18, 1859
**FRANCIS** Clara of Hoosick, NY                                 Hoosick, NY

**CLAPP** Bernard of N. White Creek, NY                          January 7, 1859
**KERRY** Julia of N. White Creek, NY

**HOLLEY** William A. of Ft. Edward, NY                          March 10, 1859
**BATES** Mary T. dau of Rev. Merritt Bates                      N. White Creek, NY

MOORE Capt. E. B. at residence of William Moore — February 16, 1859
PRATT Maria P. of Washington Co. NY — Yazoo City, Miss.

PIKE Erastus of Sandy Hill, NY — March 16, 1859
FOWLER Lizzie M. of Argyle, NY — Argyle, NY

WEISBACH Paul of Argyle, NY — March 17, 1859
TAYLOR Harriet of Greenwich, NY

SMALL James E. of Cambridge, NY — March 16, 1859
BATTY Eliza M. of Easton, NY — Easton, NY

SWEET William W. of Shushan, NY — April 10, 1859
BLOWERS Margaret of White Creek, NY — White Creek, NY

EDDY Calvin of Shaftsbury, Vt. — March 16, 1859
BOYCE Eliza J. of Shaftsbury, Vt. — White Creek, NY

VAN ORMAN Jacob of Easton, NY — April 2, 1859
HERRINGTON Louisa of Easton, NY — Easton, NY

ROTH John W. of Sandy Hill, NY — April 21, 1859
BRIERLY Louisa of Sandy Hill, NY — Sandy Hill, NY

ARMITAGE John of Coila, NY — May 3, 1859
BARBER Julia A. of Cedar Rapids, Iowa — Argyle, NY

BROWN Elijah R. of W. Troy, NY — May 10, 1859
HOUSE Laura A. of Cambridge, NY — N. White Creek, NY

WARNER Nathaniel of Easton, NY — May 8, 1859
SPRINGER Miriam of Easton, NY — Easton, NY

AYRES George W. of Greenwich, NY — May 8, 1859
MC NULTY Catherine F. of Greenwich, NY — Greenwich, NY

CLAPP Ambrose Spencer of Salem, NY — May 18, 1859
DAY Amanda of Ft. Miller, NY — Ft. Miller, NY

HANSON Albert C. of Shushan, NY — May 11, 1859
TURNER Ellen E. of Salem, NY — Salem, NY

DWELLIE Albert of Greenwich, NY — June 1, 1859
WALKER Sarah M. of Salem, NY — Salem, NY

HOYT Albert H. of Castleton, Vt. — May 26, 1859
HALL Fannie D. dau of Dr. A. Hall of Whitehall, NY

JERMAIN George W. of Lockport, NY — June 9, 1859

**WARNER** Abigail P. J. of Milwaukee, Wis.                Milwaukee, Wis.

**MC KILLIP** Dwight of Shushan, NY                       June 22, 1859
**CULVER** Mary E. of Jackson, NY

**CASSELS** Thomas of Cambridge, NY                       July 27, 1859
**GOODWIN** Margaret Jane of Easton, NY                   Easton, NY

**FORT** Gerritt of Cambridge, NY                         August 22, 1859
**VAN VECHTEN** Eunice of Cambridge, NY                   Cambridge, NY

**THOMPSON** John Banks                                   July 29, 1859
**ROBERTSON** Susan formerly of N. White Creek, NY        Preston, Wis.

**PARKER** Rev. Carson of Aversboro, NC                   September 1, 1859
**FISHER** Anna Sarah dau of John of White Creek, NY      White Creek, NY

**MC GOWAN** John of Schaghticoke, NY                     August 21, 1859
**BECROFT** Ellen of Schaghticoke, NY

**AGAN** Jacob of N. White Creek, NY                      September 6, 1859
**SEELEY** Mary M. of N. White Creek, NY                  N. White Creek, NY

**GREGORY** John Jr. of Ferrisburgh, Vt.                  August 31, 1859
**COVEY** Dora E. of Sandgate, Vt.                        Granville, NY

**STEVENS** Clark A. of Shushan, NY                       September 2/14, 1859
**RICE** Julia A. dau of Roswell of N. White Creek, NY    N. White Creek, NY

**GOODING** Hiram M. of Hoosick, NY                       September 20, 1859
**FENTON** Charlotte S. of White Creek, NY                White Creek, NY

**NOBLE** Henry of White Creek, NY                        September 20, 1859
**BARTON** Sarah M. of White Creek, NY                    White Creek, NY

**BLASHFIELD** F. M.                                      September 21, 1859
**CROWL** Mary A.                                         Salem, NY

**WOODARD** James of Jackson, NY                          September 27, 1859
**COLLINS** Sarah of Jackson, NY                          Jackson, NY

**QUACKENBUSH** John W. of Easton, NY                     September 8, 1859
**HANDY** Caroline dau of late Elisha of Easton, NY       Easton, NY

**ARMSTRONG** J. A. of Argyle, NY                         August 30, 1859
**CARL** Carrie of Argyle, NY                             Argyle, NY

**MARSHALL** John R. of Jackson, NY                       October 6, 1859
**WARNER** Jane E. of Jackson, NY                         Jackson, NY

LAWTON Clark H. of Cambridge, NY — October 1, 1859
PRATT Sarah Ann of Shaftsbury Hollow, Vt. — N. White Creek, NY

CHASE George M. formerly of White Creek, NY — October 8, 1859
KILLIAN Sally A. — Martinsville, Ind.

BLISS Norton R. of Cheshire, Mass — November 26, 1859
BRATT Ladiuska of Hoosick, NY — White Creek, NY

FISHER Stephen R. of N. White Creek, NY — December 1, 1859
MOODY Frances R. of N. White Creek, NY

WALLACE Theodore C. of Schuylerville, NY — December 6, 1859
RICE Mary J. dau of Daniel of White Creek, NY — White Creek, NY

WILSON Robert of Cambridge, NY — December 3, 1859
EDMISTON Martha of N. White Creek, NY — Cambridge, NY

MC KIE James of White Creek, NY — December 8, 1859
WHITESIDE Annie of Cambridge, NY — Cambridge, NY

ARNOLD Aaron of Pittstown, NY — December 28, 1859
WORTHINGTON Elizabeth Margaret of Pittstown, NY — Cambridge, NY

COTTRELL Stephen of Schaghticoke, NY — January 4, 1860
DANFORTH Annetta of Pittstown, NY — Cambridge, NY

PRUYN Samuel of Glens Falls, NY — January 2, 1860
BALDWIN Eliza of Cambridge, NY — Cambridge, NY

COLBY Hiram of White Creek, NY — January 5, 1860
DICKINSON Eliza — Arlington, Vt.

CHAMBERS William J. of Union Village, NY — January 7, 1860
KNAPP Sarah of Union Village, NY — Union Village, NY

BECKER Edward S. of Cambridge, NY — January 12, 1860
WAIT Mary A. of Cambridge, NY — Cambridge, NY

GILCHRIST John of Argyle, NY — January 3, 1860
CARL Abigail of Argyle, NY — Argyle, NY

WESTFALL Daniel M. of White Creek, NY — February 8, 1860
HOWE Susan M. dau of L. J. of White Creek, NY — White Creek, NY

ROBINSON Freeman of Camden Valley, NY(newspaper date) — February 10, 1860
DANA Lydia M. dau of Horatio N. — Shushan, NY

GETTY William F. of Hebron, NY — January 26, 1860

BASSETT Sarah E. of Hebron, NY      Hebron, NY

MC MILLAN David F. of Argyle, NY      February 11, 1860
EATON Alvira of Queensbury, NY      Sandy Hill, NY

WALKER John of Somonauk, Ill.      February 2, 1860
DOBBIN Margaret of Greenwich, NY      Greenwich, NY

DUEL Henry of N. Hebron, NY      February 1, 1860
STEWART Caroline of Union Village, NY      Union Village, NY

AMES Justin of Union Village, NY      February 1, 1860
BENNETT Lydia of Union Village, NY      Union Village, NY

NICKERSON William T. of Ticonderoga, NY      February 2, 1860
MAXWELL Elizabeth of Putnam, NY      Putnam, NY

COULTER Alexander of Jackson, NY      February 22, 1860
ALEXANDER Jennett of Jackson, NY

KENYON David A. of Schaghticoke, NY      February 22, 1860
VAN WOERT Mary dau of Jacob L. of Johnsonville, NY      Johnsonville, NY

LAWRENCE Rodney      February 15, 1860
SWEET Eliza J. dau of Almond of Salem, NY

DURFEE Mathew C. of Cambridge, NY      February 23, 1860
HILL Martha C. of Cambridge, NY      Easton, NY

KENYON Joseph M. of Greenwich, NY      February 4. 1860
SUTTON Loretta R. G. of Warrensburgh, NY      Granville, NY

CHANDLER Fred I. of Hartford, NY      February 6, 1860
COOPER Susan E. of Hartford, NY      Ft. Edward, NY

FORBES Andes of Ft. Edward, NY      February 9, 1860
CRAMER Esther J. of Northumberland, NY      Northumberland, NY

NICHOLS Julius E. of New York City      March 3, 1860
BANKS Nellie I. of Bennington, Vt.

HARRINGTON David B. of Shaftsbury, Vt.      March 2, 1860
MC DONALD Susan A. of Shaftsbury, Vt.      White Creek, NY

ROBERTSON William of W. Hebron, NY      March 22, 1860
ARCHIBALD Mary E. dau of late David T. of Salem, NY      Salem, NY

DUTTON Joseph of Castleton, Vt.      March 21, 1860
WRIGHT Adaliza of W. Pawlet, Vt.      W. Pawlet, Vt.

ARCHER Charles of White Creek, NY      April 5, 1860
ROBERTSON Amanda N. of White Creek, NY      Ft. Edward, NY

LEWIS Spencer G. of Centre Falls, NY      April 17, 1860
WEIR Amy of Centre Falls, NY

JACKSON David of Shushan, NY      May 8, 1860
BROUGHTON Ammeralla of Hartford, NY      Jackson, NY

OSBORN Henry S. of New York City      May 1, 1860
MC ALLISTER Sarah dau of Dr. Archibald of Salem, NY      Salem, NY

ALLEN Squire of New York City      May 17, 1860
LOOMIS Abby S. dau of A. S. NOBLE of Cambridge, NY      Cambridge, NY

HUGGINS James of Salem, NY      June 2, 1860
JOHNSON Mary of Salem, NY      Union Village, NY

SAFFORD Marvin F.      May 26, 1860
WITHERELL Mary Jane dau of Alanson

CHEESEMAN James H. of Ft. Edward, NY      May 22, 1860
WRIGHT Sarah M. dau of George of Jackson, NY      Jackson, NY

TWISS Russell P. of Cambridge, NY      June 13, 1860
GREEN Mary Jane of Cambridge, NY

PERRY Simeon S. of White Creek, NY      June 14, 1860
SLY Lydia A. dau of A. of Lee, NY      Lee, NY

WEIR Judson of Cambridge, NY      July 18/25, 1860
SPRAGUE Abbie      Cambridge, NY

BARTLETT John of Shushan, NY      July 28, 1860
REED Mary of Shushan, NY

JACKSON George E. of New Haven, Conn.      August 15, 1860
FISHER Maria E. dau of John of N. White Creek, NY      N. White Creek, NY

GIFFORD John of Hoosick, NY      August 19, 1860
CURTIS Caroline of Shaftsbury, Vt.      White Creek, NY

MEEHAN Richard of N. Arlington, Vt.      July 30, 1860
WELCH Mary of N. Arlington, Vt.      White Creek, NY

WATSON John M. of N. Bennington, Vt.      August 16, 1860
WOODS Margaret of N. Bennington, Vt.      White Creek, NY

CROCKER Charles W. of Langley, Va.      September 5, 1860

MILLER Margaret E. of Cambridge, NY      Cambridge, NY

WRIGHT Pierce      September 18, 1860
SKELLIE Mary Jane      Jackson, NY

HILL H. Alexander of Jackson, NY      September 13, 1860
CONKEY Lucy A. of Salem, NY      N. White Creek, NY

BREWER Alonzo of Union Village, NY      September 5, 1860
PAULEY Matilda of Troy, NY      Union Village, NY

WHITCOMB Mortimer of White Creek, NY      September 26, 1860
SHAW Lucy A. of White Creek, NY      White Creek, NY

GAGE Samuel D. of Eagle Bridge, NY      September 29, 1860
FOWLER Julia of Cambridge, NY

BROWNELL Charles of Chillicothe, Ohio      September 25, 1860
BARNETT Ruth of Hoosick, NY      Hoosick, NY

ROSEBROOK John M. of Hoosick, NY      September 26, 1860
SWEET Mary of Hoosick, NY      Hoosick, NY

LAMPER Carves of Sandgate, Vt.      October 10, 1860
STILL Helen of Sandgate, Vt.      Sandgate, Vt.

SLOAN William of Salem, NY      October 11, 1860
WALKER Jesamine of Salem, NY      Shushan, NY

MC ANDLES Samuel of Jackson, NY      October 21, 1860
FAXON Hatty of Jackson, NY      Jackson, NY

BARTON Mial P. of N. White Creek, NY      October 23, 1860
RICH Hattie A. of N. White Creek, NY

HILL Elisha of Shaftsbury, Vt.      November 3, 1860
BEVIS Martha A. of Sandgate, Vt.      White Creek, NY

KIRKHAM Rev. G. C. of Hoosick Falls, NY      October 24, 1860
AGAN Sarah E. of Hoosick, NY

CHASE Dr. Aaron B. of Indianna      October 16, 1860
PRESSEL Ellen A. of Bloomington

GAINER Hiram of Ela, Ill.      November 1, 1860
FISHER Harriet C. dau of John of N. White Creek, NY

CRAWFORD Sansom of Petersburgh, NY      November 21, 1860
BRIMMER Eveline of Petersburgh, NY

NORTON Albert A. of Bennington, Vt.                    November 29, 1860
WADSWORTH Helen of Bennington, Vt.                     White Creek, NY

KERR Michael of Jackson, NY                            November 28, 1860
ASHTON Lydia M. of Ash Grove, NY

LARMON William C. of Cambridge, NY                     December 5, 1860
ALMA Hannah L. of Cambridge, NY                        Cambridge, NY

DOBBIN James of Argyle, NY                             December 12, 1860
LEIGH Frances I. dau of James S. of Argyle, NY         Argyle, NY

CURTIS F. of E. Greenwich, NY                          December 4, 1860
JORDAN Martha of E. Greenwich, NY                      Union Village, NY

MC ALLISTER James of Salem, NY                         December 4, 1860
FOSTER Anna of Salem, NY                               Salem, NY

MC KINNEY John of Salem, NY                            December 4, 1860
FERGUSON Martha of Salem, NY                           Salem, NY

HODGES Mc Rea of Jackson, NY                           December 20, 1860
WOODWORTH Anna M. of Shushan, NY                       Shushan, NY

HOYT William M. of Arlington, Vt.                      December 31, 1860
HURD C. E. of E. Salem, NY

LATIMER James of Argyle, NY                            December 31, 1860
HUNTER Mary of Argyle, NY                              Argyle, NY

BRISTOL Seth W. of Argyle, NY                          January 1, 1861
PENDERGAST Margaret of Argyle, NY                      Argyle, NY

WILSON John of Easton, NY                              December 31, 1860
SHERWOOD Frances of Easton, NY                         N. White Creek, NY

BROWN William O. of Farihaven, Vt.                     January 2, 1861
VALENTINE Emily M. of Jackson, NY                      Jackson, NY

MAYNARD X. I. of White Creek, NY                       December 19, 1860
BROMLEY Jennie A.                                      Pawlet, Vt.

GILCHRIST Lewis A. of Ft. Edward, NY                   January 9, 1861
ROZZELL Louisa C. of Ft. Edward, NY                    Ft. Edward, NY

FISK George W. Jr. of Hoosick Falls, NY                January 23, 1861
AMES Lucy E. of White Creek, NY                        White Creek, NY

STEVENSON William J. of Cambridge, NY                  January 24, 1861

WARNER Sarah M. of White Creek, NY

    White Creek, NY

GILBERT Edward W. of Shushan, NY
BEEBE Carrie Y. of Salem, NY

    January 19, 1861
    Coila, NY

COMER E. of White Creek, NY
RICH Hattie R. of Salem, NY

    February 6, 1861
    Salem, NY

BUCK Charles of Arlington, Vt.
HOYT Anna Jane of Arlington, Vt.

    January 21, 1861
    Arlington, Vt.

BECKER Nathaniel K. of Cambridge, NY
BEADLE Philena of Easton, NY

    February 13/14, 1861
    Easton, NY

HAXTON Horace W. of Cambridge, NY
WICKES Fanny E. of Schaghticoke, NY

    January 29, 1861
    Cambridge, NY

BURCH Thomas F. of Cambridge, NY
BURCH Emily of Easton, NY

    January 30, 1861
    Cambridge, NY

LYON Charles of E. Salem, NY
HATCH S. A. of Manchester, Vt.

    February 6, 1861
    Manchester, Vt.

GIBSON Cyrus O. of Hoosick, NY
OSTRANDER Sarah Amelia of Hoosick, NY

    February 13, 1861
    Hoosick, NY

DURRIN Alden of Queensbury, NY
MC CLELLAN Anna Mary of Jackson, NY

    March 5, 1861

DURRIN Arden of Queensbury, NY
MC CLELLAN Libbie N. of Jackson, NY

    March 5, 1861

WEST Richard of E. Salem, NY
BALDWIN Kate of Jackson, NY

    February 27, 1861
    Camden, NY

NARAMORE Martin of Burlington, Vt.
HAXTON Annie M. of Cambrdige, NY

    March 14, 1861
    Cambridge, NY

SWEET William O.
ROBINSON Melissa Y. dau of Ira of Camden, NY

    March 15, 1861
    Shushan, NY

COULTER James Jr. of Cambridge, NY
SQUIRES B. E. of W. Arlington, Vt.

    March 18, 1861
    W. Arlington, Vt.

FOWLER Francis of White Creek, NY
VAN VECHTEN Eva of White Creek, NY

    March 22, 1861
    Salem, NY

LONG Edward of Cambridge, NY
RICH Sarah A. of Cambridge, NY

    April 2, 1861

MC COY Robert E. of the Ft. Edward Vol.     May 2, 1861
MORGAN Julia dau of Carlos of Glens Falls, NY  Glens Falls, NY

GROESBECK William H. of Ft. Edward (newspaper date) May 24, 1861
HEATH Mary A. dau of Stephen G.

NEWTON John M. of Cincinnati, Ohio     June 1, 1861
GRAHAM Lavina dau of George of Cincinnati, Ohio Cincinnati, Oh.

HURD Reuben of Sandgate, Vt.       May 30, 1861
WILSON Maria of Hebron, NY       Hebron, NY

HOWARD Rev. A. L. of Dover, Vt.      July 4, 1861
STETSON Frances of Racket Settlement    White Creek, NY

BEADLE Thomas D. Jr. of Troy, NY     July 2, 1861
FORT Elizabeth dau of Lewis of Easton, NY   Easton, NY

WELLING N. B of Easton, NY       July 3, 1861
HARRINGTON Anna C. of Easton, NY    Easton, NY

ROWLAND Amasa of White Creek, NY    July 4, 1861
BENTLEY Eliza Ann of White Creek, NY

BULL Stephen of Hebron, NY       July 26, 1861
HEART Miss of Hebron, NY        Hebron, NY

KETCHUM Dr. of Manchester, Vt.     August 7, 1861
GRAY Eliza dau of H. C.         White Creek, NY

AUSTIN George of Salem, NY       August 1, 1861
BILLINGS Caroline of Salem, NY      Union Village, NY

RICE George of Salem, NY        August 16, 1861
SMITH Anna of Jackson, NY

RILEY Patrick of Cambridge, NY      August 18, 1861
CUMMINGS Eliza of Cambridge, NY     Hoosick Falls, NY

KELLOGG John B. of Troy, NY      September 3, 1861
KELLOGG Anna dau of Palmer V. of Utica, NY  Utica, NY

RUSSELL Henry of N. White Creek, NY    September 18, 1861
WHITCOMB Hannah C. of N. White Creek, NY  N. White Creek, NY

JOHNSON Rev. W. M. of Stillwater, NY    October 3, 1861
WARNER Anna E. dau of Jonathan      Jackson, NY

VAN VECHTEN William W. of Cambridge, NY  October 17, 1861

**DARROW** Elizabeth of Cambridge, NY                    Cambridge, NY

**HAWTHORNE** Ira of Salem, NY                    October 15, 1861
**CORNLEY** Mary of Salem, NY                    White Creek, NY

**BURGESS** Loam J. of Hoosick, NY                    October 13, 1861
**RANDALL** Eliza M. of White Creek, NY

**KENYON** Clarence D. of White Creek, NY                    November 6, 1861
**COTTRELL** Mary E. of White Creek, NY

**AKIN** H. B.                    November 20, 1861
**HOUGHTON** Nancy J. dau of Andrew of Buskirks Bridge                    Buskirks Bridge, NY

**ROBERTSON** William W. of Jackson, NY                    November 20, 1861
**MC LEAN** Bell of Jackson, NY                    Jackson, NY

**MUZZY** William L.                    November 28, 1861
**ARCHER** Sarah J. of Cambridge, NY                    Saratoga Springs, NY

**SCUDDER** B. of Delaware Co. NY                    December 12, 1861
**HOYT** Mrs. W. D. of Arlington, Vt.                    Arlington, Vt.

**BUCK** Ransom of Jackson, NY                    December 18, 1861
**MONCRIEF** Isabella of E. Salem, NY

**MAXWELL** Walter F. of Kenesha, Wis.                    December 19, 1861
**ROBINSON** Annie M.

**PARKER** George W. of White Creek, NY                    January 1, 1862
**PRATT** Olive A. of White Creek, NY

**ARCHER** James H. of Cambridge, NY                    January 9, 1862
**TRIPP** Julia dau of Anthony of Cambridge, NY

**ROBINSON** Alexander B. of Argyle, NY                    December 31, 1861
**WALLACE** Mrs. Hannah of W. Hebron, NY

**BENNETT** James Jr. of Ft. Edward, NY                    January 7, 1862
**BETTS** Lida of Moreau, NY

**PIKE** J. R. of Ft. Edward, NY                    January 15, 1862
**POTTER** Mary Jane of Ft. Edward, NY                    Ft. Edward, NY

**FULLER** Lewis C. son of Freeman of N. White Creek, NY                    January 23, 1862
**FOSTER** Jennie S. dau of Robert L. of Shushan, NY

**HASKINS** Abel N. of Battenville, NY                    January 21, 1862
**WEED** Charlotte F. of Rupert, Vt.                    Salem, NY

| | |
|---|---|
| **BROWNELL** Daniel W. of Easton, NY | February 13, 1862 |
| **CAIN** Mary E. of Cambridge, NY | White Creek, NY |
| | |
| **MC CLAUGHRY** Thomas of E. Greenwich, NY | March 5, 1862 |
| **STONE** Sophia W. of White Creek, NY | White Creek, NY |
| | |
| **GREEN** Alexander of Cambridge, NY | March 13, 1862 |
| **CULVER** Frances S. of Cambridge, NY | Coila, NY |
| | |
| **WILSON** Eli of Hebron, NY | March 18, 1862 |
| **HEDGES** Mrs. Julia of Cambridge, NY | Cambridge, NY |
| | |
| **FLACK** George H. of Argyle, NY | March 18, 1862 |
| **FOSTER** Martha R. of Ashgrove, NY | Ashgrove, NY |
| | |
| **MC DOUAL** Alexander of Coila, NY | April 1, 1862 |
| **SCULLION** Mary of Coila, NY | |
| | |
| **WARNER** Abner of Jackson, NY | April 3, 1862 |
| **CAMERON** Jennie of Coila, NY | |
| | |
| **ELDRIDGE** Harvey L. of White Creek, NY | April 24, 1862 |
| **HUNT** Sarah of White Creek, NY | White Creek, NY |
| | |
| **TRIPP** Lewis of White Creek, NY | June 1, 1862 |
| **BURGESS** Freelove of White Creek, NY | White Creek, NY |
| | |
| **STEVENS** Simon L. of Greenwich, NY | June 6, 1862 |
| **RUSSELL** Helen C. dau of William A. of Salem, NY | Salem, NY |
| | |
| **VAN RENSALAER** John of White Creek, NY | June 5, 1862 |
| **POWERS** Eunice A. of White Creek, NY | Eagle Bridge, NY |
| | |
| **MC FARLAND** William of Jackson, NY | September 11, 1862 |
| **WOODWORTH** Wealthy Ann dau of Charles of Jackson, NY | |
| | |
| **SIPPERLEY** A. F. of Hoosick, NY | September 25, 1862 |
| **WARNER** Susie H. of Hoosick, NY | White Creek, NY |
| | |
| **WAIT** Wayland W. of Chicago, Ill. | September 16, 1862 |
| **GORDON** Emma formerly of Schaghticoke, NY | Fairhaven, Conn. |
| | |
| **SHAW** Charles H. of Hoosick Falls, NY | September 24, 1862 |
| **WELCH** Mary E. of Hoosick Falls, NY | White Creek, NY |
| | |
| **PRIESTLY** James of Hoosick Falls, NY   (newspaper date) | October 10, 1862 |
| **CRANE** Mary A. of Hoosick Falls, NY | |
| | |
| **BRUNETT** Thomas of White Creek, NY | October 23, 1862 |

**BOWEN** Fidelia of White Creek, NY

**BATEY** Stephen                                           November 13, 1862
**IVES** Mary D.                                            S. Easton, NY

**WHITNEY** Josiah S.                                       November 19, 1862
**MOTROS** Nancy                                            White Creek, NY

**HASTELL** Isaac Mack                                      November 27, 1862
**SHERMAN** Hannah Victoria dau of Levi of Pittstown, NY    Pittstown, NY

**MATTERSON** James T. of Shaftsbury, Vt.                   November 25, 1862
**TINKHAM** Ann of Shaftsbury, Vt.                          White Creek, NY

**SWEET** John T. of Hoosick, NY                            November 29, 1862
**GOODWIN** Minerva M. of Hoosick, NY                       White Creek, NY

**IVES** Frederick D. of Easton, NY                         December 23, 1862
**GIFFORD** Susannah R. of Easton, NY                       Easton, NY

**FOSTER** Anderson S. of Salem, NY                         December 18, 1826
**MC GEOCH** Jennie dau of George of Jackson, NY

**DONAHUE** Galloway of Harmony, NY                         December 25, 1862
**DURFEE** Mary E. of Cambridge, NY                         Cambridge, NY

**HAXTON** William E. of Cambridge, NY                      December 30, 1862
**RUNDELL** Ruth of Cambridge, NY                           Cambridge, NY

**VAUGHN** Carnel of Arlington Vt.                          January 7, 1863
**WALLACE** Condercia of White Creek, NY

**JOSLIN** Gilbert F. of Hoosick, NY                        February 15, 1863
**GALLOWAY** Anna of Cambridge, NY

**KENYON** T. M. fo Cambridge, NY                           February 18, 1863
**STARR** A. M. of Cambridge, NY                            Cambridge, NY

**VALENTINE** Joseph of Jackson, NY                         February 19, 1863
**KETCHUM** Mrs. Clarissa B. of Argyle, NY                  Argyle, NY

**RANDLES** Caleb of Jackson, NY                            February 25, 1863
**DECKER** Anna M. of Cambridge, NY                         Cambridge, NY

**JOHNSON** Hiram of Union Village, NY                      April 18, 1863
**LAMPMAN** Sarah Elizabeth of Union Village, NY            Union Village, NY

**CARTWRIGHT** Aaron of Leroy, NY                           April 29, 1863
**NORTON** Sarah M. of Union Village, NY                    Union Village, NY

WEBB William A. of Illinois

April 29, 1863

WATERS Mrs. Eleanor M. of Union Village, NY

Union Village, NY

WALLACE George S. of White Creek, NY

May 28, 1863

PRATT Cynthia M. of Cambridge, NY

Cambridge, NY

ROBERSON Henry H. of Gillford, Minn.

May 14, 1863

WHITCOMB Lydia of Lakeville, NY

Lake, NY

KING John of Salem, NY

June 2, 1863

SHEPPARD Elizabeth of Norfolk, NY

Saratoga Springs, NY

BURROUGHS Lewis Z. of Cambridge, NY

June 2, 1863

EDIE Annie L. of Cambridge, NY

Greenwich, NY

MC CORD C. W. of New York City

June 23, 1863

HOLDEN Evelyn dau of William of Jackson, NY

E. Salem, NY

WEST Julius of Salem, NY

July 2, 1863

BURR Maggie of Salem, NY

RANNEY William T. late of 24th Reg. NYS Vol.

July 3, 1863

LAWTON Jerusha of White Creek, NY

LIVINGSTON W. A. of Cambridge, NY

June 29, 1863

WELCH Margaret A. of Cambridge, NY

Shushan, NY

BARNES William W. of Salem, NY

June 29, 1863

SWEET Sarah M. of Salem, NY

Shushan, NY

JOHNSON Elijah of Shaftsbury, Vt.

June 28, 1863

MATHEWS Aron of Bennington, Vt.

White Creek, NY

SLOCUM George A. of N. White Creek, NY

August 17, 1863

MOSSY Mattie W. of N. White Creek, NY

N. White Creek, NY

BURKE George F. of Greenwich, NY

August 29, 1863

ARCHIBALD Fannie E. of Greenwich, NY

White Creek, NY

COOK Henry of White Creek, NY

September 9, 1863

ARNOLD Mary of White Creek, NY

JOHNSON John of Shaftsbury, Vt.

September 14, 1863

WELLS Mellina M. of Bennington, Vt.

White Creek, NY

HOYT Ron C. of Sandgate, Vt.

September 3/23, 1863

HURD Emeline of Sandgate, Vt.

White Creek, NY

BROWN Hiram W. of Jackson, NY

September 23, 1863

**THOMAS** Parmelia of Easton, NY
Cambridge, NY

**HERRINGTON** Arnold Jr. of White Creek, NY
**HERRINGTON** Sarah of Arlington, Vt.
September 26, 1863
White Creek, NY

**HASTINGS** George of Salem, NY
**GILCHRIST** Nancy M. of Cambridge, NY
September 28, 1863
Argyle, NY

**BENTLEY** Ralph of Manchester, Vt.
**WOODWARD** Julia of Arlington, Vt.
September 29, 1863
White Creek, NY

**WARKIN** Milos D. of White Creek, NY
**AGAN** Maria C. of White Creek, NY
September 24, 1863

**KILBURN** Aandrew J. of Manchester, Vt.
**SMITH** Lucy Ann of Asherolot, NH
October 4, 1863
Cambridge, NY

**CONKEY** Jason A. of Arlington, Vt.
**PARISH** Fannie of Salem, NY
October 3, 1863
Salem, NY

**DOIG** William J. of Jackson, NY
**ROBERSON** Mary Eliza of Jackson, NY
October 8, 1863
Jackson, NY

**NICHOLSON** William of N. White Creek, NY
**BENEDICT** Caroline E. dau of Timothy of Belvidere, Ill.
October 12, 1863
Belvidere, Ill.

**WILSON** L. M. of the 2nd Vet. Cal.
**WALKER** Louisa of Troy, NY
October 20, 1863
Troy, NY

**MOYNIHAN** John of Salem, NY
**MC CORMICK** Kate of Salem, NY
October 28, 1863
White Creek, NY

**EDDY** Luther of Troy, NY
**YATES** Electa B. dau of late James of Pittstown, NY
October 29, 1863
Pittstown, NY

**COLE** Felix of Bennington, Vt. (44th Vt. St. Vol.)
**BEEBE** Carrie of E. Greenwich, NY
November 14, 1863
White Creek, NY

**HOLLENBECK** Daniel of Hoosick, NY
**ARMSTRONG** Sarah of Hoosick, NY
November 24, 1863
Cambridge, NY

**HOLDEN** William Henry son of William of Jackson, NY
**THOMPSON** Cornelia dau of William of Jackson, NY
December 1, 1863
Jackson, NY

**ALLEN** David of Cambridge, NY
**MORSE** Alice of Lansingburgh, NY
December 2, 1863
Lansingburgh, NY

**HAWLEY** Charles T. of White Creek, NY
**WARNER** Fannie S. of White Creek, NY
December 9, 1863
White Creek, NY

SHAW John of Argyle, NY     December 10, 1863
COULTER Kate of Cambridge, NY     White Creek, NY

HUNT Clark of Salem, NY     December 22, 1863
LYON Susan of Salem, NY

MASON Herbert A. Sgt. in Potomac Army    (newspaper date) January 1, 1864
SHERMAN Emily J. dau of Levi of Pittstown, NY     Pittstown, NY

BURBY Henry Clay of N. White Creek, NY     January 1, 1864
CURTIS Eleanor dau of John B. of N. White Creek, NY     N. White Creek, NY

AUSTIN William of Salem, NY     December 31, 1863
SLOCUM Nellie of Manchester, Vt     Salem, NY

AUSTIN Alexander of Salem, NY     December 22, 1863
CURTIS Lucinda of Rupert, Vt.     Salem, NY

AUSTIN Abner of Salem, NY     December 31, 1863
JORDAN Frances E. of Jackson, NY     Salem, NY

POMEROY E. R. of Chicago, Ill.     December 22, 1863
HASTINGS M. F. of Salem, NY     Salem, NY

SKINNER Nathan of Cambridge, NY     December 23, 1863
MC FARLAND Martha E. dau of John of Salem, NY     Salem, NY

PITNEY Eddie H. of Jackson, NY     January 7, 1864
AKIN Aramantha of N. White Creek, NY     N. White Creek, NY

CONNOR Henry of Salem, NY     January 25, 1864
HOLDEN Eva of Chester, NY     Cambridge, NY

ENGLISH Charles W. of Cambridge, NY     January 13, 1864
HILLMAN Harriet J. of Cambridge, NY     Cambridge, NY

AUSTIN William A. of Cambridge, NY     February 17, 1864
HAXTON Martha J. of Cambridge, NY     Cambridge, NY

HOWARD Nathan of Rutland, Vt.     February 23, 1864
CHAPPELL Mrs. Margaret of Rutland, Vt.     Poultney, Vt.

WARNER Charles S. of the 123rd Reg.     March 1, 1864
GREEN Anna of Cambridge, NY     Cambridge, NY

HEDGES Samuel of Jackson, NY     March 2, 1864
BUCKLEY E. of Cambridge, NY     Cambridge, NY

SKELLIE Alexander of Cambridge, NY     February 2, 1864

**ARNOTT** Nancy of Jackson, NY

**MAXWELL** William of Washington Co., NY     January 14, 1864
**MC ARTHUR** Mary of Washington Co., NY     Binghamton, Iowa

**BAKER** Theodore J. of Nevada, Cal.     March 22, 1864
**BUCKLEY** Sarah E. dau of Ezra of Schaghticoke, NY     Schaghticoke, NY

**SHERMAN** George W. of Union Village, NY     March 28, 1864
**MC ENERY** Nancy of Cambridge, NY

**DOUDAL** Bartholomew of Jackson, NY     March 27, 1864
**MC FARLAND** Lizzie of Jackson, NY     White Creek, NY

**RYAN** Patrick of Hoosick, NY     March 28, 1864
**SHEA** Gennie of Hoosick, NY

**MULLEN** Mathew of Salem, NY     March 30, 1864
**BEVENS** Mary of Salem, NY

**WHALEN** Edwin of Salem, NY     March 23, 1864
**BARNES** Mary Elizabeth of Salem, NY

**BURKE** Colon M. of Salem, NY     March 25, 1864
**FOSTER** Annie Jane of Salem, NY

**DUNTON** Josiah of White Creek, NY     May 4, 1864
**ROSS** Phebe of White Creek, NY     Cambridge, NY

**TOWNE** Edwin of Northumberland, NY     April 30, 1864
**ESMANN** Carrie E. of Cambridge, NY     White Creek, NY

**HILL** George M. of Easton, NY     May 11, 1864
**GREEN** Margaret of Cambridge, NY

**HUNT** John L. of Cambridge, NY     May 24, 1864
**GALLOWAY** M. A. of Cambridge, NY     Cambridge, NY

**MELTON** Major     May 12, 1864
**JENKINS** Louise of Cambridge, NY     New York City

**WOOD** John Quincey Adams of Vermont     June 7, 1864
**COBB** Diantha of Vermont

**AUSTIN** George A. of Hoosick, NY     July 4, 1864
**GOODING** Vashta E. of Hoosick, NY     White Creek, NY

**BARNES** Rev. C. R. of Franklin, NJ     July 5, 1864
**DARROW** Carrie dau of Hiram of Cambridge, NY     Cambridge, NY

**JOLES** William F. M. of Sandwich, Ill.  
**MUZZY** Mary Jane formerly of White Creek, NY  
August 6, 1864  
Sandwich, Ill.

**HORTON** Abraham A. of Ft. Ann, NY  
**LYON** Mary of Ft. Ann, NY  
August 16, 1864  
Cambridge, NY

**PRATT** Charles Wesley of White Creek, NY  
**SWEET** Hannah A. of White Creek, NY  
September 5, 1864

**BAKER** Charles C. of the 11th NY Heavy Artillery  
**UTLEY** Sarah dau of Squire of N. Western, NY  
September 14, 1864  
N. Western, NY

**HENRY** Walter of Buskirks Bridge, NY  
**PRUYN** Maria dau of Francis of Buskirks Bridge, NY  
September 20, 1864  
Buskirks Bridge, NY

**SHERMAN** Justus of Cambridge, NY  
**DOOLITTLE** Harriet of Pittstown, NY  
September 20, 1864  
Cambridge, NY

**DUNHAM** Henry M. of Jackson, NY  
**HILLMAN** Sarah E. of Jackson, NY  
September 27, 1864  
Jackson, NY

**SWEET** Freeborn of White Creek, NY  
**WINCHELL** Emma E. of White Creek, NY  
August 7, 1864  
Cambridge, NY

**KENYON** Charles of White Creek, NY  
**SMITH** Rhoby Jane of White Creek, NY  
August 17, 1864

**MOSELY** Charles L. of Hoosick, NY  
**LANGWORTHY** Augusta L. of Hoosick, NY  
August 17, 1864

**JONES** Hiram S. of Berlin, NY            (newspaper date)  
**HEWITT** Hannah M. Petersborough, NY  
October 7, 1864  
White Creek, NY

**PADDOCK** Merritt C. of Hoosick, NY  
**JOSLIN** Elsie M. of Hoosick, NY  
September 15, 1864

**GILMAN** Dr. Charles O. T. of Salem, NY  
**BLINN** Hattie E. dau of Col. M. W. of N. Granville, NY  
October 4, 1864  
N. Granville, NY

**BURTIS** John H.  
**THOMASON** Mary G. dau of J. B. of New York City  
October 5, 1864  
New York City

**WHITE** John W. of Jackson, NY  
**FENTON** Hattie A. of N. White Creek, NY  
October 13, 1864

**SHILAND** Albert of Cambridge, NY  
**SHERMAN** Minnie dau of Lemuel of Cambridge, NY  
December 5, 1864  
Cambridge ,NY

**ROBERTSON** David of Cambridge, NY  
January 10, 1865

**PRATT** Mary F. of Cambridge, NY	Cambridge, NY

**BOWMAN** Jeffray of Sunderland, Vt.	January 21, 1865
**WARNER** Hattie A. of Sunderland, Vt.	Cambridge, NY

**FERGUSON** Sam F. of Salem, NY	February 1, 1865
**SCOTT** Maggie A. dau of W. M. of Cambridge, NY	Cambridge, NY

**VALENTINE** Warren E. of Jackson, NY	February 8, 1865
**CENTER** Carrie A. dau of Sheldon of White Creek, NY	White Creek, NY

**BAILEY** Francis S. of White Creek, NY late of 93rd Reg.	February 22, 1865
**ELLIS** Mary Ida dau of Alexander of White Creek, NY

**QUA** William C. of White Creek, NY	February 23, 1865
**HOWE** Annie E. dau of Eli of Jackson, NY

**ESMOND** Gordon D. of Pittstown, NY	March 8, 1865
**LARMON** Mary of Cambridge, NY

**MARTIN** John W. of Cambridge, NY	May 4, 1865
**SAXBURY** Sarah M. of White Creek, NY	White Creek, NY

**WALLACE** Truman J. of Hoosick Falls, NY	May 9, 1865
**CARPENTER** Mary M. dau of Caleb of Keene, NH	Keene, NH

**CULVER** Charles G. of Sandwich, Ill. (105th Reg. Ill. Vol.)	July 11, 1865
**BARNES** Maria of Sandwich, Ill.	Sandwich, Ill.

**EATON** William F. of Arlington, Vt.	August 9, 1865
**EVANS** M. Janette of Washington DC	Rutland, Vt.

**BROWN** Anderson of Salem, NY	August 29, 1865
**JOHNSON** Lillie of Shushan, NY	Shushan, NY

**WRIGHT** Benjamin R. of Cambridge, NY	September 6, 1865
**HILL** Margaret G. of Cambridge, NY	Coila, NY

**JULLIAND** Frederick of Greene, NY	September 6, 1865
**CROCKER** H. M. of White Creek, NY	White Creek, NY

**CROMACK** S. M. of Bennington, Vt.	August 24, 1865
**TITUS** Carrie of Ballston Spa, NY	Cambridge, NY

**LAMBERT** David C. of N. White Creek, NY	September 12, 1865
**KERR** Eliza of Jackson, NY

**MC FARLAND** George H. formerly of Cambridge, NY	October 11, 1865
**MONEYPENNY** Rosina H. of New York City	New York City

SAYLES Arnold of Salem, NY       October 16, 1865
SCERLES Kate of Cohoes, NY       Troy, NY

HICKS Sanford of Sunderland, NY       October 28, 1865
BUCK Julia E. of Sunderland, Vt.       White Creek, NY

WHITE Albert C. Jr. of New York City       October 25, 1865
SELLICK Camille A. dau of late P. M.       Union Village, NY

WOODARD Frank of Hebron, NY       November 23, 1865
SMITH Caroline A. of Hebron, NY

BURDICK Phillip T. of Troy, NY       November 30, 1865
GOODRICH Mary E. of Salem, NY       Troy, NY

FISK Perrin B. of Shushan, NY       November 30, 1865
HEATH Mrs. Hannah M. of Shushan, NY       Shushan, NY

NEWCOMB John L. of Cambridge, NY       November 26, 1865
WINNIE Harriet of Cambridge, NY

MC COLLUM J. A. of S. Argyle, NY       November 29, 1865
ALEXANDER Belle of E. Greenwich, NY       E. Greenwich, NY

COWAN George of Jackson, NY       December 6, 1865
WILSON Mary J. of Cambridge, NY       Cambridge, NY

MC ARTHUR James of Salem, NY       December 5, 1865
ALEXANDER Mary of Jackson, NY       Jackson, NY

DOUGAN Mathew of W. Hebron, NY       December 7, 1865
BRANT Mary of W. Hebron, NY       Belcher, NY

TULL J. W. of Green, NY       December 6, 1865
BROWNELL D. M. of Cambridge, NY       White Creek, NY

CALVERT William of Lockport, NY       December 13, 1865
WEIR R. Amanda of Cambridge, NY       Cambridge, NY

CONGHEY William of Canada formerly of Cambridge, NY       December 8, 1865
ALLEN Emily M. of Sunderland, Vt.       Sunderland, Vt.

BROWN Orlando H. of Pittstown, NY       December 13, 1865
MILLER Miranda of Pittstown, NY       White Creek, NY

RUSSELL William A. of Salem, NY       November 15, 1865
FOX Mattie dau of Dr. A Fox late of Fitchburg, Mass.       New Ipswich, NH

HAWKINS Warren F. of White Creek, NY       December 20, 1865

**QUA** Mattie J. dau of Abner of White Creek, NY

**MC MORRIS** James T. of Jackson, NY                        December 19, 1865
**MC GEOCH** Anna J. of W. Hebron, NY                        W. Hebron, NY

**DARROW** Peter H. of Cambridge, NY                         December 21, 1865
**DURFEE** Anna of Cambridge, NY                             Cambridge, NY

**CASE** Buckley of Bennington, Vt.                          December 25, 1865
**GREENLEAF** Henrietta of Bennington, Vt.                   White Creek, NY

**LIDDLE** David S. of Argyle, NY                            December 20, 1865
**MC NEIL** Annie of Argyle, NY

**MC MAHON** John                                            December 30, 1865
**O'BRIEN** Annie                                            Cambridge, NY

**COULTER** W. J. of Clinton, Mass. formerly White Creek     December 19, 1865
**CRAVER** Celina                                            Graniteville, Mass.

**SAFFORD** Ezra of Easton, NY                               January 17, 1866
**SIMPSON** Elizabeth B. of Jackson, NY                      Jackson, NY

**FONDA** D. I. of Cohoes, NY                                January 24, 1866
**ARNOLD** E. S. dau of Jesse of White Creek, NY             White Creek, NY

**SHALER** William of Salem, NY                              January 24, 1866
**PRATT** Seraph H. of Cambridge, NY                         Cambridge, NY

**BINNINGER** W. S.                                          January 24, 1866
**VALENTINE** Hattie A. dau of Daniel formerly of Shushan    Milwaukee, Wis.

**GIFFORD** Gideon W. formerly of Cambridge, NY              January 11, 1866
**HUGHES** Sarah M. dau of A. M. of Columbia, Tenn.

**RICE** Clark of Cambridge, NY                              January 24, 1866
**ROBERTSON** Anna M. dau of George of Cambridge, NY

**WHYTE** Archibald of Argyle, NY                            January 24, 1866
**MC COLLUM** Ann Eliza of Argyle, NY

**NILES** Walter C. of White Creek, NY                       January 18, 1866
**BRIGGS** Josephine dau of George W. of White Creek, NY     White Creek, NY

**HOVER** Anderson D. of Cambridge, NY                       February 1, 1866
**STANTON** Anna M. of Cambridge, NY

**BEVERIDGE** Andrew of Hebron, NY                           February 1, 1866
**MC CONNELL** Mary J. dau of James of Hebron, NY            Hebron, NY

**FERGUSON** Samuel of Cambridge, NY      February 1, 1866
**ALLEN** Ruth of Cambridge, NY      Cambridge, NY

**HOLLENBECK** Harvey of Hoosick, NY      February 7, 1866
**WILCOX** Harriet of Hoosick, NY      Hoosick, NY

**ARNOLD** Anson J. of Parma, NY      January 31, 1866
**MC GEOCH** Mary E. of Jackson, NY

**GRAHAM** Walter of Cambridge, NY      February 20, 1866
**MARTIN** Ida C. of Cambridge, NY

**ADAMS** Daniel of N. White Creek, NY      February 11, 1866
**DOLL** Julia A. of Rockland, NY      Rockland, NY

**ELDRIDGE** Deroy of White Creek, NY      January 16, 1866
**WING** Mary Frances of Shushan, NY      Shushan, NY

**MYERS** David of Schaghticoke, NY      February 21, 1866
**BANKER** Hattie dau of John of Schaghticoke, NY      Schaghticoke, NY

**MACK** James of Salem, NY      February 20, 1866
**PRUYN** Sarah of Ft. Miller, NY

**PETTIT** George W. of Troy, NY with the 125th NY Vol.      February 4, 1866
**WEIR** Maggie E. of Cambridge, NY      Shushan, NY

**AKIN** Charles C. of Johnsonville, NY      February 28, 1866
**ROSS** Jane of Johnsonville, NY      N. White Creek, NY

**RIDDLE** William of E. Greenwich, NY      January 30, 1866
**DOBBIN** Sarah of E. Greenwich, NY      E. Greenwich, NY

**SHIELDS** Thomas      February 1, 1866
**TIERNEY** Ellena      Cambridge, NY

**HALPIN** William Joseph      February 7, 1866
**GANNOR** Johanna Maria

**LOFTISS** Michael      March 5, 1866
**MALOY** Mary

**TINKEY** Daniel of Argyle, NY      March 6, 1866
**WILLETT** Nancy Jane of Argyle, NY

**AMES** Alva of Shaftsbury, Vt.      January 26, 1866
**BENNETT** Henrietta of Shaftsbury, Vt.

**BROWN** Francis E. of White Creek, NY      February 27, 1866

**BENNETT** Martha of Shaftsbury, NY

**MARSHALL** W. J. of Cambridge, NY
**MILLER** Sarah of Jackson, NY

March 13, 1866
Jackson, NY

**WHITLOCK** W. J. of Hebron, NY
**COON** Martha of Salem, NY

April 25, 1866
Salem, NY

**GROESBECK** Edward E. of Ft. Edward, NY
**EASTMAN** Elizabeth of Ft. Ann, NY

April 25, 1866
Ft. Ann, NY

**INFIELD** John C. of Ft. Edward, NY
**BRADLEY** Catherine of Comstocks Landing, NY

April 24, 1866
Comstocks Landing

**DURKEE** Alonzo of Hebron, NY
**LUNDY** Sarah E. of Hebron, NY

May 12, 1866
Salem, NY

**ORCUTT** Edwin of Shushan, NY
**REED** Mararet M. of E. Greenwich, NY

May 8, 1866
E. Greenwich, NY

**LEE** Chester of Granville, NY
**WHITCOMB** Eliza of Granville, NY

May 18, 1866
Granville, NY

**GILBERT** Joseph of Cambridge, NY
**CULVER** Alice of Cambridge, NY

June 24, 1866
Cambridge, NY

**BAKER** Gideon of Union Village, NY
**NEILSON** Ann Aurelia dau of Charles

June 24, 1866
Bemis Heights, NY

**COOK** Nathan of Wells, Vt.
**CONE** Anna Isabella of Wells, Vt.

July 3, 1866
Poultney, Vt.

**SAUNDERS** Edwin P. of Middletown, Vt.
**HOUGHTON** Mary J. of Middletown, Vt.

July 4, 1866
Poultney, Vt.

**PERRY** Abner J. of Wells, Vt.
**GOODSPEED** Luna L. of Pawlet, Vt.

July 4, 1866
Poultney, NY

**STAFFORD** William C. of Granville, NY
**CHENEY** Adeline A. of Rutland, Vt.

July 3, 1866
Rutland, Vt.

**MC CARTY** James
**JOHNSON** Mary C. dau of William of Hartford, NY

August 1, 1866
Hartford, NY

**CHAPLIN** George W. of Rutland, Vt.
**CAMPBELL** Maggie of Fairhaven, Vt.

August 14, 1866
Cambridge, NY

**WOODARD** Edwin S. Lieut. Commander US Navy
**HAWLEY** Mary E. dau of Rev. E. Hawley

August 9, 1866
Ft. Plain, NY

RUSSELL Solomon W. Jr. of Salem, NY      August 16, 1866
DIXON Anna A. of N. Wales, Va.      N. Wales, Va.

CREIGHTON George of Salem, NY      August 15, 1866
WHITE Elizabeth of Salem, NY      Salem, NY

DUEL A. of Hebron, NY      August 16, 1866
RUMBLIN Eliza of Hebron, NY      Hebron, NY

WILCOX Henry E. of Rochester, NY      September 5, 1866
RICE H. Josie of Jackson, NY      Jackson, NY

THOMPSON Smith of Pittstown, NY      September 5, 1866
BURCH Ellen of Easton, NY      Cambridge, NY

HILL James of Coila, NY      September 5, 1866
STEVENS Julia dau of C. Stevens of Greenwich, NY      Greenwich, NY

WEEKS John of Coila, NY      September 15, 1866
PARKER Anna of Troy, NY

GILBERT Charles W. of Cambridge, NY      September 5, 1866
HODGES Weltha A. of Spencerport, Vt.      Spencerport, NY

PORTER Charles of Cambridge, NY      September 25, 1866
ALEXANDER Mrs. Mary dau of Col. Elisha BILLINGS      Jackson, NY

MAYNARD X. J. of Cambridge, NY      September 30, 1866
RICE Mary J. of Cambridge, NY      White Creek, NY

COMAN Seymour      October 9, 1866
TILLOTSON Mrs. Eunice B. dau of John BARNARD      Union Village, NY

STEVENS Charles A. of New York City      October 16, 1866
VAUGHN Beulah A. dau of Thomas T. of Whitehall, NY      Whitehall, NY

TOLEMAN W. J. of Salem, NY      October 1, 1866
CHARTER Jennie of Salem, NY      Poultney, Vt.

EDGERTON Edward M. of Rutland, Vt.      October 3, 1866
DYER Belle of Poultney, Vt.      Poultney, Vt.

MC CARTHY Samuel of Birmingham, Iowa      October 16, 1866
LOURIE Margaret of Cambridge, NY      Cambridge, NY

FENTON George J. of Albany, NY      October 17, 1866
BROCKWAY Cornelia of Albany, NY      Albany, NY

HOWDEN James P. of Cambridge, NY      October 18, 1866

**SMITH** Addie Mary of Cambridge, NY                          Cambridge, NY

**HUBBARD** Henry L. of Geneva, Ill.                          October 24, 1866
**SLOCUM** Mrs. Mattie W. formerly of Cambridge, NY           Geneva, Ill.

**SWEET** Charles of Whitehall, NY                            October 21, 1866
**ASHLEY** Elizabeth of Ft. Ann, NY                           Ft. Ann, NY

**PORTER** William R. of Whitehall, NY                        October 24, 1866
**SNODY** Mary B. of Whitehall, NY                            Whitehall, NY

**PEMBER** Joseph of Caldwell, NY                             October 18, 1866
**WILLIAMS** Mahala J. of Caldwell, NY                        Sandy Hill, NY

**WHITNEY** George H. of Sandy Hill, NY                       October 11, 1866
**FASSETT** Eliza M. of Sandy Hill, NY                        Sandy Hill, NY

**PROUDFIT** Alexander son of John A. of New Brunswick        October 17, 1866
**COOPER** Annie dau of J. Logan **SMITH** of New Castle, Del  New Castle, Del.

**QUA** Abner of Cambridge, NY                                November 14, 1866
**SCOTT** Mrs. Charlotte S. of Cambridge, NY                  Cambridge, NY

**MC VAY** John                                               November 10, 1866
**MC CARTY** Mary                                             Sandy Hill, NY

**ROBINSON** Chauncey H. of Pawlet, Vt.                       November 13, 1866
**LEWIS** Mary E. of Rutland, Vt.                             Rutland, Vt.

**BECKETT** James of Hampton, NY                              November 13, 1866
**PROUTY** Edna S. of Hampton, NY                             Granville, NY

**BARTON** Henry H. of Ft. Edward, NY                         November 13, 1866
**TAYLOR** Nancy E. of Ft. Edward, NY                         Gloversville, NY

**FLEMING** William S. of E. Salem, NY                        November 7, 1866
**MC ARTHUR** Isabella of E. Salem, NY                        E. Salem, NY

**HAGGARD** James of Belcher, NY                              November 14, 1866
**CLAPP** Keziah of Belcher, NY                               Belcher, NY

**SHERMAN** Alexander M. of Cambridge, NY                     December 5, 1866
**SIMPSON** Fannie of Cambridge, NY                           Cambridge, NY

**DURHAM** William of Salem, NY                               November 16, 1866
**ELLIOTT** Addie of Salem, NY                                Salem, NY

**DONALDSON** M. of Hartford, NY                              December 12, 1866
**LIESY** Mary J. of Hartford, NY                             Sandy Hill, NY

WAIT William of Sandy Hill, NY
WARWICK Antoinette of Amsterdam, NY

December 12, 1866
Amsterdam, NY

MORSE Hiram G. of Granville, NY
ASHWELL Jennie E. of New York City

December 4, 1866
New York City

FINCH Alonzo J.
FRENCH Maggie

December 12, 1866

BARTHOLOMEW William of Whitehall, NY
MERRIAM Mary L. of Whitehall, NY

December 18, 1866
Whitehall, NY

SHARPE Henry of Hebron, NY
DENNISON Sarah of Salem, NY

December 25, 1866

BRIDGEFORD William of Glens Falls, NY
CAREY Catherine of Glens Falls, NY

December 19, 1866
Sandy Hill, NY

DENNISON William of Salem, NY
NICHOLS Susan of Argyle, NY

December 9, 1866
Argyle, NY

WILLARD George W. of Poultney, Vt.
THOMPSON Grace A. of Hartford, NY

December 19, 1866
Hartford, NY

GREGORY Samuel of Whitehall, NY
REYNOLDS Elizabeth of Whitehall, NY

December 23, 1866
Whitehall, NY

DERRICK D. W. of Lansingburgh, NY
JILLSON A. E. of Whitehall, NY

December 24, 1866
Whitehall, NY

DOBIE David F. of Plattsburgh, NY
JILLSON Harriet L. only dau of N. T. of Whitehall, NY

December 26, 1866
Whitehall, NY

WRIGHT John M. of E. Whitehall, NY
SEARS Lucy M. of E. Whitehall, NY

December 26, 1866

EVERTS Palmer D. of Granville, NY
PERRY Elizabeth A. of Easton, NY

December 20, 1866
Easton, NY

BAKER William of Salem, NY
DOYLE Margaret of Salem, NY

December 11, 1866
Salem, NY

CASEY Edward of Salem, NY
TREMBLE Kate of Salem, NY

December 25, 1866
Salem, NY

CLARK Freeman M. of Jackson, NY
ANTHONY Nancy M. of Cambridge, NY

December 25, 1866
Cambridge, NY

CLARK Richard G. of Essex, NY

December 25, 1866

**BENTLEY** Hattie of Ft. Ann, NY

**WHITMORE** Thomas of Ft. Ann, NY          December 27, 1866
**BRAYTON** Jennie of Ft. Ann, NY

**PARKER** James of Ft. Ann, NY             December 31, 1866
**PARDO** Mary B. of Ft. Ann, NY

**HAY** Henry of Greenwich, NY              January 6, 1867
**TULL** Abbie of Greenwich, NY             Union Village, NY

**MILLS** Frederick of Ft. Edward, NY       January 1, 1867
**STOVER** Mary E. of Ft. Edward, NY        Ft. Edward, NY

**CLARK** Merritt W. of Granville, NY       January 1, 1867
**MARTLING** Fannie M. of Whitehall, NY     N. Granville, NY

**KARNOHAN** Samuel of Jackson, NY          January 12, 1867
**NICHOLS** Mary Ann of Jackson, NY         Salem, NY

**JACKSON** Ezra P. of Sandy Hill, NY       January 12, 1867
**JOHNSON** Lucy A. of Sandy Hill, NY       Sandy Hill, NY

**BROWN** William H. of Granville, NY       January 13, 1866
**SIMPSON** Mary A. of Queensbury, NY

**BURTON** James of Hartford, NY            January 17, 1867
**SMITH** Mary of Hartford, NY              Ft. Edward, NY

**SMITH** Eugene of Ft. Edward, NY          December 24, 1866
**CALL** Emma M. of Ft. Edward, NY          Ft. Edward, NY

**MC MILLAN** Benjamin of Hebron, NY        December 31, 1866
**GILCHRIST** Nancy M. of Argyle, NY        Argyle, NY

**LESTER** Samuel A. of Argyle, NY          January 1, 1867
**HALL** Maggie E. of Hebron, NY            Hebron, NY

**COOK** Warren T. of Ft. Edward, NY        January 24, 1867
**BIBBINS** Georgianna of Ft. Edward, NY    Sandy Hill, NY

**MC GUIRE** M. of Ft. Ann, NY              January 27, 1867
**MURPHY** L. of Ft. Ann, NY                Whitehall, NY

**REID** William J. of S. Argyle, NY        January 31, 1867
**ARMSTRONG** Mattie J. of S. Argyle, NY    S. Argyle, NY

**STEWART** David of Salem, NY              January 24, 1867
**STAFFORD** Ellen of Greenwich, NY         Argyle, NY

THORNTON Sidney of Lyman, NH
FRANCISCO Ellen of Whitehall, NY

January 25, 1867
Whitehall, NY

HILLS Jesse M. of Hartford, NY
GRAHAM Sarah J. of Ft. Ann, NY

February 7, 1867
Ft. Ann, NY

MC GEOCH John of Jackson, NY
FOSTER Susan F.

February 12, 1867
Salem, NY

MOSELY Myron W. of Hoosick, NY
CENTH Lucena A. of White Creek, NY

December 12, 1866
White Creek, NY

PIERCE John S. of White Creek, NY
STANLEY Sarah A. of Shaftsbury, NY

January 17, 1867
Shaftsbury, NY

SAUNDERS Joseph J. of Grafton, NY
FORD Mary Jane of Grafton, NY

January 22, 1867
Grafton, NY

ROWLAND Amasa P. of White Creek, NY
HAIGHT Harriet A. of White Creek, NY

January 31, 1867
Cambridge, NY

CROMACK Frank of Bennington, Vt.
MATHEWS Sarah F. of Bennington, Vt.

February 6, 1867
White Creek, NY

ALLEN William R. of Chicago, Ill.
PRATT Almira of Cambridge, NY

February 20, 1867
Cambridge, NY

MC NISH Andrew B. of Cambridge, NY
BROWNELL Addie A. of Cambridge, NY

February 20, 1867
Cambridge, NY

STOVER Wesley of Pittstown, NY
WILKS Emma A. of Valley Falls, NY

February 13, 1867
Valley Falls, NY

DUEL Hiram of Sliborough, NY
HICKS Elmery of Sliborough, NY

February 12, 1867
Sliborough, NY

DUEL Richard of Granville, NY
HICKS Abby of Granville, NY

February 12, 1867

LEWIS William of Granville, NY
BROWN Ellen of Granville, NY

February 14, 1867

VAUGHN Richard of Kingsbury, NY
NEWTON Mary L. of Kingsbury, NY

February 16, 1867
Kingsbury, NY

SHELDON Orville of Ft. Ann, NY
STEWART Julia M. of Ft. Ann, NY

February 20, 1867
Ft. Ann, NY

SIBLE Ezra of Stillwater, NY

February 20, 1867

**MC NAUGHTON** S. Libbie of Schuylerville, NY — Schuylerville, NY

**WILLIAMS** Willis H. of Shushan, NY — February 20, 1867
**SHEDD** Helen S. of Shushan, NY — Shushan, NY

**MARTIN** William of Cambridge, NY — March 7, 1867
**MC ARTHUR** Margaret of Salem, NY

**HENRY** George W. of Granville, NY — February 27, 1867
**ROOT** Helen M. of Bennington, Vt. — Bennington, Vt.

**DECKER** Charles of Cambridge, NY — (newspaper date) — March 29, 1867
**STORY** Emily F. of Cambridge, NY — Cambridge, NY

**BRIGGS** George of White Creek, NY — March 21, 1867
**RUSSELL** Mary F. of White Creek, NY — White Creek, NY

**ARNOLD** C. W. of Cambridge, NY — March 31, 1867
**SEARLES** Rose of Cohoes, NY — White Creek, NY

**ROBEDEAU** C. T. of Ft. Edward, NY — March 28, 1867
**WINN** Nellie M. of Ft. Edward, NY — Ft. Edward, NY

**FOSMIRE** J. F. — March 27, 1867
**MC ALLISTER** Ann — Sandy Hill, NY

**MARTIN** Simeon of Shaftsbury, Vt. — April 4, 1867
**DUNLOP** Mrs. Sarah of White Creek, NY — Cambridge, NY

**GREEN** A. H. of Granville, NY — April 10, 1867
**GOODSPEED** Leonora E. of Wells, Vt. — Wells, Vt.

**MOTLEY** Francis of Sugar Grove, NY — April 2, 1867
**GRAVES** Emma of Rupert, Vt. — Rupert, Vt.

**MARROW** G. E. of Detroit, Mi. — April 11, 1867
**GIFFORD** Sarah M. of Coila, NY — Detroit, Mi.

**DENNIS** B. C. of Sandy Hill, NY — April 16, 1867
**BURDICK** Mrs. E. J. of Sandy Hill, NY — Sandy Hill, NY

**MEEKER** M. — April 16, 1867
**CORNING** Florence — Ft. Ann, NY

**GILLETTE** C. L. of Whitehall, NY — May 1, 1867
**ADAMS** Ada of Whitehall, NY

**SKIFF** Allen of Coila, NY — May 8, 1867
**CULVER** Sarah of Coila, NY — Coila, NY

GRAY Henry of Cambridge, NY      May 7, 1867
BUEL Anna of Troy, NY

STEPHENS Melvin J. of Shelburne Falls, Mass.      May 8, 1867
MC NAUGHTON Esther J. dau of Gen. John Mc Naughton      Salem, NY

BURKE James of Salem, NY      May 16, 1867
GANSWORTH Helen of Salem, NY      Salem, NY

WINEGAR Horace      May 15, 1867
FITCH Amanda      Ft. Ann, NY

STEWART Joseph of Cambridge, NY      May 28, 1867
COULTER Annie M. of Cambridge, NY      Cambridge, NY

ACKER Theodore of Sing Sing, NY   (newspaper date)    June 7, 1867
NEWMAN Abbie L. of White Creek, NY      Cohoes, NY

LYONS Edward of Whitehall, NY      May 27, 1867
CARPENTER Louisa of Whitehall, NY      Whitehall, NY

COMFORT J. E. Md. of Sandy Hill, NY      May 23, 1867
RANDALL Lucy A. dau of S. S. of Morrisania, NY      New York City

BUELL A. A. of Whitehall, NY      June 5, 1867
VAUGHN Mary L. dau of T. T. of Whitehall, NY      Whitehall, NY

LEWIS E. A.      June 3, 1867
MOSHER Jennie P.      Ft. Ann, NY

GIBBS T. Z. Md.      June 5, 1867
SKINNER M. J. of Ft. Ann, NY

CARPENTER Hudson of S. Granville, NY      June 20, 1867
SMITH Caroline of S. Granville, NY      N. Hebron, NY

ANDREWS Marcus of Hoosick, NY      June 12, 1867
TABER Sarah of White Creek, NY

SMITH John E. of Cambridge, NY      June 19, 1867
NORTON Abbie dau of G. F. of Cambridge, NY      Cambridge, NY

LANE William H. Jr. of Burlington, Vt.      June 12, 1867
STANTON Mary E. dau of William BROWN of Salem, NY      Salem, NY

BILLINGER Jacob H. of Ogdensburgh, NY      June 18, 1867
SMITH Hannah A. of Salem, NY      Salem, NY

HAWKINS Jason L. of Granville, Ill.      June 16, 1867

**HARKNESS** Lydia of Granville, NY

Granville, NY

**GRISWOLD** Samuel K.
**EDDY** Mattie B. dau of W. S.

June 11, 1867
Whitehall, NY

**DECKER** William W.
**DUNTON** Charlotte Ann

June 30, 1867
Cambridge, NY

**REED** John of Argyle, NY
**WHEATON** Gathie of Argyle, NY

July 1, 1867
Cambridge, NY

**DORRENCE** Hugh of S. Granville, NY
**SPRAGUE** Mrs. Melissa of W. Rupert, Vt.

July 4, 1867
Granville, NY

**NEWMAN** J. L. of Cambridge, NY
**CONKEY** Katie J. of Cambridge, NY

July 8, 1867
W. Hebron, NY

**JOHNSON** Nathan
**WRIGHT** Alice

July 4, 1867
Sandy Hill, NY

**ROSS** Ervin
**WILLAR** Jennie

July 4, 1867

**WALLACE** William of Sandy Hill, NY
**HILL** Aseneth of Sandy Hill, NY

July 6, 1867

**DUEL** Hiram of S. Granville, NY
**MOORE** Amelia of S. Granville, NY

July 6, 1867
S. Granville, NY

**NELSON** Horatio of Ft. Ann, NY
**BROUGHTON** Hattie of Ft. Ann, NY

July 14, 1867
Ft. Ann, NY

**COOPER** William E. of Kingsbury, NY
**DEWEY** Frances E. of Kingsbury, NY

July 31, 1867
Kingsbury, NY

**BARTON** Henry O. of Cambridge, NY
**BAILEY** Louisa of Cambridge, NY

July 31, 1867
Salem, NY

**DIBBLE** Charles V. of Battenville, NY
**MC LEAN** J. H. of Jackson, NY

August 13, 1867
E. Salem, NY

**GOODRICH** Charlie L. of Mohawk, NY
**WHITTAKER** Josephine of Jackson, NY

August 20, 1867
Cambridge, NY

**FRAZIER** John of Salem, NY
**MITCHELL** Jane of Hebron, NY

August 20, 1867
Cambridge, NY

**DENNISON** Thomas of Argyle, NY
**GALBRAITH** Mary of Argyle, NY

September 11, 1867

| | |
|---|---|
| **KING** Benjamin of Sandy Hill, NY<br>**SWEET** Mary A. of Sandy Hill, NY | September 2, 1867 |
| **PRIEST** Henry of Cambridge, NY<br>**COOK** Mary of Cambridge, NY | September 5, 1867<br>Union Village, NY |
| **SWEET** George M. of White Creek, NY<br>**LEE** Sarah M. of Cambridge, NY | September 11, 1867<br>Cambridge, NY |
| **PRATT** Dr. Morris of Buskirks Bridge, NY<br>**ALLEN** Adia of N. Adams, Mass. | September 25, 1867<br>N. Adams, Mass. |
| **MERRITT** Jacob<br>**COOLEY** Sarah I., dau of L. M. of Hoosick Falls, NY | September 25, 1867<br>Hoosick Falls, NY |
| **MC ARTHUR** Symmers of Jackson, NY<br>**CLEVELAND** Fannie L. of Greig, NY | September 10, 1867<br>Greig, NY |
| **TEN EYCK** Jonas S. of Cohoes, NY<br>**BROWN** Christina of Schaghticoke, NY | September 25, 1867<br>Schaghticoke, NY |
| **SWEET** Emery T. of N. Hoosick, NY<br>**MOSELY** Nettie of White Creek, NY | September 25, 1867<br>White Creek, NY |
| **MOSHER** Henry W. of Lansingburgh, NY<br>**GILLESPIE** Mary H. of Lansingburgh, NY | September 25, 1867<br>Lansingburgh, NY |
| **BASCOM** W. F.<br>**BUELL** Clara E. dau of J. T. of Whitehall, NY | September 25, 1867<br>Whitehall, NY |
| **DAWSON** William of Whitehall, NY<br>**HAVENS** Mrs. J. D. of Ft. Henry, NY | September 24, 1867 |
| **CULVER** Jonathan L. of Cambridge, NY<br>**MITCHELL** Isabella of Cambridge, NY | September 16, 1867<br>Salem, NY |
| **BENNETT** Phennor of Shaftsbury, Vt.<br>**SURDAM** Lucy J. of Shaftsbury, Vt. | August 17, 1867<br>White Creek, NY |
| **HEWITT** Morgan P. of White Creek, NY<br>**DYER** Frances M. dau of John E. of White Creek, NY | September 19, 1867<br>White Creek, NY |
| **CORBETT** Simeon of White Creek, NY<br>**BENNETT** Josephine of White Creek, NY | September 19, 1867<br>White Creek, NY |
| **WRIGHT** George H. of White Creek, NY<br>**BROWNELL** Pemina Augusta of White Creek, NY | September 19, 1867<br>White Creek, NY |
| **GALUSHA** John F. of Ft. Edward, NY | October 10, 1867 |

**TOWNE** Betsey of Ft. Edward, NY — Ft. Edward, NY

**ELLIS** George — October 7, 1867
**ROBERTS** Mrs. Lydia A. — Ft. Edward, NY

**ANDREWS** Cleveland D. of Arlington, Vt. — October 15, 1867
**NELSON** Maggie of Salem, NY

**FASSETT** George C. of Sandy Hill, NY — October 21, 1867
**TALLMAN** Annie M. of Sandy Hill, NY — Sandy Hill, NY

**DOOAY** James of Hebron, NY — October 16, 1867
**DOOAY** Sarah of Hebron, NY — Salem, NY

**STEWART** James of Hartford, NY — October 31, 1867
**MC CARTER** Elizabeth of Hartford, NY

**BEATTIE** Alexander of Watertown, NY — November 13, 1867
**MC KNIGHT** Hannah dau of George of Heborn, NY — Hebron, NY

**PERRY** John H. of Argyle, NY — November 13, 1867
**JOHNSON** Margaret J. of Argyle, NY — Argyle, NY

**BISHOP** Arp of Dalton, Mass. — November 27, 1867
**HERRINGTON** Charlotte dau of John of White Creek, NY — White Creek, NY

**HEATON** M. B. of Troy, NY — November 14, 1867
**MC LEAN** Lucie H. of Jackson, NY — Jackson, NY

**BEEBE** David G. — December 12, 1867
**SHALER** Anna E.

**WILLIAMS** Milton E. of Greenwich, NY — December 14, 1867
**MILLS** Mary S. of White Creek, NY — White Creek, NY

**WOODWORTH** George of Jackson, NY — December 25, 1867
**ROBERTSON** Maria G. of Cambridge, NY — Cambridge, NY

**COOPER** George of Sterling, NY — January 1, 1868
**PARISH** Susan of Jackson, NY

**WAIT** George of Salem, NY — December 31, 1867
**EDIE** Mary A. of Salem, NY — Shushan, NY

**HENRY** Peter of Salem, NY — January 1, 1868
**PROCTOR** Lucinda A. of Salem, NY — Salem, NY

**HERRINGTON** Allen A. of White Creek, NY — December 11, 1867
**WOOD** Mary Jane of White Creek, NY — White Creek, NY

MC GEOCH William of Jackson, NY  
HUNT Mary F. of White Creek, NY

January 1, 1868  
White Creek, NY

RICE Marcus D. of Cambridge, NY  
ARCHIBALD Mary J. of Cambridge, NY

January 1, 1868  
Salem, NY

SMITH William F. of Salem, NY  
HILL Celia of Hoosick Falls, NY

January 1, 1868  
Hoosick Falls, NY

ALEXANDER Orlando of E. Greenwich, NY  
HALL Mary C. of E. Greenwich, NY

December 31, 1867  
E. Greenwich, NY

RUSSELL George of Bennington, Vt.  
PADDOCK Malinda of Bennington, Vt.

January 3, 1868

ARNOLD D. E.  
HODGE Alice E.

January 15, 1868  
White Creek, NY

KING Ira of Jackson, NY  
DOANE Sarah M. of White Creek, NY

January 22, 1868  
White Creek, NY

FORT J. W. of Easton, NY  
BROWNELL Alice of Cambridge, NY

February 12, 1868  
Cambridge, NY

SHALER Andrew of Jackson, NY  
HAXTON Mary A. dau of Jeremiah of Cambridge, NY

February 5, 1868

COY Chauncey P. of Hebron, NY  
KENNEDY Mary of Hebron, NY

February 11, 1868

WYMAN Walter E. of White Creek, NY  
SURDAM Bella of Hoosick, NY

February 4, 1868  
Hoosick, NY

HOAG Stephen B. of Galesburg, Wis.  
BUTTS Zadie of White Creek, NY

February 5, 1868  
White Creek, NY

COULTER George of Jackson, NY  
DARROW Allie dau of Hiram formerly of Cambridge, NY

February 11, 1868  
Plainfield, NJ

STAPLES Clarence of N. Granville, NY  
BROWN Isabel of N. Granville, NY

February 4, 1868  
N. Granville, NY

HART Thomas of Battle Creek, Mi.  
SEARLES Kitty of N. Granville, NY

February 6, 1868  
N. Granville, NY

MASON Frederick of Granville, NY  
HICKS Sarah of Granville, NY

January 29, 1868  
Granville, NY

GAVETT Asahel of Argyle, NY

March 4, 1868

**FISHER** Fanny of White Creek, NY

White Creek, NY

**BALDWIN** Rollin of Sunderland, Vt.
**GRAHAM** Eleanor W. of Manchester, Vt.

March 10, 1868
Coila, NY

**ANDREWS** David B. of Hebron, NY
**WINSLOW** Josephine of Pawlet, Vt.

March 4, 1868
Salem, NY

**WILLIAMSON** Thomas of Argyle, NY
**WILSON** Marthaette of Argyle, NY

February 27, 1868

**ASHLEY** John H. of W. Hebron, NY
**WILSON** Nancy of Argyle, NY

February 27, 1868

**DEWEY** Robert of Hebron, NY
**MUNSON** Amanda of Hebron, NY

March 5, 1868

**REYNOLDS** William B. of Hartford, NY
**BRAYTON** Sarah E. of Hartford, NY

March 17, 1868
N. Argyle, NY

**IRWIN** John of S. Argyle, NY
**WATSON** Lizzie E. of S. Argyle, NY

March 4, 1868

**EDIE** George of E. Salem, NY
**ARMSTRONG** Nannie Bell of S. Argyle, NY

March 10, 1868

**KENYON** Clark H. of Greenwich, NY
**MILLS** Sarah M. of White Creek, NY

March 24, 1868
White Creek, NY

**BERRY** Ward L. of Cambridge, NY
**SKINNER** Mary A. of Cambridge, NY

March 25, 1868
Cambridge, NY

**MC KINNEY** James of Cambridge, NY
**ODBERT** Florence of Cambridge, NY

April 5, 1868
Cambridge, NY

**WRIGHT** Gilbert of White Creek, NY
**FULLMAN** Eva L. of Webster, NY

March 25, 1868
Webster, NY

**PRIEST** John H. of Hoosick, NY
**SPAULDING** Mary L. of Hoosick, NY

April 23, 1868
Hoosick, NY

**MC COLT** Oscar of Roundout, NY
**SHAW** Mrs. Helen of Salem, NY

April 28, 1868
Cambridge, NY

**BURDICK** Eugene of Shushan, NY
**BURDICK** Mrs. Judith M. of Shushan, NY

April 25, 1868
Shushan, NY

**SMALL** James
**EDIE** Sarah Martha

May 26, 1868
Shushan, NY

FRASER Walter of Salem, NY
MITCHELL Mary of Salem, NY

May 20, 1868
W. Hebron, NY

MATHEWS Horace P. of Salem, NY
MORRISON Nellie L. of Salem, NY

May 21, 1868
Salem, NY

ALEXANDER George of Jackson, NY
LEE Emma J. of White Creek, NY

June 3, 1868
White Creek, NY

GREEN Charles of Cambridge, NY
PERKINS Mrs. Orville of Cambridge, NY

May 13, 1868
Cambridge, NY

CROCKER B. Porter of Cambridge, NY
WESTON S. Josephine of Cohoes, NY

June 11, 1868
Cohoes, NY

ELLIS Ira M. of Cambridge, NY
CONGDON Mary E. of N. Hartford, NY

June 28, 1868
N. Hartford, NY

HAWKINS Newman of Ft. Edward, NY
WENTWORTH Mary E. of Granville, NY

July 5, 1868
Hoosick Falls, NY

CHATFIELD Col. H. S. of New York City
TOWNE Sarah M. of Cambridge, NY

July 29, 1868
Cambridge, NY

KING J. W. of Cobleskill, NY
POWELL Lottie E. of Salem, NY

August 5, 1868
Shushan, NY

GILCHRIST John
WHITE Ella

August 20, 1868
Argyle, NY

WILLIAMSON John of Hebron, NY
CAMPBELL Mary Ann of Hebron, NY

September 2, 1868
Hebron, NY

MC CLELLAN Donald of Hebron, NY
MC CLELLAN Libbie of Cambridge, NY

September 10, 1868
Cambridge, NY

BAKER George R. of Granville, NY
REYNOLDS Jennie R. of Granville, NY

September 8, 1868
Granville, NY

REYNOLDS Oliver Jr. of Granville, NY
BLOSSOM Georgie G. of Pawlet, Vt.

September 8, 1868
Pawlet, Vt.

HARVEY John of Ft. Ann, NY
VAUGHEL Adelia E. of Plattsburgh, NY

September 9, 1868
Ft. Ann, NY

FLOWERS Dewitt
CROWL Abba of Salem, NY

September 15, 1868
Salem, NY

MC GEOCH W. J. of Greenwich, NY

September 17, 1868

**MC MORRIS** Elizabeth J. of Jackson, NY        Jackson, NY

**JOHNSON** Henry G. of Greenwich, NY      September 17, 1868
**MC MORRIS** Anna of Jackson, NY        Jackson, NY

**RICE** Clark      September 21, 1868
**BUCK** Martha M.      Cambridge, NY

**PRATT** Phillip E. of Cambridge, NY      September 23, 1868
**BROWN** Sybil A. of Bennington, Vt.      Bennington, Vt.

**WHITE** D. M. of Argyle, NY      September 17, 1868
**SHANNON** E. of Argyle, NY      Argyle, NY

**PARSONS** Emery C. of Hartford, Conn.      September 30, 1868
**CROSBY** Kate G. of Hartford, Conn.      Cambridge, NY

**WAIT** Albert of Salem, NY      September 24, 1868
**DOWNS** Mrs. Hattie of Bennington, Vt.      Bennington, Vt.

**MAHAFFY** David of Salem, NY      September 24, 1868
**HENRY** Annie of Argyle, NY      Argyle, NY

**CADY** J. of Chicago, Ill.      October 3, 1868
**WRIGHT** Sarah C. of Cambridge, NY      White Creek, NY

**BROWNELL** Jonathan of Cambridge, NY      October 13, 1868
**BURNHAM** Phebe Ann of Cambridge, NY      Cambridge, NY

**FISHER** D. Wesley of Cambridge, NY      October 8, 1868
**BLAIR** Eliza J. of Cambridge, NY      Cambridge, NY

**CASE** William J. of Pittstown, NY      October 15, 1868
**CULVER** Sarah M. of Cambridge, NY      Cambridge, NY

**SEWELL** Robert of Easton, NY      October 15, 1868
**RANDALL** Ruth A. of Cambridge, NY      Cambridge, NY

**HASKINS** W. E. of Jackson, NY    (newspaper date)      October 30, 1868
**TAYLOR** Sarah J. of St. John, New Brunswick,      Salem, NY

**CENTER** Arnold C. of Cambridge, NY      October 28, 1868
**SWEET** Ida C. of Cambridge, NY      Cambridge, NY

**COTTRELL** Arthur of White Creek, NY      October 28, 1868
**WHITCOMB** Nellie of White Creek, NY      White Creek, NY

**STERLING** Henry of Verona, NY      October 20, 1868
**WELLS** Sarah B. of Berlin, NY      Berlin, NY

LONG Berry of Cambridge, NY  
KINNEY Charlotte L. of Schaghticoke, NY

November 11, 1868  
Schaghticoke, NY

LAMB William P. of Whitehall, NY  
FULLERTON Julia of Argyle, NY

November 10, 1868  
Argyle, NY

DAVIS Albert of Stoddard, NY          (newspaper date)  
TOWNE Rosetta of Sullivan, NH formerly of Cambridge, NY

December 11, 1868  
Sullivan, NH

SNYDER Charles G. of Ft. Edward, NY  
RAMSEY Margaret A. of Ft. Edward, NY

December 3, 1868  
Ft. Edward, NY

STODDARD Anson of Ft. Edward, NY  
TILFORD Emma of Ft. Edward, NY

December 3, 1868  
Ft. Edward, NY

LARKIN George W. of E. Greenwich, NY  
HULETT Altie J. of Pawlet, Vt.

December 1, 1868  
Granville, NY

CONKLIN John of Cambridge, NY  
FAY Susan of Cambridge, NY

December 3, 1868  
Cambridge, NY

COWAN George of Jackson, NY  
TILFORD Mary J. of Jackson, NY

December 16, 1868  
Jackson, NY

BACHELDER Mr. ____  
WILSEY H. A.

December 9, 1868  
Ft. Ann, NY

KIRK George of Troy, NY  
WATERS Kate M. of Lewiston, Pa.

December 8, 1868  
Salem, NY

WIGGINS John of Argyle, NY  
MANNING Zipporah of Greenwich, NY

December 24, 1868

HOWELL Walter S. of Florida, NY  
BROWNELL Jennie of Cambridge, NY

December 29, 1868  
Cambridge, NY

CLOSSON Robert E. of Cambridge, NY  
HATCH Mary A. of Jackson, NY

December 30, 1868  
Jackson, NY

ABBOTT Elisha  
DENNIS Libbie

December 24, 1868  
Greenwich, NY

BROWN Frederick L. of Ft. Ann, NY  
DAILEY Eliza J. of Sandy Hill, NY

December 17, 1868  
Sandy Hill, NY

GILBERT Edward J. of Fairhaven, Vt.  
ROGERS Addie of Hebron, NY

December 25, 1868  
Granville, NY

MACK Josiah D. of Salem, NY

December 30, 1868

**PERRY** Mary J. of Salem, NY

Salem, NY

**LEE** William H. of Cambridge, NY
**MARTIN** Sarah E. of Battenville, NY

December 24, 1868

**POLLOCK** John W.
**SHAW** Libbie

December 27, 1868
Argyle, NY

**BRANT** Jacob of Argyle, NY
**MC GEOCH** Frances of Argyle, NY

November 3, 1868
Argyle, NY

**CHAMBERLAIN** John M. of Hebron, NY
**MUNSON** Mrs. Nancy of Hebron, NY

December 31, 1868

**DINNING** Robert of N. Argyle, NY
**MURRAY** Margaret of N. Argyle, NY

January 5, 1869
N. Argyle, NY

**MC MILLAN** John of S. Argyle, NY
**CURTIS** Christina of S. Argyle, NY

December 25, 1868
S. Argyle, NY

**MC CLELLAN** John T. of Hebron, NY
**REID** Amanda of S. Argyle, NY

December 29, 1868
S. Argyle, NY

**DINGS** Charles N.
**BAIN** Hannah of S. Argyle, NY

December 30, 1868
S. Argyle, NY

**WHITTAKER** Orrin C. of Easton, NY
**BARBER** Jennie L. of Cambridge, NY

December 31, 1868
Cambridge, NY

**MC ROBERTS** Robert of Albany, NY
**HILL** Emma of Jackson, NY

January 8, 1869
Jackson, NY

**HANNA** Jacob A. of Hebron, NY
**HOLMES** Mariette of Hebron, NY

December 30, 1868
Cambridge, NY

**BROWNELL** Kenyon R. of Cambridge, NY
**KENYON** Julina H. of Cambridge, NY

January 26, 1869

**HICKS** Hiland J. of Hebron, NY
**SMITH** Freelove A. of Hebron, NY

January 19, 1869
Salem, NY

**GRAY** George W. of Wilton, NY
**BUCK** Carrie of Corinth, NY

January 27, 1869
Cambridge, NY

**HERRINGTON** Artemus C. of White Creek, NY
**PIERCE** Julia E. of White Creek, NY

February 4, 1869
Cambridge, NY

**GRAHAM** William S. of Putnam, NY
**NEWBURY** Mary E.

January 28, 1869
Greenwich, NY

| | |
|---|---|
| **STEWART** Reuben of Jackson, NY | January 28, 1869 |
| **SHERMAN** Jennie F. of Greenwich, NY | Greenwich, NY |
| | |
| **CRAMER** E. P. of Cambridge, NY | February 11, 1869 |
| **MAYNARD** Ruby of Cambridge, NY | Cambridge, NY |
| | |
| **SMITH** Ervin S. of Hebron, NY | February 9, 1869 |
| **HICKS** Stella A. of Hebron, NY | Salem, NY |
| | |
| **HOXIE** Florence of Easton, NY | February 11, 1869 |
| **SKIFF** Rhoda dau of John of Easton, NY | Easton, NY |
| | |
| **ROXBURY** Daniel of Cambridge, NY | February 10, 1869 |
| **SULLIVAN** Clara of Troy, NY | Troy, NY |
| | |
| **FOSTER** James of Cambridge, NY | February 13, 1869 |
| **HILL** Nancy of Coila, NY | |
| | |
| **REYNOLDS** William V. E. of Easton, NY | February 17, 1869 |
| **COLLAMER** Melinda A. of Greenwich, NY | Greenwich, NY |
| | |
| **BACON** Edward L. of Cambridge, NY | January 30, 1869 |
| **VARNUM** Amelia J. of Cambridge, NY | Greenwich, NY |
| | |
| **STOVER** Charles H. of Greenwich, NY | February 11, 1869 |
| **GREEN** Lydia Ann of Greenwich, NY | Greenwich, NY |
| | |
| **QUA** George E. | February 18, 1869 |
| **BARKLEY** Julia of Argyle, NY | Argyle, NY |
| | |
| **DEACON** William of Hebron, NY | February 16, 1869 |
| **MC GEOCH** Hattic dau of William of Argyle, NY | Argyle, NY |
| | |
| **SMITH** Robert | February 16, 1869 |
| **SAFFORD** Jane E. | Argyle, NY |
| | |
| **STYLES** Samuel of Hartford, NY | March 2, 1869 |
| **MILLARD** Anna E. of Easton, NY | Greenwich, NY |
| | |
| **REYNOLDS** Harvey of Hebron, NY | February 24, 1869 |
| **MC EACHRON** Jane of Argyle, NY | Argyle, NY |
| | |
| **LOOP** George T. of Sandy Hill, NY | February 23, 1869 |
| **KILBURN** Eva M. of Ft. Ann, NY | Ft. Ann, NY |
| | |
| **STEVENSON** William D. of Troy, NY | March 3, 1869 |
| **WALLACE** Lizzie L. of N. Argyle, NY | N. Argyle, NY |
| | |
| **ENGLISH** Alexander L. of Cambridge, NY | March 10, 1869 |

**RICE** Libbie M. of Cambridge, NY

**MC CALL** John of Keokuk, Iowa                                    March 10, 1869
**FISHER** Jennie of Cambridge, NY                              White Creek, NY

**CLOFF** Elijah of Greenwich, NY                                   March 2, 1869
**MC EACHRON** Anna of Argyle, NY

**PITNEY** Samuel of Eagle Bridge, NY                           March 11, 1869
**ELWELL** Rebecca of Troy, NY                                    Cambridge, NY

**CONNELLY** Hugh of Hebron, NY          (newspaper date)    March 19, 1869
**LUKE** Agnes of Hebron, NY                                        Hebron, NY

**SHANKLAND** John of Bangor, Wis.                              March 15, 1869
**CUMMINGS** Ellen A. of Putnam, NY                            Putnam, NY

**RODGERS** Anson of Coose Co. Oregon                          March 13, 1869
**DILLINGHAM** Elizabeth K. dau of Otis                        Granville, NY

**FULLER** John N. of White Creek, NY                           March 15, 1869
**RANDALL** Florence of Jackson, NY                             Jackson, NY

**HARVEY** Albert L. of Ft. Ann, NY                               March 16, 1869
**JOHNSON** Margaret of Whitehall, NY                          Whitehall, NY

**WILLIAMS** D. W. of N. Argyle, NY                              March 18, 1869
**ROBINSON** F. A. of Galesville, NY                             Galesville, NY

**CLARK** Henry W.                                                    March 23, 1869
**GUILDER** Elsie Jane                                               Granville, NY

**SHALER** Julius of Jackson, NY                                  March 18,1869
**HALL** Miss ____ of Greenwich, NY                            E. Greenwich, NY

**CONGDON** Duncan of Salem, NY                                April 6, 1869
**BARTLETT** Minnie of Salem, NY                                Shushan, NY

**GRISWOLD** Alfred H. of Whitehall, NY                       March 30, 1869
**BECK** Mrs. Susan of Arlington, Vt.                            Arlington, Vt.

**MC CONNELL** Thomas of Washington Co. NY               March 23, 1869
**GAYLORD** Fannie dau of Henry of Brooklyn, NY         Brooklyn, NY

**ROBERTSON** Francis of Salem, NY                            April 6, 1869
**MARSH** Jennie E. of Arlington, Vt.                            Greenwich, NY

**SHAW** George of Greenwich, NY                              April 8, 1869
**LEE** Addie of Ft. Miller, NY                                     Greenwich, NY

HENRY Solomon of Syracuse, NY
TINKEY Margaret of Argyle, NY
March 24, 1869

BAIN Alfred H. of Argyle, NY
PARKER Maryette of Jackson, NY
March 25, 1869
Sandy Hill, NY

CROSBY Frederick W. of Chicago, Ill.
NORTON Jennie A. of Chicago, Ill.
March 31, 1869
Chicago. Ill.

ENGLISH William L. of Cambridge, NY
MILLER Jane A. of Cambridge, NY
April 21, 1869
White Creek, NY

EDWARDS John Quincey of Plattsburgh, NY
COOK Emma V. dau of B. T. of Whitehall, NY
April 14, 1869
Whitehall, NY

ROBERSON Francis of Camden, NY
MARSH Jennette of Chunks Brook, NY
April 6, 1869
Greenwich, NY

MC NEIL Archibald of E. Greenwich, NY
HOME Addie of Troy, NY
April 21, 1869
Troy, NY

STOVER J. B. of N. Greenwich, NY
MASON Jennie L. of Greenwich, NY
May 2, 1869
Greenwich, NY

DAWLEY George of Greenwich, NY
HYDE Mrs. Eliza of Greenwich, NY
May 2, 1869
Greenwich, NY

LAW William
LAW Eliza Agnes dau of David E. of Salem, NY
May 5, 1869

PATTERSON J. C. of Cambridge, NY
JUDD Jennie of Brooklyn, NY
May 11, 1869
Cambridge, NY

HILLMAN E. D. formerly of Greenwich, NY
SPENCER Della of Rochester, Mi.
April 20, 1869
Rochester, Mi.

BEST Walter of Brooklyn, NY
THOMPSON Mattie F. of Salem, NY
April 26, 1869
Brooklyn, NY

KIERNAN George D. of Whitehall, NY
LANDON Mary of Whitehall, NY
May 3, 1869
Whitehall, NY

SHULTZ William F. of Whitehall, NY
BLATCHLEY Charlotte of Whitehall, NY
May 6, 1869
Saratoga Springs, NY

COMISKEE Patrick of Cambridge, NY
LUDDY Ann of Cambridge, NY
May 25, 1869
Cambridge, NY

FORD Timothy of Cambridge, NY
May 25, 1869

| | |
|---|---|
| **LYNCH** Bridget of Cambridge, NY | Cambridge, NY |
| | |
| **SANDERSON** Harvey J. of Cambridge, NY | May 1, 1869 |
| **LOVEJOY** Jessie of Cambridge, NY | Greenwich, NY |
| | |
| **LASHER** Alonzo of Greenwich, NY | May 22, 1869 |
| **MC DONALD** Mary of Greenwich, NY | Greenwich, NY |
| | |
| **VANDENBURGH** Edwin of White Creek, NY | May 26, 1869 |
| **CLINT** Maggie E. of Poestenskill, NY | Poestenskill, NY |
| | |
| **BENNETT** James W. of Greenwich, NY | May 27, 1869 |
| **GREEN** Sarah of Greenwich, NY | Greenwich, NY |
| | |
| **GIBSON** James Jr. | June 8,1869 |
| **COWAN** Jennie E. dau of Hugh formerly of Cambridge, NY | Salem, NY |
| | |
| **LIDDLE** Leonard M. of Salem, NY | June 9, 1869 |
| **FREEMAN** Lottie dau of Marvin of Salem, NY | Salem, NY |
| | |
| **GRAHAM** Sylvester W. of Ft. Edward, NY | June 1, 1869 |
| **PARTRIDGE** Susan J. of Ft. Edward, NY | Ft. Edward, NY |
| | |
| **LOUDON** Charles H. of Ft. Edward, NY | May 26, 1869 |
| **RAMSEY** Nellie S. of Ft. Edward, NY | Ft. Edward, NY |
| | |
| **WRIGHT** Ira G. of Whitehall, NY | June 2, 1869 |
| **REDDING** Julia M. of Poultney, Vt. | Poultney, Vt. |
| | |
| **BURDETT** Allen M. of Whitehall, NY | June 1, 1869 |
| **KING** Martha E. of Madrid, NY | Whitehall, NY |
| | |
| **WEEKS** H. B. of Rutland, Vt. | June 8, 1869 |
| **STAPLES** Elizabeth of N. Granville, NY | N. Granville, NY |
| | |
| **SQUIRES** Fred C. of Bennington, Vt. | June 9, 1869 |
| **KNAPP** Lucy of M. Granville, NY | |
| | |
| **JOHNSTON** Albert J. of Canojoharie, NY | June 22, 1869 |
| **CAMPBELL** Eliza J. dau of late Rev. Peter Campbell | Cambridge, NY |
| | |
| **FARRELL** Thomas of Troy, NY | June 20, 1869 |
| **FLYNN** Ellen of S. Easton, NY | S. Easton, NY |
| | |
| **WOLFE** Job of Greenwich, NY | June 29, 1869 |
| **POTTER** Emma of Greenwich, NY | Greenwich, NY |
| | |
| **GIFFORD** Lewis of Cambridge, NY | July 1, 1869 |
| **ENGLISH** Mary L. of Cambridge, NY | Greenwich, NY |

| | |
|---|---|
| **LEWIS** William of Schuylerville, NY | July 3, 1869 |
| **DECKER** Mary A. of Battenville, NY | |
| | |
| **PARKER** Henry of Cambridge, NY | July 6, 1869 |
| **TRIPP** Mary J. of Cambridge, NY | Hoosick, NY |
| | |
| **PERKINS** Newman of Mishawaka, Ind. | July 7, 1869 |
| **STARBUCK** Cecelia of S. Easton, NY | Cambridge, NY |
| | |
| **FORREST** Daniel of Salem, NY | July 7, 1869 |
| **JOHNSON** Maria of Hartford, NY | Hartford, NY |
| | |
| **FOOTE** Charles H. of Pt. Henry, NY | June 30, 1869 |
| **SMITH** Mary T. dau of Justin A. of Whitehall, NY | Whitehall, NY |
| | |
| **KEEFER** Jerome of E. Greenwich, NY | June 28, 1869 |
| **LYON** Henrietta of New York City | Jersey City, NJ |
| | |
| **KELSEY** Don A. of Whitehall, NY | July 18, 1869 |
| **DAVISON** M. A. of Whitehall, NY | Whitehall, NY |
| | |
| **NORTON** Milon P. of Burkirks Bridge, NY | July 27, 1869 |
| **BARTLETT** G. O. of Cambridge, NY | Cambridge, NY |
| | |
| **WALLER** Elisha of Greenwich, NY | July 24, 1869 |
| **PLATT** Amanda D. of Greenwich, NY | Greenwich, NY |
| | |
| **PHILLIPS** Joseph N. of Brooklyn, NY | July 1, 1869 |
| **CHASE** Fannie E. of White Creek, NY | White Creek, NY |
| | |
| **DOTY** Charles H. of Ft. Edward, NY | July 29, 1869 |
| **TOOMBS** Sarah J. of Ft. Edward, NY | Argyle, NY |
| | |
| **ELLSWORTH** Erastus of Easton, NY | August 3, 1869 |
| **EDDY** Frank T. C. of Greenwich, NY | Greenwich, NY |
| | |
| **SPARHAWK** Edward of Greenwich, NY | July 29, 1869 |
| **RICHARDS** Lucinda of Greenwich, NY | Greenwich, NY |
| | |
| **MC DOWELL** James of Greenwich, NY | August 4, 1869 |
| **GAMBOL** Sarah C. of Greenwich, NY | |
| | |
| **BARDEN** James H. of Argyle, NY | August 18, 1869 |
| **NELSON** Eliza M. of Whitehall, NY | Whitehall, NY |
| | |
| **BARNES** Wallace of Hoosick Falls, NY | August 18, 1869 |
| **BROUGHTON** Alice dau of Ira | Salem, NY |
| | |
| **FULLER** Lewis C. of White Creek, NY | September 1, 1869 |

**STEELE** Nettie dau of Thomas of E. Salem, NY

Salem, NY

**STACKHOUSE** J. of Cambridge, NY
**WISWELL** Hattie F. of Easton, NY

September 1, 1869
Easton, NY

**CLARK** George of Coila, NY
**MILLER** Rachel of Jackson, NY

September 8, 1869

**STEELE** Thomas of Blairstown, Iowa
**CROWL** Louise dau of A. Crowl of Salem, NY

September 14, 1869

**COWAN** John of Jackson, NY
**MC FARLAND** Catherine of Jackson, NY

September 15, 1869

**SMITH** James Y. of Cambridge, NY
**DANFORTH** Mrs. Martha E. of Eagle Bridge, NY

September 16, 1869
Eagle Bridge, NY

**DONALDSON** James of Salem, NY
**LARKIN** Emma of E. Greenwich, NY

September 21, 1869
E. Greenwich, NY

**SMILEY** Thomas of Hickory, Pa.
**MC ARTHUR** Mary E. of Jackson, NY

September 23, 1869
Jackson, NY

**CREIGHTON** William A. of Salem, NY
**REID** Emma E. of E. Greenwich, NY

September 28, 1869
E. Greenwich, NY

**SOPER** Edgar B.of Schaghticoke, NY
**EDIE** Maria L. of Easton, NY

September 27, 1869

**MATHEWS** George W. of Fairhaven, Vt.
**SAFFORD** Sarah H. of Salem, NY

September 30, 1869
Salem, NY

**ELDRIDGE** Dewitt Phill of Washington DC
**WALLACE** Aggie of Cambridge, NY

October 12, 1869
Cambridge, NY·

**MC GEOCH** Robert of S. Argyle, NY
**MC CLELLAN** Mrs. Mary Jane of Hebron, NY

September 21, 1869
N. Argyle, NY

**SMITH** Charles of Battenville, NY
**SMITH** Frankie L. of Battenville, NY

October 4, 1869
Battenville, NY

**MC FARLAND** John of Jackson, NY
**SKELLIE** Harriet of N. Argyle, NY

October 6, 1869
N. Argyle, NY

**WADE** Thomas R. of Argyle, NY
**HARSHA** Louise M. dau of James C. of Argyle, NY

October 13, 1869
Argyle, NY

**LEWIS** Nathaniel of Middletown, Vt.
**CRAMER** Lucy C. of Cambridge, NY

October 18, 1869
White Creek, NY

CRARY A. M. of Sunderland, Vt.
ALLEN Hattie of Sunderland, Vt.

October 11, 1869
Salem, NY

HARRINGTON William S. of Easton, NY
SPRINGER Mary E. of Easton, NY

October 24, 1869
S. Cambridge, NY

KENNEDY L. W. Md. of Cambridge, NY
GRAY Fannie dau of H. C. Md. of Cambridge, NY

October 27, 1869
Cambridge, NY

GOODING Bradford of Hoosick, NY
ROBINSON Susannah of Salem, NY

October 25, 1869
Cambridge, NY

WEIR George H. of Greenwich, NY
MOWRY Sarah G. of Greenwich, NY

October 21, 1869

DALTON T. Lloyd of Brooklyn, NY       (newspaper date)
WAIT Mary A. dau of N. W. of Sandy Hill, NY

October 29, 1869
Sandy Hill, NY

HILL Henry H. of Warrensburgh, NY
HERRINGTON Carrie of Kingsbury, NY

October 16, 1869
Kingsbury, NY

MORRELL Fitzland of Sandy Hill, NY
HOLDEN Elizabeth of Corinth, NY

October 10, 1869
Sandy Hill, NY

GOUNDRY George of Ft. Edward, NY
ANDREWS Lydia L. of Glens Falls, NY

October 24, 1869
Sandy Hill, NY

MAXWELL John of Jackson, NY
MC GEOCH Jane E. of E. Greenwich, NY

October 29, 1869
E. Greenwich, NY

MC LEAN W. C. formerly of Cambridge, NY
OSTLER Mary A. of Sarpy Co., Neb.

October 27, 1869

BLASHFIELD A. of Chatham, NY
MARTIN Mary Eliza dau of Josephus of Salem, NY

October 19, 1869
Salem, NY

ALMY B. A. of Middleville, Mi. formerly Buskirks Bridge
SYLVESTER M. of Yankee Springs, Mi.

October 10, 1869
Middleville, Mi.

BROWN Isaac of W. Ft. Ann, NY
STEVENSON Mrs. Mary of Ft. Edward, NY

November 16, 1869
Ft. Edward, NY

MOORE William A. of Alexandria, Va.
DUNHAM Carrie A. of Jackson, NY

November 11, 1869
Jackson, NY

MOORE John H.
LINCOLN Mary A.

November 16, 1869
Cambridge, NY

LINCOLN David W. of Hebron, NY

November 16, 1869

**BURKE** Fannie R. of Hebron, NY                                    Cambridge, NY

**BILLINGS** William H. of Jackson, NY                               November 17, 1869
**MC LEAN** Martha J. of Jackson, NY                                 Jackson, NY

**SHIELDS** Frank of Salem, NY                                       November 23, 1869
**NUGENT** Mary of Salem, NY                                         Salem, NY

**RUPPANNER** James of Cohoes, NY                                    November 16, 1869
**MC NULTY** Catherine of Ft. Edward, NY                             Ft. Edward, NY

**WITHERELL** Edward of Connecticutt                                 November 23, 1869
**LAPHAM** Susan F. of Ft. Edward, NY                                Ft. Edward. NY

**HOAG** Charles B. of Salem, NY                                     November 18, 1869
**WILBER** Elizabeth A. of Salem, NY                                 Easton, NY

**CHASE** Alonzo of Walworth, NY                                     November 25, 1869
**FALES** Elizabeth A. of Poultney, Vt.                              Poultney, Vt.

**WATT** William D.                                                  November 25, 1869
**MAGEE** Sarah L. dau of Calvin of Salem, NY                        Salem, NY

**ROOD** F. A. of Poultney, NY                                       December 8, 1869
**MEEKER** Elvira E. dau of Rev. C. Meeker of Hebron, NY             Hebron, NY

**DAWLEY** George R. of Easton, NY                                   December 3, 1869
**BROOKS** Addie of Easton, NY                                       Easton, NY

**MC DOUGAL** Daniel of Argyle, NY                                   December 7, 1869
**ROBBINS** Helen of Greenwich, NY

**HUNSIKER** James A. of Patterson, NJ                               December 14, 1869
**GLASS** Alice W. of Cambridge, NY                                  Cambridge, NY

**OSTERHOUT** Oscar J. of Hoosick Falls, NY                          December 23, 1869
**ROBERTSON** Belle of Hoosick Falls, NY                             Cambridge, NY

**SAFFORD** D. H. of Salem, NY                                       December 22, 1869
**MC CURDY** Agnes M. dau of late Daniel of Salem, NY                Salem, NY

**BEATTIE** William J. of Salem, NY          (newspaper date)        December 24, 1869
**HUTTON** Mrs. Mary J. of Salem, NY                                 Salem, NY

**TRACY** J. of Dresden, NY                                          November 11, 1869
**BARBER** A. of Dresden, NY

**UPTON** Richard                                                    December 8, 1869
**CARPENTER** Mary J. of Whitehall, NY

JOHNSON Albert
KINNER H. Augusta dau of John A. of Whitehall, NY

December 16, 1869
Whitehall, NY

HEATH Henry L. of Greenwich, NY
COLE Mattie of Greenwich, NY

December 22, 1869
Greenwich, NY

ALEXANDER Orlando of Jackson, NY
WATERS Mary E. of Coila, NY

December 22, 1869
Coila, NY

CHASE Henry of Easton, NY
PARKMAN S. Augusta of Troy, NY

December 28, 1869
Troy, NY

CULVER George P. of Elizabeth, NJ
BAKER Lucy C. dau of I. V. of Comstocks Landing, NY

December 23, 1869
Comstocks Landing

MC EACHRON Phillip
SMITH Mattie

December 28, 1869
Hebron, NY

BAIN Alexander
GILCHRIST Jennett

December 28, 1869
Argyle, NY

BRAYMER Daniel of Missouri
WOODARD N. A. of Hebron, NY

December 29, 1869
Salem, NY

KINCAID Milo
DAY Julia L.

December 28, 1869
N. Granville, NY

MORLIN Charles of Poultney, Vt.
WRAY Betsey of Ft. Ann, NY

December 28, 1869

LEE Henry of Bald Mountain, NY
SCHULTZ Aurelia of Greenwich, NY

December 28, 1869
Greenwich, NY

PATNAUD Julius of Greenwich, NY
LA POINTE Matilda of Greenwich, NY

December 28, 1869
Greenwich, NY

BURCH Robert of Hebron, NY
SMITH Almira of Hebron, NY

December 25, 1869
Greenwich, NY

MC GANN William of Granville, NY
SMITH Marilla W. of Hebron, NY

December 25, 1869
Greenwich, NY

EYCLESHYMER Peter J. of Pittstown, NY
DARROW Rebecca of S. Easton, NY

December 28, 1869
S. Easton, NY

MOSS Montgomery C. of Sandy Hill, NY
ADAMS Clara C. of Sandy Hill, NY

December 29, 1869
Sandy Hill, NY

CRAWFORD John N. of Kingsbury, NY

January 1, 1870

**TANNER** Marion of Kingsbury, NY                    Sandy Hill, NY

**PATTISON** George of Ft. Ann, NY          January 1, 1870
**PALMER** Amanda of Ft. Ann, NY            Sandy Hill, NY

**PARKS** Solomon H. of Moreau, NY          January 4, 1870
**BUCK** Laura J.                            Kingsbury, NY

**LANT** William of S. Argyle, NY           December 28, 1869
**LANT** Amanda of S. Argyle, NY            S. Argyle, NY

**SMART** J. S.                             January 13, 1870
**SHERMAN** Elizabeth dau of Zina of Cambridge, NY    Cambridge, NY

**HERRINGTON** Truman R. of Easton, NY      January 1, 1870
**HERRINGTON** Mary Ann of Easton, NY       Greenwich, NY

**SLOCUM** Joseph P. of Manchester, Vt.     January 11, 1870
**HURD** Sarah I. of Sandgate, Vt.

**GETTY** James A.                          January 11, 1870
**WILLIAMSON** Sarah E. of Argyle, NY       Argyle, NY

**LANGWORTHY** Heman of Middlebury, Vt.     January 2, 1870
**CRAY** Eva of Kingsbury, NY               Kingsbury, NY

**DEVINE** Robert of Jackson, NY            January 12, 1870
**WILSON** Maggie of E. Salem, NY           E. Salem, NY

**GREEN** William of Cambridge, NY          January 13, 1870
**MC CLELLAN** Belle dau of William of Coila, NY    Coila, NY

**HASKINS** Myron of Woolmington, Vt.       January 19, 1870
**WAIT** Mina of Shushan, NY                Shushan, NY

**COULTER** Alexander B. of Jackson, NY     January 20, 1870
**SELFRIDGE** Cornelia of Jackson, NY       Jackson, NY

**MILLER** Miron H. of Greenwich, NY        January 19, 1870
**ROBERSON** Fannie of Easton, NY           Easton, NY

**WHITNEY** Charles of Whitehall, NY        January 14, 1870
**MAYFIELD** Adeline of Whitehall, NY       Whitehall, NY

**BINNINGER** Abraham of Salem, NY          January 25, 1870
**ROBERTSON** Maggie of Cambridge, NY       Cambridge, NY

**COOK** Calvin E. of Sunderland, Vt.       January 1, 1870
**COFFINGER** Lydia of Sunderland, Vt.      E. Salem, NY

THOMPSON James A. son of Col. A. of Jackson, NY
COULTER Cordelia dau of James of Jackson, NY

February 10, 1870

ANTHONY James W. of Smyrna, Cal.
BARKER Mary E. of Easton, NY

February 15, 1870
Easton, NY

GORDON John of Argyle, NY
LINDSAY Mary of Argyle, NY

February 10, 1870
Argyle, NY

WEAVER A. of Milton, Wis.
THOMPSON Christeann of Chester, NY

February 10, 1870
Chester, NY

DAWLEY Morgan of Greenwich, NY
KIPP Martha Jane of Greenwich, NY

February 14, 1870
Greenwich, NY

MARTIN Hugh of White Creek, NY
WEIR Martha of Jackson, NY

February 17, 1870

CORLISS Nathan of Easton, NY
PARKER Angeline C. dau of I. G.

February 22, 1870
Greenwich, NY

NILES Walter G. of White Creek, NY
SISSON Maggie dau of I. Sisson of White Creek, NY

February 24, 1870
White Creek, NY

ROBINSON Oscar of Rutland, Vt.
MOORE Lou of Smiths Basin, NY

February 20, 1870
Smiths Basin, NY

HUDSON Stephen of Lowberryville, NY
BOTTELL Eliza of Lowberryville, NY

March 6, 1870
Greenwich, NY

KENYON Ambrose of Greenwich, NY
CURRY Carrie M. of Greenwich, NY

March 15, 1870
Galesville, NY

CORNELL John C. of Argyle, NY
MC DOUGAL Libbie of Argyle, NY

March 2, 1870
N. Argyle, NY

SHALER Andrew of Jackson, NY
SALISBURY Cornelia of Jackson, NY

March 30, 1870
Jackson, NY

HUTTON William of Greenwich, NY
TEFFT Ann Eliza of Greenwich, NY

March 23, 1870
Greenwich, NY

CLARK Thomas B. of Greenwich, NY
WRIGHT Alice M. of Greenwich, NY

March 30, 1870
Greenwich, NY

GLEASON Daniel of Greenwich, NY
MC DURFEE Mary L. of Greenwich, NY

April 7, 1870
Greenwich, NY

POWELL Warren H. of Syracuse, NY

April 6, 1870

**QUA** Mary A. of S. Argyle, NY — S. Argyle, NY

**STILES** Samuel of Hartford, NY
**RICKERT** Martha M. of Easton, NY — April 22, 1870 Greenwich, NY

**HENRY** William of Greenwich, NY
**WHITMAN** Amanda M. of Arlington, Vt. — April 23, 1870 Arlington, Vt.

**FERGUSON** Alexander of S. Argyle, NY
**MC CALL** Eliza of S. Argyle, NY — April 19, 1870 S. Argyle, NY

**CARRIGAN** J. M. of Hartford, NY
**DAISY** Sarah of Hartford, NY — May 1, 1870 Hartford, NY

**BROWN** Warren H. of Hartford, NY
**BULLIONS** Julia S. of Cambridge, NY — April 20, 1870 New York City

**NELLIS** Daniel W. of Topeka, Kansas
**COCHRANE** M. J. dau of A. G & Cella G. of Galesville — May 17, 1870 Galesville, NY

**STOVER** George of New York City
**WELLS** Sarah Ann dau of Joseph of N. Easton, NY — May 18, 1870 N. Easton, NY

**SAFFORD** John of Greenwich, NY
**ROSE** Elizabeth J. of Greenwich, NY — May 11, 1870 Greenwich, NY

**MC FARLAND** John of Salem, NY
**HOPKINS** Mary of Salem, NY — May 17, 1870 Salem, NY

**ALEXANDER** William of Greenwich, NY
**MC EACHRON** Jennie of Argyle, NY — May 19, 1870 Argyle, NY

**LAW** George R.
**JOHNSON** Mrs. Louisa — May 19, 1870 Coila, NY

**MC LEAN** Francis of Washington DC
**KENYON** Mary J. of N. Cambridge, NY — May 20, 1870 N. Cambridge, NY

**STORY** Charles H. of New York City
**WELLS** Sarah A. dau of James of Easton, NY — May 18, 1870

**HILLMAN** John F. of Greenwich, NY
**WINNIE** Katie M. of Saratoga, NY — May 18, 1870 Grangerville, NY

**ALLEN** John of Hebron, NY
**HILL** Laurie A. of Hebron, NY — May 26, 1870 Hebron, NY

**FISK** Perrin H. of Shushan, NY
**GLEASON** Mary E. of Shushan, NY — May 25, 1870 W. Rupert, Vt.

**JOHNSON** William of Ft. Edward, NY
**WING** Jennie of Ft. Edward, NY

May 29, 1870
Granville, NY

**HARRINGTON** Richard of Easton, NY
**HARRINGTON** Ellen F. of Easton, NY

May 28, 1870
Cambridge, NY

**MARTIN** Harvey J. of Salem, NY
**KETCHUM** Mary of Cambridge, NY

June 15, 1870
Cambridge, NY

**JOHNSON** Henry A. of Shaftsbury, Vt.
**GOODING** Maggie H. of White Creek, NY

June 20, 1870
White Creek, NY

**LAMB** George
**FELLOWS** Mary dau of T. E.

June 16, 1870
N. Granville, NY

**PENDERGRASS** Joseph of Argyle, NY
**EVOY** Kattie M. of Argyle, NY

June 16, 1870

**NEWELL** Henry of Londonderry, Vt.
**MANLY** Mattie B. of Granville, NY

June 23, 1870
Granville, NY

**WILLS** Judson of Hampton, NY
**TURK** Polly Ann of Hampton, NY

June 19, 1870
Granville, NY

**LEE** Elisha H. of Greenwich, NY
**GREEN** Mary E. of Cambridge, NY

July 4, 1870
Cambridge, NY

**FRASER** Lawrence of Whitehall, NY
**MC DONALD** Bridget of Pittsfield, Mass.

July 3, 1870
Salem, NY

**FIFIELD** Frank N. of Salem, NY
**NARAMORE** Hannah L. of Fairhaven, Vt.

June 22, 1870
Fairhaven, Vt.

**LARKIN** Peter B. of Hebron, NY
**FRASER** Mary of Hebron, NY

July 4, 1870
Greenwich, NY

**BROWN** George L. of Greenwich, NY
**JACKSON** Mary E. of Jackson, NY

June 24, 1870

**GRAY** Henry of Palatine, NY
**KENERSON** Marilla of Easton, NY

June 3, 1870
Cambridge, NY

**PLACE** Charles S. of Greenwich, NY
**HILLMAN** Jennie L. of Greenwich, NY

July 4, 1870
Greenwich, NY

**BARNES** William of Greenwich, NY
**BREWER** Mary of Greenwich, NY

June 29, 1870
Shushan, NY

**HERRINGTON** William of Easton, NY    (newspaper date)    July 15, 1870

**HILLMAN** Lucy of Jackson, NY — Greenwich, NY

**DUEL** Malcolm of Cambridge, NY — July 10, 1870
**GARRICK** Jane M. of Cambridge, NY — S. Granville, NY

**BIGELOW** Charles E. — July 19, 1870
**WYATT** Lucella M. of Cambridge, NY — Buskirks Bridge, NY

**DEXTER** John of Albany, NY — July 31, 1870
**SNOWDEN** Sarah A. of Salem, NY

**PHARMAR** John A. of Ft. Miller, NY — August 9, 1870
**COPP** Mary A. of Ft. Miller, NY — Greenwich, NY

**TINGUE** Charles of Cambridge, NY — August 23, 1870
**GIFFORD** Nellie S. of Cambridge, NY — Shushan, NY

**HOVER** Walter — August 17, 1870
**WADE** Eveline — White Creek, NY

**LINDLOFF** Henry C. of Cohoes, NY — September 3, 1870
**FAIRBANKS** Mary E. of Greenwich, NY — Greenwich, NY

**LEE** John F. of Johnsonville, NY — September 8, 1870
**GIFFORD** Annie M. of Cambridge, NY

**GATES** John L. of New York City — September 14, 1870
**PARSONS** Mrs. Mary M. of Shaftsbury, Vt. — Shaftsbury, Vt.

**RODELL** Nelson of Greenwich, NY — September 14, 1870
**MANOR** Rosanna of Greenwich, NY

**DECKER** Heman of Battenville, NY — September 13, 1870
**CHAPIN** Ann Eliza of Battenville, NY — Greenwich, NY

**BARKLEY** Charles H. of Argyle, NY — September 1, 1870
**MC DOUGAL** Jane C. of Argyle, NY — Argyle, NY

**DURHAM** George of Salem, NY — September 15, 1870
**REYNOLDS** Ella of Salem NY — E. Greenwich, NY

**BROWN** William of Greenwich, NY — September 20, 1870
**BROWNELL** Sarah J. of Cambridge, NY

**CENTER** Sheldon W. of Cambridge, NY — August 3, 1870
**BUTLER** Jennie of Batavia, NY — Buskirks Bridge, NY

**MOSELY** Howard S. of Hoosick, NY — September 21, 1870
**CROSS** Electa D. of Hoosick, NY — Hoosick, NY

**MC INTYRE** J. H. of Rutland, Vt.
**BARTLETT** Viola E. of Salem, NY

September 21, 1870
Greenwich, NY

**WOOSTER** Charles of Momence, Ill.
**LOVEJOY** Lydia M. of Cambridge, NY

September 28, 1870

**CORNELL** Henry of N. Argyle, NY
**NORTHUP** Jennie of N. Argyle, NY

September 5, 1870
N. Argyle, NY

**MONTEITH** James of Hebron, NY
**MC NEIL** Catherine of Hebron, NY

September 8, 1870
N. Argyle, NY

**BROWNELL** Myron C. of Cambridge, NY
**EDIE** Maggie of Coila, NY

October 27, 1870
Saratoga Springs, NY

**AUSTIN** Orrin of Salem, NY
**COX** Addie H. of Brooklyn, NY

October 20, 1870
Brooklyn, NY

**HYDE** James T. of Salem, NY
**JOHNSON** Delia M. of Albany, NY

October 12, 1870
Albany, NY

**RICE** D. C. of Greenwich, NY      (newspaper date)
**BAYLE** Mary A. of Greenwich, NY

November 11, 1870
Greenwich, NY

**BAUMES** Peter of Greenwich, NY
**KENDALL** Maria L. of Greenwich, NY

November 2, 1870
Greenwich, NY

**SQUIRES** Charles W. of Sandgate, Vt.
**COVEY** Marie of Sandgate, Vt.

November 15, 1870
White Creek, NY

**GALLOWAY** John of Cambridge, NY
**HUNT** Libbie of Cambridge, NY

November 15, 1870

**JENNENS** B. W. E. of Salt Lake City, Utah
**NEWBURY** Jennie

November 15, 1870
Galesville, NY

**GARRISON** Augustus of Greenwich, NY
**BRACKETT** Maria of Greenwich, NY

November 12, 1870
Greenwich, NY

**BEATTIE** Marcus J. of Salem, NY
**BROUGHTON** Fannie of Salem, NY

November 9, 1870
Salem, NY

**MC KIE** E. J. of Cambridge, NY
**SHORTT** Jennie of Cambridge, NY

November 22, 1870
Cambridge, NY

**SEYMOUR** Morris J.
**BURT** Hannah of Sodus, NY

November 23, 1870
White Creek, NY

**BURTON** Albert E.

November 23, 1870

**BURCH** Frances E.                                                     N. Hebron, NY

**GALUSHA** Frank of Argyle, NY                                         November 17, 1870
**STODDARD** Flora of Ft. Edward, NY                                    Ft. Edward, NY

**SHAW** Alvin of Cambridge, NY                                         November 27, 1870
**WOLFE** Carrie of Greenwich, NY                                       Ft. Edward, NY

**BENNETT** Romain of White Creek, NY                                   November 28, 1870
**BONPLON** Rosa H. of Shaftsbury, Vt.

**BURCH** Russell of S. Easton, NY                                      November 30, 1870
**STARBUCK** Lydia of S. Easton, NY                                     Cambridge, NY

**DICKINSON** J. W. of Kansas City, Mo.                                 November 8, 1870
**HALL** Julia of Kansas City, Mo.                                      Kansas City, Mo.

**CURTIS** John B. of White Creek, NY                                   December 1, 1870
**SMITH** Emily of Hebron, NY

**WALSH** J. D. of Maysville, Ky. formerly of Battenville, NY           October 22, 1870
**BRIGHT** Charlotte E. of Lexington, Ky.                               Lexington, Ky.

**RICHARDSON** Edward B.                                                December 8, 1870
**MC LAREN** Mary dau of Re. D. C. Mc Laren                             Geneva, NY

**HOAG** Levi of Troy, NY                                               December 13, 1870
**DILLINGHAM** Ruth G. of Granville, NY                                 Granville, NY

**DINGS** James of N. Argyle, NY                                        December 7, 1870
**LANT** Mrs. Ann of N. Argyle, NY                                      N. Argyle, NY

**HANDY** Seth P.                                                       December 14, 1870
**BAKER** Harriet M. widow of Robert                                    Easton, NY

**SAFFORD** J. Leroy                                                    December 19, 1870
**GRIFFIN** Mary M.                                                     S. Argyle, NY

**MC CLENATHAN** Julius of Sandgate, Vt.                                November 30, 1870
**GALE** Emma of Sandgate, Vt.                                          Shushan, NY

**WOODCOCK** William of W. Pawlet, Vt.                                  December 14, 1870
**GALE** Clarissa E. of Sandgate, Vt.

**MONTGOMERY** William S. of Shushan, NY                                December 20, 1870
**JACKSON** Mary E. of Shushan, NY                                      Shushan, NY

**ANDREWS** Ernest E. of Arlington, Vt.                                 December 21, 1870
**CONKEY** Cornelia A. of E. Salem, NY                                  E. Salem, NY

**WYMAN** James G. of Arlington, Vt.
**PERKINS** Libbie of Manchester, Vt.

December 21, 1870
E. Salem, NY

**KENYON** William M. of Cambridge, NY
**HERRINGTON** Mary of Easton, NY

December 21, 1870
Easton, NY

**HARKNESS** Edward P. of Greenwich, NY
**EDWARDS** Mary J. of Greenwich, NY

December 15, 1870

**HASWELL** Robert S. of Hoosick, NY
**PRUYN** Amanda dau of late William

December 26, 1870
Cambridge, NY

**MC EACHRON** Archibald of Argyle, NY
**POWELL** Mrs. Esther M. of Argyle, NY

December 21, 1870

**CHAPMAN** O. H. of Hebron, NY
**POWELL** Sarah M. of Hebron, NY

December 27, 1870

**LINDSAY** George of Hebron, NY
**QUA** Eliza of Hebron, NY

January 2, 1871

**REED** Harvey T. of Pittstown, NY
**O'BERNE** Annie of N. Cambridge, NY

January 2, 1871
N. Cambridge, NY

**MONROE** Warner
**ANDREWS** D. Jane

December 29, 1870
Shaftsbury, Vt.

**RICHEY** George H. of Rupert, Vt.
**MAYNARD** Emma S. of Rupert, Vt.

January 2, 1871
Troy, NY

**MONIHAN** Andrew of Salem, NY
**WALSH** Kate of Salem, NY

January 4, 1871
Salem, NY

**CRAIG** James J. of Salem, NY
**SHAW** Jennie of W. Hebron, NY

January 4, 1871
W. Hebron, NY

**SMITH** Russell of Hartford, NY
**EDGERTON** Hattie J. dau of late Rev. C. H. of Hartford

January 3, 1871
Hartford, NY

**GILMAN** Dr. E. R. of N. Hebron, NY
**ROWAN** Josie H. of Danbury, Conn.

December 29, 1870
Danbury, Conn.

**SMITH** Charles O. ot Hebron, NY
**ROGERS** Jane Ornette of Hebron, NY

January 11, 1871
Greenwich, NY

**CAMPBELL** Andrew A. of Cambridge, NY
**DAY** Amelia A. of Cambridge, NY

January 23, 1871
Greenwich, NY

**MC LEAN** Alanson of Jackson, NY

January 25, 1871

**MC LEAN** Anna E. of Jackson, NY

**SKINNER** Fortunatus of Cambridge, NY          January 25, 1871
**LANGWORTHY** Frances S. of Greenwich, NY       Greenwich, NY

**VAN BUREN** George W. of Easton, NY            January 25, 1871
**JONES** Lizzie of Greenwich, NY                Greenwich, NY

**STEWART** Norman F. of Jackson, NY             January 18, 1871
**MILLER** Anna C. of Battenville, NY            Battenville, NY

**WITBECK** Henry of Easton, NY                  January 18, 1871
**RATHBONE** Mary P. of Easton, NY               Greenwich, NY

**DARBY** A. L. of Hoosick Falls, NY             January 27, 1871
**ASHTON** Janett of Ash Grove, NY               Ash Grove, NY

**BEATTIE** J. of Hebron, NY                     January 31, 1871
**MC MULLEN** Mary Agnes of N. Argyle, NY        N. Argyle, NY

**SAFFORD** Charles H. of Greenwich, NY          February 15, 1871
**SPENCER** Jennie E. of Greenwich, NY           Greenwich, NY

**GREEN** John Q. of Jackson, NY                 February 9, 1871
**TEFFT** Emma of Salem, NY                      Salem, NY

**SKINNER** Lemuel F. of Cambridge, NY           February 15, 1871
**MC MILLAN** Lydia of Jackson, NY               Jackson, NY

**FASSETT** A. S. of Cambridge, NY               February 15, 1871
**CULVER** Sarah A. of Cambridge, NY             Cambridge, NY

**AUSTIN** George A. of Greenwich, NY            February 15, 1871
**STOVER** Mary of Lagrange, NY                  Greenwich, NY

**JOHNSON** Charles G. of Granville, NY          March 2, 1871
**CLOUGH** Mary dau of Stephen of Granville, NY  Granville, NY

**NEWMAN** J. M. Jr. of Troy, NY                 March 9, 1871
**FIELD** Annie Augusta of Mt. Pleasant, NY      Mt. Pleasant, NY

**HULETT** Aaron of Shaftsbury, Vt.              March 9, 1871
**TURNER** Anna Eliza of White Creek, NY         White Creek, NY

**EVANS** John of Ft. Ann, NY                    March 16, 1871
**STARKS** Frank of Ft. Ann, NY

**BROWN** Charles of Ft. Ann, NY                 March 10, 1871
**BROWN** Miss ____ of Ft. Ann, NY               Ft. Ann, NY

| | |
|---|---|
| MOORE William T. of St. Charles, Minn. | March 7, 1871 |
| RICE Ella M. dau of O. K. of Greenwich, NY | Greenwich, NY |
| | |
| TUCKER Franklin of Greenwich, NY | March 22, 1871 |
| TEFFT Jane of Greenwich, NY | Greenwich, NY |
| | |
| MARTIN William R. of Washington Co. NY | March 14, 1871 |
| LANT Eliza J. of Washington, Co. NY | |
| | |
| BENNETT Albert of Ft. Edward, NY | March 24, 1871 |
| CRANDALL Adeline of Moreau, NY | |
| | |
| SISSON Merritt of Hoosick, NY | January 24, 1871 |
| SURDAM Zetta of Hoosick, NY | |
| | |
| FRISBEE Gilbert J. of Westport, NY | February 9, 1871 |
| TABER Maggie of White Creek, NY | |
| | |
| CROSS Wait J. of Wolcott, NY | March 15, 1871 |
| SCRIVER Hannah M. of Hoosick, NY | |
| | |
| HELTON William of New York City | March 28, 1871 |
| MC AUL Maggie of Hartford, NY | Hartford, NY |
| | |
| PORTER Eddy of Cambridge, NY | April 5, 1871 |
| MANDERSON Helen of Cambridge, NY | Cambridge, NY |
| | |
| SCHAUBER E. D. of Schenectady, NY | April 5, 1871 |
| PATTERSON Anna A. formerly of Cambridge, NY | Schenectady, NY |
| | |
| MILLER Stephen R. of Ft. Ann, NY | March 29, 1871 |
| STEWART Helen of Wallingford, Vt. | |
| | |
| LYTLE Abram of Salem, NY | March 26, 1871 |
| BEATTIE Mary of Salem, NY | Farmer Village, NY |
| | |
| POOR David of the Troy Conference | April 13, 1871 |
| CONKEY Mrs. Sarah | Green Island, NY |
| | |
| WILSON John Q. of Hebron, NY | April 12, 1871 |
| NESBIT Helen | Lee, NY |
| | |
| BURNHAM R. W of Saratoga Springs, NY | April 2, 1871 |
| MC GWYER Widow M. of Easton, NY | Saratoga, NY |
| | |
| HOLT Merritt C. of Albany, NY | April 21, 1871 |
| SMITH Mrs. Martha of N. Bennington, Vt. | Cambridge, NY |
| | |
| ELDRIDGE Ahira of Cambridge, NY | April 27, 1871 |

**BAKER** Mrs. Rebecca of Cambridge, NY — Cambridge, NY

**WELCH** Albert of Cambridge, NY — April 26, 1871
**LA BARRON** Julia Ann of Cambridge, NY — Hoosick, NY

**BEATTIE** Thomas G. of Salem, NY — April 23, 1871
**SPRAGUE** Jennie of E. Bennington, Vt. — Greenwich, NY

**INGALLS** George F. of Granville, NY — April 26, 1871
**COZZENS** Ella M. dau of Earl M. of Greenwich, NY — Greenwich, NY

**MC ARTHUR** Robert E. of Shushan, NY — April 15, 1871
**CHILLIS** Ella of Sandgate, Vt. — Salem, NY

**WHITCOMB** Charles of Salem, NY — April 20, 1871
**SYKES** Elizabeth of Montreal, Canada — E. Rupert, Vt.

**JOHNSON** C. E. of Sandy Hill, NY — April 25, 1871
**BELL** Sarah of Johnstown, NY — Johnstown, NY

**MULLEN** Andrew J. of Ft. Edward, NY — May 2, 1871
**FOSTER** Libbie of Ft. Edward, NY — Greenwich, NY

**DAWLEY** George E. of Greenwich, NY — May 25, 1871
**KILDA** Jennie of Ballston, NY — Galesville, NY

**BATTIE** Joseph of Easton, NY (newspaper date) — June 9, 1871
**BUCKLEY** Rebecca E. of Greenwich, NY — Greenwich, NY

**HARRIS** Frank — June 1, 1871
**SHERRILL** Julia dau of George of Sandy Hill, NY

**ESTY** Eldridge G. of Fairhaven, Vt. — June 7, 1871
**GILLIS** Jane Agnes of Salem, NY — Salem, NY

**DWYER** S. of Hebron, NY — June 7, 1871
**BRADFORD** A. of Hebron, NY — Salem, NY

**METCALF** J. E. of Ft. Ann, NY — June 6, 1871
**NEEDHAM** Eliza S. of Middlebury, Vt. — Bristol, Vt.

**ANDREWS** Rev. J. H. of S. Argyle, NY — June 27, 1871
**MARSHALL** Mary of Jackson, NY — Jackson, NY

**GUILE** Charles H. of Hoosick, NY — July 2, 1871
**CARTER** Lucy M. of Hoosick, NY — White Creek, NY

**SARVIS** Millard of Coveville, NY — July 2, 1871
**HARRINGTON** Sarah E. of Easton, NY — Greenwich, NY

PRESTON William L. of N. Bennington, Vt.            July 10, 1871
KNAPP Ella S. of N. Bennington, Vt.            White Creek, NY

WOODARD James of Cambridge, NY            July 4, 1871
KENYON Anna of Sandgate, Vt.            Shushan, NY

PEMBER Albert J. of Granville, NY            July 3, 1871
LAMB Janett of Wells, Vt.            S. Granville, NY

MILLER S. C. of Green Island, NY            July 10, 1871
MC FARLAND Camlia of Hebron, NY            Green Island, NY

PETTIGREW Elon G. of Ludlow, Vt.            August 3, 1871
MAYNARD Jennie R. of Cambridge, NY

STARBUCK Herbert A. of White Creek, NY            August 3, 1871
COTTRELL Emma of White Creek, NY

BRAYTON Marcus M. of White Creek, NY            August 9, 1871
TURNER Susie H. of White Creek, NY            Cambridge, NY

WALDO Homer H.            August 15, 1871
FLETCHER Mary E.            Wallingford, Vt.

WHITAKER Benjamin of Greenwich, NY            August 10, 1871
WILBER Anna E. of Greenwich, NY            Greenwich, NY

MAGEE Austin of Salem, NY            August 22, 1871
GRAY Mary S. of Salem, NY            Greenwich, NY

JOHNSON O. D. of Salem, NY            August 25, 1871
BOWKER Mary J. of Granville, NY            Greenwich, NY

STREETER Dr. M. H. of Pawlet, Vt.            August 17, 1871
WARNER Sarah of Pawlet, Vt.            Salem, NY

HOYT Frank E.            September 6, 1871
RICE Emma E. dau of Daniel of Cambridge, NY            Cambridge, NY

KNISKERN A. P. of Hobart, NY            September 6, 1871
HOYT Fannie of W. Arlington, Vt.            Cambridge, NY

HICKS Frank E. of Granville, NY            September 6, 1871
WAIT Ida J. of Granville, NY

PRATT William H. of Hoosick, NY            September 9, 1871
MC CARTHY Mrs. Elizabeth (MOLES) of Salem, NY            Salem, NY

SMITH William of Easton, NY            September 13, 1871

**TRAVIS** Mary F. of Easton, NY                    Easton, NY

**WEST** Henry of Cambridge, NY                    September 13, 1871
**SHAW** Frances of Cambridge, NY                    N. Bennington, Vt.

**MILLER** George W. of Cambridge, NY                    September 28, 1871
**HITCHCOCK** Ella W. of Cambridge, NY

**MC DONALD** Elihu A. of Glastonbury, Vt.                    September 30, 1871
**MOFFITT** Agness of Arlington, Vt.                    White Creek, NY

**HARRINGTON** Jermod of Glastonbury, Vt.                    September 30, 1871
**MC DONALD** Laurie of Glastonbury, Vt.                    White Creek, NY

**ARCHIBALD** Willie M. of Cambridge, NY                    October 4, 1871
**SKIFF** Etta of Cambridge, NY

**ROACH** John of Buskirks Bridge, NY                    October 1, 1871
**WOOD** Madora M. of Cambridge, NY                    Cambridge, NY

**MC CLELLAN** Warren L.                    October 11, 1871
**SHILAND** Sarah W. dau of William                    Coila, NY

**PRATT** George W. of Salem, NY                    October 3, 1871
**WHITCOMB** Charlotte E. of Salem, NY                    Salem, NY

**MC WHORTER** John H. formerly Cambridge          (news. date) October 20, 1871
**SMITH** Lucy E. of Sandwich, Ill.                    Sandwich, Ill.

**STEWART** Allen of Jackson, NY                    November 9, 1871
**COCHRANE** Anna E. dau of Rev. A. G.                    Galesville, NY

**SNYDER** Phillip M. of Grangerville, NY                    October 11, 1871
**COFFIN** Anna E. of Victory Mills, NY

**JEFFREY** W. E. of Bennington, Vt.                    October 21, 1871
**STREETER** Mary L. of Bennington, Vt.                    White Creek, NY

**MC ARTHUR** Samuel of Salem, NY                    November 15, 1871
**FOWLER** Sarah T. of Cambridge, NY                    Cambridge, NY

**WALLIS** Marquis D.                    November 16, 1871
**JOHNSON** Josephine dau of J. B. of White Creek, NY                    White Creek, NY

**BARBER** Martin I.                    November 11, 1871
**VERNUM** Mary E. of Cambridge, NY                    Cambridge, NY

**SPROUT** John W. of Pittstown, NY                    November 15, 1871
**LUSTIE** Louisa of Greenwich, NY                    Salem, NY

TATRO Charles of Salem, NY
SHIPLEY Cornelia E. of Salem, NY

November 14, 1871
Salem, NY

BARNETT Warren of Salem, NY
NORTON Emma E. of Salem, NY

November 16, 1871
Salem, NY

SHILAND Edwin of Coila, NY
SKELLIE Eliza J. of Cambridge, NY

November 29, 1871

LANNON John of E. Camden, NY
COMSTOCK Rachel of Albany, NY

November 30, 1871
Albany, NY

DONAHUE Lewis
MACUMBER Emeline

December 8, 1871
Wells Bridge

FADALAY Milton M. of Camden, NJ
DUNHAM Anna M. formerly of Jackson, NY

November 29, 1871
Alexandria, Va.

PETTEYS Lewis of Cambridge, NY
HERRINGTON Hettie E. of Greenwich, NY

December 17, 1871
Greenwich, NY

DOOLITTLE Chester R. of Easton, NY
LITTLE Melvina of Greenwich, NY

December 21, 1871
Greenwich, NY

DOBBIN William of Shushan, NY
FISHER Josephine M. of Pittstown, NY

December 27, 1871
Pittstown, NY

BRIGGS Alexander of Easton, NY
WAIT Mettie of Easton, NY

December 20, 1871

SMITH Henry of Jackson, NY
MALONEY Elizabeth of Jackson, NY

December 23, 1871

MATTISON James of Arlington, Vt.
BARBER Mary E. of Sandgate, Vt.

December 24, 1871

WEST Edward of Jackson, NY
BUCK Catherine L. of Jackson, NY

December 26, 1871

No 1872 issues available

LINDSAY JamesDecember 24, 1872
LANT AnnieN. Argyle, NY

BALDWIN John of Schaghticoke, NYJanuary 1, 1873
BAKER Lucinda D. of Shushan, NY

MC MACKIN James of Cambridge, NY
HERRINGTON Patience A. of Cambridge, NY

January 1, 1873

**BURGESS** Abraham E. of Argyle, NY
**RICE** Mary of Argyle, NY

January 1, 1873

**BINGHAM** Henry of Bennington, Vt.
**LORING** Fannie T. of Bennington, Vt.

January 2, 1873
Bennington, Vt.

**KANE** John of Greenwich, NY
**GLEAN** Mrs. Jane Ann of Galesville, NY

December 30, 1872
Galesville, NY

**BROWN** Henry J. of Ft. Ann, NY
**FISHER** Sylvia J. of Ft. Ann, NY

January 1, 1873
Ft. Ann, NY

**MC LEAN** Andrew of Hebron, NY
**MULLEN** Mary Ann of Hebron, NY

December 24, 1872
Salem, NY

**AYERS** Horace J. of Hebron, NY
**HICKS** Ella R. of Hebron, NY

January 7, 1873
Hartford, NY

**BACON** Benjamin F. of Sunderland, Vt.
**NIDO** Delia of Sunderland, Vt.

January 1, 1873
Cambridge, NY

**GRAHAM** Andrew of Victor, NY
**MC EACHRON** Mary R. of Waterman, Ill.

December 26, 1872
Waterman, Ill.

**CATHCART** Franklin of Pawlet, Vt.
**HASKINS** Frances of Pawlet, Vt.

January 1, 1873
N. Granville, NY

**COOMBS** William of Corinth, NY   (newspaper date)
**AYERS** Jennie of Easton, NY

January 17, 1873
S. Corinth, NY

**GREEN** Leroy of Greenwich, NY
**GAMBLE** Emma F. of Greenwich, NY

January 12, 1873
Greenwich, NY

**CORNELL** S. A. of Easton, NY
**WEIR** H. Louise of Cambridge, NY

January 22, 1873
Cambridge, NY

**KING** A.
**HERRINGTON** Emelie E. of Greenwich, NY

January 22, 1873
Cambridge, NY

**ENSIGN** D. T. of Greenwich, NY
**DOWNIE** C. of Schaghticoke, NY

January 23, 1873
Greenwich, NY

**BARRINGER** Dennis of Saratoga, NY
**TATRO** Nellie of Salem, NY

January 30, 1873
Salem, NY

**DAVEY** C. F. of New York City
**COWAN** Minerva L. formerly of Whitehall, NY

January 22, 1873
Tarrytown, NY

**NORDHAM** E. B. of Ripley, NY
**BRAYTON** M. L. of Hartford, NY

January 28, 1873
Hartford, NY

BEEBE James H. of Shushan, NY  
SMITH Mary A. of Shushan, NY  
February 4, 1873  
Shushan, NY

WYMAN J. of Arlington, Vt.        (newspaper date)  
CONKEY Mary E. of Sandgate, Vt.  
February 14, 1873  
Shushan, NY

WEST Samuel M. Jr. of Arlington, Vt.  
LATHROP Mary H. dau of Eli B. of Manchester, Vt.  
February 10, 1873  
Manchester, Vt.

JUDSON Eugene M. of Sunderland, Vt.  
BOARDMAN Lucy E. of Arlington, Vt.  
February 11, 1873  
Arlington, Vt.

BENNETT Abel of White Creek, NY  
O'DELL Cynthia of White Creek, NY  
February 25, 1873  
White Creek, NY

HURD Zadoc of Arlington, Vt.  
DAVIS Alma of Arlington, Vt.  
February 20, 1873  
Arlington, Vt.

COPELAND John J. of Salem, NY  
BAKER Phebe A. of Cambridge, NY  
February 26, 1873  
Cambridge, NY

EDIE J. Judson of Greenwich, NY  
BRYANT Mary E. of Greenwich, NY  
February 20, 1873  
Greenwich, NY

PAGMAN John J. of Whitehall, NY  
ALLEN Janette of Whitehall, NY  
February 27, 1873  
Whitehall, NY

BENTLEY Ira of Manchester, Vt.  
PECK Eliza of Sandgate, Vt.  
February 27, 1873  
Sandgate, Vt.

BOSWORTH H. M. of New York City  
ANDREWS Lizzie D. of Troy, NY  
February 26, 1873  
Troy, NY

COON Clarence L. of Gansevort, NY  
LAWRENCE Ida F. dau of Harlow of Gansevort, NY  
March 12, 1873  
Gansevort, NY

DEDRICK Herbert P. of New York City  
HURD Julia Frances of Arlington, Vt.  
March 18, 1873  
Arlington, Vt.

FISHER George H. of Greenwich, NY  
STEVENS Emma K. of Jackson, NY  
March 20, 1873  
Jackson, NY

FOSTER Nathan Henry of Easton, NY  
GILLIS Sarah Frances of Salem, NY  
March 19, 1873  
Salem, NY

FERGUSON Samuel  
CALLEN Mary  
March 19, 1873  
Salem, NY

LANGWORTHY Charles L. formerly of Greenwich, NY        March 20, 1873

**LANGWORTHY** Frances A. dayu of Dr. B. of Brooklyn          Brooklyn, NY

**CRANDALL** Frank L. of Greenwich, NY          April 27, 1873
**BENNETT** Matilda M. of Greenwich, NY          Schaghticoke, NY

**SKEENE** Charles of Stillwater, NY          April 24, 1873
**SHONTS** Sarah of Mechanicsville, NY          Mechanicsville, NY

**THOMPSON** James E. of Pittsfield, Mass.          May 14, 1873
**WEBB** Alice of Greenwich, NY          Greenwich, NY

**TANNER** Col. A. H. of Whitehall, NY          May 26, 1873
**HALL** Mary dau of Sheriff O. S. Tanner of Salem, NY          Salem, NY

**CHERRY** John W. of E. Greenwich, NY          June 4, 1873
**JOHNSON** Frankie of Sterling Valley, NY

**WILSON** Robert of Granville, NY          June 11, 1873
**BLOOMINGDALE** Mary of Stillwater, NY          Stillwater, NY

**SIMMONS** Thomas of Eagle Bridge, NY          June 18, 1873
**CUBIT** Emma L.

**SAFFORD** G. T. of Salem, NY          June 18, 1873
**TURNER** Lucy M. of Salem, NY          Shushan, NY

**CAMPBELL** William O. of E. Arlington, Vt.          August 2, 1873
**HAYDEN** Lizzie of E. Arlington, Vt.          Buskirks Bridge,
NY

**FISHER** William G. of Denver, Col.          August 21, 1873
**CHERRY** Frank M. dau of Alexander          Saratoga Springs,
NY

**GOULD** Frank of Burlington, Vt.          August 21, 1873
**MOODY** Anna          Oneonta, NY

**WATKINS** John of Granville, NY          September 3, 1873
**GRAVES** Cornie B. of Granville, NY          Granville, NY

**SIMMONS** Alfred of Ft. Ann, NY          August 17, 1873
**BUTLER** Jennette of Dresden, NY          Whitehall, NY

**GRANGER** George E. of Granville, NY          August 30, 1873
**INGLESTON** Elmira of Hydesville, Vt.          Whitehall, NY

**SARGENT** Frank R. of Ft. Ann, NY          September 3, 1873
**SIMMONS** S. Etta of Ft. Edward, NY          Ft. Edward, NY

**DOUBET** Joseph of Whitehall, NY          September 15, 1873

**RIVETT** Louisa of Whitehall, NY

Whitehall, NY

**FULLER** Edwin J.
**RICE** Albertine dau of H. Niles Rice of Cambridge, NY

September 17, 1873
Cambridge, NY

**PERKINS** William H. of Rupert, Vt.
**WOODARD** Lucinda J. of Rupert, Vt.

July 5, 1873
White Creek, NY

**HUBBARD** Charles of Shushan, NY
**WRIGHT** Adeline of Shushan, NY

July 22, 1873
Cambridge, NY

**BENTLEY** Jay of Sunderland, Vt.
**STONE** Pamelia A. of Sunderland, Vt.

July 27, 1873
Cambridge, NY

**HILL** Hiram C. of Greenwich, NY
**WILCOX** Levina C. of Greenwich, NY

September 11, 1873
Greenwich, NY

**COLLINS** X. W.
**JOHNSON** Grace

October 9, 1873
Rupert, Vt.

**MC ARTHUR** Archibald of Jackson, NY
**THOMPSON** Sarah M. formerly of Jefferson Co. Pa.

October 1, 1873
Jackson, NY

**CRONKHITE** Tunis J.
**AUSTIN** Mrs. Jane

October 6, 1873
White Creek, NY

**FARR** Charles of Wallingford, Vt.
**AERO** Emma of Wallingford, Vt.

October 13, 1873
Whitehall, NY

**SHAFER** Mitchell of Blairstown, Ill.
**BEATTIE** Almira of Salem, NY

October 15, 1873
Salem, NY

**DELAVERGNE** Isaac of Easton, NY
**WHITE** Mrs. Ann of Greenwich, NY

October 22, 1873
Greenwich, NY

**TURNER** Royal of Pittstown, NY
**HUNT** Lavina J. of Schaghticoke, NY

October 24, 1873
Schaghticoke, NY

**DE PUY** Alexander
**HUNT** Mary C.

October 24, 1873
Schaghticoke, NY

**HOLMES** Adam of Westford, Vt.
**TABOR** Elizabeth of White Creek, NY

October 7, 1873
White Creek, NY

**BUSH** Sidney
**HUGHES** Frank A.

October 30, 1873
S. Argyle, NY

**YOUNG** Alfred M. of E. Greenwich, NY
**NEWTON** Mary L. dau of Charles L.

October 28, 1873
Troy, NY

**CROSBY** Charles E.
**BENTLEY** Phebe L.

November 21, 1873
Arlington, Vt.

**BARBY** Alexander of Williamstown, Mass.
**SIMPSON** Louisa A. of Williamstown, Mass.

November 22, 1873
White Creek, NY

**CORBETT** Albert of Shushan, NY
**ORCUTT** Ruth M. of Shushan, NY

November 27, 1873
Shushan, NY

**MOORE** John K. of Cambridge, NY
**MONTGOMERY** Martha E. of Salem, NY

November 27, 1873
Salem, NY

**STEELE** Daniel T. of Salem, NY
**THOMAS** Jennie of Salem, NY

November 19, 1873
Salem, NY

**MC GRATH** Edward
**MC DONNELL** Kate

November 26, 1873
Whitehall, NY

**LAVINE** William James of Argyle, NY
**GRANT** Estella M. of Windsor, Conn.

December 2, 1873
Argyle, NY

**MONTGOMERY** William M. of Galesville, NY
**HOVER** Janette of W. Arlington, Vt.

November 28, 1873
Argyle, NY

**DEVOE** Thomas
**MC QUARRIE** Sarah Jane

December 17, 1873
Argyle, NY

**LOY** Edward of Argyle, NY
**MC LAY** Maggie of Argyle, NY

December 4, 1873
Argyle, NY

**SMITH** Merritt H. of W. Pawlet, Vt.
**MILLER** Clara E. of Rutland, Vt.

December 17, 1873
Whitehall, NY

**MC GILL** John of W. Hebron, NY
**MC EACHRON** Elizabeth of Argyle, NY

December 18, 1873
E. Greenwich, NY

**MILLIMAN** Pierce
**TODD** Almirine

December 23, 1873
N. Argyle, NY

**BRIDGE** Andrew
**SANFORD** Frances of Whitehall, NY

December 20, 1873
Whitehall, NY

**JOSLIN** Grove
**HERRINGTON** Ida M.

December 24, 1873

**SMITH** William
**WADE** Elizabeth

December 20, 1873
Easton, NY

**SKINNER** Lemuel of Cambridge, NY
**RIDER** Mrs. Anna (**FITCH**)

December 24, 1873
Fitchs Point, NY

CONLEE James H. of Oshkosh, Wis.
BURDICK Addie

December 23, 1873
Centre Falls, NY

MC GILL William of Troy, NY
ARNOLD Martha of White Creek, NY

December 24, 1873
White Creek, NY

ASHLEY William of Whitehall, NY
LA PLANT Selina of Whitehall, NY

December 27, 1873
Whitehall, NY

PARKER Henry of Cambridge, NY
PETERS Eliza Ann of Waterford, NY

December 30, 1873
Shushan, NY

SIMPSON John C. of Jackson, NY
VOLENTINE Henrietta C. of Jackson, NY

January 1, 1874
Jackson, NY

CARPENTER J. Niles of N. Hoosick, NY
SWEET Estella of N. Hoosick, NY

December 23, 1873
N. Hoosick, NY

BREWER George L. of Hoosick Falls, NY
LADD Eunice of Hoosick Falls, NY

December 24, 1873

WAIT Charles E. of W. Hebron, NY
TEFFT Emma E. of N. Petersburg, NY

January 1, 1874
N. Petersburg, NY

MYERS James B. of Hoosick Falls, NY
BARBER Mary E. of Hoosick Falls, NY

January 1, 1874

MC KNIGHT Charles
VOLENTINE Mrs. Sarah of Saratoga Springs, NY

January 1, 1874
Ft. Edward, NY

SMITH Charles
TURNER Maggie

January 1, 1874
Ft. Edward, NY

HYNEMAN Jacob of Schuylerville, NY
CHASE Calista A. of W. Ft. Ann, NY

January 1, 1874
W. Ft. Ann, NY

SMITH John D. of Argyle, NY
SHAW Maria of Watson, NY

January 1, 1874
Schenectady, NY

COLLINS William C. of Medina, Ohio
SEARS Emma L. of Jackson, NY

January 30, 1874
Jackson, NY

ACKERS William J. of Whitehall, NY
FITZGERALD Katie of Whitehall, NY

January 21, 1874
Whitehall, NY

LA RONE Caliste of Sandy Hill, NY
ANDETTE Olive of Sandy Hill, NY

January 26, 1874
Sandy Hill, NY

GETTY Theodore of Granville, NY

January 21, 1874

**WHITING** Harriet Adelle dau of Edmund C. of Pawlet, Vt.   Pawlet, Vt.

**WOODBECK** Walter C. of Davenport, NY   January 21, 1874
**NELSON** Emma of Davenport, NY

**MC CANDLES** Harvey   January 28, 1874
**MC NEIL** Mary of S. Argyle, NY   S. Argyle, NY

**CLARK** R. W. of Huntington, Mass.   January 26, 1874
**DOWNS** Laura of Hartford, NY   M. Granville, NY

**HAWLEY** H. T. Md. of Tittabawasee, Mi.   February 11, 1874
**BROWN** Marion A. of Cambridge, NY   Tittabawasee, Mi.

**KINNEY** John M. of Argyle, NY   February 13, 1874
**ALLISON** Laura A. of Rochester, NY   Rochester, NY

**TRUMBULL** Titus S. of Greenwich, NY   February 17, 1874
**DEAN** Marietta of Greenwich, NY   Greenwich, NY

**SWEET** John T. of N. Hoosick, NY   December 31, 1873
**GREEN** Achsah S. of N. Hoosick, NY   White Creek, NY

**DWINNELL** George W. of White Creek, NY   February 5, 1874
**BRAYTON** Jane M. of White Creek, NY   White Creek, NY

**BARKER** George Jr. of White Creek, NY   February 19, 1874
**DYER** Ruth J. dau of John of White Creek, NY   White Creek, NY

**EDGERTON** John of Hebron, NY   (newspaper date)   February 24, 1874
**MAYNARD** Florence of Hebron, NY   Hebron, NY

**TEMPLE** John of Albany, NY   February 26, 1874
**PALMER** Martha B. of Hoosick Falls, NY   Hartford, NY

**DOBBIN** Melvin M. of Shushan, NY   March 4, 1874
**VOLENTINE** Anna M. of Jackson, NY   Shushan, NY

**YARTER** Levi of Sandy Hill, Ny   March 14, 1874
**RIVETT** Emma of Hartford, NY   Hartford, NY

**HANKS** Martin   March 11, 1874
**COOK** Florence   Lake, NY

**ELWELL** Alexander of Shaftsbury, Vt.   March 17, 1874
**MORSE** Rebecca of Shaftsbury, Vt.   White Creek, NY

**COLBY** Abner W. of Jackson. NY   March 21, 1874
**PRATT** Julia L. of Jackson, NY   Cambridge, NY

HARRIS Frederick M. of Boston, Mass.  March 10, 1874
WARREN Julia E. of Hampton, NY  Hampton, NY

WRIGHT Joseph of Warrensburgh, NY  March 16, 1874
WHITE Mary of Crown Point, NY  Whitehall, NY

CARLTON Horton of Granville, NY  March 18, 1874
SMITH Ada of Comstocks Landing, NY  Comstocks Landing

HUGGINS John of Argyle, NY  March 19, 1874
FLACK Louisa of Argyle, NY  Hebron, NY

WILSON Ira C. of Hampton, NY  March 18, 1874
ANDREWS Emma G. of Ft. Edward, NY  Ft. Edward, NY

HEDGER D. F of Ft. Ann, NY  March 18, 1874
WEBSTER Mary L. of Hartford, NY  Ft. Edward, NY

HEDGER James of Ft. Ann, NY  March 24, 1874
COLLINS Mary A. of Jackson, NY  Salem, NY

VAUGHN Edward D.  March 31, 1874
JENKINS Sarah M.  Kingsbury, NY

HOYT E. F. of Sandgate, Vt.  April 9, 1874
COVEY Verona E. dau of John B. of Sandgate, Vt.  Salem, NY

PHILLIPS Nathan of Shaftsbury, Vt.  April 12, 1874
BECKER Ann Eliza of Shaftsbury, Vt.  White Creek, NY

MATTISON Hiram of Shaftsbury, Vt.  April 4, 1874
TWITCHELL Ella of Shaftsbury, Vt.  White Creek, NY

SANTERS Robert of Sandgate, Vt.  April 12, 1874
SMITH Jessie of Camden, NY  Shushan, NY

JOHNSTON John George of Hebron, NY  April 15, 1874
CAMPBELL Rachel of Hebron, NY  N. Argyle, NY

NELSON Dr. J. E.  (newspaper date)  May 8, 1874
MOORE Lydia of Wells River, Vt.  Wells River, Vt.

BLACKMER John C. of Manchester, Vt.  May 7, 1874
PRATT Jennie E. of Cambridge, NY  Cambridge, NY

LAMPMAN Charles of Greenwich, NY  March 28, 1874
YOUNG Electa of Greenwich, NY  Greenwich, NY

HAMMOND John C. of St. Louis, Mo.  May 19, 1874

**FISHER** Carrie dau of H. K. of Chili, NY

N. Chili, NY

**MARTIN** Alonzo C.
**MC NUTT** Mary F. of Ft. Ann, NY

May 20, 1874
Ft. Ann, NY

**AGAN** J. L. of Cambridge, NY
**LUCE** Bertie L. of Stowe, Vt.

June 3, 1874
Stowe, Vt.

**BURGESS** Nairn of N. Hoosick, NY
**DUNDON** Ann of N. Hoosick, NY

June 9, 1874
White Creek, NY

**ROBINSON** Richard of Chicago, Ill.
**COON** Abbie dau of James F.

June 14, 1874
Whitehall, NY

**BRIMMER** George R. of Eagle Bridge, NY
**FISH** Vashti A. of Eagle Bridge, NY

June 18 1874
N. Hoosick, NY

**BUCK** Lemuel A.
**YOUNG** Alice B. dau of Charles H.

June 23, 1874
W. Arlington, Vt.

**BUCK** David F.
**FLEMING** Agnes A. dau of Thomas

June 24, 1874
W. Arlington, Vt.

**BELL** Eugene of Salem, NY
**JORDAN** Julia of Salem, NY

June 27, 1874
Greenwich, NY

**HOE** James E. of Shaftsbury, Vt.
**FISHER** Cynthia of Shaftsbury, Vt.

June 27, 1874
White Creek, NY

**STILL** Jerome of Sandgate, Vt.
**BENTLEY** Sybil of Sandgate, Vt.

July 8, 1874
Shushan, NY

**PRATT** Franklin of Jackson, NY
**VERNUM** Sarah A. of Cambridge, NY

June 20, 1874
Jackson, NY

**CONANT** A. of Granville, NY
**CAREY** Mrs. Mary of Coila, NY

July 15, 1874
Coila, NY

**WILSON** Edward of Whitehall, NY
**BOICE** Frances M. of Ft. Ann, NY

July 8, 1874
Shushan, NY

**GREEN** Charles
**SHARP** Mary A. of Putnam, NY

July 3, 1874
Putnam, NY

**NICHOLS** Calvin of Granville, NY
**DAVIS** Mrs. Barbara Ann of Granville, NY

July 1, 1874
Granville, NY

**TOWNSEND** L. D. of Wallingford, Vt.
**BAKER** Mrs. Eliza A. of Granville, NY

July 16, 1874
Granville, NY

CARRINGTON Ira F. of Ft. Ann, NY
LARKIN Rose E. of Hartford, NY

July 8, 1874
Hartford, NY

INGRAHAM Lyman of Lake, NY
CURTIS Mrs. Almira of Lake, NY

July 15, 1874
Lake, NY

RANDALL Nelson of Ripley, NY
BRAYTON E. E. of Hartford, NY

July 30, 1874
Hartford, NY

OATMAN Benjamin of Argyle, NY
WOODELL Mary of Hartford, NY

August 4, 1874
Hartford, NY

HARRINGTON Martin H. of Jackson, NY
LARRABEE Gertrude of Shushan, NY

August 17, 1874
White Creek, NY

MEAGHER Michael of Hoosick Falls, NY
TRACY Elnora of Cambridge, NY

August 16, 1874
Cambridge, NY

FAULK John Q. of Marion, Mi.
TAYLOR Inez O. of Belcher, NY

August 16, 1874
Williamstown, Mi.

MOSS F. D. of Belcher, NY
CASSELS Isabelle of Belcher, NY

August 20, 1874
Belcher, NY

INGLEE R. J. of Machias, Mi.
NICHOLS Luana of Kingsbury, NY

September 1, 1874
Kingsbury, NY

BAIN William Henry of Argyle, NY
FRENCH Jane of Argyle, NY

September 1, 1874
Argyle, NY

SMITH Sanford of Argyle, NY
TAYLOR Lucy of Argyle, NY

August 27, 1874
Ft. Edward, NY

COON John R. of Lake, NY
BREESON Jennie of N. Argyle, NY

August 19, 1874
Schuylerville, NY

KILBURN R. J. of Rutland, Vt.
MC DONALD N. V. of Hampton, NY

August 29, 1874
Hampton, NY

KELLY George E. of Westhaven, Vt.
BARTHOLOMEW Mattie E. of Dresden, NY

September 2, 1874
Dresden, NY

RUDD Ebb S. of Hoosick, NY
CARPENTER Mary A. of Hoosick, NY

September 8, 1874
White Creek, NY

HURD Albert of Sandgate, Vt.     (newspaper date)
RAY Lydia of Cambridge, NY

October 2, 1874
Cambridge, NY

GILLIS John B. of Salem, NY

September 22, 1874

**THOMPSON** Belle of Manchester, Vt.                    Manchester, Vt.

**RIGLEY** John of Westchester, NY                       August 29, 1874
**SWEET** Mrs. Clara E. of Whitehall, NY                 Whitehall, NY

**LITTLE** Asa W.                                        September 3, 1874
**ABRAMS** Mary A. of Castleton, Vt.                     Whitehall, NY

**HALL** John W. of Whitehall, NY                        September 24, 1874
**BENJAMIN** Josephine dau of Samuel of Whitehall, NY    Whitehall, NY

**CARPENTER** C. Henry of Cambridge, NY                  October 7, 1874
**HARSHA** Nettie E. of Cambridge, NY                    Cambridge, NY

**PERKINS** Walter Edward                                October 7, 1874
**MATTISON** Effie Pamelia dau of Eben of Sunderland, Vt. Sunderland, Vt.

**RAYMOND** Charles M. of Bordentown, NY                 September 30, 1874
**LANSING** Kate dau of Abram C. of Salem, NY            Bordentown, NY

**LYONS** John of Amsterdam, NY                          October 14, 1874
**HOPE** Delina of Ft. Edward, NY                        Ft. Edward, NY

**BUTTON** Andrew                                        October 18, 1874
**WHITE** Emeline                                        Greenwich, NY

**WILSON** Charles H. of Salem, NY    (newspaper date)   October 30, 1874
**RICHARDS** Georgie dau of George of Potsdam, NY        Potsdam, NY

**LENOIS** Francis                                       October 27, 1874
**LORTIE** Mary Aurelia                                  Whitehall, NY

**INGLEE** Charles B. of Whitehall, NY                   October 24, 1874
**RODD** E. J. of Whitehall, NY                          Whitehall, NY

**TOBIA** George                                         October 21, 1874
**CARVER** Hattie                                        Pawlet, Vt.

**CANE** William of Whitehall, NY                        November 2, 1874
**GRANT** Ann of Grand Isle, Vt.                         Whitehall, NY .

**ROLLIN** James of White Creek, NY   (newspaper date)   November 13, 1874
**MONROE** Emma Ida of White Creek, NY                   Cambridge, NY

**RIPWELL** John of Hoosick Falls, NY  (newspaper date)  November 20, 1874
**MULDOON** Annie of Hoosick Falls, NY                   Hoosick Falls, NY

**THEUSIC** Peter of Hoosick Falls, NY                   November 17, 1874
**NEWMAN** Rosanna of Hoosick Falls, NY                  Hoosick Falls, NY

MC LEAN Leroy Md.
ORR Anna E. dau of William of Troy, NY

November 24, 1874
Troy, NY

CULL Thomas of Middletown, Ohio
KENNEDY Fannie Gray of Cambridge, NY

November 26, 1874
White Creek, NY

GANNON James H. of Ft. Ann, NY
RICE Helen Adelaide of Ft. Ann, NY

November 24, 1874
Ft. Ann, NY

TILFORD John of Whitehall, NY
TEFFT Mrs. Annis of Whitehall, NY

November 18, 1874
Whitehall, NY

BILLINGS Henry
WARNER Lillie A.

November 25, 1874
Troy, NY

CHAMBERLAIN Lauren J. of Gloversville, NY
MC LEAN Sarah M. dau of Ebenezer of Anaquasicoke, NY

December 1, 1874
Anaquasicoke, NY

BLANCHARD J. B. of Putnam, NY
ROOT Jennie of Putnam, NY

November 16, 1874
Putnam, NY

BISHOP Elliot of Woodford, Vt.
HARVEY Charlotte of Searsbury, Vt.

October 28, 1874
White Creek, NY

MATTISON Norman of Glastonbury, Vt.
MC DONALD Angela of Glastonbury, Vt.

November 26, 1874
White Creek, NY

FARR Charles formerly of Ft. Edward, NY
KING Mary of Greenfield, NY

November 25, 1874
Ft. Edward, NY

THOMPSON James A. of E. Tawas, Mi.
BUCK Etta M. dau of Samuel of W. Arlington, Vt.

December 9, 1874
W. Arlington, Vt.

ALLEN Robert of Jackson, NY
DEVINE Mary of Jackson, NY

December 10, 1874
Jackson, NY

GILES Fred
BLOSSOM Lucy

December 16, 1874
N. Pawlet, Vt.

MILLER Lewis N. of Beatrice, Neb.
CAVANAUGH Katie of Eagle Bridge, NY

December 22, 1874
Eagle Bridge, NY

CONKLIN Andrew of Argyle, NY
WIET Elizabeth of Argyle, NY

December 20, 1874
Hartford, NY

CRANSTON William of Shaftsbury, Vt.
MORSE Rebecca of Shaftsbury, Vt.

December 30, 1874
White Creek, NY

HILL Levi of Shaftsbury, Vt.

January 3, 1875

**CAREY** Mary of Shaftsbury, Vt.

White Creek, NY

**PRIEST** Alansing H. of White Creek, NY
**MACK** Laura A. of W. Arlington, Vt.

January 2, 1875
White Creek, NY

**CHASE** Edgar B. of Buskirks Bridge, NY
**SISSON** Emma J. of Eagle Bridge, NY

January 20, 1875
Eagle Bridge, NY

**ROUSE** George of Argyle, NY
**MC CLOY** Mary Jane of Argyle, NY

January 28, 1875
Argyle, NY

**SLOAN** Edward
**MATHEWS** Carrie

January 27, 1875
Argyle, NY

**SULLIVAN** John of Hoosick Falls, NY
**SULLIVAN** Mary of Hoosick Falls, NY

February 1, 1875
Hoosick Falls, NY

**NEWMAN** Thomas of Hoosick Falls, NY
**STAPLETON** Anna of Hoosick Falls, NY

February 3, 1875
Hoosick Falls, NY

**NOLT** Barney of Hoosick, NY
**BALDWIN** Sarah Jane of Hoosick, NY

February 17, 1875
Hoosick, NY

**PALMER** J. E. of New York City
**STEVENS** Effie M. of Jersey City, NJ
(both formerly of Cambridge, NY)

March 24, 1875
Jersey City, NJ

**BENTLEY** Sam
**SULLIVAN** Mary

March 27, 1875
Hoosick Falls, NY

**BALDWIN** William Skidmore of Whitehall, NY
**WOOD** Anne of New York City

March 31, 1875
New York City

**BROWN** M. W. of Hebron, NY
**CAMPBELL** Emma L. of Hebron, NY

May 26, 1875
Hebron, NY

**NELSON** George H.                    (newspaper date)
**VAUGHN** Ida J.

June 25, 1875
Ft. Ann, NY

**JONES** Morris M. of Salem, NY
**JONES** Margaret of Salem, NY

June 14, 1875
Salem, NY

**WHITLOCK** W. J. of Salem, NY
**PATRICK** Mary A. of Salem, NY

August 4, 1875
Belcher, NY

**SYKES** Seth B. of Manchester, Vt.
**WEAVER** Eunice of Manchester, Vt.

August 11, 1875
Salem, NY

**CURTIS** S. W. of Cambridge, NY
**CAMPBELL** Isabella of E. Yozza, Ontario, Canada

August 25, 1875
E. Yozza, Ontario

MILLER Norman L. of Saginaw, Mi.
RICHARDS Camelia H. dau of George of White Creek, NY

September 23, 1875
White Creek, NY

WILBER Jonathan of Johnsonville, NY
STACK Frances of Clarks Mills, NY

September 18, 1875
N. Easton, NY

BALDWIN Edwin J. of Whitehall, NY
AINSWORTH Fannie M. of Albany, NY

September 29, 1875
Albany, NY

FISH George Henry of Whitehall, NY
COLLINS Alice of Whitehall, NY

October 26, 1875
Whitehall, NY

DICKINSON Seymour of Ft. Edward, NY
SAFFORD Helen D. of Ft. Edward, NY

November 11, 1875
Easton, NY

BURCH Welling W. of Schaghticoke, NY
WAIT Jessie F. of Easton, NY

November 24, 1875
Easton, NY

FLEMING John
ALLEN Emma

November 24, 1875
N. Hebron, NY

BLODGETT William of Whitehall, NY
DAVIS Mary E. of Whitehall, NY

December 6, 1875
Whitehall, NY

ABBOTT Leonard J. of Pittstown, Mass.
HERRINGTON Lucie F. of Hoosick, NY

December 30, 1875
Hoosick, NY

DERBY Henry of Easton, NY
MOTT Sarah of Easton, NY

January 2, 1876
Easton, NY

CORNELL Edwin T. of S. Cambridge, NY
OLIN Ella E. of S. Cambridge, NY

January 1, 1876
Coila, NY

COLBURN Charles of Cornwall, Vt.
DENNISON Mararet of Hebron, NY

December 27, 1875
Hebron, NY

COOK Northup E. of Ft. Edward, NY
PARISH Abigail E. of Ft. Edward, NY

December 22, 1875
Ft. Edward, NY

BELCHER John of Ft. Edward, NY
MACK Kate of Ft. Edward, NY

December 30, 1875
Ft. Edward, NY

GATES Philander Jr. of White Creek, NY
EATON Mary Jane of Easton, NY

January 1, 1876
White Creek, NY

HARRINGTON Edward of W. Hoosick, NY
HAVILAND Jane A. of w. Hoosick, NY
NY

January 22, 1876
Buskirks Bridge,

**MC CLARTY** David of S. Hartford, NY
**BARKER** Marie W. of S. Hartford, NY
January 15, 1876
S. Hartford, NY

**HAY** W. of Slateville, NY
**MC COTTER** Mrs. Sophrona of Hebron, NY
January 27, 1876
Hebron, NY

**CLOSSON** Robert E. of Cambridge, NY
**MOFFITT** Mary J. of Cambridge, NY
January 19, 1876
Coila, NY

**WELLING** Jerome B. of Cambridge, NY
**PRATT** Mary Libbie of Cambridge, NY
January 27, 1876
Cambridge, NY

**BAKER** David of Easton, NY
**MERRITT** J. Annette of Easton, NY
December __, 1875
Greenwich, NY

**SHERRILL** Robert of Sandy Hill, NY
**BAKER** Celestia F. of Sandy Hill, NY
February 14, 1876
Sandy Hill, NY

**BLANCHARD** Newel of Ft. Ann, NY    (newspaper date)
**GRANT** Louise of Whitehall, NY
March 3, 1876
Dresden, NY

**BULSON** Ludowick of Greenwich, NY
**ROBBINS** Libbie of Lansingburgh, NY
February 26, 1876
Lansingburgh, NY

**CHASE** Reuben of Bennington, Vt.
**SENDELL** Emma of Shaftsbury, Vt.
March 3, 1876
White Creek, NY

**HENNING** Thomas
**MC CLOY** Anna
February 10, 1876
Hebron, NY

**QUINN** Thomas
**CLOSH** Mary E.
March 15, 1876
Hebron, NY

**DERBY** Theodore
**CORNELL** Sarah
March 15, 1876
Sandy Hill, NY

**CLARK** Robert G. of Argyle, NY
**CUNNINGHAM** Frank A. of Belcher, NY
March 30, 1876
Belcher, NY

**PARISH** Seth of Ft. Edward, NY
**ROBINSON** Caroline of Whitehall, NY
March 27, 1876
Whitehall, NY

**THOMAS** Clark of Vly Summit, NY
**QUACKENBUSH** Mary L. of Easton, NY
March 29, 1876
Easton, NY

**STEVENS** William of Glens Falls, NY
**HUNT** Jennie of Ft. Ann, NY
April 5, 1876
Ft. Ann, NY

**SMITH** Dennis M. of Cambridge, NY
**WORTH** Emma J. of Cambridge, NY
April 20, 1876
Cambridge, NY

**HERRON** Patsy
**ENNIS** Eliza
April 20, 1876
Greenwich, NY

**FARR** Carmi C.
**ROWELL** Emma W.
April 27, 1876
Ft. Ann, NY

**ALDEN** Charles S. formerly of Cambridge, NY
**HICKS** Alzora of Cohoes, NY
June 29, 1876
Cohoes, NY

**MACY** Abram W. of the Friends Seminary of Easton, NY
**VAN SICKLE** Ella C.
July 12, 1876
S. Livonia, NY

**DEYDE** Nelson of Poultney, Vt.
**WHITCOMB** Nellie of Poultney, Vt.
August 16, 1876
Whitehall, NY

**GILCHRIST** Frank of Hartford, NY
**WHITTEMORE** Minnie C. of Hartford, NY
August 31, 1876
Hartford, NY

**DAVIS** John of Bennington, Vt
**FRENCH** Levina of Bennington, Vt.
NY
September 2, 1876
Buskirks Bridge,

**BOSWORTH** B. A.
**BROWN** M.
September 12, 1876
Hoosick, NY

**ANGELL** Frank of Greenfield, NY
**LANNON** Agnes of Schuylerville, NY
September 12, 1876
Schuylerville, NY

**MC GEOCH** George E. of Jackson, NY
**MC MILLAN** Libbie of Jackson, NY
September 13, 1876
Jackson, NY

**REED** J. Erwin Md. of Canajoharie, NY
**SMITH** Helen Frances dau of John C. of White Creek, NY
September 17, 1876
Bennington, Vt.

**AUSTIN** Truman E. of Whitehall, NY
**MILLETT** Annie L. of Whitehall, NY
September 3, 1876
Whitehall, NY

**SHEPHERD** Lorenzo of Hartford, Conn.
**MORRIS** Louisa of Pawlet, Vt.
September 16, 1876
Granville, NY

**PITTS** Roland of W. Rutland, Vt.
**LITCHFIELD** Marcia of Rutland, Vt.
September 19, 1876
Granville, NY

**BAIN** James E. of Argyle, NY
**WALLACE** Josie C. of Eagle Bridge, NY
September 28, 1876

**MC MORRIS** John A. of Jackson, NY    (newspaper date)
**SELFRIDGE** Maggie of Jackson, NY
October 6, 1876

| | |
|---|---|
| **BLAIR** Henry of Williamstown, Mass. | September 29, 1876 |
| **PRIEST** Julia of Cambridge, NY | Shushan, NY |
| | |
| **MC GOWAN** Owen | October 3, 1876 |
| **MC NEILY** Eliza | Whitehall, NY |
| | |
| **COTTRELL** Harvey T. of White Creek, NY (newspaper date) | October 13, 1876 |
| **WAIT** Sarah M. of White Creek, NY | |
| | |
| **MARCH** Charles B. of N. Hoosick, NY | October 5, 1876 |
| **FOWLER** Alice L. of Cambridge, NY | Cambridge, NY |
| | |
| **WHITE** Thomas of W. Hebron, NY | October 4, 1876 |
| **LUKE** Jennie of W. Hebron, NY | Argyle, NY |
| | |
| **CRANDALL** Washington N. | October 2, 1876 |
| **WAIT** Susie B. | Easton, NY |
| | |
| **SWIFT** Willis of Ft. Ann, NY | October 3, 1876 |
| **GRAHAM** Malvina of Ft. Ann, NY | Ft. Ann, NY |
| | |
| **COLE** Charles H. of Arlington, Vt. | October 8, 1876 |
| **ANDREWS** Ettie of Arlington, Vt. | White Creek, NY |
| | |
| **WILSEY** Almond C. of Whitehall, NY | October 11, 1876 |
| **SAWYER** Virginia M. of Whitehall, NY | Ft. Ann, NY |
| | |
| **ROBERTSON** W. L. of Lincoln, Neb. | October 17, 1876 |
| **SKINNER** Anna I. of N. Greenwich, NY | N. Greenwich, NY |
| | |
| **CUNNINGHAM** R. J. | October 3, 1876 |
| **COCHRANE** Jennie B. of Newburgh, NY | |
| | |
| **WITHERELL** Manly B. of Shushan, NY | October 15, 1876 |
| **MC MILLAN** May of Shushan, NY | Shushan, NY |
| | |
| **ROGERS** Charles M. | October 18, 1876 |
| **MUNSON** Carrie A. | Hebron, NY |
| | |
| **REID** Thomas of Arlington, Vt. | October 30, 1876 |
| **BISHOP** Addie of Cambridge, NY | Cambridge, NY |
| | |
| **CHASE** Edmond W. of Dresden, NY | October 25, 1876 |
| **CHAPIN** Hattie E. of Dresden, NY | Ft. Ann, NY |
| | |
| **LARMON** William of Salem, NY | October 26, 1876 |
| **ACKLEY** Victoria of Salem, NY | Salem, NY |
| | |
| **NORTON** Amos | October 23, 1876 |
| **HULL** Josephine | Granville, NY |

HALL Samuel J. of Cambridge, NY  
LIVINGSTON Julia of Cambridge, NY     October 26, 1876  
    Cambridge, NY

THAYER Edwin of Arlington, Vt.  
MOFFITT Laura of Arlington, Vt.     October 29, 1876  
    White Creek, NY

HUBBELL Silas S. of Ft. Edward, NY  
BROWN Annie G. of Chicago. Ill.     November 8, 1876  
    Ft. Edward, NY

ELDER Mathew of Ft. Edward, NY  
BRISTOL Hattie of Ft. Edward, NY     November 7, 1876  
    Ft. Edward, NY

WOOD Harry of Salem, NY  
BEVIN Mary E. of Salem, NY     November 16, 1876  
    Cambridge, NY

RIGHTMIRE Frank L. of Seneca Castle, NY(newspaper date)     November 24, 1876  
DE LONG Adeline U. of Pawlet, Vt.     Granville, NY

JAMES Frederick A. of N. Cambridge, NY  
BROWNELL Flora N. of Easton, NY     November 18, 1876

SCOTT W. A. of Salem, NY  
GREEN Abbie J. of Jackson, NY     November 27, 1876  
    Jackson, NY

BROWNELL Dennis of Easton, NY  
NORTON Ida E. of Salem, NY     November 29, 1876

BRUST Frank L. of Troy, NY  
BURDICK Carrie E. of Saratoga Springs, NY     November 22, 1876  
NY     Saratoga Springs,

PIERSON William of Ft. Edward, NY  
ACKLEY Lavada of Ft. Ann, NY     December 7, 1876  
    Ft. Ann, NY

WYATT Frederick of Cambridge, NY  
GREEN Rachel of Cambridge, NY     November 21, 1876  
    Cambridge, NY

HOLTON Thomas E. of Johnsonville, NY     (newspaper date) January 19, 1877  
HANAMAN Mary F. of Johnsonville, NY     Cambridge, NY

CRAMPTON Henry A. of Middletown, Vt.  
WILLIAMS Carrie A. of Middletown, Vt.     January 2, 1877  
    Middletown, Vt.

THOMAS Orrin J. of Middletown, Vt.  
HARSHA Susan A. of Middletown, Vt.     January 2, 1877  
    Middletown, Vt.

SPEER Rev. J. A. of W. Hebron, NY  
BLACK Nettie of Pittsburg, Pa.     December 27, 1876  
    Pittsburg, Pa.

NICHOLS Scott of Argyle, NY
WINN Jennie of Hartford, NY

January 9, 1877
Sandy Hill, NY

ALEXANDER James of Sandy Hill, NY
BOYCE Mrs. Caroline of Sandy Hill, NY

January 7, 1877
Sandy Hill, NY

HUGGINS Levi
MC GEOCH Ella

January 17, 1877
S. Argyle, NY

BAIN Abram
MC DOUGAL Emma

December 26, 1876
Argyle, NY

PETTEYS Jacob of Cambridge, NY
EDIE Mary of Easton, NY

January 17, 1877
Cambridge, NY

BEAGLE Robert of Shaftsbury, Vt.
BARTLETT Sally of Shaftsbury, Vt.

February 1, 1877
White Creek, NY

MILLER Mathias of Harts Falls, NY
MC DERMOTT Catherine of Easton, NY

January 20, 1877
Troy, NY

HEWITT Dr. Adelbert of Ft. Edward, NY
INGERSOLL Hattie C. of Austerlitz, NY

February 5, 1877
Austerlitz, NY

KINNE Asa of Rupert, Vt.
MC FARLAND Mary of Hebron, NY

February 27, 1877
Granville, NY

HOLLEY George of Ft. Ann, NY
HODGE Sarah of S. Hartford, NY

February 15, 1877
S. Hartford, NY

WOOD Edgar of Cambridge, NY
CLOSSON Phebe of Cambridge, NY

February 28, 1877
Cambridge, NY

MAHAFFY James of Argyle, NY
MC GEOCH Mary of Argyle, NY

March 6, 1877
Argyle, NY

CLOUGH Pitt M. of Belcher, NY
HARRISON Maggie J. of Jackson, NY

March 7, 1877
Shushan, NY

LAW Robert R. of Cambridge, NY
WOODARD M. J. of E. Greenwich, NY

March 15, 1877
E. Greenwich, NY

PATTERSON John of Argyle, NY
CAMPBELL Minnie of Argyle, NY

March 15, 1877
Argyle, NY

IRWIN Samuel of Argyle, NY
ROBINSON Jane of Hebron, NY

March 15, 1877
Hebron, NY

TAFT Andrew J. of Whitehall, NY
WILSON Sarah of Whitehall, NY

March 16, 1877
Whitehall, NY

LACKEY Merton R. of St Albans, Vt.
DOUGLAS Mary of Putnam, NY

February 27, 1877
Putnam, NY

SMITH James.Ellis of Granville, NY
GRANGER Lucy of Granville, NY

March 15/18, 1877
Granville, NY

BURNETT A. M. of Salem, NY
LOURIE Nancy of Salem, NY

March 7, 1877
W. Hebron, NY

SHELDON Smith
LEWIS Maria

March 13, 1877
Rupert, Vt.

MC LEAN Ebenezer of Jackson, NY
GILLETTE Mrs. Sarah of Jackson, NY

March 14, 1877

MOSHER Frederick D. of Eagle Bridge, NY
STEWART May D. of Eagle Bridge, NY

March 20, 1877
Eagle Bridge, NY

SLATTERGOOD Thomas of Whitehall, NY
BRANNOCK A of Whitehall, NY

April 3, 1877
N. Granville, NY

BARDEN Fred W. of Glens Falls, NY
RICE Fannie A. of M. Granville, NY

May 3, 1877
Glens Falls, NY

HALL W. D. of Argyle, NY
CUTHBERT Maggie of Argyle, NY

May 30, 1877
Argyle, NY

CHANDLER Lyman
MC KIE Belle

June 5, 1877
Cambridge, NY

CLARK L. M. Md.          (newspaper date)
BARKER Mrs. Agnes

June 8, 1877
Cambridge, NY

PIERCE Milton of White Creek, NY
DICKINSON Clara of Shaftsbury, Vt.

May 31, 1877
Cambridge, NY

DURKEE Ira S. of S. Cambridge, NY
TRIPP Satie S. of S. Cambridge, NY

June 6, 1877
S. Cambridge, NY

REARDON Thomas of Whitehall, NY
EARLE Emma H. of Whitehall, NY

May 24, 1877
Whitehall, NY

BELDON Arthur J. of Sommerset, Vt.
WERNER Iva H. ot Dover, Vt.

May 23, 1877
White Creek, NY

SKELLIE James of Hartford, NY
RAMSEY Martha of Troy, NY

June 16, 1877
Ft. Edward, NY

GOODSPEED Hosea A. of N. Ira, Vt.

July 4, 1877

**HARRINGTON** M. Louisa of Kingsbury, NY     Kingsbury, NY

**LINDSAY** James G. of Kingsbury, NY     July 3, 1877
**OATLEY** Mrs. Laura A. of Salem, NY     Salem, NY

**REED** Charles F. of Whitehall, NY     July 5, 1877
**PERRY** Nettelia of Whitehall, NY     Whitehall, NY

**PALMER** A. K. of W. Ft. Ann, NY     July 5, 1877
**BISHOP** Irene of W. Ft. Ann, NY     W. Ft. Ann, NY

**GREEN** Myron T. of Danby, Vt.     July 4, 1877
**COREY** Lettie of Danby, Vt.     Granville, NY

**BAKER** Franklin of White Creek, NY     July 7, 1877
**BENNETT** Sarah L. of White Creek, NY     White Creek, NY

**CRANDALL** George of Durkeetown, NY     July 9, 1877
**SMITH** Mary dau of Phillip of Argyle, NY     Sandy Hill, NY

**KIRKHAM** Frank of Sandy Hill, NY     July 6, 1877
**HIBBARD** Minnie E. of Sandy Hill, NY     Sandy Hill, NY

**RICE** Jerome B.     July 19, 1877
**CHANDLER** Laura J.     Cambridge, NY

**RIVETT** George of M. Granville, NY     July 10, 1877
**AVERILL** Jessie L. of N. Granville, NY     Ft. Ann, NY

**REID** Robert Jr.     July 11, 1877
**YOUNG** Sarah E. of Hebron, NY     N. Argyle, NY

**RUSSELL** Charles A. of Boston, Mass.     August 1, 1877
**JONES** Lillie E. of Greenwich, NY     Cambridge, NY

**GETTY** Addison of Salem, NY     July 26, 1877
**CRANE** Harriet J. of Phoenix, NY     Phoenix, NY

**BLACKBURN** William of Hoosick Falls, NY     August 11, 1877
**EDDY** Eliza of S. Easton, NY     Cambridge, NY

**DECKER** John G. of Jackson, NY     August 30, 1877
**HORTON** Hattie of Jackson, NY     Shushan, NY

**SHAW** John B. of Granville, NY     September 5, 1877
**THAYER** Hulda M. of Fairhaven, Vt.     W. Troy, NY

**SHELDON** Shiland H. of Winhall, Vt.     September 5, 1877
**MARKS** Addie R. dau of Ira of N. Pawlet, Vt.     N. Pawlet, Vt.

WAKEFIELD David J. of Ticonderoga, NY
CLARK Agnes of Crown Point, NY
September 8, 1877
Putnam, NY

WHITNEY Myron of Adamsville, NY    (newspaper date)
SLOCUM Hattie of Hartford, NY
October 12, 1877
Hartford, NY

FAXON W. S. of Little Rock, Ill.
NEWELL Marion of Little Rock, Ill.
September 25, 1877
Little Rock, Ill.

LE VANN Arthur of Jackson, NY
CLARK Martha E. of Ft. Ann, NY
October 28, 1877
Ft. Ann, NY

STRAIN James
SMITH Mary
October 25, 1877
Argyle, NY

WOODARD Martin of Hebron, NY
RAE Jimmy H. H. of Portageville, NY
October 24, 1877
Salem, NY

CONKLIN James M. of Chicago, Ill.
CLEMENTS Hattie A. of Queensbury, NY
October 17, 1877
Queensbury, NY

BLAISDELL George M. of Smiths Basin, NY
YOUNG Mary L. of Smiths Basin, NY
October 27, 1877
Kingsbury, NY

LOCKHART W. S.
REMINGTON Frances of Sandy Hill, NY
October 16, 1877
Albany, NY

CURTIS Mr. ___ of Meredith, Conn.
MC NISH Maggie of Salem, NY
November 13, 1877
Shushan, NY

WEED Bernice of Pawlet, Vt.
ROOT Stella of Rupert, Vt.
November 12, 1877
Rupert, Vt.

ROGERS Geroge E. of Troy, NY
HARRIS Delia dau of J. F.
November 15, 1877
Ft. Edward, NY

AUSTIN John of Cambridge, NY    (newspaper date)
MEEKER Sarah A.
December 14, 1877
Cambridge, NY

ADAMS G. H.    (newspaper date)
TRICKETT Lillie
December 14, 1877
S. Glens Falls, NY

MARSHALL Charles of Durkeetown, NY
DAVENPORT Alta of Moreau, NY
January 2, 1878
Moreau, NY

PETTIT George W. of Troy, NY
CHISHOLM Jennie M. of Cohoes, NY
December 24, 1877
Cohoes, NY

RICE James of Bennington, Vt.
January 9, 1878

**MORSE** Harriet of Bennington, Vt.                     White Creek, NY

**BRISTOL** Merritt                                       December 16, 1877
**DIXON** Frances                                         S. Argyle, NY

**MILLER** James                                          December 18/20,
1877
**MC ELWAIN** Maggie                                      N. Argyle, NY

**TAYLOR** William of Ft. Edward, NY                      January 23, 1878
**WHALEY** Mary of Ft. Edward, NY                         Ft. Edward, NY

**NEWTON** George W. of Kingsbury, NY                     January 30, 1878
**YARTER** Carrie of Kingsbury, NY                        Kingsbury, NY

**MULLIGAN** James                                        February 5, 1878
**O'DONNELL** Mary                                        Cambridge, NY

**WATERS** Elijah of Easton, NY                           March 6, 1878
**BALDWIN** Mary Frances of Buskirks Bridge, NY           Coila, NY

**MC CONEY** Xaviar of Hartford, NY                       February 28, 1878
**WHALEY** Hannah of Ft. Miller, NY                       Ft. Miller, NY

**HANKY** Robert of Kanes Falls, NY                       March 16, 1878
**EASTMAN** Louise of Kanes Falls, NY

**HOWE** Horace P. of Comstocks, NY                       April 21, 1878
**MILLER** Melissa A. of Comstocks, NY                    Sandy Hill, NY

**GREEN** Horace W. of Eagle Bridge, NY                   June 20, 1878
**ATWOOD** Alcie of Hoosick Falls, NY                     Cambridge, NY

**HIBBARD** George S. of Rupert, Vt.                      June 18, 1878
**BARNARD** Mary A. dau of J. H. of Corinth, NY           Corinth, NY

**BARRINGER** Sylvester of Troy, NY                       October 13, 1878
**CUTTER** Mary E. of Ft. Ann, NY                         Ft. Ann, NY

**VAUGHN** Parker of Arlington, Vt.                       October 21, 1878
**STEVENSON** Margaret L. of Arlington, Vt.               White Creek, NY

**GAMBLE** Melvin E.                                      October 16, 1878
**REYNOLDS** Ella J.                                      Sandy Hill, NY

**BELDEN** James M. of Syracuse, NY                       October 24, 1878
**VAN ZILE** Bessie of Troy, NY                           Troy, NY

**COPELAND** Clarence E.                                  October 26, 1878
**VAUGHN** Delia                                          Ft. Ann, NY

| | |
|---|---|
| **GORMAN** Weal<br>**BRIGGS** Carrie | October 26, 1878<br>Ft. Ann, NY |
| **SLADD** Charles H. of W. Hoosick, NY<br>**LINK** Susie A. of Cambridge, NY | November 13, 1878<br>Cambridge, NY |
| **LINCOLN** Fayette J. of Dana, Mass.<br>**HARSHA** S. Libbie of Coila, NY | November 6, 1878<br>Dana, Mass. |
| **SHAW** John of Sandy Hill, NY<br>**JACKSON** Mrs. Laura of Sandy Hill, NY | November 12, 1878<br>Sandy Hill, NY |
| **BULL** Henry C. of Granville, NY<br>**BROWN** Jennie | November 20, 1878<br>Granville, NY |
| **HILLS** Noah G. of Granville, NY<br>**HILLS** Mrs. Charles L. of Granville, NY | November 16, 1878<br>Hartford, NY |
| **MC DONALD** Manuel 2nd<br>**HARDEN** Anna | November 20, 1878<br>Hartford, NY |
| **LEVENWAY** Ransom W.<br>**PATNEAU** Ida | December 7, 1878<br>Whitehall, NY |
| **CHAPLIN** Orrin A.<br>**PATNEAU** Alma | December 7, 1878<br>Whitehall, NY |
| **O'HARA** James of Tarport, Pa.<br>**MC KEE** Minnie of S. Glens Falls, NY | December 10, 1878<br>S. Glens Falls, NY |
| **MINTON** Andrew of Smiths Basin, NY (newspaper date)<br>**WAIT** Miss ____ of Ft. Ann, NY | January 3, 1879 |
| **PORTER** Charles H. of Poultney, Vt.<br>**MC FADDEN** Alice of Wells, Vt. | January 1, 1879<br>N. Granville, NY |
| **HICKS** Joseph of Slyborough, NY<br>**POTTER** Ellen of M. Granville, NY | January 8, 1879<br>Granville, NY |
| **EMERSON** Frank V. of Taftsville, Vt.<br>**BAKER** Mary L. dau of Lewis N. | December 25, 1878<br>Ft. Ann, NY |
| **TOOHEY** Frank of Walloomsac, NY<br>**MC DUNN** Lizzie of Walloomsac, NY | April 13, 1879<br>Hoosick Falls, NY |
| **WHITMORE** J. M. of Ira, Vt.<br>**LOGAN** Matilda of Ira, Vt. | July 3, 1879<br>Hampton, NY |
| **BAILEY** Robert M. son of Dr. T. H. of Adrian, Mi. | June 26, 1879 |

**STRONG** Laura M. of Cambridge, NY — Sandy Hill, NY

**MC LAUGHLIN** Milton E. of Glens Falls, NY — June 30, 1879
**HAWKS** Ida J. of Sandy Hill, NY — Sandy Hill, NY

**KENNER** John of Illinois — July 9, 1879
**MOREY** Millie formerly of Stillwater, NY

**ROSS** Andrew of Vergennes, Vt. — June 12, 1879
**WRIGHT** Carrie E. dau of Rev. Stephen of Glens Falls, NY — Glens Falls, NY

**WRIGHT** William G. of Bennington, Vt. — August 6, 1879
**HOBBS** Mac F. dau of late Jonathan of Hampton, NY — Rowley, Mass.

**TURNER** Elbridge of Shaftsbury, Vt. — September 6, 1879
**HORTON** Jane of Cambridge, NY — W. Cambridge, NY

**DOANE** John W. — September 3, 1879
**HOVER** Georgie B. — Cambridge, NY

**CLUTE** James of Milton, NY — September 18, 1879
**ROXBURY** M. Rose of Cambridge, NY — Cambridge, NY

**OUTERSON** James T. of Sandy Hill, NY — September 24, 1879
**WEAVER** Margaret E. of Sandy Hill, NY — Sandy HIll, NY

**GOODSPEED** George S. of Wells, Vt.   (newspaper date) — October 3, 1879
**CULVER** Lizzie A. of Pawlet, Vt. — Ft. Edward, NY

**DE FOREST** A. D. of Ft. Edward, NY — October 2, 1879
**WING** Lucy L. of Glens Falls, NY — Glens Falls, NY

**CORLEW** William W. of Dresden, NY — September 28, 1879
**NOBLE** Emma B. of Dresden, NY — Ft. Ann, NY

**KENYON** William M. of Cambridge, NY — September 30, 1879
**HILLMAN** Anna L. of Broadalbin, NY — Broadalbin, NY

**HUMPHREY** R. J. of Poultney, Vt. — October 14, 1879
**SPOONER** Ella of Poultney, Vt. — Poultney, Vt.

**BARBER** Edward of Easton, NY — October 22, 1879
**GANNON** Susie of Summit, NY

**ADAMS** Frederick M. of Bennington, Vt. — October 28, 1879
**BABCOCK** Nettie C. of Cambridge, NY — Cambridge, NY

**BROWN** A. H. of Rexford, Pa. — October 22, 1879
**GREENOUGH** Nellie of Whitehall, NY — Whitehall, NY

MC CLELLAN Robert of Galena
GARFIELD Mrs. Clara (DENNISON) of Jacksonville

October 1, 1879
Jacksonville

PIERCE Herbert A. of White Creek, NY
LOOMIS Lillian S. of White Creek, NY

October 30, 1879
Cambridge, NY

BROWNELL Benjamin of Cambridge, NY
HILL Marion of Summit, NY

November 18, 1879

GRANGER Charles P. of Pittsford, Vt.
BUTLER Nellie A. of Pittsford, Vt.

December 11, 1879
Hampton, NY

KEYES John of W. Hebron, NY
MC QUEEN Libbie H. of W. Galway, NY

December 15, 1879
W. Galway, NY

BROWN Mac J. of Whitehall, NY
ADAMS Ida of Whitehall, NY

December 17, 1879
Whitehall, NY

LAKE Albert of Jamestown, NY
BAIN Emma of Argyle, NY

December 10, 1879
Argyle, NY

## WHITEHALL CHRONICLE
### September 1851 - February 10, 1877
Scattered issues

KEYES Charles E. of Gansevort, NY
BURKBY Elizabeth of Gansevort, NY

August 26, 1851
Whitehall, NY

MOORE William W. of Shoreham, Vt.
HAMMOND Jennie dau of Charles of Crown Pt., NY

September 9, 1851
Crown Point, NY

WINEGAR Russell of Ft. Ann, NY
BENJAMIN Mary Ann of Ft. Ann, NY

September 15, 1851
Ft. Ann, NY

DE LE BARRE Isaac of Dorset, Vermont
WINTERS Mary A. of Whitehall, NY

January 29, 1856
Whitehall, NY

GODDARD Charles A. of Worcester, Mass.
FREEMAN Martha A. adopted dau of Leonard TRACY

February 5, 1856
Whitehall, NY

EMPEY David of Ft. Ann, NY          (newspaper date)
FLACK Helen of N. Granville, NY

February 8, 1856
N. Granville, NY

ROSS Hosea B. of Cornwall, NY
GROVES Mary A. of Middlebury, Vt.

January 29, 1856
Middlebury, Vt.

MC FARLAND Joseph of Greenwich, NY
ARMSTRONG Christiana of Argyle, NY

January 31, 1856
Argyle, NY

| | |
|---|---|
| **LITTLE** Alexander of Salem, NY | February 20, 1856 |
| **CUMMINGS** Ann of Whitehall, NY | Whitehall, NY |
| | |
| **STICKLES** Israel F. of Schuyler Falls, NY | February 25, 1856 |
| **WHITE** Mary dau of Rev. J. D. of Whitehall, NY | Whitehall, NY |
| | |
| **STAFFORD** Seymour F. of Whitehall, NY | February 21, 1856 |
| **GEORGE** Cynthia P. of Whitehall, NY | Whitehall, NY |
| | |
| **WHITMORE** George R. | March 4, 1856 |
| **NIMS** Frances Ann dau of Warren | Ft. Ann, NY |
| | |
| **GOSS** Lauriston H. of Whitehall, NY | March 6, 1856 |
| **WILSON** Barbara J. of Whitehall, NY | |
| | |
| **POTTER** Charles W. of Granville, NY | March 5, 1856 |
| **BURDICK** Martha Jane of Granville, NY | M. Granville, NY |
| | |
| **FINCH** Henry M. | March 19, 1856 |
| **DOUGLAS** Martha Jane | Whitehall, NY |
| | |
| **MC MURRAY** William J. of Argyle, NY | March 5, 1856 |
| **SHIELL** Margaret of Putnam, NY | Putnam, NY |
| | |
| **CUMMINGS** William A. | March 12, 1856 |
| **EASTON** Calista Frances | Putnam, NY |
| | |
| **HUTTON** Robert H. | March 27, 1856 |
| **CUMMINGS** Mary Isabella | Putnam, NY |
| | |
| **GOLDSMITH** David P. of Poultney, Vt. | April 16, 1856 |
| **HOPKINS** Alice A. of Poultney, Vt. | Whitehall, NY |
| | |
| **RENNIE** Robert of Whitehall, NY | March 25, 1856 |
| **WILDIC** Margaret of Whitehall, NY | Whitehall, NY |
| | |
| **HOOKER** Martin P. of Hampton, NY | March 20, 1856 |
| **PARKHILL** Jane H. of Benson, Vt. | Benson, Vt. |
| | |
| **PECK** G. H. of Syracuse, NY | May 5, 1856 |
| **WELLER** Lizzie S. of Ft. Ann, NY | Ft. Ann, NY |
| | |
| **CAMPBELL** William J. of Burlington, Vt. (newspaper date) | July 4, 1856 |
| **GRIFFITH** Grace W. of Burlington Vt. | Whitehall, NY |
| | |
| **KNIGHT** H. H. of Whitehall, NY | July 8, 1856 |
| **WALKER** M. M. of Whitehall, NY | Whitehall, NY |
| | |
| **GREGG** Thomas of Whitehall, NY | July 5, 1856 |
| **KENNEDY** Ellen of Whitehall, NY | Whitehall, NY |

**COZZENS** Stephen of Whitehall, NY
**FOSDICK** Clarrie of Whitehall, NY

July 23, 1856
Whitehall, NY

**NASH** Charles S. of Granville, NY
**HATCH** Mary Lucinda of Whitehall, NY

July 15, 1856
Granville, NY

**KING** D. Harvey of Chicago, Ill.
**COLEMAN** Susan Anna of Whitehall, NY

July 31, 1856

**MURRAY** William H. of Whitehall, NY
**WHITNEY** Marion C. of Whitehall, NY

September 4, 1856
Whitehall, NY

**MASON** Daniel M. of Ft. Ann, NY
**WELLS** Harriet M. of Ft. Ann, NY

September 8, 1856
Ft. Ann, NY

**CLARK** Henry G. of Granville, NY
**SHERMAN** Flora E. of W. Rupert, Vt.

October 9, 1856
W. Rupert, Vt.

**BARNAM** Moses J. of Ft. Ann, NY
**STURDEVANT** Sarah A. late of Como, Ill.

September 24, 1856
Ft. Ann, NY

**SNOW** William of Orange, NJ
**CREE** Mary of Whitehall, NY

October 24, 1856
Whitehall, NY

**FAULKENBURY** D. L. of Whitehall, NY
**THOMSON** S. Jeannin of Fortsville, NY

October 25, 1856
Fortsville, NY

**REYNOLDS** Werden P. of Manchester
**PURDY** Nancy P. of Manchester

October 21, 1856
Factory Point, Vt.

**COLE** Andrew of Jackson, NY
**HITCHCOCK** Miriam M. of Westhaven, Vt.

October 23, 1856
Westhaven, Vt.

**SHELDON** John of Essex Co. NY
**WALLACE** Julia Ann

November 23, 1856
Whitehall, NY

**FULLERTON** Willam Henry of Hebron, NY
**AVERY** Janette E. of Granville, NY

December 24, 1856
Granville, NY

**ROOT** Sidney D. of Whitehall, NY
**CLOSE** Maria A. of Saratoga Springs, NY
NY

January 13, 1857
Saratoga Springs,

**LILLIE** Robert S.
**MC LAUGHLIN** Jane

January 15, 1857
Putnam, NY

**STEVENS** Lafayette of Whitehall, NY
**SIMONS** Marinda A. of Whitehall, NY

April 14, 1857
Whitehall, NY

| | |
|---|---|
| **GOODMAN** Eleazer Jr. of Glens Falls, NY<br>**BLOUNT** Jane E. of Whitehall, NY | June 1, 1857<br>Whitehall, NY |
| **PROUTY** Levi of Hampton, NY<br>**ALLEN** Emily F. of Whitehall, NY | May 27, 1857<br>Whitehall, NY |
| **LING** Lorenzo of Pulaski, NY<br>**LIVINGSTON** C. A. of Saratoga Springs, NY<br>NY | May 28, 1857<br>Saratoga Springs, |
| **DUNCAN** Joshua of Granville, NY<br>**GRAY** Frances of Granville, NY | May 31, 1857<br>Granville, NY |
| **MC MULLEN** James H. of Castleton, Vt.<br>**ROCKWELL** Lizzie of Saratoga, NY | August 25, 1859 |
| **CULL** John of Whitehall, NY<br>**DAVIS** Mrs. Sarah of Whitehall, NY | March 22, 1860<br>Whitehall, NY |
| **WILSON** William of Whitehall, NY<br>**WORDEN** Jerusha of Whitehall, NY | December 13, 1860<br>Whitehall, NY |
| **FADDEN** J. A. of Benson, Vt.<br>**DORSEY** Sarah A. of Whitehall, NY | December 25, 1860<br>Whitehall, NY |
| **HIGLEY** C. W.<br>**AVERY** Calista | August 17, 1862<br>Hartford, NY |
| **BUTLER** Winfield of Whitehall, NY<br>**SEARLES** Mary of Whitehall, NY | August 12, 1862<br>Whitehall, NY |
| **COUSE** Abijah of New York City<br>**JOHNSON** Nellie of New York City | August 12, 1862<br>Whitehall, NY |
| **GILLETTE** Oscar<br>**BARRETT** Emily | January 1, 1863<br>Dresden, NY |
| **PECOR** Basil W.<br>**WHEELER** Martha C. of Whitehall, NY | January 8, 1863<br>Whitehall, NY |
| **MAY** Earl H.<br>**BURROUGHS** Julia A. | January 13, 1863<br>M. Granville, NY |
| **GRANT** Andrew Jr. of Whitehall, NY<br>**MC FARRAS** Nancy of Whitehall, NY | January 13, 1863<br>Whitehall, NY |
| **MANVILLE** Marcus M. of Whitehall, NY<br>**PAYNE** Carrie of Moreau, NY | January 21, 1863<br>Moreau, NY |
| **IVES** George of Ticonderoga, NY | February 21, 1864 |

STEVENS E. of Putnam, NY
Putnam, NY

COATS George
BURNETT Mrs. Emeline of Putnam, NY
March 1, 1864
Putnam, NY

WARD William of Norumberland, NY
WETHERBEE Polly M. of Dresden, NY
March 6, 1864
Putnam, NY

NEDDO Phillip of Whitehall, NY
PRATT Sarah J. of Whitehall, NY
May 3, 1864
Whitehall, NY

AUSTIN W. A. R. of Westhaven, Vt.
COLLINS Josephine of Whitehall, NY
February 18, 1874
Whitehall, NY

MONROE James of Saratoga, NY
HILLMAN Fanny D.
February 16, 1874
S. Wilton, NY

CARLTON Horton of Middle Granville, NY
SMITH Ada dau of Nathan of Comstocks Landing, NY
March 18, 1874
Comstocks Landing

HARRIS Frederick M. of Boston, Ma.
WARREN Julia E. of Hampton, NY
March 10, 1874
Hampton, NY

HANKS Marlin of Lakeville, NY
COOK P. A. of Lakeville, NY
March 11, 1874
Lakeville, NY

WRIGHT Joseph of Warrensburgh, NY
WHITE Mary of Crown Point, NY
March 16, 1874
Whitehall, NY

BADGER D. Stephen of Ft. Ann, NY
WEBSTER Mary L. of Hartford, NY
March 18, 1874
Ft. Edward, NY

WILSON Ira C. of Hampton, NY
ANDREWS Emma G. of Ft. Edward, NY
March 18, 1874
Ft. Edward, NY

ANDRUS Edward D. of Poultney, Vt.
NEWBURY Grace A. (COON) of Ft. Ann, NY
March 24, 1874
Ft. Ann, NY

VAUGHN Edward D. of Kingsbury, NY
JENKINS Sarah M. of Kingsbury, NY
March 31, 1874
Kingsbury, NY

COLERIDGE John of Ft. Edward, NY
ARNDT Lina of Ft. Edward, NY
March 27, 1874
Ft. Edward, NY

WILLIE W. H. of Ft. Edward, NY
MARTIN Lizzie of Ft. Edward, NY
April 12, 1874
Ft. Edward, NY

VALIQUETTE Lewis of Rutland Vt.
O'MARA Winifred of Whitehall, NY
May 12, 1874
Whitehall, NY

| | |
|---|---|
| **METCALF** Benjamin of Ft. Edward, NY<br>**STATIA** Mary of Whitehall, NY | May 27, 1874<br>Whitehall, NY |
| **ANSON** Frank of Milwaukee, Wis.<br>**GRISWOLD** Mollie A. of Whitehall, NY | June 2, 1874<br>Whitehall, NY |
| **ALLARD** Jasper H. of Sherburne, Vt.<br>**WILLARD** Lizzie W. of Sherburne, Vt. | June 1, 1874<br>at Yule House |
| **DAY** William A. of Rutland, Vt.<br>**WING** Mary of Rutland, Vt. | June 10, 1874 |
| **SHANKS** William of Carlisle, NY<br>**OSGOOD** Hattie H. dau of Rev. David of Arglye, NY | June 10/11, 1874<br>Argyle, NY |
| **SUDDARD** David H. of Ticonderoga, NY<br>**BENSON** Harriet A. of Fairhaven, Vt. | July 14, 1874 |
| **SCOTT** Ezra of Weston, Vt.<br>**HANINGTON** Sarah E. of Fairhaven, Vt. | July 4, 1874<br>Granville, NY |
| **CROSEN** Daniel of Hebron, NY<br>**ANDREWS** Emma of Hebron, NY | July 4, 1874<br>Granville, NY |
| **RATHBUN** Allen of Easton, NY<br>**NORTON** Mary E. of Granville, NY | July 4, 1874 |
| **GREER** Charles of Benson, Vt.<br>**SHARP** Mary Ann of Putnam, NY | July 2, 1874 |
| **WILSON** Edward of Whitehall, NY<br>**BOICE** Frances M. of Ft. Ann, NY | July 8, 1874<br>Shushan, NY |
| **CRANDALL** Valorous C. of Ft. Ann, NY<br>**ELLSWORTH** Mary J. of Caldwell, NY | July 11, 1874<br>Bolton, NY |
| **CONANT** Alonzo of M. Granville, NY<br>**CARY** Mrs. ____ of Coila, NY | July 15, 1874<br>Coila, NY |
| **RANDALL** Nelson of Ripley, NY<br>**BRAYTON** E. E. of Hartford, NY | July 30, 1874<br>Hartford, NY |
| **OATMAN** Benjamin of Argyle, NY<br>**WOODALL** Mary of Hartford, NY | August 4, 1874<br>Hartford, NY |
| **GOODRICH** E. R.<br>**WHIPPLE** Sarah | August 4, 1874<br>Fairhaven, Vt. |
| **INGLES** P. G. of Machias, NY<br>**NICHOLS** Luana of Kingsbury, NY | September 1, 1874<br>Kingsbury, NY |

KILBURN R. J. of Rutland, Vt.
MC DONALD N. V. of Hampton, NY

August 29, 1874
Hampton, NY

KELLEY George E. of Westhaven, Vt.
BARTHOLOMEW Matty E. of Dresden, NY

September 2, 1874
Dresden, NY

TANNER Morgan B. of Bolton, NY
PIKE Abbie M. of Ft. Edward, NY

September 15, 1874
Ft. Edward, NY

HALL John W.
LANDON Mrs. Josephine

September 24, 1874
Whitehall, NY

BAILEY Charles H. of Hoosick Falls, NY
BLANCHARD Emma F. of Whitehall, NY

September 30, 1874
Whitehall, NY

RIGLEY John of Westchester, NY
SWEET Clara E. of Whitehall, NY

August 29, 1874
Whitehall, NY

LITTLE Asa W. of Castleton, Vt.
ABRAMS Mary A. of Castleton, Vt.

September 3, 1874
Whitehall, NY

PARO Alfred of Whitehall, NY
RINGER Jennie of Whitehall, NY

September 30, 1874
Whitehall, NY

LYONS John of Whitehall, NY
HOPE Delina

October 14, 1874
Whitehall, NY

RENOIS Francis
LORTIE Mary Aurelia

October 27, 1874
Whitehall, NY

INGLEE W. B. of Whitehall, NY
RODD E. J. of Whitehall, NY

October 24, 1874
Whitehall, NY

CAIN William of Whitehall, NY
GRANT Ann of Grand Isle, Vt.

November 2, 1874
Whitehall, NY

WILKINSON Dr. A. of Alpina, Mi.
SHEPARDSON Frankie of Whitehall, NY

November 18, 1874
Whitehall, NY

## WHITEHALL DEMOCRAT
### January 6, 1847 - February 20, 1847

KELLOGG John Jr. of Benson, Vt.
GIBBS Emeline Jane of Benson, Vt.

January 3, 1847
Benson, Vt.

NELSON George of Crown Point, NY
WHITING Josephine of Orwell, Vt.

January 4, 1847
Orwell, Vt.

**MERRITT** Michael P.
**REYNOLDS** Mrs. Jane Ann

December 30, 1846
M. Granville, NY

**SWEET** William H. of Granville, NY
**TOWNE** Mary Jane of Whitehall, NY

January 6, 1847
Whitehall, NY

**WICKER** Charles L. of Orwell, Vt.
**ROYCE** Helen of Orwell, Vt.

January 15, 1847
Orwell, Vt.

**MANLY** Reuben son of John E. of Benson, Vt.
**WHITE** Maria of Benson, Vt.

December 20, 1846
Benson, Vt.

**BARRETT** David B. of Dresden, NY
**WICKER** Pyra A. of Westhaven, Vt.

January 14, 1847
Westhaven, Vt.

## WHITEHALL TIMES
### June 25, 1864 - December 27, 1882
Scattered issues

**COOPE** John E. of Blackington, Mass.
**WILBUR** Annie E. of Greenwich, NY

August 17, 1871
Greenwich, NY

**PRATT** Almon of Whitehall, NY    (newspaper date)
**BELDEN** Viola of Westhaven, Vt.

February 14, 1877

# INDEX

ABBOTT 26, 58, 139, 298, 363, 401
ABEEL 57, 70, 182, 233, 261
ABELL 246, 263
ABRAMS 145, 398, 419
ACKER 355
ACKERMAN 91
ACKERS 393
ACKINS 246
ACKLEY 20, 76, 82, 143, 162, 278, 280, 297, 305, 404, 405
ADAMS 9, 19, 30, 32, 57, 85, 86, 97, 98, 125, 126, 146, 149, 150, 155, 167, 218, 224, 246, 247, 265, 272, 319, 347, 354, 373, 409, 412, 413
ADDAM 303
AELITT 81
AERO 391
AGAN 39, 80, 322, 328, 332, 340, 396
AGATE 88
AINSLEE 37
AINSWORTH 401
AKESTER 258
AKIN 35, 137, 180, 304, 336, 341, 347
ALDEN 61, 63, 403
ALDOUS 271
ALDRICH 40
ALEXANDER 6, 44, 160, 205, 217, 276, 294, 299, 330, 345, 349, 359, 361, 373, 376, 406
ALLARD 418
ALLBRIGHT 2
ALLEN 33, 34, 39, 44, 70, 77, 83, 96, 107, 113, 115, 121, 138, 145, 158, 164, 172, 176, 177, 183, 185, 194, 196, 197, 198, 209, 214, 220, 221, 224, 252, 260, 269, 279, 284, 291, 297, 298, 302, 306, 307, 322, 331, 340, 345, 347, 353, 357, 371, 376, 389, 399, 401, 416
ALLISON 72, 102, 394
ALLORD 234
ALMA 333
ALMY 189, 262, 371
ALSTON 84, 223
ALVORD 48, 293
AMBLER 111
AMES 6, 87, 148, 185, 190, 206, 257, 313, 330, 333, 347
AMIDON 35, 39, 66, 70, 76, 87, 101, 154, 257, 310
AMMOND 246
AMOREUX 89
ANDERSON 69, 96, 109, 137, 181, 189, 195, 273
ANDETTE 110, 393
ANDRESS 87, 106
ANDREWS 7, 12, 43, 44, 51, 55, 62, 93, 110, 117, 118, 123, 135, 140, 157, 163, 164, 189, 235, 239, 289, 305,

309, 355, 358, 360, 371, 380, 381, 384, 389, 395, 404, 417, 418
ANDRUS 22, 113, 311, 417
ANGELL 116, 403
ANGUS 181
ANSON 418
ANTHONY 25, 73, 90, 149, 171, 199, 217, 351, 375
ARCHER 153, 177, 306, 331, 336
ARCHIBALD 77, 92, 94, 241, 243, 278, 288, 330, 339, 359, 386
ARLING 91
ARMINGTON 206
ARMITAGE 279, 327
ARMSTRONG 7, 27, 28, 170, 173, 201, 217, 266, 292, 306, 308, 321, 322, 324, 326, 328, 340, 352, 360, 413
ARNDT 417
ARNOLD 177, 242, 324, 329, 339, 346, 347, 354, 359, 393
ARNOTT 135, 170, 255, 318, 342
ARTHUR 158, 169
ASHBY 50
ASHE 141
ASHLEY 72, 125, 261, 310, 350, 360, 393
ASHTON 26, 31, 294, 318, 324, 333, 382
ASHWELL 351
ATHERTON 53
ATKINS 137
ATWATER 214, 274
ATWELL 56, 232
ATWOOD 28, 31, 36, 106, 151, 154, 171, 208, 259, 264, 410
AUBERY 131
AURINGER 131
AUSTIN 2, 30, 31, 53, 59, 86, 88, 107, 110, 117, 137, 141, 161, 166, 207, 212, 237, 245, 249, 268, 282, 296, 300, 315, 322, 326, 335, 341, 342, 379, 382, 391, 403, 409, 417
AVERILL 408
AVERY 142, 178, 277, 300, 415, 416
AXTELL 35, 49, 119
AYERS 141, 388
AYLIFFE 95
AYLSWORTH 1, 184, 310
AYRES 253, 327
AYREY 187
BABCOCK 20, 123, 218, 225, 238, 252, 265, 316, 412
BACHELDER 21, 52, 67, 252, 257, 363
BACHELOR 251
BACON 190, 276, 289, 365, 388
BADGER 260, 417
BADGLEY 104
BAGG 162
BAIL 172
BAILEY 4, 17, 59, 91, 113, 114, 123, 173, 176, 226, 233, 247, 255, 256, 284, 344, 356, 411, 419

BAILLIE 44
BAIN 20, 21, 28, 38, 45, 63, 92, 119, 126, 132, 151, 188, 194, 213, 218, 231, 243, 253, 255, 308, 323, 364, 367, 373, 397, 403, 406, 413
BAKER 1, 8, 10, 13, 19, 22, 33, 46, 48, 49, 58, 64-66, 68, 76, 78, 88, 94, 96, 99, 106, 119, 125-127, 136, 140, 142, 156, 172, 186, 199, 203, 205, 215, 221, 226, 228, 234, 238-240, 246, 248, 271, 289, 309, 314, 319, 321, 342, 343, 348, 351, 361, 373, 380, 384, 387, 389, 396, 402, 408, 411
BALCH 98
BALDRIDGE 83
BALDWIN 19, 21, 24, 33, 48, 68, 81, 145, 152, 169, 227, 244, 246, 323, 329, 334, 360, 387, 400, 401, 410
BALEY 295
BALL 91, 117, 204, 243
BALLOU 63
BANARD 289, 292
BANCROFT 52, 298, 325
BANE 128
BANKER 173, 283, 303, 347
BANKS 330
BANNISTER 36
BARBER 8, 9, 25, 41, 55, 56, 62, 76, 85, 95, 109, 131, 138, 149, 153, 157, 170, 193, 194, 218, 245, 248, 252, 263, 267, 278, 295, 307, 312, 314, 317, 321, 322, 327, 364, 372, 386, 387, 393, 412
BARBOUR 83
BARBY 392
BARCLAY 293
BARDEN 80, 88, 100, 159, 205, 250, 369, 407
BARDWELL 195, 199, 200
BARESE 302
BARKER 3, 20, 26, 47, 52, 99, 103, 105, 108, 131, 144, 168, 176, 210, 236, 253, 273, 274, 282, 298, 303, 306, 310, 375, 394, 402, 407
BARKLEY 80, 87, 102, 111, 134, 161, 221, 222, 365, 378
BARLOW 230
BARNAM 415
BARNARD 16, 36, 171, 188, 191, 210, 213, 246, 349, 410
BARNES 18, 25, 125, 132, 163, 202, 280, 308, 315, 339, 342, 344, 369, 377
BARNETT 42, 105, 201, 282, 332, 387
BARNEY 49, 293
BARNHART 319
BARNUM 299
BARON 178

271, 274, 277, 344, 355, 372, 393, 397, 398
CARR 6, 57, 86, 106, 113, 127, 150, 212, 219, 249, 254
CARRIER 38
CARRIGAN 376
CARRINGTON 102, 397
CARROL 314
CARROLL 114, 124
CARRUTH 271
CARSON 11, 141, 193, 204, 222, 309
CARSWELL 1, 10, 11, 16, 20, 42, 55, 63, 86, 90, 140, 166, 182, 186, 195, 202, 214, 270, 273
CARTER 16, 37, 40, 102, 118, 186, 235, 245, 259, 272, 290, 293, 384
CARTWRIGHT 338
CARUTHERS 6, 29, 30, 167
CARVER 230, 398
CARY 52, 59, 104, 130, 307, 418
CASAVANT 78
CASE 93, 105, 253, 346, 362
CASEY 110, 351
CASS 241
CASSELS 45, 328, 397
CASTLE 114
CATHCART 388
CAULKINS 157, 185
CAVANAUGH 232, 399
CAVIENOR 63
CAW 158
CELSIS 228
CENTER 226, 253, 316, 319, 344, 362, 378
CENTH 353
CHALK 62
CHALLES 179
CHALMERS 49, 288
CHAMBERLAIN 16, 21, 23, 38, 187, 198, 217, 277, 290, 364, 399
CHAMBERS 17, 23, 137, 165, 185, 302, 329
CHAMPAYNE 86
CHANDLER 56, 171, 220, 330, 407, 408
CHAPIN 45, 65, 87, 116, 155, 166, 171, 181, 206, 309, 378, 404
CHAPLIN 348, 411
CHAPMAN 22, 81, 98, 122, 147, 162, 174, 181, 262, 300, 381
CHAPPELL 13, 341
CHARTER 349
CHARTIER 172
CHASE 3, 14, 15, 19, 40, 43, 88, 97, 127, 202, 207, 232, 235, 269, 270, 273, 282, 303, 306, 320, 329, 332, 369, 372, 373, 393, 400, 402, 404
CHATFIELD 361
CHATTIN 14
CHAUBIN 235
CHEESBRO 19
CHEESEMAN 331

CHENEY 64, 132, 145, 314, 348
CHERRY 29, 160, 390
CHESTNUT 119
CHILLIS 384
CHIPMAN 323
CHISHOLM 409
CHOATE 61
CHRISTIE 21
CHUBB 15, 202, 236, 296
CHURCH 1, 52, 76, 136, 283, 292, 300
CHURCHILL 60, 63, 94, 321
CISCO 6
CLAGHORN 32
CLANCY 135, 226
CLAPP 26, 29, 136, 203, 276, 278, 279, 290, 297, 316, 322, 326, 327, 350
CLARK 3, 8, 12, 18, 20, 23, 25, 33, 41, 42, 47, 52, 57, 59, 66, 68, 71, 72, 79, 84, 89, 90, 108, 117, 121, 124, 127, 133, 138, 146, 153, 157, 158, 161, 163, 168, 171-173, 176, 179, 184, 186, 187, 190, 201, 202, 207, 225, 226, 229, 243, 248, 251, 256, 272, 294, 301, 305, 310, 313, 351, 352, 366, 370, 375, 394, 402, 407, 409, 415
CLAY 38
CLEARWATER 314
CLEAVER 67
CLEGG 112, 151
CLEMENT 63, 191, 239, 321
CLEMENTS 73, 87, 92, 95, 101, 154, 156, 266, 409
CLEMMONS 140, 226
CLENDON 78
CLEVELAND 19, 20, 38, 41, 45, 95, 154, 183, 278, 283, 289, 305, 357
CLINT 368
CLOFF 366
CLOSE 415
CLOSH 402
CLOSSON 184, 217, 224, 363, 402, 406
CLOUGH 55, 196, 277, 382, 406
CLOW 299
CLUFF 57, 264
CLUM 218
CLUTE 136, 197, 226, 412
COAN 303
COATS 146, 246, 252, 268, 417
COBB 106, 292, 342
COBINE 58
COBURN 72
COCAKLY 259
COCHRANE 376, 386, 404
COCRANE 234
CODAIR 104
CODMAN 86
CODNER 241
COFFIN 58, 96, 104, 107, 112, 136, 172, 183, 386
COFFINGER 147, 374
COGSHALL 268, 280, 324
COLBURN 61, 401

COLBY 209, 309, 329, 394
COLE 37, 41, 42, 66, 67, 81, 93, 156, 173, 176-178, 210, 235, 239, 258, 278, 295, 302, 340, 373, 404, 415
COLEMAN 53, 57, 117, 120, 133, 207, 226, 233, 275, 415
COLER 5
COLERIDGE 417
COLESTON 296
COLLAMER 50, 54, 55, 155, 251, 365
COLLETT 75
COLLIGAN 310
COLLINS 41, 92, 104, 162, 175, 177, 191, 204, 259, 260, 276, 278, 280, 290, 294, 308, 326, 328, 391, 393, 395, 401, 417
COLTON 4, 42, 86, 125, 141
COLVIN 45, 96, 119, 145
COMAN 349
COMBS 122, 168
COMEGYS 38
COMER 98, 334
COMERFORD 227
COMFORT 355
COMISKEE 259, 367
COMSTOCK 6, 7, 93, 153, 195, 273, 279, 387
CONANT 94, 182, 322, 396, 418
CONATY 242
CONE 2, 237, 348
CONERY 101, 197
CONGDON 18, 111, 147, 191, 256, 361, 366
CONGER 103
CONGHEY 345
CONGLOND 117
CONKEY 7, 38, 276, 297, 332, 340, 356, 380, 383, 389
CONKLIN 47, 70, 130, 177, 222, 223, 272, 363, 399, 409
CONLEE 58, 135, 162, 223, 297, 393
CONLEY 281
CONNEL 320
CONNELLY 73, 113, 227, 366
CONNOR 45, 110, 206, 212, 341
CONVERSE 100
CONWAY 96, 112, 253
COOK 10, 17, 25, 26, 31, 40, 55, 78, 83, 122, 128, 132, 142, 154, 158, 165, 172, 185, 193, 197, 206, 216, 238, 262, 280, 289, 296, 298, 300, 303, 339, 348, 352, 357, 367, 374, 394, 401, 417
COOKINGHAM 231
COOL 99, 113, 118, 126
COOLEY 12, 89, 161, 164, 295, 357
COOLIDGE 80, 136
COOMBS 388
COON 15, 33, 79, 85, 136, 151, 155, 159, 160, 219, 245, 274, 290, 318, 323, 348, 389, 396, 397, 417

Made in the USA
Columbia, SC
25 January 2025

52602486R00246